Red Hat® Linux® Networking and System Administration

Second Edition

Terry Collings and Kurt Wall

WILEY

Wiley Publishing, Inc.

Red Hat® Linux® Networking and System Administration, Second Edition

Published by
Wiley Publishing, Inc.
10475 Crosspoint Boulevard
Indianapolis, IN 46256
www.wiley.com

Copyright © 2004 by Red Hat, Inc.

Published by Wiley Publishing, Inc., Indianapolis, Indiana

Published simultaneously in Canada

Library of Congress Control Number:

ISBN: 0-7645-4498-5

Manufactured in the United States of America

10 9 8 7 6 5 4 3 2

Red Hat® Linux® Networking and System Administration

Second Edition

Credits

ACQUISITIONS EDITOR
Debra Williams Cauley

DEVELOPMENT EDITOR
Scott Amerman

RED HAT TECHNICAL EDITOR
Chip Turner

RED HAT PRESS LIAISONS
Chris Grams
Jeremy Hogan
Stephanie Jordan

PRODUCTION EDITOR
Eric Newman

COPY EDITOR
C. M. Jones

EDITORIAL MANAGER
Kathryn A. Malm

VICE PRESIDENT & EXECUTIVE GROUP PUBLISHER
Richard Swadley

VICE PRESIDENT AND EXECUTIVE PUBLISHER
Robert Ipsen

EXECUTIVE EDITORIAL DIRECTOR
Mary Bednarek

PROJECT COORDINATOR
Erin Smith

GRAPHICS AND PRODUCTION SPECIALISTS
Beth Brooks
Joyce Haughey
Jennifer Heleine
LeAndra Hosier
Michael Kruzil
Kristin McMullan

QUALITY CONTROL TECHNICIANS
Laura Albert
Susan Moritz
Brian H. Walls

PERMISSIONS EDITOR
Carmen Krikorian

MEDIA DEVELOPMENT SPECIALIST
Greg Stafford

PROOFREADING AND INDEXING
TECHBOOKS Production Services

About the Authors

Terry Collings is the Instructional Technologist at Muhlenberg College in Allentown, Pennsylvania, where he is responsible for researching and implementing emerging technology in an educational environment. He is also the system administrator for all Red Hat Linux servers on campus.

Terry is an adjunct faculty member at Lehigh Carbon Community College, where he currently teaches A + and Network + certification courses. He has taught courses on Unix, Linux, TCP/IP, and Novell Netware.

Terry is the co-author of *Linux Bible* and contributing writer to *Linux Weekend Crash Course*, and he has been a technical editor for the following books: *KDE Bible, The Samba Book, Unix Weekend Crash Course, Red Hat Linux 9 For Dummies*, and *Solaris 9 For Dummies*.

Kurt Wall first touched a computer in 1980 when he learned FORTRAN on an IBM mainframe of forgotten vintage; things have improved since then. A professional technical writer by trade and a historian by training, Kurt has a diverse work history. These days, Kurt works for TimeSys Corporation in Pittsburgh, Pennsylvania. His primary responsibility is managing TimeSys's Content Group or, as it is known in-house, the artists' colony. In addition to directing production of the technical and end-user documentation for TimeSys's embedded Linux operating system and development tools, he writes much of the documentation for TimeSys's embedded Linux products. Kurt's secondary duties include making sure the marketing department take their daily Linux clue pills. Kurt has written all or parts of 15 books on Linux system administration and programming topics. In his spare time, he has no spare time.

Kurt, who dislikes writing about himself in the third person, receives entirely too much e-mail at kwall@kurtwerks.com.

Preface

Red Hat produces the most popular distribution of Linux currently in use. It is a robust, reliable operating system that can run on a variety of hardware, from personal computers to large mainframes. Linux in general, and Red Hat Enterprise Linux in particular, is a very powerful operating system that can be used at the enterprise level as a full-fledged server. It functions equally well at the enterprise-workstation level for typical user applications, as well as on home PCs. For those of us dissatisfied with the reliability and security of other commercially available operating systems, Red Hat Enterprise Linux is a pleasant alternative.

How This Book Is Organized

This book is divided into five parts, each covering a specific area of functionality in a typical Red Hat Linux system. In this book, the second edition, we have added five chapters that cover areas we discussed in the first edition or that explore material not covered in the first edition. We also want to note that this book is useful for advanced users of Fedora, the open source community–based Linux project supported by Red Hat.

Part I: System and Network Administration Defined

This part sets the stage and defines the role of a system administrator, beginning with an explanation of the duties of a system administrator and continuing through installing your system and finishing with descriptions of the file system and system configuration files. Chapter 1 explains some of the common tasks an administrator may perform, such as installing servers and application software, managing user accounts, and backing up and restoring files. Chapter 2 details the steps involved in planning and implementing a network, including security and disaster-recovery considerations. Chapter 3 covers all the steps required to install Red Hat Enterprise Linux on a local system using the most typical installation method. Chapter 4 gives you instructions on using Kickstart to perform system installations on remote systems. Chapter 5 teaches you about the startup and shutdown process of your system, including the GRUB boot loader and the init process. In Chapter 6, you explore the details of the file system hierarchy and learn about other supported file systems. Part I ends with Chapter 7, which lists the system and network configuration files and explains the purpose of each file.

Part II: Network Services

This part of the book is where you learn about the networking services available in Red Hat Enterprise Linux. Beginning with Chapter 8, you learn about the X Window system used to provide a graphical working environment as well as font management. Chapter 9 tells you how to configure your printers to use the Common Unix Printing System (CUPS), the default printing system used by Red Hat Enterprise Linux. In Chapter 10, you learn about the TCP/IP protocol suite and how to configure it on your system. Chapter 11 explains the configuration of the Network File System (NFS) used to share files with other Linux or Unix computers on your network. Chapter 12 gives you the details about the Network Information System (NIS) and configuration instructions. If you have computers running Microsoft Windows NT, 2000, or XP, you will want to read Chapter 13 to learn how to share files with them using Samba. Chapter 13 also provides instructions on connecting a client to Novell networks so you can share files with these systems as well. Chap-ter 14 is for those of you who want to connect your Linux systems to computers running the Mac OS. The last chapter in this part, Chapter 15, gives you some helpful tips for optimizing the services discussed in Part II.

Part III: Internet Services

Internet services are somewhat different from network services on an internal network, and Chapter 16 begins this part by explaining what we mean by Internet services. Included in this chapter is an explanation of the Xinetd and TCP wrappers configuration files. Chapter 17 explains the Lightweight Directory Access Protocol (LDAP) used for network authentication. The ability to convert domain names to IP addresses is a fundamental part of providing Internet services. Chapter 18 explains how to configure BIND on your system to provide this service. The next three chapters provide installation and configuration instructions for three commonly used Internet services. Chapter 19 describes the process of sending e-mail and how to configure Sendmail, the most commonly used mail transfer agent, as well as Postfix, which is quickly gaining popularity. Chapter 20 explains setting up an FTP server on your system. Chapter 21 covers the most widely used Web server, Apache, and explains the configuration process. The last chapter in Part III, Chapter 22, provides some optimization information for the services covered in this part of the book.

Part IV: System Maintenance

The goal of this part of the book is to provide enough information so you have a fundamental understanding of the tasks required to maintain your system and ensure that it runs well. Chapter 23 explains the Red Hat Network, a service available from Red Hat that you can use to keep your system current. You can register your systems with Red Hat and then receive automatic notifications of updated or new software that can be installed. Sometimes it is advantageous to upgrade or recompile your kernel for your specific needs. Chapter 24 discusses the pros and cons of making changes and provides instructions to recompile your kernel. If you would rather do your system configuration from a command prompt rather than using many of the available GUI tools, Chapter 25 is for you. This chapter provides command prompt configuration instructions, as well as instructions to create scripts to automate many routine administration tasks. Chapter 26 tells you all you need to know to effectively manage the users and groups on your system. In Chapter 27, you learn how to install and upgrade software packages on your system. And in the last chapter in this part, Chapter 28, you explore the process of backing up the files on your system and how to restore them.

Part V: System Security and Problem Solving

Most of the last part of the book deals with securing your system, with a final chapter on general system troubleshooting. Maintaining a secure system is a critical area of concern for system administrators. Chapter 29 explains the basic steps involved in security, including establishing a security policy for your organization. Continuing the discussion, Chapter 30 addresses local (host-based) security. In Chapter 31, you find an explanation of firewalls and Internet security and the risks involved with connections from outside your network. Chapter 32 looks at ways to monitor your system for potential, attempted, and actual security compromises using the tools available in a standard system installation. The last chapter in this part, Chapter 33, lists some problems you may encounter during normal operation of your system and the steps to take to solve the problems discussed.

What's on the Web Site

As well as a CD-ROM that is included at the back of the book (see instructions for usage in the "What's on the CD-ROM" appendix), this book includes a companion Web site:

```
www.wiley.com/compbooks/collings
```

The site contains files for the code appearing throughout the book, as well as links to the primary vendors discusssed in the book.

How to Use This Book

Our intention in this book is to cover the Red Hat Enterprise Linux operating system in enough detail to provide the answers you need. The book is divided into the parts previously discussed to make it easy for you to go to the specific part for the topic you need to learn about. You can use the book as a reference for whatever you need to know about a particular topic.

Using This Book's Icons

Look for the following margin icons to help you get the most out of this book:

Tips provide special information or advice.

 Caution icons warn you of a potential problem or error.

 Cross-references direct you to related information in another section or chapter.

 Notes highlight areas of interest or special concern related to a topic.

Conventions

This book uses the following conventions for explanations of how to do things on your computer:

◆ *Italic type* introduces new technical terms. It also indicates replaceable arguments that you should substitute with actual values – the context makes clear the distinction between new terms and replaceable arguments.

◆ **Bold** shows a command you type.

◆ `Monospaced text` distinguishes commands, options, and arguments from surrounding explanatory content.

◆ Keys to press in combination are shown as in this example: Ctrl+Alt+Delete means to press all three keys at the same time.

◆ The term *click* means to press the left mouse button once. *Double-click* means to press the left button twice in quick succession. *Right-click* means to press the right mouse button once. *Drag* means to hold down the left mouse button and move the mouse while holding down the button.

Acknowledgments

Terry Collings: My first thought when I was asked to write the second edition of this book was Wow! It appears that we did a good enough job on the first edition that many people bought the book and found it useful. So to everyone who bought our book and made it possible for us to do another edition, here's a big thank you!

Thanks to Kurt Wall, my co-author, for again doing a great job in our collaboration on this new edition. Kurt is very easy to work with, and I hope I'll have a chance to work with him again.

This book would not have been possible without the hard work of everyone at John Wiley & Sons, especially our acquisitions editor, Debra Williams Cauley, and our development editor, Scott Amerman. Debra and Scott are both consummate professionals who were always there to answer our questions or concerns and make sure we kept on track. Thanks go to our copy editor, technical editor, and production staff at Wiley for ensuring that our book is technically accurate and grammatically correct.

I would like to extend my thanks to all those at Red Hat who participated in the technical-editing process. Their help was critical in ensuring our technical accuracy.

Finally, I would like to thank my wife, Nancy, who, in addition to giving me her support and encouragement while I worked on this book, gave me something incredibly precious. She gave me a new daughter, Sabrina, who was born just as I began work on this new edition.

Kurt Wall: I'm grateful to my co-author, Terry Collings, for asking me to work on this book. Terry's thanked me in the past for getting him started writing Linux books; he may yet curse me. As usual, the staff at Wiley has been terrific, despite the fact that they drove us to meet an insane deadline. Debra Williams Cauley, the Voice of Deadlines Missed, is just a doll; Scott Amerman is the long-suffering development editor who had to cope with metric boatloads of work when I submitted my material late; C. M. Jones, the book's copy editor, kept me from sounding illiterate, which is no mean feat. The unnamed others who converted the manuscript into printable copy never get enough credit. Thanks to you all. Red Hat Software earns mention here for supporting this book and, naturally, for providing the subject matter. I'm especially appreciative of the outstanding work Chip Turner of Red Hat Software did as our technical editor. Huzzah, Chip! Thanks. Any mistakes are mine, mine, I tell you, all mine!

Kudos to Marta Justak, principal of Justak Literary Services and my agent. Marta has always represented me well, and this book is no exception. Even while she was throwing crystal vases on the floor, Marta managed to keep me on task. Words fail to express my gratitude, Marta.

I work with an incredibly talented group of people at TimeSys. I learn something new from each of them every day. In particular, these people deserve credit for their friendship and support: Bill "Hot Sauce" von Hagen, my former boss; my Trusty Minions, Erin "Label Mamma" Kelly, Michaela "Eeyore" Jencka, and Kate "I Hate the Web" Tabasko. Everyone should have the opportunity to work with people they truly like. Thanks to you all!

Above all, if I have any talent as a writer, credit goes to the God who gave me the talent, provided me the opportunities to develop and use it, and kept me sober long enough to do so. Thanks and Amen.

Contents at a Glance

Contents

Part I

System and Network Administration Defined

Chapter 1

Duties of the System Administrator

IN THIS CHAPTER

- ◆ The Linux system administrator
- ◆ Installing and configuring servers
- ◆ Installing and configuring application software
- ◆ Creating and maintaining user accounts
- ◆ Backing up and restoring files
- ◆ Monitoring and tuning performance
- ◆ Configuring a secure system
- ◆ Using tools to monitor security

LINUX IS A MULTIUSER, multitasking operating system from the ground up. In this regard the system administrator has flexibility – and responsibility – far beyond those of other operating systems. Red Hat has employed innovations that extend these duties even for the experienced Linux user. In this chapter, we briefly look at those responsibilities, which we'll cover in more detail in later chapters.

The Linux System Administrator

Using Linux involves much more than merely sitting down and turning on the machine. Often you hear talk of a "steep learning curve" but that discouraging phrase can be misleading. Instead, Linux is quite different from the most popular commercial operating systems in a number of ways. While it is no more difficult to learn than other operating systems, it is likely to seem very strange even to the experienced administrator of other systems. In addition, the sophistication of a number of parts of the Red Hat distribution has increased by an order of magnitude, so even an experienced Linux administrator is likely to find much that is new and unfamiliar. Fortunately, there are new tools designed to make system administration easier than ever before.

Make no mistake: Every computer in the world has a system administrator. It may be – and probably is – true that the majority of system administrators are those who decided what software and peripherals were bundled with the machine when it was shipped. That status quo remains because the majority of users who acquire computers for use as appliances probably do little to change the default values. But the minute a user decides on a different wallpaper image or adds an application that was acquired apart from the machine itself, he or she has taken on the role of system administration.

The highfalutin title of system administrator brings with it some responsibilities. No one whose computer is connected to the Internet, for instance, has been immune to the effects of poorly administered systems, as demonstrated by the Distributed Denial of Service (DDoS) and e-mail macro virus attacks that have shaken the online world in recent years. The scope of these acts of computer vandalism (in some cases, computer larceny) would have been greatly reduced if system administrators had a better understanding of their duties.

Linux system administrators are likely to understand the necessity of active system administration more than those who run whatever came on the computer, assuming that things came properly configured from the factory. The user or enterprise that decides on Linux has decided, too, to assume the control that Linux offers, and the responsibilities that this entails.

By its very nature as a modern, multiuser operating system, Linux requires a degree of administration greater than that of less robust, home-market systems. This means that even if you use just a single machine connected to the Internet by a dial-up modem – or not even connected at all – you have the benefits of the same system employed by some of the largest businesses in the world, and will do many of the same things that IT professionals employed by those companies are paid to do. Administering your system does involve a degree of learning but it also means that in setting up and configuring your own system you gain skills and understanding that raise you above mere "computer user" status. The Linux system administrator does not achieve that mantle by purchasing a computer but by taking full control of what the computer does and how it does it.

You may end up configuring a small home or small office network of two or more machines, perhaps including ones that are not running Linux. You may be responsible for a business network of dozens of machines. The nature of system administration in Linux is surprisingly constant, no matter how large or small your installation. It merely involves enabling and configuring features you already have available.

By definition, the Linux system administrator is the person who has "root" access, which is to say the one who is the system's "super user" (or root user). A standard Linux user is limited to whatever he or she can do with the underlying engine of the system. But the root user has unfettered access to everything – all user accounts, their home directories, and the files therein; all system configurations; and all files on the system. A certain body of thought says that no one should ever log in as "root," because system administration tasks can be performed more easily and safely through other, more specific means, which we discuss in due course. Because the system administrator has full system privileges, your first duty is to know what you're doing, lest you break something.

By definition, the Linux system administrator is the person who has "root" access — the one who is the system's "super user."

The word *duty* implies a degree of drudgery; in fact, it's a manifestation of the tremendous flexibility of the system measured against the responsibility to run a tight organization. These duties do not so much constrain you, the system administrator, as free you to match the job to the task. Let's take a brief look at them.

Installing and Configuring Servers

When you hear the word *server* to describe a computer, you probably think of a computer that offers some type of service to clients. The server may provide file or printer sharing, File Transfer Protocol (FTP) or Web access, or e-mail processing tasks. Don't think of a server as a standalone workstation; think of it as a computer that specifically performs these services for many users.

In the Linux world, the word *server* has a broader meaning than what you might be used to. For instance, the standard Red Hat graphical user interface (GUI) requires a graphical layer called XFree86. This is a server. It runs even on a stand-alone machine with one user account. It must be configured. (Fortunately, Red Hat has made this a simple and painless part of installation on all but the most obscure combinations of video card and monitor; gone are the days of anguish as you configure a graphical desktop.)

Likewise, printing in Linux takes place only after you configure a print server. Again, this has become so easy as to be nearly trivial.

In certain areas the client-server nomenclature can be confusing, though. While you cannot have a graphical desktop without a server, you can have Web access without a Web server, FTP access without running an FTP server, and e-mail capabilities without ever starting a mail server. You may well want to use these servers, all of which are included in Red Hat; then again, maybe not. Whenever a server is connected to other machines outside your physical control, there are security implications to consider. You want your users to have easy access to the things they need but you don't want to open up the system you're administering to the whole wide world.

Whenever a server is connected to machines outside your physical control, security issues arise. You want users to have easy access to the things they need but you don't want to open up the system you're administering to the whole wide world.

Linux distributions used to ship with all imaginable servers turned on by default. Just installing the operating system on the computer would install and configure – with default parameters – all the services available with the distribution. This was a reflection of an earlier, more innocent era in computing when people did not consider vandalizing other people's machines to be good sportsmanship. Unfortunately, the realities of this modern, more dangerous world dictate that all but the most essential servers remain turned off unless specifically enabled and configured. This duty falls to the system administrator. You need to know exactly which servers you need and how to employ them, and to be aware that it is bad practice and a potential security nightmare to enable services that the system isn't using and doesn't need. Fortunately, the following pages show you how to carry out this aspect of system administration easily and efficiently.

Installing and Configuring Application Software

Although it is possible for individual users to install some applications in their home directories – drive space set aside for their own files and customizations – these applications are not available to other users without the intervention of the system administrator. Besides, if an application is to be used by more than one user, it probably needs to be installed higher up in the Linux file hierarchy, which is a job that only the system administrator can perform. (The administrator can even decide which users may use which applications by creating a "group" for that application and enrolling individual users in that group.)

New software packages might be installed in /opt if they are likely to be upgraded separately from the Red Hat distribution itself. Doing this makes it simple to retain the old version until you are certain that the new version works and meets your expectations. Some packages may need to go in /usr/local or even /usr if they are upgrades of packages installed as part of Red Hat. (For instance, there are sometimes security upgrades of existing packages.) The location of the installation usually matters only if you compile the application from source code; if you use a Red Hat Package Manager (RPM) application package, it automatically goes where it should.

Configuration and customization of applications is to some extent at the user's discretion, but not entirely. "Skeleton" configurations – administrator-determined default configurations – set the baseline for user employment of applications. If there are particular forms, for example, that are used throughout an enterprise, the system administrator would set them up or at least make them available by adding them to the skeleton configuration. The same applies to configuring user desktops and in even deciding what applications should appear on user desktop menus. For instance, your company may not want to grant users access to the games that ship with modern Linux desktops. You may also want to add menu items for newly installed or custom applications. The system administrator brings all this to pass.

Creating and Maintaining User Accounts

Not just anyone can show up and log on to a Linux machine. An account must be created for each user and — you guessed it — no one but the system administrator can do this. That's simple enough.

But there's more. It involves decisions that either you or your company must make. You might want to let users select their own passwords, which would no doubt make them easier to remember but which probably would be easier for a malefactor to crack. You might want to assign passwords, which is more secure in theory but increases the likelihood that users will write them down on a conveniently located scrap of paper — a risk if many people have access to the area where the machine(s) is located. You might decide that users must change their passwords periodically — something you can configure Red Hat Enterprise Linux to prompt users about.

What happens to old accounts? Suppose someone leaves the company. You probably don't want him or her to gain access to the company network, but you also don't want to delete the account wholesale, only to discover later that essential data resided nowhere else.

To what may specific users have access? It might be that there are aspects of your business that make Web access desirable, but you don't want everyone spending their working hours surfing the Web. If your system is at home, you may wish to limit your children's access to certain Web sites.

These and other issues are part of the system administrator's duties in managing user accounts. Whether the administrator or his or her employer establishes policies governing accounts, these policies should be delineated — preferably in writing for a company — for the protection of all concerned.

Backing Up and Restoring Files

Until computer equipment becomes infallible, until people lose the desire to harm others' property, and — truth be told — until system administrators become perfect, there is considerable need to back up important files so that the system can be up and running again with minimal disruption in the event of hardware, security, or administration failure. Only the system administrator may do this. (Because of its built-in security features, Linux doesn't allow users even to back up their own files to removable disks.)

It's not enough to know that performing backups is your job. You need to formulate a strategy for making sure your system is not vulnerable to catastrophic disruption. This is not always obvious. If you have a high-capacity tape drive and several good sets of restore disks, you might make a full system backup every few days. If you are managing a system with scores of users, you might find it more sensible to back up user accounts and system configuration files, figuring that reinstallation from the distribution CDs would be quicker and easier than getting the basics off a tape archive. (Don't forget about applications you install separately from your Red Hat distribution, especially those involving heavy customization.)

Once you decide *what* to back up, you need to decide *how frequently* to perform backups, whether to maintain a series of incremental backups – adding only files that have changed since the last backup – or multiple full backups, and *when* these backups should be performed. Do you trust an automated, unattended process? If you help determine which equipment to use, do you go with a redundant array of independent disks (RAID), which is to say multiple hard drives all containing the same data as insurance against the failure of any one of them, in addition to other backup systems? (A RAID is not enough because hard drive failure is not the only means by which a system can be brought to a halt.)

You don't want to become complacent or foster a lackadaisical attitude among users. Part of your strategy should be to maintain perfect backups without ever needing to resort to them. This means encouraging users to keep multiple copies of their important files in their home directories so that you won't be asked to mount a backup to restore a file that a user corrupted. (If your system is a standalone one then, as your own system administrator, you should make a habit of backing up your configuration and other important files.)

Restoring files from your backup media is no less important than backing them up in the first place. Be certain you can restore your files if the need arises by testing your restore process at least once during a noncritical time.

Chances are good that even if you work for a company, you'll be the one making these decisions. Your boss just wants a system that runs perfectly, all the time. Backing up is only part of the story, however. You need to formulate a plan for bringing the system back up after a failure. A system failure could be caused by any number of problems, either related to hardware or software (application, system configuration) trouble, and could range from a minor inconvenience to complete shutdown.

Hardware failures caused by improper configuration can be corrected by properly configuring the device. Sometimes hardware failures are caused by the device itself, which typically requires replacing the device. Software failures caused by improperly configured system files are usually corrected by properly configuring those files. An application can cause the system to fail for many reasons and may require a lot of research on the part of the administrator to find the root of the problem.

If you are the administrator of servers and workstations for a business, you should have a disaster recovery plan in place. Such a plan takes into account the type of data and services provided and how much *fault tolerance* your systems require – that is, how long your systems could be down and what effect that would have on your company's ability to conduct business. If you require 100 percent fault tolerance, meaning your systems must be online 24/7, then disaster recovery is unnecessary as your systems never go down and there is no disaster from which to recover. Most organizations, though, cannot afford such a high level of fault tolerance; they are willing to accept less stringent standards. Based on the level of fault tolerance you require, your disaster recovery plan should list as many possible failures as you can anticipate and detail the steps required to restore your systems. In Chapter 2, we describe fault tolerance and disaster recovery in more detail.

 TIP   Backing up is only part of the story. You need to formulate a disaster recovery plan to bring your system back up in the event of a failure.

Monitoring and Tuning Performance

The default installation of Red Hat Enterprise Linux goes a long way toward capitalizing on existing system resources. There is no "one size fits all" configuration, however. Linux is infinitely configurable, or close to it.

On a modern standalone system, Linux runs pretty quickly. If it doesn't, there's something wrong – something the system administrator can fix. Still, you might want to squeeze one last little bit of performance out of your hardware – or a number of people might be using the same file server, mail server, or other shared machine, in which case seemingly small improvements in system performance add up.

System tuning is an ongoing process aided by a variety of diagnostic and monitoring tools. Some performance decisions are made at installation time, while others are added or tweaked later. A good example is the use of the hdparm utility, which can increase throughput in IDE drives considerably; but for some high-speed modes a check of system logs shows that faulty or inexpensive cables can, in combination with hdparm, produce an enormity of nondestructive but system-slowing errors.

Proper monitoring allows you to detect a misbehaving application that consumes more resources than it should or fails to exit completely upon closing. Through the use of system performance tools you can determine when hardware – such as memory, added storage, or even something as elaborate as a hardware RAID – should be upgraded for more cost-effective use of a machine in the enterprise or for complicated computational tasks such as three-dimensional rendering.

Possibly most important, careful system monitoring and diagnostic practices give you an early heads-up when a system component is showing early signs of failure, so that you can minimize any potential downtime. Combined with the resources for determining which components are best supported by Red Hat Enterprise Linux, performance monitoring can result in replacement components which are far more robust and efficient in some cases.

In any case, careful system monitoring plus wise use of the built-in configurability of Linux allows you to squeeze the best possible performance from your existing equipment, from customizing video drivers to applying special kernel patches or simply turning off unneeded services to free memory and processor cycles.

TIP   To squeeze the best performance from your equipment, monitor your system
        carefully and use Linux's built-in configurability wisely.

Configuring a Secure System

If there is a common thread in Linux system administration, it is the security of the computer and data integrity.

What does this mean? Just about everything. The system administrator's task, first and foremost, is to make certain that no data on the machine or network are likely to become corrupted, whether by hardware or power failure, by misconfiguration or user error (to the extent that the latter can be avoided), or by malicious or inadvertent intrusion from elsewhere. It means doing all the tasks described throughout this chapter, and doing them well, with a full understanding of their implications.

No one involved in computing has failed to hear of the succession of increasingly serious attacks on machines connected to the Internet. For the most part, these attacks have not targeted Linux systems. That doesn't mean Linux systems have been entirely immune, either to direct attack or to the effects of attacks on machines running other operating systems. In one Distributed Denial of Service (DDoS) attack aimed at several major online companies, for instance, many "zombie" machines – those that had been exploited so that the vandals could employ thousands of machines instead of just a few – were running Linux that had not been patched to guard against a well-known security flaw. In the various "Code Red" attacks during the summer of 2001, Linux machines themselves were invulnerable, but the huge amount of traffic generated by this "worm" infection nevertheless prevented many Linux machines from accomplishing much Web-based work for several weeks, so fierce was the storm raging across the Internet. And few e-mail users have been immune from receiving at least some "SirCam" messages – nonsensical messages from strangers with randomly selected files attached from their machines. While this infection did not corrupt Linux machines per se, as it did those running MS Windows, anyone on a dial-up Internet connection who had to endure downloading several megabytes of infected mail each day would scarcely describe himself or herself as unaffected by the attack.

Depending on how a Linux machine is connected, and to what, the sensitivity of the data it contains and the uses to which it is put, security can be as simple as turning off unneeded services, monitoring the Red Hat security mailing list to make sure that all security advisories are followed, and otherwise engaging in good computing practices to make sure the system runs robustly. It's almost a full-time job involving levels of security permissions within the system and systems to which it is connected; elaborate firewalls to protect not just Linux machines but machines that, through their use of non-Linux software, are far more vulnerable; and physical security – making sure no one steals the machine itself!

For any machine connected to another machine, security means hardening against attacks and making certain no one else uses your machine as a platform for launching attacks against others. If you run Web, FTP, or mail servers, it means giving access to only those who are entitled to it, while locking out everyone else. It means making sure that passwords are not easily guessed and not made available to unauthorized persons. It means that disgruntled former employees no longer have access to the system and that no unauthorized person may copy files from your machines.

Security is an ongoing process. The only really secure computer is one that contains no data, is unplugged from networks and power supplies, has no keyboard attached, and resides in a locked vault. While that is theoretically true, it implies that security diminishes the usefulness of the machine. Your job as system administrator is to strike the right balance between maximum utility and maximum safety, all the while bearing in mind that confidence in a secure machine today means nothing about the machine's security tomorrow.

In the chapters that follow, you learn about the many tools that Red Hat provides to help you guard against intrusion, even to help you prevent intrusion into non-Linux machines that may reside on your network. Linux is designed from the beginning with security in mind. In all your tasks you should maintain that same security awareness.

TIP Your job as system administrator is to strike the right balance between maximum utility and maximum safety, all the while bearing in mind that confidence in a secure machine today means nothing about the machine's security tomorrow.

Using Tools to Monitor Security

People who, for purposes of larceny or to amuse themselves, like to break into computers — they're called "crackers" — are a clever bunch. If there is a vulnerability in a system, they will find it. Fortunately, the Linux development community is quick to find potential exploits and to create ways of slamming the door shut before crackers can enter. Fortunately, too, Red Hat is diligent in making available new, patched versions of packages in which potential exploits have been found. Your first and best security tool, therefore, is making sure that whenever a security advisory is issued, you download and install the repaired package. This line of defense can be annoying but it is nothing compared to rebuilding a compromised system.

As good as the bug trackers are, sometimes their job is reactive. Preventing the use of your machine for nefarious purposes and guarding against intrusion are, in the end, your responsibility alone. Red Hat equips you with tools to detect and deal with unauthorized access of many kinds. As this book unfolds, you'll learn how to install and configure these tools and how to make sense of the warnings they provide. Pay careful attention to those sections and do what they say. If your machine is connected to the Internet, you will be amazed at the number of attempts made to break into your machine. You'll be struck by how critical the issue of security is.

Summary

As you, the system administrator, read this book, bear in mind that your tasks are ongoing and that there is never a machine that is completely tuned, entirely up-to-date, and utterly secure for very long. The pace of Linux development is quite rapid, so it's important to keep current in the latest breakthroughs. This book gives you the very best information as to the Red Hat distribution you're using and tells you all you need to know about getting the most from it. Even more than that, you should read it with an eye toward developing a Linux system administrator's point of view, an understanding of how the system works as opposed to the mere performance of tasks. As the best system administrators will tell you, system administration is a state of mind.

Chapter 2

Planning the Network

IN THIS CHAPTER

- ◆ Deciding what kind of network you need

- ◆ Planning and implementing security

- ◆ Planning for fault tolerance and disaster recovery

- ◆ Writing it down — good records can save your job

WHILE YOU CAN SET UP a Red Hat Enterprise Linux network on the fly, your time will be spent most efficiently if you plan your network. Preparation reduces confusion not just now but in the future, makes provision for expansion later on, and assures that you make the best use of your resources, both budgetary and system-related. Although setting up a huge network of hundreds of nodes requires planning beyond the scope of this chapter, we explore here the fundamentals of planning and preparing for your new network installation.

Deciding What Kind of Network You Need

By definition and right out of the box, Linux is a network operating system. It is also nearly infinitely configurable: You can tailor a network to meet your precise needs. That is a tremendous strength but it can also be daunting when compared with systems that are more limited. As the philosopher James Burnham said, where there is no alternative, there is no problem.

Before you install Red Hat Enterprise Linux on anything other than a standalone box just to take a look at it, you would be well-advised to consider what kind of network you want to install, what it will be used for, what kinds of connections to the outside world it will have, and whether it is something you're likely to expand later.

Questions to ask include the following:

- ◆ What services do you wish to provide within your local network?

- ◆ Will your network be made up entirely of Linux machines or will boxes running other operating systems be connected to it?

◆ What devices (printers, scanners, and DSL, cable modem, or T-1 connections) do you plan to share?

◆ Do you intend to host a Web site or an FTP site?

◆ What security implications do you foresee?

◆ How many machines will make up your network?

It makes sense now to take notes and answer these questions. You can find details about setting up your network elsewhere in this book. But careful planning now lets you chart a clear path to developing a quick and efficient network and, perhaps even more important, helps you make sure that your network is secure from both internal and external mischief.

To learn more about setting up your network, see Chapters 10–13.

For example, many people who now enjoy DSL or cable Internet service wish to set up small networks purely to allow sharing of that broadband connection. A permanent Internet connection demands that you pay more attention to security, which means making sure you don't accidentally run any easily exploited services. If the network includes easily exploited operating systems, security becomes even more of a concern. Perhaps you will decide to set up a firewall on your Linux machine (or even set up a Linux box solely for firewall purposes). Or you might decide to employ one of the firewall-gateway-router network appliances that are gaining popularity and simply attach a hub to the appliance and attach each machine on the "network" to that hub. Such a network may not be big but it may be all you need or want.

A good rule of thumb is to provide the services your network needs — and *only* those it needs.

Chances are good that you want to do more. Even if your needs are modest at first, adding services is simple in Red Hat Linux. Some features, such as printer sharing, you'll probably set up at the beginning.

Before you do anything else, decide the physical layout, or *topology*, of your network – how machines are connected – and whether you want a peer-to-peer or client/server network. These details matter because on the one hand you can over-build your network so that your equipment isn't used efficiently; on the other hand you can underestimate the demands on the network and end up slowing down one or more machines to near uselessness.

Understanding topologies

Your network will probably be one of the first two of the following four commonly used topologies (at least for starters): star, bus, ring, and tree.

STAR TOPOLOGY

Think of this system as resembling a power strip with various devices plugged into it. In this case, instead of a power strip you have a network hub, and instead of devices requiring electricity you have devices needing and providing data. These devices might include computers, network-equipped printers, cable or DSL modems, a local network backbone, or even other hubs. Star topology networks are connected by "twisted pair" cabling, which looks like the cabling used in modular phone systems. Twisted pair cables and other devices are rated according to category (typically just called "cat"): Cat 3 uses two pairs of twisted wires as the standard for regular telephone service. Star topology networks usually use cat 5 twisted pair cabling, which has four twisted pairs and terminates in connectors called RJ-45s. (Your phone is connected with RJ-11s.) You may have up to 1,024 "nodes" – distinct machines or devices – on a star topology network, at speeds of up to 100MB per second. The newest networking technology provides even faster speeds. Figure 2-1 shows an example of a star topology network.

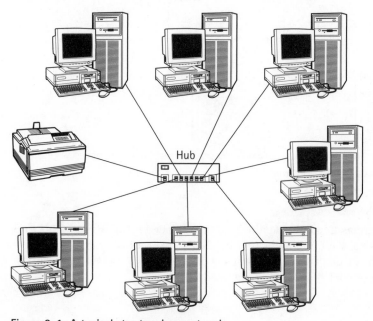

Figure 2-1: A typical star topology network

BUS TOPOLOGY

If star topology resembles a power strip with many devices plugged into it, bus topology physically resembles strings of old-fashioned Christmas tree lights, hooked together one after another. Of course, on your network there's a lot more going on than what happens on a string of lights. On a bus topology network one machine is plugged to the next, which is plugged to the next, and so on. Two types of coaxial cable hold bus topology networks together: RG-8, often called thicknet because of the thickness of the cable, and RG-58, often called thinnet because it is thinner than RG-8. RG-8 is familiar at least in general form to anyone involved in amateur radio or anyone who has ever hooked up cable television. With this kind of topology, each end of the cable is specifically terminated by use of a "terminating resistor."

Bus topology networks are limited to 30 machines. They were a very common style in early networks. While considered highly reliable, bus topology networks are not very fault tolerant because the failure of any device on the cable causes the entire network to fail. Also, their potential bandwidth (data-handling capacity) is limited to 10MB per second. Nearly all modern networks use some type of star topology with cat 5 or better cabling. Figure 2-2 shows a typical bus topology network.

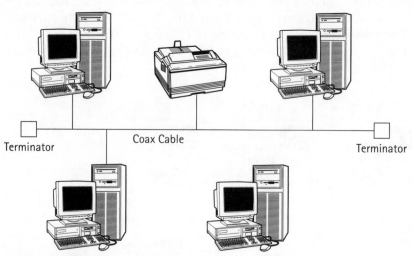

Terminator   Coax Cable   Terminator

Figure 2-2: A typical bus topology network

RING TOPOLOGY

Imagine those Christmas tree lights again. This time the end of the string plugs into its beginning, creating a loop. Popularized by IBM's Token Ring system, ring networks are relatively difficult to set up but do offer high bandwidth capabilities. Figure 2-3 shows a typical ring topology network.

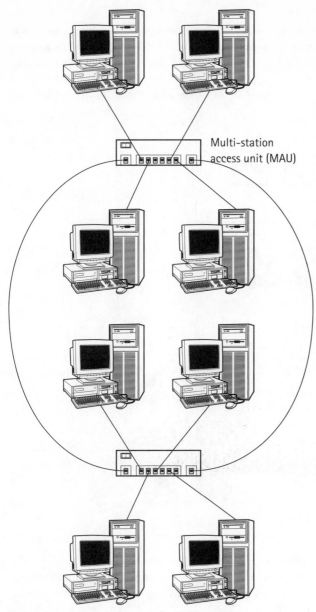

Multi-station access unit (MAU)

Figure 2-3: A typical ring topology network

TREE TOPOLOGY

Although you almost certainly won't undertake this system at the outset, you should know about it anyway. A tree network involves a high-speed "backbone" that is connected in the fashion of bus topology. However, instead of connecting individual machines, it connects groups of star topology subnetworks. Many network backbones use fiber-optic cabling to achieve high throughput. Figure 2-4 shows a typical tree topology.

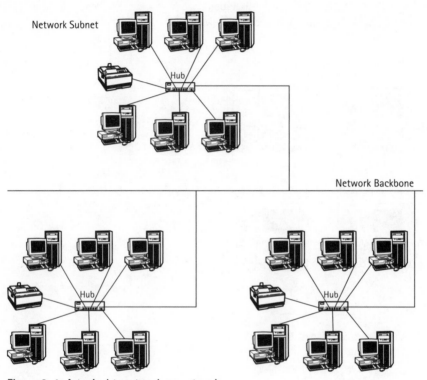

Figure 2-4: A typical tree topology network

Ultimately, your choice of network is determined by the equipment you already own and the amount of money you have to spend. If you are setting up a new network, speed, ease of configuration, and relatively low cost all argue in favor of establishing a star topology network.

Client/server or peer-to-peer?

In a *client/server* network, machines are dedicated to performing a variety of functions, in some ways like the old mainframe/dumb terminal days. You might, for instance, have a print server that handles print jobs for every computer on the network – a highly useful arrangement if, for example, yours is an enterprise that prepares many invoices, contracts, or other documents. Or you might have a file server, whose sole purpose is to serve up "boilerplate" documents or the contents of a huge database, or to serve as the repository of a big project on which many people collaborate. If your enterprise has an online presence, you may wish to dedicate one machine (or more) as a Web server, and perhaps one or more machines as an FTP (File Transfer Protocol) server, so that people can download (and upload) files. You'll probably need some kind of mail server to handle both external e-mail and messages sent within the network. Clients are machines connected to such a network. They are not servers; instead, they rely on network services provided by the server machines. Clients are usually full, freestanding workstations, although it is possible to connect dumb terminals – monitor, keyboard, pointing device – to such a network in some circumstances. In order to use the services provided by the server(s), clients need to have accounts on the desired server(s) and must log in to those accounts.

A *peer-to-peer* network resembles a client/server network in that the machines are wired to each other and some services are shared. But in a peer network, those shared items – a CD reader, perhaps, or a printer – reside on machines that are also used for other purposes. If you have a very small, low-traffic network, a peer-to-peer system might be right for you because it requires no dedicated server machine(s). Peer networking can prove impractical for high-volume operations because, for instance, multiple big print jobs will keep the poor soul who shares his printer from getting much else done.

What's in the mix?

If you are only a little bit familiar with Red Hat Enterprise Linux, your exposure to it has probably relied on industry press reports extolling its suitability as a server operating system. There is no doubt that it is indeed superb for this purpose. Don't make the mistake, though, of thinking that this is *all* it is good for. Red Hat Enterprise Linux comes with a full range of powerful and secure server applications. (Secure by industry standards, although security is a process, not a state of being.) It also comes with powerful, attractive, and easy-to-use graphical desktops and a wide range of productivity applications, communications tools, and – yes – even amusements, which make it an ideal client or peer operating system as well.

Your network may be a mixed marriage of machines of different architectures and operating systems. For instance, your graphics design department would probably rather paint with their fingers on a cave wall than use anything other than a Macintosh. Meanwhile your legacy applications, boilerplate documents, and relations with paying customers dictate that you maintain one or more Windows machines. In these cases, choose a client/server arrangement with a secure Red Hat box serving as a firewall between your network and the outside world, a mail server (it is now easy with Linux to filter out e-mail attachments of the sort that have caused so much disruption of Windows networks in recent years), a Web server if you have a presence in that milieu, and even perhaps a print server.

Although many peer functions can be performed on a mixed network, your job as system administrator is much easier if you undertake the more straightforward client/server approach with a mixed installation. Additionally, if your network includes machines running Windows and is connected to the Internet, you would be irresponsible not to set up a firewall and let Linux handle Web, FTP, and mail services. History has shown that Linux is more secure in its fundamental architecture. Beyond that, however, there are thousands of eyes constantly searching for and fixing potential security exploits. Red Hat is often first to make these fixes available, usually before the exploits are known to the cracker crowd.

 If your network includes machines running Windows and is connected to the Internet, set up a firewall and let Linux handle your Web, FTP, and mail services.

A client/server network acts very much like a small Internet: Just about any machine can connect to it and make use of its services, irrespective of its architecture or operating system.

Determining system requirements

Depending on the kind of network you choose, you need, of course, computers and any devices you intend to connect to the hub (if you're using a star-topology network). Don't forget an appropriate and supported Ethernet card for each machine — two for your firewall machine because it has one line in from the outside world and one line out to the rest of your network. You also need the appropriate cabling and, if you go the recommended star topology route, one or more hubs to support the network.

Red Hat Enterprise Linux has excellent support for a broad range of Ethernet cards. Still, there are some factors to take into consideration. If you have old, eight-bit Ethernet adapters, now is the time to replace them. They are slow and often difficult to configure. Now that 100Mbps cards are quite inexpensive, it's probably not a good idea to invest in a slower card that's slightly cheaper. Be sure to check the Red Hat hardware database at www.redhat.com/support/hardware/ before buying new cards — in fact, it's a good idea to go here to make sure that the ones you do have are fully supported if you're upgrading to Red Hat Linux. (You don't need to do this for Windows machines connected to an existing network because as long as they're properly configured for use with Windows, and as long as you continue to use Windows with them, they will work on your network, even though it's served by Red Hat machines. Of course, if you use eight-bit or older, slow peer network cards and you're going to star architecture, you need to replace them too.)

TIP If you have old, non-PCI Ethernet adapters, now is the time to replace them.

At this stage, you need to decide which headaches you're willing to accept and which ones might more sensibly be placed elsewhere. An example of this is Web and FTP hosting. For a few dollars per month, you can arrange for your Web site (and FTP site, if you have one) to be hosted by a large and secure commercial enterprise. Although it's fun to host your own site, it may be much more cost-effective to outsource those duties. The best ones have strict security rules — assigned passwords and administrator access by SSH or other highly secure methods only — and offer very high bandwidth and professional administration. With such an arrangement, you can still have your own domain and still use your own local mail server, with mail downloaded from your hosting company. (Your own SMTP mail server for outgoing mail remains on a local machine.) For many smaller companies, the cost of outsourcing is more than covered by the ability to use a low-cost cable or DSL service whose terms of use prohibit Web and FTP servers, meaning that you gain an extra level of professional service at no cost — quite a bargain. Of course, if your enterprise is of sufficient size that you have a T-1 line and a huge server farm, there's little to gain by not hosting your site yourself.

Planning and Implementing Security

We cannot overstate the importance of computer security. Practically every day there are new stories of large and small systems' being cracked by vandals and other criminals. Enterprises have been held hostage as criminals threatened to release the credit card numbers of thousands or hundreds of thousands of customers. Not long ago, the entire Internet was slowed drastically because hundreds of thousands of machines, many of whose owners weren't even aware they were running Web server software, were hijacked by a series of increasingly vicious and efficient "worm" programs that tried to corrupt other machines. The attack grew to the point where there were so many machines at work scanning the Internet for potential victims that much of the Internet's bandwidth — practically all of it in some places — was consumed. System administrators who allow machines under their control to be vulnerable to this kind of attack, when there is an alternative, are certainly not doing their job as completely as they should be.

Addressing external and internal threats

The threats from the outside world are very real and very frightening. The extent to which data on your network are safe from prying eyes or random acts of destruction is entirely up to you. But your concerns cannot stop there. While cracker attacks get all the press, there are security concerns just as real that you can find within your own network – whether it's a 500-node affair in an enterprise or a 3-node setup at home.

Imagine the damage that a disgruntled employee could do – or, for that matter, a child disappointed at being grounded. Imagine what harm a dishonest employee could bring about, upon gaining access to company accounts or company secrets – or a troubled teenager who finds your credit card number (which you should *never* put on your computer).

There is also the security issue of a user who simply makes a mistake that could have destroyed crucial data or brought down the entire system had certain security safeguards not been in place.

Take advantage of all the multiple lines of defense available, no matter the size of your network – even if you have a single standalone system that is physically accessible to others or that is connected to the Internet. Otherwise, assume that anything on your network (or the machines on it) is accessible to anyone else in the world who is a little bit determined to get it. Part V deals with security issues in great detail, but much of your security policy needs to be established before you install the network.

To learn more about security, see Chapters 29–32.

Formulating a security policy

What should your security policy consist of? It should encompass an effective password policy, general security rules, security updates, and an appropriate firewall system.

AN EFFECTIVE PASSWORD POLICY

Although the method brings grumbles from users, assigned, random passwords made up of a combination of numbers and uppercase and lowercase letters, all with no discernable meaning, are safest. (This procedure includes, most especially, the root account password.)

Who has access to what? Red Hat Enterprise Linux allows you to create special groups and assign users to them. This means that some users might have access to devices such as CD burners and modems, while others would not. You may have sensitive situations in which you do not want users to send files or even carry them from the building on a floppy disk. You can provide increased security by using groups. Although you don't necessarily have to set this up first thing, it's important to plan for and good to keep in mind.

GENERAL SECURITY RULES

A server that isn't running cannot be used to crack your system. If you're not using a server application, don't run it. Change all passwords periodically. Be prompt in removing network access of any employee who is discharged. Employ intrusion detection software and check your logs regularly for anything unusual.

SECURITY UPDATES

Do you subscribe to the Red Hat Linux security mailing list? (Find it at `www.redhat.com/mailing-lists/linux-security/index.html`.) Have you established a procedure that makes sure that every security update is downloaded and installed? Luckily for you, Red Hat has created the Red Hat Network, a program intended to help keep your system updated with the latest security updates.

Learn how to use the Red Hat Network in Chapter 23.

AN APPROPRIATE FIREWALL SYSTEM

If yours is a standalone box on a broadband connection, the bare minimum is an Internet firewall-gateway-router appliance plus iptables. If you run a Web site, set up a separate firewall machine. (The more experienced administrator could go so far as to create a custom firewall on a bootable CD and then boot the firewall machine from that CD. It is impossible to install a root kit on a CD, and the machine can have a hard drive for logging purposes.)

Security is a process — a matter of constantly outwitting people who wish your network ill. Red Hat Enterprise Linux goes a long way toward helping you beat crackers to the punch. It's up to you to make sure that your machine is not just buttoned up tightly today but continues to be secure tomorrow and the day after.

Planning for Recovery from Disasters

Rare is the professional system administrator who hasn't been awakened in the middle of the night or who had to work an entire weekend to recover from some tremendous mishap. Likewise, rare is the owner of a standalone machine who hasn't spent frantic hours trying with varying degrees of success to recover from a catastrophic failure of hardware, software, or execution.

When you plan your systems it is critical to keep in mind two important terms: fault tolerance and disaster recovery. Fault tolerance is the system's ability to respond automatically to various conditions that can affect system operation and resolve the condition. By responding automatically to a problem, fault tolerance reduces the effect of the problem on the system. Properly implemented fault tolerance is transparent to users of the system. They will continue to work, totally unaware that any problem has occurred.

Disaster recovery is the ability to restore functionality to the system after a failure has occurred. The system administrator must implement this process; it does not occur automatically. The goal of disaster recovery is to restore full functionality as quickly as possible. Depending on the degree of fault tolerance your systems have, disaster recovery may not be necessary at all.

Planning for fault tolerance and disaster recovery require that you assess the needs of your systems. The following two questions are the most important ones you should ask:

- How critical are the systems to daily operation?
- Could the systems be down and not affect operations?

Obviously, if your systems are used for business, they could not be down for long, if at all. You must determine how vital a given system is to your operation. Vital systems require greater fault tolerance than nonvital systems. Be sure to keep in mind that greater fault tolerance costs more than less fault tolerance. Another important consideration is the amount of money available for building fault tolerance into your system. Balance your need for fault tolerance with the amount of money you can spend on it.

Clustering solutions

If your systems must be up 24/7, you have to rely on a clustering solution for your fault tolerance. You basically have two choices for clustering: failover clustering and true clustering. Both of these solutions are costly to implement and require a great deal of configuration. Configuring these types of systems are well beyond the scope of this book but a brief description of the two types of clustering is useful.

Failover clustering typically requires two systems. The first system is the active system that responds to service requests. The second, failover system is an exact copy of the first system that is connected to the first system by a dedicated link. The second system uses the dedicated link to listen for a signal — called a heartbeat — from the first system at a specified interval. The second system does nothing but listen to the heartbeat signal from the first system. If the second system does not receive the signal, it assumes that the first system has gone offline and immediately begins accepting requests for services. When the first system comes back online, the second system returns to monitoring the heartbeat signal.

True clustering uses multiple systems, usually more than two, that act as a single system. Network services run on each system and requests for services are distributed between the systems. Each system is connected to every other system by a dedicated link. Unlike the second system in failover clustering that only listens for the heartbeat, the systems in true clustering handle requests for services. If a system does go down, the requests for service are just sent to the other systems, which take up the slack. Both clustering solutions do not employ disaster recovery. Because they must be up 100 percent of the time, there is no disaster from which to recover, except perhaps the disaster to your budget because the cost of implementing such a system is quite high.

Disaster recovery

For systems that do not require 100 percent uptime, disaster recovery is the method used. A typical solution is to configure an identical system and keep it ready for service. Placing the other system into service requires intervention by the administrator and no services will be possible during this time. Service can usually be restored fairly quickly using this method and the cost is less than a clustering solution.

The least costly method (in hardware) of dealing with system problems is to fix them after they have occurred. Here you shut down the system until it is fixed; no services are available during the repair. For example, if the hard drive in your system crashes, you simply replace the hard drive. This is the least costly method of dealing with a system problem.

System administrators who plan their network well may not be able to prevent disasters entirely, but they greatly reduce the likelihood of such events taking place and make complete or near-complete recovery a quick and orderly process.

Planning for recovery ideally involves considering everything bad that can possibly happen and figuring out a way around it. However, that which is ideal often does not square with what's practical, especially when it involves spending money to guard against an infinitesimal likelihood. Fortunately, the things that save you from likely disasters save you from the most unlikely ones, too.

Just as security planning requires attention to threats from outside and inside the network, there are two parts to disaster planning. The first is doing everything you can to prevent a catastrophe from taking place.

Only you, or other administrators at your organization, know how important your system is and how much money is budgeted to keep it running. Chances are good that an uninterruptible power supply (UPS) that keeps the network up long enough to save and close files and shut down the system in an orderly fashion fits within the available budget. A good UPS system is especially useful if your enterprise has a generator backup that kicks on in the event of power failure because generators do not always start instantly and, when they do, the electricity provided is not always clean enough for computer use. A battery backup can protect you from both of these potential problems. If your enterprise is important enough to have an emergency generator, it's probably important enough to keep the network running.

Renegade electricity is one of the worst enemies of system reliability. Small power strips with surge suppression are better than nothing, but more robust power conditioning is needed if really important equipment and data are to be protected. In fact, be sure to protect all lines from the outside world that attach to your computer or its peripherals, be they phone lines or cable or DSL connections. Likewise, put the peripherals themselves on protected circuits.

Second, formulate a regular (daily or better) backup scheme, with one set of backups stored in a safe place off site as protection against loss of data in the event of fire, flood, tornado, or other physical disaster. One way of making this process relatively painless, albeit an expensive one, is to rent storage from a commercial operation whose business is storing other people's data. The best firms are very responsive and secure.

Redundancy is also important. Make sure your plans don't put critical data on only one machine. That way, in the event of a machine failure, a replacement machine with a copy of your critical data can be put online very quickly. This is some, but not all, of the theory behind RAID (redundant array of independent disks) systems, in which multiple hard drives in the same machine contain the same data. RAID is good protection in case any one drive fails (the best RAIDs allow hot-swapping of drives so that a replacement can be added without bringing the system down), but it also allows for much faster data access, making it especially useful for file server machines. Don't be lulled into complacency by a RAID, though — there are computer failure modes that can render an entire system useless. In keeping with Murphy's law, the worst failures and calamities occur at the worst possible time — just before the rollout of a new product, just as the monthly billing is scheduled to go out, in the middle of the worst blizzard in 10 years, or most of the computer staff is on vacation or out sick. You need to establish an emergency response policy that takes these examples, and there are many others, into account. This involves convincing your employer of the necessity of sufficient staff to guard against such horrors, or even the employment of an outside firm to augment your own staff in the event of an especially ill-timed disaster. If your company follows the latter route, it's well worth the investment of time and money to make sure that the outside firm's representatives tour and learn your network on a day when everything is working smoothly.

Some of this planning is far more elaborate than anything you're likely to undertake if you have only a small household network or a very small office; on the other hand, if you're in a very large enterprise, data security and system integrity involve issues and procedures far beyond the scope of this book. Everything mentioned in this section, however, can be scaled to fit any network.

Writing It Down – Good Records Can Save Your Job

A very important part of network planning is to put it all down on paper and to save that piece of paper. Working out your network's design is best done by actually diagramming the network, making multiple diagrams to explore different strategies. Once you settle on a design, draw a more formal diagram. Sometimes it's a good idea to save your discarded designs as well, with a note on each version explaining why it wasn't chosen. Formalizing the network design and saving the discarded ideas is useful for several reasons. It bolsters your decisions in case you're second-guessed, it demonstrates that you considered all the possibilities, and the formal diagram is a valuable tool should someone need to administer the system in your absence.

A written security policy is essential in the enterprise, and not a bad idea even for a home network. An additional security file you should always keep is a full security log. Such a record might begin by detailing what security measures you have designed into the system. It should include copies of any security notices you have received, as well as an initialed notation of when the recommended security patch was applied. If log files show an attempted crack of your network, hard copies of the relevant portions should be kept there, too.

When users or management complain about how you have the system so tight that it seems inconvenient even for them to log in, there's nothing like proving that the system is regularly under attack – and it will be, by port scanners and others – to demonstrate the wisdom of tight security. One very big company has made huge amounts of money by putting user convenience over security, and many companies have paid a high price for adopting their products. Your Red Hat system costs a very small amount of user inconvenience in exchange for greatly enhanced system security. It's useful to be able to prove that the threat is real.

A security log is also the place to keep copies of any security-related e-mail messages from within the company, from log listings of employees who have decided to "go exploring" (which is sometimes but not always a sign of bad intent) to exchanges with management over the implementation of new security features. This file is not something for general consumption, but it's very important. Keep a copy locked away at work, and it won't hurt to keep a copy safely off site, too.

To learn more about writing a security policy, see Chapter 29.

While your security log should detail actions you have taken to prevent disaster and actions you have recommended in that regard, your plan of action in the event of a catastrophe should also be committed to paper and should be well known and easily available. If you are the sole administrator, it is far better to work out your plan of action calmly and ahead of time, which of course you will have done. But under the stress of an actual emergency, it is easy to forget important details. Having a specific plan on paper right in front of you is a big help and a great stress reliever. Your action plan should be sufficiently detailed so that if the disaster takes place while you are away, any competent system administrator can use it to bring the system back up. If you are part of a larger department, include the assignments of others in restoring the system. In either case, someone who is completely trusted and who is never on vacation at the same time you are should know the root's password. Alternately, the password can be placed in a sealed envelope inside the company safe — the one time it is allowable to put a password on paper.

TIP Keep a hard copy of your security log in a safe place!

We're all happy with the idea of the paperless office, but until computers become perfectly reliable, paper — as a roadmap indicating where you are and how you arrived there — will remain necessary.

Summary

In this chapter you learned the importance of planning your network before you begin to construct it, discovered some of the options available to you, and found out some of the reasons why you might choose one over another. You learned that network security is a never-ending task made easier by careful planning and that threats can come both from outside the network and from among its users. Working to prevent catastrophic failures and having a plan to recover from them is something you've learned to do. You now know the importance of putting it all on paper as you proceed, too.

Chapter 3

Standard Installation

IN THIS CHAPTER

◆ Exploring your PC's components

◆ Checking for supported hardware

◆ Starting the installation

◆ Configuring Red Hat Enterprise Linux installation

◆ Selecting packages to install

THIS CHAPTER EXPLAINS the steps necessary to install Red Hat Enterprise Linux on a single system. You begin by making a list of your PC's hardware. You use this hardware inventory later when you begin the installation.

 When you purchase an official Red Hat Enterprise Linux boxed set, you are eligible for installation support from Red Hat. Also, an online installation manual is available on the Red Hat Web site at www.redhat.com/docs.

Exploring Your PC's Components

Before installing Red Hat Enterprise Linux, you should compile a list of the hardware components in your computer. Linux supports different types of hardware through software components called *device drivers*, similar to other operating systems. A driver is required for each type of peripheral device; depending on the age of your hardware, a driver may not be available. If your hardware is current, meaning less than two years old, the drivers you need are probably available and included with the distribution. If you need a driver that is not included with the distribution, searching the Internet usually provides you with a solution.

You can install and run Red Hat Enterprise Linux even if no Linux drivers are available for certain devices. Of course, those devices won't function, but this may not be a problem for you depending on the device. To be able to install Red Hat

Enterprise Linux, you must have a compatible processor, bus type, floppy disk, hard disk, video card, monitor, keyboard, mouse, and CD-ROM drive. If you are planning to use a graphical user interface (GUI) such as GNOME or KDE, you must ensure that XFree86 (the X Window System for Linux) supports the mouse, video card, and monitor. Nearly all devices made within the past two years are supported.

The following sections briefly describe the PC hardware supported by Red Hat Enterprise Linux. Your hardware list should contain information about the hardware described here before you begin to install Red Hat Enterprise Linux on your PC.

Processor

The *central processing unit (CPU)* – or just *the processor* – is an integrated circuit chip that performs nearly all control and processing functions in the PC. Red Hat Enterprise Linux runs on an Intel 80386 processor or newer, as well as compatibles made by AMD or Cyrix. However, you probably don't want to use any processor older than a Pentium-class processor. Red Hat Linux also supports motherboards with multiple processors that use the *symmetric multiprocessing (SMP)* Linux kernel.

Bus

The *bus* provides the electrical connection between the processor and its peripherals. Several types of PC buses exist on the motherboard with slots to accept peripheral components. Each of the slots is colored to help in its identification. The most recent is the *Peripheral Component Interconnect (PCI)* bus, and it is found on all current production motherboards. The PCI slot is white, and is available in 32- and 64-bit form as well as 33 and 64 MHz. Another type of slot is also used by the PCI bus, the *Accelerated Graphics Port (AGP)*; it is a special slot on the motherboard designed to accept an AGP graphics card. The AGP slot is brown. Another is the *Industry Standard Architecture (ISA)* bus, formerly called the AT bus because IBM introduced it in the IBM PC-AT computer in 1984. The ISA bus is black. Other, less frequently encountered buses because of their aging status include *Extended Industry Standard Architecture (EISA)*; *VESA local (VL-bus)*; and *Micro Channel Architecture (MCA)*. Red Hat Enterprise Linux supports all of these buses.

Memory

Referred to as *random-access memory,* or *RAM*, memory is not a consideration in determining compatibility. For good performance though, you need at least 64MB of RAM for a text install, and 128MB for a graphical install. If you are planning to run the X Window System to be able to use a GUI on the PC, you need even more memory because the X Window System manages the graphical interface through an X server, which is a large program that needs a lot of memory to run efficiently. Red Hat recommends 192MB for a graphical installation.

If you are buying a new PC, it probably comes with 128MB or more RAM. If you can afford it, buy as much RAM as you can. The more RAM a system has, the more efficiently it runs multiple programs (because the programs can all fit in memory). Red Hat Linux can use a part of the hard disk as virtual memory. Such disk-based memory, called *swap space*, is much slower than physical memory.

Video card and monitor

If you are not planning to use the X Window system, any video card works. Red Hat Enterprise Linux supports all video cards in text mode. If you are planning to use the X Window system, be sure to find a video card that is supported by *XFree86,* which is the version of the X Window System used in Red Hat Linux. You can save yourself a lot of aggravation if your video card is supported by XFree86.

Your choice of monitors depends on your use of the X Window system. For text mode displays, typically used on servers, any monitor will do. If you are setting up a workstation, or using the X Window system on your server, choose a monitor that supports the display resolution you use. Resolution is expressed in terms of the number of picture elements, or *pixels*, horizontally and vertically (such as 1024 × 768).

XFree86's support for a video card depends on the *video chipset* — the integrated circuit that controls the monitor and causes the monitor to display output. You can find out the name of the video chipset used in a video card from the card's documentation.

Your video card's name may not be in the list at the Red Hat site. The important thing to note is the name of the video chipset. Many popular video cards made by different manufacturers use the same video chipsets. Look for the name of the video chipsets listed at the Red Hat site. In nearly all cases, the Red Hat installation program automatically detects the video chipset as it sets up the X Window System.

Hard drive

Red Hat Enterprise Linux supports any IDE hard drive that your PC's *Basic Input/Output System (BIOS)* supports, as long as the system BIOS supports the hard drive without any additional drivers.

For hard drives connected to your PC through a *SCSI (Small Computer System Interface)* controller card, Red Hat Linux must have a driver that enables the SCSI controller to access and use the hard drive.

As for the size (storage capacity) of the drive, most new systems seem to have drives 20GB or larger. You should buy the highest capacity drive you can afford.

Floppy disk drive

Linux drivers use the PC BIOS to access the floppy disk drive, so any floppy disk drive is compatible with Red Hat Enterprise Linux. The Red Hat installation program can be started from the CD-ROM if your PC has one and is able to boot from it. If not, you have to boot Red Hat Linux from a floppy disk drive during the installation, so you need a high-density 3.5-inch (1.44MB capacity) floppy disk drive. You can also avoid booting from a floppy if you can boot your PC under MS-DOS (not an MS-DOS window under Windows 95/98/2000), and you can access the CD-ROM from the DOS command prompt.

Keyboard and mouse

Red Hat Enterprise Linux supports any keyboard that already works with your PC. The mouse, however, needs explicit support in Red Hat Linux. You need a mouse if you want to configure and run XFree86, the X Window System for Linux. Red Hat Linux supports most popular mice, including the commonly found PS/2 and USB mouse. Red Hat Linux also supports touch pad devices, such as ALPS GlidePoint, as long as they are compatible with one of the supported mice.

SCSI controller

The Small Computer System Interface, commonly called *SCSI* (and pronounced "skuzzy"), is a standard way of connecting many types of peripheral devices to a computer. SCSI is used in many kinds of computers, from servers to high-end UNIX workstations to PCs. Typically, you connect hard drives and CD-ROM drives through a *SCSI controller*. To use a SCSI device on your PC, you need a SCSI controller card that plugs into one of the bus connector slots on your PC's bus.

If you want to access and use a SCSI device under Linux, you have to make sure that Red Hat Linux supports your SCSI controller card.

CD/DVD-R/RW drive

CD-R (compact disc read-only) drives are popular because each CD-ROM can hold up to 650MB of data, a relatively large amount of storage compared with a floppy disk. CD-ROMs are reliable and inexpensive to manufacture. Vendors can use a CD-ROM to distribute a large amount of information at a reasonable cost..

DVD-ROM drives are found already installed on many new systems. DVD-ROM discs are capable of storing up to 4.7GB and are most frequently used to record digital video, but can be used to hold any data.

CD-RW and DVD-R/RW and DVD+R/RW drives are used to create CDs and DVDs, respectively. Either of these types of drives can be used in your Red Hat system. The most important consideration is the bus that the drive will use. Any IDE/ATAPI compatible drive, as well as SCSI drives, will work with Red Hat Enterprise Linux.

Sound card

If you are configuring a server, you probably aren't too interested in playing sounds. But with Red Hat Enterprise Linux you can play sound on a sound card to enjoy multimedia programs and games. If you have a sound card, you can also play audio CDs. Nearly all sound cards available today, whether built into the mother-board or a separate card that plugs into a bus socket, are supported.

Network card

A *network interface card (NIC)* is necessary if you connect your Red Hat Linux PC to a *local area network (LAN)*, which is usually an Ethernet network. If you are config-uring a server, you certainly want to configure at least one network card. Red Hat Enterprise Linux supports a variety of Ethernet network cards. ARCnet and IBM's Token Ring network are also supported. Check the hardware list on the Red Hat site to see if your NIC is supported. Nearly all NICs currently in use are supported.

For any Red Hat Linux PC connected to a network, you need the following information:

♦ Host name of the PC

♦ Domain name of the network

♦ Internet Protocol (IP) address of the PC (or, if the IP address is provided by a DHCP server, the server's address)

♦ Address of the gateway

♦ IP address of name servers

 If you plan to use DHCP to obtain your IP information, you do not need to specify the IP information in the above list.

Checking for Supported Hardware

To check if Red Hat Enterprise Linux supports the hardware in your PC, follow these steps:

1. Make a list of the make, model, and other technical details of all hardware installed in your PC. Most of this information is in the manuals that came with your hardware. If you don't have the manuals, and you already have an operating system on the PC, you may be able to obtain this informa-tion from that operating system.

2. Go to the Red Hat Web site at `www.redhat.com/hardware`. Compare your hardware list to the list of hardware that the latest version of Red Hat Linux supports. If the components listed earlier are supported, you can prepare to install Red Hat.

You do not need a boot disk if you can start your PC from your CD-ROM drive. The first installation disk is a bootable CD-ROM and can be used to start the installation process. If you can boot from your CD-ROM, skip to the Starting the Red Hat Linux Installation section. If you are unable to boot from your CD-ROM drive, continue to the next section, Creating the Red Hat Boot Disk, and then go to the Installation section.

Creating the Red Hat Boot Disk

To boot Red Hat Enterprise Linux for the first time and start the Red Hat Linux installation program, you need a Red Hat boot disk. For this step, you should turn on your PC without any disk in the A drive and run Windows as usual.

You do not need a boot disk if you can start your PC under MS-DOS (not an MS-DOS window in Windows 95) and access the CD-ROM from the DOS command prompt. If you run Windows 95/98, restart the PC in MS-DOS mode. However, you may not be able to access the CD-ROM in MS-DOS mode because the startup files (`AUTOEXEC.BAT` and `CONFIG.SYS`) may not be configured correctly. To access the CD-ROM from DOS, you typically must add a CD-ROM driver in `CONFIG.SYS` and add a line in `AUTOEXEC.BAT` that runs the MSCDEX program. Try restarting your PC in MS-DOS mode and see if the CD-ROM can be accessed.

The Red Hat boot disk starts your PC and the Red Hat Linux installation program. After you install Red Hat Linux, you no longer need the Red Hat boot disk (except when you want to reinstall Red Hat Linux from the CD-ROMs).

The Red Hat boot disk contains an initial version of the Red Hat Linux installation program that you use to start Red Hat Enterprise Linux, prepare the hard disk, and load the rest of the installation program. Creating the Red Hat boot disk involves using a utility program called `RAWRITE.EXE` to copy a special file called the Red Hat Linux *boot image* to a disk.

To create the Red Hat boot disk under Windows, follow these steps:

1. In Windows 95/98/ME open an MS-DOS window (select Start →
   Programs → MS-DOS Prompt). In Windows 2000 or XP, select Start →
   Run and enter **cmd** in the dialog box.

2. In the MS-DOS window, enter the following commands at the MS-DOS
   prompt. (Our comments are in parentheses and your input is in boldface.)

   ```
   d:    (use the drive letter for the CD-ROM drive)
   cd \dosutils
   rawrite
   Enter disk image source file name: \images\boot.img
   Enter target diskette drive: a
   Please insert a formatted diskette into drive A: and press -
   ENTER- :
   ```

3. As instructed, you should put a formatted disk into your PC's A drive and
   press Enter. RAWRITE.EXE copies the boot-image file to the disk.

When the DOS prompt returns, remove the Red Hat boot disk from the floppy drive
and label it as a Red Hat boot disk.

Starting the Installation

To start the Red Hat Linux installation, power up the PC and put the Red Hat
Installation CD-ROM 1 (and the boot disk if you created one) into your PC's
CD-ROM drive (and floppy drive if applicable). The PC boots Red Hat Linux and
begins running the Red Hat installation program. The Red Hat installation program
controls the installation of the operating system.

 If you are using a boot disk that you created, be sure to place the first installation CD-ROM in the CD-ROM drive after you start the PC. The installation
program looks for the Red Hat Linux CD-ROMs to start the installation in
graphical mode. If the installation program can't find the CD-ROM, the installation program starts in text mode and prompts for it.

A few moments after you start the boot process, an initial screen appears. The
screen displays a welcome message and ends with a boot: prompt. The welcome
message tells you that more information is available by pressing one of the function
keys F1 through F5.

If you want to read the help screens, press the function key corresponding to the help you want. If you don't press any keys after a short delay, the boot process proceeds with the loading of the Linux kernel into the PC's memory. To start booting Red Hat Enterprise Linux immediately, press Enter. After the Linux kernel loads, it automatically starts the Red Hat Linux installation program. This, in turn, starts the X Window System, which provides a graphical user interface for the installation.

You should compile all the configuration information explained earlier in this chapter before you begin. If the installation program detects your hardware, installing Red Hat Linux from the CD-ROM on a fast (200 MHz or better) Pentium PC should take 30 to 40 minutes.

 During installation, the Red Hat installation program tries to determine the hardware in your PC and alters the installation steps as required. For example, if the installation program detects a network card, the program displays the appropriate network configuration screens. If a network card is not detected, the network configuration screens are not displayed. So, depending on your specific hardware, the screens you see during installation may differ from those shown in this section.

 If you run into any problems during the installation, refer to Chapter 33 to learn how to troubleshoot common installation problems.

You go through the following steps before moving on to disk setup and installation:

1. The installation program starts the X Window System and displays a list of languages to use during the installation in a graphical installation screen, as shown in Figure 3-1. Use your mouse to select the language you want to use for installation and then click the Next button to proceed to the next step.

 In the graphical installation, each screen has online help available on the left side of the screen. You can read the help message to learn more about what you are supposed to select in a specific screen.

Figure 3-1: Choosing the installation language

2. The installation program displays a list of keyboard language layouts, as shown in Figure 3-2. Select a keyboard language layout appropriate to the language you desire.

3. The installation program displays a screen (see Figure 3-3) from which you can configure the mouse in your system. The various mouse types are listed in a tree structure organized alphabetically by manufacturer. You need to know your mouse type and whether it is connected to the PC's serial port or the PS/2 port. If your mouse type appears in the list, select it. Otherwise, select a generic mouse type. Most new PCs have a PS/2 mouse, and some may even have a USB mouse. Finally, for a two-button mouse, you should select the Emulate 3 Buttons option. Because many X applications assume that you use a three-button mouse, you should select this option. On a typical two-button mouse, you can simulate a middle-button click by pressing both buttons simultaneously. On a Microsoft IntelliMouse, the wheel acts as the middle button.

If you select a mouse with a serial interface, you are asked to specify the serial port where the mouse is connected. For COM1, specify /dev/ttyS0 as the device; for COM2, the device name is /dev/ttyS1.

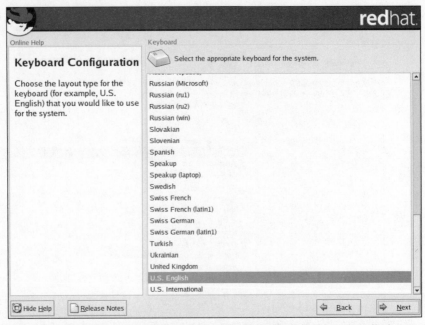

Figure 3-2: Selecting a keyboard configuration during Red Hat Linux installation

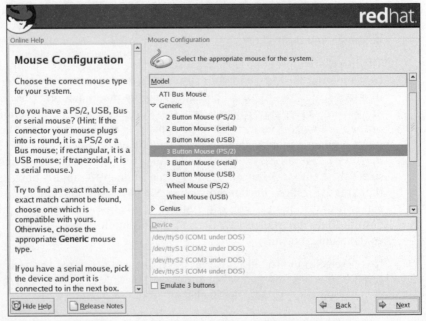

Figure 3-3: Configuring your mouse during Red Hat Linux installation

4. The installation program displays a welcome message that provides some helpful information, including a suggestion that you access the online manuals at www.redhat.com. Click the Next button to proceed.

5. The installation program displays a screen asking if you want to install a new system or upgrade an older Red Hat installation.

    For a new installation, the installation program requires you to select the installation type: *Workstation, Server,* or *Custom.* The Workstation and Server installations simplify the installation process by partitioning the disk in a predefined manner. A Workstation-class installation deletes all currently existing Linux-related partitions. A Server-class installation deletes all existing disk partitions, including any existing Windows partitions. Regardless of the installation type chosen, you will still be given the opportunity to change the system partitions if you desire. For maximum flexibility (so you can specify how the disk is used), select the Custom installation.

The next major phase of installation involves partitioning the hard disk.

Partitioning the Hard Disk

Red Hat Enterprise Linux requires you to partition and prepare a hard disk before you can begin installation. For a new PC, you usually do not perform this step because the vendor normally takes care of preparing the hard disk and installing Windows and all other applications on the hard disk. Because you are installing Red Hat Enterprise Linux from scratch, however, you have to perform this crucial step yourself. As you see in the following sections, this task is just a matter of following instructions.

The Red Hat Linux installation program offers you several choices for partitioning your hard drive. You can choose to have the installation program automatically partition your disk, you can choose to use Disk Druid, or you can use fdisk. For this installation, choose Disk Druid, a utility program that enables you to partition the disk and, at the same time, specify which parts of the Linux file system you want to load on which partition.

Before you begin to use Disk Druid to partition your disk, you need to know how to refer to the disk drives and partitions in Linux. Also, you should understand the terms *mount points* and *swap partition*. In the next three sections, you learn these terms and concepts and then proceed to use Disk Druid.

Naming disks and devices

If you are experienced with Unix or Linux, this section and the two following are quite basic to you. If you are already familiar with Unix and Linux file systems and naming conventions, skip to the section titled "Preparing Disk Partition." The first step is to understand how Red Hat Enterprise Linux refers to the various disks. Linux treats all devices as files and has actual files that represent each device. In Red Hat Linux, these *device files* are located in the /dev directory. If you are new to UNIX, you may not yet know about UNIX file names. But you'll learn more as you continue to use Red Hat Linux. If you know how MS-DOS file names work, you find that Linux file names are similar. However, they have two exceptions: they do not use drive letters (such as A and C) and they substitute the slash (/) for the MS-DOS backslash (\) as the separator between directory names.

Because Linux treats a device as a file in the /dev directory, the hard disk names start with /dev. Table 3-1 lists the hard disk and floppy drive names that you may have to use.

TABLE 3-1 HARD DISK AND FLOPPY DRIVE NAMES

Name	Description
/dev/hda	First Integrated Drive Electronics (IDE) hard drive (the C drive in DOS and Windows) connected to the first IDE controller as the master drive
/dev/hdb	Second (IDE) hard drive connected to the first IDE controller as the slave drive
/dev/hdc	First (IDE) hard drive connected to the second IDE controller as the master drive
/dev/hdd	Second (IDE) hard drive connected to the second IDE controller as the slave drive
/dev/sda	First Small Computer System Interface (SCSI) drive
/dev/sdb	Second SCSI drive
/dev/fd0	First floppy drive (the A drive in DOS)
/dev/fd1	Second floppy drive (the B drive in DOS)

When Disk Druid displays the list of partitions, the partition names take the form hda1, hda2, and so on. Linux constructs each partition name by appending the partition number (1 through 4 for the four primary partitions

on a hard disk) to the disk's name. Therefore, if your PC's single IDE hard drive
has two partitions, notice that the installation program uses hda1 and hda2
as the names of these partitions.

Mounting a file system on a device

In Red Hat Enterprise Linux, you use a physical disk partition by associating it with
a specific part of the file system. This arrangement is a hierarchical directory — a
directory tree. If you have more than one disk partition (you may have a second
disk with a Linux partition), you can use all of them in Red Hat Linux under a single directory tree. All you have to do is decide which part of the Linux directory
tree should be located on each partition — a process known in Linux as *mounting a
file system on a device*. (The disk partition is a device.)

The term *mount point* refers to the directory you associate with a disk partition or any other device.

Suppose you have two disks on your PC and you have created Linux partitions
on both disks. Figure 3-4 illustrates how you can mount different parts of the Linux
directory tree (the *file system*) on these two partitions.

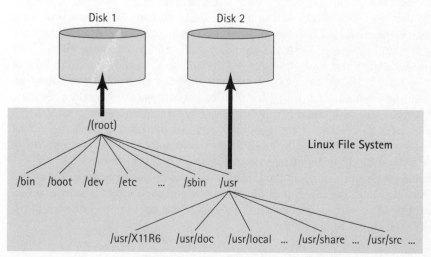

Figure 3-4: Mounting the Red Hat Linux file system on two disk partitions

Understanding the swap partition

Most advanced operating systems support the concept of *virtual memory*, in which part of your system's hard disk functions as an extension of the physical memory (RAM). When the operating system runs out of physical memory, it can move (or swap out) the contents of currently unneeded parts of RAM to make room for a program that needs more memory. When the operating system needs to access anything in the swapped-out data, it has to find something else to swap out and then it swaps in the required data from disk. This process of swapping data back and forth between the RAM and the disk is also known as *paging*.

Because the disk is much slower than RAM, the system's performance is slower when the operating system has to perform a lot of paging. However, virtual memory enables you to run programs that you otherwise can't run.

Red Hat Enterprise Linux supports virtual memory and can make use of a swap partition. When you create the Linux partitions, you should also create a swap partition. With the Disk Druid utility program, described in the next section, creating a swap partition is easy. Simply mark a partition type as a swap device, choose the size, and let Disk Druid perform the necessary tasks.

Preparing disk partitions

After you select Custom installation, a screen prompts you for the method you want to use to partition the disk – the choices are automatically partition or manually partition with Disk Druid. You should select Disk Druid and click the Next button. You should then see the Disk Druid screen (as shown in Figure 3-5).

Before beginning to partition the drive, consider exactly how you want to create the partitions. Most people typically create one partition on the drive to be used as the root (/) partition. This works well in most cases, but it can cause some problems. If the root partition should become full, the system could crash. Many times the partition fills up because of system logging, e-mail, and print queue files. These files are all written to the /var directory by default, so it would be a good idea to create a separate partition for /var to prevent the root partition from filling up with system logs, e-mail, and print files. You might also want to create a separate partition for your user's home directories if you have a large number of users.

You also need to create a swap partition. A swap partition is used for virtual memory to hold data that is too large to fit into system RAM. Your swap partition should be at least 32MB or two times your system's RAM, whichever is larger.

Disk Druid gathers information about the hard drives on your system and displays a list of disk drives in the lower part of the screen and the current partition information for one of the drives in the Partitions area in the upper part. For each partition, Disk Druid shows seven fields:

◆ **Device** refers to the partition's device name. For example, `hda1` is the first partition on the first IDE drive.

◆ **Mount Point/RAID/Volume** indicates the directory where the partition will be mounted. For example, if you have only one partition for the entire Linux file system, the mount point is the root directory (/). For the swap partition, this field shows `<Swap>`. If this field appears as `<not set>`, you have to specify a mount point. To do so, select the partition and click the Edit button.

◆ The **Type** field shows the partition's file type, such as ext3, swap, or DOS.

◆ The **Format** field shows a check mark if the partition will be formatted and is blank if the partition will not be formatted.

◆ The **Size** field shows the amount of disk space the partition is using.

◆ **Start** and **End** are the beginning and ending cylinders on the hard drive used by the partition.

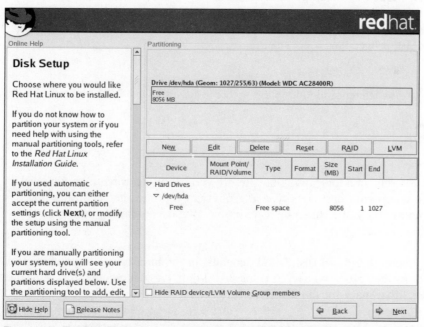

Figure 3-5: The Disk Druid screen from the Red Hat Linux installation program

If there are no partitions defined, the table in the Partitions list is empty. You have to add new partitions by clicking the Add button.

You perform specific disk setup tasks in Disk Druid through the six buttons that run across the middle of the screen. Specifically, the buttons perform the following actions:

◆ **New** enables you to create a new partition, assuming there is enough free disk space available. When you click this button, another dialog box appears in which you can fill in information necessary to create a partition.

◆ **Edit** enables you to alter the attributes of the partition currently highlighted in the Partitions list. You make changes to the current attribute in another dialog box that appears when you click the Edit button.

◆ **Delete** removes the partition currently highlighted in the Partitions list.

◆ **Reset** causes Disk Druid to ignore any changes that you may have made.

◆ **RAID** sets up a *RAID (Redundant Array of Independent Disks)* device – a technique that combines multiple disks to improve reliability and data transfer rates. There are several types of RAID configurations. This button is active only if your system has the hardware necessary to support a RAID device.

    The reference to RAID in this section is for a software RAID configuration.

◆ **LVM** sets up a logical volume. Before you can use this feature, you need to set up your partitions type as a physical volume. Then choosing this option lets you create a logical volume to make managing the physical disks easier.

Exactly what you do in Disk Druid depends on the hard drives in your PC and the partitions they already have. For this discussion, we assume you are using the entire hard drive space for the Red Hat installation.

Setting up the partitions

To prepare a new hard drive to install Red Hat Enterprise Linux, you have to perform the following steps in Disk Druid.

Create a new partition for the Linux file system. To do this, click the New button on the Disk Druid screen. You should see a dialog box (see Figure 3-6) containing the following fields, which you need to fill in:

♦ **Mount Point** shows the place in the file system where the partition will be mounted. You can enter a mount point or click the down arrow to open the drop-down menu and choose a mount point from the list.

♦ **File System Type** is the type of filesystem you want the partition to be. Click on the down arrow to open the drop-down menu and choose the filesystem type. The most common choices here are ext2, ext3, and swap.

♦ **Allowable Drives** shows the installed hard drives. A check mark in the box means that the drive is available for creating partitions. Click to highlight the drive you want to use for the partitions.

♦ **Size (MB)** is the field where you can set the size of the partition. The default size is 100MB but you can set the size to whatever you desire.

♦ **Additional Size Options** lets you set other size restrictions by clicking on the radio button. Fixed Size is the default. If you choose Fill All Space Up To, you need to enter a number in the field provided. Fill to Maximum Allowable Size will use all remaining space on the drive.

♦ **Force to Be a Primary Partition** lets you set the drive as either a primary or logical partition. Primary partitions are the first four partitions on the hard drive.

♦ **Check for Bad Blocks,** if checked, will cause the installation program to do a physical scan of the drive to find and mark any blocks that may be bad. This prevents the system from attempting to write data to such areas of the disk. Keep in mind that checking this box will slow down the installation process depending on the size of your hard drive.

After you have filled in the field with your choices, click OK to return to the Disk Druid main screen.

Create another new partition and set it as a Linux swap space. To do this, click the New button in the Disk Druid screen (refer to Figure 3-5). In the dialog box shown in Figure 3-6, enter the size of the partition. Click the list of partition types and select Linux Swap as the type. When you do so, <Swap Partition> appears in the Mount Point field. Enter the size of the swap partition and any other parameters you desire. Next, click OK to define the new partition and return to the Disk Druid screen.

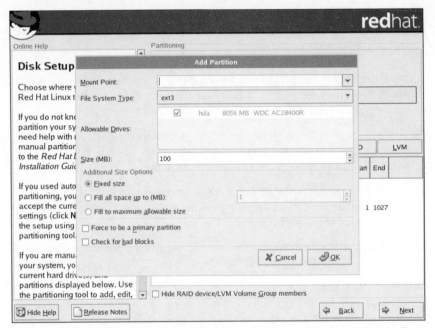

Figure 3-6: The Add Partition dialog box in which you establish the attributes of a new partition

After you finish specifying the partitions in Disk Druid, the Disk Druid screen will display the details: partition number, file type, size, and starting and ending cylinders. A check mark in the Format column indicates that the partition will be formatted. If you wish to change the mount point of the partition, highlight it and click the Edit button. If you want to make any other changes to the partition, you will have to delete it and create a new one. If you are satisfied with your selections, click Next.

If you have multiple disk partitions mounted on different directories of the Linux file system and you are upgrading an existing installation, you do not have to format any partitions in which you want to preserve existing data. For example, if you have all user directories on a separate disk partition mounted on the /home directory, you do not have to format that partition.

You have now completed the disk preparation phase of the installation. The installation program performs the actual formatting of the partitions after it asks for some more configuration information, including the packages you want to install.

Configuring the Installation

After you prepare the disk partitions with Disk Druid and specify which partitions to format, the installation program moves on to some configuration steps. The typical configuration steps are as follows:

- Install GRUB

- Configure the network

- Set the time zone

- Set the root password and add user accounts

- Configure password authentication

The following sections guide you through each of these configuration steps.

Installing the boot loader

The Red Hat installation program displays the Boot Loader Configuration screen (see Figure 3-7), which asks you where you want to install the boot loader. A boot loader is a program that resides on your disk and starts Red Hat Enterprise Linux from the hard disk. Red Hat provides *GRUB (Grand Unified Bootloader)* as the default boot loader.

The GRUB boot loader is selected as the default choice on this screen. Clicking on the Change Boot Loader button lets you choose LILO, a different boot loader, instead of GRUB, or choose not to install any boot loader.

 If you choose not to install one of the boot loaders, you should definitely create a boot disk. Otherwise you can't start Red Hat Linux.

In the center of the Boot Loader screen is a box that shows any operating systems, if there are any, that were detected on your system. The Red Hat Linux system will be shown as the default system. If you want to boot another system as the default, click on the box in front of the other operating system's name. There are three options available:

- **Add:** If an operating system was not detected and you wish to add it manually

- **Edit:** If you want to change the name of the operating system

- **Delete:** To remove an operating system from the list that you've highlighted

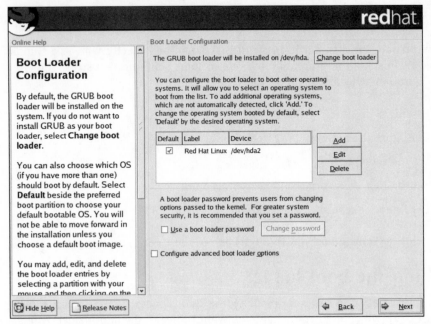

Figure 3-7: The Boot Loader Configuration screen enables you to specify which operating systems to boot.

The next item on this screen gives you the option to use a boot loader password. Using a boot loader password prevents someone from entering kernel commands which could affect system security or operation. If your servers are not accessible to anyone except you or other trusted administrators, you may not need a boot loader password, but if you want good security for your system, using a boot loader password is a good idea. To enable this feature, click the Use a Boot Loader Password checkbox, click the Change Password button, and enter the password.

The last option on this page gives you the opportunity of choosing the location of the boot loader and passing additional parameters to the kernel. If you want to do either of these, click the option and then click Next. The Advanced Boot Loader Configuration screen, shown in Figure 3-8, will appear.

The choices for the boot loader location are as follows:

◆ Master Boot Record (MBR), which is located in the first sector of your PC's hard disk

◆ First sector of the boot partition where you loaded Red Hat Linux

You should install the boot loader in the MBR unless you are using another operating system loader such as System Commander or OS/2 Boot Manager. You can also change the drive order by clicking on the Change Drive Order button. This is only necessary if you want your drives to appear in a different order or if they are not listed in the correct order. As shown on the screen following the option Force LBA32, this option is usually not required and is necessary only if you put the boot loader beyond the first 1024 cylinders on your hard drive.

The screen includes a text field labeled General Kernel Parameters that enables you to enter any special options that Red Hat Linux may need as it boots. Your need for special options depends on what hardware you have.

The remainder of the Boot Loader Configuration screen gives you the option to select the disk partition from which you want to boot the PC. A table then lists the Linux partition and any other partitions that may contain another operating system. If your system has a Linux partition and a DOS partition (that actually has Windows 95/98 installed on it), the table shows both of these entries. Each entry in that table is an operating system that the boot loader can boot.

After you install the boot loader, whenever your PC boots from the hard disk, the boot loader runs and displays a screen showing the operating systems that you can boot. The default selection will be highlighted and will boot automatically after a few seconds. You may move the highlight bar to the name of another operating system to boot. (The Boot label column in the table in the center section of Figure 3-7 shows the names you may enter at the boot loader prompt.)

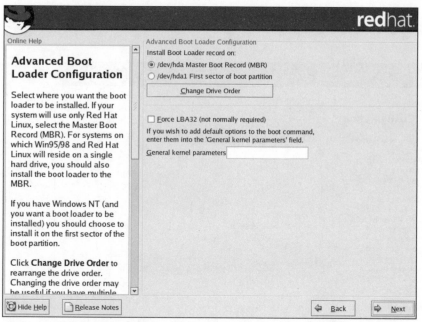

Figure 3-8: The Advanced Boot Loader Configuration screen specifies where you can change the location of the boot loader and enter kernel parameters.

When booting the PC, if you enter nothing at the boot loader screen, the boot loader waits for a few seconds and boots the default operating system. The default operating system is the one with a check mark in the Default column in Figure 3-7. In this case, Red Hat Linux is the default operating system.

All of the instructions in this section are for your information if you choose to change any of the default settings. You can essentially accept the default selections on this screen and click the Next button to proceed to the next configuration step.

Configuring the network

If the Linux kernel detects a network card, the Red Hat installation program displays the Network Configuration screen (see Figure 3-9), which enables you to configure the local area network (LAN) parameters for your Linux system.

This step is not for configuring dial-up networking. You need to perform this step if your Linux system is connected to a TCP/IP LAN through an Ethernet card.

If the Red Hat installation program does not detect your network card and you have a network card installed on the PC, you should restart the installation and type **expert** at the boot prompt. Then you can manually select your network card. See Chapter 33 for more information on troubleshooting.

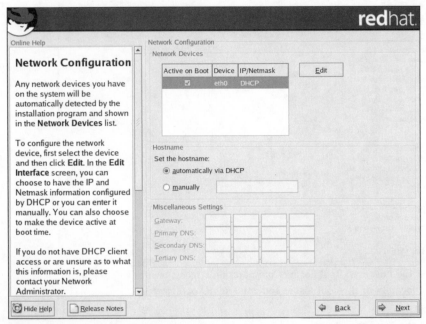

Figure 3-9: The Network Configuration screen enables you to configure the local area network.

The Network Configuration screen (Figure 3-9) displays a list of the network card(s) installed on your system and detected by the Linux kernel. The network cards are labeled eth0, eth1, and so on. If your system has only one Ethernet card, you see only eth0. Figure 3-9 shows that only one network card has been detected. The default selections for the network card are Active on Boot and Configure Using DHCP. If you want to enter an IP address manually for your network card or disable the card on boot, click the Edit button to open the Edit Interface dialog box shown in Figure 3-10.

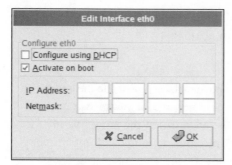

Figure 3-10: You can set the IP address for your network card manually using this screen.

To disable DHCP remove the check mark from the box and enter an IP address and net mask into the appropriate boxes. To enable DHCP click the option to place the check mark there.

To disable the card on boot, remove the check mark from the box. To enable the card on boot, click the option to place the check mark there.

The Hostname section of the Network Configuration screen shown in Figure 3-9 lets you choose how your system host name will be set. The choices are as follows:

◆ **Automatically via DHCP:** This is the default setting. Your PC will obtain its IP address and other network information from a *Dynamic Host Configuration Protocol (DHCP)* server.

◆ **Manually:** If you choose this option, you must provide a host name.

Select DHCP only if a DHCP server is running on your local area network. If you choose DHCP, your network configuration is set automatically and you can skip the rest of this section. You should leave the Activate on Boot button selected so that the network is configured whenever you boot the system.

If you have disabled DHCP, you will need to enter the IP address and net mask manually for the network card by editing the card. In addition, you have to enter certain parameters for the TCP/IP configuration in the text input fields for host name and the Miscellaneous Settings section shown in Figure 3-9.

The Network Configuration screen asks for the following key parameters:

◆ The host name of your Linux system (for a private LAN, you can assign your own host name without worrying about conflicting with any other existing systems on the Internet)

◆ IP address of the *gateway* (the system through which you might go to any outside network)

◆ IP address of the primary name server

◆ IP address of a secondary name server (if available)

◆ IP address of a ternary name server (if available)

If you have a private LAN (one that is not directly connected to the Internet), you may use an IP address from a range designated for private use. Common IP addresses for private LANs are the addresses in the range 192.168.1.1 through 192.168.1.254. Chapter 10 provides more in-depth information about TCP/IP networking and IP addresses.

After you enter the requested parameters, click Next to proceed to the next configuration step.

Configuring the firewall

By default, the installation program configures a firewall to isolate your system from other systems on the network. You can choose the level of security settings to allow or prohibit other users from using services on your system by making selections in the Firewall Configuration screen shown in Figure 3-11.

On this screen you can choose three levels of security: High, Medium, or No Firewall (meaning no security). Depending on your choice, different services may or may not be allowed access. Refer to the Help section on the left side of the screen for a description of services allowed for each level.

After making your selections, click Next to continue.

Choosing additional languages

The Additional Language Support screen, shown in Figure 3-12, is where you select the default language to be used on your system.

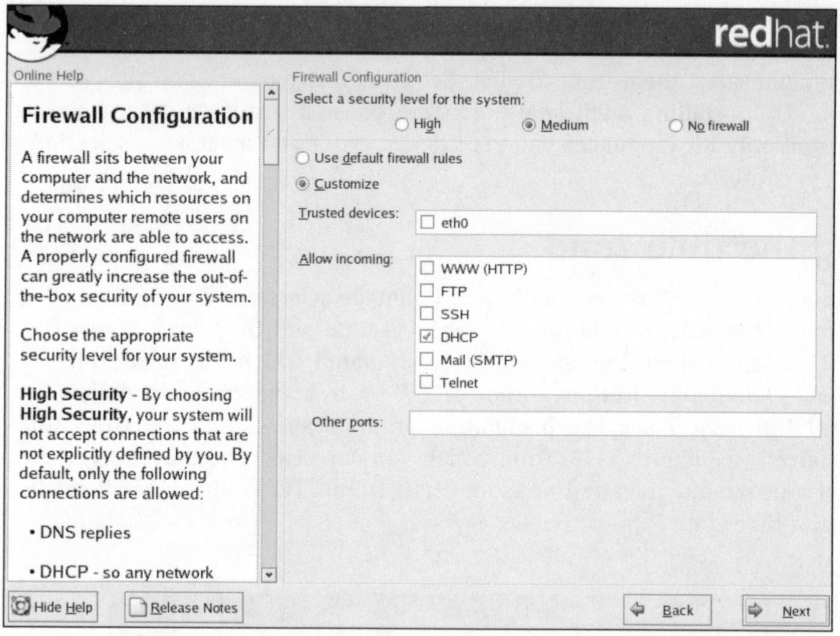

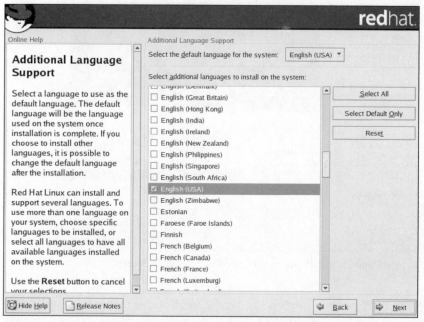

Figure 3-11: The Firewall Configuration screen lets you choose your security level.

Figure 3-12: On the Additional Language Support screen you set the default language for your system as well as additional languages you may use.

The language you chose to use for system installation earlier in the installation process will be shown as the default language. If you desire to use other languages as well, you can select them from the list. Select as many other languages as you desire. Note that installing additional languages consumes storage space on your disk, so install only the languages you plan to use. After you make your selections, click Next to continue.

Setting the time zone

After completing the default and additional language selection, you have to select the *time zone* – the difference between your local time and *Greenwich Mean Time (GMT)* or UTC (the current time in Greenwich, England) which was selected by the *International Telecommunication Union (ITU)* as a standard abbreviation for *Coordinated Universal Time*. The installation program shows you the Time Zone Selection screen (see Figure 3-13) from which you can select the time zone, either in terms of a geographic location or as an offset from UTC. Figure 3-13 shows the selection of a time zone.

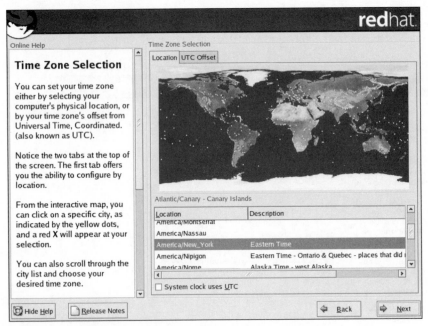

Figure 3-13: Select your time zone using the Time Zone Selection screen.

Notice that there are two tabs on the Time Zone Selection screen: Location and UTC Offset. Initially, the screen shows the Location tab, which enables you to pick a time zone by simply clicking your geographic location. As you move the mouse over the map, the currently selected location's name appears in a text field. If you want, you can also select your location from a long list of countries and regions. If you live on the east coast of the United States, for example, select USA/Eastern. Of course, the easiest way is to simply click the eastern United States on the map.

If the world view of the map is too large for you to select your location, click the View button on top of the map. A drop-down list of views appears with several choices. Click the appropriate view for your location.

The other way to set a time zone is to specify the time difference between your local time and UTC. Click the UTC Offset tab to select the time zone this way.

For example, if you live in the eastern part of the United States, select UTC-05:00 as the time zone. The –05:00 indicates that the eastern part of the U.S. is five hours behind UTC time. This tab also lets you activate Daylight Savings Time. After you select your time zone, click the Next button to proceed to the next configuration step.

Setting the root password

After selecting the time zone, the installation program displays the Set Root Password screen (see Figure 3-14) in which you set the root password.

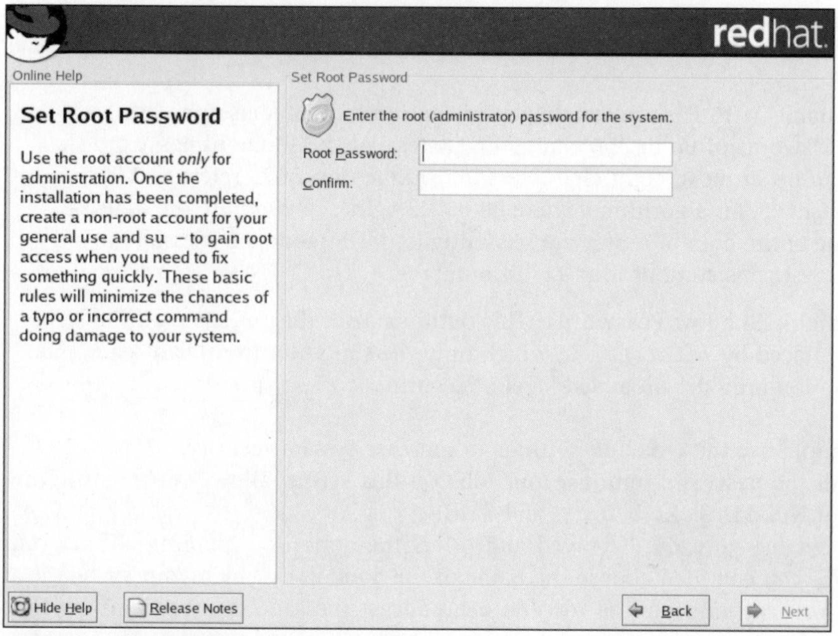

Figure 3-14: Setting the root password

The root user is the *superuser* in Linux. Because the superuser can do anything in the system, you should assign a password that only you can remember, and that others cannot guess easily. Typically, make the password at least eight characters long, include a mix of letters and numbers, and (for good measure) throw in some special characters such as + or *. Remember that the password is case-sensitive.

Type the password on the first line and then reenter the password on the next line. Each character in the password appears as an asterisk (*) on the screen for security reasons. Both entries must match before the installation program accepts the password. The installation program displays a message when it accepts the root password.

You must enter the root password before you can proceed with the rest of the installation. After you do so, click Next to continue with the installation.

Configuring password authentication

The installation program displays the Authentication Configuration screen, shown in Figure 3-15, from which you can configure the password authentication options. You can enable or disable several options. Of these, the first two are already selected:

◆ **Enable MD5 Passwords:** Select this option to enable users to use long passwords of up to 256 characters instead of the standard password that can be, at most, eight characters long. Note that *MD5* refers to *Message Digest 5*, an algorithm developed by RSA, Inc. to compute the digest of the entire data of a message. Essentially, MD5 reduces a message to a digest consisting of four 32-bit numbers.

◆ **Enable Shadow Passwords:** This option causes the /etc/psswd file to be replaced by /etc/shadow, which only the superuser (root) can read. This option provides an added level of security.

You should use these default settings to increase system security.

Beneath the password options, four tabs on this screen allow you to configure options for NIS, LDAP, Kerberos 5, and SMB.

The NIS tab is already displayed and offers the option of enabling NIS. If you enable NIS, you can then choose the name of the domain to which your system is a member. You can also choose to send a broadcast message to search for an NIS server on your network. If you choose not to send a broadcast message, you can enter the name of a specific server.

Chapter 12 explains the installation and configuration of the Network Information Service (NIS). Chapters 29 and 31 provide information about network security and its implementation.

Use the LDAP tab to set options for *Lightweight Directory Access Protocol (LDAP)*. With LDAP, you can organize information about users on your system into an LDAP directory that can be used for system authentication. From the LDAP screen you can enable LDAP and set the following options:

◆ **LDAP Server:** Specify the IP address of an LDAP server on your network

◆ **LDAP Base DN:** Search for user information by using its Distinguished Name (DN)

◆ **Use TLS Lookups:** Send encrypted user names and passwords to an LDAP server before authentication

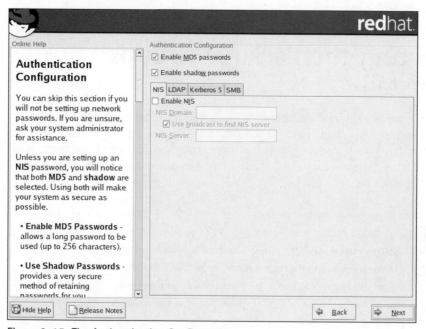

Figure 3-15: The Authentication Configuration screen

The Kerberos 5 tab opens the Kerberos 5 configuration screen. Use Kerberos 5 to provide secure network authentication services for your network. You can enable Kerberos 5 from this screen and set the following options:

◆ **Realm:** Enables you to choose to access a network running Kerberos 5

◆ **KDC:** With this option, you can access a *Key Distribution Center (KDC)* to obtain a Kerberos ticket

◆ **Admin Server:** Using this option, you can access a server running the Kerberos 5 admin program

The final tab on the Authentication Configuration screen is SMB. *Server Message Block (SMB)* is the protocol used on Microsoft networks for file sharing. Clicking on the SMB tab opens the SMB configuration screen, where you can enable SMB and choose the following options:

◆ **SMB Server:** Shows the name of the SMB server you will use

◆ **SMB Workgroup:** Shows the name of the workgroup containing the SMB server or servers

After you have finished setting your configuration options on the Authentication Configuration screen, click Next to proceed to the next configuration step.

Selecting the Package Groups to Install

After you complete the key configuration steps, the installation program displays a screen from which you can select the Red Hat Linux package groups that you want to install. After you select the package groups, take a coffee break while the Red Hat installation program formats the disk partitions and copies all selected files to those partitions.

 If you selected a custom installation as your install type, you will see the screen shown in Figure 3-16. If you chose any other installation type, you will see a screen listing the most commonly installed packages for the installation type you chose. You can accept the default on that page or you can select your own packages, which will then show you the screen in Figure 3-16.

Red Hat uses special files called *packages* to bundle files that make up specific software. For example, all configuration files, documentation, and binary files for the Perl programming language come in a Red Hat package. You use a special program called *Red Hat Package Manager (RPM)* to install, uninstall, and get information about packages. Chapter 27 shows you how to use RPM. For now, just remember that a package group is made up of several Red Hat packages.

Figure 3-16 shows the Package Group Selection screen with the list of package groups that you can elect to install. An icon, a descriptive label, and a radio button for enabling or disabling identify each package group.

Some of the components are already selected, as indicated by the checked boxes. This is the minimal set of packages that Red Hat recommends for installation for the class of installation (Workstation, Server, or Custom) you have chosen. You can, however, install any or all of the components. Scroll up and down the list and click the mouse on an entry to select or deselect that package group.

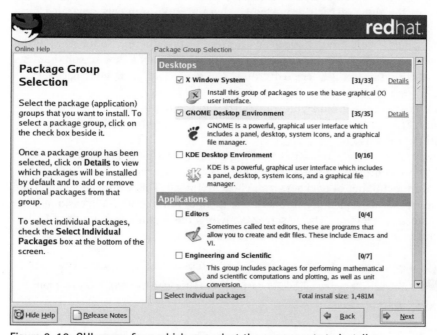

Figure 3–16: GUI screen from which you select the components to install

In an actual Red Hat Linux installation, you install exactly those package groups that you need. Each package group requires specific packages to run. The Red Hat installation program automatically checks for any package dependencies and shows you a list of packages that are required but that you have not selected. In this case, you should install the required packages. Install only those packages that you think you will need immediately after starting the system. Installing too many packages could expose your system to security risks. You can always add packages later.

Because each package group is a collection of many different Red Hat packages, the installation program also gives you the option of selecting individual packages. If you click the Select Individual Packages option, which appears below the list in Figure 3-16, and then click Next, the installation program takes you to other screens where you can select individual packages. If you are installing Red Hat Enterprise Linux for the first time, you really do not need to go down to this level of detail to install specific packages. Simply pick the components that you think you need from the screen shown in Figure 3-16.

Notice to the right of each group name there are two numbers separated by a slash. For instance, next to the X Window System is 31/33. This means that 31 of the 33 packages in this group have been selected for installation. To the right of the numbers is a link labeled Details. Clicking on this link opens a new screen that lists the packages that are in the selected group. You can select or deselect packages as desired.

After you select the groups you want, click Next to continue with the rest of the installation. The installation program now presents the About to Install screen, as shown in Figure 3-17.

If you are absolutely sure that everything is correct and you are ready to install, click Next to continue with the installation. The time required for installation depends on the number of packages you chose to install. This would be a good time to take a break, but remember to check the installation's progress occasionally as you will need to change CDs. A screen showing the installation progress is displayed to show you how the installation is proceeding.

You can always install additional packages later with the RPM utility program, described in Chapter 27.

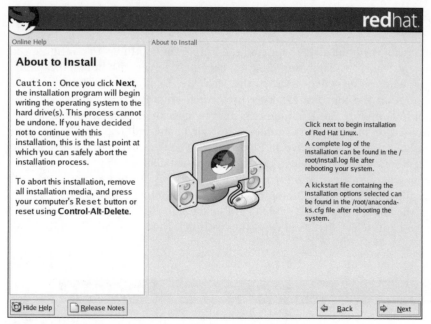

Figure 3-17: The About to Install screen gives you one last chance to cancel the installation process.

Creating a Boot Disk

The next step in the installation is to create a boot disk. After all the packages are installed, you will see the Boot Disk Creation screen where you will be given the option of creating a boot disk. By default, the choice to create the boot disk is selected. It is a good idea to create a boot disk to use in case you have problems starting your system. This disk is the emergency boot disk that you can use to start Red Hat Enterprise Linux if something happens to the hard disk or you do not install the LILO or GRUB boot loader.

Insert a blank disk into your PC's floppy drive and click Next. The installation program copies the Linux kernel and some other files to the disk.

Creating a boot disk erases all existing data on the floppy disk.

Configuring the X Window System

After you create the boot disk, the installation program continues to configure the X Window System. The installation program uses an X server with minimal capability that can work on all video cards. In this step, the installation program prepares the configuration file that the X server uses when your system reboots. You can choose not to configure the X Window System by checking the appropriate box.

The installation program tries to detect the video card and displays the result in the X Configuration screen shown in Figure 3-18. The detected card appears as the selected item in a long list of video cards. In most installations the correct card for your system will be selected and the parameters necessary for proper operation will be already filled in. Sometimes, though, you may need to make another selection. If you know the exact name of the video card or the name of the video chipset used in the video card, select that item from the list. Click Next to continue to the next screen.

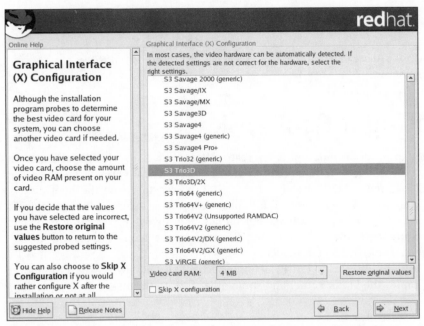

Figure 3-18: On this X Configuration screen you can choose your video card.

The installation program tries to detect the monitor and displays the Monitor Configuration screen (see Figure 3-19) with the result, whether or not it succeeds.

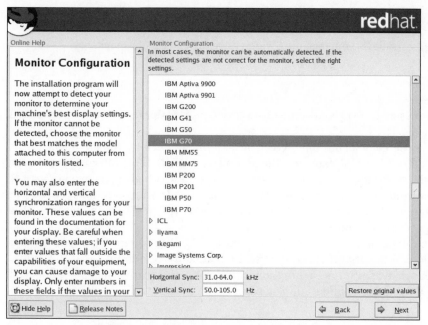

Figure 3-19: Result of detecting the monitor displayed in the X Configuration screen

If the installation program displays a wrong monitor or a generic one as the choice, try to find your monitor in the list of monitors. If you are unable to find a suitable monitor, enter a range of values for the two parameters that appear along the bottom of the screen:

◆ **Horizontal Sync:** The number of times per second the monitor displays a horizontal raster line, in kilohertz (KHz). A typical range might be 30–64 KHz.

◆ **Vertical Sync:** How many times per second the monitor displays the entire screen, in hertz (Hz). Also known as *vertical refresh rate*, the typical range is 50–90 Hz.

Typically, the monitor's documentation includes all this information. Other places to get information about your monitor include your Microsoft Windows setup, your system's Windows driver, your computer vendor's Web site, or the Norton System Information tool. Click Next after you have made your selections.

Do not specify a horizontal synchronization range that is beyond the capabilities of your monitor. A wrong value can damage the monitor.

The next screen displayed is the Customize Graphics Configuration screen shown in Figure 3-20.

Choose the color depth and screen resolution by clicking on the down arrow next to the setting and choosing the setting you desire. You can also accept the default choice for a graphical login type or choose a text login type by clicking the button in front of the text option. After you have made your selections, click Next to continue to the final screen. The Congratulations screen shown in Figure 3-21 is the final screen you will see.

All you have to do now is click on Next and be sure to remove any disks that may still be in the drives. The system will reboot and begin to load Red Hat Linux. When the system restarts, a program called First Boot will run and guide you through a few more configuration steps.

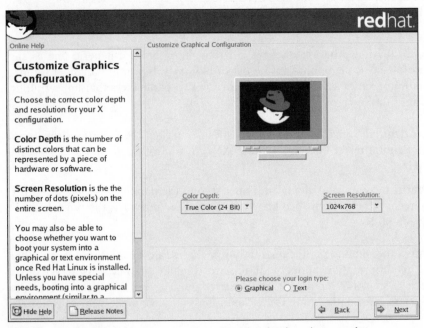

Figure 3-20: On this screen you can select the color depth and screen size.

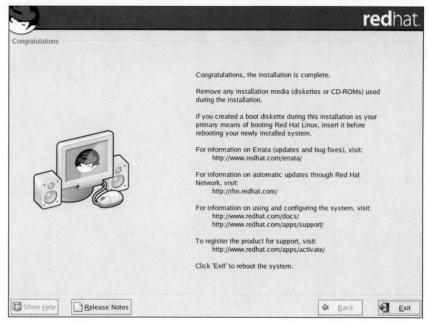

Figure 3-21: This screen tells you that you have successfully installed Red Hat Linux.

Summary

In this chapter you learned how to install Red Hat Enterprise Linux. You began by examining the hardware on your system and making a list of the components. You checked for hardware compatibility by referring to the Red Hat Web site. You learned how to partition your hard drive and you chose the type of system you wanted to install. Finally, you chose the packages you wanted on your system and configured the X server.

Chapter 4

Kickstart Installation

IN THIS CHAPTER

- ◆ Using Kickstart
- ◆ Configuring the Kickstart file (ks.cfg)
- ◆ Starting a Kickstart installation
- ◆ Configuring Kickstart using the graphical interface

AS A SYSTEM ADMINISTRATOR, one of your jobs is installing and configuring Red Hat on other computers. This could be time consuming if you have many servers and clients to administer. To make your job easier, a program is available that automates the Red Hat installation process. This program is called Kickstart. With Kickstart you can create and store configuration files for your server or client installations and then use these files to perform your installations and upgrades. Installations and upgrades can be done from a local CD-ROM or using NFS, FTP, HTTP, or a hard drive. If you are installing across the network, you need to have a DHCP server for each network segment.

The next section of this chapter explains the rules for creating and using the ks.cfg file and calling it when starting your installation.

 It is possible to configure the Kickstart file using a graphical interface. If you would rather use the graphical interface, go to the "Configuring Kickstart Using the Graphical Interface" section later in this chapter.

Configuring the Kickstart File (ks.cfg)

The file Kickstart uses to read the configuration information for the automated installation is called ks.cfg. A Kickstart configuration file, named anaconda-ks.cfg, is created during a system installation and is placed in the /root directory. This file contains the system configuration information for the system on which the file is located. If you are planning to install other systems with the same configuration, you can use this file to provide their configuration. If you need to make changes to the configuration, you can use any text-editing program to edit the ks.cfg file to make modifications as necessary for your installation.

Shown in Listing 4-1 is the ks.cfg file I created when I installed my system. You can refer to this file for comparison with the format discussed.

Listing 4-1: The anaconda-ks.cfg file created during system installation

```
# Kickstart file automatically generated by anaconda.

install
lang en_US.UTF-8
langsupport --default en_US.UTF-8 zh_CN.GB18030 en_US.UTF-8
ru_RU.UTF-8 tr_TR.UTF-8
keyboard us
mouse genericps/2 --device psaux --emulthree
xconfig --card "NVIDIA GeForce 2 MX (generic)" --videoram 32768 --
hsync 30-70 --vsync 50-100 --resolution 1280x960 --depth 24
--startxonboot  --defaultdesktop gnome
rootpw --iscrypted $1$tdX49zfJ$489pPVmTP3vxS3pFtbJ8S/
firewall --enabled --port=nfs:udp --port=nfs:udp --port=http:tcp --
port=ftp:tcp --port=ssh:tcp
authconfig --enableshadow --enablemd5
timezone America/New_York
bootloader --location=mbr --append hdc=ide-scsi
# The following is the partition information you requested
# Note that any partitions you deleted are not expressed
# here so unless you clear all partitions first, this is
# not guaranteed to work
#clearpart --all --drives=hda
#part /boot --fstype ext3 --size=100 --ondisk=hda
#part / --fstype ext3 --size=1024 --grow --ondisk=hda
#part swap --size=512 --grow --maxsize=1024 --ondisk=hda

%packages
@ office
@ mysql
@ system-tools
@ smb-server
@ base-x
@ graphics
```

```
@ web-server
@ rhel-as
@ development-tools
@ russian-support
@ printing
@ text-internet
@ kde-desktop
@ server-cfg
@ dialup
@ sound-and-video
@ turkish-support
@ admin-tools
@ chinese-support
@ gnome-desktop
@ ftp-server
@ kernel-development
@ graphical-internet
-sane-frontends
kernel
-xsane-gimp
shapecfg
mod_auth_mysql
festival
php-mysql
grub
-xsane
kdegraphics
kdemultimedia
mrtg
-tux

%post
```

The `ks.cfg` file consists of three sections:

- ◆ Command section — Contains options affecting the installation and is a required section
- ◆ Packages section — Contains the list of packages to be installed
- ◆ %pre and %post section — Contains scripts to be run before (%pre section) or after (%post section) the installation

These sections must be listed in `ks.cfg` in the preceding order. Items within a section can be in any order. In addition to the sections are some rules that must be followed.

♦ Any missing but required items will stop the installation, and the program will prompt for the information. Be sure to check your file for required items, since having to reply to prompts for information defeats the purpose of automated installation.

♦ Any item not required does not need to be included in the file.

It is a good idea to include comments in your file for future reference. You can include comments by placing a pound sign (#) at the beginning of the comment line.

If you are performing an upgrade, the `ks.cfg` file needs to contain only the language, language support, installation method, the device specification if needed for the installation, the keyboard type, the word *upgrade*, and the boot-loader configuration. Other items will be ignored, including packages. You cannot install packages using the upgrade method.

Kickstart Commands

The most commonly used commands, shown in Listing 4-1, are described next. The commands are shown in the discussion in the order in which they appear in the listing. Many of the commands have options that are listed and explained with their corresponding commands. Each explanation specifies whether the command is required or optional. For a complete listing of Kickstart commands and options, you can go to the Red Hat Web site at `http://www.redhat.com/docs/manuals/linux/RHL-9-Manual/custom-guide/s1-kickstart2-options.html`.

♦ `install` — An optional command that tells the system to do a new install. This is the default, so it isn't necessary to include this command for a new install. You need to specify the installation method on the line following this command. Installation methods can be cdrom, harddrive, nfs, or url and take the following formats:

- ■ cdrom

- ■ `harddrive --partition=your partition --dir=/your directory path` (Be sure to enter the information appropriate to your system for partition and dir.)

- ■ `nfs --server=your server --dir=/your directory path` (Be sure to enter the information appropriate to your system for partition and dir.)

- ■ `url --url http://your server/dir` (Use this for http.)

- ■ `url --url ftp://your username:password@your server/dir` (Use this for ftp.)

◆ `lang` — is required and specifies the language to use for the installation in the format shown.

◆ `Lang en_US.UTF-8`

◆ `langsupport` — is required and specifies the language to be used on the system. If you are installing more than one language, as shown in Listing 4-1, you must use the default option to specify a default language. The format is:

◆ `langsupport --default en_US .UTF-8` (other languages as desired)

◆ `keyboard` — Is required and is used to set the system keyboard type in the format

- ■ keyboard us

◆ `mouse` — is required and is used to specify the mouse configuration in the format.

- ■ `mouse --device=ttyS0` (device where mouse id located) `--emulthree` (used for 3 button emulation) `genericps/2` (specifies type of mouse)

◆ `xconfig` — Is optional — if it is not specified, you will have to manually configure X after the system is installed. If you are not installing X, you should not use this option. The format for this optional command is:

- ■ `xconfig --card` (card type) `--videoram` (specify amount on card) `--hsync` (specify values) `--vsync` (specify values) `--resolution` (specify values) `--depth` (specify value) `startxonboot` (use this if you want to start x when the system boots) `--defaultdesktop gnome` (or kde)

◆ `rootpw` — Is required and sets the root password for the system in the format

  ■ `rootpw --iscrypted` (indicates an encrypted password) `password`

◆ `firewall` — Is optional and specifies the level of protection offered by the firewall in the format

  ■ `firewall level` (specify one of low, medium, or high) `--port=`specify port allowed through firewall (the --port option can be repeated for as many ports as you want to allow through)

◆ `authconfig` — Is required and is used to set the authentication options for the system in the format

  ■ `authconfig --enablemd5 --enableshadow` (There are many options available for this required item. You should refer to the Red Hat site referenced earlier in this section for a complete list.)

◆ `timezone` — Is required and is used to set the system timezone in the format

  ■ `timezone America/New_York` (specify your location)

◆ `bootloader` — Is required and is used to specify the location of the boot loader and to pass any kernel options. The default boot loader is GRUB, but you can pass an option to request LILO instead. The format of this command is:

  ■ `bootloader --location=mbr` (specify your location) `--useLilo` (use this if you want to use LILO) `--append=`(specify your kernel options here)

◆ `clearpart` — Is optional and is used to tell the system to remove partitions from the system. You can pass options to clear Linux partitions, all partitions, or you can list specific drives to clear all their partitions. The format for this command is:

  ■ `clearpart --linux` (or you can pass) `--all` (or you can pass) `--drives=`(specify the drives here)

◆ `Part` — Is required for new installs and is ignored if used with an upgrade. With this command, you set up the partitions on your system. You should carefully examine Listing 4-1 to see the format for this command and refer to the Red Hat site previously listed for the complete list of options.

Selecting Packages

For a new system install, you must choose the packages that you want to install. You do this by using the %packages command. Packages can be listed individually or as groups. You can see a list of package groups by looking at /base/comps.xml on the first Red Hat Installation CD-ROM.

Each group has an id, user visibility value, name, description, and package list. In the package list, the packages marked *mandatory* are always installed if the group is selected, the packages marked *default* are selected by default if the group is selected, and the packages marked *optional* must be specifically selected even if the group is selected to be installed.

In most cases, it is necessary to list only the desired groups, not individual packages. Note that the core and base groups are always selected by default, so it is not necessary to specify them in the %packages section.

As you can see, groups are specified, one to a line, starting with an @ symbol, a space, and then the full group name as given in the comps.xml file. You can specify individual packages by just listing the name of the package with no additional characters.

You can also decide not to install a package by placing a minus sign in front of the package name you don't want to install. Listing 4-1 shows several packages that have been selected not to install.

There are three options that you can pass to the %package command:

◆ --resolvedeps — Automatically resolves any dependencies and installs the packages. This is the recommended option, since not using it causes the installation to stop and prompt for a response.

◆ --ignoredeps — Installs the selected packages and ignores any unresolved dependencies. This might cause the packages you install not to function if they require other packages.

◆ --ignoremissing — Makes the installation ignore missing packages and groups and not prompt for a response.

The %pre and %post Section

These two commands allow you to pass commands to the installation program to run on the system. The %pre command passes the commands to the system after the ks.cfg file is parsed but before the installation starts. A good example of using this command can be found at http://www.redhat.com/docs/manuals/linux/RHL-9-Manual/custom-guide/s1-kickstart2-preinstallconfig.html.

The %post command passes commands to the system after the Kickstart installation has finished. This could be useful for running commands to install additional software or to make system configuration changes such as starting or stopping services. Some examples of using this command can be found at http://www.redhat.com/docs/manuals/linux/RHL-9-Manual/custom-guide/s1-kickstart2-postinstallconfig.html.

Creating Bootable Diskettes

Before you can begin a Kickstart installation, there are a few additional details that must be taken care of.

◆ You must place a copy of the configuration file in one of three locations. The file can be placed on a bootable floppy, a bootable CD-ROM, or on a network drive.

◆ You need to make the installation tree available. The installation tree is a copy of the Red Hat Linux CD-ROMs with the same directory structure. For a CD-ROM installation, you can put the Installation CD #1 into the CD-ROM drive. For a hard drive or network installation, you need to have the ISO images of the binary Red Hat Linux CD-ROM accessible from those locations.

◆ If you are planning to use a bootable floppy or CD-ROM to start the Kickstart installation, you will have to make those bootable disks. Also, if you are planning to place the ks.cfg file on a bootable floppy or CD-ROM, you can do it when you create the bootable floppy or CD-ROM.

 You need to be logged in as the root user (or su to become root) to create the bootable disks.

CREATING A BOOTABLE FLOPPY
To create a bootable floppy, follow these instructions:

1. Place the Red Hat Linux Installation CD-ROM #1 into your CD-ROM drive.

2. From a terminal prompt, mount the CD-ROM and change into the /images directory. (Be sure to use the correct path for your system.)

```
mount /mnt/cdrom
cd /mnt/cdrom/images
```

3. Place a floppy disk into your floppy drive. At a terminal prompt, enter:

   ```
   dd=ifbootdisk.img of=/dev/fd0 bs=1440k
   ```

4. If you want a copy of your Kickstart configuration file, `ks.cfg`, on your bootable floppy, copy the `ks.cfg` file that you created to the bootable floppy.

CREATING A BOOTABLE CD-ROM
To create a bootable CD-ROM, follow these instructions.

1. Place the Red Hat Linux Installation CD-ROM #1 into your CD-ROM drive.

2. From a terminal prompt, mount the CD-ROM with the following command: (Be sure to use the correct path for your system.)

   ```
   mount /mnt/cdrom
   ```

3. Copy the isolinux directory from the CD-ROM to a directory on your hard drive. You should create a temporary directory for this purpose. I created a directory called `/root/tempdir` on my system to use for an example. Be sure to use the correct path for your system. Use the following command:

   ```
   cp -r isolinux/ /root/tempdir/
   ```

4. If you want a copy of your Kickstart configuration file, `ks.cfg`, on your bootable CD-ROM, copy the `ks.cfg` file that you created to the /isolinux directory on your hard drive at the location where you created it.

   ```
   cp /root/ks.cfg /tempdir/isolinux/
   ```

5. Change to the temporary directory that you created:

   ```
   cd /root/tempdir
   ```

6. Use the `chmod` command to be sure the files you copied have the correct permissions.

   ```
   chmod u+w isolinux/*
   ```

7. Create the ISO image file with this command. (The command should be entered on one line.)

   ```
   mkisofs -o file.iso -b isolinux.bin -c boot.cat -no-emul-boot
   \-boot-load-size 4 -boot-info-table -R -J -v -T isolinux/
   ```

8. The last step is writing the image file you created, `file.iso` to a CD-ROM using the process you would normally use to write to a CD-ROM.

Starting a Kickstart Installation

When you are ready to begin your installation, boot the system from a Red Hat Linux boot disk, and enter a special boot command at the boot prompt. If the Kickstart file resides on the boot disk, the proper boot command is:

```
linux ks=floppy
```

or enter

```
linux ks=cdrom:/ks.cfg
```

If, on the other hand, the Kickstart file resides on a server, the appropriate boot command is:

```
linux ks=<file location>
```

Anaconda looks for a Kickstart file if the ks command line argument is passed to the kernel. The ks command can take a number of forms:

- ks=floppy — The installation program looks for the file ks.cfg on a VFAT file system on the floppy in drive /dev/fd0.

- ks=hd:<device>:/<file> — The installation program mounts the file system on <device> (which must be VFAT or ext2), and looks for the Kickstart configuration file as <file> in that file system (for example, ks=hd:sda3:/mydir/ks.cfg).

- ks=file:/<file> — The installation program tries to read the file <file> from the file system; no mounts are done. This is normally used if the Kickstart file is already on the initrd image.

- ks=nfs:<server:>/<path> — The installation program looks for the Kickstart file on the NFS server <server>, as file <path>. The installation program uses DHCP to configure the Ethernet card.

- ks=http:<server:>/<path> — The installation program looks for the Kickstart file on the http server <server>, as file <path>. The installation program uses DHCP to configure the Ethernet card.

- ks=cdrom:/<path> — The installation program looks for the Kickstart file on CD-ROM, as file <path>.

◆ `ks` — When `ks` is specified without additional command line parameters, the DHCP bootServer field of the configuration file is used to obtain the name of the NFS server. This information is also used to configure the Ethernet card using DHCP and to find the location of the Kickstart file. The Kickstart file can be found in one of three locations:

■ If the bootfile starts with a /, and DHCP is configured, the installation program looks in the root directory on the NFS server for the bootfile.

■ If the bootfile does not start with a /, and DHCP is configured, the installation program looks in the `/kickstart` directory on the NFS server for the file.

■ When no bootfile is listed, the IP address of the PC receiving the installation is checked for the file.

If you are planning to install Kickstart across your network, you must have a DHCP server properly configured to provide IP information to the system on which you are doing the installation. Chapter 10 describes setting up a DHCP server.

Configuring Kickstart Using the Graphical Interface

For many people, especially those accustomed to MS Windows, using a text editor to do system configuration seems outdated and difficult. Even though an experienced administrator can often perform the configuration quickly by editing the configuration files manually, some people would rather just click and fill in boxes. If this is you, you're in luck because Red Hat Linux does have a graphical tool called Kickstart Configurator. Using an easy to follow interface, the program asks the same questions asked during installation and then creates a Kickstart file from your answers.

To start the Kickstart Configurator, choose main menu → System Tools → Kickstart. The Kickstart Configurator window shown in Figure 4-1 appears.

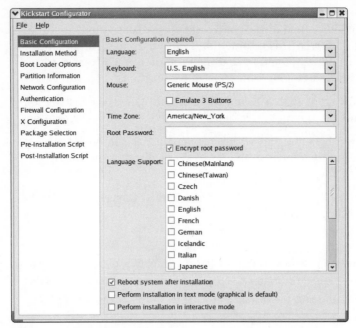

Figure 4–1: The Kickstart Configurator program window showing the
Basic Configuration screen

Basic Configuration Screen

When the Kickstart Configurator window opens, the Basic Configuration screen is
shown on the right side. On the left side of the window is a list showing the other
configuration screens. Clicking an item in the list will open the appropriate screen
on the right side of the Kickstart Configurator window. Beginning with the basic
configuration, the fields are:

◆ **Language:** Choose the language to use on the system by clicking the
down arrow on the right side of the field, and choose the language by
clicking it.

◆ **Keyboard:** Choose the language for the keyboard layout by clicking the
down arrow on the right side of the field, and choose the language by
clicking it.

◆ **Mouse:** Choose the type of mouse on your system by clicking the down
arrow on the right side of the field and by choosing the appropriate
mouse. If you have a two-button mouse and want to emulate a three-
button mouse, check the box to emulate three buttons.

◆ **Time zone:** Choose the appropriate time zone for your location by clicking
the down arrow on the right side of the field and choosing the location.

◆ **Root password:** Enter the password for the root user. Notice that it will be encrypted by default unless you remove the check from the box.

◆ **Language support:** Choose additional languages you want to install on your system by checking the box in front of the language name.

◆ **Reboot system after installation:** By default, the system reboots unless you remove the check from the box.

◆ **Perform installation in text mode:** By default, the installation is in graphical mode unless you remove the check from the box.

◆ **Perform installation in interactive mode:** Place a check in this box if you want to use interactive mode during the installation. This method lets you see the options selected for installation one screen at a time. You need to press *next* to continue at each screen.

Installation Method Screen

Click Installation Method from the list on the left side of the window. The Installation Method screen opens on the right side of the window.

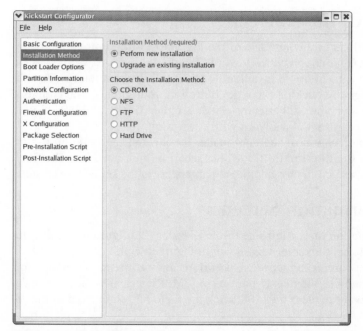

Figure 4–2: The Kickstart Configurator program window showing the Installation Method screen

On the Installation Methods screen, you can pick the type of installation you will be performing. You can choose to do a new installation or an upgrade by clicking the radio button in front of your choice.

You are also able to choose the type of media you will be using for the installation. The default choice is CD-ROM. Other choices are:

◆ NFS: If you choose this method, two additional fields will appear where you need to enter the name of the NFS server and the directory to use.

◆ FTP: If you choose this method, four additional fields will appear. You need to enter the name of the FTP server and the directory to use in two of the fields. You are also given the opportunity to show an FTP username and password by clicking on the checkbox and entering in the appropriate information.

◆ HTTP: If you choose this method, two additional fields will appear where you need to enter the name of the HTTP server and the directory to use.

◆ Hard Drive: If you choose this method, two additional fields will appear where you need to enter the partition of the hard drive and the directory to use.

Boot Loader Options Screen

Click Boot Loader Options on the left side of the Kickstart Configurator window to open the Boot Loader Options screen as shown in Figure 4-3.

On this screen, you can choose to install or not to install the boot loader you will use to boot your system by clicking the radio button of your choice. You can also select which boot loader you will use by clicking either GRUB or LILO. If you choose GRUB, you can also set a password with encryption.

You can choose the location of the boot loader by clicking the radio button in front of either Master Boot Record (MBR) or first sector of boot partition. The final field of this screen allows you to pass additional parameters to the kernel if necessary.

Partition Information Screen

Click Partition Information on the left side of the Kickstart Configurator window to open the Partition Information screen as shown in Figure 4-4.

On this screen, you can create your disk partitions and set the mount points for your directories. By default, the master boot record (MBR) is cleared during installation. If you do not want to clear the MBR, click the radio button in front of the *do not clear MBR* line.

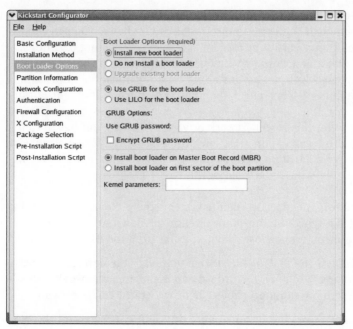

Figure 4-3: The Kickstart Configurator program window showing the Boot Loader Options screen

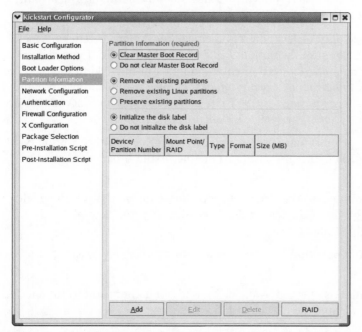

Figure 4-4: The Kickstart Configurator program window showing the Partition Information screen

Also by default, all existing partitions are removed during the installation. If you do not want to do this, click the radio button in front of your choice. You can choose to remove only existing Linux partitions, or you can keep the existing partitions.

If you are installing on a new hard drive, you will want to keep the default setting of initialize the disk label. If you are installing on a previously used drive and want to keep the existing drive label, check the radio box in front of *do not initialize the disk label.*

The partition window on this screen is currently empty, since you haven't created any partitions yet. To create a partition, click the Add button at the bottom of the screen. You should see a Partition Options dialog box (refer to Figure 4-5) containing the following fields, which you need to fill in.

- **Mount Point** shows the place in the file system where the partition will be mounted. You can type a mount point or click the down arrow to open the drop-down menu and choose a mount point from the list.

- **File System Type** is the type of file system you want the partition to be. Click the down arrow to open the drop-down menu, and choose the file system type. The most common choices here are ext2, ext3, and swap.

- **Allowable Drives** shows the installed hard drives. A checkmark in the box means that the drive is available for creating partitions. Click to highlight the drive you want to use for the partitions.

- **Size(MB)** is the field where you can set the size of the partition. The default size is 100 megabytes, but you can set the size to whatever you desire.

- **Additional size options** lets you set other size restrictions by clicking the radio button in front of the option. *Fixed size* is the default. If you choose *grow to maximum of,* you need to enter a number in the field to the right of the choice. *Fill all unused space on disk* will use all remaining space on the drive. *Use recommended swap size* is grayed out and not selectable unless the file system type selected is *swap.*

- **Force to be a primary partition** lets you set the drive as either a primary or logical partition. Primary partitions are the first four partitions on the hard drive.

- **Make partition on specific drive** lets you choose the hard drive on which to create the partition. Just enter the drive identifier; for example, hda would be the first ide drive.

- **Use an existing partition** lets you specify using an already existing partition.

- **Format partition** is checked as the default. If you do not want to format the partition, remove the check mark from the box.

After you have filled in the fields with your choices, click the OK button to return to the partition information screen. You will see the partition information you have chosen displayed in the partition window.

Mount Point:
File System Type: ext3
Size (MB): 1
Additional Size Options
Fixed size
Grow to maximum of (MB): 1
Fill all unused space on disk
Use recommended swap size
Force to be a primary partition (asprimary)
Make partition on specific drive (ondisk)
Drive : (for example: hda or sdc)
Use existing partition (onpart)
Partition : (for example: hda1 or sdc3)
Format partition
Cancel
OK

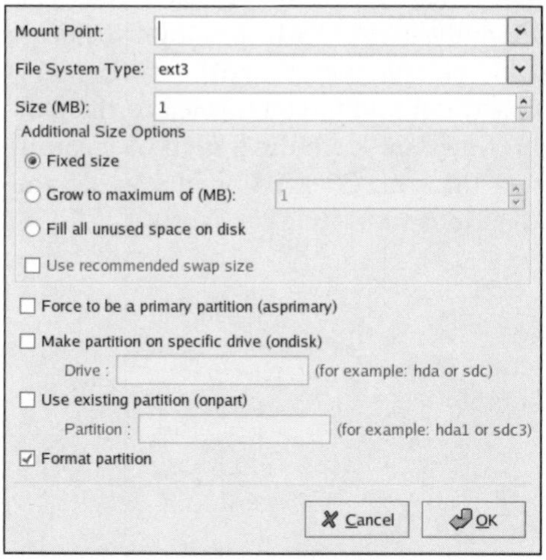

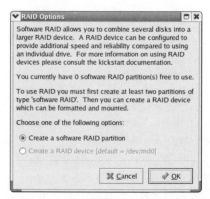

Figure 4-5: The Partition Options dialog box in which you fill in the attributes of a new partition

You can also create software RAID partitions if you desire. To create a software RAID partition, click the RAID button at the bottom of the partition information screen. You will see the RAID options dialog box as shown in Figure 4-6.

RAID Options
Software RAID allows you to combine several disks into a larger RAID device. A RAID device can be configured to provide additional speed and reliability compared to using an individual drive. For more information on using RAID devices please consult the kickstart documentation.
You currently have 0 software RAID partition(s) free to use.
To use RAID you must first create at least two partitions of type 'software RAID'. Then you can create a RAID device which can be formatted and mounted.
Choose one of the following options:
Create a software RAID partition
Create a RAID device [default = /dev/md0]
Cancel
OK

Figure 4-6: The RAID Options dialog box gives you information about creating RAID partitions.

As shown on the RAID Options dialog, you need to have two software Raid partitions to be able to create a RAID device. The only option you have on this dialog is to accept the option to create a software RAID partition; click Next to continue. A Partition Options dialog box like the one seen in Figure 4-5 appears with software RAID already selected as the file system type. Enter the remaining options as you do when creating a partition earlier. Click OK, and the first RAID partition is shown on the partition window. Click RAID again, and create another RAID partition.

After you have created the second RAID partition and have returned to the partition information window, click RAID again. Now you have the option of creating a RAID device that has already been selected for you. Click OK, and you see the Make RAID Device dialog box as shown in Figure 4-7.

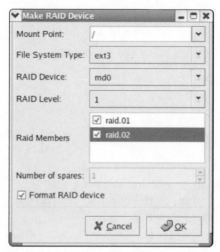

Figure 4-7: The Make RAID Device dialog box
gives you choices about creating RAID devices.

The fields on this dialog box are explained as follows:

◆ **Mount Point** shows the place in the file system where the partition will be mounted. You can type a mount point or click the down arrow to open the drop-down menu and choose a mount point from the list.

◆ **File System Type** is the type of file system you want the partition to be. Click the down arrow to open the drop-down menu, and choose the file system type. The most common choices here are ext2, ext3, swap, and vfat.

◆ **RAID Device** shows the identifier for the RAID device. By default, md0 is selected. To change this selection, click the down arrow to the right of the field and select a different identifier.

- ◆ **RAID Level** is the field where you can choose the RAID level you want to use. The choices here are levels 0, 1, and 5. See Chapter 6 for an explanation of RAID levels.

- ◆ **RAID Members** lets you select the partitions that will be a part of the RAID device. In Figure 4-7, the two partitions created previously are shown. Click the box in front of the partition to select it.

- ◆ **Number of spares** lets you specify another partition to use as a spare if you are using RAID level 1 or 5. You need to create an additional software RAID partition for each spare you select.

- ◆ **Format RAID device** is checked as the default. If you do not want to format the device, remove the check mark from the box.

After you have made your selections, click OK to create the RAID device. You should now see the device listed on the Partition Information window.

Network Configuration

Click Network Configuration on the left side of the Kickstart Configurator window to open the Network Configuration screen as shown in Figure 4-8.

Figure 4-8: The Kickstart Configurator program window showing the Network Configuration screen

On this screen, you can configure a network card if you desire. Click Add Network Device, and you see the Network Device Information dialog box shown in Figure 4-9.

Figure 4-9: The Network Device Information dialog box is where you configure your network interface card.

In this dialog box, the first network interface card is shown as eth0, and the network type is shown as DHCP. If you are using DHCP on your network, you can accept the defaults for this device. If you want to use a static IP address, click the down arrow in the network type field and choose static IP. You need to fill in the appropriate network information in the fields at the bottom of the dialog box.

Click OK to return to the Network Configuration window, and your device is shown in the list. If you want to configure additional network interfaces, click Add Network Device and make your choices.

Authentication

Click Authentication on the left side of the Kickstart Configurator window to open the Authentication screen as shown in Figure 4-10.

By default, *use shadow passwords* and *MD5* are selected. Both of these options provide increased system security and should be used unless you have good reason not to use them. If you want to use any of the other services available from this screen, click the tab for the service you want to use, and click the enable box for that service. You need to enter the appropriate options for the service you have chosen.

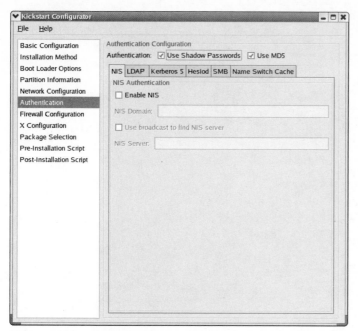

Figure 4-10: The Kickstart Configurator program window showing the Authentication screen

Firewall Configuration

Click Firewall Configuration on the left side of the Kickstart Configurator window to open the Firewall Configuration screen as shown in Figure 4-11.

From this screen, you can set the level of security you want on your system. If you choose High, only DNS, DHCP, and passive FTP will be allowed through the firewall. High is a good choice for a system that needs Internet connectivity but will not be running any servers.

Choosing Medium security allows remote systems to access your system on ports that you configure for a particular service. Choosing Disabled allows remote systems to access any services on your system that are running.

You can always click Customize and select the incoming services that you want to allow. In addition, you can set a device as a Trusted device. Any traffic received by a trusted device is not subject to the firewall rules.

Figure 4–11: The Kickstart Configurator program window showing the Firewall Configuration screen

X Configuration

Click X Configuration on the left side of the Kickstart Configurator window to open the X Configuration screen as shown in Figure 4-12.

If you wish to configure the X Window system, click the Configure the X Window System check box. After you do this, the three tabs become selectable, and you need to enter the appropriate information for each tabbed screen.

The first tab, labeled **General**, is where you can set the color depth of the system and the screen resolution. Click the down arrow next to the fields and choose the desired values from the drop-down lists. Also choose the default desktop, either Gnome or KDE. Gnome is selected as the default choice. Finally, you can decide if you want the X Window system to start at system boot. Choosing this option gives the user a graphical login window instead of a console login terminal.

Clicking the **Video Card** tab opens a new screen, shown in Figure 4-13, that gives you the opportunity to select a video card for your system.

The default selection here is to have the installation program probe for the video card installed in the system. You can disable this option by removing the check from the check box. If you disable probing for the video card, you will have to select the appropriate card from the list of cards and set the amount of video memory.

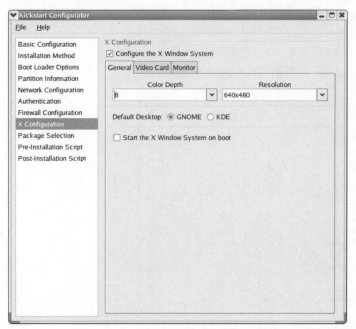

Figure 4-12: The Kickstart Configurator program window showing the X Configuration screen

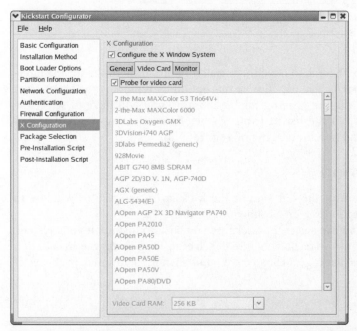

Figure 4-13: The Kickstart Configurator program window showing the X Configuration Video Card screen

Clicking the **Monitor** tab opens a new screen, shown in Figure 4-14, that gives you the opportunity to select a video card for your system.

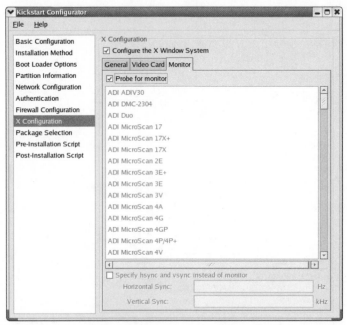

Figure 4–14: The Kickstart Configurator program window showing the X Configuration Monitor screen

The default selection here is to have the installation program probe for the monitor installed in the system. You can disable this option by removing the check from the check box. If you disable probing for the monitor, you will have to select the appropriate monitor from the list of cards. Rather than selecting a monitor, you may set the vertical and horizontal sync of your monitor.

Package selection

Click Package selection on the left side of the Kickstart Configurator window to open the Package Selection screen as shown in Figure 4-15.

From this screen, you can select the packages you wish to install on your system. Click the box in front of the package name to select it. By default, the installation automatically resolves package dependencies and installs additional packages if required. You can choose to ignore dependencies by selecting this option, and no additional packages will be installed to resolve dependency problems. There is a possibility that your selected packages may not work with unresolved dependencies, so it is best to let the installation program automatically resolve the dependency.

Figure 4-15: The Kickstart Configurator program window showing the Package Selection screen

Pre-Installation Script

Click Pre-Installation Script on the left side of the Kickstart Configurator window to open the Pre-Installation Selection screen as shown in Figure 4-16.

If you want to have commands run on your system before the installation starts, you can enter them in the area indicated on the screen. The system parses the Kickstart file and then runs your commands before beginning the installation. You can have your script interpreted by the scripting language of your choice by selecting the Use an Interpreter option and entering the interpreter to use.

Figure 4-16: The Kickstart Configurator program window showing the Pre-Installation Script screen

Post-Installation Script

Click Post-Installation Script on the left side of the Kickstart Configurator window to open the Post-Installation screen as shown in Figure 4-17.

If you want to have commands run on your system after the installation ends, you can enter them in the area indicated on the screen. If you desire, you can have the post-install script run outside of the chroot environment by selecting this option. Also, you can have your script interpreted by the scripting language of your choice by selecting the Use an Interpreter option and entering the interpreter to use.

Summary

In this chapter, you learned about installing Red Hat using the Kickstart program. First, you learned about the Kickstart configuration file and how to configure it manually. Then you learned about the Red Hat program called Kickstart Configurator. Using Kickstart Configurator, you can automate the creation of the Kickstart configuration file using an easy to follow graphical interface.

Figure 4-17: The Kickstart Configurator program window showing the Post-Installation Script screen

Chapter 5

System Startup and Shutdown

IN THIS CHAPTER

◆ Understanding the boot process

◆ Using GRUB

◆ Running programs at boot time

◆ Init runlevels

◆ Shutting down the system

AN IMPORTANT AND POWERFUL ASPECT of Red Hat Enterprise Linux is the open method it uses for starting and stopping the operating system. During boot time, Red Hat Enterprise Linux loads programs in a specific and configurable order. Once booted, you are free to change the configuration files controlling the boot process as well as the configuration files for the programs started at boot time.

Similarly, system shutdown gracefully terminates processes in an organized and configurable way, although customization of this process is rarely required. Understanding how the boot and shutdown processes work not only allows you to easily customize Red Hat Enterprise Linux to your needs but makes it easier to troubleshoot problems related to starting or shutting down your system.

In addition, the initialization process that Red Hat Enterprise Linux uses allows for multiple configurations, or *runlevels*, to be created on a single machine. This allows the administrator to switch between modes and to define a single mode as the default.

Understanding the Boot Process

Following are the basic stages of the boot process for an x86 system:

1. The system BIOS checks the system and launches the first-stage boot loader on the MBR of the primary hard disk.

2. The first-stage boot loader loads itself into memory and launches the second-stage boot loader from the /boot/ partition.

3. The kernel is loaded into memory, which in turn loads any necessary modules and mounts the root partition read-only.

4. The kernel hands control of the boot process to the `/sbin/init` program.

5. The `/sbin/init` program loads all services and user-space tools and mounts all partitions listed in `/etc/fstab`.

6. The user is presented with a login prompt for the freshly booted Linux system.

Because configuration of the boot process is more common than the customization of the shutdown process, the remainder of this chapter discusses in detail how the boot process works and how it can be customized to suit your needs.

A Detailed Look at the Boot Process

The beginning of the boot process varies depending on the platform on which you are booting your system. However, once the kernel is found and loaded by the system, the default boot process is identical across all architectures. In the example that follows, the system is an x86 computer.

THE BIOS

When an x86 computer is booted, the processor looks at the end of system memory for the Basic Input/Output System, or BIOS, program and runs it. The BIOS not only controls the first step of the boot process but also provides the lowest-level interface to peripheral devices before the operating system takes over. For this reason, it is written into read-only, permanent memory and is always available for use. Other platforms use different programs to perform low-level tasks roughly equivalent to those of the BIOS on an x86 system. For instance, Itanium-based computers use the Extensible Firmware Interface (EFI) Shell, while Alpha systems use the SRM console.

Once loaded, the BIOS tests the system, looks for and checks peripherals, and locates a valid device with which to boot the system. Usually, it first checks any floppy drives and CD-ROM drives present for bootable media; then it looks to the system's hard drives. The order of the drives searched for booting can often be controlled with a setting in BIOS. Often, the first hard drive set to boot is the C drive or the master IDE device on the primary IDE bus. The BIOS loads whatever program is residing in the first sector of this device, called the Master Boot Record, or MBR, into memory. The MBR is only 512 bytes and contains machine-code instructions for booting the machine, along with the partition table. Once found and loaded, the BIOS passes control to whatever program is on the MBR.

THE BOOT LOADER

This section looks at the boot process for the x86 platform. Depending on your system's architecture, the boot process may differ slightly. Please see the section

"Differences in the Boot Process of Other Architectures" later in this chapter for a brief overview of non-x86 boot processes.

Linux boot loaders for the x86 platform are broken into at least two stages. The first stage is a small machine code binary on the MBR. Its sole job is to locate the second stage boot loader and load the first part of it into memory. Under Red Hat Linux, you can install one of two boot loaders: GRUB or LILO. GRUB is the default boot loader, but LILO is available for those who require it for their hardware setup or who prefer it.

If you are using LILO under Red Hat Linux, the second stage boot loader uses information on the MBR to determine what boot options are available to the user. This means that when a configuration change is made or you upgrade your kernel manually, you must run the /sbin/lilo -v command to write the appropriate information to the MBR. GRUB, on the other hand, can read ext2 partitions and therefore simply loads the configuration file /boot/grub/grub.conf when the second stage loader is called.

TIP   If you upgrade the kernel using the Red Hat Update Agent, the MBR or the /boot/grub/grub.conf file will be updated automatically. For more information on Red Hat Network (RHN), see http://rhn.redhat.com.

Once the second-stage boot loader is in memory, it presents the user with the Red Hat Linux initial graphical screen showing the different operating systems or kernels it has been configured to boot. If you have only Red Hat Linux installed and have not changed anything in the /etc/lilo.conf or /boot/grub/grub.conf files, you will see only one option for booting. If you have configured the boot loader to boot other operating systems, this screen gives you the opportunity to select them. Use the arrow keys to highlight the operating system and press Enter. If you do nothing, the boot loader will load the default selection.

NOTE   If you installed Symmetric Multi-Processor (SMP) kernel support, you will see more than one option the first time you boot your system. Under LILO, you will see linux and linux-up. Under GRUB, you will see Red Hat Linux (kernel version) and Red Hat Linux (kernel version-smp). The linux or Red Hat Linux (kernel version-smp) option is the SMP kernel. If you experience any problems with the SMP kernel, select the linux-up or non-SMP kernel upon rebooting. If you need to alter the command-line arguments to the kernel, see the section on GRUB later in this chapter. For information on changing the runlevel at the GRUB or LILO prompt, see the section "Init Runlevels" in this chapter.

Once the second-stage boot loader has determined which kernel to boot, it locates the corresponding kernel binary in the /boot/ directory. The proper binary is the /boot/vmlinuz-2.4.x-xx file that corresponds to the boot loader's settings. Next, the boot loader places the appropriate initial RAM disk image, called an initrd, into memory. The initrd image is used by the kernel to load any drivers not compiled into it that are necessary to boot the system. This is particularly important if you have SCSI hard drives or are using the ext3 file system.

 Do not remove the /initrd/ directory from the file system for any reason. Removing this directory causes your system to fail with a kernel panic error message at boot time.

Once the kernel and the initrd image are loaded into memory, the boot loader hands control of the boot process to the kernel.

THE KERNEL

When the kernel loads, it immediately initializes and configures the computer's memory. Next, it configures the various hardware attached to the system, including all processors and I/O subsystems, as well as any storage devices. It then looks for the compressed initrd image in a predetermined location in memory, decompresses it, mounts it, and loads all necessary drivers. Next, it initializes file-system-related virtual devices, such as LVM or software RAID, before unmounting the initrd disk image and freeing all the memory it once occupied.

After the kernel has initialized all the devices on the system, it creates a root device, mounts the root partition read-only, and frees unused memory. At this point, with the kernel loaded into memory, the system is operational. However, with no user applications to give the user the ability to provide meaningful input to the system, not much can be done with it. To set up the user environment, the kernel starts the /sbin/init command.

THE /sbin/init PROGRAM

The init program coordinates the rest of the boot process and configures the environment for the user. When the init command starts, it becomes the parent or grandparent of all of the processes that start up automatically on a Red Hat system. First, it runs the /etc/rc.d/rc.sysinit script, which sets the environment path, starts swap, checks the file systems, and so on. Basically, rc.sysinit takes care of everything that a system needs to have done at initialization.

For example, most systems use a clock, so on them rc.sysinit reads the /etc/sysconfig/clock configuration file to initialize the clock. If special serial-port processes must be initialized, rc.sysinit executes the /etc/rc.serial file.

The init command then runs the /etc/inittab script, which describes how the system should be set up in each SysV init runlevel. Among other things, /etc/inittab sets the default runlevel.

For details on making an initrd, see the section about converting to an ext3 file system in Chapter 6.

Next, the init command sets the source function library, /etc/rc.d/init.d/ functions, for the system. This spells out how to start or kill a program and how to determine the process identification number (PID) of a program. The init program starts all of the background processes by executing /etc/rc.d/rc and passing it the new runlevel.

When booting to runlevel 5, the init program looks in the /etc/rc.d/rc5.d/ directory to determine which processes to start and stop. Following is an example listing for a runlevel 5, /etc/rc.d/rc5.d/ directory:

```
K01pppoe -> ../init.d/pppoe
K05innd -> ../init.d/innd
K10ntpd -> ../init.d/ntpd
K15httpd -> ../init.d/httpd
K15mysqld -> ../init.d/mysqld
K15pvmd -> ../init.d/pvmd
K16rarpd -> ../init.d/rarpd
K20bootparamd -> ../init.d/bootparamd
K20nfs -> ../init.d/nfs
K20rstatd -> ../init.d/rstatd
K20rusersd -> ../init.d/rusersd
K20rwalld -> ../init.d/rwalld
K20rwhod -> ../init.d/rwhod
K25squid -> ../init.d/squid
K28amd -> ../init.d/amd
K30mcserv -> ../init.d/mcserv
K34yppasswdd -> ../init.d/yppasswdd
K35dhcpd -> ../init.d/dhcpd
K35smb -> ../init.d/smb
K35vncserver -> ../init.d/vncserver
K45arpwatch -> ../init.d/arpwatch
K45named -> ../init.d/named
K50snmpd -> ../init.d/snmpd
K54pxe -> ../init.d/pxe
K55routed -> ../init.d/routed
K60mars-nwe -> ../init.d/mars-new
K61ldap -> ../init.d/ldap
K65kadmin -> ../init.d/kadmin
K65kprop -> ../init.d/kprop
```

```
K65krb524 -> ../init.d/krb524
K65krb5kdc -> ../init.d/krb5kdc
K75gated -> ../init.d/gated
K80nscd -> ../init.d/nscd
K84ypserv -> ../init.d/ypserv
K90ups -> ../init.d/ups
K96irda -> ../init.d/irda
S05kudzu -> ../init.d/kudzu
S06reconfig -> ../init.d/reconfig
S08ipchains -> ../init.d/ipchains
S10network -> ../init.d/network
S12syslog -> ../init.d/syslog
S13portmap -> ../init.d/portmap
S14nfslock -> ../init.d/nfslock
S18autofs -> ../init.d/autofs
S20random -> ../init.d/random
S25netfs -> ../init.d/netfs
S26apmd -> ../init.d/apmd
S35identd -> ../init.d/identd
S40atd -> ../init.d/atd
S45pcmcia -> ../init.d/pcmcia
S55sshd -> ../init.d/sshd
S56rawdevices -> ../init.d/rawdevices
S56xinetd -> ../init.d/xinetd
S60lpd -> ../init.d/lpd
S75keytable -> ../init.d/keytable
S80isdn -> ../init.d/isdn
S80sendmail -> ../init.d/sendmail
S85gpm -> ../init.d/gpm
S90canna -> ../init.d/canna
S90crond -> ../init.d/crond
S90FreeWnn -> ../init.d/FreeWnn
S90xfs -> ../init.d/xfs
S95anacron -> ../init.d/anacron
S95firstboot -> ../init.d/firstboot
S97rhnsd -> ../init.d/rhnsd
S99local -> ../rc.local
S99mdmonitor -> ../init.d/mdmonitor
```

As you can see, none of the scripts that actually start and stop the services are located in the /etc/rc.d/rc5.d/ directory. Rather, all of the files in /etc/rc.d/ rc5.d/ are symbolic links pointing to scripts located in the /etc/rc.d/init.d/ directory. Symbolic links are used in each of the rc directories so that the runlevels can be reconfigured by creating, modifying, and deleting the symbolic links without affecting the actual scripts they reference.

A symbolic link is a type of file that points to another file in the file system.

The name of each symbolic link begins with either a *K* or an *S*. The *K* links are processes that are killed on that runlevel, and those beginning with an *S* are started. The `init` command first stops all of the *K* symbolic links in the directory by issuing the `/etc/rc.d/init.d/ command stop` command, where `command` is the process to be killed. It then starts all of the S symbolic links by issuing `/etc/rc.d/ init.d/ command start`.

After the system is finished booting, you can log in as root and execute these same scripts to start and stop services. For instance, the command `/etc/rc.d/init.d/httpd stop` stops the Apache Web server.

Each of the symbolic links is numbered to dictate start order. You can change the order in which the services are started or stopped by changing this number. Symbolic links that have the same number are started alphabetically.

In the preceding example `/etc/rc.d/rc5.d/` directory, the `init` command kills `pppoe`, `innd`, `ntpd`, `httpd`, `mysqld`, `pvmd`, `rarpd`, `bootparamd`, `nfs`, `rstatd`, `rusersd`, `rwalld`, `rwhod`, `squid`, `amd`, `mcserv`, `yppasswdd`, `dhcpd`, `smb`, `vncserver`, `arpwatch`, `named`, `snmpd`, `pxe`, `routed`, `mars-nwe`, `ldap`, `kadmin`, `kprop`, `krb524`, `krb5kdc`, `gated`, `nscd`, `ypserv`, `ups`, and `irda`. After all processes are killed, `init` looks into the same directory and finds start scripts for `kudzu`, `reconfig`, `ipchains`, `portmap`, `nfslock`, `autofs`, `random`, `netfs`, `apmd`, `identd`, `atd`, `pcmcia`, `sshd`, `rawdevices`, `xinetd`, `lpd`, `keytable`, `isdn`, `sendmail`, `gpm`, `canna`, `crond`, `FreeWnn`, `xfs`, `anacron`, `firstboot`, `rhnsd`, and `mdmonitor`.

The last thing the init program does is run any scripts located in `/etc/rc.d/ rc.local` (see the section "Running Programs at Boot Time" in this chapter for more on customizing the `rc.local` file). At this point, the system is considered to be operating at runlevel 5.

After the `init` command has progressed through the appropriate `rc` directory for the runlevel, the `/etc/inittab` script forks a `getty` process for each virtual console (login prompts) allocated to the runlevel. Runlevels 2 through 5 get all six virtual consoles, while runlevel 1 (single-user mode) gets only one, and runlevels 0 and 6 get none. The `getty` process opens communication pathways to tty devices, sets their modes, prints the login prompt, gets the user name, and initiates the login process for the user. In runlevel 5, `/etc/inittab` runs a script called `/etc/X11/ prefdm`. The `prefdm` script runs the preferred X display manager – gdm if you are running GNOME or kdm if you are running KDE – based on the contents of the `/etc/sysconfig/desktop/` directory.

Finally, the `init` command runs the `/etc/rc.d/rc.local` script. At this point, you should be looking at a login prompt. This is the sequence of events that occurs when the system starts. Next, we take a more detailed look at GRUB, the default boot loader.

Using GRUB

As you saw in the previous section, in order for a Red Hat system to boot properly, a boot loader – typically either GRUB or LILO – must be invoked in order for the operating system to be loaded and initialized. The default boot loader for Red Hat Linux is GRUB, the *GRand Unified Boot* loader. In addition to loading the Red Hat operating system, GRUB allows for multiple boot options to be configured. For example, GRUB can be used in a dual-boot situation, where both Red Hat Linux and another operating system like Windows are available. GRUB can also be used to pass boot-time arguments to the kernel.

GRUB is typically used only on Intel-compatible x86 architectures. If your architecture differs, see the available documentation at `http://www` `.redhat.com`.

GRUB and the x86 Boot Process

This section discusses the specific role GRUB plays when booting an x86 system. GRUB loads itself into memory in the following stages:

1. The Stage 1 or primary boot loader is read into memory by the BIOS from the MBR1. The primary boot loader exists on less than 512 bytes of disk space within the MBR. The only thing it does is load the Stage 1.5 or Stage 2 boot loader.

2. The Stage 1.5 boot loader is read into memory by the Stage 1 boot loader only if necessary. Some hardware requires an intermediate step to get to the Stage 2 boot loader. This is sometimes true when the `/boot` partition is above the 1024-cylinder head of the hard drive or when using LBA mode. The Stage 1.5 boot loader is found either on the `/boot` partition or on a small part of the MBR and the `/boot` partition.

3. The Stage 2 or secondary boot loader is read into memory. The secondary boot loader displays the GRUB menu and command environment. This interface allows you to select which operating system or Linux kernel to boot, pass arguments to the kernel, or look at system parameters, such as available RAM.

4. The secondary boot loader reads the operating system or kernel and `initrd` into memory. Once GRUB determines which operating system to start, it loads it into memory and hands control of the machine to that operating system.

The boot method used to boot Red Hat Linux is called the direct loading method because the boot loader loads the operating system directly. There is no intermediary between the boot loader and the kernel.

The boot process used by other operating systems may differ. For example, Microsoft's operating systems, as well as various other proprietary operating systems, are loaded using a chain loading boot method. Under this method, the MBR simply points to the first sector of the partition holding the operating system. There it finds the files necessary to actually boot that operating system. GRUB supports both direct and chain loading boot methods, allowing it to boot almost any operating system.

During installation, Microsoft's DOS and Windows installer completely overwrites the MBR, destroying any existing boot loader. If creating a dual-boot system, it is best to install the Microsoft operating system first. If you do overwrite your boot loader, you can run `grub-install /dev/hda` from an emergency boot disk to restore it.

Features of GRUB

A number of features make GRUB preferable to other boot loaders available for the x86 architecture. Following is a list of some of the more important features:

◆ GRUB provides a true command-based, pre-OS environment on x86 machines. This affords the user maximum flexibility in loading operating systems with certain options or gathering information about the system. For years, many non-x86 architectures have employed pre-OS environments that allow system booting from a command line. While some command features are available with LILO and other x86 boot loaders, GRUB is more feature rich.

◆ GRUB supports Logical Block Addressing (LBA) mode. LBA places the addressing conversion used to find files in the hard driver's firmware, and it is used on many IDE and all SCSI hard devices. Before LBA, boot loaders could encounter the 1024-cylinder BIOS limitation, where the BIOS could not find a file after that cylinder head of the disk. LBA support allows GRUB to boot operating systems from partitions beyond the 1024-cylinder limit, so long as the system BIOS supports LBA mode. Most modern BIOS revisions support LBA mode.

◆ GRUB can read `ext2` partitions. This allows GRUB to access its configuration file, `/boot/grub/grub.conf`, every time the system boots, obviating the need for the user to write a new version of the first-stage boot loader to MBR when configuration changes are made. The only time a user needs to reinstall GRUB on the MBR is when the physical location of the `/boot` partition is moved on the disk. For details on installing GRUB to the MBR, see the next section.

Installing GRUB

If GRUB was not installed during the installation process, you can install it afterwards, and it will automatically become the default boot loader. Before installing GRUB, make sure you have the latest GRUB package available, or use the GRUB package from the installation CD-ROMs.

For instructions on installing packages, see Chapter 27.

Once the GRUB package is installed, open a root shell `prompt` and run the command `/sbin/grub-install location`, where `location` is the location where GRUB Stage 1 boot loader should be installed. The following command installs GRUB to the MBR of the master IDE device on the primary IDE bus, also known as the C drive:

```
/sbin/grub-install /dev/hda
```

The next time you boot the system, you should see the GRUB graphical boot loader menu before the kernel loads.

GRUB Terminology

When configuring GRUB, it is important to understand the way in which it refers to devices on any particular system. The device naming conventions differ from typical Linux `/dev` entries, and the GRUB syntax must be understood if advanced or unusual configurations, such as setting up a dual-boot system, are to be included on your system.

DEVICE NAMES

The first hard drive of a system is called (`hd0`) by GRUB. The first partition on that drive is called (`hd0,0`), and the fifth partition on the second hard drive is called (`hd1,4`). In general, the naming convention for file systems when using GRUB breaks down in the following way:

```
( <type-of-device> <bios-device-number> , <partition-number> )
```

The parentheses and comma are very important to the device naming conventions. The `type-of-device` refers to whether a hard disk (`hd`) or floppy disk (`fd`) is being specified. The `bios-device-number` is the number of the device according to the system's BIOS, starting with 0. The primary IDE hard drive is numbered 0, while the secondary IDE hard drive is numbered 1. The ordering is roughly equivalent to the way the Linux kernel arranges the devices by letters, where *a* in `hda` relates to 0, *b* in `hdb` relates to 1, and so on.

GRUB's numbering system for devices starts with 0, not 1. Failing to make this distinction is one of the most common mistakes that new GRUB users make.

The `partition-number` relates to the number of a specific partition on a disk device. Like the `bios-device-number`, the partition numbering starts at 0. While most partitions are specified by numbers, if a system uses BSD partitions, they are signified by letters, such as *a* or *c*.

GRUB uses the following rules when naming devices and partitions:

◆ It does not matter if system hard drives are IDE or SCSI. All hard drives start with `hd`. Floppy disks start with `fd`.

◆ To specify an entire device without respect to its partitions, simply omit the comma and the partition number. This is important when telling GRUB to configure the MBR for a particular disk. For example, (`hd0`) specifies the MBR on the first device, and (`hd3`) specifies the MBR on the fourth device.

◆ If a system has multiple drive devices, it is very important to know the drive boot order set in the BIOS. This is rather simple to do if a system has only IDE or SCSI drives, but if there is a mix of devices, it can become confusing.

FILE NAMES

When typing commands to GRUB involving a file, such as a menu list to use when allowing the booting of multiple operating systems, it is necessary to include the name of the file immediately after specifying the device and partition. A sample file specification to an absolute file name is organized as follows:

```
( <type-of-device> <bios-device-number> , <partition-number> \
)/path/to/file
```

Most of the time, a user specifies files by the directory path on that partition, plus the file name. It is also possible to specify files to GRUB that do not actually appear in the file system, such as a chain loader that appears in the first few blocks of a partition. To specify these files, you must provide a blocklist, which tells GRUB, block by block, where the file is located in the partition. Since a file can comprise several different sets of blocks, there is a specific way to write blocklists. Each file's section location is described by an offset number of blocks and then a number of blocks from that offset point, and the sections are put together in a comma-delimited order. Consider the following blocklist:

```
0+50,100+25,200+1
```

This blocklist tells GRUB to use a file that starts at the first block on the partition and uses blocks 0 through 49, 99 through 124, and 199. Knowing how to write blocklists is useful when using GRUB to load operating systems that use chain loading, such as Microsoft Windows. It is possible to leave off the offset number of blocks if starting at block 0. As an example, the chain-loading file in the first partition of the first hard drive would have the following name:

```
(hd0,0)+1
```

The following shows the `chainloader` command with a similar blocklist designation at the GRUB command line after setting the correct device and partition as root:

```
chainloader +1
```

GRUB'S ROOT FILE SYSTEM

Some users are confused by the use of the term "root file system" with GRUB. It is important to remember that GRUB's root file system has nothing to do with the Linux root file system. The GRUB root file system is the root partition for a particular device. GRUB uses this information to mount the device and load files from it.

With Red Hat Linux, once GRUB has loaded its root partition, which equates to the `/boot` partition and contains the Linux kernel, the `kernel` command can be executed with the location of the kernel file as an option. Once the Linux kernel boots, it sets its own root file system. The original GRUB root file system and its mounts are forgotten; they existed only to boot the kernel file. Refer to the root and kernel commands in the "GRUB Commands" section of this chapter for more information.

GRUB Interfaces

GRUB features three interfaces, each of which provides a different level of functionality. Each of these interfaces allows users to boot operating systems and move among interfaces within the GRUB environment.

MENU INTERFACE

If GRUB was automatically configured by the Red Hat Linux installation program, this is the interface shown by default. A menu of operating systems or kernels pre-configured with their own boot commands are displayed as a list, ordered by name.

Use the arrow keys to select an option other than the default selection, and press the Enter key to boot it. Alternatively, a timeout period is set, so that GRUB starts loading the default option.

From the menu interface, type **e** to enter the entry editor interface or **c** to load a command-line interface. See the "Command-Line Interface" section of this chapter for more information on configuring this interface.

MENU ENTRY EDITOR INTERFACE

To access the menu entry editor, type **e** at the boot loader menu. The GRUB commands for that entry are displayed here, and users may alter these command lines before booting the operating system by adding a command line (**o** inserts the new line after the current line and **O** before it), editing one (**e**), or deleting one (**d**).

After all changes are made, type **b** to execute the commands and boot the operating system. The Esc key discards any changes and reloads the standard menu interface. Type **c** to load the command-line interface.

COMMAND–LINE INTERFACE

The command line is the most basic GRUB interface, but it is also the one that grants the most control. The command line makes it possible to type any relevant GRUB commands followed by the Enter key to execute them. This interface features some advanced shell-like features, including Tab key completion, based on context, and Ctrl key combinations when typing commands, such as Ctrl-a to move to the beginning of a line and Ctrl-e to move to the end of a line. In addition, the arrow, Home, End, and Delete keys work as they do in the `bash` shell. See the "GRUB Commands" section for a list of common commands.

ORDER OF INTERFACE USE

When the GRUB environment loads the second-stage boot loader, it looks for its configuration file. When found, it uses the configuration file to build the menu list, and it displays the boot menu interface. If the configuration file cannot be found, or if the configuration file is unreadable, GRUB will load the command-line interface to allow users to manually type the commands necessary to boot an operating system.

If the configuration file is not valid, GRUB will print the error and ask for input. This can be very helpful, because users can then see precisely where the problem occurred and fix it in the file. Pressing any key reloads the menu interface, where it is then possible to edit the menu option and correct the problem based on the error reported by GRUB. If the correction fails, the error is reported and GRUB will begin again.

GRUB Commands

GRUB allows a number of useful commands in its command-line interface. Some of the commands accept options after their name, and these options should be separated from the command and other options on that line by space characters. The following is a list of useful commands:

◆ boot — Boots the operating system or chain loader that has been previously specified and loaded.

◆ chainloader filename — Loads the specified file as a chain loader. To grab the file at the first sector of the specified partition, use +1 as the file's name.

◆ displaymem — Displays the current use of memory, based on information from the BIOS. This is useful to determine how much RAM a system has prior to booting it.

◆ initrd filename — Enables users to specify an initial RAM disk to use when booting. An initrd is necessary when the kernel needs certain modules in order to boot properly, such as when the root partition is formatted with the ext3 file system.

◆ install stage-1 install-disk stage-2 p config-file — Installs GRUB to the system MBR.

This command can be configured in several different ways. However, it is required to specify a stage-1, which signifies a device, partition, and file where the first boot loader image can be found, such as (hd0,0)/grub/ stage1. In addition, specify the disk where the stage 1 boot loader should be installed, such as (hd0). The stage-2 section tells the stage 1 boot loader where the stage 2 boot loader is located, such as (hd0,0)/grub/ stage2. The p option tells the install command that a menu configuration file is being specified in the config-file section, such as (hd0,0)/grub/ grub.conf.

The install command overwrites any other information in the MBR. If install is executed, any information (other than GRUB information) used to boot other operating systems will be lost. Make sure you know what you are doing before executing this command.

◆ kernel kernel-filename option-1 option-N — Specifies the kernel file to load from GRUB's root file system when using direct loading to boot the operating system. Options can follow the kernel command and are passed to the kernel when it is loaded. For Red Hat Linux, an example kernel command looks like the following:

```
kernel /vmlinuz root=/dev/hda5
```

This line specifies that the vmlinuz file is loaded from GRUB's root file system, such as (hd0,0). An option is also passed to the kernel specifying that the root file system for the Linux kernel when it loads should be on hda5, the fifth partition on the first IDE hard drive. Multiple options may be placed after this option, if needed.

- `root device-and-partition` — Configures GRUB's root partition to be the particular device and partition, such as (hd0,0), and mounts the partition so that files can be read.

- `rootnoverify device-and-partition` — Does the same thing as the `root` command but does not mount the partition.

Commands other than these are available. Type **info grub** for a full list of commands.

GRUB Menu Configuration File

The configuration file, which is used to create the list in GRUB's menu interface of operating systems to boot, essentially allows the user to select a preset group of commands to execute. The commands given in the previous "GRUB Commands" section of this chapter can be used, as well as some special commands available only in the configuration file.

SPECIAL CONFIGURATION FILE COMMANDS

The following commands can be used only in the GRUB menu configuration file:

- `color normal-color selected-color` — Configures specific colors for the foreground and background of the GRUB menu. Use simple color names, such as red/black. For example:

  `color red/black green/blue.`

- `default title-name` — The default entry title name that will be loaded if the menu interface times out.

- `fallback title-name` — If used, the entry title name to try if the first attempt fails.

- `hiddenmenu` — If used, prevents the GRUB menu interface from being displayed, loading the default entry when the timeout period expires. The user can see the standard GRUB menu by pressing the Esc key.

- `password password` — If used, prevents the user who does not know the password from editing the entries for this menu option. It is possible to specify an alternate menu configuration file after the password, so that, if the password is known, GRUB will restart the second stage of the boot loader and use this alternate configuration file to build the menu. If this alternate file were left out of the command, a user who knows the password would be able to edit the current configuration file.

- `timeout` — If used, sets the interval, in seconds, before GRUB loads the entry designated by the default command.

◆ `splashimage` — Specifies the location of the splash screen image to be used when GRUB boots.

◆ `title` — Sets a title to be used with a particular group of commands used to load an operating system. The # character can be used to place comments in the menu configuration file.

CONFIGURATION FILE STRUCTURE

The GRUB menu interface's configuration file is `/boot/grub/grub.conf`. The commands to set the global preferences for the menu interface are placed at the top of the file, followed by the different entries for each of the operating systems or kernels listed in the menu. A very basic GRUB menu configuration file designed to boot either Red Hat Linux or Microsoft Windows 2000 might look as follows:

```
default=0
timeout=10
splashimage=(hd0,0)/grub/splash.xpm.gz

# section to load linux
title Red Hat Linux (2.4.18-5.47)
            root (hd0,0)
            kernel /vmlinuz-2.4.18-5.47 ro root=/dev/sda2
            initrd /initrd-2.4.18-5.47.img

# section to load Windows 2000
title windows
            rootnoverify (hd0,0)
            chainloader +1
```

This file tells GRUB to build a menu with Red Hat Linux as the default operating system, set to autoboot it after 10 seconds. Two sections are given, one for each operating system entry, with commands specific to this system's disk partition table.

 The default is specified as a number. This refers to the first title line GRUB comes across. If you want Windows to be the default, change the `default=` value to `1`.

Running Programs at Boot Time

The file `/etc/rc.d/rc.local` script is run by the `init` command at boot time, or when changing runlevels, after all other initialization is complete. You can use this file to add commands necessary for your environment. For instance, you can start additional daemons or initialize a printer.

In addition, if you require serial port setup at boot time, you can create and edit /etc/rc.serial. This script runs setserial commands to configure the system's serial ports. See the setserial man page for more information.

Differences in the Boot Processes of Other Architectures

Once the Red Hat Linux kernel loads and hands off the boot process to the init command, the same sequence of events occurs on every architecture. So the main difference among each architecture's boot process is in the application used to find and load the kernel. For example, the Alpha architecture uses the aboot boot loader, while the Itanium architecture uses the ELILO boot loader.

SysV init

SysV init is a standard process used by Red Hat Linux to control which software the init command launches or shuts off on a given runlevel. SysV init was chosen because it is easier to use and more flexible than the traditional BSD-style init process. The configuration files for SysV init are in the /etc/rc.d/ directory. Within this directory are the rc, rc.local, and rc.sysinit scripts as well as the following directories:

- init.d
- rc0.d
- rc1.d
- rc2.d
- rc3.d
- rc4.d
- rc5.d
- rc6.d

The /init.d directory contains the scripts used by the init command when controlling services. Each of the numbered directories represents one of the six default runlevels configured by default under Red Hat Linux. For more information on runlevels, see the section "Init Runlevels" in this chapter.

The default runlevel is listed in /etc/inittab. To find out the default runlevel for your system, look for the line similar to the one that follows near the top of /etc/inittab:

```
id:3:initdefault:
```

The default runlevel listed in the preceding example is 3, as the number after the first colon indicates. If you want to change it, edit /etc/inittab as root.

Be very careful when editing /etc/inittab. Simple typos can cause your system to become unbootable. If this happens, you will either need a boot diskette for your system or you will need to enter rescue mode to boot your computer and fix the file.

Init Runlevels

The idea behind operating different services at different runlevels revolves around the fact that different systems can be used in a different ways. Some services cannot be used until the system is in a particular state, or mode, such as being ready for more than one user or having networking available. There are times when you may want to operate the system at a lower mode, such as fixing disk-corruption problems in runlevel 1, when no other users can possibly be on the system, or leaving a server in runlevel 3 without an X session running. In these cases, running services that depend upon a higher system mode to function does not make sense, because they will not work correctly anyway.

By already having each service assigned to start when its particular runlevel is reached, you ensure an orderly startup process and can quickly change the mode of the machine without worrying about which services to manually start or stop. Generally, Red Hat Linux operates in runlevel 3 or runlevel 5 – both full multiuser modes. The following runlevels are defined in Red Hat Linux:

◆ 0 – Halt

◆ 1 – Single-user mode

◆ 2 – Not used (user-definable)

◆ 3 – Full multiuser mode

◆ 4 – Not used (user-definable)

◆ 5 – Full multiuser mode (with an X-based login screen)

◆ 6 – Reboot

The default runlevel for a system to boot into and stop in is configured in /etc/inittab. Feel free to configure runlevels 2 and 4 as you see fit. Many users configure those runlevels in a way that makes the most sense for them while leaving the standard runlevels 3 and 5 alone. This allows them to quickly move in and out of their custom configuration without disturbing the normal set of features at the standard runlevels.

If your machine gets into a state where it will not boot because of a bad /etc/inittab or will not let you log in because you have a corrupted /etc/passwd or if you have simply forgotten your password, you can boot into single-user mode. If you are using LILO, you can enter single-user mode by typing linux single at the LILO boot: prompt. If you are using GRUB as your boot loader, you can enter single-user mode using the following steps.

1. In the graphical GRUB boot loader screen, select the Red Hat Linux boot label and type **e** to edit it.

2. Arrow down to the kernel line and type **e** to edit it.

3. At the prompt, type **single** and press Enter.

4. You are returned to the GRUB screen with the kernel information. Type **b** to boot the system into single-user mode.

5. A very bare system will boot, and you will have a command shell from which you can fix things.

If this does not work, you will need to boot by typing **linux init=/bin/bash** at the LILO boot: prompt. Doing so places you at a shell prompt; note that no file systems other than the root file system are mounted, and the root file system is mounted in read-only mode. To mount it in read-write mode (to allow editing of a broken /etc/inittab, for example) do:

```
mount -n /proc
mount -o rw,remount /
```

Initscript Utilities

The /sbin/chkconfig utility is a simple command-line tool for maintaining the /etc/rc.d/init.d directory hierarchy. It relieves system administrators of having to directly manipulate the numerous symbolic links in the directories under /etc/rc.d. In addition, there is /sbin/ntsysv, which provides a text-based interface that you may find easier to use than chkconfig's command-line interface.

If you prefer a graphical interface, use the Services Configuration Tool program, which can be invoked using the redhat-config-services command. All of these utilities must be run as root.

Shutting Down the System

The command to bring the system down is shutdown and uses the following syntax:

```
/sbin/shutdown [-t sec.] [-arkhncfF] time [warning message]
```

You can refer to the man page for shutdown to get all the details for the `shutdown` command. To access the man page for `shutdown`, type the following command:

`man shutdown`

Shutdown is an orderly process for bringing the system down. Logged-in users receive notification that the system is coming down, and new users are prevented from logging in. All running processes receive the SIGTERM signal, allowing for a clean, orderly shutdown of the running processes. The shutdown program signals the init program to change to a different runlevel depending on the shutdown command. Runlevel 0 is used for a system shutdown, and runlevel 6 is used for a system reboot. Some examples of commonly used shutdown commands with explanations of their meanings are shown as follows.

 Typically, only the root user can issue the `shutdown` command.

`/sbin/shutdown -h now`

(This command immediately begins the shutdown process and halts the system.)

`/sbin/shutdown -r now`

(This command immediately begins the shutdown process and reboots the system.)

Summary

In this chapter, you learned about the procedure Red Hat Enterprise Linux uses to start and stop the system. Each step of the boot process was explained in the order in which it occurs, and the programs that run at each step were listed. In addition, you learned about boot loaders and their significance in starting the system. The GRUB boot loader was explained in detail to give you a better understanding of how it works. The role of the init process and runlevels in the system were also explained. Finally, you learned how to gracefully bring the system down using the `shutdown` command.

Chapter 6

The File System Explained

IN THIS CHAPTER

- ◆ Understanding the file system structure
- ◆ Special file locations
- ◆ Working with Linux-supported file systems
- ◆ Memory and virtual file systems
- ◆ Linux disk management
- ◆ What is RAID?

THIS CHAPTER BEGINS with a description of the file system structure and an explanation of the directories and the files they contain. Following the look at the file system structure are the file system commands, essential to proper file system management. In addition to the native Linux file system, Red Hat Enterprise Linux supports many other file system types. This chapter explains the other file system types and ends with a discussion of Linux disk management.

Understanding the File System Structure

Understanding the organization, or layout, of the file system is one of the most important aspects of system administration. For administrators, programmers, users, and installed software, knowing how and where the files are stored on the system is critical for proper system operation. A standard should be in place that specifies locations for specific types of data. Fortunately, Red Hat has chosen to follow the standards outlined in the Filesystem Hierarchy Standard (FHS). This section briefly explains the FHS and its relevance to proper system administration. For the complete standard, refer to http://www.pathname.com/fhs.

The FHS provides specific requirements for the placement of files in the directory structure. Placement is based on the type of information contained in the file. Two categories of file information exist: shareable or unshareable, and variable or static. Shareable files are files that can be accessed by other hosts, and unshareable files can be accessed only by the local system. Variable files contain information that can change at any time on their own, without anyone actually changing the file. A log file is an example of such a file. A static file contains information that does not change unless a user changes it. Program documentation and binary files are examples of static files. Figure 6-1 shows the organization of the file system on a typical Red Hat Linux system. Following the figure is an explanation of each directory and the types of files it may contain.

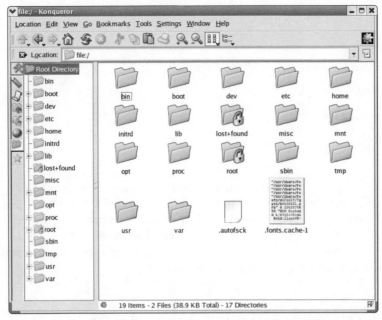

Figure 6-1: The file-system organization for a typical Red Hat Linux system

As shown in the illustration, the file system is organized in a flat, hierarchical file system. Linux's method of mounting its file systems in a flat, logical, hierarchical method has advantages over the file system mounting method used by Windows. Linux references everything relative to the root file system point /, whereas Windows has a different root mount point for every drive.

If you have a / partition that fills up in Linux, you can create another file system called /usr/local and move your data from / to the new file system definition. This practice frees up space on the / partition, and is an easy way to bring your system back up to a fully functional state.

This trick wouldn't work on a Windows machine, because Windows maps its file locations to static device disk definitions. You would have to change programs' file references from c:\ to d:\, and so forth. Linux's file system management is another good reason to use Linux on your production servers instead of Windows.

The / Directory

The / directory is called the *root* directory and is typically at the top of the file system structure. In many systems, the / directory is the only partition on the system and all other directories are mounted under it. Figure 6-1 shows a file system with the / directory mounted as the only partition, with all other directories mounted beneath it. The primary purpose of the / directory is booting the system, and to correct any problems that might be preventing the system from booting. According to the FHS, the / directory must contain, or have links to, the following directories:

◆ bin — This directory contains command files for use by the system administrator or other users. The bin directory can not contain subdirectories.

◆ boot — On Red Hat systems, this is the directory containing the kernel, the core of the operating system. Also in this directory are files related to booting the system, such as the bootloader.

◆ dev — This directory contains files with information about devices, either hardware or software devices, on the system.

◆ etc — This directory and its subdirectories contain most of the system configuration files. If you have the X Window System installed on your system, the X11 subdirectory is located here. Networking related files are in the subdirectory sysconfig. Another subdirectory of etc is the skel directory, which is used to create files in users' home directories when the users are created.

◆ home — This directory contains the directories of users on the system. Subdirectories of home will be named for the user to whom they belong.

◆ lib — The shared system files and kernel modules are contained in this directory and its subdirectories.

◆ mnt — This directory is the location of the mount point for temporary file systems, such as a floppy or CD.

◆ opt — This directory and its subdirectories are often used to hold applications installed on the system.

◆ proc — Information about system processes is included in this directory.

◆ root — This is the home directory of the root user. Don't confuse this with the / directory, which has the same name.

◆ sbin — Contained in this directory are system binaries used by the system administrator or the root user.

◆ tmp — This directory contains temporary files used by the system.

- ◆ usr — This directory is often mounted on its own partition. It contains shareable, read-only data. Subdirectories can be used for applications, typically under /usr/local.

- ◆ var — Subdirectories and files under var contain variable information, such as system logs and print queues.

Special File Locations

Red Hat extends the FHS structure slightly to accommodate special files used by Red Hat Linux. Most files pertaining to the Red Hat Package Manager (RPM) are kept in the /var/lib/rpm/ directory.

The /var/spool/up2date/ directory contains files used by Red Hat Update Agent, including RPM header information for the system. This location may also be used to temporarily store RPMs downloaded while updating your system. For more information on Red Hat Update Agent and Red Hat Network, see the Red Hat Network Web site at https://rhn.redhat.com/.

Another location specific to Red Hat Linux is the /etc/sysconfig/ directory. This directory stores a variety of configuration information. Many scripts that run at boot time use the files in this directory. See Chapter 7 for more information on what is within this directory and the role these files play in the boot process.

Finally, one more directory worth noting is the /initrd/ directory. It is empty, but it is used as a critical mount point during the boot process.

Do not remove the /initrd/ directory for any reason. Removing this directory will cause your system to fail to boot with a kernel panic error message.

Working with Linux-Supported File Systems

Linux is a very flexible operating system that has a long history of interoperability with other systems on a number of different hardware platforms. A consequence of this friendliness to other operating systems is that Linux can read and write to several different file systems that originated with other operating systems much different from Linux. This section details the different file systems supported and where they originated.

One reason that Linux supports so many file systems is because of the design of its Virtual File Systems (VFS) layer. The VFS layer is a data abstraction layer between the kernel and the programs in userspace that issue file system commands.

Programs that run inside the kernel are in *kernelspace*. Programs that don't run inside the kernel are in *userspace*.

The VFS layer avoids duplication of common code between all file systems. It provides a fairly universal backward compatible method for programs to access all of the different forms of file support. Only one common, small API set accesses each of the file system types, to simplify programming file system support.

Support for these file systems come standard in Red Hat Enterprise Linux. They are compiled into the kernel by default. If for some reason your kernel does not currently support these file systems, a kernel recompile with the proper options turned on should enable you to access all these file systems.

The ext3 File System

The ext3, or third extended file system has been the default file system on all Red Hat Linux versions since version 7.2. ext3 replaces the venerable ext2 file system. Data is easily converted between the two file systems, and ext3 adds several new features, most notably journaling, which permits better maintenance of data integrity. The ext3 file system is essentially an enhanced version of the ext2 file system. These improvements provide the following advantages.

AVAILABILITY

After an unexpected power failure or system crash (also called an unclean system shutdown), each mounted ext2 file system on the machine must be checked for consistency by the e2fsck program. This is a time-consuming process that can delay system boot time significantly, especially with large volumes containing a large number of files. During this time, any data on the volumes is unreachable.

The journaling provided by the ext3 file system means that this sort of file system check is no longer necessary after an unclean system shutdown. The only time a consistency check occurs using ext3 is in certain rare hardware-failure cases, such as hard-drive failures. The time to recover an ext3 file system after an unclean system shutdown does not depend on the size of the file system or the number of files; rather, it depends on the size of the journal used to maintain consistency. The default journal size takes about a second to recover, depending on the speed of the hardware.

DATA INTEGRITY

The ext3 file system provides stronger data integrity in the event that an unclean system shutdown occurs. The ext3 file system allows you to choose the type and level of protection that your data receives. By default, Red Hat Linux configures ext3 volumes to keep a high level of data consistency with regard to the state of the file system.

SPEED

Despite writing some data more than once, `ext3` has a higher throughput in most cases than `ext2` because `ext3`'s journaling optimizes hard-drive head motion. You can choose from three journaling modes to optimize speed, but doing so means tradeoffs with regard to data integrity.

EASY TRANSITION

It is easy to change from `ext2` to `ext3` and gain the benefits of a robust journaling file system without reformatting. See the "Converting to an Ext3 File System" section of this chapter for more on how to perform this task. If you perform a fresh installation of Red Hat Linux, the default file system assigned to the system's Linux partitions is `ext3`. If you upgrade from a version of Red Hat Linux that uses `ext2` partitions, the installation program allows you to convert these partitions to `ext3` partitions without losing data. See the section "Converting to an Ext3 File System."

The following sections walk you through the steps for creating and tuning `ext3` partitions. If you have ext2 partitions and are running Red Hat Linux 8.0 or later, you can skip the partitioning and formatting sections below and go directly to the next section.

Creating an ext3 File System

After installation, it is sometimes necessary to create a new `ext3` file system. For example, if you add a new disk drive to a Red Hat Linux system, you may want to partition the drive and use the `ext3` file system. The steps for creating an `ext3` file system are as follows:

1. Create the partition using parted or fdisk.

2. Format the partition with the `ext3` file system using mkfs.

3. Label the partition using e2label.

4. Create the mount point.

5. Add the partition to `/etc/fstab`.

Converting to an ext3 File System

The tune2fs program can add a journal to an existing `ext2` file system without altering the data already on the partition. If the file system is already mounted while it is being transitioned, the journal will be visible as the file `.journal` in the root directory of the file system. If the file system is not mounted, the journal will be hidden and will not appear in the file system at all.

To convert an `ext2` file system to `ext3`, log in as root and type:

```
/sbin/tune2fs -j /dev/hdbX
```

In the preceding command, replace /dev/hdb with the device name and X with the partition number. After doing this, be certain to change the partition type from ext2 to ext3 in /etc/fstab. If you are transitioning your root file system, you will have to use an initrd image (or RAM disk) to boot. To create this, run the mkinitrd program. For information on using the mkinitrd command, type **man mkinitrd**. Also make sure your GRUB or LILO configuration loads the initrd image. If you fail to make this change, the system will still boot, but the file system will be mounted as ext2 instead of ext3.

Reverting to an ext2 File System

Because ext3 is relatively new, some disk utilities do not yet support it. For example, you may need to shrink a partition with resize2fs, which does not yet support ext3. In this situation, it may be necessary to temporarily revert a file system to ext2. To revert a partition, you must first unmount it by logging in as root and typing:

```
umount /dev/hdbX
```

In the preceding command, replace /dev/hdb with the device name and X with the partition number. For the remainder of this section, the sample commands will use hdb1 for these values. Next, change the file system type to ext2 by typing the following command as root:

```
/sbin/tune2fs -O ^has_journal /dev/hdb1
```

Check the partition for errors by typing the following command as root:

```
/sbin/e2fsck -y /dev/hdb1
```

Then mount the partition again as an ext2 file system by typing:

```
mount -t ext2 /dev/hdb1 /mount/point
```

In the preceding command, replace /mount/point with the mount point of the partition. Next, remove the .journal file at the root level of the partition by changing to the directory where it is mounted and by typing:

```
rm -f .journal
```

You now have an ext2 partition. If you permanently change the partition to ext2, remember to update the /etc/fstab file.

ext2

ext2 was the standard file system for Linux until the introduction of ext3. The ext2 implementation has not changed much since it was introduced with the 1.0

kernel back in 1993. Since then, a few new features have been added. One of these was sparse super blocks, which increases file system performance.

ext2 was designed to make it easier for new features to be added, so that it can constantly evolve into a better file system. Users can take advantage of new features without reformatting their old ext2 file systems. ext2 has the added bonus of being designed to be POSIX compliant. New features that are still in the development phase are access control lists, undelete, and on-the-fly compression.

ext2 is flexible, can handle file systems up to 4TB large, and supports long filenames up to 1,012 characters long. In case user processes fill up a file system, ext2 normally reserves about 5 percent of disk blocks for exclusive use by root so that root can easily recover from that situation. Modern Red Hat boot and rescue diskettes now use ext2 instead of minix.

reiserfs

The Reiser file system is a journaling file system designed for fast server performance, especially in directories containing thousands of files. It is more space efficient than most other file systems, because it does not take up a minimum of one block per file. If you write a bunch of really small files to disk, reiserfs squeezes them all into one block instead of writing one small file to one block like other file systems do. Reiserfs also does not have fixed space allocation for inodes, which saves about 6 percent of your disk space.

SystemV

Linux currently provides read support for SystemV partitions, and write support is experimental. The SystemV file system driver currently supports AFS/EAFS/EFS, Coherent FS, SystemV/386 FS, Version 7 FS, and Xenix file systems.

ufs

ufs is used in Solaris and early BSD operating systems. Linux provides read support, and write support is experimental.

FAT

FAT is one of a few different file systems used with Windows over the years. Almost every computer user has used FAT at one time or another, since it was the sparse base operating system at the heart of all Windows operating systems.

FAT was originally created for QDOS and used on 360K (double density, double sided) floppy disks. Its address space has since been extended from 12 bit to 32 bit, so it can handle very large file systems. There have been four versions of FAT since its beginnings: FAT12, FAT16, VFAT, and FAT32. Nowadays, it's possible to create FAT32 file systems over a terabyte in size.

Do not confuse a FAT file system with a FAT32 file system. They are named similarly but are two different beasts!

NTFS

NTFS is the next generation of HPFS. It comes with all versions of Microsoft operating systems beginning with Windows NT. Unlike FAT, it is a b-tree file system, meaning it has a performance and reliability advantage, including journaling, and support for encryption and compression, over FAT.

IBM JFS

IBM JFS is an easy to use journaling file system created by IBM. It is designed for high-throughput server environments. This is the same file system that will be provided in AIX version 5.1. Linux support for JFS was written by IBM. IBM has contributed quite a bit of code to the Linux cause, and is a staunch supporter of Linux. They have also decided to make Linux their main server file system in the future.

SGI XFS

SGI's Extended File System (XFS) is SGI's newest file system for all Silicon Graphics systems, from workstations to their supercomputer line (before they sold that line to Terra computers.) It has been available for use on Linux since May 2001.

XFS is designed for high performance. It rapidly recovers from system crashes and can support extremely large disk farms (it can handle files as large as a million terabytes.) It is one of a few journaling file systems that have had a proven track record in production environments for several years now.

 Its other features include access control lists, volume management, guaranteed rate I/O, and journaling for faster recovery. XFS can be backed up while still in use, which comes in handy since it reduces system administration time. This is a fast file system, and now you can read it with your Red Hat Linux machine.

Nonstandard Linux File Systems

Support for these file systems needs to be explicitly compiled into the Linux kernel, since kernel support for them is not configured by default.

FREEVxFS

VxFS is the Veritas file system developed by the Veritas Corporation. It is used in SCO UnixWare, HP-UX, Solaris, and other systems. Some of its features include access control lists, journaling, online backup, and support for files up to 2TB large.

Three different versions of VxFS are in use. Version 1 is the original VxFS that is not commonly used anymore. Version 2 includes support for filesets and dynamic inode allocation. Version 4 is the latest version, and it supports quotas and large files.

GNU utilities available for Linux called VxTools can read VxFS versions 2 and 4. The tools included in the VxTools package are `vxmount`, `vxumount`, `vxls`, `vxcat`, `vxidump`, `vxcd`, and `vxpwd`. Currently there is only read support in Linux for VxFS file systems.

GFS

GFS is Sistina's Global File System. It is a clustered journaling file system for SANs that enables multiple servers to have read/write access to a single file system on shared SAN devices.

GFS is scalable, since storage devices and servers can be added without taking the system down or taking the disks offline. It also makes a single image of all the data in the SAN, so that if a server fails it can be removed and replaced while the load is rebalanced amongst the remaining servers.

In a proper cluster setup, all nodes in the cluster share the same storage devices through a fiber channel, SCSI hookup, or network block device. Each node sees the file system as being local to their machine, and GFS synchronizes files across the cluster. GFS is fully symmetric, so no server is a bottleneck or single point of failure. GFS uses regular UNIX-style file semantics.

Memory and Virtual File Systems

These file systems do not exist on disk in the same way that traditional file systems do. They either exist entirely in system memory, or they are virtual because they are an interface to system devices, for example.

cramfs

`cramfs` is designed to cram a file system onto a small ROM, so it is small, simple, and able to compress things well. The largest file size is 16MB, and the largest file system size is 256MB.

Since `cramfs` is so compressed, it isn't instantly updateable. The `mkcramfs` tool needs to be run to create or update a `cramfs` disk image. The image is created by compressing files one page at a time, so this enables random page access. The metadata is not compressed, but it has been optimized to take up much less space than other file systems. For example, only the low 8 bits of the gid are stored. This saves space but also presents a potential security issue.

tmpfs

tmpfs is structured around the idea that whatever is put in the /tmp file system is accessed again shortly. tmpfs exists solely in memory, so what you put in temp doesn't persist between reboots.

Creating /tmp as an in-memory file system is a performance boost but is rarely used in Linux because of the performance available by the traditional Linux file system. But for those who feel that they need the performance gains of storing /tmp in memory, this option is now available in Linux.

ramfs

ramfs is basically cramfs without the compression.

romfs

This is a read-only file system that is mostly used for the initial RAM disks of installation disks. It was designed to take up very little space, so you could fit a kernel and some useful code into a small boot disk, without having the file system overhead taking up too much precious space in memory or on the disk.

The kernel on the disk has only this file system linked into it, and then it can load any modules it needs later, after bootup. After the kernel is loaded, it can call other programs to help determine what SCSI drivers are needed, if any, or what IDE or floppy drives should be accessed after bootup. This method is perfect for rescue diskettes or installation diskettes, where all that is really required is that a very bare minimum kernel be loaded into memory, so after initial boot it can then load from CD-ROM whatever ext2 modules or other drivers are necessary to mount the system's regular drives.

The romfs file system is created with a program called genromfs.

/proc

The Linux kernel has two primary functions: to control access to physical devices on the computer and to schedule when and how processes interact with these devices. The /proc/ directory contains a hierarchy of special files that represent the current state of the kernel — allowing applications and users to peer into the kernel's view of the system.

Within the /proc/ directory, one can find a wealth of information about the system hardware and any processes currently running. In addition, some of the files within the /proc/ directory tree can be manipulated by users and applications to communicate configuration changes to the kernel.

A Virtual File System

Under Linux, all data is stored as files. Most users are familiar with the standard types of regular files. But the /proc/ directory contains other types of files that do not correspond with the typical file system. For this reason, /proc/ is often referred to as a virtual file system.

These virtual files have unique qualities. Most of them are listed as zero bytes, yet when one is viewed, it can contain a large amount of information. In addition, most of the time and date settings on virtual files reflect the current time and date, indicative of the fact they are constantly changing.

Virtual files such as `interrupts`, `/proc/meminfo`, `/proc/mounts`, and `/proc/partitions` provide an up-to-the-moment glimpse of the system's hardware. Others, like `/proc/file systems` and the `/proc/sys/` directory, provide system configuration information and interfaces. For organizational purposes, files containing information on a similar topic are grouped into virtual directories and subdirectories. For instance, `/proc/ide/` contains information for all physical IDE devices. Likewise, process directories contain information about each running process on the system.

Viewing Virtual Files

By using the `cat`, `more`, or `less` commands on files within the `/proc/` directory, you can immediately access an enormous amount of information about the system. For example, if you want to see what sort of CPU your computer has, type `cat /proc/cpuinfo`, and you will see something similar to Listing 6-1.

When viewing different virtual files in the `/proc/` file system, you will notice that some of the information is easily understandable while some is not human-readable. This is in part why utilities exist to pull data from virtual files and display it in a useful way. Some examples of such applications are lspci, apm, free, and top.

 Some of the virtual files in the `/proc/` directory are readable by the root user only.

Changing Virtual Files

As a general rule, most virtual files within the `/proc/` directory are read-only. However, some can be used to adjust settings in the kernel. This is especially true for files in the `/proc/sys/` subdirectory. To change the value of a virtual file, use the `echo` command and a > symbol to redirect the new value to the file. For instance, to change your hostname on the fly, you can type:

```
echo bob.subgenius.com > /proc/sys/kernel/hostname
```

Other files act as binary or boolean switches. For instance, if you type **cat /proc/sys/net/ipv4/ip_forward**, you will see either a 0 or a 1. A 0 indicates that the kernel is not forwarding network packets. By using the `echo` command to change the value of the `ip_forward` file to 1, you can immediately turn packet forwarding on.

TIP

Another command used to alter settings in the /proc/sys/ subdirectory is /sbin/sysctl.

For a listing of some of the kernel configuration files available in /proc/sys/, see the "/proc/sys" section later in this chapter.

Top-level Files in the proc File System

Following is a list of some of the more useful virtual files in the top level of the /proc/ directory.

NOTE

In most cases, the content of files listed in this section will not be the same on your machine. This is because much of the information pertains to the hardware on which you are running Red Hat Linux.

/proc/apm

This file provides information about the state of the Advanced Power Management (APM) system and is used by the apm command. If the system with no battery is connected to an AC power source, this virtual file looks similar to this:

```
1.16 1.2 0x07 0x01 0xff 0x80 -1% -1 ?
```

Running the apm -v command on such a system results in output similar to this:

```
APM BIOS 1.2 (kernel driver 1.16)
AC on-line, no system battery
```

For systems that do not use a battery as a power source, apm is able to do little more than put the machine in standby mode. The apm command is much more useful on laptops. For example, the following output is from the command cat /proc/apm on a laptop running Red Hat Linux while plugged into a power outlet:

```
1.16 1.2 0x03 0x01 0x03 0x09 100% -1 ?
```

When the same laptop is unplugged from its power source for a few minutes, the contents of the apm file change to something like this:

```
1.16 1.2 0x03 0x00 0x00 0x01 99% 1792 min
```

The `apm -v` command will now yield more useful data, such as the following:

```
APM BIOS 1.2 (kernel driver 1.16)
AC off-line, battery status high: 99% (1 day, 5:52)
```

/proc/cmdline

This file shows the parameters passed to the kernel at the time it is started. A sample `/proc/cmdline` file looks like this:

```
ro root=/dev/hda2
```

This tells us the filesystem is mounted read-only — signified by `ro` — off of the second partition on the first IDE device (`/dev/hda2`).

/proc/cpuinfo

This virtual file identifies the type of processor used by your system. Listing 6-1 is an example of the output you'll typically see from `/proc/cpuinfo`.

Listing 6-1: Output from cat /proc/cpuinfo

```
processor          : 0
vendor_id          : AuthenticAMD
cpu family         : 5
model              : 9
model name         : AMD-K6(tm) 3D+ Processor
stepping           : 1
cpu MHz            : 400.919
cache size         : 256 KB
fdiv_bug           : no
hlt_bug            : no
f00f_bug           : no
coma_bug           : no
fpu                : yes
fpu_exception      : yes
cpuid level        : 1
wp                 : yes
flags              : fpu vme de pse tsc msr mce cx8 pge mmx syscall  \
                     3dnow k6_mtrr
bogomips           : 799.53
```

◆ `processor` — Provides each processor with an identifying number. If you have only one processor, you will see only a 0.

◆ `cpu family` — Authoritatively tells you the type of processor you have in the system. If your computer is an Intel-based system, simply place the number in front of "86" to determine the value. This is particularly helpful if you are wondering about the architecture of an older system such as the 586, 486, or 386. Because some RPM packages are compiled for each of these particular architectures, this value enables you to determine which package to install.

◆ model name — Gives you the common name of the processor, including its project name.

◆ cpu MHz — Shows the processor's precise speed, in megahertz, to the thousandth decimal point.

◆ cache size — Tells you the amount of level 2 memory cache available to the processor.

◆ flags — Defines a number of different processor attributes, such as the presence of a floating-point unit (FPU) and the ability to process MMX instructions.

/proc/devices

This file displays the various character and block devices currently configured for use with the kernel. It does not include devices whose modules are not loaded into the kernel. Listing 6-2 is a sample output from this virtual file.

Listing 6-2: Output from cat /proc/devices

```
Character devices:
      1 mem
      2 pty
      3 ttyp
      4 ttyS
      5 cua
      7 vcs
     10 misc
     14 sound
     29 fb
     36 netlink
    128 ptm
    129 ptm
    136 pts
    137 pts
    162 raw
    254 iscsictl
Block devices:
      1 ramdisk
      2 fd
```

Continued

Listing 6-2 *(Continued)*

```
  3 ide0
  9 md
 22 ide1
```

The output from /proc/devices includes the major number and name of the device and is broken into two major sections: character devices and block devices. Character devices are similar to block devices, except for two basic differences.

Block devices have a buffer available, allowing them to order requests before dealing with them. This is important for devices designed to store information — such as hard drives — because the ability to order the information before writing it to the device allows it to be placed in a more efficient order. Character devices do not require buffering.

The other difference is that block devices can send and receive information in blocks of a size configured per device. Character devices send data with no pre-configured size. For more information about devices, see /usr/src/linux-2.4/ Documentation/devices.txt.

/proc/dma

This file contains a list of the registered ISA direct memory access (DMA) channels in use. A sample /proc/dma file looks like this:

```
4: cascade
```

/proc/execdomains

This file lists the execution domains currently supported by the Linux kernel, along with the range of personalities they support.

```
0-0      Linux                [kernel]
```

Think of execution domains as the "personality" for a particular operating system. Because other binary formats, such as Solaris, UnixWare, and FreeBSD, can be used with Linux, programmers can change the way the operating system treats particular system calls from these binaries by changing the personality of the task. Except for the PER_LINUX execution domain, different personalities can be implemented as dynamically loadable modules.

/proc/fb

This file contains a list of frame buffer devices, with the frame buffer device number and the driver that controls it. Typical output of /proc/fb for systems that contain frame buffer devices looks similar to this:

```
0 VESA VGA
```

/proc/filesystems

This file displays a list of the file system types currently supported by the kernel. Sample output from a generic kernel's /proc/filesystems file looks similar to Listing 6-3.

Listing 6-3: Output from cat /proc/filesystems

```
nodev           rootfs
nodev           bdev
nodev           proc
nodev           sockfs
nodev           tmpfs
nodev           shm
nodev           pipefs
                ext2
nodev           ramfs
                iso9660
nodev           devpts
                ext3
nodev           autofs
nodev           binfmt_misc
```

The first column signifies whether the file system is mounted on a block device. Those beginning with nodev are not mounted on a device. The second column lists the name of the file systems supported. The mount command cycles through these file systems when one is not specified as an argument.

/proc/interrupts

This file records the number of interrupts per IRQ on the x86 architecture. A standard /proc/interrupts file looks similar to Listing 6-4.

Listing 6-4: Output from cat /proc/interrupts

```
  0:    80448940        XT-PIC      timer
  1:      174412        XT-PIC      keyboard
  2:           0        XT-PIC      cascade
  8:           1        XT-PIC      rtc
 10:      410964        XT-PIC      eth0
 12:       60330        XT-PIC      PS/2 Mouse
 14:     1314121        XT-PIC      ide0
 15:     5195422        XT-PIC      ide1
NMI:           0
ERR:           0
```

For a multiprocessor machine, this file may look slightly different, as shown in Listing 6-5.

Listing 6-5: Output from cat /proc/interrupts with a multi-processor system

```
            CPU0           CPU1
  0:   1366814704            0      XT-PIC      timer
  1:          128          340      IO-APIC-edge        keyboard
  2:            0            0      XT-PIC      cascade
  8:            0            1      IO-APIC-edge         rtc
 12:         5323         5793      IO-APIC-edge        PS/2 Mouse
 13:            1            0      XT-PIC      fpu
 16:     11184294     15940594      IO-APIC-level Intel \
                                    EtherExpress \ Pro 10/100 Ethernet
 20:      8450043     11120093      IO-APIC-level megaraid
 30:        10432        10722      IO-APIC-level aic7xxx
 31:           23           22      IO-APIC-level aic7xxx
NMI:            0
ERR:            0
```

The first column refers to the IRQ number. Each CPU in the system has its own column and its own number of interrupts per IRQ. The next column reports the type of interrupt, and the last column contains the name of the device that is located at that IRQ. Each type of interrupt seen in this file, although each interrupt is architecture-specific, means something a little different. For x86 machines, the following values are common:

◆ XT-PIC — This is the old AT computer interrupts.

◆ IO-APIC-edge — The voltage signal on this interrupt transitions from low to high, creating an edge where the interrupt occurs, and is signaled only once. This kind of interrupt, as well as the IO-APIC-level interrupt, is seen only on systems with processors from the 586 family and higher.

◆ IO-APIC-level — Generates interrupts when its voltage signal goes high until the signal goes low again.

/proc/iomem

Listing 6-6 shows you the current map of the system's memory for each physical device.

Listing 6-6: Output from cat/proc/iomem

```
00000000-0009fbff : System RAM
0009fc00-0009ffff : reserved
000a0000-000bffff : Video RAM area
000c0000-000c7fff : Video ROM
```

```
000f0000-000fffff : System ROM
00100000-07ffffff : System RAM
  00100000-00291ba8 : Kernel code
  00291ba9-002e09cb : Kernel data
e0000000-e3ffffff : VIA Technologies, Inc. VT82C597 [Apollo VP3]
e4000000-e7ffffff : PCI Bus #01
  e4000000-e4003fff : Matrox Graphics, Inc. MGA G200 AGP
  e5000000-e57fffff : Matrox Graphics, Inc. MGA G200 AGP
e8000000-e8ffffff : PCI Bus #01
  e8000000-e8ffffff : Matrox Graphics, Inc. MGA G200 AGP
ea000000-ea00007f : Digital Equipment Corporation DECchip 21140 [FasterNet]
  ea000000-ea00007f : tulip
ffff0000-ffffffff : reserved
```

The first column displays the memory registers used by each of the different types of memory. The second column tells the kind of memory located within those registers. In particular, this column tells you which memory registers are used by the kernel within the system RAM or, if you have multiple Ethernet ports on your NIC, the memory registers assigned for each port.

/proc/ioports

The output of /proc/ioports provides a list of currently registered port regions used for input or output communication with a device. This file can be quite long, with a beginning similar to Listing 6-7.

Listing 6-7: Output from cat /proc/ioports

```
0000-001f : dma1
0020-003f : pic1
0040-005f : timer
0060-006f : keyboard
0070-007f : rtc
0080-008f : dma page reg
00a0-00bf : pic2
00c0-00df : dma2
00f0-00ff : fpu
0170-0177 : ide1
01f0-01f7 : ide0
02f8-02ff : serial(auto)
0376-0376 : ide1
03c0-03df : vga+
03f6-03f6 : ide0
03f8-03ff : serial(auto)
0cf8-0cff : PCI conf1
```

Continued

Listing 6-7 *(Continued)*

```
d000-dfff : PCI Bus #01
e000-e00f : VIA Technologies, Inc. Bus Master IDE
  e000-e007 : ide0
  e008-e00f : ide1
e800-e87f : Digital Equipment Corporation DECchip 21140 [FasterNet]
  e800-e87f : tulip
```

The first column gives the IO port address range reserved for the device listed in the second column.

/proc/isapnp

This file lists Plug and Play (PnP) cards in ISA slots on the system. This is most often seen with sound cards but may include any number of devices. A /proc/ isapnp file containing a Soundblaster entry looks similar to Listing 6-8.

Listing 6-8: Output from cat /proc/isapnp

```
Card 1 'CTL0070:Creative ViBRA16C PnP' PnP version 1.0 Product version 1.0
    Logical device 0 'CTL0001:Audio'
    Device is not active
    Active port 0x220,0x330,0x388
    Active IRQ 5 [0x2]
    Active DMA 1,5
    Resources 0
        Priority preferred
        Port 0x220-0x220, align 0x0, size 0x10, 16-bit address decoding
        Port 0x330-0x330, align 0x0, size 0x2, 16-bit address decoding
        Port 0x388-0x3f8, align 0x0, size 0x4, 16-bit address decoding
        IRQ 5 High-Edge
        DMA 1 8-bit byte-count compatible
        DMA 5 16-bit word-count compatible
        Alternate resources 0:1
            Priority acceptable
            Port 0x220-0x280, align 0x1f, size 0x10, 16-bit address decoding
            Port 0x300-0x330, align 0x2f, size 0x2, 16-bit address decoding
            Port 0x388-0x3f8, align 0x0, size 0x4, 16-bit address decoding
            IRQ 5,7,2/9,10 High-Edge
            DMA 1,3 8-bit byte-count compatible
            DMA 5,7 16-bit word-count compatible
```

This file can be quite long, depending on the number of devices displayed and their resource requirements. Each card lists its name, PnP version number, and product version number. If the device is active and configured, this file will also reveal the port and IRQ numbers for the device. In addition, to ensure better compatibility, the card will specify preferred and acceptable values for a number of different parameters. The goal here is to allow the PnP cards to work around one another and avoid IRQ and port conflicts.

/proc/kcore

This file represents the physical memory of the system and is stored in the core file format. Unlike most /proc/ files, kcore displays a size. This value is given in bytes and is equal to the size of physical memory (RAM) used plus 4KB. The contents of this file are designed to be examined by a debugger, such as gdb; they are not human-readable.

 Do not view the /proc/kcore virtual file. The contents of the file will scramble text output on the terminal. If you accidentally view this file, press Ctrl+C to stop the process; then type **reset** to bring back the command-line prompt.

/proc/kmsg

This file is used to hold messages generated by the kernel. These messages are then picked up by other programs, such as /sbin/klogd.

/proc/ksyms

This file holds the kernel-exported symbol definitions used by the module tools to dynamically link and bind loadable modules.

```
e003def4 speedo_debug [eepro100]
e003b04c eepro100_init [eepro100]
e00390c0 st_template [st]
e002104c RDINDOOR [megaraid]
e00210a4 callDone [megaraid]
e00226cc megaraid_detect [megaraid]
```

The first column lists the memory address for the kernel function, the second column refers to the name of the function, and the last column reveals the name of the loaded module.

/proc/loadavg

This file provides a look at load average on the processor over time and additional data used by uptime and other commands. A sample /proc/loadavg file looks similar to this:

```
0.20 0.18 0.12 1/80 11206
```

The first three entries measure CPU utilization of the last 1-, 5-, and 10-minute periods. The fourth column shows the number of currently running processes and the total number of processes. The last column displays the last process ID used.

/proc/locks

This file displays the files currently locked by the kernel. The content of this file contains internal kernel debugging data and can vary tremendously, depending on the use of the system. A sample /proc/locks file for a lightly loaded system looks similar to this:

```
1: FLOCK  ADVISORY  WRITE 807 03:05:308731 0 EOF c2a260c0 c025aa48 c2a26120
2: POSIX  ADVISORY  WRITE 708 03:05:308720 0 EOF c2a2611c c2a260c4 c025aa48
```

Each lock has its own line that starts with a unique number. The second column refers to the class of lock used, with FLOCK signifying the older-style UNIX file locks from a flock system call and POSIX representing the newer POSIX locks from the lockf system call. The third column can have two values. ADVISORY means that the lock does not prevent other people from accessing the data; it prevents only other attempts to lock it. MANDATORY means that no other access to the data is permitted while the lock is held. The fourth column reveals whether the lock is allowing the holder READ or WRITE access to the file, and the fifth column shows the ID of the process holding the lock. The sixth column shows the ID of the file being locked, in the format of MAJOR-DEVICE:MINOR-DEVICE:INODE-NUMBER. The seventh column shows the start and end of the file's locked region. The remaining columns point to internal kernel data structures used for specialized debugging and can be ignored.

/proc/mdstat

This file contains the current information for multiple-disk software RAID configurations. If your system does not contain such a configuration, your /proc/mdstat file will look similar to this:

```
Personalities :
read_ahead not set
unused devices: none
```

This file remains in the state above unless you create a software RAID or md device. In that case, you can view /proc/mdstat to give you a picture of what is currently happening with your mdX RAID devices. The following /proc/mdstat file shows a system with its md0 configured as a RAID 1 device. It is currently resyncing the disks:

```
Personalities : [linear] [raid1]
read_ahead 1024 sectors
```

```
md0: active raid1 sda2[1] sdb2[0] 9940 blocks [2/2] [UU] resync=1% \
finish=12.3min
algorithm 2 [3/3] [UUU]
unused devices: none
```

/proc/meminfo

This is one of the more commonly used files in the /proc/ directory, as it reports plenty of valuable information about the current RAM usage on the system. A system with 256MB of RAM and 384MB of swap space will likely have a /proc/meminfo file similar to Listing 6-9.

Listing 6-9: Output from cat /proc/meminfo

```
            total:      used:     free:  shared:    buffers:   cached:
Mem:    261709824 253407232 8302592        0    120745984  48689152
Swap:   402997248      8192 402989056
MemTotal:        255576 kB
MemFree:           8108 kB
MemShared:            0 kB
Buffers:         117916 kB
Cached:           47548 kB
Active:          135300 kB
Inact_dirty:      29276 kB
Inact_clean:        888 kB
Inact_target:         0 kB
HighTotal:            0 kB
HighFree:             0 kB
LowTotal:        255576 kB
LowFree:           8108 kB
SwapTotal:       393552 kB
SwapFree:        393544 kB
```

Much of the information here is used by the free, top, and ps commands. In fact, the output of the free command is even similar in appearance to the contents and structure of /proc/meminfo. But looking directly at /proc/meminfo reveals more details:

♦ Mem — Displays the current state of physical RAM in the system, including a full breakdown of total, used, free, shared, buffered, and cached memory utilization in bytes.

♦ Swap — Displays the total, used, and free amounts of swap space, in bytes.

♦ MemTotal — Total amount of physical RAM, in kilobytes.

♦ MemFree — The amount of physical RAM, in kilobytes, left unused by the system.

◆ MemShared — Unused with 2.4 and later kernels but left in for compatibility with earlier kernel versions.

◆ Buffers — The amount of physical RAM, in kilobytes, used for file buffers.

◆ Cached — The amount of physical RAM, in kilobytes, used as cache memory.

◆ Active — The total amount of buffer or page cache memory, in kilobytes, that is in active use.

◆ Inact_dirty — The total amount of buffer or cache pages, in kilobytes, that might be free and available.

◆ Inact_clean — The total amount of buffer or cache pages in kilobytes that are definitely free and available.

◆ Inact_target — The net amount of allocations per second, in kilobytes, averaged over one minute.

◆ HighTotal and HighFree — The total and free amount of memory, respectively, that is not directly mapped into kernel space. The HighTotal value can vary based on the type of kernel used.

◆ LowTotal and LowFree — The total and free amount of memory, respectively, that is directly mapped into kernel space. The LowTotal value can vary based on the type of kernel used.

◆ SwapTotal — The total amount of swap available, in kilobytes.

◆ SwapFree — The total amount of swap free, in kilobytes.

/proc/misc

This file lists miscellaneous drivers registered on the miscellaneous major device, which is device number 10:

```
135 rtc
  1 psaux
134 apm_bios
```

The first column is the minor number of each device, and the second column shows the driver in use.

/proc/modules

This file displays a list of all modules loaded into the kernel. Its contents will vary based on the configuration and use of your system, but it should be organized in a similar manner to this sample /proc/modules file output:

```
ide-cd                  27008      0 (autoclean)
cdrom                   28960      0 (autoclean) [ide-cd]
soundcore                4100      0 (autoclean)
agpgart                 31072      0 (unused)
binfmt_misc              5956      1
iscsi                   32672      0 (unused)
scsi_mod                94424      1 [iscsi]
autofs                  10628      0 (autoclean) (unused)
tulip                   48608      1
ext3                    60352      2
jbd                     39192      2 [ext3]
```

The first column contains the name of the module. The second column refers to the memory size of the module, in bytes. The third column tells you whether the module is currently loaded (1) or unloaded (0). The final column states if the module can unload itself automatically after a period without use (autoclean) or if it is not being utilized (unused). Any module with a line containing a name listed in brackets ([and]) tells you that this module depends upon another module's presence in order to function.

/proc/mounts

This file provides a quick list of all mounts in use by the system:

```
rootfs / rootfs rw 0 0
/dev/hda2 / ext3 rw 0 0
/proc /proc proc rw 0 0
/dev/hda1 /boot ext3 rw 0 0
none /dev/pts devpts rw 0 0
none /dev/shm tmpfs rw 0 0
none /proc/sys/fs/binfmt_misc binfmt_misc rw 0 0
```

The output found here is similar to the contents of /etc/mtab, except that /proc/mount can be more current. The first column specifies the device that is mounted, with the second column revealing the mount point. The third column tells the file system type, and the fourth column tells you if it is mounted read-only (ro) or read-write (rw). The fifth and sixth columns contain dummy values designed to match the format used in /etc/mtab.

/proc/mtrr

This file refers to the current Memory Type Range Registers (MTRRs) in use with the system. If your system's architecture supports MTRRs, your mtrr might look something like this:

```
reg00: base=0x00000000 (     0MB), size=    64MB: write-back, count=1
```

MTRRs are used with the Intel P6 family of processors (Pentium II and higher), and they are used to control processor access to memory ranges. When using a video card on a PCI or AGP bus, a properly configured /proc/mtrr file can increase performance by more than 150 percent. Most of the time, this value is properly configured for you. For more information on MTRRs and manually configuring this file, please see http://web1.linuxhq.com/kernel/v2.3/doc/mtrr.txt.html.

/proc/partitions

Most of the information here is of little importance to the user, except for the following columns:

◆ major — The major number of the device with this partition. The major number corresponds with the block device ide0 in /proc/devices.

◆ minor — The minor number of the device with this partition. This serves to separate the partitions into different physical devices and relates to the number at the end of the name of the partition.

◆ #blocks — Lists the number of physical disk blocks contained in a particular partition.

◆ name — The name of the partition.

/proc/pci

This file contains a full listing of every PCI device on your system. Depending on the number of PCI devices you have, /proc/pci can get rather long. An example of this file on a basic system looks similar to Listing 6-10.

Listing 6-10: Output from cat /proc/pci

```
Bus      0, device      0, function      0:
 Host bridge:Intel Corporation 440BX/ZX - 82443BX/ZX Host bridge (rev 3).
         Master Capable.        Latency=64.
         Prefetchable 32 bit memory at 0xe4000000 [0xe7ffffff].
Bus      0, device      1, function      0:
 PCI bridge:Intel Corporation 440BX/ZX - 82443BX/ZX AGP bridge (rev 3).
         Master Capable.        Latency=64.     Min Gnt=128.
Bus      0, device      4, function      0:
 ISA bridge: Intel Corporation 82371AB PIIX4 ISA (rev 2).
Bus      0, device      4, function      1:
 IDE interface: Intel Corporation 82371AB PIIX4 IDE (rev 1).
         Master Capable.        Latency=32.
         I/O at 0xd800 [0xd80f].
```

```
Bus       0, device      4, function        2:
  USB Controller: Intel Corporation 82371AB PIIX4 USB (rev 1).
        IRQ 5.
        Master Capable.         Latency=32.
        I/O at 0xd400 [0xd41f].
  Bus       0, device      4, function        3:
   Bridge: Intel Corporation 82371AB PIIX4 ACPI (rev 2).
        IRQ 9.
  Bus       0, device      9, function        0:
   Ethernet controller: Lite-On Communications Inc LNE100TX (rev 33).
        IRQ 5.
        Master Capable.         Latency=32.
        I/O at 0xd000 [0xd0ff].
        Non-prefetchable 32 bit memory at 0xe3000000 [0xe30000ff].
  Bus       0, device     12, function        0:
   VGA compatible controller: S3 Inc. ViRGE/DX or /GX (rev 1).
        IRQ 11.
        Master Capable.         Latency=32.    Min Gnt=4.Max Lat=255.
        Non-prefetchable 32 bit memory at 0xdc000000 [0xdfffffff].
```

   This output shows a list of all PCI devices, sorted in the order of bus, device, and function. Beyond providing the name and version of the device, this list gives you detailed IRQ information so you can quickly look for conflicts.

TIP   To get a more readable version of this information, type `lspci -vb`.

/proc/slabinfo

This file gives information about memory usage on the slab level. Linux kernels later than 2.2 use slab pools to manage memory above the page level. Commonly used objects have their own slab pools. The following is a portion of a typical /proc/slabinfo virtual file:

```
slabinfo - version: 1.1
kmem_cache                  64      68      112     2     2     1
nfs_write_data               0       0      384     0     0     1
nfs_read_data                0     160      384     0    16     1
nfs_page                     0     200       96     0     5     1
ip_fib_hash                 10     113       32     1     1     1
journal_head                51    7020       48     2    90     1
revoke_table                 2     253       12     1     1     1
```

```
revoke_record              0        0        32      0      0      1
clip_arp_cache             0        0       128      0      0      1
ip_mrt_cache               0        0        96      0      0      1
```

The values in this file occur in the following order: cache name, number of active objects, number of total objects, size of the object, number of active slabs (blocks) of the objects, total number of slabs of the objects, and the number of pages per slab. Note that *active* in this case means that an object is in use. Therefore, an active object is in use, and an active slab contains one or more active objects.

/proc/stat

This file keeps track of a variety of different statistics about the system since it was last restarted. The content of /proc/stat, which can be quite long, begins something like this:

```
cpu   1139111 3689 234449 84378914
cpu0 1139111 3689 234449 84378914
page 2675248 8567956
swap 10022 19226
intr 93326523 85756163 174412 0 3 3 0 6 0 1 0 428620 0 60330 0 1368304 \ 5538681
disk_io: (3,0):(1408049,445601,5349480,962448,17135856)
ctxt 27269477
btime 886490134
processes 206458
```

Some of the more popular statistics include:

- ◆ cpu — Measures the number of jiffies (1/100 of a second) that the system has been in user mode, user mode with low priority (nice), system mode, and the idle task, respectively. The total for all CPUs is given at the top, and each individual CPU is listed below with its own statistics.

- ◆ page — The number of memory pages the system has written in and out to disk.

- ◆ swap — The number of swap pages the system has brought in and out.

- ◆ intr — The number of interrupts the system has experienced.

- ◆ btime — The boot time, measured in the number of seconds since January 1, 1970, otherwise known as the epoch.

/proc/swaps

This file measures swap space and its utilization. For a system with only one swap partition, the output of /proc/swap may look similar to this:

```
Filename          Type          Size        Used        Priority
/dev/hda6         partition     136512      20024       -1
```

While some of this information can be found in other files in the /proc/ directory, /proc/swap provides a snapshot of every swap file name, type of swap space, the total size, and the amount of this space that is in use (in kilobytes). The priority column is useful when multiple swap files are in use. The lower the priority, the more likely the swap file is to be used.

/proc/uptime

This file contains information about how long the system has been on since its last restart. The output of /proc/ uptime is quite minimal:

```
350735.47 234388.90
```

The first number tells you the total number of seconds the system has been up. The second number tells you how much of that time the machine has spent idle in seconds.

/proc/version

This file tells you the versions of the Linux kernel and gcc, as well as the version of Red Hat Linux installed on the system:

```
Linux version 2.4.18-0.40 (user@foo.redhat.com)(gcc version 2.96 20000731
(Red Hat Linux 7.2 2.96-102)) #1 Tue May 28 04:28:05 EDT 2002
```

This information is used for a variety of purposes, including the version data presented when a user logs in.

Directories in /proc/

Common groups of information concerning the kernel are grouped into directories and subdirectories within the /proc/ directory.

Process Directories

Every /proc/ directory contains a number of directories and their numerical names. A listing of them may start off like this:

```
dr-xr-xr-x     3 root        root        0 Feb 13 01:28 1
dr-xr-xr-x     3 root        root        0 Feb 13 01:28 1010
```

```
dr-xr-xr-x      3 xfs          xfs           0 Feb 13 01:28 1087
dr-xr-xr-x      3 daemon       daemon        0 Feb 13 01:28 1123
dr-xr-xr-x      3 root         root          0 Feb 13 01:28 11307
dr-xr-xr-x      3 apache       apache        0 Feb 13 01:28 13660
dr-xr-xr-x      3 rpc          rpc           0 Feb 13 01:28 637
dr-xr-xr-x      3 rpcuser      rpcuser       0 Feb 13 01:28 666
```

These directories are called process directories, as they are named after a program's process ID and contain information specific to that process. The owner and group of each process directory are set to the user running the process. When the process is terminated, its /proc/ process directory vanishes. Each process directory contains the following files. A brief description of the files follows.

```
-r--r--r--      1 terry        terry         0 Oct 27 09:35 cmdline
lrwxrwxrwx      1 terry        terry         0 Oct 27 09:35 cwd ->
                                             /home/terry
-r--------      1 terry        terry         0 Oct 27 09:35 environ
lrwxrwxrwx      1 terry        terry         0 Oct 27 09:35 exe -> /usr/
                                             local/mozilla/mozilla-bin
dr-x------      2 terry        terry         0 Oct 27 09:35 fd
-r--r--r--      1 terry        terry         0 Oct 27 09:35 maps
-rw-------      1 terry        terry         0 Oct 27 09:35 mem
-r--r--r--      1 terry        terry         0 Oct 27 09:35 mounts
lrwxrwxrwx      1 terry        terry         0 Oct 27 09:35 root -> /
-r--r--r--      1 terry        terry         0 Oct 27 09:35 stat
-r--r--r--      1 terry        terry         0 Oct 27 09:35 statm
-r--r--r--      1 terry        terry         0 Oct 27 09:35 status
```

♦ The cmdline file contains the command issued when starting the process.

♦ Next is a symlink to the current working directory for the process.

♦ Gives a list of the environment variables for the process. The environment variable is given in all uppercase characters, and the value is in lowercase characters.

♦ A symlink to the executable of this process.

♦ A directory containing all of the file descriptors for a particular process. These are given in numbered links:

```
total 0
lrwx------      1 root    root    64 May     8 11:31 0 -> /dev/null
lrwx------      1 root    root    64 May     8 11:31 1 -> /dev/null
lrwx------      1 root    root    64 May     8 11:31 2 -> /dev/null
lrwx------      1 root    root    64 May     8 11:31 3 -> /dev/ptmx
```

```
lrwx------    1 root    root    64 May    8 11:31  4 ->
                                           socket:[7774817]
lrwx------    1 root    root    64 May    8 11:31 5 -> /dev/ptmx
lrwx------    1 root    root    64 May    8 11:31 6 ->
                                           socket:[7774829]
lrwx------    1 root    root    64 May    8 11:31 7 -> /dev/ptmx
```

◆ Contains memory maps to the various executables and library files associated with this process. This file can be rather long, depending upon the complexity of the process. Sample output from the sshd process begins like this:

```
/usr/sbin/sshd
08086000-08088000 rw-p 0003e000 03:03 391479
/usr/sbin/sshd
08088000-08095000 rwxp 00000000 00:00 0
40000000-40013000 r-xp 00000000 03:03 293205
lib/ld-2.2.5.so
40013000-40014000 rw-p 00013000 03:03 293205
/lib/ld-2.2.5.so
40031000-40038000 r-xp 00000000 03:03 293282
/lib/libpam.so.0.75
40038000-40039000 rw-p 00006000 03:03 293282
/lib/libpam.so.0.75
40039000-4003a000 rw-p 00000000 00:00 0
4003a000-4003c000 r-xp 00000000 03:03 293218
/lib/libdl-2.2.5.so
4003c000-4003d000 rw-p 00001000 03:03 293218
/lib/libdl-2.2.5.so
```

◆ The memory held by the process. This file cannot be read by the user.

◆ A link to the root directory of the process.

◆ The status of the process.

◆ The status of the memory in use by the process. Following is a sample /proc/statm file:

```
    263 210 210 5 0 205 0
```

The seven columns relate to different memory statistics for the process. From left to right, they report the following aspects of the memory used:

1. Total program size, in kilobytes

2. Size of memory portions, in kilobytes

3. Number of pages that are shared

4. Number of pages that are code

5. Number of pages of data/stack

6. Number of pages that are libraries

7. Number of dirty pages

◆ The status of the process is a more readable form than stat or statm. Sample output for sshd looks similar to Listing 6-11.

Listing 6-11: Output from cat /proc/(process ID)/status

```
Name: sshd
State: S (sleeping)
Tgid: 797
Pid: 797
PPid: 1
TracerPid: 0
Uid: 0 0 0 0
Gid: 0 0 0 0
FDSize: 32
Groups:
VmSize:         3072 kB
VmLck:             0 kB
VmRSS:           840 kB
VmData:          104 kB
VmStk:            12 kB
VmExe:           300 kB
VmLib:          2528 kB
SigPnd: 0000000000000000
SigBlk: 0000000000000000
SigIgn: 8000000000001000
SigCgt: 0000000000014005
CapInh: 0000000000000000
CapPrm: 00000000fffffeff
CapEff: 00000000fffffeff
```

Other than the process' name and ID, the state such as S (sleeping) or R (running) and user/group ID running the process are available, as well as much more detailed data regarding memory usage.

/proc/self/

The /proc/self/ directory is a link to the currently running process. This allows a process to look at itself without having to know its process ID. Within a shell environment, a listing of the /proc/self/ directory produces the same contents as listing the process directory for that process.

/proc/bus/

This directory contains information specific to the various buses available on the system. So, for example, on a standard system containing ISA, PCI, and USB buses, current data on each of these buses is available in its directory under /proc/bus/. The contents of the subdirectories and files available vary greatly on the precise configuration of your system. However, each of the directories for each of the bus types has at least one directory for each bus of that type. These individual bus directories, usually signified with numbers, such as 00, contain binary files that refer to the various devices available on that bus.

 IF you have USB devices connected to your system, they will be shown as a separately mounted file system called usbdevfs. The usbdevfs file system will be mounted on /proc/bus/usb.

So, for example, a system with a USB bus but no USB devices connected to it has a /proc/bus/usb/ directory containing several files:

```
total 0
dr-xr-xr-x     1 root      root       0 May    3 16:25 001
-r--r--r--     1 root      root       0 May    3 16:25 devices
-r--r--r--     1 root      root       0 May    3 16:25 drivers
```

The /proc/bus/usb/ directory contains files that track the various devices on any USB buses, as well as the drivers required to use them. The /proc/bus/usb/ 001/ directory contains all devices on the first USB bus. By looking at the contents of the devices file, you can identify the USB root hub on the motherboard:

```
T:    Bus=01 Lev=00 Prnt=00 Port=00 Cnt=00 Dev#=    1 Spd=12    MxCh= 2
B:    Alloc=    0/900 us ( 0%), #Int=    0, #Iso=    0
D:    Ver= 1.00 Cls=09(hub   ) Sub=00 Prot=00 MxPS= 8 #Cfgs=         1
P:    Vendor=0000 ProdID=0000 Rev= 0.00
S:    Product=USB UHCI Root Hub
S:    SerialNumber=d400
C:* #Ifs= 1 Cfg#= 1 Atr=40 MxPwr=            0mA
I:    If#= 0 Alt= 0 #EPs= 1 Cls=09(hub    ) Sub=00 Prot=00 Driver=hub
E:    Ad=81(I) Atr=03(Int.) MxPS=      8 Ivl=255ms
```

/proc/driver/

This directory contains information for some drivers in use by the kernel. A common file found here is `rtc`, which provides output from the driver for the system's Real Time Clock (RTC), the device that keeps the time while the system is switched off. Sample output from `/proc/driver/rtc` looks like this:

```
rtc_time : 01:38:43
rtc_date : 1998-02-13
rtc_epoch : 1900
alarm     : 00:00:00
DST_enable : no
BCD       : yes
24hr      : yes
square_wave : no
alarm_IRQ : no
update_IRQ : no
periodic_IRQ : no
periodic_freq : 1024
batt_status : okay
```

For more information about the RTC, review `/usr/src/linux-2.4/Documentation/rtc.txt`.

/proc/fs

This directory shows which file systems are exported. If you are running an NFS server, you can type **cat /proc/fs/nfs/exports** to view the file systems being shared and the permissions granted for those file systems. For more on sharing file system with NFS, see Chapter 20.

/proc/ide/

This directory holds information about IDE devices on the system. Each IDE channel is represented as a separate directory, such as `/proc/ide/ide0` and `/proc/ide/ide1`. In addition, a `drivers` file is available, providing the version number of the various drivers used on the IDE channels:

```
ide-cdrom version 4.59
ide-floppy version 0.97
ide-disk version 1.10
```

Many chipsets also provide an informational file in this directory that gives additional data concerning the drives connected through the channels. For example, a generic Intel PIIX4 Ultra 33 chipset produces a `/proc/ide/piix` file that will tell you whether DMA or UDMA is enabled for the devices on the IDE channels:

```
Intel PIIX4 Ultra 33 Chipset.
--------- Primary Channel ------- Secondary Channel --------

                enabled             enabled
------------- drive0 ---- drive1 ---- drive0 ---- drive1 ---

DMA enabled:    yes        no         yes        no
UDMA enabled:   yes        no         no         no
UDMA enabled:   2          X          X          X
UDMA
DMA
PIO
```

Navigating into the directory for an IDE channel, such as ide0, provides additional information. The channel file provides the channel number, while the model tells you the bus type for the channel (such as pci).

The Device Directory

Within each IDE channel directory is a device directory. The name of the device directory corresponds to the drive letter in the /dev/ directory. For instance, the first IDE drive on ide0 would be hda.

 There is a symlink to each of these device directories in the /proc/ide/ directory.

Each device directory contains a collection of information and statistics. The contents of these directories vary according to the type of device connected. Some of the more useful files common to many devices are:

♦ cache — The device's cache.

♦ capacity — The capacity of the device, in 512-byte blocks.

♦ driver — The driver and version used to control the device.

♦ geometry — The physical and logical geometry of the device.

♦ media — The type of device, such as a disk.

◆ `model` — The model name or number of the device.

◆ `settings` — A collection of current parameters of the device. This file usually contains quite a bit of useful technical information. A sample settings file for a standard IDE hard disk looks similar to Listing 6-12.

Listing 6-12: Output from cat /proc/ide/hda/settings

name	value	min	max	mode
----	-----	---	---	----
bios_cyl	784	0	65535	rw
bios_head	255	0	255	rw
bios_sect	63	0	63	rw
breada_readahead	4	0	127	rw
bswap	0	0	1	r
current_speed	66	0	69	rw
file_readahead	0	0	2097151	rw
ide_scsi	0	0	1	rw
init_speed	66	0	69	rw
io_32bit	0	0	3	rw
keepsettings	0	0	1	rw
lun	0	0	7	rw
max_kb_per_request	64	1	127	rw
multcount	8	0	8	rw
nice1	1	0	1	rw
nowerr	0	0	1	rw
number	0	0	3	rw
pio_mode	write-only	0	255	w
slow	0	0	1	rw
unmaskirq	0	0	1	rw
using_dma	1	0	1	rw

/proc/irq/

This directory is used to set IRQ to CPU affinity, which allows you to connect a particular IRQ to only one CPU. Alternatively, you can exclude a CPU from handling any IRQs. Each IRQ has its own directory, allowing for individual configuration of each IRQ. The `/proc/irq/prof_cpu_mask` file is a bitmask that contains the default values for the `smp_affinity` file in the IRQ directory. The values in `smp_affinity` specify which CPUs handle that particular IRQ. `/usr/src/linux-2.4/Documentation/filesystems/proc.txt` contains more information.

/proc/net/

This directory provides a comprehensive look at various networking parameters and statistics. Each of the files covers a specific range of information related to networking on the system. Following is a partial listing of these virtual files:

- `arp` – Contains the kernel's ARP table. This file is particularly useful for connecting a hardware address to an IP address on a system.

- `atm` – A directory containing files with various Asynchronous Transfer Mode (ATM) settings and statistics. This directory is primarily used with ATM networking and ADSL cards.

- `dev` – Lists the various network devices configured on the system, complete with transmit and receive statistics. This file will quickly tell you the number of bytes each interface has sent and received, the number of packets inbound and outbound, the number of errors seen, the number of packets dropped, and more.

- `dev_mcast` – Displays the various `Layer2` multicast groups each device is listening to.

- `igmp` – Lists the IP multicast addresses that this system joined.

- `ip_fwchains` – If ipchains are in use, this virtual file reveals any current rule.

- `ip_fwnames` – If ipchains are in use, this virtual file lists all firewall chain names.

- `ip_masquerade` – Provides a table of masquerading information under ipchains.

- `ip_mr_cache` – List of the multicast routing cache.

- `ip_mr_vif` – List of multicast virtual interfaces.

- `netstat` – Contains a broad yet detailed collection of networking statistics, including TCP time-outs, SYN cookies sent and received, and much more.

- `psched` – List of global packet scheduler parameters.

- `raw` – List of raw device statistics.

- `route` – Displays the kernel's routing table.

- `rt_cache` – Contains the current routing cache.

- `snmp` – List of Simple Network Management Protocol (SNMP) data for various networking protocols in use.

- `sockstat` – Provides socket statistics.

- `tcp` – Contains detailed TCP socket information.

- `tr_rif` – The token ring RIF routing table.

- `udp` – Contains detailed UDP socket information.

- `unix` – Lists UNIX domain sockets currently in use.

- `wireless` – Lists wireless interface data.

/proc/scsi/

This directory is analogous to the `/proc/ide/` directory, only it is for connected SCSI devices. The primary file in this directory is `/proc/scsi/scsi`, which contains a list of every recognized SCSI device. From this listing, the type of devices, as well as the model name, vendor, SCSI channel and ID data, is available. For example, if a system contains a SCSI CD-ROM, tape drive, hard drives, and RAID controller, this file will look similar to this:

```
Attached devices:
Host: scsi1 Channel: 00 Id: 05 Lun: 00
  Vendor: NEC          Model: CD-ROM DRIVE:466 Rev: 1.06
  Type:     CD-ROM              ANSI SCSI revision: 02
Host: scsi1 Channel: 00 Id: 06 Lun: 00
  Vendor: ARCHIVE       Model: Python 04106-XXX Rev: 7350
  Type:     Sequential-Access    ANSI SCSI revision: 02
Host: scsi2 Channel: 00 Id: 06 Lun: 00
  Vendor: DELL          Model: 1x6 U2W SCSI BP    Rev: 5.35
  Type:     Processor            ANSI SCSI revision: 02
Host: scsi2 Channel: 02 Id: 00 Lun: 00
  Vendor: MegaRAID      Model: LD0 RAID5 34556R Rev: 1.01
  Type:     Direct-Access        ANSI SCSI revision: 02
```

Each SCSI driver used by the system has its own directory in `/proc/scsi/`, which contains files specific to each SCSI controller using that driver. So, for the example system above, `aic7xxx` and `megaraid` directories are present, as those two drivers are being utilized. The files in each of the directories typically contain IO address range, IRQ, and statistics for the particular SCSI controller using that driver. Each controller can report a different type and amount of information. The Adaptec AIC-7880 Ultra SCSI host adapter's file in this example system produces the output shown in Listing 6-13.

Listing 6-13: Output from cat /proc/scsi/aic7xxx/settings

```
Adaptec AIC7xxx driver version: 5.1.20/3.2.4
Compile Options:
     TCQ Enabled By Default : Disabled
     AIC7XXX_PROC_STATS     : Enabled
     AIC7XXX_RESET_DELAY    : 5

Adapter Configuration:
     SCSI Adapter: Adaptec AIC-7880 Ultra SCSI host adapter
     Ultra Narrow Controller  PCI MMAPed I/O Base: 0xfcffe000
 Adapter SEEPROM Config: SEEPROM found and used.
         Adaptec SCSI BIOS: Enabled
                     IRQ: 30
```

```
                SCBs: Active 0, Max Active 1, Allocated 15,
                     HW 16, Page 255
                  Interrupts: 33726
             BIOS Control Word: 0x18a6
          Adapter Control Word: 0x1c5f
          Extended Translation: Enabled
Disconnect Enable Flags: 0x00ff
         Ultra Enable Flags: 0x0020
 Tag Queue Enable Flags: 0x0000
Ordered Queue Tag Flags: 0x0000
Default Tag Queue Depth: 8
     Tagged Queue By Device array for aic7xxx host instance 1:

{255,255,255,255,255,255,255,255,255,255,255,255,255,255,255,255}
    Actual queue depth per device for aic7xxx host instance 1:
          {1,1,1,1,1,1,1,1,1,1,1,1,1,1,1,1}


Statistics:

(scsi1:0:5:0)
   Device using Narrow/Sync transfers at 20.0 MByte/sec, offset 15
      Transinfo settings: current(12/15/0/0), goal(12/15/0/0),
user(12/15/0/0)
      Total transfers 0 (0 reads and 0 writes)
        < 2K      2K+     4K+     8K+    16K+    32K+    64K+    128K+
Reads:   0        0       0       0       0       0       0       0
Writes:  0        0       0       0       0       0       0       0


(scsi1:0:6:0)
      Device using Narrow/Sync transfers at 10.0 MByte/sec, offset
15
      Transinfo settings: current(25/15/0/0), goal(12/15/0/0),
user(12/15/0/0)
      Total transfers 132 (0 reads and 132 writes)
        < 2K      2K+     4K+     8K+    16K+    32K+    64K+    128K+
Reads:   0        0       0       0       0       0       0       0
Writes:  0        0       0       1      131      0       0       0
```

From this screen, you can see the transfer speed to the various SCSI devices connected to the controller based on channel ID, as well as detailed statistics concerning the amount and sizes of files read or written by that device. For instance, from the output above you can see that this controller is communicating with the CD-ROM at 20 megabytes per second, while the tape drive is connected at only 10 megabytes per second.

/proc/sys/

The /proc/sys/ directory is different from others in /proc/; it not only provides information about the system but allows you to make configuration changes to the kernel. This allows the administrator of the machine to immediately enable and disable kernel features.

 Use caution when changing settings on a production system using the various files in the /proc/sys/ directory. Changing the wrong setting may render the kernel unstable, requiring a reboot of the system. For this reason, be sure you know the valid options for that file and the expected outcome before attempting to change a value in /proc/sys/.

A good way to determine if a particular file can be configured or is designed only to provide information is to list it with the -l flag in the terminal. If the file is writable, you may use it to configure the kernel. For example, a partial listing of /proc/sys/fs looks like this:

```
-r--r--r--    1 root    root    0 May 10 16:14 dentry-state
-rw-r--r--    1 root    root    0 May 10 16:14 dir-notify-enable
-r--r--r--    1 root    root    0 May 10 16:14 dquot-nr
-rw-r--r--    1 root    root    0 May 10 16:14 file-max
-r--r--r--    1 root    root    0 May 10 16:14 file-nr
```

In this listing, the files dir-notify-enable and file-max can be written to and, therefore, can be used to configure the kernel. The other files only provide feedback on current settings. Changing a value within a /proc/sys/ file is done by echoing the new value into the file. For example, to enable the System Request Key on a running kernel, type the command:

```
echo 1 > /proc/sys/kernel/sysrq
```

This will change the sysrq file's value from 0 (off) to 1 (on). The purpose of the System Request Key is to allow you to immediately instruct the kernel to do a number of important activities by using a simple key combination, such as immediately shutting down or restarting a system, syncing all mounted file systems, or dumping important information to your console. This feature is most useful when using a development kernel or if you are experiencing system freezes. However, it is considered a security risk for an unattended console and is therefore turned off by default under Red Hat Linux. Refer to /usr/src/linux-2.4/Documentation/ sysrq.txt for more information on the System Request Key.

A few `/proc/sys/` configuration files contain more than one value. In order to correctly send new values to them, place a space character between each value passed with the `echo` command, such as in this example:

```
echo 4 2 45 > /proc/sys/kernel/acct
```

 Any configuration changes you make using the `echo` command will disappear when the system is restarted. To make your configuration changes take effect at the time the system is booted, be sure to make the appropriate changes to your system start-up files.

The `/proc/sys/` directory contains several subdirectories controlling different aspects of a running kernel.

/proc/sys/dev/

This directory provides parameters for particular devices on the system. Most systems have at least two directories, `cdrom` and `raid`, but customized kernels can have others, such as `parport`, which provides the ability to share one parallel port between multiple device drivers. The `cdrom` directory contains a file called `info`, which reveals a number of important CD-ROM parameters as shown in Listing 6-14.

Listing 6-14: Output from cat /procsys/dev/cdrom/info

```
CD-ROM information, Id: cdrom.c 3.12 2000/10/18

drive name:             hdc
drive speed:            32
drive # of slots:       1
Can close tray:         1
Can open tray:          1
Can lock tray:          1
Can change speed:       1
Can select disk:        0
Can read multisession:  1
Can read MCN:           1
Reports media changed:  1
Can play audio:         1
Can write CD-R:         0
Can write CD-RW:        0
Can read DVD:           0
Can write DVD-R:        0
Can write DVD-RAM:      0
```

This file can be quickly scanned to discover the qualities of an unknown CD-ROM, at least in the eyes of the kernel. If multiple CD-ROMs are available on a system, each device is given its own column of information.

Various files in /proc/sys/dev/cdrom, such as autoclose and checkmedia, can be used to control the system's CD-ROM. Use the echo command to enable or disable these features. If RAID support is compiled into the kernel, a /proc/sys/ dev/raid/ directory will be available with at least two files in it: speed_limit_ min and speed_limit_max. The settings of these files determine how much to accelerate the RAID device for particularly I/O-intensive tasks, such as resyncing the disks.

/proc/sys/fs/

This directory contains an array of options and information concerning various aspects of the file system, including quota, file handle, inode, and dentry information. The binfmt_misc directory is used to provide kernel support for miscellaneous binary formats. The important files in /proc/sys/fs include:

◆ dentry-state — Provides the status of the directory cache. The file looks similar to this:

```
57411 52939 45 0 0 0
```

The first number reveals the total number of directory cache entries, while the second number displays the number of unused entries. The third number tells the number of seconds between when a directory has been freed and when it can be reclaimed, and the fourth measures the pages currently requested by the system. The last two numbers are not used and currently display only zeros.

◆ dquot-nr — Shows the maximum number of cached disk quota entries.

◆ file-max — Allows you to change the maximum number of file handles that the kernel will allocate. Raising the value in this file can resolve errors caused by a lack of available file handles.

◆ file-nr — Displays the number of allocated file handles, used file handles, and the maximum number of file handles.

◆ overflowgid and overflowuid — Define the fixed group ID and user ID, respectively, for use with file systems that support only 16-bit group and user IDs.

◆ super-max — Controls the maximum number of superblocks available.

◆ super-nr — Displays the current number of superblocks in use.

/proc/sys/kernel/

This directory contains a variety of different configuration files that directly affect the operation of the kernel. Some of the most important files are:

- ◆ acct — Controls the suspension of process accounting based on the percentage of free space available on the file system containing the log. By default, the file looks like this:

  ```
  4 2 30
  ```

  The second value sets the threshold percentage of free space when logging will be suspended, while the first value dictates the percentage of free space required for logging to resume. The third value sets the interval in seconds that the kernel polls the file system to see if logging should be suspended or resumed.

- ◆ cap-bound — Controls the capability bounding settings, which provide a list of capabilities for any process on the system. If a capability is not listed here, then no process, no matter how privileged, can use that capability. The idea is to make the system more secure by ensuring that certain things cannot happen, at least beyond a certain point in the boot process. The various values that are possible here are beyond the scope of this book, so consult the kernel documentation for more information.

- ◆ ctrl-alt-del — Controls whether Ctrl+Alt+Del will gracefully restart the computer using init (value 0) or force an immediate reboot without syncing the dirty buffers to disk (value 1).

- ◆ domainname — Allows you to configure the system's domain name, such as subgenius.com.

- ◆ hostname — Allows you to configure the system's hostname, such as bob.subgenius.com.

- ◆ hotplug — Configures the utility to be used when a configuration change is detected by the system. This is primarily used with USB and Cardbus PCI. The default value of /sbin/hotplug should not be changed unless you are testing a new program to fulfill this role.

- ◆ modprobe — Sets the location of the program to be used to load kernel modules when necessary. The default value of /sbin/modprobe signifies that kmod will call it to actually load the module when a kernel thread calls kmod.

- ◆ msgmax — Sets the maximum size of any message sent from one process to another. This value is set to 8,192 bytes by default. Be careful about raising this value, as queued messages between processes are stored in non-swappable kernel memory. Any increase in msgmax would increase RAM requirements for the system.

- ◆ msgmnb — Sets the maximum number of bytes in a single message queue. The default is 16,384.

- ◆ msgmni — Sets the maximum number of message queue identifiers. The default is 16.

◆ osrelease — Lists the Linux kernel release number. This file can be altered only by changing the kernel source and recompiling.

◆ ostype — Displays the type of operating system. By default, this file is set to Linux, and this value can be changed only by changing the kernel source and recompiling.

◆ overflowgid and overflowuid — Define the fixed group ID and user ID, respectively, for use with system calls on architectures that support only 16-bit group and user IDs.

◆ panic — Defines the number of seconds the kernel will postpone rebooting when the system experiences a kernel panic. By default, the value is set to 0, which disables automatic rebooting after a panic.

◆ printk — This file controls a variety of settings related to printing or logging error messages. Each error message reported by the kernel has a loglevel associated with it that defines the importance of the message. The loglevel values break down in this order:

■ 0 — Kernel emergency. The system is unusable.

■ 1 — Kernel alert. Action must be taken immediately.

■ 2 — Condition of the kernel is considered critical.

■ 3 — General kernel error condition.

■ 4 — General kernel warning condition.

■ 5 — Kernel notice of a normal but significant condition.

■ 6 — Kernel informational message.

■ 7 — Kernel debug-level messages.

Four values are found in the printk file:

6 4 1 7

Each of these values defines a different rule for dealing with error messages. The first value, called the console loglevel, defines the lowest priority of messages that will be printed to the console. (Note that the lower the priority, the higher the loglevel number.) The second value sets the default loglevel for messages without an explicit loglevel attached to them. The third value sets the lowest possible loglevel configuration for the console loglevel. The last value sets the default value for the console loglevel.

◆ rtsig-max — Configures the maximum number of POSIX realtime signals that the system may have queued at any one time. The default value is 1,024.

- ◆ rtsig-nr — The current number of POSIX realtime signals queued by the kernel.

- ◆ sem — This file configures semaphore settings within the kernel. A semaphore is a System V IPC object that is used to control utilization of a particular process.

- ◆ shmall — Sets the total amount of shared memory that can be used at one time on the system, in bytes. By default, this value is 2,097,152.

- ◆ shmmax — Sets the largest shared memory segment size allowed by the kernel, in bytes. By default, this value is 33,554,432. However, the kernel supports much larger values than this.

- ◆ shmmni — Sets the maximum number of shared memory segments for the whole system. By default, this value is 4,096.

- ◆ sysrq — Activates the System Request Key, if this value is set to anything other than the default of 0.

- ◆ threads-max — Sets the maximum number of threads to be used by the kernel, with a default value of 2,048.

- ◆ version — Displays the date and time the kernel was last compiled. The first field in this file, such as #3, relates to the number of times a kernel was built from the source base.

The random directory stores a number of values related to generating random numbers for the kernel.

/proc/sys/net/

This directory contains assorted directories concerning various networking topics. Various configurations at the time of kernel compilation make available different directories here, such as appletalk, ethernet, ipv4, ipx, and ipv6. Within these directories, you can adjust the assorted networking values for that configuration on a running system.

 Given the wide variety of possible networking options available with Linux and the great amount of space required to discuss them, only the most common /proc/sys/net/ directories will be discussed.

The core directory contains a variety of settings that control the interaction between the kernel and networking layers. The most important files there are:

◆ message_burst — The amount of time in tenths of a second required to write a new warning message. This is used to prevent Denial of Service (DoS) attacks. The default setting is 50.

◆ message_cost — Also used to prevent DoS attacks by placing a cost on every warning message. The higher the value of this file (default of 5), the more likely the warning message will be ignored. The idea of a DoS attack is to bombard your system with requests that generate errors and fill up disk partitions with log files or require all of your system's resources to handle the error logging. The settings in message_burst and message_cost are designed to be modified based on your system's acceptable risk versus the need for comprehensive logging.

◆ netdev_max_backlog — Sets the maximum number of packets allowed to queue when a particular interface receives packets faster than the kernel can process them. The default value for this file is 300.

◆ optmem_max — Configures the maximum ancillary buffer size allowed per socket.

◆ rmem_default — Sets the receive socket buffer's default size in bytes.

◆ rmem_max — Sets the receive socket buffer's maximum size in bytes.

◆ wmem_default — Sets the send socket buffer's default size in bytes.

◆ wmem_max — Sets the send socket buffer's maximum size in bytes.

The /ipv4 directory contains additional networking settings. Many of these settings, used in conjunction with one another, are very useful in preventing attacks on the system or using the system to act as a router.

An erroneous change to these files may affect your remote connectivity to the system.

Here are some of the most important files in the /proc/sys/net/ipv4/ directory:

◆ icmp_destunreach_rate, icmp_echoreply_rate, icmp_paramprob_rate, and icmp_timeexeed_rate — Set the maximum ICMP send packet rate, in hundredths of a second, to hosts under certain conditions. A setting of 0 removes any delay and is not a good idea.

◆ icmp_echo_ignore_all and icmp_echo_ignore_broadcasts — Allows the kernel to ignore ICMP ECHO packets from every host or only those originating from broadcast and multicast addresses, respectively. A value of 0 allows the kernel to respond, while a value of 1 ignores the packets.

- ◆ `ip_default_ttl` – Sets the default Time To Live (TTL), which limits the number of hops a packet may make before reaching its destination. Increasing this value can diminish system performance.

- ◆ `ip_forward` – Permits interfaces on the system to forward packets to one other. By default, this file is set to 0. Setting this file to 1 will enable network packet forwarding.

- ◆ `ip_local_port_range` – Specifies the range of ports to be used by TCP or UDP when a local port is needed. The first number is the lowest port to be used, and the second number specifies the highest port. Any systems that expect to require more ports than the default 1,024 to 4,999 should use the 32,768 to 61,000 range in this file.

- ◆ `tcp_syn_retries` – Provides a limit on the number of times your system will retransmit a SYN packet when attempting to make a connection.

- ◆ `tcp_retries1` – Sets the number of permitted retransmissions attempting to answer an incoming connection. Default of 3.

- ◆ `tcp_retries2` – Sets the number of permitted retransmissions of TCP packets. Default of 15.

The `/usr/src/linux-2.4/Documentation/networking/ip-sysctl.txt` file contains a complete list of files and options available in the `/proc/sys/net/ipv4/` directory. A number of other directories that exist within the `/proc/sys/net/ipv4/` directory cover specific topics.

The `conf` directory allows each of the system interfaces to be configured in different ways, including the use of default settings for unconfigured devices (in the `default` subdirectory) and settings that override all special configurations (in the `all` subdirectory). In order to control connections between direct neighbors, meaning any other system directly connected to your system, the `neigh` directory allows special configurations for each interface. This will allow you to treat differently systems that you trust more because of their relative proximity to your system. At the same time, it also makes it easy to put strict rules in place for systems several hops away.

Routing over IPV4 also has its own directory, `route`. Unlike `conf` and `neigh`, the `route` directory contains specifications that apply to routing with any interfaces on the system. Many of these settings, such as `max_size`, `max_delay`, and `min_delay`, relate to controlling the size of the routing cache. To clear the routing cache, simply write any value to the `flush` file. Additional information about these directories and the possible values for their configuration files can be found in `/usr/src/linux-2.4/Documentation/filesystems/proc.txt`.

/proc/sys/vm/

This directory facilitates the configuration of the Linux kernel's virtual memory (VM) subsystem. The kernel makes extensive and intelligent use of virtual memory, which is commonly called swap space. The following files are commonly found in the `/proc/sys/vm/` directory:

◆ bdflush — Sets various values related to the bdflush kernel daemon.

◆ buffermem — Allows you to control the percentage amount of total system memory to be used for buffer memory. Typical output for this file looks like this:

```
2        10        60
```

The first and last values set the minimum and maximum percentage of memory to be used as buffer memory, respectively. The middle value sets the percentage of system memory dedicated to buffer memory where the memory management subsystem will begin to clear buffer cache more than other kinds of memory to compensate for a general lack of free memory.

◆ kswapd — Sets various values concerned with the kernel swap-out daemon, kswapd. This file has three values:

```
512 32 8
```

The first value sets the maximum number of pages that kswapd will attempt to free in a single attempt. The larger this number, the more aggressively the kernel can move to free pages. The second value sets the minimum number of times that kswapd attempts to free a page. The third value sets the number of pages kswapd attempts to write in a single attempt. Proper tuning of this final value can improve performance on a system using a lot of swap space by telling the kernel to write pages in large chunks, minimizing the number of disk seeks.

◆ max_map_count — Configures the maximum number of memory map areas a process may have. In most cases, the default value of 65,536 is appropriate.

◆ overcommit_memory — When this is set to the default value of 0, the kernel estimates the amount of memory available and fails requests that are blatantly invalid. Unfortunately, since memory is allocated using a heuristic rather than a precise algorithm, it can sometimes overload the system. If overcommit_memory is set to 1, the potential for system overload is increased, but so is the performance for memory-intensive tasks, such as those used by some scientific software.

◆ pagecache — Controls the amount of memory used by the page cache. The values in pagecache are percentages, and they work in a similar way as buffermem to enforce minimums and maximums of available page cache memory.

◆ page-cluster — Sets the number of pages read in a single attempt. The default value of 4, which actually relates to 16 pages, is appropriate for most systems.

◆ pagetable_cache — Controls the number of page tables that are cached on a per-processor basis. The first and second values relate to the minimum and maximum number of page tables to set aside, respectively.

The `/usr/src/linux-2.4/Documentation/sysctl/vm.txt` file contains additional information on these various files.

/proc/sysvipc/

This directory contains information about System V IPC resources. The files in this directory relate to System V IPC calls for messages (`msg`), semaphores (`sem`), and shared memory (`shm`).

/proc/tty/

This directory contains information about the available and currently used tty devices on the system. Originally called a teletype device, character-based data terminals are called tty devices. In Linux, there are three different kinds of tty devices. Serial devices are used with serial connections, such as over a modem or using a serial cable. Virtual terminals create the common console connection, such as the virtual consoles available when pressing Alt+F at the system console. Pseudo terminals create a two-way communication that is used by some higher level applications, such as X11. The `drivers` file is a list of the current tty devices in use as shown in Listing 6-15.

Listing 6-15: Output from cat /proc/tty/devices

```
serial        /dev/cua      5     64-127    serial:callout
serial        /dev/ttyS     4     64-127    serial
pty_slave     /dev/pts      136   0-255     pty:slave
pty_master    /dev/ptm      128   0-255     pty:master
pty_slave     /dev/ttyp     3     0-255     pty:slave
pty_master    /dev/pty      2     0-255     pty:master
/dev/vc/0     /dev/vc/0     4         0     system:vtmaster
/dev/ptmx     /dev/ptmx     5         2     system
/dev/console  /dev/console  5         1     system:console
/dev/tty      /dev/tty      5         0     system:/dev/tty
unknown       /dev/vc/%d    4     1-63      console
```

The `/proc/tty/driver/serial` file lists the usage statistics and status of each of the serial tty lines. In order for tty devices to be used in a similar way as network devices, the Linux kernel enforces line discipline on the device. This allows the driver to place a specific type of header with every block of data transmitted over the device, making it possible for the remote end of the connection to be able to see that block of data as just one in a stream of data blocks. SLIP and PPP are common line disciplines, and each is commonly used to connect systems to one other over a serial link. Registered line disciplines are stored in the `ldiscs` file, with detailed information available in the `ldisc` directory.

Using sysctl

The sysctl command is used to view, set, and automate kernel settings in the /proc/sys/ directory. To get a quick overview of all settings configurable in the /proc/sys/ directory, type the sysctl a command as root. This will create a large, comprehensive list, a small portion of which looks something like this:

```
net.ipv4.route.min_delay = 2
kernel.sysrq = 0
kernel.sem = 250          32000          32          128
```

This is the same basic information you would see if you viewed each of the files individually. The only difference is the file location. The /proc/sys/net/ipv4/route/min_delay file is signified by net.ipv4.route.min_delay, with the directory slashes replaced by dots and the proc.sys portion assumed.

The sysctl command can be used in place of echo to assign values to writable files in the /proc/sys/ directory. For instance, instead of using this command:

```
echo 1 > /proc/sys/kernel/sysrq
```

you can use this sysctl command:

```
sysctl -w kernel.sysrq="1"
kernel.sysrq = 1
```

 TIP You could also edit the sysctl.conf file to make the changes you desire and then run sysctl -p to reload the file.

While quickly setting single values like this in /proc/sys/ is helpful during testing, it does not work as well on a production system, as all /proc/sys/ special settings are lost when the machine is rebooted. To preserve the settings that you want to make permanently to your kernel, add them to the /etc/sysctl.conf file. Every time the system boots, the init program runs the /etc/rc.d/rc.sysinit script. This script contains a command to execute sysctl using /etc/sysctl.conf to dictate the values passed to the kernel. Any values added to /etc/sysctl.conf will take effect each time the system boots.

Linux Disk Management

This section explains some basics about disk partitioning and disk management under Linux. To see how your Linux disks are currently partitioned and what file systems are on them, look at the /etc/fstab file.

In Listing 6-16, you can see what a simple /etc/fstab file looks like.

Listing 6-16: Output from cat /etc/fstab

```
[terry@terry terry]$ cat /etc/fstab
LABEL=/                /               ext3     defaults                    1 1
LABEL=/boot1           /boot           ext3     defaults                    1 2
none                   /dev/pts        devpts   gid=5,mode=620              0 0
none                   /proc           proc     defaults                    0 0
none                   /dev/shm        tmpfs    defaults                    0 0
/dev/hdb3              swap            swap     defaults                    0 0
/dev/cdrom            /mnt/cdrom       iso9660  noauto,owner,kudzu,ro 0 0
/dev/fd0             /mnt/floppy       auto     noauto,owner,kudzu      0 0
/dev/hdb5           /mnt/drive2root    auto     defaults                    0 0
/dev/hdb2           /mnt/drive2home    auto     defaults                    0 0
/dev/sda1            /mnt/thumb        auto     noauto,user,owner        0 0
```

TIP To see how your Linux disks are currently partitioned and what file systems are on them, look at the /etc/fstab file. You could also use the fdisk -l command to obtain partition information about your disks.

Partitioning an x86 Machine

When partitioning an x86 PC, you need to be mindful of the limitations present in the x86 architecture. You are allowed to create 4 primary partitions. Primary partitions are the only partitions that are bootable. You can create more partitions if you make logical partitions.

Logical partitions are set into a primary partition. So if you choose to make logical partitions, you are allowed to make only three primary partitions for operating system use, and the fourth partition is dedicated to hosting the logical partitions.

Mounting Other OS Partitions/Slices

Not only can Linux read other operating systems' file systems; it can mount disk drives from other systems and work with their partition tables. However, it is necessary to compile two options into the kernel to do this. You must have the file system support and the file partitioning support turned on in the kernel. Usually file system support is compiled as a module by default, but disk partition support usually has to be explicitly compiled.

Some common partitioning schemes that Linux supports are: x86 partitions, BSD disklabel, Solaris x86, Unixware, Alpha, OSF, SGI, and Sun.

Mounting other operating systems' partitions is helpful if you need to put a Sun hard disk into a Linux machine, for example. You may need to do this if the original Sun system has gone bad, and you need to recover the information that was on its disk, or if it's the target of a forensic computer crime investigation, and you need to copy the disk contents to another machine to preserve evidence. This method takes advantage of the fact that copying a large amount of data is much faster across a SCSI connection than across a network.

If you need to copy a large amount of raw disk data across a network, you can use the Network Block Daemon, which enables other machines to mount a disk on your machine as if it were on their machine.

TIP   When running the Network Block Daemon, make sure that you have the appropriate partition support compiled into the kernel.

Metadevices

Virtual block devices that are made up of other block devices are referred to in this book as a metadevice. An example of a metadevice is a disk array that makes many disks look like one large disk. When a disk that's mounted as a regular block device dies, then the data on it becomes unavailable. If a disk dies in a metadevice, the metadevice is still up. As long as the criteria are met for the minimum number of working devices in the metadevice, the metadevice still functions.

LOGICAL VOLUMES

Logical Volume Manager (LVM) enables you to be much more flexible with your disk usage than you can be with conventional old-style file partitions. Normally if you create a partition, you have to keep the partition at that size indefinitely.

For example, if your system logs have grown immensely, and you've run out of room on your /var partition, increasing a partition size without LVM is a big pain. You would have to get another disk drive, create a /var mount point on there too, and copy all your data from the old /var to the new /var disk location. With LVM in place, you could add another disk, and then assign that disk to be part of the /var partition. Then you'd use the LVM file system resizing tool to increase the file system size to match the new partition size.

Normally you might think of disk drives as independent entities, each containing some data space. When you use LVMs, you need a new way of thinking about disk space. First you have to understand that space on any disk can be used by any file system. A Volume Group is the term used to describe various disk spaces (either whole disks or parts of disks) that have been grouped together into one volume.

Volume groups are then bunched together to form Logical volumes. Logical volumes are akin to the historic idea of partitions. You can then use a file system creation tool such as `fdisk` to create a file system on the logical volume. The Linux kernel sees a logical volume in the same way it sees a regular partition.

Some Linux tools for modifying logical volumes are `pvcreate` for creating physical volumes, `vgcreate` for creating volume groups, `vgdisplay` for showing volume groups, and `mke2fs` for creating a file system on your logical volume.

What Is RAID?

RAID is a method in which information is spread across several disks, using techniques such as disk striping (RAID Level 0), disk mirroring (RAID Level 1), and disk striping with parity (RAID Level 5) to achieve redundancy, lower latency and/or increased bandwidth for reading from or writing to disks, and maximize the ability to recover from hard-disk crashes.

The underlying concept of RAID is that data may be distributed across each drive in the array in a consistent manner. To do this, the data must first be broken into consistently sized chunks (often 32K or 64K in size, although different sizes can be used). Each chunk is then written to a hard drive in RAID according to the RAID level used. When the data is to be read, the process is reversed, giving the illusion that multiple drives are actually one large drive.

Who Should Use RAID?

Anyone who needs to keep large quantities of data on hand (such as a system administrator) can benefit by using RAID technology. Primary reasons to use RAID include:

- ◆ Enhanced speed
- ◆ Increased storage capacity using a single virtual disk
- ◆ Lessened impact of a disk failure

Hardware RAID versus Software RAID

There are two possible RAID approaches: hardware RAID and software RAID.

HARDWARE RAID

The hardware-based system manages the RAID subsystem independently from the host and presents to the host only a single disk per RAID array. An example of a hardware RAID device is one that connects to a SCSI controller and presents the

RAID arrays as a single SCSI drive. An external RAID system moves all RAID-handling "intelligence" into a controller located in the external disk subsystem. The whole subsystem is connected to the host via a normal SCSI controller and appears to the host as a single disk.

RAID controllers also come in the form of cards that act like a SCSI controller to the operating system but handle all of the actual drive communications themselves. In these cases, you plug the drives into the RAID controller just as you would into a SCSI controller, but then you add them to the RAID controller's configuration, and the operating system never knows the difference.

SOFTWARE RAID

Software RAID implements the various RAID levels in the kernel disk (block device) code. It offers the cheapest possible solution, as expensive disk controller cards or hot-swap chassis are not required. A hot-swap chassis allows you to remove a hard drive without having to power down your system. Software RAID also works with cheaper IDE disks as well as SCSI disks. With today's fast CPUs, software RAID performance can easily beat the performance of hardware RAID.

Reliable hotswap support in Linux requires Single Connection Attach (SCA) SCSI disk enclosures. The general solution is to have extra disks already in the system and to remove them via software when they go bad, adding the spare disk to the RAID array. Without SCA, a reboot is necessary to actually physically add/remove devices.

The MD driver in the Linux kernel is an example of a RAID solution that is completely hardware independent. The performance of a software-based array is dependent on the server CPU performance and load. For information on configuring Software RAID in the Red Hat installation program, refer to the "Software RAID Configuration" section of this chapter.

For those interested in learning more about what software RAID has to offer, here is a brief list of the most important features:

♦ Threaded rebuild process

♦ Kernel-based configuration

♦ Portability of arrays between Linux machines without reconstruction

♦ Backgrounded array reconstruction using idle system resources

♦ Hotswappable drive support

♦ Automatic CPU detection to take advantage of certain CPU optimizations

RAID Levels and Linear Support

RAID supports various configurations, including levels 0, 1, 4, 5, and linear. These RAID types are defined as follows.

LEVEL 0

RAID level 0, often called "striping," is a performance-oriented striped data mapping technique. This means the data being written to the array is broken down into strips and written across the member disks of the array, allowing high I/O performance at low inherent cost but providing no redundancy. The storage capacity of a level 0 array is equal to the total capacity of the member disks in a hardware RAID or the total capacity of member partitions in a software RAID.

LEVEL 1

RAID level 1, or "mirroring," has been used longer than any other form of RAID. Level 1 provides redundancy by writing identical data to each member disk of the array, leaving a "mirrored" copy on each disk. Mirroring remains popular because of its simplicity and high level of data availability. Level 1 operates with two or more disks that may use parallel access for high data-transfer rates when reading but more commonly operate independently to provide high I/O transaction rates. Level 1 provides very good data reliability and improves performance for read-intensive applications but at a relatively high cost. The storage capacity of the level 1 array is equal to the capacity of one of the mirrored hard disks in a hardware RAID or one of the mirrored partitions in a software RAID.

RAID level 1 comes at a high cost because you write the same information to all of the disks in the array, which wastes drive space. For example, if you have RAID level 1 set up so that your root (/) partition exists on two 40GB drives, you have 80GB total but are able to access only 40GB of that 80GB. The other 40GB acts like a mirror of the first 40GB.

LEVEL 4

Level 4 uses parity concentrated on a single disk drive to protect data. Level 4 is better suited to transaction I/O than large file transfers. Because the dedicated parity disk represents an inherent bottleneck, level 4 is seldom used without accompanying technologies such as write-back caching. Although RAID level 4 is an option in some RAID partitioning schemes, it is not an option allowed in Red Hat Linux RAID installations. The storage capacity of hardware RAID level 4 is equal to the capacity of member disks, minus the capacity of one member disk. The storage capacity of software RAID level 4 is equal to the capacity of the member partitions, minus the size of one of the partitions if they are of equal size.

Parity information is calculated based on the contents of the rest of the member disks in the array. This information can then be used to reconstruct data when one disk in the array fails. The reconstructed data can then be used to satisfy I/O requests to the failed disk before it is replaced and to repopulate the failed disk after it has been replaced.

RAID level 4 takes up the same amount of space as RAID level 5, but level 5 has more advantages. For this reason, level 4 is not supported under Red Hat Enterprise Linux.

LEVEL 5

This is the most common type of RAID. By distributing parity across some or all of an array's member disk drives, RAID level 5 eliminates the write bottleneck inherent in level 4. The only performance bottleneck is the parity calculation process. With modern CPUs and software RAID, that usually is not a very big problem. As with level 4, the result is asymmetrical performance, with reads substantially outperforming writes. Level 5 is often used with write-back caching to reduce the asymmetry. The storage capacity of hardware RAID level 5 is equal to the capacity of member disks, minus the capacity of one member disk. The storage capacity of software RAID level 5 is equal to the capacity of the member partitions, minus the size of one of the partitions if they are of equal size.

LINEAR RAID

Linear RAID is a simple grouping of drives to create a larger virtual drive. In linear RAID, the chunks are allocated sequentially from one member drive, going to the next drive only when the first is completely filled. This grouping provides no performance benefit, as it is unlikely that any I/O operations will be split among member drives. Linear RAID also offers no redundancy and, in fact, decreases reliability: If a member drive fails, the entire array cannot be used. The capacity is the total of all member disks.

Software RAID Configuration

Software RAID can be configured during the graphical installation of Red Hat Linux or during a kickstart installation. You can use fdisk or Disk Druid to create your RAID configuration, but these instructions will focus mainly on using Disk Druid to complete this task. Before you can create a RAID device, you must first create RAID partitions, using the following step-by-step instructions.

TIP If you are using fdisk to create a RAID partition, remember that instead of creating a partition as type 83, which is Linux native, you must create the partition as type fd (Linux RAID). Also, for best performance, partitions within a given RAID array should span identical cylinders on drives.

1. On the Disk Partitioning Setup screen, select Manually partition with Disk Druid.

2. In Disk Druid, choose New to create a new partition.

   You will not be able to enter a mount point (you will be able to do that once you have created your RAID device).

3. Choose software RAID from the File System Type pull-down menu.

4. For Allowable Drives, select the drive(s) on which RAID will be created. If you have multiple drives, all drives will be selected here, and you must deselect those drives that will not have the RAID array on them.

5. Enter the size that you want the partition to be.

6. Select Fixed size to make the partition the specified size, select Fill all space up to (MB) and enter a size in MBs to give range for the partition size, or select Fill to maximum Using RAID.

Summary

Linux supports many file systems. It supports those from other operating systems, remote file systems, memory file systems, CD-ROM file systems, virtual file systems, and metadevice file systems. This makes Linux very good at managing and accessing any file or file systems that you may ever come across in a multiplatform environment.

Chapter 7

Red Hat System Configuration Files

IN THIS CHAPTER

◆ Becoming familiar with the system configuration files

◆ Becoming familiar with the network configuration files

◆ Managing the init scripts

THIS CHAPTER DESCRIBES the file system and configuration files in a typical Red Hat Enterprise Linux server.

The system configuration files in the /etc directory are the first places a system administrator goes after installing a system to set it up. The /etc directory is probably the most often visited directory by a system administrator after his or her own home directory and /var/log.

All of the systemwide important configuration files are found either in /etc or in one of its many subdirectories. An advantage to keeping all system configuration files under /etc is that it's easier to restore configurations for individual programs, as opposed to having all the system's configurations rolled up into a monstrous registry hive like some operating systems.

 Be vigilant that your files in /etc are modifiable only by appropriate users. Generally, this means being modifiable only by root.

Because these files are so important and their contents so sensitive (everything from users' hashed passwords to the host's ssh key are stored in /etc), it is important to keep the file permissions set properly on everything in /etc. Almost all files should be owned by root, and *nothing* should be world writable. Most files should have their file permissions set to user readable and writable, and group and world readable, like this:

```
-rw-r--r--    1 root      root          172 Aug  6 02:03 hosts
```

Some notable exceptions are files such as /etc/shadow, where users' hashed passwords are stored, and /etc/wvdial.conf, which stores dial-up account names and passwords. These files' permissions should be set to owned by root, and read by root only, like this:

```
-rw-------    1 root      root            1227 Sep  2 13:52 /etc/shadow
```

The /etc/sysconfig directory contains configuration scripts written and configured by Red Hat and Red Hat administration tools. /etc/sysconfig contains both system and networking configuration files. Putting these files in /etc/sysconfig distinguishes them from other /etc configuration files not designed by Red Hat. You should keep these files in a separate directory so that the risk of other developers writing configuration files with the same names and putting them in the same place as existing config files is reduced.

Examining the System Configuration Files

The Red Hat system configuration files can fall within a few different functions. Some specify system duties, such as logging and automatically running programs with cron. Some set default configurations for important programs such as sendmail and Bash. And many other system configuration files are responsible for arranging the appearance of the system, such as setting the colors that show up when a directory listing is shown and the banners that pop up when someone logs in. This section discusses the more important system configuration files on your Red Hat system.

Systemwide Shell Configuration Scripts

These files determine the default environment settings of system shells and what functions are started every time a user launches a new shell.

The files discussed next are located in /etc. These configuration files affect all shells used on the system. An individual user can also set up a default configuration file in his or her home directory that affects only his or her shells. This ability is useful in case the user wants to add some extra directories to his or her path or some aliases that only he or she use.

When used in the home directory, the names are the same, except they have a. in front of them. So /etc/bashrc affects bash shells systemwide, but /home/kelly/.bashrc affects only the shells that the user kelly starts.

SHELL CONFIG SCRIPTS: bashrc, csh.cshrc, zshrc

Bashrc is read by bash, csh.cshrc is read by tcsh, and zshrc is read by zsh. These files are read every time a shell is launched, not just upon login, and they determine the settings and behaviors of the shells on the system. The following are places to put functions and aliases.

profile   This file is read by all shells except tcsh and csh upon login. Bash falls back to reading it if there is no bash_profile. Zsh looks for zprofile, but if there is none, it reads profile as well. Listing 7-1 shows a typical /etc/profile file.

Listing 7-1: A typical /etc/profile file

```
# /etc/profile

# System wide environment and startup programs
# Functions and aliases go in /etc/bashrc

if ! echo $PATH | /bin/grep -q "/usr/X11R6/bin" ; then
  PATH="$PATH:/usr/X11R6/bin"
fi

PATH=$PATH:/sbin:/usr/sbin:/usr/local/sbin

ulimit -S -c 1000000 > /dev/null 2>&1
if [ `id -gn` = `id -un` -a `id -u` -gt 14 ]; then
        umask 002
else
        umask 022
fi

USER=`id -un`
LOGNAME=$USER
MAIL="/var/spool/mail/$USER"

HOSTNAME=`/bin/hostname`
HISTSIZE=1000

if [ -z "$INPUTRC" -a ! -f "$HOME/.inputrc" ]; then
        INPUTRC=/etc/inputrc
fi

export PATH USER LOGNAME MAIL HOSTNAME HISTSIZE INPUTRC

for i in /etc/profile.d/*.sh ; do
        if [ -x $i ]; then
                . $i
        fi
done

unset i
```

profile is a good place to set paths because it is where you set environmental variables that are passed to child processes in the shell. If you want to change the default path of your shells in profile, modify the following line:

```
PATH=$PATH:/sbin:/usr/sbin:/usr/local/sbin
```

Do not add too many paths to this line; users can set their own paths using a .profile in their home directories. More default paths than are necessary can pose a security risk. For example, a user named katie may want to run her own version of pine that she keeps in her home directory.

In that case, she may want to have /home/$USER or /home/katie at the beginning of her path so that when she types **pine**, the version in her home directory is found by the shell first, before finding the copy of pine in /usr/bin/pine. Generally, putting /home/$USER or any other directory whose contents are not controlled by root in /etc/profile is not a good idea.

The reason for this warning is that a rogue user or cracker can compile a backdoor, a way to enter the system unexpectedly, or corrupted version of a program and somehow get it in a user's home directory, perhaps even by mailing it to the user. If users' paths are set to check their home directories first, they may think they are running a system program but instead are unknowingly running an alternate version.

On the other hand, if this path modification is set only in katie's .profile, only she runs this risk. She should also be aware of this risk since she has to perform the extra step of adding this path modification herself.

Another useful variable to change in the system profile is the number of user commands saved in the .history file in the user's directory. This command history is especially useful, since you can scroll through your previous commands by using the up and down arrows. To change the number of commands saved in the .history file, modify this line:

```
HISTSIZE=1000
```

bash, tcsh, zsh, AND THEIR CONFIG FILE READ ORDERS

The shells read a few configuration files when starting up. It is good to know which files are read in what order, so that you know where to set variables that will only apply to certain users.

bash   bash reads the following files on startup: /etc/profile, ~/.bash_profile, ~/.bash_login, and ~/.profile. Upon logout, bash reads ~/.bash_logout.

tcsh   tcsh reads the following files when starting up: /etc/csh.cshrc, then /etc/csh.login. After these come the config files in the user's home directory: ~/.tcshrc (or if not present, ~/.cshrc), ~/.history, ~/.login, ~/.cshdirs.

zsh   zsh reads the following when starting up: /etc/zshenv, ~/.zshenv, /etc/zprofile, ~/.zprofile, /etc/zshrc, ~/.zshrc, **and** /etc/zlogin.

Nonlogin shells also read ~/.bashrc. Upon logout, zsh reads the ~/.zlogout and /etc zlogout files.

System Environmental Settings

The files discussed in this section deal with system environmental settings.

motd

This file contains the message that users see every time they log in. It's a good place to communicate messages about system downtime and other things that users should be aware of. On the other hand, you can put amusing quotes here to entertain your users. Usually, the motd contains a message like:

```
Welcome to Generic University's Unix mail system.
This system is monitored. Unauthorized use prohibited.
System downtime scheduled this Sunday night from 10pm to 1am.
```

TIP motd is a plain-text file, but variables can be placed into the script to customize what users see when they log in. You can customize the output based on the user group, user type, or user ID number.

dir_colors

Red Hat Linux enables you to view file listings in color, as long as you are using a terminal program that supports colors. This file specifies which colors should be used to display what kinds of files. By default, executable files are green, directories are dark blue, symlinks are light blue, and regular files are white.

issue

Whatever is in this file shows up as a prelogin banner on your console. By default, this file tells what version of Red Hat is running on the system and the kernel version.
   The default file looks like this:

```
Red Hat Linux release 7.2 (Enigma)
Kernel \r on an \m
```

So when you log in, you see this message:

```
Red Hat Linux release 7.2 (Enigma)
Kernel 2.4.10 on an i686
```

issue.net

This file generally contains the same thing as /etc/issue. It shows up when you attempt to telnet into the system. Because it shows up to people who are connecting to your system over the Internet, you should change this message to include a warning such as "Access is being monitored. Unauthorized access is prohibited." Displaying this warning is good practice because if you want to prosecute intruders, it helps your case to show that you warned them that unauthorized access was prohibited.

ALIASES

/etc/mail/aliases is the e-mail aliases file for the sendmail program, and postfix uses /etc/postfix/aliases. By default, it contains many system account aliases. The aliases file sends mail for all the basic system accounts such as bin, daemon, and operator to root's mailbox.

Other common e-mail aliases, for example, send all of root's mail to the user who commonly acts as root. So if taleen acts as root most of the time, she can alias root's mailbox to her mailbox. This way, she doesn't need to log in as root to read important system mail.

To do this, she'd put the following line in the aliases file:

```
root:          taleen
```

Or if she wants to send all root mail to her account on a remote machine, the line will read:

```
root:          taleen@buffy.xena.edu
```

Whenever you make changes to this file, you need to run the newaliases command to have the changes take affect in sendmail.

fstab

fstab contains important information about your file systems, such as what file system type the partitions are, where they are located on the hard drive, and what mount point is used to access them.

This information is read by vital programs such as mount, umount, and fsck. mount runs at start time and mounts all the file systems mentioned in the fstab file, except for those with noauto in their line. If a partition you want to access is not listed in this file, you have to mount it manually. This can get tedious, so it's better to list all of your file systems in fstab. However, you should not put nfs file systems into the fstab file.

When fsck is run at bootup, it also checks all the file systems listed in fstab for consistency. It then fixes corrupted file systems, usually because they were not umounted properly when the system crashed or suddenly lost power. File systems with an fs_passno value of 0 (the number in the last column) are not checked at boot time. As you can see in Listing 7-2, almost all file systems are checked at startup except for the floppy drive, which is not checked by fsck at bootup.

The fstab line has six fields, and each field represents a different configuration value. The first field describes the remote file system. The second field is the mount point used to access the file system. The third field describes the file system type.

The fourth field is the place for any mount options you may need. The fifth field is 0 or 1 to determine if dump backs up this file system. The final field sets the order in which `fsck` checks these file systems.

Listing 7-2: A typical fstab file

```
# LABEL=/              /             ext3    defaults                  1 1
# LABEL=/boot          /boot         ext2    defaults                  1 2
/dev/hda5              /             ext3    defaults                  1 1
/dev/hda2             /boot         ext2    defaults                  1 2
/dev/fd0             /mnt/floppy    auto    noauto,owner              0 0
none                 /proc         proc    defaults                  0 0
none                 /dev/shm      tmpfs   defaults                  0 0
none                 /dev/pts      devpts  gid=5,mode=620            0 0
/dev/hda3             swap          swap    defaults                  0 0
/dev/hda1            /mnt/dos       vfat    noauto                    0 0
/dev/cdrom           /mnt/cdrom    iso9660 noauto,owner,kudzu,ro 0 0
/dev/cdrom1          /mnt/cdrom1   iso9660 noauto,owner,kudzu,ro 0 0
/SWAP                 swap          swap    defaults                  0 0
```

grub.conf

GRUB stands for the modest acronym GRand Unified Bootloader. It is the default boot loader used by Red Hat Linux.

A big difference between lilo and grub is that lilo usually offers a simple graphical interface, while grub offers a much more elaborate graphical interface. When you make a change to `lilo.conf`, you must rerun lilo, but when you change `grub.conf`, you do not have to rerun grub. At boot time, they both operate in the same fashion, giving you a basic choice between which installed kernels you want to run.

Listing 7-3 shows a typical `grub.conf` file.

Listing 7-3: A typical GRUB configuration file

```
# grub.conf generated by anaconda
#
# Note that you do not have to rerun grub after making changes to
     this file
# NOTICE:  You have a /boot partition.  This means that
#          all kernel and initrd paths are relative to /boot/, eg.
#          root (hd0,1)
#          kernel /vmlinuz-version ro root=/dev/sda8
#          initrd /initrd-version.img
#boot=/dev/sda
default=0
timeout=10
splashimage=(hd0,1)/grub/splash.xpm.gz
```

Continued

Listing 7-3 *(Continued)*

```
title Red Hat Linux (2.4.16)
        root (hd0,1)
        kernel /vmlinuz-2.4.16 ro root=/dev/hda5 hdd=ide-scsi
title Red Hat Linux (2.4.9-13)
        root (hd0,1)
        kernel /vmlinuz-2.4.9-13 ro root=/dev/hda5 hdd=ide-scsi
        initrd /initrd-2.4.9-13.img
title DOS
        rootnoverify (hd0,0)
        chainloader +1
```

As you can see, the default=0 line indicates that the first kernel section (2.4.16) should be booted by default. grub starts its counting at 0 instead of 1. The title line contains the label that will be shown in the boot menu for that kernel. The root line specifies that Linux will be booted off the first hard drive. The kernel line indicates the kernel's location on the file system.

In the DOS title section, notice that grub is calling a chain loader to be used for loading DOS. This is because grub doesn't support loading DOS; grub uses a chain loader to load any operating system that it doesn't support.

See Chapter 5 for a detailed explanation of GRUB.

cron FILES

cron is a daemon that executes commands according to a preset schedule that a user defines. It wakes up every minute and checks all cron files to see what jobs need to be run at that time. cron files can be set up by users or by the administrator to take care of system tasks. Basically, users edit their crontab files by telling cron what programs they'd like run automatically and how often they'd like to run them.

You should never manually edit the files in the /var/spool/cron directory.

User crontab files are stored in /var/spool/cron/. They are named after the user they belong to. System cron files are stored in the following subdirectories of the /etc directory:

- ◆ cron.d
- ◆ cron.daily
- ◆ cron.hourly
- ◆ cron.monthly
- ◆ cron.weekly

crontab in the /etc directory is sort of the master control file set up to run all the scripts in the cron.daily directory on a daily basis, all the scripts in the cron.hourly directory on an hourly bases, and so on with cron.monthly and cron.weekly.

cron.d is where system maintenance files that need to be run on a different schedule than the other /etc cron files are kept. By default, a file in cron.d called sysstat runs a system activity accounting tool every 10 minutes, 24 × 7.

Chapter 25 explains the cron command in more detail.

syslog.conf

The syslog daemon logs any notable events on your local system. It can store these logs in a local file or send them to a remote log host for added security. It can also accept logs from other machines when acting as a remote log host. These options and more, such as how detailed the logging should be, are set in the syslog.conf file.

Listing 7-4 is an excerpt that demonstrates the syntax and logic of the syslog .conf file. The first entry specifies that all messages that are severity-level info or higher should be logged in the /var/log/messages file.

Also indicated by the first entry is that any mail, news, private authentication, and cron messages should be logged elsewhere. Having separate log files makes it easier to search through logs if they are separated by type or program. The lines following this one specify the other places where those messages should be logged.

Authentication privilege messages contain somewhat sensitive information, so they are logged to /var/log/secure. That file can be read by root only, whereas /var/log/messages is sometimes set to be readable by everyone or at least has less stringent access control. By default, /var/log/messages is set to be read by root only as well.

All mail messages are logged to /var/log/maillog, and cron messages are saved at /var/log/cron. uucp and critical-level news daemon log messages are saved to /var/log/spooler. All of these log files are set by default to be readable by root only. Emergency messages are sent to all the log files listed in the syslog .conf file, including to the console.

Listing 7-4: An excerpt from the /etc/syslog.conf file

```
# Log anything (except mail) of level info or higher.
# Don't log private authentication messages!
*.info;mail.none;news.none;authpriv.none;cron.none        /var/log/messages

# The authpriv file has restricted access.
authpriv.*                                                /var/log/secure

# Log all the mail messages in one place.
mail.*                                                    /var/log/maillog


# Log cron stuff
cron.*                                                    /var/log/cron

# Everybody gets emergency messages
*.emerg                                                           *

# Save news errors of level crit and higher in a special file.
uucp,news.crit                                            /var/log/spooler
```

ld.so.conf

This configuration file is used by ldconfig, which configures dynamic linker run-time bindings. It contains a listing of directories that hold shared libraries. Shared library files typically end with .so, whereas static library files typically end with .a, indicating they are an archive of objects.

You may need to edit this file if you've installed a program that has installed a shared library to a different library directory that is not listed in the ld.so.conf file. In this case, you get an error at runtime that the library does not exist.

An additional troubleshooting step to take in that case is to run ldd on the executable in question, which prints shared library dependencies. The output would look something like this:

```
[root@terry root]# ldd /bin/bash
libtermcap.so.2 => /lib/libtermcap.so.2 (0x40026000)
libdl.so.2 => /lib/libdl.so.2 (0x4002a000)
libc.so.6 => /lib/tls/libc.so.6 (0x42000000)
/lib/ld-linux.so.2 => /lib/ld-linux.so.2 (0x40000000)
[
```

You can see a default listing of library directories in Listing 7-5.

Listing 7-5: A typical ld.so.conf file

```
/usr/lib
/usr/kerberos/lib
```

```
/usr/X11R6/lib
/usr/lib/mysql
/usr/local/lib
/usr/local/lib/oms/plugins

/usr/i486-linux-libc5/lib
/usr/lib/sane
/usr/lib/qt-1.45/lib

/usr/lib/qt-3.0.0/lib
/usr/lib/qt-2.3.1/lib


/usr/lib/wine
```

logrotate.conf

`logrotate.conf` and the files within `logrotate.d` determine how often your log files are rotated by the logrotate program. logrotate can automatically rotate, compress, remove, and mail your log files. Log files can be rotated based on size or on time, such as daily, weekly, or monthly.

As you can see from the `default logrotate.conf` file shown in Listing 7-6, most of the options set for how and when to rotate the system logs are pretty self-explanatory.

For every program that has a separate log rotation configuration file in `log rotate.d`, and uses `syslogd` for logging, there should be a logrot config file for all log entries in `/etc/syslog.conf`, as well as logfiles produced by external applications, such as apache. This is because syslog needs to save log entries for these programs in separate files so that their log files can be rotated independently of one another.

Listing 7-6: The logrotate.conf file

```
# see "man logrotate" for details
# rotate log files weekly
weekly

# keep 4 weeks worth of backlogs
rotate 4

# create new (empty) log files after rotating old ones
create

# uncomment this if you want your log files compressed
#compress
```

Continued

Listing 7-6 *(Continued)*

```
# RPM packages drop log rotation information into this directory
include /etc/logrotate.d

# no packages own lastlog or wtmp -- we'll rotate them here
/var/log/wtmp {
    monthly
    create 0664 root utmp
    rotate 1
}
```

The /etc/sysconfig/ Directory

The following information outlines some of the files found in the /etc/sysconfig/ directory, their functions, and their contents. This information is not intended to be complete, as many of these files have a variety of options used only in very specific or rare circumstances. The /usr/share/doc/initscripts-version-number/ sysconfig.txt file contains a more authoritative listing of the files found in the /etc/sysconfig directory and the configuration options available.

Files in the /etc/sysconfig/ Directory

The following files are normally found in the /etc/sysconfig/ directory:

amd	identd	radvd
apmd	init	rawdevices
arpwatch	ipchains	redhat-config-users
authconfig	iptables	redhat-logviewer
cipe	irda	samba
clock	keyboard	sendmail
desktop	kudzu	soundcard
dhcpd	mouse	squid
firstboot	named	tux
gpm	netdump	ups
harddisks	network	vncservers
hwconf	ntpd	xinetd
i18n	pcmcia	

It is possible that your system may be missing a few of the preceding files if the corresponding programs that need the files are not installed. Next, we take a look at each file.

/etc/sysconfig/amd

The `/etc/sysconfig/amd` file contains various parameters used by amd, allowing for the automounting and automatic unmounting of file systems.

/etc/sysconfig/apmd

The `/etc/sysconfig/apmd` file is used by apmd as a configuration for what things to start/stop/change on suspend or resume. It is set up to turn on or off apmd during startup, depending on whether your hardware supports Advanced Power Management (APM) or if you choose not to use it. APM is a monitoring daemon that works with power management code within the Linux kernel. It can alert you to a low battery if you are using Red Hat Linux on a laptop, among other things.

/etc/sysconfig/arpwatch

The `/etc/sysconfig/arpwatch` file is used to pass arguments to the arpwatch daemon at boot time. The arpwatch daemon maintains a table of Ethernet MAC addresses and their IP address pairings. For more information about the parameters you can use in this file, type **man arpwatch**. By default, this file sets the owner of the `arpwatch` process to the user `pcap`.

/etc/sysconfig/authconfig

The `/etc/sysconfig/authconfig` file sets the kind of authorization to be used on the host. It contains one or more of the following lines:

- ◆ `USEMD5=value`, where `value` is one of the following:
  - ■ `yes` — MD5 is used for authentication.
  - ■ `no` — MD5 is not used for authentication.
- ◆ `USEKERBEROS=value`, where `value` is one of the following:
  - ■ `yes` — Kerberos is used for authentication.
  - ■ `no` — Kerberos is not used for authentication.
- ◆ `USELDAPAUTH=value`, where `value` is one of the following:
  - ■ `yes` — LDAP is used for authentication.
  - ■ `no` — LDAP is not used for authentication.

/etc/sysconfig/clock

The `/etc/sysconfig/clock` file controls the interpretation of values read from the system clock. Earlier releases of Red Hat Linux used the following values (which are deprecated):

- CLOCKMODE=*value*, where *value* is one of the following:

  - GMT — Indicates that the clock is set to Universal Time (Greenwich Mean Time).

  - ARC — Indicates the ARC console's 42-year time offset is in effect (for Alpha-based systems only).

Currently, the correct values are:

- UTC=value, where value is one of the following boolean values:

  - true — Indicates that the hardware clock is set to Universal Time.

  - Any other value indicates that it is set to local time.

- ARC=value, where value is the following:

  - true — Indicates the ARC console's 42-year time offset is in effect.

  - Any other value indicates that the normal UNIX epoch is assumed (for Alpha-based systems only).

- ZONE=filename — Indicates the timezone file under /usr/share/zoneinfo that /etc/localtime is a copy of, such as: ZONE="America/New York". Identifies the timezone file copied into /etc/localtime, such as ZONE= "America/New York". Timezone files are stored in /usr/share/zoneinfo.

/etc/sysconfig/desktop

The /etc/sysconfig/desktop file specifies the desktop manager to be run, such as:

```
DESKTOP="GNOME"
```

/etc/sysconfig/dhcpd

The /etc/sysconfig/dhcpd file is used to pass arguments to the dhcpd daemon at boot time. The dhcpd daemon implements the Dynamic Host Configuration Protocol (DHCP) and the Internet Bootstrap Protocol (BOOTP). DHCP and BOOTP assign hostnames to machines on the network. For more information about the parameters you can use in this file, type **man dhcpd**.

/etc/sysconfig/firstboot

Beginning with Red Hat Linux 8.0, the first time you boot the system, the /sbin/ init program calls the etc/rc.d/init.d/firstboot script. This allows the user to install additional applications and documentation before the boot process completes. The /etc/sysconfig/firstboot file tells the firstboot command not to run on subsequent reboots. If you want firstboot to run the next time you boot the system, simply remove /etc/sysconfig/firstboot and execute chkconfig -- level 5 firstboot on.

/etc/sysconfig/gpm

The `/etc/sysconfig/gpm` file is used to pass arguments to the gpm daemon at boot time. The gpm daemon, which is used only on consoles, is the mouse server that allows mouse acceleration and middle-click pasting. For more information about the parameters you can use in this file, type **man gpm**. By default, it sets the mouse device to `/dev/mouse`.

/etc/sysconfig/harddisks

The `/etc/sysconfig/harddisks` file allows you to tune your hard drive(s). You can also use `/etc/sysconfig/hardiskhd[a-h]`, where `a-h` are the unique identifiers for the desired drive, to configure parameters for specific drives.

Do not make changes to this file lightly. If you change the default values stored here, you could corrupt all of the data on your hard drive(s).

The `/etc/sysconfig/harddisks` file may contain the following:

♦ `USE_DMA=1`, where setting this to 1 enables DMA. However, with some chipsets and hard-drive combinations, DMA can cause data corruption. Check with your hard-drive documentation or manufacturer before enabling this.

♦ `Multiple_IO=16`, where a setting of 16 allows for multiple sectors per I/O interrupt. When enabled, this feature reduces operating system overhead by 30 to 50 percent. Use with caution.

♦ `EIDE_32BIT=3` enables (E)IDE 32-bit I/O support to an interface card.

♦ `LOOKAHEAD=1` enables drive read-lookahead.

♦ `EXTRA_PARAMS=` specifies where extra parameters can be added.

/etc/sysconfig/hwconf

The `/etc/sysconfig/hwconf` file lists all the hardware that kudzu detected on your system, as well as the drivers used, vendor ID, and device ID information. The kudzu program detects and configures new and/or changed hardware on a system. The `/etc/sysconfig/hwconf` file is not meant to be manually edited. If you do edit it, devices can suddenly show up as added or removed.

/etc/sysconfig/i18n

The `/etc/sysconfig/i18n` file sets the default language, such as:

```
LANG="en_US"
```

/etc/sysconfig/identd

The `/etc/sysconfig/identd` file is used to pass arguments to the identd daemon at boot time. The identd daemon returns the username of processes with open TCP/IP connections. Some services on the network, such as FTP and IRC servers, will complain and cause slow responses if identd is not running. But in general, identd is not a required service, so if security is a concern, you should not run it. For more information about the parameters you can use in this file, type **man identd**. By default, the file contains no parameters.

/etc/sysconfig/init

The `/etc/sysconfig/init` file controls how the system will appear and function during the boot process. The following values may be used:

- ♦ `BOOTUP=`*value*, where *value* is one of the following:

    - ■ `BOOTUP=color` means the standard color boot display, where the success or failure of devices and services starting up is shown in different colors.

    - ■ `BOOTUP=verbose` means an old-style display, which provides more information than purely a message of success or failure.

    - ■ Anything else means a new display, but without ANSI formatting.

- ♦ `RES_COL=`*value*, where *value* is the number of the column of the screen to start status labels. It defaults to 60.

- ♦ `MOVE_TO_COL=`*value*, where *value* moves the cursor to the value in the `RES_COL` line. It defaults to ANSI sequences output by `echo -e`.

- ♦ `SETCOLOR_SUCCESS=`*value*, where *value* sets the color to a color indicating success. It defaults to ANSI sequences output by `echo -e`, setting the color to green.

- ♦ `SETCOLOR_FAILURE=`*value*, where *value* sets the color to one indicating failure. It defaults to ANSI sequences output by `echo -e`, setting the color to red.

- ♦ `SETCOLOR_WARNING=`*value*, where value sets the color to one indicating warning. It Defaults to ANSI sequences output by `echo -e`, setting the color to yellow.

- ♦ `SETCOLOR_NORMAL=`*value*, where *value* sets the color to "normal." It defaults to ANSI sequences output by `echo -e`.

- ♦ `LOGLEVEL=`*value*, where *value* sets the initial console logging level for the kernel. The default is 7; 8 means everything (including debugging); 1 means nothing except kernel panics. syslogd will override this once it starts.

◆ PROMPT=*value*, where *value* is one of the following boolean values:

yes — Enables the key check for interactive mode.

no — Disables the key check for interactive mode.

/etc/sysconfig/ipchains

The `/etc/sysconfig/ipchains` file contains information used by the kernel to set up ipchains packet-filtering rules at boot time or whenever the service is started. This file is modified by typing the command **/sbin/service ipchains save** when valid ipchains rules are in place. You should not manually edit this file. Instead, use the `/sbin/ipchains` command to configure the necessary packet filtering rules and then save the rules to this file using **/sbin/service ipchains save**.

Use of ipchains to set up firewall rules is not recommended, as it is deprecated and may disappear from future releases of Red Hat Linux. If you need a firewall, use iptables instead.

/etc/sysconfig/iptables

Like `/etc/sysconfig/ipchains`, the `/etc/sysconfig/iptables` file stores information used by the kernel to set up packet-filtering services at boot time or whenever the service is started. You should not modify this file by hand unless you are familiar with how to construct iptables rules. The simplest way to add rules is to use the `/usr/sbin/lokkit` command or the gnome-lokkit graphical application to create your firewall. Using these applications automatically edits this file at the end of the process.

If you wish, you can manually create rules using `/sbin/iptables` and then type **/sbin/service iptables save** to add the rules to the `/etc/sysconfig/iptables` file. Once this file exists, any firewall rules saved there are persisted through a system reboot or a service restart.

For more information on iptables, see Chapter 31.

/etc/sysconfig/irda

The `/etc/sysconfig/irda` file controls how infrared devices on your system are configured at startup. The following values may be used:

- ◆ IRDA=`value`, where `value` is one of the following boolean values:

  - yes – irattach will be run, which periodically checks to see if anything is trying to connect to the infrared port, such as another notebook computer attempting to make a network connection. For infrared devices to work on your system, this line must be set to yes.

  - no – irattach will not be run, preventing infrared device communication.

- ◆ DEVICE=value, where value is the device (usually a serial port) that handles infrared connections.

- ◆ DONGLE=value, where value specifies the type of dongle being used for infrared communication. This setting exists for people who use serial dongles rather than real infrared ports. A dongle is a device attached to a traditional serial port to communicate via infrared. This line is commented out by default because notebooks with real infrared ports are far more common than computers with add-on dongles.

- ◆ DISCOVERY=value, where value is one of the following boolean values:

  - yes – Starts irattach in discovery mode, meaning it actively checks for other infrared devices. This needs to be turned on in order for the machine to be actively looking for an infrared connection (meaning the peer that does not initiate the connection).

  - no – Does not start irattach in discovery mode.

/etc/sysconfig/keyboard

The /etc/sysconfig/keyboard file controls the behavior of the keyboard. The following values may be used:

- ◆ KEYBOARDTYPE=sun|pc, which is used on SPARCs only. sun means a Sun keyboard is attached on /dev/kbd, and pc means a PS/2 keyboard is connected to a PS/2 port.

- ◆ KEYTABLE=file, where file is the name of a keytable file. For example: KEYTABLE="us". The files that can be used as keytables start in /usr/lib/kbd/keymaps/i386 and branch into different keyboard layouts from there, all labeled file.kmap.gz. The first file found beneath /usr/lib/kbd/keymaps/i386 that matches the KEYTABLE setting is used.

/etc/sysconfig/kudzu

The /etc/sysconfig/kuzdu allows you to specify a safe probe of your system's hardware by kudzu at boot time. A safe probe is one that disables serial port probing.

- ◆ SAFE=*value*, where *value* is one of the following:

  - ■ yes – kuzdu does a safe probe.

  - ■ no – kuzdu does a normal probe.

/etc/sysconfig/mouse

The /etc/sysconfig/mouse file is used to specify information about the available mouse. The following values may be used:

- ◆ FULLNAME=*value*, where *value* refers to the full name of the kind of mouse being used.

- ◆ MOUSETYPE=*value*, where *value* is one of the following:

  - ■ microsoft – A Microsoft mouse.

  - ■ mouseman – A MouseMan mouse.

  - ■ mousesystems – A Mouse Systems mouse.

  - ■ ps/2 – A PS/2 mouse.

  - ■ msbm – A Microsoft bus mouse.

  - ■ logibm – A Logitech bus mouse.

  - ■ atibm – An ATI bus mouse.

  - ■ logitech – A Logitech mouse.

  - ■ mmseries – An older MouseMan mouse.

  - ■ mmhittab – An mmhittab mouse.

- ◆ XEMU3=*value*, where *value* is one of the following boolean values:

  - ■ yes – The mouse has only two buttons, but three mouse buttons should be emulated.

  - ■ no – The mouse already has three buttons.

- ◆ XMOUSETYPE=*value*, where *value* refers to the kind of mouse used when X is running. The options here are the same as those provided by the MOUSETYPE setting in this same file.

- ◆ DEVICE=*value*, where value is the mouse device. In addition, /dev/mouse is a symbolic link that points to the actual mouse device.

/etc/sysconfig/named

The /etc/sysconfig/named file is used to pass arguments to the named daemon at boot time. The named daemon is a Domain Name System (DNS) server, which implements the Berkeley Internet Name Domain (BIND) version 9 distribution. This server maintains a table of which hostnames are associated with IP addresses on the network. Currently, only the following values may be used:

◆ ROOTDIR=/some/where, where /some/where refers to the full directory path of a configured chroot environment under which named will run. This chroot environment must first be configured. Type **info chroot** for more information on how to do this.

◆ OPTIONS="value", where value is any option listed in the man page for named except -t. In place of -t, use the preceding ROOTDIR line.

For more information about what parameters you can use in this file, type **man named**. By default, the file contains no parameters.

For detailed information on how to configure a BIND DNS server, see Chapter 18.

/etc/sysconfig/netdump

The /etc/sysconfig/netdump file is the configuration file for the /etc/init.d/ netdump service. The netdump service sends both oops data and memory dumps over the network. In general, netdump is not a required service, so you should run it only if you absolutely need to. For more information about what parameters you can use in this file, type **man netdump**.

/etc/sysconfig/network

The /etc/sysconfig/network file is used to specify information about the desired network configuration. The following values may be used:

◆ NETWORKING=value, where value is one of the following boolean values:

 ■ yes — Networking should be configured.

 ■ no — Networking should not be configured.

◆ HOSTNAME=value, where value should be the Fully Qualified Domain Name (FQDN), such as hostname.domain.com, but can be whatever hostname you want.

For compatibility with older software that people might install (such as trn), the /etc/HOSTNAME file and the /etc/sysconfig/network file should contain the same value.

◆ GATEWAY=*value*, where *value* is the IP address of the network's gateway.

◆ GATEWAYDEV=*value*, where *value* is the gateway device, such as eth0.

◆ NISDOMAIN=*value*, where *value* is the NIS domain name.

/etc/sysconfig/ntpd

The /etc/sysconfig/ntpd file is used to pass arguments to the ntpd daemon at boot time. The ntpd daemon sets and maintains the system clock to synchronize with an Internet standard time server. It implements version 4 of the Network Time Protocol (NTP). For more information about what parameters you can use in this file, point a browser at the following file: /usr/share/doc/ntp-*version*/ntpd. htm (where *version* is the version number of ntpd). By default, this file sets the owner of the ntpd process to the user ntp.

/etc/sysconfig/pcmcia

The /etc/sysconfig/pcmcia file is used to specify PCMCIA configuration information. The following values may be used:

◆ PCMCIA=*value*, where *value* is one of the following:

  ■ yes — PCMCIA support should be enabled.

  ■ no — PCMCIA support should not be enabled.

◆ PCIC=*value*, where *value* is one of the following:

  ■ i82365 — The computer has an i82365-style PCMCIA socket chipset.

  ■ tcic — The computer has a tcic-style PCMCIA socket chipset.

◆ PCIC_OPTS=*value*, where *value* is the socket driver (i82365 or tcic) timing parameters.

◆ CORE_OPTS=*value*, where *value* is the list of pcmcia_core options.

◆ CARDMGR_OPTS=*value*, where *value* is the list of options for the PCMCIA cardmgr (such as -q for quiet mode, -m to look for loadable kernel modules in the specified directory, and so on). Read the cardmgr man page for more information.

/etc/sysconfig/radvd

The /etc/sysconfig/radvd file is used to pass arguments to the radvd daemon at boot time. The radvd daemon listens for router requests and sends router advertisements for the IP version 6 protocol. This service allows hosts on a network to dynamically change their default routers based on these router advertisements. For more information about what parameters you can use in this file, type **man radvd**. By default, this file sets the owner of the radvd process to the user radvd.

/etc/sysconfig/rawdevices

The `/etc/sysconfig/rawdevices` file is used to configure raw device bindings, such as:

```
/dev/raw/raw1 /dev/sda1
/dev/raw/raw2 8 5
```

/etc/sysconfig/redhat-config-users

The `/etc/sysconfig/redhat-config-users` file is the configuration file for the graphical application User Manager. Under Red Hat Linux 8.0, this file is used to filter out system users such as root, daemon, and lp. This file is edited via the Preferences → Filter system users and groups pull-down menu in the User Manager application and should not be edited manually.

/etc/sysconfig/redhat-logviewer

The `/etc/sysconfig/redhat-logviewer` file is the configuration file for the graphical, interactive log viewing application Log Viewer. This file is edited via the Edit → Preferences pull-down menu in the Log Viewer application and should not be edited manually.

/etc/sysconfig/samba

The `/etc/sysconfig/samba` file is used to pass arguments to the smbd and the nmbd daemons at boot time. The smbd daemon offers file-sharing connectivity for Windows clients on the network. The nmbd daemon offers NetBIOS-over-IP naming services. For more information about what parameters you can use in this file, type **man smbd**. By default, this file sets smbd and nmbd to run in daemon mode.

/etc/sysconfig/sendmail

The `/etc/sysconfig/sendmail` file allows messages to be sent to one or more recipients, routing the message over whatever networks are necessary. The file sets the default values for the Sendmail application to run. Its default values are to run as a background daemon, and to check its queue once an hour in case something has backed up and stalled the process. The following values may be used:

- ◆ `DAEMON=value`, where `value` is one of the following boolean values:
  - ■ `yes` – Sendmail should be configured to listen to port 25 for incoming mail. `yes` implies the use of Sendmail's `-bd` options.
  - ■ `no` – Sendmail should not be configured to listen to port 25 for incoming mail.
- ◆ `QUEUE=1h`, which is given to Sendmail as `-q$QUEUE`. The `-q` option is not given to Sendmail if `/etc/sysconfig/sendmail` exists and `QUEUE` is empty or undefined.

/etc/sysconfig/soundcard

The `/etc/sysconfig/soundcard` file is generated by sndconfig and should not be modified. The sole use of this file is to determine what card entry in the menu to pop up by default the next time sndconfig is run. Sound card configuration information is located in the `/etc/modules.conf` file. It may contain the following:

- ◆ `CARDTYPE=`*value*, where *value* is set to, for example, `SB16` for a Soundblaster 16 sound card.

/etc/sysconfig/squid

The `/etc/sysconfig/squid` file is used to pass arguments to the squid daemon at boot time. The squid daemon is a proxy caching server for Web client applications. For more information on configuring a squid proxy server, use a Web browser to open the `/usr/share/doc/squid-`*version*`/` directory (replace *version* with the squid version number installed on your system). By default, this file sets squid to start in daemon mode and sets the amount of time to forcefully shut down squid when it is still active or serving requests.

/etc/sysconfig/tux

The `/etc/sysconfig/tux` file is the configuration file for the Red Hat Content Accelerator (formerly known as TUX), the kernel-based Web server. For more information on configuring the Red Hat Content Accelerator, use a Web browser to open the `/usr/share/doc/tux-`*version*`/tux/index.html` file (replace *version* with the version number of TUX installed on your system). The parameters available for this file are listed in `/usr/share/doc/tux-version/tux/parameters.html`.

/etc/sysconfig/ups

The `/etc/sysconfig/ups` file is used to specify information about any Uninterruptible Power Supplies (UPS) connected to your system. A UPS can be very valuable for a Red Hat system because it gives you time to correctly shut down the system in the case of power interruption. The following values may be used:

- ◆ `SERVER=`*value*, where *value* is one of the following:
  - ▪ `yes` – A UPS device is connected to your system.
  - ▪ `no` – A UPS device is not connected to your system.
- ◆ `MODEL=`*value*, where value must be one of the following or set to `NONE` if no UPS is connected to the system:
  - ▪ `apcsmart` – For an APC SmartUPSTM or similar device.
  - ▪ `fentonups` – For a Fenton UPSTM.
  - ▪ `optiups` – For an OPTI-UPSTM device.
  - ▪ `bestups` – For a Best PowerTM UPS.

- `genericups` — For a generic brand UPS.

- `ups-trust425+625` — For a TrustTM UPS.

◆ `DEVICE=`*value*, where *value* specifies where the UPS is connected, such as `/dev/ttyS0`.

◆ `OPTIONS=`*value*, where *value* is a particular command that needs to be passed to the UPS.

/etc/sysconfig/vncservers

The `/etc/sysconfig/vncservers` file configures the way the Virtual Network Computing (VNC) server starts up. VNC is a remote display system which allows you to view a desktop environment not only on the machine where it is running but across different networks on a variety of architectures. It may contain the following:

◆ `VNCSERVERS=value`, where `value` is set to something like `1:fred` to indicate that a VNC server should be started for user fred on display :1. User fred must have set a VNC password using vncpasswd before attempting to connect to the remote VNC server.

Note that when you use a VNC server, your communication with it is unencrypted, and so it should not be used on an untrusted network. For specific instructions concerning the use of SSH to secure the VNC communication, see `http://www.uk.research.att.com/vnc/sshvnc.html`. To find out more about SSH, see Chapter 24.

/etc/sysconfig/xinetd

The `/etc/sysconfig/xinetd` file is used to pass arguments to the xinetd daemon at boot time. The xinetd daemon starts programs that provide Internet services when a request to the port for that service is received. For more information about what parameters you can use in this file, type **man xinetd**. For more information on the xinetd service, see Chapter 21.

Directories in the /etc/sysconfig/ Directory

The following directories are normally found in `/etc/sysconfig/`.

apm-scripts

This contains the Red Hat APM `suspend/resume` script. You should not edit this file directly. If you need customization, simply create a file called `/etc/sysconfig/apm-scripts/apmcontinue` and it will be called at the end of the script. Also, you can control the script by editing `/etc/sysconfig/apmd`.

cbq

This directory contains the configuration files needed to do Class Based Queuing for bandwidth management on network interfaces.

NETWORKING

This directory is used by the Network Administration Tool (`redhat-config-network`), and its contents should not be edited manually.

For more information about configuring network interfaces using the Network Administration Tool, see Chapter 10.

NETWORK-SCRIPTS

This directory contains the following network-related configuration files:

- Network configuration files for each configured network interface, such as `ifcfg-eth0` for the `eth0` Ethernet interface.

- Scripts used to bring up and down network interfaces, such as ifup and ifdown.

- Scripts used to bring up and down ISDN interfaces, such as ifup-isdn and ifdown-isdn.

- Various shared network function scripts that should not be edited directly.

rhn

This directory contains the configuration files and GPG keys for Red Hat Network. No files in this directory should be edited by hand. For more information on Red Hat Network, see the Red Hat Network Web site at `https://rhn.redhat.com`.

Examining the Network Configuration Files

This section discusses the following topics:

- Files to change when setting up a system or moving the system

- Starting up network services from xinetd

- Starting up network services from the rc scripts

- Other important network configuration files in the `/etc/sysconfig` directory

Files to Change When Setting Up a System or Moving the System

Whenever you set up a system to work on a new network, either because you've just installed Red Hat or you're moving the machine from one location to another, a set of files need to be modified to get it working on the new network.

You need to:

◆ Set up the IP addresses of your network interfaces. Make changes to:

`/etc/sysconfig/network-scripts/ifcfg-eth0`

`/etc/sysconfig/network-scripts/ifcfg-eth1`

◆ Set up the hostname of your machine. Make changes to:

`/etc/sysconfig/network`

`/etc/hosts`

◆ Set up the DNS servers to reference. Make changes to:

`/etc/resolv.conf`

◆ Make a local file of hostname to IP address mappings. Make changes to:

`/etc/hosts`

◆ Set up the device order from which hostnames are looked up. Make changes to:

`/etc/nsswitch.conf`

Chapter 18 explains the Domain Name System (DNS) and how to set it up on your network.

Red Hat Enterprise Linux provides a handy graphical tool for configuring your network settings called the Red Hat Network Administration tool. Start up the Network Administration tool while in X-Window, and enjoy an interface very similar to the Windows control panel for networks.

SETTING UP THE IP ADDRESS

The first thing you should do is set an IP address on your network interfaces. This step provides your computer with an identity on the network. If you haven't set the

IP address already in the installation process, you need to edit the configuration files by hand.

To set the IP address on your first Ethernet interface eth0, edit the /etc/sysconfig/network-scripts/ifcfg-eth0 file. A copy of this file is shown in Listing 7-7.

Insert your interface's IP address on the line that says:

```
IPADDR="192.168.1.10"
```

You should also check that the rest of the lines look all right, but pay special attention to the following two lines:

```
BROADCAST=192.168.1.255
NETMASK="255.255.255.0"
```

Listing 7-7: The /etc/sysconfig/network-scripts/ifcfg-eth0 file

```
DEVICE="eth0"
BOOTPROTO="none"
BROADCAST=192.168.1.255
IPADDR="192.168.1.10"
NETMASK="255.255.255.0"
NETWORK=192.168.1.0
ONBOOT="yes"
USERCTL=no
```

SETTING UP THE HOSTNAME

Once you've picked your hostname, you need to put it into two different places: /etc/sysconfig/network and /etc/hosts.

In /etc/sysconfig/network, shown next, change the line that says:

```
HOSTNAME="buffy"
```

This is the /etc/sysconfig/network file:

```
NETWORKING=yes
HOSTNAME="buffy"
GATEWAY="192.168.1.1"
GATEWAYDEV="eth0"
FORWARD_IPV4="yes"
```

You also need to modify the /etc/hosts file. Change the first line in the file, which would look something like this:

```
127.0.0.1       buffy    localhost.localdomain localhost locala localb localc
```

SETTING UP THE DNS NAME RESOLUTION

Now you should be able to communicate with the other hosts on the network. However you won't be able to talk to them unless you know their IP addresses, because you haven't set up what DNS servers you should reference to map hostnames to IP addresses.

The program that resolves hostnames to IP addresses reads a file called `resolv.conf`, so you need to put your DNS server IP addresses there. Generally, you need one nameserver, but you can include up to three, if you'd like. Specifying more than one name server is important. If the first one on the list is not responding, your computer tries to resolve against the next one on the list, until it finds one that is responding.

Edit `/etc/resolv.conf` to contain a list of nameservers, like so:

```
nameserver 1.2.3.4
nameserver 1.2.3.5
nameserver 1.2.3.6
```

MAKING A LOCAL FILE OF HOSTNAME TO IP ADDRESS MAPPINGS

Linux gives you the ability to store a list of hostnames and their corresponding IP addresses in `/etc/hosts`, so that you don't have to look them up in DNS every time you use them. While you shouldn't do this with every hostname you ever use, one of the advantages gained by configuring often-used hostnames in this way includes the ability to alias a fully qualified hostname to a shorter version of itself. So instead of typing **ssh foo.xena.edu** every time you want to ssh to that machine, you can just type **ssh foo**, and have it connect to the same host.

Another useful example occurs if you're monitoring several servers' network services from a monitoring host. If you're monitoring ssh connectivity to certain servers, for example, and your DNS server stops responding, then the monitoring software may report that all your hosts are down. This happens because the monitoring software tries to connect to the server via its hostname, and gets no response because DNS is not providing it with an IP address to connect to. In this case it looks like your whole network fell over, when the real problem is that your DNS service is not responding properly.

To keep this kind of scenario from happening, you should put the hostnames and IP addresses of all your monitored servers in `/etc/hosts`. This way, your monitoring software looks into `/etc/hosts` to get the proper IP addresses, instead of relying on DNS.

The only caveat to keep in mind when putting hosts in `/etc/hosts` is that if the hostname's IP address changes for whatever reason, the hosts file does not automatically update to reflect that change. If you start getting connection errors when connecting to a host in the `/etc/hosts` file, you should do an `nslookup` on the host and update your `/etc/hosts` file accordingly.

Your `/etc/hosts` file should contain IP address to hostname mappings that follow this format:

```
IP_address canonical_hostname aliases
```

So that the lines look like this:

```
192.168.1.66    foo.xena.edu      foo
192.168.1.76    buffy.xena.edu    buffy
152.2.210.81    sunsite.unc.edu   sunsite
```

SETTING UP NAME SERVICE RESOLUTION ORDER

Now that you've set up your DNS servers and hosts file, you need to tell your Linux server which method it should use first to look up hostnames.

The place to set up this configuration is in the /etc/nsswitch.conf file. Edit the following line:

```
hosts:      files nisplus dns
```

The order of the words *files*, *nisplus*, and *dns* determines which method is checked first. Files refers to the /etc/hosts file, nisplus refers to any nisplus servers you may have on your network, and dns refers to any DNS servers you have set up your machine to reference.

As you can see in Listing 7-8, the /etc/nsswitch.conf file contains some other useful settings. Other useful settings are the following two lines, which specify whether the server should authenticate users off the local password file or off the network's NIS plus service:

```
passwd:     files nisplus
shadow:     files nisplus
```

Listing 7-8: The /etc/nsswitch.conf file

```
#
# /etc/nsswitch.conf
#
# An example Name Service Switch config file. This file should be
# sorted with the most-used services at the beginning.
#
# The entry '[NOTFOUND=return]' means that the search for an
# entry should stop if the search in the previous entry turned
# up nothing. Note that if the search failed due to some other reason
# (like no NIS server responding) then the search continues with the
# next entry.
#
```

Continued

Listing 7-8 *(Continued)*

```
# Legal entries are:
#
#       nisplus or nis+        Use NIS+ (NIS version 3)
#       nis or yp              Use NIS (NIS version 2), also called YP
#       dns                    Use DNS (Domain Name Service)
#       files                  Use the local files
#       db                     Use the local database (.db) files
#       compat                 Use NIS on compat mode
#       hesiod                 Use Hesiod for user lookups
#       [NOTFOUND=return]      Stop searching if not found so far
#


# To use db, put the "db" in front of "files" for entries you want to be
# looked up first in the databases
#
# Example:
#passwd:    db files nisplus nis
#shadow:    db files nisplus nis
#group:     db files nisplus nis

passwd:     files nisplus
shadow:     files nisplus
group:      files nisplus

#hosts:     db files nisplus nis dns
hosts:      files nisplus dns

# Example - obey only what nisplus tells us...
#services:   nisplus [NOTFOUND=return] files
#networks:   nisplus [NOTFOUND=return] files
#protocols:  nisplus [NOTFOUND=return] files
#rpc:        nisplus [NOTFOUND=return] files
#ethers:     nisplus [NOTFOUND=return] files
#netmasks:   nisplus [NOTFOUND=return] files

bootparams: nisplus [NOTFOUND=return] files

ethers:     files
netmasks:   files
networks:   files
protocols:  files nisplus
rpc:        files
services:   files nisplus
```

```
netgroup:    files nisplus

publickey:   nisplus

automount:   files nisplus
aliases:     files nisplus
```

Starting Up Network Services from xinetd

xinetd is the replacement for inetd. xinetd is started on bootup, and listens on ports designated in the /etc/xinetd.conf for incoming network connections. When a new connection is made, xinetd starts up the corresponding network service.

You should disable any unnecessary services from being started from xinetd as part of securing your machine. The way to do this is to edit that service's configuration file. xinetd's main configuration file is /etc/xinetd.conf. At the end of the xinetd.conf file is a line that indicates that all the files in the /etc/xinetd.d are also included in the configuration. This means that you need to go through the files in that directory as well in order to turn off any services you don't want.

So, to disable telnet, you would look in /etc/xinetd.d for a file called telnet. The telnet file is shown in Listing 7-9. Edit the line in the config file that says disable = no, and change that to disable = yes, as it appears in Listing 7-9. Once that line is set to disable = yes, the service is disabled and does not start up the next time you boot up.

Listing 7-9: The telnet config file in the xinetd.d directory

```
/etc/xinetd.d/telnet

# default: on
# description: The telnet server serves telnet sessions; it uses \
#        unencrypted username/password pairs for authentication.
service telnet
{
        flags           = REUSE
        socket_type     = stream
        wait            = no
        user            = root
        server          = /usr/sbin/in.telnetd
        log_on_failure  = USERID
        disable         = yes
}
```

An automated tool, called chkconfig, manages what services are started from xinetd and the rc scripts. You can read more about chkconfig in the section called "Managing rc Scripts Using chkconfig."

Starting Up Network Services from the rc Scripts

Network services that are not started out of `xinetd` are started out of the rc scripts at boot time. Network services started at the default boot level 3 (multiuser networked mode) are started out of the `/etc/rc3.d` directory. If you look in that directory, you should see a file with the name of the service you want to stop or start. The script to start the service starts with an S, and the kill script starts with a K.

So for example, ssh is started from `/etc/rc3.d /S55sshd`, and killed upon shutdown from `/etc/rc6.d/K25sshd`. Runlevel 6 is the shutdown level, so that's why its kill script is located in the `rc6.d` directory.

Detailed information on managing all of the services started at boot time can be found in the section "Managing the Init Scripts" later in this chapter.

 See Chapter 5 for details about the system startup process.

Other Important Network Configuration Files in the /etc/sysconfig Directory

You can use the files listed in this section to create routes to other hosts, either on your own network, or on outside networks. You also can use these files to set up firewall rules for your network to either allow or disallow connections to your network.

STATIC-ROUTES

If you want to set up some static routes on your machine, you can do so in the static-routes file. This config file has lines that follow the format of:

```
network-interface net network netmask netmask gw gateway
```

iptables

iptables is the next generation Linux firewall. It supercedes the ipchains firewall. It can use ipchains rules as a component of its firewall filtering, but iptables and ipchains cannot be run at the same time.

This is the file where the iptables rules are stored. iptables syntax is very similar to the ipchains syntax, which is briefly explained by the following example.

ipchains

ipchains is a Linux firewall that is now being superceded by iptables. The GUI interface that configures the ipchains firewall rules is firewall-config. The ipchains rules are stored in the ipchains file.

When you install Red Hat, it asks if you would like to set up a host-based firewall. If you select a medium or heavy security host-based firewall, a default set of iptables rules installs according to your preferences.

The following is a simplified configuration file. The gist of this configuration is that all incoming traffic to privileged ports (those below 1024) is dropped except for ssh traffic. The first line accepts all traffic from the loopback interface. The second line accepts all incoming TCP traffic to the ssh port. The third line drops all incoming TCP traffic to ports between 1 and 1024. The last line drops all incoming UDP traffic to ports between 1 and 1024.

```
-A INPUT -i lo -j ACCEPT
-A INPUT -p tcp --dport 22 -p tcp -j ACCEPT
-A INPUT -p tcp -s ! 192.168.1.0/24 --dport 1:1024 -j DROP
-A INPUT -p udp -s ! 192.168.1.0/24 --dport 1:1024 -j DROP
```

Network Configuration Files in /etc/sysconfig/network-scripts

You can use the files in this directory to set the parameters for the hardware and software used for networking. The scripts contained here are used to enable network interfaces and set other network related parameters.

ifcfg-networkinterfacename

A few files fall into this specification. Red Hat specifies a separate configuration file for each network interface. In a typical Red Hat install you might have many different network interface config files that all follow the same basic syntax and format.

You could have ifcfg-eth0 for your first Ethernet interface, ifcfg-irlan0 for your infrared network port, ifcfg-lo for the network loop-back interface, and ifcfg-ppp0 for your PPP network interface.

ifup AND ifdown

These files are symlinks to /sbin/ifup and /sbin/ifdown. In future releases, these symlinks might be phased out. But for now, these scripts are called when the network service is started or stopped. In turn, ifup and ifdown call any other necessary scripts from within the network-scripts directory. These should be the only scripts you call from this directory.

You call these scripts with the name of the interface that you want to bring up or down. If these scripts are called at boot time, then "boot" is used as the second argument. For instance, to bring your Ethernet interface down and then up again after boot, you would type:

```
ifup eth0
ifdown eth0
```

Managing the init Scripts

This section discusses the following topics:

◆ Managing rc scripts by hand

◆ Managing rc scripts using `chkconfig`

Init scripts determine what programs start up at boot time. Red Hat and other Unix distributions have different runlevels, so there are a different set of programs that are started at each runlevel.

Usually Red Hat Linux starts up in multiuser mode with networking turned on. These are some of the other runlevels available:

◆ 0 – Halt

◆ 1 – Single-user mode

◆ 2 – Multiuser mode, without networking

◆ 3 – Full multiuser mode

◆ 4 – Not used

◆ 5 – Full multiuser mode (with an X-based login screen)

◆ 6 – Reboot

The system boots into the default runlevel set in `/etc/inittab` (see Listing 7-10).

In Red Hat Linux, the default boot level is 3. When booting into an X-windows login, the default boot level is 5.

Listing 7-10: A default /etc/inittab file

```
#
# inittab       This file describes how the INIT process should set up
#               the system in a certain run-level.
#
# Author:       Miquel van Smoorenburg, <miquels@drinkel.nl.mugnet.org>
#               Modified for RHS Linux by Marc Ewing and Donnie Barnes
#

# Default runlevel. The runlevels used by RHS are:
#   0 - halt (Do NOT set initdefault to this)
#   1 - Single user mode
```

```
#    2 - Multiuser, without NFS (The same as 3, if you do not have networking)
#    3 - Full multiuser mode
#    4 - unused
#    5 - X11
#    6 - reboot (Do NOT set initdefault to this)
#
id:5:initdefault:

# System initialization.
si::sysinit:/etc/rc.d/rc.sysinit

l0:0:wait:/etc/rc.d/rc 0
l1:1:wait:/etc/rc.d/rc 1
l2:2:wait:/etc/rc.d/rc 2
l3:3:wait:/etc/rc.d/rc 3
l4:4:wait:/etc/rc.d/rc 4
l5:5:wait:/etc/rc.d/rc 5
l6:6:wait:/etc/rc.d/rc 6


# Things to run in every runlevel.
ud::once:/sbin/update

# Trap CTRL-ALT-DELETE
ca::ctrlaltdel:/sbin/shutdown -t3 -r now

# When our UPS tells us power has failed, assume we have a few minutes
# of power left.  Schedule a shutdown for 2 minutes from now.
# This does, of course, assume you have powerd installed and your
# UPS connected and working correctly.
pf::powerfail:/sbin/shutdown -f -h +2 "Power Failure; System Shutting Down"

# If power was restored before the shutdown kicked in, cancel it.
pr:12345:powerokwait:/sbin/shutdown -c "Power Restored; Shutdown Cancelled"

# Run gettys in standard runlevels
1:2345:respawn:/sbin/mingetty tty1
2:2345:respawn:/sbin/mingetty tty2
3:2345:respawn:/sbin/mingetty tty3
4:2345:respawn:/sbin/mingetty tty4
5:2345:respawn:/sbin/mingetty tty5
6:2345:respawn:/sbin/mingetty tty6

# Run xdm in runlevel 5
# xdm is now a separate service
x:5:respawn:/etc/X11/prefdm -nodaemon
```

Managing rc Scripts by Hand

If you want to configure what services are started at boot time, you need to edit the rc scripts for the appropriate runlevel. The default runlevel is 3, which is full multi-user mode. So to change what services are started in the default runlevel, you should edit the scripts found in /etc/rc3.d.

When you look at a directory listing of the rc directories, notice that the files either start with S or K. The files that start with S are startup files, and the files that start with K are kill files. The S scripts are run in the numerical order listed in their filenames. It should be mentioned that if a startup script is set to S15, the K script should be K85 (or in general, SN becomes SM with M = 100 - n; the idea being the last started service is the first killed).

Note that case is important. Scripts that do not start with a capital S do not run upon startup. So one good way to keep scripts from starting up at boot time without deleting them is to rename the file with a small s at the beginning instead of a capital S. This way you can always put the script back into the startup configuration by capitalizing the initial letter.

When the system starts up, it runs through the scripts in the rc directory of the runlevel it's starting up in. So when the system starts up in runlevel 3, it runs the scripts in the /etc/rc3.d directory.

Looking at the directory listing included in Listing 7-11, you can see that the first few services start in this order: kudzu, reconfig, iptables, and network. That is because their scripts are named S05kudzu, S06reconfig, S08iptables, and S10network, respectively.

Kudzu is called first because it detects new hardware. Reconfig runs to put into effect any changes made with the chkconfig tool. Iptables then starts up the built-in firewall. Network then brings up the system's network interfaces. As you can see, the order in which these services are started makes a lot of sense, and their order is enforced by the way their rc startup scripts are named. All of the files in rc#.d are symboliclinks to /etc/init.d scripts and the names are used here only to affect what services start or stop and the ordering of those services. Editing the rc3.d/httpd file will affect rc5.d/httpd.

Listing 7-11: A directory listing of the r3.d directory

```
[root@buffy rc3.d]# ls
K05innd         K20rwhod        K50xinetd       K74ypserv       K92ipvsadm      S60lpd
K08vmware       K25squid        K54pxe          K74ypxfrd       K92upsd         S83iscsi
K09junkbuster   K28amd          K55routed       K75gated        K96irda         S90crond
K10fonttastic   K30mcserv       K61ldap         K75netfs        S05kudzu        S90xfs
K12mysqld       K30sendmail     K65identd       K84bgpd         S06reconfig     S91atalk
K15gpm          K34yppasswdd    K65kadmin       K84ospf6d       S08iptables     S95anacron
K15httpd        K35smb          K65kprop        K84ospfd        S10network      S97rhnsd
K15postgresql   K35vncserver    K65krb524       K84ripd         S12syslog       S99linuxconf
```

```
K16rarpd        K40mars-nwe    K65krb5kdc    K84ripngd      S17keytable    S99local
K20bootparamd   K45arpwatch    K73ypbind     K85zebra       S20random      S99wine
K20nfs          K45named       K74apmd       K86nfslock     S28autofs
K20rstatd       K46radvd       K74nscd       K87portmap     S40atd
K20rusersd      K50snmpd       K74ntpd       K91isdn        S55sshd
K20rwalld       K50tux         K74ups        K92ipchains    S56rawdevices
[root@buffy rc3.d]#
```

The S scripts are started in this order until they have all been started. When the system shuts down, the corresponding K, or kill scripts are run to shut down the services started from the rc directory. In general, every S script should have a corresponding K script to kill the service at shutdown.

If you can't find the corresponding K script in the startup directory, it is probably located in the shutdown directory. When the system is shut down, it enters runlevel 6. So most of the K scripts are in /etc/rc6.d. A typical /etc/rc6.d directory listing is shown in Listing 7-12.

Listing 7-12: The file contents of the /etc/rc6.d directory

```
[root@buffy rc6.d]# ls
K00linuxconf    K16rarpd        K34yppasswdd    K55routed     K74nscd       K85zebra
K03rhnsd        K20bootparamd   K35atalk        K60atd        K74ntpd       K86nfslock
K05anacron      K20iscsi        K35smb          K60crond      K74ups        K87portmap
K05innd         K20nfs          K35vncserver    K60lpd        K74ypserv     K88syslog
K05keytable     K20rstatd       K40mars-nwe     K61ldap       K74ypxfrd     K90network
K08vmware       K20rusersd      K44rawdevices   K65identd     K75gated      K91isdn
K09junkbuster   K20rwalld       K45arpwatch     K65kadmin     K75netfs      K92ipchains
K10wine         K20rwhod        K45named        K65kprop      K80random     K92ipvsadm
K10xfs          K25squid        K46radvd        K65krb524     K84bgpd       K95kudzu
K12mysqld       K25sshd         K50snmpd        K65krb5kdc    K84ospf6d     K95reconfig
K15gpm          K28amd          K50tux          K72autofs     K84ospfd      K96irda
K15httpd        K30mcserv       K50xinetd       K73ypbind     K84ripd       S00killall
K15postgresql   K30sendmail     K54pxe          K74apmd       K84ripngd     S01reboot
```

If you ever need to restart a service that's started from an rc directory, an easy way to do it properly is to run its startup script with the restart option. This procedure enables all the proper steps to be followed (configuration files read, lock files released, and so forth) when the service starts up again. So to restart syslog, for example, run the following command from the rc directory:

```
[root@buffy rc3.d]# ./S12syslog restart
Shutting down kernel logger:                              [  OK  ]
Shutting down system logger:                              [  OK  ]
Starting system logger:                                   [  OK  ]
Starting kernel logger:                                   [  OK  ]
```

Managing rc Scripts Using chkconfig

Red Hat comes with a useful tool called chkconfig. It helps the system administrator manage rc scripts and xinetd configuration files without having to manipulate them directly. It is inspired by the `chkconfig` command included in the IRIX operating system.

Type **chkconfig --list** to see all the services chkconfig knows about, and whether they are stopped or started in each runlevel. An abridged example output is shown in the following listing. The chkconfig output can be a lot longer than that listed here, so be prepared to pipe it through less or more.

The first column is the name of the installed service. The next seven columns each represent a runlevel, and tell you whether that service is turned on or off in that runlevel.

Since xinetd is started on the system whose chkconfig output is excerpted, at the end of chkconfig's report is a listing of what xinetd started services are configured to begin at boot time. The listing is abridged, since a lot of services can be started from xinetd, and there's no need to show all of them.

Listing 7-13 shows how chkconfig can be an effective tool for handling all your network services and controlling which ones get started up at boot time. This is the output of `chkconfig --list`:

Listing 7-13: Output from chkconfig --list

```
atd            0:off   1:off   2:off   3:on    4:on    5:on    6:off
rwhod          0:off   1:off   2:off   3:off   4:off   5:off   6:off
keytable       0:off   1:on    2:on    3:on    4:on    5:on    6:off
nscd           0:off   1:off   2:off   3:off   4:off   5:off   6:off
syslog         0:off   1:off   2:on    3:on    4:on    5:on    6:off
gpm            0:off   1:off   2:on    3:off   4:off   5:off   6:off
kudzu          0:off   1:off   2:off   3:on    4:on    5:on    6:off
kdcrotate      0:off   1:off   2:off   3:off   4:off   5:off   6:off
lpd            0:off   1:off   2:on    3:on    4:on    5:on    6:off
autofs         0:off   1:off   2:off   3:on    4:on    5:on    6:off
sendmail       0:off   1:off   2:on    3:off   4:off   5:off   6:off
rhnsd          0:off   1:off   2:off   3:on    4:on    5:on    6:off
netfs          0:off   1:off   2:off   3:off   4:off   5:off   6:off
network        0:off   1:off   2:on    3:on    4:on    5:on    6:off
random         0:off   1:off   2:on    3:on    4:on    5:on    6:off
rawdevices     0:off   1:off   2:off   3:on    4:on    5:on    6:off
apmd           0:off   1:off   2:on    3:off   4:off   5:off   6:off
ipchains       0:off   1:off   2:off   3:off   4:off   5:off   6:off

<snip>
```

```
xinetd based services:
        rexec:  off
        rlogin: off
        rsh:    off
        chargen:        off
        chargen-udp:    off
        daytime:        off
        daytime-udp:    off
        echo:   off
        echo-udp:       off
        time:   off
        time-udp:       off
        finger: off
        ntalk:  off
        talk:   off
        telnet: off
        wu-ftpd:        on
        rsync:  off
        eklogin:        off
        gssftp: off
        klogin: off
```

To turn a service off or on using chkconfig, use this syntax:

```
chkconfig -level[0-6](you must choose the runlevel) servicename
off|on|reset
```

So to turn off the ftp daemon turned on previously, type:

```
chkconfig wu-ftpd off
```

To turn on xinetd, type:

```
chkconfig xinetd on
```

Run `chkconfig --list` again to see if the service you changed has been set to the state you desire. Changes you make with chkconfig take place the next time you boot up the system. You can always start, stop, or restart a service by running `service (service name)` from a terminal prompt.

Summary

All systemwide configuration files are located in /etc. So if you want to change something across the system, look in /etc and its subdirectories first. If you're at a loss in terms of figuring out which configuration file you need to edit, try grepping for keywords in /etc.

To change configuration variables for one or a few users, you can usually edit configuration files within the individual users' home directories. Most configuration files in home directories start with a . so you need to look for them with the ls -a command.

Be mindful of configuration file permissions, to ensure that unauthorized parties cannot modify them. Flat out instant root access for unauthorized parties is one possible outcome of a modified configuration file. A more likely outcome is that a configuration file modification would make it easier for a system compromise to take place.

You can either edit startup files by hand, or by using one of Red Hat's useful system administration tools such as chkconfig. You should at least know the format of the startup files and where they are, so that if automatic tools can't do the job for some reason, you can always change things yourself.

Part II

Network Services

Chapter 8

X Servers and Clients

IN THIS CHAPTER

◆ The power of X

◆ XFree86

◆ XFree86 configuration file

◆ Desktop environments and window managers

◆ Runlevels

◆ Fonts

THE HEART OF RED HAT ENTERPRISE LINUX IS THE KERNEL, but for many users, the face of the operating system is the graphical environment provided by the X Window System, also called X. This chapter is an introduction to the behind-the-scenes world of XFree86, the open-source implementation of X provided with Red Hat Enterprise Linux.

The Power of X

Linux began as a powerful, server-based operating system, excelling at efficiently processing complicated programs requiring high CPU utilization and handling requests from hundreds or thousands of clients through network connections. However, because of its openness and stability, Linux has quickly developed into a popular GUI-based operating system for workstations, both in the home and in the workplace.

In the Unix world, windowing environments have existed for decades, predating many of the current mainstream operating systems. The X Window System is now the dominant graphical user interface (GUI) for Unix-like operating systems. To create this GUI for the user, X uses a client/server architecture. An X server process is started, and X client processes can connect to it via a network or local loopback interface. The server process handles the communication with the hardware, such as the video card, monitor, keyboard, and mouse. The X client exists in the user space, issuing requests to the X server.

On all Red Hat Linux systems — Enterprise Advanced Server, Workstation, and Fedora — the XFree86 server fills the role of the X server. As a large-scope open-source software project, with hundreds of developers around the world, XFree86 features rapid development, a wide degree of support for various hardware devices and architectures, and the ability to run on different operating systems and platforms.

Most desktop users are unaware of the XFree86 server running on their system. They are much more concerned with the particular desktop environment in which they spend most of their time. The installation program does an excellent job of configuring your XFree86 server during the installation process, ensuring that X performs optimally when first started.

The X server performs many difficult tasks using a wide array of hardware, requiring detailed configuration. If some aspect of your system changes, such as the monitor or video card, XFree86 will need to be reconfigured. In addition, if you are troubleshooting a problem with XFree86 that cannot be solved using a configuration utility, such as the X Configuration Tool (`redhat-config-xfree86`), you may need to access its configuration file directly.

The X Configuration Tool is capable of configuring XFree86 while the X server is active. To activate the configuration program from the command line, type `redhat-config-xfree86`. To start the X Configuration Tool while in an active X session, go to the Main Menu Button (on the Panel) → System Settings → Display. After using the X Configuration Tool during an X session, you will need to log out of the current X session and log back in for the changes to take effect.

XFree86

The base X Window System is XFree86 version 4.3, which includes the various necessary X libraries, fonts, utilities, documentation, and development tools.

Red Hat no longer provides the older XFree86 version 3 server packages. Before upgrading to the latest version of Red Hat Linux, be sure that your video card is compatible with XFree86 version 4 by checking the Red Hat Hardware Compatibility List located at `http://hardware.redhat .com/hcl/`.

The X server includes many cutting-edge XFree86 technology enhancements such as hardware 3D acceleration support, the XRender extension for antialiased fonts, a modular driver-based design, support for modern video hardware and input devices, and many other features. The installation program installs the base components of XFree86. You may choose to install any optional XFree86 packages.

The X Window System resides primarily in two locations in the file system: the /usr/X11R6/ directory and the /etc/X11/ directory.

/usr/X11R6/ Directory

This directory contains X client binaries (the bin directory), assorted header files (the include directory), libraries (the lib directory), man pages (the man directory), and various other X documentation (the /usr/X11R6/lib/X11/doc/ directory).

/etc/X11/ Directory

The /etc/X11/ directory hierarchy contains all of the configuration files for the various components that make up the X Window System. This includes configuration files for the X server itself, the X font server (xfs), the X Display Manager (xdm), and many other base components.

Display managers such as gdm and kdm, as well as various window managers and other X tools, also store their configuration in this hierarchy. XFree86 version 4 server is a single binary executable (/usr/X11R6/bin/XFree86). This server dynamically loads various X server modules at runtime from the /usr/X11R6/lib/modules/ directory, including video drivers, font engine drivers, and other modules as needed. Some of these modules are automatically loaded by the server, whereas some are optional features that you must specify in the XFree86 server's configuration file, /etc/X11/XF86Config, before they can be used. The video drivers are located in the /usr/X11R6/lib/modules/drivers/ directory. The DRI hardware accelerated 3D drivers are located in the /usr/X11R6/lib/modules/dri/ directory.

XFree86 Server Configuration Files

The XFree86 server configuration files are stored in the /etc/X11/ directory. The XFree86 version 4 server uses /etc/X11/XF86Config. When Red Hat Linux is installed, the configuration files for XFree86 are created using information gathered during the installation process.

Although there is rarely a need to manually edit these files, it is useful to know about the various sections and optional parameters they contain. Each section begins with a *section-name* line and ends with an EndSection line. Within each of the sections, you will find several lines containing an option name and at least one option value, occasionally seen in quotes. The following list explores the most useful sections of an XFree86 version 4 file and the roles of various popular settings.

DEVICE

This specifies information about the video card used by the system. You must have at least one Device section in your configuration file. You may have multiple Device sections in the case of multiple video cards or multiple settings that can run a single card. The following options are required or widely used:

◆ BusID – Specifies the bus location of the video card. This option is necessary only for systems with multiple cards and must be set so that the Device section uses the proper settings for the correct card.

◆ Driver – Tells XFree86 which driver to load in order to use the video card.

◆ Identifier – Provides a unique name for this video card. Usually, this name is set to the exact name of the video card used in the Device section.

◆ Screen – An optional setting used when a video card has more than one head, or connector, to go out to a separate monitor. If you have multiple monitors connected to one video card, separate Device sections must exist for each of them with a different Screen value for each Device section. The value that this option accepts is a number starting at 0 and increasing by 1 for each head on the video card.

◆ VideoRam – The amount of RAM available on the video card in kilobytes. This setting is not normally necessary, since the XFree86 server can usually probe the video card to autodetect the amount of video RAM. But since there are some video cards that XFree86 cannot correctly autodetect, this option allows you to specify the amount of video RAM.

DRI

Direct Rendering Infrastructure (DRI) is an interface that primarily allows 3D software applications to take advantage of the 3D hardware acceleration capabilities on modern supported video hardware. In addition, DRI can improve 2D hardware acceleration performance when using drivers that have been enhanced to use the DRI for 2D operations. This section is ignored unless DRI is enabled in the Module section.

Since different video cards use DRI in different ways, before changing any DRI values, read the /usr/X11R6/lib/X11/doc/README.DRI file for specific information about your particular video card.

FILES

This section sets paths for services vital to the XFree86 server, such as the font path. Common options include:

◆ FontPath – Sets the locations where the XFree86 server can find fonts. Different fixed paths to directories holding font files can be placed here, separated by commas. By default, Red Hat Linux uses xfs as the font server and points FontPath to unix/:7100. This tells the XFree86 server to obtain font information by using Unix-domain sockets for interprocess communication (IPC). See the "Fonts" section of this chapter for more information concerning XFree86 and fonts.

- ◆ ModulePath — Allows you to set up multiple directories to use for storing modules loaded by the XFree86 server.

- ◆ RgbPath — Tells the XFree86 server where the RGB color database is located on the system. This database file defines all valid color names in XFree86 and ties them to specific RGB values.

INPUTDEVICE

This configures an input device such as a mouse or keyboard used to convey information to the system using the XFree86 server. Most systems have at least two InputDevice sections: keyboard and mouse. Each section includes these two lines:

- ◆ Driver — Tells XFree86 the name of the driver to load to use the device.

- ◆ Identifier — Sets the name of the device, usually the name of the device followed by a number, starting with 0 for the first device. For example, the first keyboard InputDevice would have an Identifier of Keyboard0.

Most InputDevice sections contain lines assigning specific options to that device. Each of these lines starts with Option and contains the name of the option in quotes, followed by the value to assign to that option. Mice usually receive options such as Protocol, PS/2, and Device, which designates the mouse to use for this section. The InputDevice section is well commented, allowing you to configure additional options for your particular devices by uncommenting certain lines.

MODULE

This tells the XFree86 server which modules from the /usr/X11R6/lib/modules/ directory to load. Modules provide the XFree86 server with additional functionality.

Be careful when editing these values. Changes made to the modules can prevent your X server from starting.

MONITOR

This refers to the type of monitor the system uses. While one Monitor section is the minimum, there may be several Monitor sections, one for each monitor the machine uses.

Be careful when manually editing values in the options of the Monitor section. Inappropriate values in this section can damage or destroy your monitor. Consult the documentation that comes with your monitor for the safe operating parameters available.

The following options are usually configured during installation or when using the X Configuration Tool:

- `HorizSync` — Tells XFree86 the range of horizontal sync frequencies compatible with the monitor in kHz. These values are used as a guide by the XFree86 server so that it knows whether to use a particular `Modeline` entry's values with this monitor.

- `Identifier` — Provides a unique name for this monitor, usually numbering each monitor starting at 0. The first monitor would be named `Monitor0`, the second `Monitor1`, and so on.

- `Modeline` — Used to specify the video modes that the monitor uses at particular resolutions, with certain horizontal sync and vertical refresh resolutions. `Modeline` entries are usually preceded by a comment that explains what the mode line specifies. If your configuration file does not include comments for the various mode lines, you can scan over the values (also called *mode descriptions*) to determine what the mode line is attempting to do. See the XF86Config man page for detailed explanations of each mode description section.

- `ModelName` — An optional parameter that displays the model name of the monitor.

- `VendorName` — An optional parameter that displays the name of the vendor that manufactured the monitor.

- `VertRefresh` — Lists the vertical refresh range frequencies supported by the monitor, in kHz. These values are used as a guide by the XFree86 server so that it knows whether to use a particular `Modeline` entry's values with this monitor.

SCREEN

This binds together a particular `Device` and `Monitor` that can be utilized as a pair and contain certain settings. You must have at least one `Screen` section in your configuration file. The following options are common:

- `DefaultDepth` — Tells the `Screen` section the default color depth to try, in bits. The default is 8; specifying 16 provides thousands of colors, and 32 displays millions of colors.

- `Device` — Signifies the name of the `Device` section to use with this `Screen` section.

- `Identifier` — Identifies the `Screen` section so that it can be referred to by a `ServerLayout` section and be utilized.

- `Monitor` — Reveals the name of the `Monitor` section to be used with this `Screen` section.

You may also have a `Display` subsection within the `Screen` section that tells the XFree86 server the color depth (`Depth`) and resolution (`Mode`) to try first when using this particular monitor and video card.

SERVERFLAGS

This contains miscellaneous global XFree86 server settings. These settings may be overridden by options placed in the `ServerLayout` section. Among the most useful settings are:

- `DontZap` — Prevents the use of the `Ctrl-Alt-Backspace` key combination to immediately terminate the XFree86 server.

- `DontZoom` — Prevents cycling through configured video resolutions using the `Ctrl-Alt-Keypad-Plus` and `Ctrl-Alt-Keypad-Minus` key combinations.

SERVERLAYOUT

This binds a `Screen` section with the necessary `InputDevice` sections and various options to create a unified collection of preferences used by the XFree86 server as it starts. If you have more than one `ServerLayout` section, and the one to use is not specified on the command line when you bring up the XFree86 server, the first `ServerLayout` section in the configuration file is used. The following options are used in a `ServerLayout` section:

- `Identifier` — A unique name used to describe this `ServerLayout` section.

- `InputDevice` — The names of any `InputDevice` sections to be used with the XFree86 server. Most users will have only two lines here, `Keyboard0` and `Mouse0`, the first keyboard and mouse configured for the system. The options `CoreKeyboard` and `CorePointer` refer to the fact that these are the preferred keyboard and mouse, respectively, to use with the XFree86 server.

- `Screen` — The name of the `Screen` section to use. The number to the left of the name of the `Screen` section refers to the particular screen number to use in a multihead configuration. For standard single-head video cards, this value is 0. The numbers to the right give the *X* and *Y* absolute coordinates for the upper-left corner of the screen, by default 0 0. Following is an example of a typical screen entry:

```
Screen          0     "Screen0" 0 0
```

For more information, refer to the XF86Config man page.

To review the current configuration of your XFree86 server, type the `xset -q` command. This provides you with information about the keyboard, pointer, screen saver, and font paths.

Desktop Environments and Window Managers

The configuration of an XFree86 server is useless until accessed by an X client that will use it to display a program using the hardware controlled by the X server. X clients are programs designed to take advantage of the X server's hardware, usually to provide interactivity with a user.

You do not have to run a complicated window manager in conjunction with a particular desktop environment to use X client applications. Assuming that you are not already in an X environment and do not have an .xinitrc file in your home directory, type the xinit command to start X with a basic terminal window (the default xterm application). This basic environment utilizes your keyboard, mouse, video card, and monitor with the XFree86 server, using the server's hardware preferences. Type **exit** at the xterm prompt to leave this basic X environment.

Of course, most computer users require more features and utility from their GUIs. Developers have added layers of features to create highly developed and interactive environments that utilize the full power of the XFree86 server. These layers break into two fundamental groups based on their purpose.

Window Managers

Window managers are X client programs that control the way other X clients are positioned, resized, or moved. Window managers can also provide title bars to windows, keyboard focus by keyboard or mouse, and user-specified key and mouse-button bindings. Window managers work with a collection of different X clients, wrapping around the program, making it look a certain way and appear on the screen in a particular place. Five window managers are included with the Red Hat Linux versions:

♦ twm — The minimalist Tab Window Manager, which provides the most basic toolset of any of the window managers.

♦ mwm — *mwm* stands for Motif Window Manager. It is a simple and efficient stand-alone window manager that supports custom themes.

♦ kwin — The kwin window manager is the default window manager for KDE.

♦ metacity — The metacity window manager is the default window manager for the GNOME desktop.

♦ sawfish — sawfish was the default window manager for GNOME until the release of Red Hat Linux 8. It can be used as a stand-alone or with a desktop environment.

These window managers can be run as individual X clients to gain a better sense of their differences. Type the `xinit path-to-window-manager` command, where `path-to-window-manager` is the location of the window manager binary file. The binary file can be found by typing **which window-manager-name** or by looking for the name of the window manager in a `bin` directory.

Desktop Environments

A desktop environment brings together assorted X clients that can be run together using similar methods, utilizing a common development environment. Desktop environments are different from window managers, which control only the appearance and placement of X client windows. Desktop environments contain advanced features that allow X clients and other running processes to communicate with one another. This allows all applications written to work in that environment to commonly integrate and be used in new ways, such as permitting drag-and-drop behavior with text.

GNOME is the default desktop environment for Red Hat Linux, using the GTK2 base widget toolkit and miscellaneous other widgets that extend the base functionality. KDE, another desktop environment, uses a different toolkit called Qt. GNOME and KDE both contain advanced productivity applications, such as word processors, spreadsheets, and control panel devices that allow you to have complete control of the look and feel of your user experience. Both environments can run standard X client applications, and most KDE applications can run in GNOME, if the Qt libraries are installed.

When you start X using the `startx` command, a prespecified desktop environment is utilized. To change the default desktop environment used when X starts, open a terminal and type **switchdesk**. This brings up a graphical utility that allows you to select the desktop environment or window manager to use the next time X starts.

Desktop environments utilize window managers to provide consistency in appearance among different applications. KDE contains its own window manager, called kwm, specifically for this functionality.

Runlevels

Most users run X from runlevels 3 or 5. Runlevel 3 places your system in multiuser mode, with full networking capabilities. The machine boots to a text-based login prompt with all necessary preconfigured services started. Most servers are run in runlevel 3, as X is not necessary to provide any services utilized by most users. Runlevel 5 is similar to 3, except that it automatically starts X and provides a graphical login screen. Many workstation users prefer this method because they never have to see a command prompt.

The default runlevel used when your system boots can be found in the `/etc/inittab` file. If you have a line in that file that looks like `id:3:initdefault:`, your system will boot to runlevel 3. If you have a line that looks like `id:5:initdefault:`, your system is set to boot into runlevel 5. As root, change the runlevel number in this file to set a different default. Save the file and restart your system to verify that it boots to the correct runlevel.

RUNLEVEL 3: startx

When in runlevel 3, the preferred way to start an X session is to type **startx**. A front end to the `xinit` program, startx launches the XFree86 server and connects the X clients to it. Because you must already be logged in to the system at runlevel 3 to be able to type commands, startx is designed only to bring up certain X clients, such as a desktop environment, in a particular manner. It does not provide any user authentication.

When startx begins, it looks for an `.xinitrc` file in the user's home directory to define the X clients to run. If it does not find that file, it runs the system default `/etc/X11/xinit/xinitrc` script instead. The `startx` script then does the same thing with the `.xserverrc` file, looking for it in the user's home directory and then running the default `/etc/X11/xinit/xserverrc` script if it cannot be found. Since many different X clients exist, the `xinitrc` files are very important. The `xserverrc` script is less important. It sets only the X server to connect to the X clients. Since the default X server is already configured with the `/etc/X11/X` link, Red Hat Linux does not install a default `xserverrc`.

The default `xinitrc` script then looks for user-defined files and default system files, including `.Xresources`, `.Xmodmap`, and `.Xkbmap`, in the user's home directory and `Xresources`, `Xmodmap`, and `Xkbmap` in the `/etc/X11/` directory. The `Xmodmap` and `Xkbmap` files, if they exist, are used by the xmodmap utility to configure the keyboard. The `Xresources` files are read to assign specific preference values to particular applications.

After setting these options, the `xinitrc` script executes all scripts located in the `/etc/X11/xinit/xinitrc.d/` directory. One important script in this directory is `xinput`, which configures settings such as the default language to use and the desktop environment to start from (`/etc/sysconfig/desktop`).

Next, the `xinitrc` script tries to execute `.Xclients` in the user's home directory and turns to `/etc/X11/xinit/Xclients` if it cannot be found. The purpose of the `Xclients` file is to start the desktop environment or, possibly, just a basic window manager. The `.Xclients` script in the user's home directory starts the user-specified desktop environment or window manager in the `.Xclients-default` file. If `.Xclients` does not exist in the user's home directory, the standard `/etc/X11/init/Xclients` script attempts to start another desktop environment, trying GNOME first and then KDE. If a desktop environment cannot be found by this point, `Xclients` attempts the default window manager listed in the `.wm_style` file in the user's home directory. If this fails, it cycles through a predefined list of window managers.

The preferred X client applications should now have started, along with the XFree86 server. If you need more details concerning starting X in runlevel 3, refer to the startx and xinit man pages and read through the previously named scripts.

RUNLEVEL 5: prefdm

Runlevel 5 uses a slightly different method to start X. When the system starts, no one is logged in to the system by default. In order to start a session, a user must log in to the system. In runlevel 5, users authenticating themselves at the console use a display manager, a special X client that allows them to submit their login names and passwords.

Depending on the desktop environments installed on your specific Red Hat Linux system, three different display managers are available to handle the user authentication. The xdm display manager is the original X authentication tool. xdm allows you to log in and start an X session only, nothing more. The gdm display manager, designed to work with the GNOME desktop environment, and kdm display manager, used with the KDE desktop environment, allow you to set the desktop environment, or session, you would like to use after authentication. Also, you can restart or halt the system from the login screen. The gdm display manager also allows you to configure the language you would like to use.

When the system enters runlevel 5, a line in the /etc/inittab file specifies that the prefdm script is executed in order to determine the preferred display manager to bring up for user authentication. The prefdm script uses the preferences stated in the /etc/sysconfig/desktop file to find the proper display manager. If no desktop environment is specified, prefdm cycles through the gdm, kdm, and xdm display managers to find one to use. Once one is found, prefdm launches it to handle the user login.

Each of the display managers looks to the /etc/X11/xdm/Xsetup_0 file to set up the login screen. Once the user logs in to the system, the /etc/X11/xdm/ GiveConsole script runs to assign ownership of the console to the user. Then the /etc/X11/xdm/Xsession script runs to accomplish many of the tasks normally done by the xinitrc script when starting X in runlevel 3, including setting system and user resources, as well as running the scripts in the /etc/X11/xinit/ xinitrc.d/ directory.

Users can specify which desktop environment they want to utilize when they authenticate using the gdm or kdm display managers by selecting it from the Session menu. If the desktop environment is not specified in the display manager, the /etc/X11/xdm/Xsession script will check the .xsession and .Xclients files in the user's home directory to decide which desktop environment to load. As a last resort, the /etc/X11/xinit/Xclients file is used to select a desktop environment or window manager to use in the same way as runlevel 3.

When the user finishes an X session on the default display (:0) and logs out, the /etc/X11/xdm/TakeConsole script runs and reassigns ownership of the console to the root user. The original display manager, which continues running after the user logs in, takes control by spawning a new display manager. This restarts the XFree86 server, displays a new login window, and starts the entire process over again. For more information about how display managers control user authentication, read the xdm man page.

Fonts

Red Hat Linux uses xfs (X Font Server) to provide fonts to the XFree86 server and the X client applications that connect to it. While it is possible to circumvent xfs and place the paths to font directories in your XF86Config configuration file, using xfs has several advantages:

◆ It is easier to add and remove fonts, including editing the font path. The font path is a collection of paths in the file system where font files are stored. The xfs service keeps the font path out of the XFree86 configuration files, making it easier to edit.

◆ Fonts may be stored on one machine acting as a networked font server and can be shared among multiple X servers over the network. A common set of fonts can be maintained in one place and easily shared among all users.

◆ More types of fonts are supported. xfs can handle TrueType, Type1, and bitmap fonts.

The XFree86 configuration files know whether to use xfs or hard-coded font paths because of the FontPath setting in their Files sections. By default, the FontPath is set to unix/:7100. This tells the XFree86 server to connect to port 7100 using an inner-machine communication link. The xfs server listening on this port responds with font information when queried by the XFree86 server.

The xfs service must be running when X is started. If it is not, you will be returned to a command prompt with an error similar to failed to set default font path unix/:7100. Check to see if xfs is running by using the ps aux | grep xfs command. By default, xfs is set to start in runlevels 2, 3, 4, and 5, covering all runlevels where you would run X. If xfs is not running on your system, you can start it as root using the /sbin/service xfs start command. Use the /usr/sbin/ntsysv, serviceconf, or /sbin/chkconfig utilities to force it to start at the correct runlevels. For more on configuring services for a particular runlevel, refer to Chapter 6.

xfs Configuration

The /etc/rc.d/init.d/xfs script starts the xfs server. Several options can be configured in the /etc/X11/fs/config file:

- `alternate-servers` — Sets a list of alternate font servers to be used if this font server is not available. A comma must separate every font server in the list.

- `catalogue` — An ordered list of font paths to use that contain the font files. A comma must follow every font path before a new font path can be started in the list. You can use the string `:unscaled` immediately after the font path to make the unscaled fonts in that path load first. Then you can specify the entire path again so that other scaled fonts will also be loaded.

- `client-limit` — Sets the number of clients this font server will service before refusing to handle any more. The default is 10.

- `clone-self` — Decides if the font server will clone a new version of itself when the `client-limit` is hit. By default, this option is on. Set it to off to disable this feature.

- `default-point-size` — Sets the default point size for any font that does not specify this value. The value for this option is set in decipoints. The default of 120 corresponds to 12-point fonts.

- `default-resolutions` — Specifies a list of resolutions supported by the XFree86 server. Each resolution in the list must be separated by a comma.

- `deferglyphs` — Tells xfs whether to defer the loading of glyphs, images used to visually represent a font. You can disable this feature (`none`), enable this feature for all fonts (`all`), or turn this feature only for 16-bit fonts (`16`), which are largely used with Asian languages.

- `error-file` — Allows you to specify the path and file name of a location where xfs errors can be logged.

- `no-listen` — Tells xfs not to listen using a particular protocol. By default, this option is set to `tcp` to prevent xfs from listening on TCP ports, primarily for security reasons. If you plan on using xfs to serve fonts to networked workstations on a LAN, remove the `tcp` from this line.

- `port` — Specifies the TCP port that xfs will listen on if `no-listen` does not exist or is commented out.

- `use-syslog` — Tells xfs to use the system error log if set to `on`.

Adding Fonts

There has been some confusion regarding font-related issues under the X Window System in recent versions of Red Hat Linux. At the present time, there are two font subsystems, each with different characteristics.

The original (15+ years old) subsystem is referred to as the "core X font subsystem." Fonts rendered by this subsystem are not antialiased, are handled by the X server, and have names like `misc-fixed-medium-r-normal--10-100-75-75-c-60-iso8859-1`.

The newer font subsystem is known as "fontconfig" and allows applications direct access to the font files. Fontconfig is often used along with the "Xft" library, which allows applications to render fontconfig fonts to the screen with antialiasing. Fontconfig uses more human-friendly names like `Luxi Sans-10`.

Over time, fontconfig/Xft will replace the core X font subsystem. At present, applications using the Qt 3 or GTK 2 toolkits (which would include KDE and GNOME applications) use the fontconfig and Xft font subsystem; most everything else uses the core X fonts. In the future, all Red Hat Linux versions may support only fontconfig/Xft in place of the XFS font server as the default local font access method.

An exception to the font subsystem usage outlined previously is OpenOffice .org (which uses its own font rendering technology).

If you wish to add new fonts to your system, you must be aware that the steps necessary depend on which font subsystem is to use the new fonts. For the core X font subsystem, you must:

1. Create the `/usr/share/fonts/local/` directory (if it doesn't already exist):

   `mkdir /usr/share/fonts/local/`

2. Copy the new font file into `/usr/share/fonts/local/`.

3. Update the font information by issuing the following commands (note that, because of formatting restrictions, the following commands may appear on more than one line; in use, each command should be entered on a single line):

   ```
   ttmkfdir -d /usr/share/fonts/local/ -o /usr/share/fonts/local/fonts.scale
   mkfontdir /usr/share/local/
   ```

4. If you had to create `/usr/share/fonts/local/`, you must then add it to the X font server (xfs) path:

   `chkfontpath --add /usr/share/fonts/local/`

5. Restart xfs and your X session.

Adding new fonts to the fontconfig font subsystem is much easier. The new font file needs to be copied into the `/usr/share/fonts/` directory only (individual users can modify their personal font configuration by copying the font file into the ~/.fonts/directory).

After the new font has been copied, use fc-cache to update the font information cache:

```
fc-cache <directory>
```

where <directory> would be either the /usr/share/fonts/ or ~/.fonts/ directories.

Individual users may also install fonts graphically by browsing fonts:/// in Nautilus and dragging the new font files there.

If the font filename ends with .gz, it has been compressed with gzip and must be decompressed (with the gunzip command) before the fontconfig font subsystem can use the font.

You must have a fonts.dir file in your new font directory for the chkfontpath command to work correctly. The creation of the fonts.dir file, as well as any other files used by xfs with these fonts, is beyond the scope of this book.

The Red Hat Support Web site contains more information on this subject. See http://www.redhat.com/support for additional help documents.

Additional Resources

Much more can be said about the XFree86 server, the clients that connect to it, and the assorted desktop environments and window managers. Advanced users interested in tweaking their XFree86 configuration will find these additional sources of information useful.

Installed documentation:

◆ /usr/X11R6/lib/X11/doc/README — Briefly describes the XFree86 architecture and how to get additional information about the XFree86 project as a new user.

♦ `/usr/X11R6/lib/X11/doc/README.Config` — Explains the advanced configuration options open to XFree86 version 3 users.

♦ `/usr/X11R6/lib/X11/doc/RELNOTES` — For advanced users who want to read about the latest features available in XFree86.

♦ `man XF86Config` — Contains information about the XFree86 configuration files, including the meaning of and syntax for the different sections within the files.

♦ `man XFree86` — The primary man page for all XFree86 information. It details the difference between local and network X server connections, explores common environmental variables, lists command-line options, and provides helpful administrative key combinations.

♦ `man Xserver` — Describes the X display server.

Useful Web sites:

♦ `http://www.xfree86.org` — Home page of the XFree86 project, which produces the XFree86 open-source version of the X Window System. XFree86 is bundled with Red Hat Linux to control the necessary hardware and provide a GUI environment.

♦ `http://dri.sourceforge.net` — Home page of the DRI (Direct Rendering Infrastructure) project. The DRI is the core hardware 3D acceleration component of XFree86.

♦ `http://www.redhat.com/mirrors/LDP/HOWTO/XFree86-HOWTO` — A HOWTO document detailing the manual installation and custom configuration of XFree86.

♦ `http://www.gnome.org` — The home page of the GNOME project.

♦ `http://www.kde.org` — The home page of the KDE desktop environment.

Summary

In this chapter, you learned about the X window system. You examined the XF86 Config file and how to use it to configure your system's X server. Also, you learned about desktop environments and window managers. Finally, you looked at the two font subsystems currently in use on your system and learned how to add fonts to them. In the next chapter, you learn about printing and how to configure various types of printers.

Chapter 9

Printer Configuration

IN THIS CHAPTER

- ◆ Adding a local printer
- ◆ Adding a Networked CUPS (IPP) printer
- ◆ Adding a Networked Unix (LPD) zhu1haiprinter
- ◆ Adding a Networked Windows (SMB) printer
- ◆ Adding a Networked Novell (NCP) printer
- ◆ Adding a JetDirect printer
- ◆ Selecting the print driver
- ◆ Editing the printer configurations
- ◆ Managing print jobs

PRINTER CONFIGURATION HAS LONG BEEN A HEADACHE for Linux and Unix administrators. Red Hat Enterprise Linux provides the Printer Configuration Tool for streamlining the task of configuring the default printing system. The default printing system installed with Red Hat is the Common Unix Printing System (CUPS).

Printer Configuration Tool

The Printer Configuration Tool allows users to configure a printer in Red Hat Enterprise Linux. It helps maintain the /etc/printcap configuration file, print spool directories, and print filters. The Printer Configuration Tool is used to configure the CUPS printing system.

To use the Printer Configuration Tool, you must have root privileges. To start the application, select Main Menu Button (on the Panel) → System Settings → Printing, or type **redhat-config-printer at a shell prompt**. This command automatically determines whether to run the graphical or text-based version. You can also force the Printer Configuration Tool to run as a text-based application by using the command redhat-config-printer-tui from a shell prompt. To add a printer using the command-line version, refer to the "Command-Line Configuration" section of this chapter. Figure 9-1 shows the Printer Configuration Tool user interface.

Do not edit the /etc/printcap file. Each time the printer daemon (lpd) is started or restarted, a new /etc/printcap file is dynamically created.

If you want to add a printer without using the Printer Configuration Tool, edit the /etc/printcap.local file. The entries in /etc/printcap.local are not displayed in the Printer Configuration Tool but are read by the printer daemon. If you upgrade your system from a previous version of Red Hat Linux, your existing configuration file is converted to the new format used by this application. Each time a new configuration file is generated, the old file is saved as /etc/printcap.old.

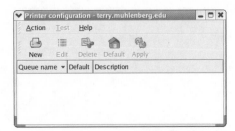

Figure 9-1: The Printer Configuration Tool

Six types of print queues can be configured:

◆ Locally-connected – A printer attached directly to your computer through a parallel or USB port.

◆ Networked CUPS (IPP) – A printer that can be accessed over a TCP/IP network using the Internet Printing Protocol (IPP)

◆ Networked Unix (LPDl) – A printer attached to a different Unix system that can be accessed over a TCP/IP network (for example, a printer attached to another Red Hat Linux system on your network).

◆ Networked Windows (SMB) – A printer attached to a different system that is sharing a printer over a SMB network (for example, a printer attached to a Microsoft Windows machine).

◆ Networked Novell (NCP) – A printer attached to a different system that uses Novell's NetWare network technology.

◆ Networked JetDirect – A printer connected directly to the network through HP JetDirect instead of to a computer.

If you add a print queue or modify an existing one, you need to restart the printer daemon for the changes to take effect.

Clicking the Apply button saves any changes you have made and restarts the printer daemon. The changes are not written to the /etc/printcap configuration file until the printer daemon (lpd) is restarted. Alternatively, you can choose File → Save Changes and then choose File → Restart lpd to save your changes and then restart the printer daemon.

If a printer appears in the main printer list with the Queue Type set to INVALID, the Printer Configuration Tool is missing options that are required for the printer to function properly. To remove this printer from the list, select it from the list and click the Delete button.

Adding a Local Printer

To add a local printer such as one attached to the parallel or USB port of your computer, click the New button in the main Printer Configuration Tool window. The window shown in Figure 9-2 will appear. Click Forward to proceed.

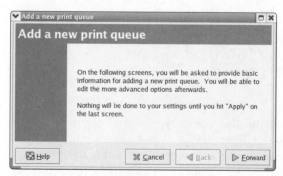

Figure 9-2: Adding a printer

You will then see the Queue Name screen shown in Figure 9-3. Enter a unique name for the printer in the Queue Name text field. This can be any descriptive name for your printer. The printer name cannot contain spaces and must begin with a letter *a* through *z* or *A* through *Z*. The valid characters are *a* through *z*, *A* through *Z*, *0* through *9*, -, and _ (underscore). You can also enter a description for the printer if you desire in the description section. When you have finished, click Forward.

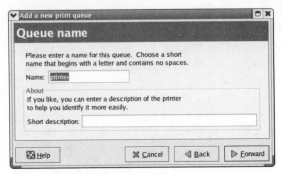

Figure 9-3: Choosing a name for the print queue

The Printer Configuration Tool attempts to detect your printer device as shown in Figure 9-4.

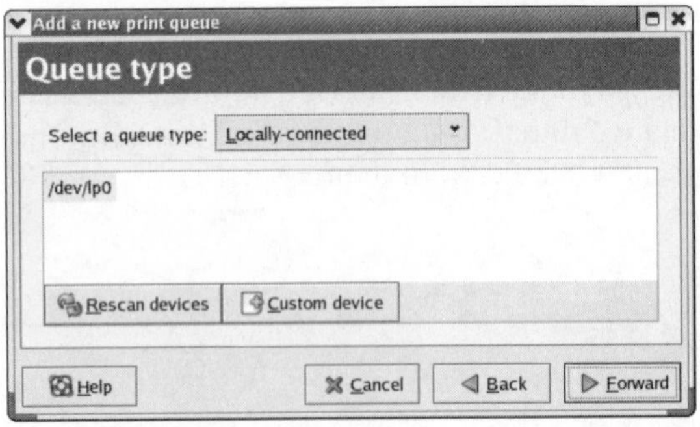

Figure 9-4: Adding a local printer

By default, *locally-connected* will be the queue type and the printer device should be shown in the list. If your printer device is not shown, click Custom Device. Type the name of your printer device and click OK to add it to the printer device list. A printer device attached to the parallel port is usually referred to as /dev/lp0. A printer device attached to the USB port is usually referred to as /dev/usblp0. Click the printer device and then Forward to continue. Refer to the section "Selecting the Printer Driver and Finishing" later in this chapter to complete the printer configuration process.

If the Printer Configuration Tool detects your printer model, it displays the recommended print driver. Skip to the section "Selecting the Print Driver and Finishing" to continue.

Adding a Networked CUPS (IPP) Printer

To add a networked CUPS printer, click the New button in the main Printer Configuration window. Figure 9-2 will appear. Click Forward to continue to the

Queue Name screen as shown in Figure 9-3. Enter the queue name and a printer description if you desire. Click Forward to continue to the Queue type screen as shown in Figure 9-4. Click the down arrow next to the queue type, and choose Networked CUPS (IPP). A new screen as shown in Figure 9-5 will appear.

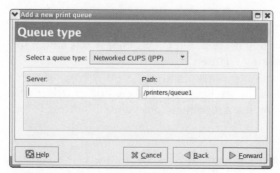

Figure 9-5: The Networked CUPS (IPP) screen is where you enter the server name and path.

On this screen, enter the server name and the path to the server. After entering this information, click Forward to continue. Refer to the section "Selecting the Printer Driver and Finishing" later in this chapter to complete the printer configuration process.

Adding a Networked Unix (LPD) Printer

To add a Networked Unix printer, such as one attached to a different Linux system on the same network, click the New button in the main Printer Configuration Tool window. The window shown in Figure 9-2 will appear. Click Forward to continue to the Queue Name screen as shown in Figure 9-3. Enter the queue name and a printer description if you desire. Click on Forward to continue to the Queue type screen as shown in Figure 9-4. Click on the down arrow next to the queue type and choose Networked Unix (LPD). A new screen as shown in Figure 9-6 will appear.

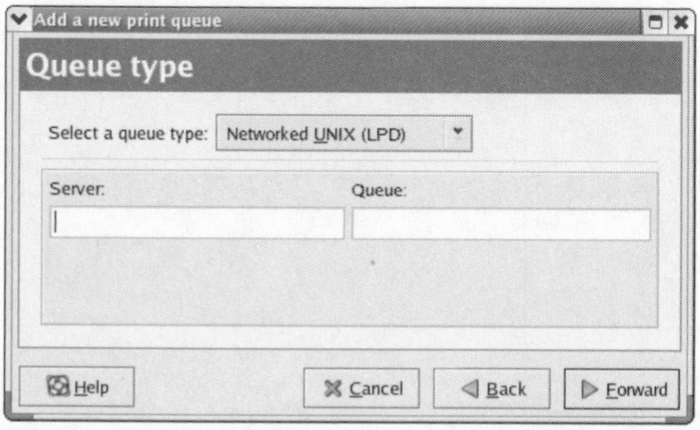

Figure 9-6: Entering the server and queue for a Networked Unix (LPD) printer

Enter the appropriate information for the text fields for the following options as shown in Figure 9-6:

- ♦ Server — The hostname or IP address of the remote machine to which the printer is attached.

- ♦ Queue — The remote printer queue. The default printer queue is usually lp. By default, the Strict RFC1179 Compliance option is not chosen. If you are having problems printing to a non-Linux lpd queue, choose this option to disable enhanced LPRng printing features.

Click Forward to continue. Refer to the section "Selecting the Printer Driver and Finishing" later in this chapter to complete the printer configuration process.

 The remote machine must be configured to allow the local machine to print on the desired queue. As root, create the file /etc/hosts.lpd on the remote machine to which the printer is attached. On separate lines in the file, add the IP address or hostname of each machine that should have printing privileges.

Adding a Networked Windows (SMB) Printer

To add a printer that is accessed using the SMB protocol (such as a printer attached to a Microsoft Windows system), click the New button in the main Printer Configuration Tool window. The window shown in Figure 9-2 will appear. Click Forward to continue to the Queue Name screen as shown in Figure 9-3. Enter the queue name and a printer description if you desire. Click Forward to continue to the Queue type screen as shown in Figure 9-4. Click the down arrow next to the queue type and choose Networked Windows (SMB). A new screen as shown in Figure 9-7 will appear.

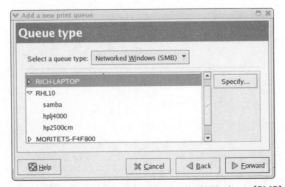

Figure 9-7: Configuring the Networked Windows (SMB) printer screen

On this screen, you see a list of shares from which you can select the networked Windows printer that you want to use. To the left of the share name is an arrow that can be clicked to expand the share listing and show any configured printers. Figure 9-7 shows the RHL10 share expanded and lists three printers. Click the printer you wish to use, and click Forward. An Authentication screen will appear as shown in Figure 9-8.

Figure 9-8: The Authentication screen for connecting to a SMB printer

Text fields for the following options appear as shown in Figure 9-8:

◆ Share – The name of the shared printer on which you want to print. This name must be the same name defined as the Samba printer on the remote Windows machine.

◆ User Name – The name of the user you must log in as to access the printer. This user must exist on the Windows system, and the user must have permission to access the printer. The default user name is typically *guest* for Windows servers and *nobody* for Samba servers.

◆ Password – The password (if required) for the user specified in the User field.

◆ Workgroup – The name of the workgroup on the machine running Samba.

After you have entered the appropriate information, click OK to continue.

The next step is to select the type of printer connected to the remote SMB system. Skip to the section "Selecting the Print Driver and Finishing" later in this chapter to continue.

If you require a username and password for an SMB (LAN Manager) print queue, they are stored unencrypted in the spool directory, which only root or lp may read. Thus, it is possible for others to learn the username and password if they have root access. To avoid this, the username and password to access the printer should be different from the username and password used for the user's account on the local Red Hat Linux system. If they are different, the only possible security compromise would be unauthorized use of the printer. If there are file shares from the SMB server, they should also use a different password from the one for the print queue.

Adding a Networked Novell (NCP) Printer

To add a Novell NetWare (NCP) printer, click the New button in the main Printer Configuration Tool window. The window shown in Figure 9-2 will appear. Click Forward to continue to the Queue Name screen as shown in Figure 9-3. Enter the queue name and a printer description if you desire. Click Forward to continue to the Queue type screen as shown in Figure 9-4. Click the down arrow next to the queue type and choose Networked Novell (NCP). A new screen as shown in Figure 9-9 will appear.

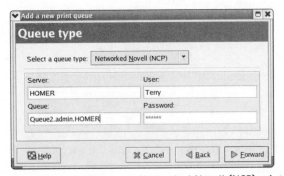

Figure 9-9: Configuring a Networked Novell (NCP) printer

Enter information for the following fields in Figure 9-9.

◆ Hostname — The hostname or IP address of the NCP system to which the printer is attached.

◆ Queue — The remote queue for the printer on the NCP system.

◆ User — The name of the user you must log in as to access the printer.

◆ Password — The password for the user specified in the User field above.

After you have entered the appropriate information, click Forward. The next step is to select the type of printer connected to the remote NCP system. Skip to the section "Selecting the Print Driver and Finishing" later in this chapter to continue.

If you require a username and password for an NCP (NetWare) print queue, they are stored. Thus, another person might learn the username and password. To avoid this, the username and password to use the printer should be different from the username and password used for the user's account on the local Red Hat Linux system. If they are different, the only possible security compromise would be unauthorized use of the printer.

Adding a Networked JetDirect Printer

To add a JetDirect printer, click the New button in the main Printer Configuration Tool window. The window shown in Figure 9-2 will appear. Click Forward to continue to the Queue Name screen as shown in Figure 9-3. Enter the queue name and a printer description if you desire. Click Forward to continue to the Queue type screen as shown in Figure 9-4. Click the down arrow next to the queue type and choose Networked JetDirect. A new screen as shown in Figure 9-10 will appear.

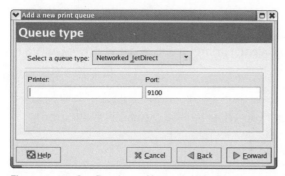

Figure 9-10: Configuring a Networked JetDirect printer

Enter the appropriate information for the following text fields as shown in Figure 9-10:

◆ PrinterIP – The hostname or IP address of the JetDirect printer.

◆ Port – The port on the JetDirect printer listening for print jobs. The default port is 9100.

After you have entered the information, click Forward. The next step is to select the type of printer connected to the JetDirect system. Skip to the next section, "Selecting the Print Driver and Finishing," to continue.

Selecting the Print Driver and Finishing

After you've selected the queue type of the printer, the next step in adding a printer is to select the print driver. You will see a window similar to the one shown in Figure 9-11.

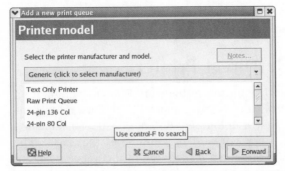

Figure 9–11: Selecting the printer manufacturer and model

Select the driver from the list. The printers are divided by manufacturers. Click the arrow beside the manufacturer for your printer. Find your printer from the expanded list, and click the arrow beside the printer name. A list of drivers for your printer will appear. Select one.

To learn more about the print drivers, go to http://www.linuxprinting .org/printer_list.cgi.

You can select a different print driver after adding a printer by starting the Printer Configuration Tool, selecting the printer from the list, clicking Edit, clicking the Driver tab, selecting a different print driver, and applying the changes.

The print driver processes the data you want to print into a format the printer can understand. Since a local printer is attached directly to your computer, you need to select a print driver to process the data sent to the printer. If you are configuring a remote printer (LPD, SMB, or NCP), the remote print server usually has its own print driver. If you select an additional print driver on your local computer, the data will be filtered more than once, and the data will be converted to a format that the printer cannot understand. To make sure the data is not filtered more than once, first try selecting Raw Print Queue or PostScript Printer if you are configuring a remote printer.

After applying the changes, print a test page to test this configuration. If the test fails, the remote print server might not have a print driver configured. Try selecting a print driver according to the manufacturer and model of the remote printer, applying the changes, and printing another test page.

Confirming Printer Configuration

The last step is to confirm your printer configuration. Click Apply to add the print queue if the settings are correct. Click Back to modify the printer configuration if necessary. Click the Apply button in the main window to save your changes to the `/etc/printcap` configuration file and restart the printer daemon. After applying the changes, print a test page to ensure that the configuration is correct. Refer to the next section, "Printing a Test Page," for details.

If you need to print characters beyond the basic ASCII set (including those used for languages such as Japanese), go to your driver options and select Prerender PostScript. Refer to the section "Modifying Existing Printers" later in this chapter for details. You can also configure options such as paper size if you edit the print queue after adding it.

Printing a Test Page

After you have configured your printer, print a test page to make sure the printer is functioning properly. To print a test page, select the printer you want to test from the printer list and select the appropriate test page from the Test pull-down menu. If you change the print driver or modify the driver options, print a test page to test the different configuration.

Modifying Existing Printers

To delete an existing printer, select the printer and click the Delete button on the toolbar. The printer will be removed from the printer list. Click Apply to save the changes and restart the printer daemon.

To set the default printer, select the printer from the printer list and click the Default button on the toolbar. The default printer icon appears in the first column of the printer list beside the default printer.

If you want to modify an imported printer's settings, note that you cannot do so directly. You must override the printer. You can override only an imported printer that has been imported using the `alchemist` libraries. Imported printers have a symbol beside them in the first column of the printer list. To override the printer, select the printer and choose File → Override Queue from the pull-down menu. After you've overridden a printer, the original imported printer will have a symbol beside it in the first column of the printer list.

After adding your printer(s), you can edit settings by selecting the printer from the printer list and clicking the Edit button. The tabbed window shown in Figure 9-12 will appear. The window contains the current values for the printer that you selected to edit. Make any changes, and click OK. Click Apply in the main Printer Configuration Tool window to save the changes and restart the printer daemon.

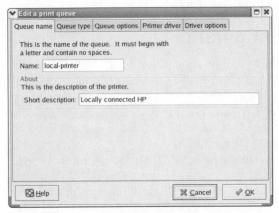

Figure 9-12: The Edit Print Queue screen

Queue Name

If you want to rename a printer, change the value of Name in the Queue Name tab. Click OK to return to the main window. The name of the printer should change in the printer list. Click Apply to save the change and restart the printer daemon.

QUEUE TYPE

The Queue Type tab shows the queue type that you selected when adding the printer and its settings. You can change the queue type of the printer or just change the settings. After making modifications, click OK to return to the main window. Click Apply to save the changes and restart the printer daemon.

Depending on which queue type you choose, you will see different options. Refer to the section of this chapter that describes your particular printer. Options unique to your printer are listed there.

QUEUE OPTIONS

On the Queue options tab screen, you can select banner pages before and after your print job. You can also set the printable area of the page. To modify filter options, highlight the option and click Edit to modify, or Delete to remove it. Click OK to accept your changes and return to the main window.

Printer Driver

The Driver tab shows which print driver is currently being used. This is the same list that you used when you added the printer. If you change the print driver, click OK to accept your changes and return to the main window. Click Apply to restart the printer daemon.

DRIVER OPTIONS

The Driver Options tab displays advanced printer options. Options vary for each print driver. Common options include:

- Select Send Form-Feed (FF) if the last page of your print job is not ejected from the printer (for example, the form feed light flashes). If selecting this option does not force the last page out of the printer, try selecting Send End-of-Transmission (EOT) instead. Some printers require both Send Form-Feed (FF) and Send End-of-Transmission (EOT) to eject the last page.

- Select Send End-of-Transmission (EOT) if sending a form-feed does not work. Refer to Send FF above.

- Select Assume Unknown Data is Text if your print driver does not recognize some of the data sent to it. Select it only if you are having problems printing. If this option is selected, the print driver will assume that any data that it cannot recognize is text and try to print it as text. If you select this option and Convert Text to PostScript, the print driver will assume the unknown data is text and then convert it to PostScript.

- Select Prerender PostScript if you are printing characters beyond the basic ASCII set (such as Japanese characters) but they are not printing correctly. This option will prerender nonstandard PostScript fonts so that they print correctly. If your printer does not support the fonts you are trying to print, try selecting this option. For example, you should select this option if you are printing Japanese fonts to a non-Japanese printer. Extra time is required to perform this action. Do not choose it unless you are having problems printing the correct fonts. You should also select this option if your printer cannot handle PostScript level 3. This option converts it to PostScript level 1.

- Convert Text to Postscript is selected by default. If your printer can print plain text, try unselecting this when printing plain text documents to decrease the time it takes to print.

- Page Size allows you to select the paper size for your printer, such as US Letter, US Legal, A3, and A4.

◆ Effective Filter Locale defaults to C. If you are printing Japanese characters, select ja_JP. Otherwise, accept the default of C.

◆ Media Source defaults to Printer default. Change this option to use paper from a different tray.

If you modify the driver options, click OK to return to the main window. Click Apply to save the changes and restart the printer daemon.

Saving the Configuration File

When you save your printer configuration using the Printer Configuration Tool, it creates its own configuration file, which is used to create the `/etc/printcap` file that the printer daemon (`lpd`) reads. You can use the command-line options to save or restore this file. If you save your `/etc/printcap` file and overwrite your existing `/etc/printcap` file with the saved file, your printer configuration will not be restored. Each time the printer daemon is restarted, it creates a new `/etc/printcap` file from the special Printer Configuration Tool configuration file. If you have configured a backup system for your configuration files, you should use the following method to save your printer configuration. If you added any custom settings in the `/etc/printcap` local file, you should save it as part of your backup system also.

To save your printer configuration, type this command as root:

```
/usr/sbin/redhat-config-printer-tui --Xexport > settings.xml
```

Your configuration is saved to the file `settings.xml`. If you save this file, you can restore your printer settings. This is useful if your printer configuration is deleted, if you reinstall Red Hat Linux and no longer have your printer configuration file, or if you want to use the same printer configuration on multiple systems. To restore the configuration, type this command as root:

```
/usr/sbin/redhat-config-printer-tui --Ximport < settings.xml
```

If you already have a configuration file (you have configured one or more printers on the system already) and you try to import another configuration file, the existing configuration file will be overwritten. If you want to keep your existing configuration and add the configuration in the saved file, you can merge the files with the following command (as root):

```
/usr/sbin/redhat-config-printer-tui --Ximport --merge < settings.xml
```

Your printer list will then consist of the printers you configured on the system as well as the printers you imported from the saved configuration file. If the imported configuration file has a print queue with the same name as an existing print queue on the system, the print queue from the imported file will override the existing printer.

After importing the configuration file (with or without the `merge` command), you must restart the printer daemon by using command `/sbin/service cups restart` or by starting the Printer Configuration Tool and clicking Apply.

Command-Line Configuration

If you do not have X installed and you do not want to use the text-based version of the Printer Configuration Tool, you can add a printer using the command line. This method is useful if you want to add a printer from a script or in the process of a kickstart installation.

Adding a Printer

To add a printer, type this command:

```
redhat-config-printer-tui --Xadd-local options
```

Following are the available options:

--device=node
Required. The device node to use. For example, `/dev/lp0`.

--make=make
Required. The `IEEE 1284 MANUFACTURER` string or the printer manufacturer's name as in the `foomatic` database if the manufacturer string is not available.

--model=model
Required. The `IEEE 1284 MODEL` string or the printer model in the foomatic database if the model string is not available.

--name=name
Optional. The name to be given to the new queue. If one is not given, a name based on the device node (such as `lp0`) will be used.

--as-default
Optional. Set this as the default queue. After adding the printer, use the following command to start/restart the printer daemon:

```
service cups restart
```

Removing a Printer

You can also remove a printer queue with the command line. To remove a printer queue, type the following command:

```
redhat-config-printer-tui --Xremove-local options
```

Following are the available options:

--device=node

Required. The device node used (for example, `/dev/lp0`).

--make=make

Required. The `IEEE 1284 MANUFACTURER` string, or (if none is available) the printer manufacturer's name as in the foomatic database.

--model=model

Required. The `IEEE 1284 MODEL` string, or (if none is available) the printer model as in the foomatic database.

After removing the printer from the Printer Configuration Tool configuration, use the following command to restart the printer daemon for the changes to take effect:

```
service cups restart
```

If you removed all printers and do not want to run the printer daemon anymore, execute the following command:

```
service cups stop
```

Managing Your Print Jobs

When you send a print job to the printer daemon, such as printing a text file from Emacs or printing an image from The GIMP, the print job is added to the print spool queue. The print spool queue is a list of print jobs that have been sent to the printer and information about each print request such as the status of the request, the username of the person who sent the request, the hostname of the system that sent the request, the job number, and more. To view the list of print jobs in the print spool, open a shell prompt and type `lpq`. The last few lines will look similar to the following:

```
Rank     Owner/ID        Class    Job Files     Size    Time
active user@localhost+902  A     902 sample.txt  2050 01:20:46
```

To cancel a print job, find the job number of the request with the command lpq and then use the command lprm job number. For example, lprm 902 would cancel the print job in the previous example. You must have proper permissions to cancel a print job. You cannot cancel print jobs that other users have started unless you are logged in as root on the machine to which the printer is attached.

You can also print a file directly from a shell prompt. For example, the command

```
lpr sample.txt
```

will print the text file sample.txt. The print filter determines what type of file it is and converts it to a format the printer can understand.

If you are using a graphical interface on your desktop, you can start the GNOME Print Manager by clicking on the Print Manager icon on the panel or by selecting it from Main Menu → System Tools. You should see a window similar to Figure 9-13.

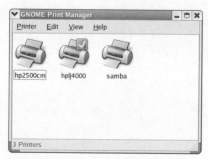

Figure 9-13: The GNOME Print Manager window

To change settings for a printer, right click it and choose Properties from the menu. The Printer Configuration Tool will open. See the section titled "Modifying Existing Printers" in this chapter for instructions on changing printer settings.

To see the print queue for the printer, double click its icon to open the queue page. To cancel a print job, highlight it and choose Edit → Cancel Document.

CUPS Configuration Interface

It is also possible to use a Web browser to configure CUPS. After starting the CUPS daemon, open a Web browser and connect to http://localhost:631 as shown in Figure 9-14.To add a printer, click Manage Printers; then click the Add Printer button. For more information, click the Help button.

To add a printer, click Manage Printers; then click the Add Printer button. For more information, click the Help button.

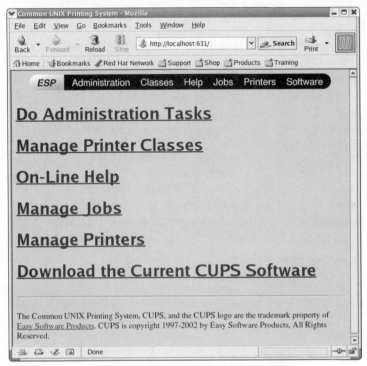

Figure 9-14: The CUPS Web browser configuration screen

Additional Resources

To learn more about printing under Red Hat Linux, refer to the following resources.
Installed documentation:

◆ man printcap — The man page for the /etc/printcap printer configuration file.

◆ man lpr — The man page for the lpr command, which allows you to print files from the command line.

◆ man lpd — The man page for the LPRng printer daemon.

◆ man lprm — The man page for the command-line utility to remove print jobs from the LPRng spool queue.

◆ man mpage — The man page for the command-line utility to print multiple pages on one sheet of paper.

◆ man cupsd — The man page for the CUPS printer daemon.

- ◆ `man cupsd.conf` — The man page for the CUPS printer daemon configuration file.

- ◆ `man classes.conf` — The man page for the class configuration file for CUPS.

Useful Web sites:

- ◆ `http://www.linuxprinting.org` — GNU/Linux Printing contains a large amount of information about printing in Linux.

- ◆ `http://www.cups.org/` — Documentation, FAQs, and pointers to newsgroups about CUPS.

Summary

In this chapter, you learned about the Common Unix Printing System (CUPS). You learned how to configure a printer connected locally to your PC, as well as how to configure several types of networked printers. Also, you looked at modifying and deleting existing printers and learned about the CUPS Web configuration interface. In Chapter 10, you examine the TCP/IP protocol suite and learn how to configure your network.

Chapter 10

TCP/IP Networking

IN THIS CHAPTER

- ◆ TCP/IP explained

- ◆ Understanding network classes

- ◆ Setting up a network interface card (NIC)

- ◆ Understanding subnetting

- ◆ Working with classless InterDomain routing (CIDR)

- ◆ Working with gateways and routers

- ◆ Configuring DHCP

- ◆ Configuring the network with the network configuration tool

- ◆ Configuring IP masquerading

THIS CHAPTER PROVIDES AN OVERVIEW of the TCP/IP protocols as they apply to networking with Red Hat Enterprise Linux. TCP/IP is complex and many books have been written on this topic alone. If you want to learn more about TCP/IP, a good place to start is to use one of the Internet search engines to search for this topic on the Internet. After the description of TCP/IP, this chapter explains how to configure such a network in a Red Hat environment.

TCP/IP Explained

TCP/IP is an acronym for Transmission Control Protocol/Internet Protocol, and refers to a family of protocols used for computer communications. TCP and IP are just two of the separate protocols contained in the group of protocols developed by the Department of Defense, sometimes called the DoD Suite, but more commonly known as TCP/IP.

In addition to Transmission Control Protocol and Internet Protocol, this family also includes Address Resolution Protocol (ARP); Domain Name System (DNS); Internet Control Message Protocol (ICMP); User Datagram Protocol (UDP); Routing Information Protocol (RIP); Simple Mail Transfer Protocol (SMTP); Telnet, and many others. These protocols provide the necessary services for basic network functionality, and you will take a closer look at them for a better understanding of how the network works.

To be able to send and receive information on the network, each device connected to it must have an address. The address of any device on the network must be unique and have a standard, defined format by which it is known to any other device on the network. This device address consists of two parts:

- The address of the network to which the device is connected

- The address of the device itself — its node or host address

Devices that are physically connected to each other (not separated by routers) would have the same network number but different node, or host numbers. This would be typical of an internal network at a company or university. These types of networks are now often referred to as *intranets*.

The two unique addresses I've been talking about are typically called the *network layer* addresses and the *Media Access Control (MAC)* addresses. Network Layer addresses are IP addresses that have been assigned to the device. The MAC address is built into the card by the manufacturer and refers to only the lowest level address by which all data is transferred between devices.

Now that you know a little about addressing, you need to learn how the address, and also the data, is transmitted across the network. This transfer is accomplished by breaking the information into small pieces of data called packets or datagrams. Why is it necessary to use packets instead of just sending the entire message as one long stream of data? There are two reasons for this — sharing resources and error correction.

Let's look at the first, sharing resources. If two computers are communicating with each other, the line is busy. If these computers were sharing a large amount of data, other devices on the network would be unable to transfer their data. When long streams of data are broken into small packets, each packet is sent individually, and the other devices can send their packets between the packets of the long stream. Since each packet is uniquely addressed and has instructions on how to reassemble it, it does not matter that it arrives in small pieces.

The second reason for breaking the data into packets is error correction. Because the data is transmitted across media that is subject to interference, the data can become corrupt. One way to deal with the corruption is to send a checksum along with the data. A checksum is a running count of the bytes sent in the message. The receiving device compares its total to the total transmitted. If these numbers are the same, the data is good; but if they are different, either the checksum or the data itself is corrupt. The receiving device then asks the sender to resend the data. By breaking the data into small packets, each with its own checksum, it is easier to ensure that a good message arrives, and if not, only a small portion needs to be resent instead of the entire message.

In the description of packets, I mentioned unique addressing and reassembly instructions. Because packets also contain data, each is made up of two parts, the *header,* which contains the address and reassembly instructions, and the *body,* which contains the data. Keeping all this information in order is the *protocol*. The protocol is a set of rules that specifies the format of the package and how it is used.

Understanding Network Classes

As stated earlier, all addresses must have two parts, the network part and the node, or host, part. Addresses used in TCP/IP networks are four bytes long, called IP addresses, and are written in standard dot notation, which means a decimal number separated by dots (for example, 192.168.1.2). The decimal numbers must be within the numeric range of 0 to 255 to conform to the one-byte requirement. IP addresses are divided into classes with the most significant being classes A, B, and C depending on the value of the first byte of the address. Table 10-1 shows valid numbers for these classes.

TABLE 10-1 NETWORK CLASSES AND THEIR IP NUMBER RANGE

Class	First Byte
Class A	0–127
Class B	128–191
Class C	192–233

The reason for the class division is to enable efficient use of the address numbers. If the division were the first two bytes to the network part as shown in Table 10-1 and the last two bytes to the host part, then no network could have more than 2^{16} hosts. This would be impractical for large networks and wasteful for small networks.

There are a few ways to assign IP addresses to the devices depending on the purpose of the network. If the network is internal, an intranet, not connected to an outside network, any class A, B, or C network number can be used. The only requirement is choosing a class that allows for the number of hosts to be connected. Although this is possible, in the real world this approach would not allow for connecting to the Internet.

A more realistic approach would be to register with one of the domain registration services and request an officially assigned network number. An organization called the InterNIC maintains a database of all assigned network numbers to ensure that each assignment is unique. After obtaining a network number, the host numbers may be assigned as required. Nearly all IP devices require manual configuration; you will look at assigning IP addresses later when you actually set up your own network. You have now seen that each device has a unique network and node address which is called an IP address. Earlier this was described as the Network Layer address. You also read about the Media Access Control, or MAC, address. The MAC address was defined as the lowest level at which communication occurs. On an Ethernet network, this address is also called the Ethernet Address. This is the address that is ultimately necessary for transmission of data. For transfer to happen, the IP address must be mapped to the Ethernet address of the device. The mechanism that makes this possible is Address Resolution Protocol or ARP.

To determine the Ethernet address of a node on the same network, the sending device sends an ARP request to the Ethernet broadcast address. The Ethernet broadcast address is a special address to which all Ethernet cards are configured to "listen." The ARP request, containing the sender's IP and Ethernet addresses, as well as the IP address it is looking for, asks each device for the Ethernet address that corresponds to a particular IP address. The device whose address matches the request sends a reply to the sender's Ethernet address. The sender is then able to send its data to the specific address it received in response to its ARP request. This process works for sending data between devices on the same network, but what about sending data to devices on different networks? For this you need a router.

Routers enable networks not physically connected to each other to communicate. A router must be connected physically to each network that wants to communicate. The sending node must be able to send its request to a router on its own network, and the receiving node must also be on a network connected to a router. The sending node sends its request to the router on its network. This router is typically called the *default gateway*, and its address must be manually configured in the sending node's configuration files. You will learn how to do this later in this chapter in the "Gateways and Routers" section.

The router receives the request from the sending node and determines the best route for it to use to transmit the data. The router has an internal program, called a *routing table*, which it uses to send the data, either to another router if the other network is not directly connected, or directly to the other network. If the destination network can not be found in the routing table, then the packet is considered undeliverable and is dropped. Typically if the packet is dropped, the router sends an ICMP Destination Unreachable message to the sender.

Routing tables can be manually configured or acquired dynamically. *Manual configuration* means that it is necessary for whoever is setting up the router to provide all the information about other networks and how to reach them. This method is impractical because of the size of the file required and constantly changing information.

Dynamic acquisition means that the router sends a message using the Routing Information Protocol (RIP) or Open Shortest Path First (OSPF) protocol. These dynamic protocols enable routers to share details with other routers concerning networks and their locations.

Ultimately, the purpose of everything you have looked at so far—packets, IP addresses, and routing—is to give users access to services such as printing, file sharing, and email.

You have had a brief look at the IP part of the TCP/IP family of protocols and have arrived at TCP. Transmission Control Protocol is encapsulated in IP packets and provides access to services on remote network devices. TCP is considered to be a stream-oriented reliable protocol. The transmission can be any size because it is broken down into small pieces as you have already seen. Data that is lost is retransmitted, and out-of-order data is reordered. The sender is notified about any data that cannot be delivered. Typical TCP services are File Transfer Protocol (FTP), Telnet, and Simple Mail Transfer Protocol (SMTP).

Setting Up a Network Interface Card (NIC)

Every Red Hat Enterprise Linux distribution includes networking support and tools that can be used to configure your network. In this section you'll learn how to configure a computer for connection to an internal and external network.

Even if the computer is not connected to outside networks, internal network functionality is required for some applications. This address is known as the loopback and its IP address is 127.0.0.1. You should check that this network interface is working before configuring your network cards. To do this, you can use the ifconfig utility to get some information. If you type **ifconfig** at a console prompt, you will be shown your current network interface configuration. Figure 10-1 illustrates the output of the `ifconfig` command.

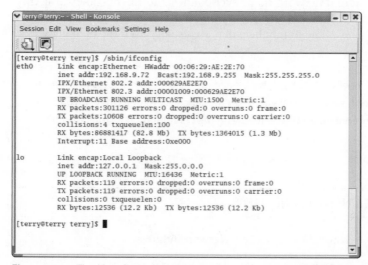

Figure 10-1: The ifconfig utility shows the current network interface configuration.

 TIP Make sure the loopback (IP address 127.0.0.1) is working before you begin to configure your network cards.

If your loopback is configured, the ifconfig shows a device called lo with the address 127.0.0.1. If this device and address are not shown, you can add the device by using the ifconfig command as follows:

```
ifconfig lo 127.0.0.1
```

You then need to use the route command to give the system a little more information about this interface. For this, type:

```
route add -net 127.0.0.0
```

You now have your loopback set up and the ifconfig command shows the device lo in its listing.

Configuring the Network Card

Configuring a network card follows the same procedure as configuring the loopback interface. You use the same command, ifconfig, but this time use the name 'eth0' for an Ethernet device. You also need to know the IP address, the netmask, and the broadcast addresses. These numbers vary depending on the type of network being built. For an internal network that never connects to the outside world, any IP numbers can be used, however there are IP numbers typically used with these networks. Table 10-2 shows the IP numbers that are usually used for such networks.

 The network interface card (NIC), if already installed, is detected and configured during system installation. You should check to determine if your card is already configured before following the configuration instructions in this section.

TABLE 10-2 RESERVED NETWORK NUMBERS

Network Class	Netmask	Network Addresses
A	255.0.0.0	10.0.0.0–10.255.255.255
B	255.255.0.0	172.16.0.0–17.31.255.255
C	255.255.255.0	192.168.0.0–192.168.255.255

If you are connecting to an existing network, you must have its IP address, netmask, and broadcast address. You also need to have the router and domain name server (DNS) addresses.

In this example, you configure an Ethernet interface for an internal network. You need to issue the command:

```
ifconfig eth0 192.168.1.1 netmask 255.255.255.0 broadcast 192.168.1.255
```

This results in the creation of device eth0 with a network address of 192.168.1.1, a netmask of 255.255.255.0, and a broadcast address of 192.168.1.255. A file is created in /etc/sysconfig/network-scripts called ifcfg-eth0. A listing of this file, shown in Figure 10-2, shows the information that you just entered. The line onboot=yes tells the kernel to configure this device at system startup.

If you want to use DHCP to obtain the required IP information for your NIC, see the section "Configuring Dynamic Host Configuration Protocol" later in this chapter.

Figure 10-2: The configuration file for the network device eth0

Configuring an Internal network

/etc/sysconfig/network also needs mentioning. Now you have a network device configured for one computer. To add additional computers to your network you need to repeat this process on the other computers you want to add. The only change is that you need to assign a different IP address. For example, the second computer on your network could have the address 192.168.1.2, the third could have 192.168.1.3, and so on.

This section does not cover the physical requirements for building a network — cabling, hubs, and so forth. A good source for this information is *Network Plus* by David Groth.

In addition to configuring the network cards on each of the computers in the network, four files on each computer need to be modified. These files are all located in the /etc directory and they are:

◆ /etc/hosts.conf

◆ /etc/hosts

◆ /etc/resolv.conf

◆ /etc/sysconfig/network

The /etc/hosts.conf file contains configuration information for the name resolver and should contain the following:

```
order hosts, bind, multi on
```

This configuration tells the name resolver to check the /etc/hosts file before attempting to query a nameserver and to return all valid addresses for a host found in the /etc/hosts file instead of just the first.

The /etc/hosts file could contain the names of all the computers on the local network, or an outside network. For a small network, maintaining this file is not difficult, but for a large network, like the Internet, keeping the file up to date is often impractical. Figure 10-3 shows a network containing two computers. The first two addresses represent the current system, and the other address represents another computer on a different network. In this example, the localhost is my PC in my office at work and the other is a PC on a different network.

The /etc/resolv.conf file provides information about nameservers employed to resolve host names. Figure 10-4 shows a typical resolv.conf file listing.

Chapter 12 discusses Domain Name Servers (DNS).

Figure 10-3: The /etc/hosts file contains a listing of the computers on your network.

Figure 10-4: The /etc/resolv.conf file contains a listing of the domain and nameservers on the network.

The `/etc/sysconfig/network` file contains two lines, as follows:

```
NETWORKING=yes
HOSTNAME=(host and domain name of your system)
```

Understanding Subnetting

You have learned how easy it is to build an internal network, but now you need to learn how to connect to the outside world. A few more steps accomplish outside connection, including configuring a router, obtaining an IP address, and actually making the connection. You begin with obtaining an IP address and subnetting.

Earlier in this chapter you saw that IP addresses used on the Internet are assigned by the InterNIC. Now you will take a closer look at the makeup of IP addresses and how they can be extended through subnetting.

IP numbers are not assigned to hosts; they are assigned to network interfaces on hosts. Even though many computers on an IP network have a single network interface and a single IP number, a single computer can have more than one network interface. In this case, each interface would have its own IP number.

It is also possible to assign more than one IP address to a single NIC. This is accomplished using the `ifconfig` and `route` commands. To add another IP address, 192.168.1.4, to eth0 issue these commands:

```
ifconfig eth0:1 192.168.1.4
route add -host 192.168.1.4 dev eth0
```

The first command binds the IP address to the virtual interface eth0:1 and the second command adds a route for the address to the actual device eth0.

Another method for adding a second IP address to a single NIC is to create an alias file. The configuration file for device eth0 is located in `/etc/sysconfig/network-scripts/ifcfg-eth0`. Copy this file to another file called `/ifcfg-eth0:1` in the same directory. Open the newly copied file and change the line that reads

```
DEVICE=eth0
```

to read

```
DEVICE=eth0:1
```

If you create an alias for your NIC, you cannot use DHCP to obtain your IP information. You must assign static IP addresses to the devices.

Even though this is true, most people refer to host addresses when referring to an IP number. Just remember, this is simply shorthand for the IP number of this particular interface on this host. Many devices on the Internet have only a single interface and thus a single IP number.

In the current (IPv4) implementation, IP numbers consist of 4 (8-bit) bytes for a total of 32 bits of available information. This system results in large numbers, even when they are represented in decimal notation. To make them easier to read and organize, they are written in what is called dotted quad format. The numbers you saw earlier in this chapter were expressed in this format, such as the internal network IP address 192.168.1.1. Each of the four groups of numbers can range from 0 to 255. The following shows the IP number in binary notation with its decimal equivalent. If the bit is set to 1 it is counted, and if set to zero it is not counted.

```
  1  +  1  +  1  +  1  +  1  +  1  +  1  +  1
128 + 64 + 32 + 16 +  8  +  4  +  2  +  1  = 255
```

The binary notation for 192.168.1.1 would be:

```
11000000.10101000.00000001.00000001
```

The dotted quad notation from this binary is:

```
(128+64) = 192.(128+32+8) = 168.(1)=1.(1) = 1
```

The leftmost bits of the IP number of a host identify the network on which the host resides; the remaining bits of the IP number identify the network interface. Exactly how many bits are used by the network ID and how many are available to identify interfaces on that network is determined by the network class. Earlier you learned that there are three classes of networks and you saw how they are composed in Table 10-1.

Class A IP network numbers use the left quad to identify the network, leaving 3 quads to identify host interfaces on that network. Class A addresses always have the farthest left bit of the farthest left byte a zero, so there are a maximum of 128 class A network numbers available, with each one containing up to 33,554,430 possible interfaces.

The network numbers 0.0.0.0, known as the default route, and 127.0.0.0, the loopback network, have special meanings and cannot be used to identify networks. You saw the loopback interface when you set up your internal network. You'll look at the default route when you set up your connection to the Internet. So if you take these two network numbers out, there are only 126 available class A network numbers.

Class B IP network numbers use the two left dotted quads to identify the network, leaving two dotted quads to identify host interfaces. Class B addresses always have the farthest left bits of the left byte set to 10. This leaves 14 bits left to specify the network address giving 32,767 available B class networks. Class B networks have a range of 128 to 191 for the first of the dotted quads, with each network containing up to 32,766 possible interfaces.

Class C IP network numbers use the left three quads to identify the network, leaving the right quad to identify host interfaces. Class C addresses always start with the farthest left 3 bits set to 1 1 0 or a range of 192 to 255 for the farthest left dotted quad. This means that there are 4,194,303 available Class C network numbers, each containing 254 interfaces.

IP addresses are also set aside for internal networks, as you saw in Table 10-2.

Interpreting IP numbers

IP numbers can have three possible meanings. The first of these is an address of a network, which is the number representing all the devices that are physically connected to each other. The second is the broadcast address of the network, which is the address that enables all devices on the network to be contacted. Finally, the last meaning is an actual interface address. Look at a Class C network for an example. For a Class C network:

◆ 192.168.3.0 is a Class C network number

◆ 192.168.3.42 is a host address on this network

◆ 192.168.3.255 is the network broadcast address

When you set up your Ethernet device, eth0, you used the ifconfig utility to pass some information that was written to the ifcg-eth0 file. One of these parameters was the network mask. The network mask is more properly called the *subnetwork mask*. However, it is generally referred to as the *network mask*, or *subnet mask*. The determining factor in subnetting is the network mask and how it is understood on a local network segment. In setting up your network card you used a netmask of 255.255.255.0. In this case, all the network bits were set to one and the host bits were set to zero. This is the standard format for all network masks. Table 10-2 shows the network masks for the three classes of networks.

You should remember two important things about the network mask. The network mask affects only the interpretation of IP numbers on the same network segment, and the network mask is not an IP number, it is used to modify how IP numbers are interpreted by the network.

The network mask affects only the interpretation of IP numbers on the same network segment.

A subnet enables you to use one IP address and split it up so that it can be used on several physically connected local networks. This is a tremendous advantage, as the number of IP numbers available is rapidly diminishing. You can have multiple subnetted networks connected to the outside world with just one IP address. By splitting the IP address, it can be used on sites that need multiple connectivity; splitting the address eliminates the problems of high traffic and difficult manageability.

The other advantages to subnetting are that different network topologies can exist on different network segments within the same organization, and overall network traffic is reduced. Subnetting also enables increased security by separating traffic into local networks. There is a limit to the number of subnets that can be created simply based on the number of times a given number can be divided. Tables 10-3, 10-5, and 10-6 show the possible numbers of subnets and hosts that can exist.

Before You Subnet Your Network

Before you can subnet your network, you need to make some choices and gather some information.

First you need to decide the number of hosts on each of your subnets so you can determine how many IP addresses you need. Earlier in this chapter you set up an Ethernet interface using the reserved internal Class C network number 192.168.1.0. You will continue to use this number for the subnetting example.

Every IP network has two addresses that cannot be used – the network IP number itself and the broadcast address. Whenever you subnetwork the IP network you are creating additional addresses that are unusable. For each subnet you create, two addresses are unusable, the subnet's network IP address and its broadcast address. Every time you subnet you are creating these two unusable addresses, so the more subnets you have, the more IP addresses you lose. The point is that you don't subnet your network more than necessary.

 TIP Don't subnet your network more than necessary.

Next you need to determine the subnetwork mask and network numbers. The network mask for an IP network without subnets is simply a dotted quad that has all the "network bits" of the network number set to '1' and all the host bits set to '0'.

So, for the three classes of IP networks, the standard network masks are shown in Table 10-2.

Subnetworking takes one or more of the available host bits and makes them appear as network bits to the local interfaces. If you wanted to divide your Class C network into two subnetworks, you would change the first host bit to one, and you would get a netmask of 11111111.11111111.11111111.10000000 or 255.255.255.128.

This would give you 126 possible IP numbers for each of our subnets. Remember that you lose two IP addresses for each subnet. If you want to have four subnetworks, you need to change the first two host bits to ones, and this would give you a netmask of 255.255.255.192. You would have 62 IP addresses available on each subnetwork. Table 10-3 shows the subnets, the subnet masks, and the available hosts for your Class C network.

TABLE 10-3 CLASS C SUBNETS AND SUBNET MASKS

Number of Bits	Number of Subnets	Subnet Mask	Number of Hosts
1*	2	255.255.255.128	126
2	4	255.255.255.192	62
3	8	255.255.255.224	30
4	16	255.255.255.240	14
5	32	255.255.255.248	6
6	64	255.255.255.252	2

Now all you need to do is assign the appropriate numbers for the network, the broadcast address, and the IP addresses for each of the interfaces and you're nearly done. Table 10-4 shows these numbers for subnetting your Class C network into two subnets.

TABLE 10-4 CREATING TWO SUBNETS FOR A CLASS C NETWORK ADDRESS

Network	Netmask	Broadcast	First IP	Last IP
192.168.1.0	255.255.255.128	192.168.1.127	192.168.1.1	192.168.1.126
192.168.1.128	255.255.255.128	192.168.1.255	192.168.1.129	192.168.1.254

Creating subnets for Class A and B networks follows the same procedure as that shown for Class C networks. Table 10-5 shows the subnets for a Class A network, and Table 10-6 shows the subnets for a Class B network.

TABLE 10-5 CLASS A SUBNETS AND SUBNET MASKS

Number of Bits	Number of Subnets	Subnet Mask	Number of Hosts
2	2	255.192.0.0	4194302
3	6	255.224.0.0	2097150
4	14	255.240.0.0	1048574
5	30	255.248.0.0	524286
6	62	255.252.0.0	262142
7	126	255.254.0.0	131070
8	254	255.255.0.0	65534
9	510	255.255.128.0	32766
10	1022	255.255.192.0	16382
11	2046	255.255.224.0	8190
12	4094	255.255.240.0	4094
13	8190	255.255.248.0	2046
14	16382	255.255.252.0	1022
15	32766	255.255.254.0	510
16	65534	255.255.255.0	254
17	131070	255.255.255.128	126
18	262142	255.255.255.192	62
19	524286	255.255.255.224	30
20	1048574	255.255.255.240	14
21	2097150	255.255.255.248	6
22	4194302	255.255.255.252	2

TABLE 10-6 CLASS B SUBNETS AND SUBNET MASKS

Number of Bits	Number of Subnets	Subnet Mask	Number of Hosts
2	2	255.255.192.0	16382
3	6	255.255.224.0	8190
4	14	255.255.240.0	4094
5	30	255.255.248.0	2046
6	62	255.255.252.0	1022
7	126	255.255.254.0	510
8	254	255.255.255.0	254
9	510	255.255.255.128	126
10	1022	255.255.255.192	62
11	2046	255.255.255.224	30
12	4094	255.255.255.240	14
13	8190	255.255.255.248	6
14	16382	255.255.255.252	2

Classless InterDomain Routing (CIDR)

CIDR was invented several years ago to keep the Internet from running out of IP addresses. The class system of allocating IP addresses can be very wasteful. Anyone who could reasonably show a need for more than 254 host addresses was given a Class B address block of 65,533 host addresses. Even more wasteful was allocating companies and organizations Class A address blocks, which contain over 16 million host addresses! Only a tiny percentage of the allocated Class A and Class B address space has ever been actually assigned to a host computer on the Internet.

People realized that addresses could be conserved if the class system was eliminated. By accurately allocating only the amount of address space that was actually needed, the address space crisis could be avoided for many years. This solution was first proposed in 1992 as a scheme called *supernetting*. Under supernetting, the class subnet masks are extended so that a network address and subnet mask could, for example, specify multiple Class C subnets with one address. For example, if you needed about a thousand addresses, you could supernet 4 Class C networks together:

```
192.60.128.0   (11000000.00111100.10000000.00000000)  Class C subnet address
192.60.129.0   (11000000.00111100.10000001.00000000)  Class C subnet address
192.60.130.0   (11000000.00111100.10000010.00000000)  Class C subnet address
192.60.131.0   (11000000.00111100.10000011.00000000)  Class C subnet address
---------------------------------------------------------
192.60.128.0   (11000000.00111100.10000000.00000000)  Supernetted Subnet address
255.255.252.0  (11111111.11111111.11111100.00000000)  Subnet Mask
192.60.131.255 (11000000.00111100.10000011.11111111)  Broadcast address
```

In this example, the subnet 192.60.128.0 includes all the addresses from 192.60.128.0 to 192.60.131.255. As you can see in the binary representation of the subnet mask, the network portion of the address is 22 bits long, and the host portion is 10 bits long.

Under CIDR, the subnet mask notation is reduced to simplified shorthand. Instead of spelling out the bits of the subnet mask, the number of 1s bits that start the mask are simply listed. In the example, instead of writing the address and subnet mask as

```
192.60.128.0, Subnet Mask 255.255.252.0
```

the network address is written simply as:

```
192.60.128.0/22
```

This address indicates starting address of the network, and number of 1s bits (22) in the network portion of the address. If you look at the subnet mask in binary, you can easily see how this notation works.

```
(11111111.11111111.11111100.00000000)
```

The use of a CIDR-notated address is the same as for a Class address. Class addresses can easily be written in CIDR notation (Class A = /8, Class B = /16, and Class C = /24).

It is currently almost impossible for you, as an individual or company, to be allocated your own IP address blocks. You will be told simply to get them from your ISP. The reason for this is the ever-growing size of the Internet routing table. Just five years ago, there were less than 5,000 network routes in the entire Internet. Today, there are over 100,000. Using CIDR, the biggest ISPs are allocated large chunks of address space, usually with a subnet mask of /19 or even smaller. The ISP's customers, often other, smaller ISPs, are then allocated networks from the big ISP's pool. That way, all the big ISP's customers, and their customers, are accessible via one network route on the Internet.

CIDR will probably keep the Internet happily in IP addresses for the next few years at least. After that, IPv6, with 128 bit addresses, will be needed. Under IPv6, even careless address allocation would comfortably enable a billion unique IP addresses for every person on earth! The complete details of CIDR are documented in RFC1519, which was released in September 1993.

 Requests for Comment (RFC) are documents containing information about computer networking and many areas of the Internet. If you want to learn more about RFCs, check out `ftp://ftp.rfc-editor.org/in-notes/rfc2555.txt`.

Gateways and Routers

You have successfully created two subnets from your Class C network, but the individual network segments cannot communicate with each other yet. You still have to configure a path for them; you do this by using a router. Earlier in this chapter, you learned that a router is necessary for separate networks to communicate with each other. You also learned that each network must be connected to a router in order for this communication to take place. This router connected to each network is called its *gateway*.

In Linux, you can use a computer with two network interfaces to route between two or more subnets. To be able to do this you need to make sure that you enable IP Forwarding. All current Linux distributions have IP Forwarding compiled as a module, so all you need to do is make sure the module is loaded. You can check this by entering the following query at a command prompt:

```
cat /proc/sys/net/ipv4/ip_forward
```

If forwarding is enabled, the number 1 is returned; if forwarding is not enabled, the number 0 is returned.

To enable IP forwarding if it is not already enabled, type the following command:

```
echo "1" > /proc/sys/net/ipv4/ip_forward
```

Continue your setup using the two subnets you previously created with the information in Table 10-4.

Assume that a computer running Linux is acting as a router for your network. It has two network interfaces to the local LANs using the lowest available IP address in each subnetwork on its interface to that network. The network interfaces would be configured as shown in Table 10-7.

TABLE 10-7 NETWORK INTERFACE CONFIGURATION

Interface	IP Address	Netmask
Eth0	192.168.1.1	255.255.255.128
Eth1	192.168.1.129	255.255.255.128

The network routing the system would use is shown in Table 10-8.

TABLE 10-8 NETWORK ROUTING CONFIGURATION

Destination	Gateway	Mask	Interface
192.168.1.0	192.168.1.1	255.255.255.128	eth0
192.168.1.128	192.168.1.129	255.255.255.128	eth1

You're nearly finished now, just one more step. Each computer on the subnet has to show the IP address for the interface that is its gateway to the other network. The computers on the first subnet, the 192.168.1.0 network, would have the gateway 192.168.1.1. Remember that you used the first IP address on this network for the gateway computer. The computers on the second subnet, 192.168.1.128, would use 192.168.1.129 as the gateway address. You can add this information using the route command as follows:

```
route add -net 192.168.1.0
```

and then type

```
route add default gw 192.168.1.129
```

This command sets up the route for local (internal) routing as well as sets up the external route for our first subnet. You need to repeat the previous commands, substituting the appropriate numbers for the second subnet and any additional subnets. You have now successfully set up two subnets and established communication between them. Next you'll look at connecting to the Internet.

Configuring Dynamic Host Configuration Protocol (DHCP)

So far, you have learned to configure a network card and assign it an IP address, subnet mask, broadcast address, and gateway. Using DHCP, you can have an IP address and the other information automatically assigned to the hosts connected to your network. This method is quite efficient and convenient for large networks with many hosts, because the process of manually configuring each host is quite time consuming. By using DHCP, you can ensure that every host on your network has a valid IP address, subnet mask, broadcast address, and gateway, with minimum effort on your part.

You should have a DHCP server configured for each of your subnets. Each host on the subnet needs to be configured as a DHCP client. You may also need to configure the server that connects to your ISP as a DHCP client if your ISP dynamically assigns your IP address.

Configuring a DHCP Client

The first step in configuring a DHCP client is to make sure the kernel recognizes the network interface card. Most cards are recognized during the installation process, and the system is configured to use the correct kernel module for the card. If you install a card after installation, Kudzu should recognize it and prompt you to configure the corresponding kernel module for it. Be sure to check the Red Hat Linux Hardware Compatibility List at `http://hardware.redhat.com/hcl/`.

To configure a DHCP client manually, you need to modify the `/etc/sysconfig/network` file to enable networking and the configuration file for each network device in the `/etc/sysconfig/network-scripts` directory. In this directory, each device should have a configuration file named `ifcfg-eth0`, where `eth0` is the network device name. The `/etc/sysconfig/network` file should contain the following line:

```
NETWORKING=yes
```

You might have more information in this file, but the `NETWORKING` variable must be set to `yes` if you want networking to start at boot time. The `/etc/sysconfig/network-scripts/ifcfg-eth0` file should contain the following lines:

```
DEVICE=eth0
BOOTPROTO=dhcp
ONBOOT=yes
```

You need a configuration file for each device that you want to configure to use DHCP. If you prefer a graphical interface for configuring a DHCP client, refer to

Chapter 13 for details on using Network Configurator to configure a network interface to use DHCP.

Configuring a DHCP Server

You can configure a DHCP server using the configuration file `/etc/dhcpd.conf`. DHCP also uses the file `/var/lib/dhcp/dhcpd.leases` to store the client lease database. Refer to the "Lease Database" section of this chapter for more information.

The first step in configuring a DHCP server is to create the configuration file that stores the network information for the clients. Global options can be declared for all clients, or options can be declared for each client system. The configuration file can contain any extra tabs or blank lines for easier formatting. The keywords are case-insensitive, and lines beginning with a hash mark (#) are considered comments.

Two DNS update schemes are currently implemented – the ad hoc DNS update mode and the interim DHCP-DNS interaction draft update mode. When these two are accepted as part of the IETF standards process, there will be a third mode – the standard DNS update method. The DHCP server must be configured to use one of the two current schemes. Version 3.0b2pl11 and previous versions used the ad hoc mode; however, it has been deprecated. If you want to keep the same behavior, add the following line to the top of the configuration file:

```
ddns-update-style ad-hoc;
```

To use the recommended mode, add the following line to the top of the configuration file:

```
ddns-update-style interim;
```

Read the `dhcpd.conf` man page for details about the different modes. There are two types of statements in the configuration file:

- Parameters – State how to perform a task, whether to perform a task, or what network configuration options to send to the client.

- Declarations – Describe the topology of the network, describe the clients, provide addresses for the clients, or apply a group of parameters to a group of declarations.

Some parameters must start with the `option` keyword and are referred to as options. Options configure DHCP options, whereas parameters configure values that are not optional or control how the DHCP server behaves. Parameters (including options) declared before a section enclosed in curly braces (`{ }`) are considered global parameters. Global parameters apply to all the sections that follow them.

If you change the configuration file, the changes will not take effect until you restart the DHCP daemon with the command `service dhcpd restart`.

In Listing 10-1, the `routers`, `subnet-mask`, `domain-name`, `domain-name-servers`, and `time-offset` options are used for any host statements declared below them. As shown in Listing 10-1, you can declare a subnet. You must include a `subnet` declaration for every subnet in your network. If you do not, the DHCP server will fail to start. In this example, there are global options for every DHCP client in the subnet and a range declared. Clients are assigned an IP address within the range.

Listing 10-1: Subnet declaration

```
subnet 192.168.1.0 netmask 255.255.255.0 {
        option routers 192.168.1.254;
        option subnet-mask 255.255.255.0;

        option domain-name "example.com";
        option domain-name-servers 192.168.1.1;

        option time-offset -18000; # Eastern Standard Time

 range 192.168.1.10 192.168.1.100;
}
```

All subnets that share the same physical network should be declared within a `shared-network` declaration as shown in Listing 10-2. Parameters within the shared network but outside the enclosed subnet declarations are considered global parameters. The name of the shared network should be a descriptive title for the network such as `test-lab` to describe all the subnets in a test lab environment.

Listing 10-2: Shared-network declaration

```
shared-network name {
      option domain-name "test.redhat.com";
      option domain-name-servers ns1.redhat.com, ns2.redhat.com;
      option routers 192.168.1.254;
      more parameters for EXAMPLE shared-network
      subnet 192.168.1.0 netmask 255.255.255.0 {
          parameters for subnet
          range 192.168.1.1 192.168.1.31;
}
        subnet 192.168.1.32 netmask 255.255.255.0 {
            parameters for subnet
```

```
        range 192.168.1.33 192.168.1.63;
    }
}
```

As demonstrated in Listing 10-3, the group declaration can be used to apply global parameters to a group of declarations. You can group shared networks, subnets, hosts, or other groups.

Listing 10-3: Group declaration

```
group {
    option routers                          192.168.1.254;
    option subnet-mask                      255.255.255.0;

    option domain-name                      "example.com";
    option domain-name-servers               192.168.1.1;

    option time-offset   -18000;      # Eastern Standard Time

    host apex {
            option host-name "apex.example.com";
            hardware ethernet 00:A0:78:8E:9E:AA;
            fixed-address 192.168.1.4;
    }

    host raleigh {
            option host-name "raleigh.example.com";
            hardware ethernet 00:A1:DD:74:C3:F2;
            fixed-address 192.168.1.6;
    }
}
```

To configure a DHCP server that leases a dynamic IP address to a system within a subnet, modify the Range Parameter section of the dhcpd.conf file with your values. Listing 10-4 shows a default lease time, maximum lease time, and network configuration values for the clients. This example assigns IP addresses in the range between 192.168.1.10 and 192.168.1.100 to client systems.

Listing 10-4: Range parameter

```
default-lease-time 600;
max-lease-time 7200;
option subnet-mask 255.255.255.0;
option broadcast-address 192.168.1.255;
option routers 192.168.1.254;
```

Continued

Listing 10-4 *(Continued)*

```
option domain-name-servers 192.168.1.1, 192.168.1.2;
option domain-name "example.com";

subnet 192.168.1.0 netmask 255.255.255.0 {
    range 192.168.1.10 192.168.1.100;
}
```

To assign an IP address to a client based on the MAC address of the network interface card, use the hardware ethernet parameter within a host declaration. As demonstrated in Listing 10-5, the host apex declaration specifies that the network interface card with the MAC address 00:A0:78:8E:9E:AA always receives the IP address 192.168.1.4. Notice that you can also use the optional parameter host-name to assign a hostname to the client.

Listing 10-5: Static IP address using DHCP

```
host apex {
        option host-name "apex.example.com";
        hardware ethernet 00:A0:78:8E:9E:AA;
        fixed-address 192.168.1.4;
}
```

You can use the sample configuration file in Red Hat Linux as a starting point and add your own custom configuration options to it. Copy it to its proper location with the command cp /usr/share/doc/dhcp-version-number/ dhcpd.conf.sample /etc/dhcpd.conf (where version-number is the DHCP version you are using).

For a complete list of option statements and what they do, refer to the dhcp-options man page.

Lease Database

On the DHCP server, the file /var/lib/dhcp/dhcpd.leases stores the DHCP client lease database. This file should not be modified manually. DHCP lease information for each recently assigned IP address is automatically stored in the lease database. The information includes the length of the lease to whom the IP address has been assigned, the start and end dates for the lease, and the MAC address of the network interface card that was used to retrieve the lease.

All times in the lease database are in Greenwich Mean Time (GMT), not local time. The lease database is recreated from time to time so that it is not too large. All known leases are saved in a temporary lease database. The `dhcpd.leases` file is renamed `dhcpd.leases~`, and the temporary lease database is written to `dhcpd.leases`.

The DHCP daemon could be killed or the system could crash after the lease database has been renamed to the backup file but before the new file has been written. If this happens, there is no `dhcpd.leases` file, which is required to start the service. Do not create a new lease file if this occurs. If you do, all the old leases will be lost, and this will cause many problems. The correct solution is to rename the `dhcpd.leases~` backup file to `dhcpd.leases` and to start the daemon.

TIP Before you start the DHCP server for the first time, it will fail unless there is an existing `dhcpd.leases` file. Use the command `touch /var/lib/dhcp/dhcpd.leases` to create the file if it does not exist.

Starting and Stopping the Server

To start the DHCP service, use the command `/sbin/service dhcpd start`. To stop the DHCP server, use the command `/sbin/service dhcpd stop`. If you want the daemon to start automatically at boot time, see Chapter 21 for information on how to manage services.

If you have more than one network interface attached to the system, but you want the DHCP server to start on only one interface, you can configure the DHCP server to start only on that device. In `/etc/sysconfig/dhcpd`, add the name of the interface to the list of `DHCPDARGS`:

```
# Command line options here

DHCPDARGS=eth0
```

This is useful if you have a firewall machine with two network cards. One network card can be configured as a DHCP client to retrieve an IP address to the Internet. The other network card can be used as a DHCP server for the internal network behind the firewall. Specifying only the network card connected to the internal network makes the system more secure because users cannot connect to the daemon via the Internet.

Other command-line options that can be specified in `/etc/sysconfig/dhcpd` are:

◆ `-p portnum` — Specify the udp port number on which `dhcpd` should listen. The default is port 67. The DHCP server transmits responses to the DHCP clients at a port number one greater than the udp port specified. For example, if you accept the default of port 67, the server listens on port 67 for requests and on port 68 for responses to the client. If you specify a port here and use the DHCP relay agent, you must specify the same port on which the DHCP relay agent should listen. See the "DHCP Relay Agent" section of this chapter for details.

◆ `-f` — Run the daemon as a foreground process. This is used mostly for debugging.

◆ `-d` — Log the DHCP server daemon to the standard error descriptor. This is used mostly for debugging. If this is not specified, the log is written to `/var/log/messages`.

◆ `-cf filename` — Specify the location of the configuration file. The default location is `/etc/dhcpd.conf`.

◆ `-lf filename` — Specify the location of the lease database file. If a lease database file already exists, it is very important that the same file be used every time the DHCP server is started. It is strongly recommended that this option be used only for debugging purposes on nonproduction machines. The default location is `/var/lib/dhcp/dhcpd.leases`.

◆ `-q` — Do not print the entire copyright message when starting the daemon.

DHCP Relay Agent

The DHCP Relay Agent allows you to relay DHCP and BOOTP requests from a subnet with no DHCP server on it to one or more DHCP servers on other subnets. When a DHCP client requests information, the DHCP Relay Agent forwards the request to the list of DHCP servers specified when the DHCP Relay Agent is started. When a DHCP server returns a reply, the reply is broadcast or unicast on the network that sent the original request. The DHCP Relay Agent listens for DHCP requests on all interfaces unless the interfaces are specified in `/etc/sysconfig/dhcrelay` with the `INTERFACES` directive. To start the DHCP Relay Agent, use the command `service dhcrelay start`.

Configuring the Network Using the Network Configuration Tool

Red Hat provides a graphical network configuration tool that you can use to configure network interface devices installed in your system. With this tool, you can configure CIPE, Ethernet, ISDN, Modem, Token Ring, Wireless, and xDSL devices. This section will cover the most common types of devices, Ethernet and modem. The Network Configuration Tool can be accessed using the menus from both GNOME and KDE, but the easiest way to start it from either desktop is from a terminal window. To start the Network Configuration Tool, enter `redhat-config-network` at a shell prompt. The window shown in Figure 10-5 will appear.

Figure 10-5: The Red Hat Network Configuration Tool main window

The main Network Configuration Tool window shown in Figure 10-5 has four tabbed pages and shows the Devices tab when the tool is started. As you can see from the figure, the Devices tab shows that the network device eth0 is active, is an ethernet device, and is already configured. The tabs allow you to further configure the devices.

 If you had a supported network interface card (NIC) installed on your system during installation of Red Hat Linux, your NIC should already be listed in the network configuration tool. Click the Hardware tab to see information about the device.

Adding an Ethernet Device

To add an ethernet device, click the New button from the toolbar, choose Ethernet connection from the Select Device Type list, and click Forward. If your NIC is shown in the Select Ethernet Device list, select it and click Forward to go to the Configure Network Settings window shown in Figure 10-7.

If your NIC is not listed, choose Other Ethernet Card and click Forward to open the Select Ethernet Adapter window as shown in Figure 10-6.

Select your card from the drop-down list in the Adapter field. If your adapter is not listed, it is an unsupported card. After choosing your card, choose the device name from the drop-down list in the Device field. You should choose eth0 for the first device, eth1 for the second, eth2 for the third, and so on. You can also enter the system resources that the adapter will use if desired. Usually, this is not necessary. Click Forward to continue to the Configure Network Settings window shown in Figure 10-7.

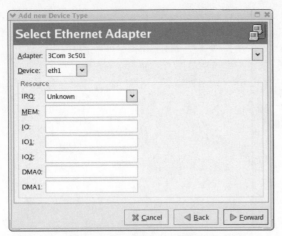

Figure 10-6: The Select Ethernet Adapter window

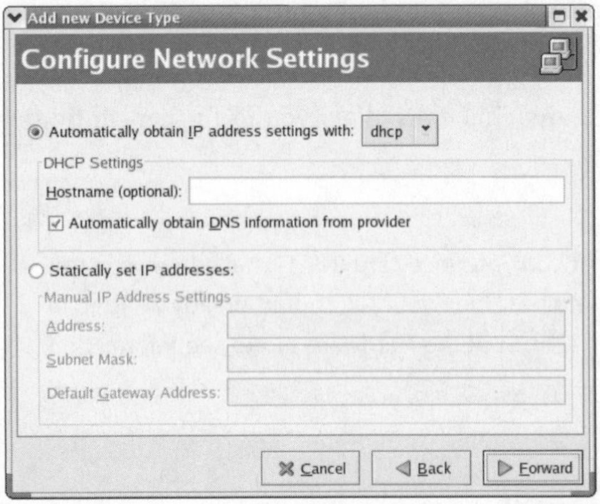

Figure 10-7: The Configure Network Settings window

In this window, you can choose whether you want to use DHCP to automatically obtain your IP address or if you want to enter a static IP address. If you choose to set your address statically, you must enter the IP address, the network mask, and the address of the default gateway. After you have made the appropriate entries, click Forward. Next, you will see a listing of your selected information. If you are satisfied with your choices, click Apply to create the device. If you want to make changes, click Back to go back to the desired window and make changes. After you click Apply, the device is created and will appear in the device list.

Although the device has been configured and added to the list of devices, it is inactive as can be seen from the device listing. By default, the device will start at boot time, but you can activate it immediately by highlighting it and then clicking the Activate button from the menu bar at the top of the window.

To edit your device configurations, highlight the device you want to edit and click the Edit button from the menu bar. Make the changes you desire and then click OK to accept your edits. You should save your configuration by clicking on File → Save after making any changes.

Adding a Modem Connection

To add a modem, click on the New button from the toolbar, choose Modem connection from the Select Device Type list, and click Forward. The configuration tool will probe your system to try to detect a modem.

 If you had a modem installed on your system during installation of Red Hat Linux, your modem should already be listed in the network configuration tool. Click the Hardware tab to see information about the device.

If you have a modem in your hardware list, the configuration tool will use that modem and will open the Select Modem window shown in Figure 10-8, with values appropriate for the modem. If no modem is found, a message will appear, stating that no modem was found. The Select Modem window shown in Figure 10-8 will appear, but the values may not be correct for the modem you have installed.

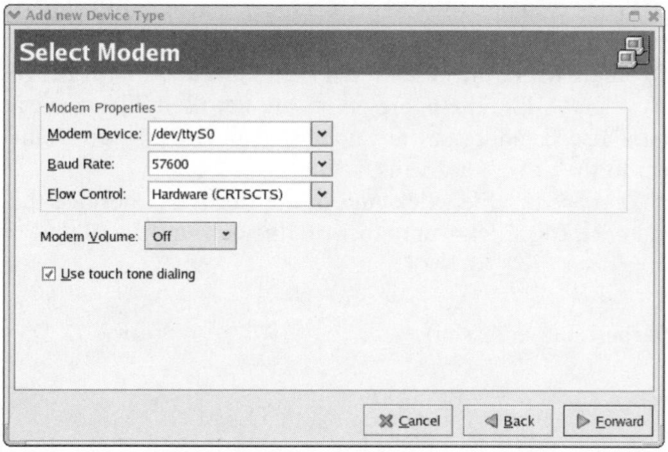

Figure 10-8: The Select Modem window

If your modem was successfully probed, you can accept the default vales for modem device, baud rate, flow control, and modem volume; otherwise, enter the values appropriate for your modem. If you don't have touch-tone dialing, remove the checkmark from the use touch tone dialing box. When you are satisfied with the settings, click Forward.

The next window to appear is the Select Provider window. Here you need to enter the name of your ISP and the telephone number you will dial to connect. Enter your login name and password that were given to you by your ISP.

Click Forward to go to the IP Settings page. Most likely, you can accept the default setting here to obtain IP addressing information automatically. Click Forward to continue.

Next, you will see a listing of your selected information. If you are satisfied with your choices, click Apply to create the device. If you want to make changes, click Back to go back to the desired window and make changes. After you click Apply, the device is created and will appear in the device list.

Although the device has been configured and added to the list of devices, it is inactive as can be seen from the device listing. By default, the device will start at boot time, but you can activate it immediately by highlighting it and then clicking the Activate button from the menu bar at the top of the window.

To edit your device configurations, highlight the device you want to edit and click the Edit button from the menu bar. Make the changes you desire and then click OK to accept your edits. You should save your configuration by clicking File → Save after making any changes.

Managing Hosts

The Hosts tab of the network configuration tool allows you to add, edit, or remove hosts to or from the /etc/hosts file. This file contains IP addresses and their corresponding hostnames. When your system tries to resolve a hostname to an IP address or determine the hostname for an IP address, it refers to the /etc/hosts file before using the nameservers (if you are using the default Red Hat configuration). If the IP address is listed in the /etc/hosts file, the nameservers are not used. If your network contains computers whose IP addresses are not listed in DNS, it is recommended that you add them to the /etc/hosts file.

To add an entry to the /etc/hosts file, click Add in the Hosts tab, provide the requested information, and click OK. Click Apply to write the entry to the file.

 Do not remove the localhost entry.

To change lookup order, edit the /etc/host.conf file. The line order hosts, bind specifies that the /etc/hosts file takes precedence over the nameservers. Changing the line to order bind, hosts configures your system to resolve hostnames and IP addresses using the nameservers first. If the IP address cannot be resolved through the nameservers, your system looks for the IP address in the /etc/hosts file.

Managing DNS Settings

The DNS tab of the network configuration tool allows you to configure the system's hostname, domain, nameservers, and search domain. Nameservers are used to look up other hosts on the network.

The nameservers section does not configure the system to be a nameserver.

If the DNS server names are retrieved from DHCP (or retrieved from the ISP of a modem connection), do not add primary, secondary, or tertiary DNS servers.

Working with Profiles

Multiple logical network devices can be created for each physical hardware device. For example, if you have one Ethernet card in your system (eth0), you can create logical network devices with different nicknames and different configuration options, all associated with eth0. Logical network devices are different from device aliases. Logical network devices associated with the same physical device must exist in different profiles and cannot be activated simultaneously. Device aliases are also associated with the same physical hardware device, but device aliases associated with the same physical hardware can be activated at the same time. Refer to the "Device Aliases" section of this chapter for details about creating device aliases.

Profiles can be used to create multiple configuration sets for different networks. A configuration set can include logical devices as well as hosts and DNS settings. After configuring the profiles, you can use the network administration tool to switch back and forth between them.

By default, there is one profile called Common. To create a new profile, click the New button in the Active Profile frame. Enter a unique name for the profile. After creating a new profile, if all the devices are not listed for all the profiles, add them by clicking the Add button. If a device already exists for the physical device, use the Copy button to copy the existing device. If you use the Add button, a network alias will be created, which is not correct. The device name should not end with a colon followed by a number.

In the list of devices, there is a column of checkboxes labeled Profile. For each profile, you can check or uncheck devices. Only the checked devices are included for the currently selected profile.

A profile cannot be activated at boot time. Only the devices in the Common profile, which are set to activate at boot time, are activated at boot time. After the system has booted, execute the following command to enable a profile (replace *profilename* with the name of the profile):

```
redhat-config-network-cmd --profile profilename
```

Device Aliases

Device aliases are virtual devices associated with the same physical hardware, but they can be activated at the same time to have different IP addresses. They are commonly represented as the device name followed by a colon and a number (for example, eth0:1). They are useful if you want to have more than one IP address for a system but the system has only one network card.

If you have configured a device such as eth0, click the Edit button for the device in the network administration tool and click the Hardware tab. To create an alias for the device, click the checkbox in front of Device Alias Number and choose the number you desire. Click OK and the alias will appear in the device list with a device name followed by a colon and the alias number.

 If you are configuring an Ethernet device to have an alias, neither the device nor the alias can be configured to use DHCP. You must configure the IP addresses manually.

Select the alias and click the Activate button to activate the alias. If you have configured multiple profiles, select which profiles in which to include it. To verify that the alias has been activated, use the command /sbin/ifconfig. The output should show the device and the device alias with a different IP address as shown in Listing 10-6.

Listing 10-6: Output from the /sbin/ifconfig command

```
eth0      Link encap:Ethernet    HWaddr 00:A0:CC:60:B7:G4
          inet addr:192.168.100.5      Bcast:192.168.100.255
Mask:255.255.255.0
          UP BROADCAST RUNNING MULTICAST      MTU:1500    Metric:1
```

```
        RX packets:161930 errors:1 dropped:0 overruns:0 frame:0
        TX packets:244570 errors:0 dropped:0 overruns:0 carrier:0
        collisions:475 txqueuelen:100
        RX bytes:55075551 (52.5 Mb)      TX bytes:178108895 (169.8 Mb)
        Interrupt:10 Base address:0x9000

eth0:1   Link encap:Ethernet    HWaddr 00:A0:CC:60:B7:G4
         inet addr:192.168.100.42      Bcast:192.168.100.255
Mask:255.255.255.0
         UP BROADCAST RUNNING MULTICAST     MTU:1500    Metric:1
         Interrupt:10 Base address:0x9000

lo       Link encap:Local Loopback
         inet addr:127.0.0.1    Mask:255.0.0.0
         UP LOOPBACK RUNNING    MTU:16436    Metric:1
         RX packets:5998 errors:0 dropped:0 overruns:0 frame:0
         TX packets:5998 errors:0 dropped:0 overruns:0
carrier:0
         collisions:0 txqueuelen:0
         RX bytes:1627579 (1.5 Mb)      TX bytes:1627579 (1.5 Mb)
```

Configuring IP Masquerading

So far, you have configured an internal network consisting of two subnets, and you configured a router for connectivity between the networks. Assuming that you made the connection to the Internet through your router, you need to make only a few configuration changes and every computer on your network can connect to the Internet through your one connection. To use a single Internet connection for multiple computers, you need to use *IP masquerading.* IP masquerading enables you to connect a TCP/IP network to the outside world using a single server and a single IP address.

Current Red Hat distributions make IP masquerading available as a module, so you need only load the module and enable the appropriate configuration. You already enabled IP forwarding when you configured your router, so you need to consider only one more item, a utility called iptables, which sets up a simple packet filtering firewall.

To learn about securing your Red Hat system for the Internet, see Chapter 31.

The iptables utility gives you enough protection for now. To set up masquerading, type the following commands:

```
iptables -P forward DENY
iptables -A forward -s 192.168.0.0/24 -j MASQ -d 0.0.0.0/0
```

Those commands are all that needs to be done to enable the firewall rules and to start masquerading.

Of course you want IP masquerading enabled whenever you boot the computer, so it's a good idea to make a script file that enables IP forwarding as well as the iptables utility. This file would ensure that forwarding and masquerading start each time the machine boots.

Be sure to include the command to start IP forwarding (shown earlier in this chapter) as well as the iptables commands shown previously.

Summary

In this chapter, you learned about the TCP/IP protocol suite and how it works to enable communication across networks. Then you learned how to configure a network interface card. You used subnetting to create two internal subnetworks and configured a router so the subnetworks could communicate with each other. You set up a Dynamic Host Configuration Protocol server to assign IP addresses to the hosts on the network. You also enabled forwarding and masquerading so that every computer on your internal network could have Internet access.

Chapter 11

The Network File System

RED HAT ENTERPRISE LINUX SERVERS are often installed to provide centralized file and print services for networks. This chapter explains how to use the Network File System (NFS) to create a file server. After a short overview of NFS, you learn how to plan an NFS installation, how to configure an NFS server, and how to set up an NFS client. You'll learn how to mount remote file systems automatically, eliminating the requirement specifically to mount nonlocal file systems before they are accessed. The final section of the chapter teaches you how to mount a system's root file system over NFS by passing the appropriate command line option to the Linux kernel at boot time.

NFS Overview

NFS is the most common method used to share files across Linux and Unix networks. It is a distributed file system that enables local access to remote disks and file systems. Indeed, in a properly designed and implemented NFS environment, NFS's operation is totally transparent to clients using remote file systems. Provided that you have the appropriate network connection, you can access files and directories that are physically located on another system or even in a different city or country using standard Linux commands. No special procedures, such as using a password, are necessary. NFS is a common and popular file sharing protocol, so NFS clients are available for many non-Unix operating systems, including the various Windows versions, MacOS, OS/2, VAX/VMS, and MVS.

Understanding NFS

NFS follows standard client/server architectural principles. The server component of NFS consists of the physical disks that contain the file systems you want to share and several daemons that make these shared file systems visible to and available for use by client systems on the network. When an NFS server is sharing a file system in this manner, it is said to be *exporting a file system*. Similarly, the shared file system is referred to as an *NFS export*. The NFS server daemons provide remote access to the exported file systems, enable file locking over the network, and, optionally, allow the server administrator to set and enforce disk quotas on the NFS exports.

On the client side of the equation, an NFS client simply mounts the exported file systems locally, just as local disks would be mounted. The mounted file system is known colloquially as an *NFS mount*.

The possible uses of NFS are quite varied. NFS is often used to provide diskless clients, such as X terminals or the slave nodes in a cluster, with their entire file system, including the kernel image and other boot files.

By far the most common use of NFS is storage for user home directories. Many sites store users' home directories on a central server and use NFS to mount the home directory when users log in or boot their systems. Usually, the exported directories are mounted as /home/username on the local (client) systems, but the export itself can be stored anywhere on the NFS server, for example, /exports/users/ username. Another common scheme is to export public data or project-specific directories from an NFS server and to enable clients to mount these remote file systems anywhere they see fit on the local system. Figure 11-1 illustrates both of these NFS uses.

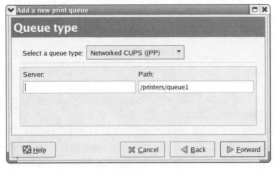

Figure 11-1: Exporting home directories and project-specific file systems

The network shown in Figure 11-1 shows a server (suppose its name is diskbeast) with 2 sets of NFS exports, user home directories in /exports/homes (/exports/ homes/u1, /exports/homes/u2, and so on) and a project directory named /proj. Figure 11-1 also illustrates a number of client systems (pear, apple, mango, and so forth). Each client system mounts /home from diskbeast. On diskbeast, the exported file systems are stored in the /exports/homes directory.

When users log in to any given system, that user's home directory is automatically mounted on /home/username on that system. So, for example, when user u1 logs in on pear, /exports/homes/u1 is mounted on pear's file system as /home/u1 (often written in host:/mount/dir format, for example, pear:/home/u1). If u1 then logs in on mango, too (not illustrated in the figure), mango also mounts /home/u1. Logging in on two systems this way is potentially dangerous because changes to files in the exported file system made from one login session might adversely affect the other login session. Despite the potential for unintended consequences, it is also very convenient for such changes to be immediately visible.

Figure 11-1 also shows that three users, u5, u6, and u7, have mounted the project-specific file system, /proj, in various locations on their local file systems. Specifically, user u5 has mounted it as /work/proj on kiwi (that is, kiwi:/work/proj in host:/mount/dir form) u6 as lime:/projects, and u7 as peach:/home/work.

NFS can be used in almost any situation requiring transparent local access to remote file systems. In fact, you can use NFS and NIS (Chapter 12, "The Network Information System," covers NIS in depth) together to create a highly centralized network environment that makes it easier to administer the network, add and delete user accounts, protect and back up key data and file systems, and give users a uniform, consistent view of the network regardless of where they log in.

As you will see in the sections titled "Configuring an NFS Server" and "Configuring an NFS Client," NFS is easy to set up and maintain and pleasantly flexible. Exports can be mounted read-only or in read-write mode. Permission to mount exported file systems can be limited to a single host or to a group of hosts using either host names with the wildcards * and ? or using IP address ranges. Other options enable strengthening or weakening of certain security options as the situation demands.

NFS Advantages and Disadvantages

Clearly, the biggest advantage NFS provides is centralized administration. It is much easier, for example, to back up a file system stored on a single server than it is to back up directories scattered across a network, on systems that are geographically dispersed, and that might or might not be accessible when the backup is made. Similarly, NFS, especially when used with NIS, makes it trivially simple to update key configuration files, provide access to shared disk space, or limit access to sensitive data.

NFS can also conserve disk space and prevent duplication of resources. Read-only file systems and file systems that change infrequently, such as /usr, can be exported as read-only NFS mounts. Likewise, upgrading applications employed by users throughout a network simply becomes a matter of installing the new application and changing the exported file system to point at the new application.

End users also benefit from NFS. When NFS is combined with NIS, users can log in from any system, even remotely, and still have access to their home directories and see a uniform view of shared data. Users can protect important or sensitive data or information that would be impossible or time consuming to recreate by storing it on an NFS mounted file system that is regularly backed up.

NFS has its shortcomings, of course, primarily in terms of performance and security. As a distributed, network-based file system, NFS is sensitive to network congestion. Heavy network traffic slows down NFS performance. Similarly, heavy disk activity on the NFS server adversely affects NFS's performance. In the face of network congestion or extreme disk activity, NFS clients run more slowly because file I/O takes longer.

If an exported file system is not available when a client attempts to mount it, the client system can hang, although this can be mitigated using a specific mount option that you will read about in the section title "Configuring an NFS Client." Another shortcoming of NFS is that an exported file system represents a single point of failure. If the disk or system exporting vital data or application becomes unavailable for any reason such as a disk crash or server failure, no one can access that resource.

NFS suffers from potential security problems because its design assumes a trusted network, not a hostile environment in which systems are constantly being probed and attacked. The primary weakness is that the NFS protocol is based on remote procedure calls (*RPC*). RPC is one of the most common targets of exploit attempts. As a result, sensitive information should never be exported from or mounted on systems directly exposed to the Internet, that is, one that is on or outside a firewall. Moreover, NFS should not be used *across* the Internet under any circumstances.

Even inside a firewall, providing all users access to all files might pose greater risks than user convenience and administrative simplicity justify. Care must be taken when exporting directories or file systems to limit access to the appropriate users and also to limit what those users are permitted to do with the data.

NFS also has quirks that can prove disastrous for unwary or inexperienced administrators. For example, when the root user on a client system mounts an NFS export, you do not want root on the client to have root privileges on the exported file system. By default, NFS prevents this, a procedure called *root squashing*, but a careless administrator might override it.

Planning an NFS Installation

Planning an NFS installation is a grand-sounding phrase that boils down to thoughtful design followed by careful implementation. Of these two steps, design is the more important because it ensures that the implementation is transparent to end users and trivial to administer. The implementation is remarkably straightforward. This section highlights the server configuration process and discusses the key design issues to keep in mind.

"Thoughtful design" consists of deciding what file systems to export to which users and selecting a naming convention and mounting scheme that maintains network transparency. When you are designing your NFS installation, you need to:

- ◆ Select the file systems to export.

- ◆ Establish which users (or hosts) are permitted to mount the exported file systems.

- ◆ Choose a naming convention and mounting scheme that maintains network transparency and ease of use.

With the design in place, implementation is a matter of configuring the exports and starting the appropriate daemons. Testing ensures that the naming convention and mounting scheme works as designed and identifies potential performance bottlenecks. Monitoring is an ongoing process to ensure that exported file systems continue to be available, network security and the network security policy remain uncompromised, and that heavy usage does not adversely affect overall performance.

A few general rules exist to guide the design process. NFS imposes restrictions based on what file systems can be exported, the design of the underlying network, the number and type of servers and clients, and the needs of each site. The following are some tips and suggestions for designing an NFS server and its exports that ease administrative overhead and reduce user confusion:

- ◆ Good candidates for NFS exports include any file system that is shared among a large number of users, such as /home, workgroup project directories, shared directories, such as /usr/share, the mail spool (/var/mail), and file systems that contain application binaries and data used by many users on the network. File systems that are relatively static, such as /usr, are also good candidates for NFS exports because there is no need to replicate the same static data and binaries across multiple machines.

- ◆ Use /home/username to mount home directories. This is one of the most fundamental directory idioms in the Linux world, so disregarding it not only antagonizes users but also breaks a lot of software that presumes user home directories live in /home. Of course, on the server, you have more leeway about where to situate the exports.

- ◆ Few networks are static, particularly network file systems, so design NFS servers with growth in mind. For example, avoid the temptation to drop all third-party software onto a single exported file system. Over time, file systems have the tendency to grow to the point that they need to be subdivided, leading to administrative headaches when client mounts must be updated to reflect a new set of exports. Instead, spread third-party applications across multiple NFS exports and export each application and its associated data separately.

◆ At large sites, distribute multiple NFS exports across multiple disks so that a single disk failure will limit the impact to the affected application.

◆ Similarly, overall disk and network performance improves if exported file systems are distributed across multiple servers rather than concentrated on a single server. If it is not possible to use multiple servers, at least try to situate NFS exports on separate physical devices and/or on separate disk controllers. Doing so reduces disk I/O contention.

When identifying the file systems to export, keep in mind the following three rules that restrict which file systems can be exported and how they can be exported. First, you can export only local file systems and their subdirectories. To express this restriction in another way, you cannot export a file system that is itself already an NFS mount. For example, if a system named diskbeast mounts /home from a server named homebeast, diskbeast cannot re-export /home. Clients wishing to mount /home from homebeast must do so directly.

The second restriction is that a subdirectory of an exported file system cannot be exported unless that subdirectory resides on a different physical disk than its parent directory. For example, suppose diskbeast, an NFS server, has the following entry in its /etc/fstab:

```
/dev/sda1 /usr/local ext3 defaults 1 2
```

If you export /usr/local, which is located on /dev/sda1, you cannot *also* export /usr/local/devtools if it is on the same disk as /usr/local. This restriction applies even if /usr/local/devtools is on a different partition (say, /dev/sda2).

NFS *clients* are free to mount /usr/local and /usr/local/devtools separately because, as you will see in the section titled "Configuring an NFS Client," client systems can mount any subdirectory of an exported file system unless specifically forbidden to do so.

If, however, diskbeast's /etc/fstab showed the following disk configuration:

```
/dev/sda1 /usr/local             ext3 defaults 1 2
/dev/sdb2 /usr/local/devtools  ext3 defaults 1 2
```

diskbeast *could* export both /usr/local and /usr/local/devtools because the file systems reside on different physical disks (/dev/sda and /dev/sdb, respectively).

The third rule is the converse of the second. If a subdirectory is exported, that subdirectory's parent directory cannot be exported unless the parent directory resides on a different physical disk. That is, if you export /usr/local/devtools, you cannot `export /usr/local` unless `/usr/local` is on a different disk device than `/usr/local/devtools`. This rule just extends the logic of the previous in the opposite direction.

Configuring an NFS Server

This section shows you how to configure an NFS server, identifies the key files and commands you use to implement, maintain, and monitor the NFS server, and illustrates the server configuration process using a typical NFS setup.

On Red Hat systems, the `/etc/exports` file is the main NFS configuration file. It lists the file systems the server exports, the systems permitted to mount the exported file systems, and the mount options for each export. NFS also maintains status information about existing exports and the client systems that have mounted those exports in `/var/lib/nfs/rmtab` and `/var/lib/nfs/xtab`. In addition to these configuration and status files, Red Hat Enterprise Linux uses the daemons and commands in the following list to execute and maintain the NFS server:

- ◆ Daemons

    - rpc.portmap

    - rpc.mountd

    - rpc.nfsd

    - rpc.statd

    - rpc.lockd

    - rpc.rquotad

- ◆ Commands and scripts

    - /etc/rc.d/init.d/nfs

    - nfstat

    - showmount

    - rpcinfo

    - exportfs

    - rpc.rquotad

NFS SERVER CONFIGURATION AND STATUS FILES

The server configuration file is `/etc/exports`, which contains a list of file systems to export, the clients permitted to mount them, and the export options that apply to client mounts. Each line in `/etc/exports` has the following format:

```
dir host(options) [host(options)] ...
```

dir specifies a directory or file system to export, *host* specifies one or more hosts permitted to mount *dir*, and *options* specifies one or more mount options. There should not be a space between the hostname and the opening parenthesis that contains the export options. *host* can be specified as a single name, an NIS netgroup, as a group of hosts using address/netmask, form, or as a group of hosts using the wildcard characters ? and *. Multiple *host* (*options*) entries, separated by whitespace, are also accepted, enabling you to specify different export options for a single *dir* depending on the host or hosts mounting *dir*.

Chapter 12 discusses NIS netgroups in detail.

When specified as a single name, *host* can be any name that DNS or the resolver library can resolve to an IP address. If *host* is an NIS netgroup, it is specified as *@groupname*. The address/netmask form enables you to specify all hosts on an IP network or subnet. In this case the netmask can be specified in dotted quad format (/255.255.252.0, for example) or as a mask length (such as /22).

You may also specify host using the wildcards * and ?, subject to the caveat that * and ? do not match the dots in a hostname. For example, the host specification *.kurtwerks.com matches all hosts in the kurtwerks.com domain, but not, for example, hosts in the subdomain guru.kurtwerks.com.

Consider the following sample /etc/exports file:

```
/usr/local    *.kurtwerks.com(ro)
/usr/devtools 192.168.1.0/24(ro)
/home         192.168.0.0/255.255.255.0(rw)
/projects     @dev(rw)
/var/mail     192.168.0.1(rw)
```

The first line permits all hosts with a name of the format *somehost*.kurtwerks. com to mount /usr/local as a read-only directory. The second line uses the address/netmask form in which the netmask is specified as a length (/24), which allows any host with an IP address in the range 192.168.1.0 to 192.168.2.255 to mount /usr/devtools read-only. The third line permits any host with an IP address in the range 192.168.0.0 to 192.168.0.255 to mount /home in read-write mode. This entry uses the address/netmask form in which the netmask is specified in dotted quad format. The fourth line permits any member of the NIS netgroup named dev to mount /projects (again, in read-write mode) The final line permits only the host whose IP address is 192.168.0.1 to mount /var/mail.

The export options, listed in parentheses after the host specification, determine the characteristics of the exported file system. Table 11-1 lists valid values for *options*, with the default values appearing in boldface.

TABLE 11-1 /ETC/EXPORTS EXPORT OPTIONS

Option	Description
secure	Requires client requests to originate from a secure (privileged) port, that is, one numbered less than 1024
insecure	Permits client requests to originate from unprivileged ports (those numbered 1024 and higher)
secure_locks	Requires that clients requesting lock operations are properly authenticated before activating the lock
insecure_locks	Disables the need for authentication before activating lock operations
ro	Exports the file system read-only, disabling any operation that changes the file system
rw	Exports the file system read-write, permitting operations that change the file system
async	Allows the server to cache disk writes to improve performance
sync	Forces the server to perform a disk write before the request is considered complete
subtree_check	If only part of a file system, such as a subdirectory, is exported, subtree checking makes sure that file requests apply to files in the exported portion of the file system
no_subtree_check	Disables subtree_check
wdelay	Allows the server to delay a disk write if it believes another related disk write may be requested soon or if one is in progress, improving overall performance
no_wdelay	Disables wdelay (must be used with the sync option)
root_squash	Maps all requests from a user ID (UID) or group ID (GID) of 0 to the UID or GID, respectively, of the anonymous user (-2 in Red Hat Linux)
no_root_squash	Disables root_squash
all_squash	Maps all requests from all UIDs or GIDs to the UID or GID, respectively, of the anonymous user

Continued

TABLE 11-1 /ETC/EXPORTS EXPORT OPTIONS *(Continued)*

Option	Description
no_all_squash	Disables all_squash
anonuid=*uid*	Sets the UID of the anonymous account to *uid*
anongid=*gid*	Sets the GID of the anonymous account to *gid*

TIP Recent versions of NFS (actually, of the NFS utilities) default to exporting directories using the sync option. This is a change from past behavior, in which directories were exported (and mounted) using the async option. This change has been made because defaulting to async violates the NFS protocol specification.

The various squash options, and the anonuid and anongid options bear additional explanation. root_squash prevents the root user on an NFS client from having root privileges on an NFS mount. The Linux security model ordinarily grants root full access to the file systems on a host. However, in an NFS environment, exported file systems are shared resources and are properly "owned" by the root user of the NFS server, not by the root users of the client systems that mount them. The root_squash option prevents NFS clients from inappropriately taking ownership of NFS exports by remapping the root UID and GID (0) on the client system to that of a less privileged user, -2. The no_root_squash option disables this behavior, but should not be used because doing so poses significant security risks. Consider the implications, for example, of letting a client system have root access to the file system containing sensitive payroll information.

The all_squash option has a similar effect to root_squash, except that it applies to all users, not just the root user. The default is no_all_squash, however, because most users that access files on NFS exported file systems are already merely mortal users, that is, their UIDs and GIDs are unprivileged, so they do not have the power of the root account. Use the anonuid and anongid options to specify the UID and GID of the anonymous user. The default UID and GID of the anonymous user is -2, which should be adequate in most cases.

subtree_check and no_subtree check also deserve some elaboration. When a file system subdirectory is exported but its parent directory is not, the NFS server must verify that the accessed file resides in the exported portion of the file system, a check that is programmatically nontrivial. This verification is called a *subtree check*. To facilitate subtree checking, the server stores file location information in the file handle given to the client that requests the file.

In most cases, storing file location information in the file handle is not a problem. However, doing so becomes potentially troublesome if a client is accessing a file that is renamed or moved *while the file is open*. Moving or renaming the file invalidates the location information stored in the file handle, so the next client I/O request on that file causes an error. Disabling the subtree check using `no_subtree_check` avoids this problem because the location information is not stored in the file handle when subtree checking is disabled. As an added benefit, disabling subtree checking improves performance because it removes the additional overhead involved in the check. The benefit is especially significant on exported file systems that are highly dynamic, such as `/home`.

Unfortunately, disabling subtree checking also poses a security risk. The subtree check routine ensures that files to which only root has access can be accessed only if the file system is exported with `no_root_squash`, even if the file itself enables more general access.

The manual page for `/etc/exports` (`man 5 exports`) recommends using `no_subtree_check` for /home because /home file systems normally experiences a high level of file renaming and moving. It also recommends leaving subtree checking enabled (the default) for file systems that are exported read-only, file systems that are largely static (such as `/usr` or `/var`), and file systems from which subdirectories, not the parent directories, are exported.

Here is a modified version of the `/etc/exports` file presented earlier.

```
/usr/local     *.kurtwerks.com(ro,secure)
/usr/devtools  192.168.1.0/24(ro,secure)
/home          192.168.0.0/255.255.255.0(rw,secure,no_subtree_check)
/projects      @dev(rw,secure,anonuid=600,anongid=600,sync,no_wdelay)
/var/mail      192.168.0.1(rw,insecure,no_subtree_check)
```

The hosts have not changed, but additional export options have been added. For example, `/usr/local`, `/usr/devtools`, `/home`, and `/project` can be accessed only from clients using secure ports (the secure option), but the server accepts requests destined for `/var/mail` from any port because the insecure option is specified. For `/projects`, the anonymous user is mapped to the UID and GID 600, as indicated by the `anonuid=600` and `anongid=600` options. Note, however, that because only members of the NIS netgroup dev are permitted to mount `/projects`, only their UIDs and GIDs are remapped.

`/home` and `/var/mail` are exported using the `no_subtree_check` option because they see a high volume of file deletion, renaming, and moving. Finally, the `sync` and `no_wdelay` options disable write caching and delayed writes to the `/project` file system. The rationale for using sync and `no_wdelay` is that the impact of data loss would be significant in the event the server crashes. However, forcing disk syncs in this manner also imposes a performance penalty because the kernel's normal disk caching and buffering heuristics cannot be applied.

Two additional files store status information about NFS exports, `/var/lib/nfs/rmtab` and `/var/lib/nfs/etab`. `/var/lib/nfs/rmtab` is the table that lists each

NFS export that is mounted by an NFS client. The daemon `rpc.mountd` (described in the section "NFS Server Daemons") is responsible for servicing requests to mount NFS exports. Each time the `rpc.mountd` daemon receives a mount request, it adds an entry to `/var/lib/nfs/rmtab`. Conversely, when mountd receives a request to unmount an exported file system, it removes the corresponding entry from `/var/lib/nfs/rmtab`. The following short listing shows the contents of `/var/lib/nfs/rmtab` on an NFS server that exports `/home` in read-write mode and `/usr/local` in read-only mode. In this case, the host with IP address 192.168.0.4 has mounted both exports:

```
$ cat /var/lib/nfs/rmtab
192.168.0.4:/home:0x00000001
192.168.0.4:/usr/local:0x00000001
```

Fields in rmtab are colon-delimited, so it has three fields: the host, the exported file system, and the mount options specified in `/etc/exports`.

Rather than try to decipher the hexadecimal options field, though, you can read the mount options directly from `/var/lib/nfs/etab`. The `exportfs` command, discussed in the subsection titled "NFS Server Scripts and Commands," maintains `/var/lib/nfs/etab`. etab contains the table of currently exported file systems. The following listing shows the contents of `/var/lib/nfs/etab` for the server exporting the `/usr/local` and `/home` file systems shown in the previous listing (the output wraps because of page width constraints).

```
$ cat /var/lib/nfs/etab
/usr/local
192.168.0.4(ro,sync,wdelay,hide,secure,root_squash,no_all_squash,
subtree_check,secure_locks,mapping=identity,anonuid=-2,anongid=-2)
/home
192.168.0.2(rw,sync,wdelay,hide,secure,root_squash,no_all_squash,
subtree_check,secure_locks,mapping=identity,anonuid=-2,anongid=-2)
```

As you can see in the listing, the format of the `etab` file resembles that of `/etc/exports`. Notice, however, that etab lists the default values for options not specified in `/etc/exports` in addition to the options specifically listed.

Most Linux systems use `/var/lib/nfs/etab` to store the table of currently exported file systems. The inquisitive reader might notice, however, that the manual page for the `exportfs` command refers to `/var/lib/nfs/xtab` as the file that contains the table of current exports. We do not have an explanation for this — it's just a fact of life that the manual page and actual usage differ.

The last two configuration files to discuss, `/etc/hosts.allow` and `/etc/hosts.deny`, are not, strictly speaking, part of the NFS server. Rather, `/etc/hosts.allow` and `/etc/hosts.deny` are access control files used by the TCP Wrappers system; you can configure an NFS server without them and the server will function perfectly (to the degree, at least, that *anything* ever functions perfectly). However, using TCP Wrappers' access control features helps enhance both the overall security of the server and the security of the NFS subsystem.

The TCP Wrappers package is covered in detail in Chapter 16, "What Are Internet Services?" Rather than preempt that discussion here, I suggest how to modify these files, briefly explain the rationale, and let you read Chapter 16 to understand the modifications in detail.

First, add the following entries to `/etc/hosts.deny`:

```
portmap:ALL
lockd:ALL
mountd:ALL
rquotad:ALL
statd:ALL
```

These entries deny access to NFS services to all hosts not explicitly permitted access in `/etc/hosts.allow`. Accordingly, the next step is to add entries to `/etc/hosts.allow` to permit access to NFS services to specific hosts. As you will learn in Chapter 16, entries in `/etc/hosts.allow` take the form

```
daemon:host_list [host_list]
```

The NFS HOWTO (`http://nfs.sourceforge.net/nfs-howto/server.html#CONFIG`) discourages use of the `ALL:ALL` syntax in `/etc/hosts.deny`, using this rationale: "While this is more secure behavior [than denying access to specific services], it may also get you in trouble when you are installing new services, you forget you put it there, and you can't figure out for the life of you why they won't work."

I respectfully disagree. The stronger security enabled by the `ALL:ALL` construct in `/etc/hosts.deny` far outweighs any inconvenience it might pose when configuring new services.

daemon is a daemon such as `portmap` or `lockd`, and *host_list* is a list of one or more hosts specified as host names, IP addresses, IP address patterns using wildcards, or address/netmask pairs. For example, the following entry permits all hosts in the kurtwerks.com domain to access the `portmap` service:

```
portmap:.kurtwerks.com
```

The next entry permits access to all hosts on the subnetworks 192.168.0.0 and 192.168.1.0

```
portmap:192.168.0. 192.168.1.
```

You need to add entries for each host or host group permitted NFS access for each of the five daemons listed in `/etc/hosts.deny`. So, for example, to permit access to all hosts in the kurtwerks.com domain, add the following entries to `/etc/host.allow`:

```
portmap:.kurtwerks.com
lockd  :.kurtwerks.com
mountd :.kurtwerks.com
rquotad:.kurtwerks.com
statd  :.kurtwerks.com
```

Note that, unlike the syntax of `/etc/exports`, a name of the form `.domain.dom` matches all hosts, including hosts in subdomains like `.subdom.domain.dom`.

NFS SERVER DAEMONS

Providing NFS services requires the services of six daemons: `/sbin/portmap`, `/usr/sbin/rpc.mountd`, `/usr/sbin/rpc.nfsd`, `/sbin/rpc.statd`, `/sbin/rpc.lockd`, and, if necessary, `/usr/sbin/rpc.rquotad`. They are generally referred to as `portmap`, `mountd`, `nfssd`, `statd`, `lockd`, and `rquotad`, respectively. Table 11-2 briefly describes each daemon's function.

TABLE 11-2 NFS SERVER DAEMONS

Daemon	Function
portmap	Enables NFS clients to discover the NFS services available on a given NFS server
mountd	Processes NFS client mount requests
nfsd	Provides all NFS services except file locking and quota management
statd	Implements NFS lock recovery when an NFS server system crashes
lockd	Starts the kernel's NFS lock manager
rquotad	Provides file system quota information NFS exports to NFS clients using file system quotas

The NFS daemons should be started in the following order to work properly:

1. `portmap`

2. `nfsd`

3. `mountd`

4. `statd`

5. `rquotad` (if necessary)

Notice that the list omits `lockd`. `nfsd` starts it on an as-needed basis, so you should rarely, if ever, need to invoke it manually. Fortunately, the Red Hat initialization script for NFS, `/etc/rc.d/init.d/nfs`, takes care of starting up the NFS server daemons for you. Should the need arise, however, you can start NFS yourself by executing the initialization script directly:

```
# /etc/rc.d/init.d/nfs start
Starting NFS services:                  [ OK ]
Starting NFS quotas:                    [ OK ]
Starting NFS daemon:                    [ OK ]
Starting NFS mountd                     [ OK ]
```

You can also use the handy service utility:

```
# service nfs start
Starting NFS services:                  [ OK ]
Starting NFS quotas:                    [ OK ]
Starting NFS daemon:                    [ OK ]
Starting NFS mountd                     [ OK ]
```

By default, the startup script starts eight copies of `nfsd` in order to enable the server to process multiple requests simultaneously. To change this value, edit `/etc/sysconfig/nfs` and add an entry resembling the following:

```
RPCNFSDCOUNT=n
```

Replace *n* with the number of nfsd processes you want to start. Busy servers with many active connections might benefit from doubling or tripling this number. If file system quotas for exported file systems have *not* been enabled on the NFS server, it is unnecessary to start the quota manager, `rquotad`, but be aware that the Red Hat initialization script starts `rquotad` whether quotas have been enabled or not.

Chapter 26 covers file-system quotas in detail.

NFS SERVER SCRIPTS AND COMMANDS

Starting and maintaining an NFS server requires surprisingly few commands. Three initialization scripts start the required daemons, `/etc/rc.d/init.d/portmap`, `/etc/rc.d/init.d/nfs`, and `/etc/rc.d/init.d/nfslock`. The `exportfs` command enables you to manipulate the list of current exports on the fly without needing to edit `/etc/exports`. The `showmount` command provides information about clients and the file systems they have mounted. The `nfsstat` command displays detailed information about the status of the NFS subsystem.

The `portmap` script starts the `portmap` daemon, frequently referred to as *the portmapper*. All programs that use RPC, such as NIS and NFS, rely on the information the portmapper provides. The Red Hat Linux boot process starts the portmapper automatically, so you rarely need to worry about it, but it is good to know the script exists. Like most startup scripts, it requires a single argument, such as `start`, `stop`, `restart`, or `status`. As you can probably guess, the `start` and `stop` arguments start and `stop` the portmapper, restart restarts it (by calling the script with the `start` and `stop` arguments, as it happens), and status indicates whether or not the portmapper is running, showing the portmapper's PID if it is running.

The primary NFS startup script is `/etc/rc.d/init.d/nfs`. Like the portmapper, it requires a single argument, `start`, `stop`, `status`, `restart`, or `reload`. `start` and `stop` start and stop the NFS server, respectively. The `restart` argument stops and starts the server processes in a single command and should be used after changing the contents of `/etc/exports`. However, it is not necessary to reinitialize the NFS subsystem by bouncing the server daemons in this way. Rather, you can use the script's `reload` argument, which causes `exportfs`, discussed shortly, to reread `/etc/exports` and to re-export the file systems listed there. Both `restart` and `reload` also update the time stamp on the NFS lock file used by the initialization script, `/var/lock/subsys/nfs`. The status argument displays the PIDs of the `mountd`, `nfsd`, and `rquotad` daemons. For example,

```
$ /etc/rc.d/init.d/nfs status
rpc.mountd (pid 4358) is running...
nfsd (pid 1241 1240 1239 1238 1235 1234 1233 1232) is running...
rpc.rquotad (pid 1221) is running...
```

The output of the command confirms that the three daemons are running and shows the PIDs for each instance of each daemon. All users are permitted to invoke the NFS initialization script with the status argument, but all the other arguments (`start`, `stop`, `restart`, and `reload`) *do* require root privileges.

NFS services also require the file locking daemons lockd and statd. As noted earlier, nfsd starts lockd itself, but you still must start statd separately. Red Hat Linux includes an initialization script for this purpose, /etc/rc.d/init.d/nfslock. It accepts almost the same arguments as /etc/rc.d/init.d/nfs, with the exception of the reload argument (because statd does not require a configuration file).

Thus, if you ever need to start the NFS server manually, the proper invocation sequence is to start the portmapper first, followed by NFS, followed by the NFS lock manager, that is:

```
# /etc/rc.d/init.d/portmap start
# /etc/rc.d/init.d/nfs start
# /etc/rc.d/init.d/nfslock start
```

Conversely, to shut down the server, reverse the start procedure:

```
# service nfslock stop
# service nfs stop
# service portmap stop
```

The example of stopping the servers uses the service utility, which is the preferred way to manipulate Red Hat Linux services. Because other programs and servers may require portmapper's service, I suggest you let it run unless you drop the system to run level 1 to perform maintenance.

You can also find out what NFS daemons are running using the rpcinfo command with the -p option. rpcinfo is a general purpose program that displays information about programs that use the RPC protocol, of which NFS is one. The -p option queries the portmapper and displays a list of all registered RPC programs. The following listing shows the output of rpcinfo -p on a fairly quiescent NFS server:

```
$ rpcinfo -p
  program vers proto   port
   100000    2   tcp    111  portmapper
   100000    2   udp    111  portmapper
   100024    1   udp  32768  status
   100024    1   tcp  32768  status
   391002    2   tcp  32769  sgi_fam
   100021    1   udp  32770  nlockmgr
   100021    3   udp  32770  nlockmgr
   100021    4   udp  32770  nlockmgr
   100011    1   udp    614  rquotad
   100011    2   udp    614  rquotad
   100011    1   tcp    617  rquotad
   100011    2   tcp    617  rquotad
   100003    2   udp   2049  nfs
```

```
100003   3   udp    2049   nfs
100005   1   udp   32772   mountd
100005   1   tcp   32825   mountd
100005   2   udp   32772   mountd
100005   2   tcp   32825   mountd
100005   3   udp   32772   mountd
100005   3   tcp   32825   mountd
```

rpcinfo's output shows the RPC program's ID number, version number, the network protocol it is using, the port number it is using, and an alias name for the program number. The program number and name (first and fifth columns) are taken from the file /etc/rpc, which maps program numbers to program names and also lists aliases for program names. At a bare minimum, to have a functioning NFS server, rpcinfo should list entries for portmapper, nfs, and mountd.

The exportfs command enables you to manipulate the list of available exports, in some cases without editing /etc/exports. It also maintains the list of currently exported file systems in /var/lib/nfs/etab and the kernel's internal table of exported file systems. In fact, the NFS initialization script discussed earlier in this subsection uses exportfs extensively. For example, the exportfs -a command initializes /var/lib/nfs/etab, synchronizing it with the contents of /etc/exports. To add a new export to etab and to the kernel's internal table of NFS exports *without* editing /etc/exports, use the following syntax:

```
exportfs -o exp_opts host:directory
```

exp_opts, *host*, and *directory* use the same syntax as that described for /etc/exports earlier in the chapter. Consider the following command:

```
# exportfs -o async,rw 192.169.0.3:/var/tmp
```

This command exports /var/tmp with the async and rw options to the host whose IP address is 192.168.0.3. This invocation is exactly equivalent to the following entry in /etc/exports:

```
/var/tmp 192.168.0.3(async,rw)
```

A bare exportfs call lists all currently exported file systems, and using -v lists currently exported file systems with their mount options.

```
# exporfs -v
/usr/local      192.168.0.4(ro,wdelay,root_squash)
/home           192.168.0.4(rw,wdelay,root_squash)
```

To remove an exported file system, use the -u option with exportfs. For example, the following command unexports the /home file system shown in the previous example.

```
# exportfs -v -u 192.168.0.4:/home
unexporting 192.168.0.4:/home
unexporting 192.168.0.4:/home from kernel
```

The showmount command queries the mount daemon, mountd, about the status of the NFS server. Its syntax is:

```
showmount [-adehv] [host]
```

Invoked with no options, showmount displays a list of all clients that have mounted file systems from the current host. Specify *host* to query the mount daemon on that host, where *host* can be a resolvable DNS host name or, as in the following example, an IP address:

```
# showmount 192.168.0.1.
Hosts on 192.168.0.1:
luther
luther.kurtwerks.com
```

Table 11-3 describes the effects of showmount's options:

TABLE 11-3 OPTIONS FOR THE SHOWMOUNT COMMAND

Option	Description
-a	Displays client host names and mounted directories in *host:directory*
-d	Displays only the directories clients have mounted
-e	Displays the NFS server's list of exported file systems
-h	Displays a short usage summary
-v	Displays showmount's version number
--no-headers	Disables displaying descriptive headings for showmount's output

The following examples show the output of showmount executed on an NFS server that has exported /home to the client named luther.kurtwerks.com, which has an IP address of 192.168.0.2, using the following entry in /etc/exports:

```
/home 192.168.0.*(rw)
```

The first command uses the -a option for the most comprehensive output, the second uses the -d option to show only the mounted directories, and the third example uses -e to show the server's export list.

```
# showmount -a
All mount points on luther.kurtwerks.com:
192.168.0.2:/home
# showmount -d
Directories on luther.kurtwerks.com:
/home
# showmount -e
Export list for luther.kurtwerks.com:
/home 192.168.0.*
```

The showmount command is most useful on potential NFS clients because they can identify the directories an NFS server is exporting. By the same token, however, this poses a security risk because, in the absence of entries in /etc/hosts.deny that forbid access to the portmapper, *any* host can obtain this information from an NFS server.

Example NFS Server

This section illustrates a simple but representative NFS server configuration. It exports two file systems, /home and /usr/local. Here are the corresponding entries in /etc/exports:

```
/home 192.168.0.*(rw,async,no_subtree_check)
/usr/local 192.168.0.*(ro)
```

With the exports configured, start the daemons (the portmapper is already running) using the initialization scripts:

```
# service nfs start
Starting NFS services:                    [ OK ]
Starting NFS quotas:                       [ OK ]
Starting NFS mountd:                       [ OK ]
Starting NFS daemon:                       [ OK ]
# service nfslock start
Starting NFS file locking services:
Starting NFS statd:                        [ OK ]
```

Next, use `rpcinfo -p` to make sure the necessary daemons are running; then finish up with `showmount -a` (or `exportfs -v`) to list the server's NFS exports:

```
# rpcinfo -p
   program vers proto   port
    100000    2   tcp    111  portmapper
    100000    2   udp    111  portmapper
    391002    2   tcp  32769  sgi_fam
    100021    1   udp  32770  nlockmgr
    100021    3   udp  32770  nlockmgr
    100021    4   udp  32770  nlockmgr
    100011    1   udp    848  rquotad
    100011    2   udp    848  rquotad
    100011    1   tcp    851  rquotad
    100011    2   tcp    851  rquotad
    100003    2   udp   2049  nfs
    100003    3   udp   2049  nfs
    100005    1   udp  32773  mountd
    100005    1   tcp  32829  mountd
    100005    2   udp  32773  mountd
    100005    2   tcp  32829  mountd
    100005    3   udp  32773  mountd
    100005    3   tcp  32829  mountd
    100024    1   udp  32774  status
    100024    1   tcp  32830  status
# showmount -a
All mount points on luther.kurtwerks.com:
192.168.0.4:/home
192.168.0.4:/usr/local
# exportfs -v
/usr/local      192.168.0.*(ro,wdelay,root_squash)
/home           192.168.0.*(rw,async,wdelay,root_squash,no_subtree_check)
```

After you have confirmed that the NFS daemons are running and that the exports are available, you are ready to configure one or more NFS clients. First, however, I'll show you how to use Red Hat's graphical tool for administering NFS exports, the NFS Server Configuration Tool.

Using the NFS Server Configuration Tool

If you prefer to use graphical tools for system administration, Red Hat Enterprise Linux includes the NFS Server Configuration Tool. It edits the `/etc/exports` file directly, so you can use the graphical tool and edit the configuration file directly using a text editor interchangeably. To start the NFS Server Configuration Tool, select Main Menu → System Settings → Server Settings → NFS Server. You can also start the tool by executing the command `redhat-config-nfs` (as root) in a terminal window. Figure 11-2 shows the NFS Server Configuration dialog box.

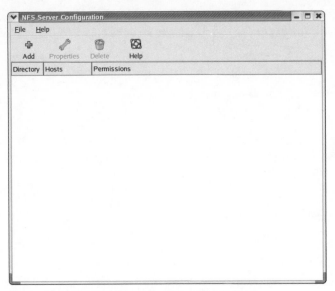

Figure 11-2: The NFS Server Configuration dialog box

To add a new export, click the Add button, which opens the Add NFS Share dialog box (see Figure 11-3). On the Basic tab, type the name of the directory you want to export in the Directory text box or use the Browse button to locate the directory to export. Use the Host(s) text box to indicate which hosts are allowed to mount this directory. Click the Read-only radio button (selected by default) or the Read/Write radio button to indicate the basic access permissions for this export.

Figure 11-3, for example, shows that /home will be exported read-write to all hosts with an IP address in the range 192.168.0.0/24. Notice that you can use the same syntax for specifying IP addresses in this NFS Server Configuration Tool that you can if you edit /etc/exports directly.

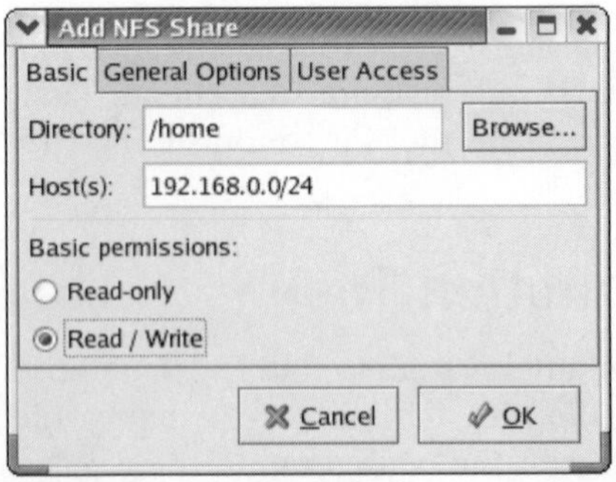

Figure 11-3: The Add NFS Share dialog box

To modify the mount options for your new NFS export, click the General Options tab. On this tab, click the checkboxes to enable the corresponding mount option. The possible mount options include

♦ Allow connections from ports 1024 and higher. This option corresponds to the insecure option listed in Table 11-1.

♦ Allow insecure file locking. This option corresponds to the insecure_locks option listed in Table 11-1.

♦ Disable subtree checking. This option corresponds to the no_subtree_check option listed in Table 11-1.

♦ Sync write operations on request. This option (enabled by default) corresponds to the sync option listed in Table 11-1.

♦ Force sync of write operations immediately. This option is only available if Sync write operations on request is enabled and corresponds to the no_wdelay option listed in Table 11-1.

Figure 11-4 shows the General Options tab. I have disabled subtree checking for the /home and have left the required sync option (Sync write operations on request) enabled.

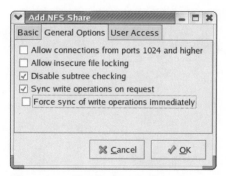

Figure 11–4: The General Options tab

The User Access tab, shown in Figure 11-5, implements the UID/GID remapping and root squashing options described earlier in this chapter. Select the Treat remote root user as local root user checkbox if you want the equivalent of no_root_squash. To remap all UIDs and GIDs to the UID and GID of the anonymous user (the all_squash option from Table 11-1), select the Treat all client users as anonymous users checkbox. As you might guess, if you want to specify the anonymous UID or GID, click the corresponding checkboxes to enable these options and then type the desired value in the matching text boxes. In Figure 11-5, I have left the user access values at their default values.

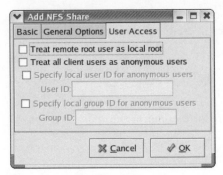

Figure 11-5: The User Access tab

When you have finished configuring your new NFS export, click the `OK` button to close the `Add NFS Share` dialog box. After a short pause, the new NFS share appears in this list of NFS exports, as shown in Figure 11-6. If you want to change the characteristics of an NFS share, select the share you want to modify and click the `Properties` button on the toolbar. This will open the `Edit NFS Share` dialog box, which has the same interface as the `Add NFS Share` dialog box.

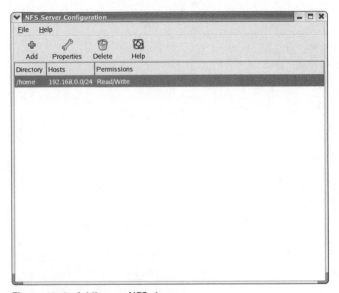

Figure 11-6: Adding an NFS share

Similarly, if you want to remove an NFS share, select the export you want to cancel and click the `Delete` button. To close the NFS Server Configuration Tool, type **Ctrl+Q** or click File → Quit on the menu bar.

Configuring an NFS Client

Configuring client systems to mount NFS exports is even simpler than configuring the NFS server itself. This section of the chapter provides a brief overview of client configuration, identifies the key files and commands involved in configuring and mounting NFS exported file systems, and shows you how to configure a client to access the NFS exports configured in the previous section.

Configuring a client system to use NFS involves making sure that the portmapper and the NFS file locking daemons `statd` and `lockd` are available, adding entries to the client's `/etc/fstab` for the NFS exports, and mounting the exports using the mount command.

As explained at the beginning of the chapter, NFS exported file systems are functionally equivalent to local file systems. Thus, as you might expect, you can use the mount command at the command line to mount NFS exports manually, just as you might mount a local file system. Similarly, to mount NFS exports at boot time, you should add entries to the file system mount table, `/etc/fstab`. As you will see in the section titled "Using Automount Services" at the end of this chapter, you can even mount NFS file systems automatically when they are first used, without having to mount them manually. The service that provides this feature is called, yup, you guessed it, the *automounter*. More on the automounter in a moment.

As a networked file system, NFS is sensitive to network conditions, so the mount command supports special options that address NFS's sensitivities and peculiarities. Table 11-4 lists the major NFS-specific options that mount accepts. For a complete list and discussion of all NFS-specific options, see the NFS manual page (`man nfs`).

TABLE 11-4 NFS-SPECIFIC MOUNT OPTIONS

Option	Description
rsize=n	Sets the NFS read buffer size to n bytes (the default is 4096)
wsize=n	Sets the NFS write buffer size to n bytes (the default is 4096)
timeo=n	Sets the RPC transmission timeout to n tenths of a second (the default is 7). Especially useful with the soft mount option
retry=n	Sets the time to retry a mount operation before giving up to n minutes (the default is 10,000)
port=n	Sets the NFS server port to which to connect to n (the default is 2049)
mountport=n	Sets the mountd server port to connect to n (no default)

Continued

TABLE 11-4 NFS-SPECIFIC MOUNT OPTIONS *(Continued)*

Option	Description
mounthost=*name*	Sets the name of the server running mountd to *name*
bg	Enables mount attempts to run in the background if the first mount attempt times out (disable with nobg)
fg	Causes mount attempts to run in the foreground if the first mount attempt times out, the default behavior (disable with nofg)
soft	Allows an NFS file operation to fail and terminate (disable with nosoft)
hard	Enables failed NFS file operations to continue retrying after reporting "server not responding" on the system, the default behavior (disable with nohard)
intr	Allow signals (such as Ctrl+C) to interrupt a failed NFS file operation if the file system is mounted with the hard option (disable with nointr). Has no effect unless the hard option is also specified or if soft or nohard is specified
tcp	Mount the NFS file system using the TCP protocol (disable with notcp)
udp	Mount the NFS file system using the UDP protocol, the default behavior (disable with noupd)
lock	Enables NFS locking and starts the statd and lockd daemons (disable with nolock)

The most commonly used and useful NFS-specific mount options are rsize=8192, wsize=8192, hard, intr, and nolock. Increasing the default size of the NFS read and write buffers improves NFS's performance. The suggested value is 8192 bytes, but you might find that you get better performance with larger or smaller values. The nolock option can also improve performance because it eliminates the overhead of file locking calls, but not all servers support file locking over NFS. If an NFS file operation fails, you can use a keyboard interrupt, usually Ctrl+C, to interrupt the operation if the exported file system was mounted with *both* the intr and hard options. This prevents NFS clients from hanging.

Like an NFS server, an NFS client needs the portmapper running in order to process and route RPC calls and returns from the server to the appropriate port and programs. Accordingly, make sure the portmapper is running on the client system using the portmap initialization script, /etc/rc.d/init.d/portmap.

In order to use NFS file locking, both an NFS server and any NFS clients need to run `statd` and `lockd`. As explained in the previous section, the simplest way to accomplish this is to use the initialization script, `/etc/rc.d/init.d/nfslock`. Presumably, you have already started `nfslock` on the server system, so all that remains is to start it on the client system.

Once you have configured the mount table and started the requisite daemons, all you need to do is mount the file systems. Chapter 6 discussed the mount command used to mount file systems, so this section shows only the mount incantations needed to mount NFS file systems. During the initial configuration and testing, it is easiest to mount and unmount NFS export at the command line. For example, to mount `/home` from the server configured at the end of the previous section, execute the following command as root:

```
# mount -t nfs luther:/home /home
```

You can, if you wish, specify client mount options using mount's `-o` option, as shown in the following example. The command wraps because of page width constraints. You should type it on a single line:

```
# mount -t nfs luther:/home /home -o rsize=8292,wsize=8192,hard,intr,nolock
```

Alternatively, you can use \ to escape the newline character:

```
# mount -t nfs luther:/home /home \
-o rsize=8292,wsize=8192,hard,intr,nolock
```

After satisfying yourself that the configuration works properly, you probably want to mount the exports at boot time. Fortunately, Red Hat Linux makes this easy because the initialization script `/etc/rc.d/init.d/netfs`, which runs at boot time, mounts all networked file systems automatically, including NFS file systems. It does this by parsing `/etc/fstab` looking for file systems of type `nfs` and mounting those file systems.

Example NFS Client

The NFS server configured in the previous section exported `/home` and `/usr/local`, so I will demonstrate configuring an NFS client that mounts those directories.

1. Clients that want to use both exports need to have the following entries in `/etc/fstab`:

   ```
   luther:/usr/local /usr/local nfs
   rsize=8192,wsize=8192,hard,intr,nolock 0 0
   luther:/home      /home       nfs
   rsize=8192,wsize=8192,hard,intr,nolock 0 0
   ```

2. Start the portmapper using the following command:

```
# service portmap start
Starting portmapper:                            [ OK ]
```

3. Mount the exports using one of the following commands:

```
# mount -a -t nfs
```

or

```
# mount /home /usr/local
```

or

```
# service netfs start
```

The first command mounts all (-a) directories of type nfs (-t nfs). The
second command mounts only the file systems /home and /usr/local.
The third command uses the service command to mount all network file
systems by invoking the netfs service. Verify that the mounts completed
successfully by attempting to access files on each file system. If everything works as designed, you are ready to go.

The next section shows you how to use the automounter to mount file systems
automatically the first time you use them.

Using Automount Services

Probably the easiest way for client systems to mount NFS exports is to use autofs,
which automatically mounts file systems not already mounted when the file system
is first accessed. autofs uses the automount daemon to mount and unmount file
systems that automount has been configured to control. Although slightly more
involved to configure than the other methods for mounting NFS file systems, autofs
setup only has to be done once.

autofs uses a set of map files to control automounting. A master map file,
/etc/auto.master, associates mount points with secondary map files that control
the file systems mounted under the corresponding mount points. For example, consider the following /etc/auto.master autofs configuration file:

```
/home /etc/auto.home
/var  /etc/auto.var --timeout 600
```

This file associates the secondary map file /etc/auto.home with the mount
point /home and the map file /etc/auto.var with the /var mount point. Thus,
/etc/auto.home defines the file systems mounted under /home and /etc/
auto.var defines the file systems mounted under /var.

Each entry in /etc/auto.master, what we'll refer to as the master map file, consists of at least two fields and possibly three fields. The first field is the mount point. The second field identifies the full path to the secondary map file that controls the map point. The third field, which is optional, consists of options that control the behavior of the automount daemon.

In the example master map file, the automount option for the /var mount point is --timeout 600, which means that after 600 seconds (10 minutes) of inactivity, the /var mount point will be umounted automatically. If a timeout value is not specified, it defaults to 300 seconds (5 minutes).

The secondary map file defines the mount options that apply to file systems mounted under the corresponding directory. Each line in a secondary map file has the general form:

```
localdir [-[options]] remotefs
```

localdir refers to the directory beneath the mount point where the NFS mount will be mounted. *remotefs* specifies the host and pathname of the NFS mount. *remotefs* is specified using the host:/path/name format described in the previous section. *options*, if specified, is a comma-separated list of mount options. These options are the same options you would use with the mount command, as discussed in Chapter 6, "The File System Explained."

Given the entry /home /etc/auto.home in the master map file, consider the following entries in /etc/auto.home:

```
kurt -rw,soft,intr,rsize=8192,wsize=8192 luther:/home/kurt
terry luther:/home/terry
```

In the first line, *localdir* is kurt, *options* is -rw,soft,intr,rsize=8192,wsize=8192, and *remotefs* is luther:/home/kurt. This means that the NFS export /home/kurt on the system named luther will be mounted in /home/kurt in read-write mode, as a soft mount, with read and write block sizes of 8192 bytes. A key point to keep in mind is that if /home/kurt exists on the local system, its contents will be temporarily replaced by the contents of the NFS mount /home/kurt. In fact, it is probably best if the directory specified by localdir does not exist because autofs will dynamically create it when it is first accessed.

The second line of the example auto.home file specifies *localdir* as terry, no *options*, and *remotefs* as the NFS exported directory /home/terry exported from the system named luther. In this case, then, /home/terry on luther will be mounted as /home/terry on the NFS client using the default NFS mount options. Again, /home/terry should not exist on the local system, but the base directory, /home, should exist.

Suppose you want to use autofs to mount a central mail queue on client systems. On the mail server (named mailbeast in this case), you would export the mail spool (usually /var/spool/mail) as described in the section "Configuring an

NFS Server." On each client that will mount this shared mail queue, create an /etc/auto.master file that resembles the following:

```
/var/spool /etc/auto.spool --timeout 600
```

This entry tells the automount daemon to consult the secondary map file /etc/auto.spool for all mounts located under /var/spool. After 600 seconds without file system activity in /var/spool/mail, autofs will automatically unmount /var/spool/mail.

 Red Hat systems provide a default /etc/auto.master map file (assuming, of course, that the autofs RPM has been installed). All of the entries are commented out using the # sign, so you can edit the existing file if you wish.

Next, create the following /etc/auto.spool file on each client that will use mailbeast's shared mail spool:

```
mail -rw,soft,rsize=8192,wsize=8192 mailbeast:/var/spool/mail
```

This entry mounts /var/spool/mail from mailbeast as /var/spool/mail on the client system. The mount options indicate that the directory will be read/write, that it will be a soft mount, and that the read and write block sizes are 8192 bytes. Recall from Table 11-4 that a soft mount means that the kernel can time out the mount operation after a period of time specified by the timeo=n option, where n is defined in tenths of a second.

Finally, as the root user, start the autofs service:

```
# /sbin/service autofs start
Starting automount:                              [ OK ]
```

After starting the autofs service, you can use the status option to verify that the automount daemon is working:

```
# /sbin/service autofs status
Configured Mount Points:
------------------------
/usr/sbin/automount --timeout 600 /var/spool file /etc/auto.mail

Active Mount Points:
--------------------
/usr/sbin/automount --timeout 600 /var/spool file /etc/auto.mail
```

As you can see under the heading Active Mount Points, the /var/spool mount point is active. You can verify this by changing to the /var/spool/mail directory and executing an ls command:

```
# cd /var/spool/mail
# ls -l
-rw-r--r--    1 root      root            0 Jun  4 22:21 kurt
-rw-------    1 1000      users      329255 Jun  4 23:36 kwall
-rw-rw----    1 root      mail         9757 Mar 23 08:17 root
```

You can also see the automount daemon at work using the mount command:

```
# mount
/dev/hda7 on / type ext3 (rw)
none on /proc type proc (rw)
usbdevfs on /proc/bus/usb type usbdevfs (rw)
/dev/hda1 on /boot type ext3 (rw)
none on /dev/pts type devpts (rw,gid=5,mode=620)
none on /dev/shm type tmpfs (rw)
automount(pid3516) on /var/spool type autofs
(rw,fd=5,pgrp=3516,minproto=2,maxproto=3)
mailbeast:/var/spool/mail on /var/spool/mail type nfs
(rw,soft,rsize=8192,wsize=8192,addr=192.168.0.1)
```

The bottom two entries show that the automount daemon is managing the /var/spool mount point and the mailbeast:/var/spool/mail is mounted on /var/spool/mail using the options specified in /etc/auto.mail.

To stop the automounter, use the stop argument to the service command:

```
# /sbin/service autofs stop
Stopping automount:                        [ OK ]
```

One of the handiest features of the autofs service is that changes made to the secondary map files go into effect almost immediately. The next time that a directory or file system managed by autofs is accessed, the automount daemon rereads the secondary map files. So, changes to the secondary map files do not require any special treatment.

However, if you change the master map file, you have to reload the configuration file using the following command:

```
/sbin/service autofs reload
```

Examining NFS Security

As explained at the beginning of the chapter, NFS has some inherent security problems that make it unsuitable for use across the Internet and potentially unsafe for use even in a trusted network. This section identifies key security issues of NFS in general and the security risks specific to an NFS server and to NFS clients and suggests remedies that minimize your network's exposure to these security risks. Be forewarned, however, that *no* list of security tips, however comprehensive, makes your site completely secure. Nor does plugging NFS security holes address other potential exploits.

General NFS Security Issues

One NFS weakness, in general terms, is the /etc/exports file. If a cracker is able to spoof or take over a *trusted address*, an address listed in /etc/exports, your mount points are accessible. Another NFS weak spot is normal Linux file system access controls that take over once a client has mounted an NFS export: Once mounted, normal user and group permissions on the files take over access control.

The first line of defense against these two weaknesses is to use host access control as described earlier in the chapter to limit access to services on your system, particularly the portmapper, which has long been a target of exploit attempts. Similarly, you should put in entries for lockd, statd, mountd, and rquotad.

More generally, wise application of IP packet firewalls, using netfilter, dramatically increases NFS server security. netfilter is stronger than NFS daemon-level security or even TCP Wrappers because it restricts access to your server at the packet level. Although netfilter is described in detail in Chapter 31, this section gives you a few tips on how to configure a netfilter firewall that plays nicely with NFS.

First, identify the ports and services NFS uses so that you know where to apply the packet filters. Table 11-5 lists the ports and protocols each NFS daemon (on both the client and server side) use.

TABLE 11-5 PORTS AND NETWORK PROTOCOLS USED BY NFS DAEMONS

Service	Port	Protocols
portmap	111	TCP, UDP
nfsd	2049	TCP, UDP
mountd	variable	TCP, UDP
lockd	variable	TCP, UDP
statd	variable	TCP, UDP
rquotad	variable	UDP

NFS over TCP is currently experimental on the server side, so you should almost always use UDP on the server. However, TCP is quite stable on NFS clients. Nevertheless, using packet filters for both protocols on both the client and the server does no harm.

Note that `mountd`, `lockd`, `statd`, and `rquotad` do not bind to any specific port; that is, they use a port number assigned randomly by the portmapper (which is one of portmapper's purposes in the first place). The best way to address this variability is to assign each daemon a specific port using the `-p` option and then to apply the packet filter to that port. Regardless of how you configure your firewall, you must have the following rule:

```
iptables -A INPUT -f -j ACCEPT
```

This rule accepts all packet fragments except the first one (which is treated as a normal packet) because NFS does not work correctly unless you let fragments through the firewall. Be sure to read Chapter 31 carefully to configure your NFS server's firewall properly.

Server Security Considerations

On the server, always use the `root_squash` option in `/etc/exports`. Actually, NFS helps you in this regard because root squashing is the default, so you should not disable it (with `no_root_squash`) unless you have an extremely compelling reason to do so. With root squashing in place, the server substitutes the UID of the anonymous user for root's UID/GID (0), meaning that a *client's* root account cannot even access, much less change, files that only the *server's* root account can access or change.

The implication of root squashing may not be clear, so permit me to make it explicit: all critical binaries and files should be owned by root, not bin, wheel, adm, or another nonroot account. The only account that an NFS client's root user cannot access is the server's root account, so critical files owned by root are much less exposed than if they are owned by other accounts.

It gets better, though. Consider the situation in which a user has root access on a system. In this case, exporting filesystems using the `all_squash` option might be worth considering. A user that has root access on a client can usually `su` to any user, and that UID will be used over NFS. Without `all_squash`, a compromised client can at least view and, if the file system is mounted read-write, update files owned by any user besides root if `root_squash` is enabled. This security hole is closed if the `all_squash` option is used.

NFS also helps you maintain a secure server through the `secure` mount option because this mount option is one of the default options `mountd` applies to all exports unless explicitly disabled using the `insecure` option. As you learn in

Chapter 16, ports 1–1024 are reserved for root's use; merely mortal user accounts cannot bind these ports. Thus, ports 1–1024 are sometimes referred to as privileged or secure ports. The secure option prevents a malevolent nonroot user from initiating a spoofed NFS dialogue on an unprivileged port and using it as a launch point for exploit attempts.

Client Security Considerations

On the client, disable SUID (set UID) programs on NFS mounts using the nosuid option. The nosuid option prevents a server's root account from creating an SUID root program on an exported file system, logging in to the client as a normal user, and then using the UID root program to become root on the client. In some cases, you might also disable binaries on mounted file systems using the noexec option, but this effort almost always proves to be impractical or even counterproductive because one of the benefits of NFS is sharing file systems that contain scripts or programs that need to be executed.

NFS version 3, the version available with Red Hat Linux (well, with version 2.4 of the Linux kernel) supports NFS file locking. Accordingly, NFS clients must run statd and lockd in order for NFS file locks to function correctly. statd and lockd, in turn, depend on the portmapper, so consider applying the same precautions for portmap, statd, and lockd on NFS clients that were suggested for the NFS server.

In summary, using TCP wrappers, the secure, root_squash, and nosuid options, and sturdy packet filters can increase the overall security of your NFS setup. However, NFS is a complex, nontrivial subsystem, so it is entirely conceivable that new bugs and exploits will be discovered.

Summary

In this chapter, you learned to configure NFS, the Network File System. First, you found a general overview of NFS, its typical uses, and its advantages and disadvantages. Next, you found out how to configure an NFS server, you identified key files and commands to use, and you saw the process with a typical real-world example. With the server configured and functioning, you then learned how to configure a client system to access NFS exported file systems, again using key configuration files and commands and simulating the procedure with a representative example. You also learned how to address NFS performance problems and how to troubleshoot some common NFS errors. The chapter's final section identified potential security problems with NFS and suggested ways to mitigate the threat.

Chapter 12

The Network Information System

IN THIS CHAPTER

- ◆ Understanding NIS
- ◆ Planning an NIS installation
- ◆ Configuring an NIS server
- ◆ Configuring an NIS client
- ◆ Strengthening NIS Security

A COMMON CHALLENGE FACING ADMINISTRATORS charged with maintaining a network of Red Hat Enterprise Linux machines is how to share information across the network while maintaining that information centrally. The Network Information Service (NIS) is one solution to such a challenge. This chapter begins by describing NIS and its security-enhanced sibling, NIS+. Once you understand a little about the problems NIS was designed to solve, you'll review some of the design issues to keep in mind when you are planning an NIS installation. Next, you learn how to configure an NIS server and an NIS client. With some NIS knowledge and experience under your belt, you'll explore NIS+, especially how it differs from and enhances plain vanilla NIS. Finally, this chapter shows you how to integrate NIS and NFS, which can significantly simplify system administration across a large or geographically dispersed network.

Understanding NIS

NIS distributes information that needs to be shared throughout a Linux network to all machines on the network. Originally developed by Sun Microsystems, NIS was first known as Yellow Pages (YP), so many commands begin with the letters yp, such as `ypserv`, `ypbind`, and `yppasswd`. Unfortunately for Sun, the phrase "Yellow Pages" was (and is) a registered trademark of British Telecom in the United Kingdom, so Sun changed the name of their Yellow Pages services to Network Information Service. Despite the name change, however, the NIS suite of utilities retained the `yp` prefixes because administrators had become accustomed to them.

The information most commonly distributed across a network using NIS consists of user database and authentication information, such as /etc/passwd and /etc/group. If, for example, a user's password entry is shared by all login hosts via the NIS password database, that user is able to log in on all login hosts on the network, all hosts, that is, that are running the NIS client programs. However, sharing authentication information is not the only use for NIS — any information that needs to be distributed across a network and that can or should be centrally administered is a viable candidate for sharing via NIS. For example, you can use NIS to distribute a company telephone directory or a listing of accounting codes.

 Do not be confused by the use of the word *database*. I use *database* in its general sense to refer to a centralized store of information, not to refer to database management systems such as Oracle or MySQL.

NIS, like NFS, uses a standard client/server architecture arrayed in one of several possible configurations. Each NIS domain must have at least one system that functions as an NIS server for that domain. An *NIS server* is a centrally administered repository for information shared across the network using NIS. *NIS clients* are programs that use NIS to query designated servers for information that is stored in the servers' databases, which are known as *maps*. NIS maps are stored in DBM format, a binary file format based on simple ASCII text files. For example, the files /etc/passwd and /etc/group can be converted directly to DBM format using an ASCII-to-DBM conversion program named makedbm.

NIS installations revolve around the notion of a domain. An NIS domain name refers to a group of systems, typically on a LAN or on only a subnet of a LAN, that use the same NIS maps. NIS domains are typically used as system management tools, a convenient method for organizing groups of machines that need to access the information shared across a network using a set of common NIS maps. Thus, an NIS domain should not be confused with an Internet or DNS domain. A DNS domain name (more specifically, a fully qualified domain name, or FQDN) is the official name that uniquely identifies a system to the Internet domain name system.

NIS servers can be further subdivided into master and slave servers. A *master server* maintains the authoritative copies of the NIS maps. A *slave server* maintains copies of the maps, which it receives from the master NIS server whenever changes are made to the databases stored on the master. In NIS configurations that use slave servers, the slaves receive copies of the DBM databases, not the ASCII source files. The yppush program notifies slave servers of changes to the NIS maps, and then the slaves automatically retrieve the updated maps in order to synchronize their databases with the master. NIS clients do not need to do this because they communicate with their designated server(s) to obtain current information. The rationale for slave servers is to provide redundancy: If the master server is unavailable for some reason, slave servers function as backups until the master is again available.

Planning an NIS Installation

Four NIS topologies are commonly used:

- ♦ A single domain with a master server, no slave servers, and one or more clients (Figure 12-1)

- ♦ A single domain with a master server, one or more slave servers, and one or more clients (Figure 12-2)

- ♦ Multiple domains, each with its own master server, no slave servers, and one or more clients (Figure 12-3)

- ♦ Multiple domains, each with its own master server, one or more slave servers, and one or more clients (Figure 12-4)

The single domain configurations are the most widely used in most situations. Figure 12-1 illustrates the single domain–single server configuration. Figure 12-2 shows the single domain–multiple server configuration.

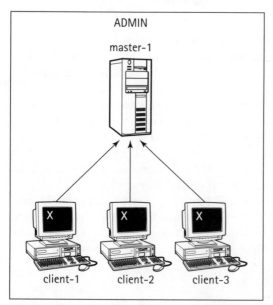

Figure 12-1: A single domain–single server NIS configuration

In Figure 12-1, the single server, master–1, responds to all queries from NIS clients (client–1, client–2, and client–3) and is the sole source of information for the domain, named admin. Figure 12-2 illustrates the same domain but includes a slave server, slave–1. In this case, client–1 and client–2 continue to query the master server, but client–3 communicates with the slave server when performing NIS queries.

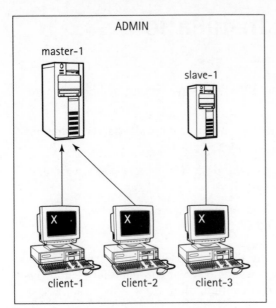

Figure 12-2: A single domain–multiple server NIS configuration

In Figure 12-2, client–3 has not specifically been configured to communicate with the slave server. Rather, it sends out NIS broadcast messages for a given domain and accepts replies from any server authoritative for that domain – the server that "wins" is the server that replies first.

At large sites or in complicated networks, you might find it necessary to have multiple NIS domains. Figures 12-3 and 12-4 illustrate such configurations. Figure 12-3 shows two domains, admin and devel, each with its own master server, master–admin and master–devel. Clients in the admin domain (client–1, client–2, and client–3) communicate only with the master-admin server, and clients in the devel domain (client–4, client–5, and client–6) communicate only with master–devel.

Figure 12-4 illustrates the same setup as Figure 12-3, except that each domain has a slave server, slave–admin, and slave–devel, and some of the clients in each domain communicate with the slave servers rather than with the master. As in the single server example, any given client communicates with the server for its domain that responds the fastest to a broadcast query.

An important caveat pertaining to NIS usage needs to be emphasized: A singleton server (one whose function is not duplicated or replicated elsewhere in the network) that relies upon NIS for key data potentially represents a single point of failure. If your network or organization relies on high availability of your network, NIS may not be an acceptable solution for information sharing.

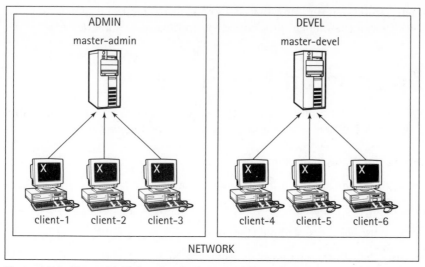

Figure 12-3: The multiple domain–single server NIS configuration

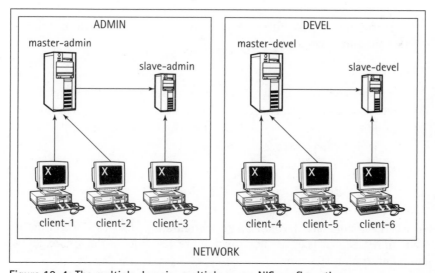

Figure 12-4: The multiple domain–multiple server NIS configuration

A complete NIS setup involves configuring at least one NIS server and one or more NIS clients. If your Red Hat system is going to be part of a network with existing NIS servers, you only need to install and configure the client programs, `ypbind`, `ypwhich`, `ypcat`, `yppoll`, and `ypmatch`. The most important program is the NIS client daemon, `ypbind`. `ypbind` is usually started from the system's startup procedure. As soon as `ypbind` is running your system has become an NIS client.

On the other hand, if your Red Hat system is going to be part of a network that does not already have NIS servers in place, you need to configure at least one NIS server, which involves configuring the `ypserv` client daemon and identifying the files that NIS distributes to client programs and, optionally, to slave servers.

Configuring an NIS Server

The simplest NIS configuration consists of a single NIS server and one or more clients. In this case, NIS server configuration involves the following steps:

1. Setting the NIS domain name.

2. Configuring and starting the server daemon, `ypbind`.

3. Initializing the NIS maps.

4. Starting the NIS password daemon.

5. Starting the NIS transfer daemon if you use slave servers.

6. Modifying the startup process to start the NIS daemons when the system reboots.

If your NIS configuration also utilizes slave servers, you need to perform configuration steps on the slave servers.

For more information about NIS configuration, see the NIS HOW-TO at the Linux Documentation Project, `http://www.linuxdoc.org/HOWTO/ NIS-HOWTO/index.html`, and the NIS Web pages at `http://www .suse.de/~kukuk/nis/`.

Key Files and Commands

Table 12-1 lists the commands, daemons, and configurations files used to configure and maintain an NIS server. They are described in greater detail as the text explains how to set up and run an NIS server.

TABLE 12-1 NIS SERVER CONFIGURATION COMMANDS AND FILES

Command	Description
nisdomainname	Sets a system's NIS domain name
ypserv	Handles the primary NIS server duties

Command	Description
ypinit	Builds and installs the NIS databases
yppasswdd	Processes user password changes in an NIS environment
ypxfrd	Speeds up the transfer of large NIS maps from master to slave servers
yppush	Propagates updated NIS maps to slave servers
/var/yp/securenets	Lists hosts permitted to access the NIS maps
/etc/ypserv.conf	Stores runtime configuration options and special host access directives

The initial step in configuring an NIS client is to set the NIS domain name. When first configuring the NIS server, the quickest way to set an NIS domain name is to use the nisdomainname command:

```
# nisdomainname nisdomain
```

Replace *nisdomain* with the name of your NIS domain. Next, reissue the *nisdomainname* command with no arguments to confirm that the NIS domain name was successfully set. These measures to set the NIS domain name are only temporary. The name set will not survive a system reboot. You learn later in this section how to set the NIS domain name permanently.

You can also use the domainname command to get and set a system's NIS domain name. In fact, you can use one of a number of similarly named commands to do so. See the domainname man page for more information.

With the NIS domain name set, at least temporarily, you can configure and start the primary NIS server daemon. The key configuration files are /var/yp/securenets and /etc/ypserv.conf. /etc/ypserv.conf is the configuration file for both ypserv, the primary NIS server daemon, and the NIS transfer daemon, ypxfrd. It contains runtime configuration options, called *option lines*, for ypserv, and host access information, called *access rules*, for both ypserv and ypxfrd. The default values in /etc/ypserv.conf, shown in the following listing, are sufficient for most NIS server configurations.

```
dns:no
*:shadow.byname:port:yes
*:passwd.adjunct.byname:port:yes
*:*:*:none
```

ypserv and ypxfrd read /etc/ypserv.conf when they start and when sent a
SIGHUP signal (for example, by kill -HUP). Entries in the file appear one per line.
Each line is made up of colon-separated fields defining either an option line or an
access rule. An option line has the following format:

option:[yes|no]

option can be either dns or xfr_check_port. dns controls whether or not the
NIS server performs a DNS lookup for hosts not listed in the host maps. The default
is no. xfr_check_port controls whether or not ypserv runs on a port numbered
less than 1024, a so-called privileged port. The default is yes. As you can see in the
default configuration file, the dns option is no. The absence of xfr_check_port
from the configuration file means that ypserv uses a privileged port.

Access rules have a slightly more complicated format:

host:map:security:mangle[:field]

- ◆ *host* – The IP address to match. Wildcards are allowed. For example, the
  entry 192.168.0. refers to all IP addresses between 192.168.0.1 and
  192.168.0.255.

- ◆ *map* – The name of a map to match or * for all maps.

- ◆ *security* – The type of security to use. Can be one of none, port, deny,
  or des. An entry of none enables access to map for host unless mangle
  is set to yes, in which case access is denied. port enables access if the
  connection is coming from a privileged port. If mangle is set to yes, access
  is enabled, but the password field is mangled. If mangle is no, access is
  denied. deny denies the matching host access to this map. des requires
  DES authentication.

- ◆ *mangle* – The type of port to use. If set to yes, field is replaced by x if the
  requesting port is unprivileged. If set to no, field is not mangled if the
  requesting port is unprivileged.

- ◆ *field* – The field number in the map to mangle. The default value if field is
  not specified is 2, which corresponds to the password field in /etc/group,
  /etc/shadow, and /etc/passwd.

Access rules are tried in order, and all rules are evaluated. If no rule matches a
connecting host, access to the corresponding map is enabled.

The most important configuration file is /var/yp/securenets, which contains netmask and network number pairs that define the lists of hosts permitted to access your NIS server maps. /var/yp/securenets contains one tuple per line of the form *m.m.m.m n.n.n.n*, where *m.m.m.m.* is a netmask, and *n.n.n.n.* is network number. A host match occurs if the IP address matches the network number and mask. For example, consider a /var/yp/securenets with these entries:

```
255.255.255.255 127.0.0.1
255.255.255.0 192.168.0.0
```

The first line indicates that the localhost (IP address 127.0.0.1) is permitted to access the NIS server. The second line specifies that any host with an IP address in the range 192.168.0.1 to 192.168.0.255 is permitted to access the NIS server. All other hosts are denied access.

Before starting the server, make sure the portmapper daemon, portmap, is running. NIS requires the portmapper because NIS uses remote procedure calls (RPC). To see if the portmapper is running, you can use the portmapper's initialization script, /etc/rc.d/init.d/portmap, or the rpcinfo command. If the portmapper is not running, you can easily start it. Using the initialization script, the command to execute and its output is:

```
# /sbin/service portmap status
portmap (pid 559) is running...
```

The output indicates the process ID (PID) of the portmapper. On the other hand, if the portmapper is not running, the output of the command looks like the following:

```
# /sbin/service portmap status
portmap is stopped
```

To start the portmapper, execute the following command:

```
# /sbin/service portmap start
Starting portmapper:                    [ OK ]
```

You can also use the rpcinfo command shown next to see if the portmapper is running:

```
# rpcinfo -p localhost
   program vers proto   port
    100000   2   tcp    111  portmapper
    100000   2   udp    111  portmapper
    100024   1   udp  32768  status
    100024   1   tcp  32768  status
    391002   2   tcp  32769  sgi_fam
```

```
100004    2    udp    909    ypserv
100004    1    udp    909    ypserv
100004    2    tcp    912    ypserv
100004    1    tcp    912    ypserv
100021    1    udp    32784  nlockmgr
100021    3    udp    32784  nlockmgr
100021    4    udp    32784  nlockmgr
```

Again, if you do not see output indicating that the portmapper is running, use the initialization script shown previously to start the portmapper. Once you have the portmapper started, start the NIS server using the command:

```
# /sbin/service ypserv start
Starting YP server services:              [ OK ]
```

Next, use the following rpcinfo invocation to make sure that the server is running:

```
# rpcinfo -u luther ypserv
program 100004 version 1 ready and waiting
program 100004 version 2 ready and waiting
```

Once the NIS server is running, you have to create something for it to serve, which means you need to create the NIS databases on the machine acting as the NIS server. The command for doing so is ypinit. ypinit builds a complete set of NIS maps for your system and places them in a subdirectory of /var/yp named after the NIS domain. As suggested earlier in this chapter, you should have only one master server per NIS domain. All databases are built from scratch, either from information available to the program at runtime or from the ASCII database files in /etc. These files include:

- ◆ /etc/passwd
- ◆ /etc/group
- ◆ /etc/hosts
- ◆ /etc/networks
- ◆ /etc/services
- ◆ /etc/protocols
- ◆ /etc/netgroup
- ◆ /etc/rpc

To create the NIS databases, execute the command /usr/lib/yp/ypinit -m.

```
# /usr/lib/yp/ypinit -m
```

The ypinit command uses the -m option to indicate that it is creating maps for the master server.

TIP Before initializing the NIS databases, you might want to make back up copies of the source text files shown in the preceding list.

If you also configure one or more slave NIS servers, you need to make sure that they can successfully communicate with the master server. From each slave server, make sure that ypwhich -m works, which means that the slave servers must also be configured as NIS clients, as described in the section "Configuring an NIS Client," later in this chapter. After configuring the slave server as described in that section, execute the command:

```
# /usr/lib/yp/ypinit -s masterhost
```

The -s option instructs ypinit to create a slave server using the databases from the master server named masterhost. An NIS database on a slave server is set up by copying an existing database from a running server. masterhost can also be a server on which the NIS maps are current and stable. Your NIS server is now up and running.

Starting the NIS Password Daemon

Because NIS is used to share authentication information, a method must exist for users to change this information on the NIS server and then to propagate the updated information out to other NIS clients and any slave servers that might be present. Similarly, when new users are added or existing users are deleted, clients and slaves must be notified of the change. The daemon that handles this requirement is yppasswdd. yppasswdd handles password changes and updating other NIS information that depends on user passwords. yppasswdd runs only on the NIS master server. Starting the NIS password daemon is a simple matter of executing its initialization script with an argument of start, as shown in the following:

```
# /sbin/service yppasswdd start
Starting YP passwd service:                [ OK ]
```

Keep in mind that NIS users are not permitted, by default, to change their full name or their login shell. You can enable NIS users to change their login information by starting yppasswdd using the -e chfn option to allow name changes or the -e chsh option to allow login shell changes.

Starting the Server Transfer Daemon

ypxfrd is used to speed up the transfer of large NIS maps from master to slave servers. Ordinarily, when a slave server receives a message from a master server that there is a new map, the slave starts ypxfr to transfer the new map. ypxfr reads the contents of a map from the master server one entry at a time. The transfer daemon, ypxfrd, speeds up the transfer process by enabling slave servers to copy the master's maps rather than building their own from scratch. As with the password daemon, you run the transfer daemon on the master server only. To start the transfer daemon, execute the command:

```
# /sbin/service ypxfrd start
```

If you need to update a map, run make in the /var/yp directory on the NIS master. This command updates a map if the source file is newer and propagates the new map out to the slave servers, if present.

Starting the NIS Servers at Boot Time

Once you have configured your NIS server, you should make the system changes persistent, which consists of permanently storing the NIS domain name in the network configuration and ensuring that the required daemons (ypserv, yppasswdd, and, if you use slave servers, ypxfrd) start and stop when the system starts and stops.

The first step is permanently saving the NIS domain name. To do this, add the following line to /etc/sysconfig/network:

```
NISDOMAIN=nisdomainname
```

Replace *nisdomainname* with the NIS domain name you selected when you initially configured your server. The networking initialization script reads /etc/sysconfig/network at boot time and picks up the domain name to use.

The next step is to run serviceconf, the new Red Hat system service configuration tool, to configure the NIS daemons to start at boot time. To do so, type serviceconf (as root) in a terminal window or click Main Menu → System Settings → Server Settings → Services. The resulting screen should resemble Figure 12-5.

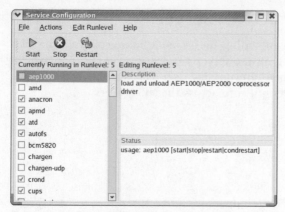

Figure 12-5: The Service Configuration main window

Scroll down to the bottom of the list, and place check marks in the boxes next to the services you want to start at boot time. In Figure 12-6, for example, you can see that the yppasswdd service has been checked, meaning it will start at boot time. The erstwhile administrator is about to enable ypserv, too. Click Save to save your changes, and then click Exit to close serviceconf.

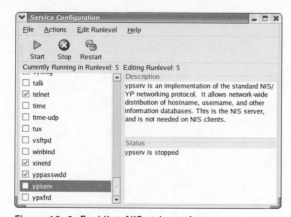

Figure 12-6: Enabling NIS at boot time

You can also use chkconfig to enable services at boot time. To start the ypserv daemons, for example, use the following command:

```
# chkconfig --levels 345 ypserv on
```

ɔnfiguring an Example NIS Server

This section illustrates the process of setting up a simple master server. The NIS domain name is kurtwerks, running on the server luther.kurtwerks.com, which has an IP address 192.168.0.4. There are no slave servers, and all hosts in the kurtwerks.com DNS domain are permitted to access the NIS server.

1. Set the NIS domain name:

```
# nisdomainname kurtwerks
# nisdomainname
kurtwerks
```

2. Edit /var/yp/securenets to permit access to the NIS server for the speci-fied hosts. The default configuration enables all hosts to have access (0.0.0.0 0.0.0.0), so change that line to read 255.255.255.0 192.168.0.0. The complete file now resembles the following:

```
255.255.255.255    127.0.0.0
255.255.255.0      192.168.0.0
```

/var/yp/securenets may not exist on your system. If not, create it.

3. Make sure that the portmapper is running:

```
# rpcinfo -u luther portmapper
    100000    2    tcp    111    portmapper
    100000    2    udp    111    portmapper
```

4. Start the primary server daemon, ypserv:

```
# /etc/rc.d/init.d/ypserv start
Starting YP server services:              [ OK ]
```

5. Confirm that ypserv is running:

```
# rpcinfo -u luther ypserv
program 100004 version 1 ready and waiting
program 100004 version 2 ready and waiting
```

6. Initialize the NIS maps:

```
#  /usr/lib/yp/ypinit -m

At this point, we have to construct a list of the hosts which
will run NIS
```

servers. luther.kurtwerks.com is in the list of NIS server
hosts. Please continue to add
the names for the other hosts, one per line. When you are
done with the
list, type a <control D>.
        next host to add: luther.kurtwerks.com
        next host to add:
The current list of NIS servers looks like this:

luther.kurtwerks.com

Is this correct? [y/n: y] y
We need a few minutes to build the databases...
Building /var/yp/kurtwerks/ypservers...
gethostbyname(): Success
Running /var/yp/Makefile...
gmake[1]: Entering directory `/var/yp/kurtwerks'
Updating passwd.byname...
Updating passwd.byuid...
Updating group.byname...
Updating group.bygid...
Updating hosts.byname...
Updating hosts.byaddr...
Updating rpc.byname...
Updating rpc.bynumber...
Updating services.byname...
Updating services.byservicename...
Updating netid.byname...
Updating protocols.bynumber...
Updating protocols.byname...
Updating mail.aliases...
gmake[1]: Leaving directory `/var/yp/kurtwerks'
luther.kurtwerks.com has been set up as a NIS master server.

Now you can run ypinit -s luther.kurtwerks.com on all slave
servers.

7. Start the password daemon, yppasswdd:

```
# /sbin/service yppasswdd start
Starting YP passwd services:                [ OK ]
```

8. Confirm that yppasswd is running:

```
# rpcinfo -u luther yppasswd
program 100009 version 1 ready and waiting
```

9. Edit /etc/sysconfig/network and add the following line, commenting out or deleting any other line that begins with NISDOMAIN:

```
NISDOMAIN=kurtwerks
```

10. Use the Service Configuration tool, as explained earlier, to configure ypserv and yppasswdd to start at boot time.

11. Reboot the server to make sure the daemons start.

If you run slave servers, repeat steps 7 and 8 for the transfer daemon, ypxfrd (that is, start ypxfrd and make sure it is running). Also make sure to set ypxfrd to start at boot time in step 10. Your shiny new NIS master server is now up and running and ready to answer requests from NIS clients.

Configuring an NIS Client

After you have successfully configured at least one master NIS server, you are ready to configure one or more NIS clients. The general procedure for setting up an NIS client involves the following steps:

1. Set the NIS domain name.

2. Configure and start the NIS client daemon.

3. Test the client daemon.

4. Configure the client's startup files to use NIS.

5. Reboot the client.

The following subsections describe these steps in detail and discuss the command and configuration file syntax. Note that there is some overlap between configuring a client and a server, so discussion emphasizes client configuration tasks. The final subsection configures an example NIS client to illustrate the process of setting up a no-frills NIS client system that connects to the server configured at the end of the previous section.

Setting the NIS Domain Name

The initial step in configuring an NIS client is to set the NIS domain name. As explained in the previous section, execute the following command to set it:

```
# nisdomainname nisdomain
```

As before, replace *nisdomain* with the name of your NIS domain.

Configuring and Starting the Client Daemon

The NIS client daemon, `ypbind` uses a configuration file named `/etc/yp.conf` that specifies which NIS servers clients should use and how to locate them, a process known as binding the client to the server. NIS clients can use one of three methods to bind the server, and the type of entry in `/etc/yp.conf` controls how binding takes place. The simplest entry takes the form:

```
ypserver nisserverip
```

This entry tells clients to use the server whose IP address is *nisserverip*. An example of this kind of entry might be:

```
ypserver 192.168.0.4
```

A somewhat more flexible approach enables clients to broadcast a query for the server to contact for a given NIS domain. This method saves tedious editing of client configuration files if (or, perhaps, when) the IP address of the NIS server changes. This entry takes the form shown here, where *nisdomain* is the name of the NIS domain of which the local host is a member.

```
domain nisdomain broadcast
```

An example entry for broadcast clients might resemble the following:

```
domain kurtwerks broadcast
```

Finally, if client systems are members of multiple NIS domains or they can connect to one of several servers for the same NIS domain, the following form enables you to associate a given server with a given NIS domain:

```
domain nisdomain server nisserverip
```

This type of entry in `/etc/yp.conf` associates the NIS domain *nisdomain* with the NIS server (either master or slave) whose IP address is *nisserverip*. One example of this type of entry might be:

```
domain kurtwerks server 192.168.0.4
domain kurtwerks server 192.168.0.2
domain bookbeast server 192.168.0.2
```

The first two lines identify two servers as the NIS servers for the kurtwerks NIS domain. The second and third lines indicate that the NIS server whose IP address is 192.168.0.2 serves two NIS domains, kurtwerks, and bookbeast.

TIP If the client system can resolve host names to IP addresses without NIS (if, for example, the client runs a caching name server or has an entry in `/etc/hosts` for the NIS server), you can use a host name instead of an IP address, but your best bet is to use IP addresses in `/etc/yp.conf` to minimize problems that might arise if name lookup services become inoperable for some reason.

To set up the client's NIS servers, you can edit `/etc/yp.conf` directly or use the Authentication Configuration tool, a graphical tool for configuring user authentication. You can even use `authconfig`, a text mode equivalent of the Authentication Configuration tool. The following procedure shows you how to use the Authentication Configuration program to configure a client system to use NIS:

1. Select Main Menu → System Settings → Authentication to open the Authentication Configuration tool shown in Figure 12-7.

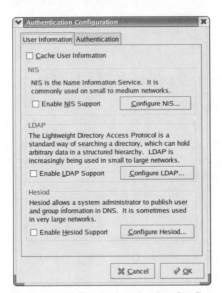

Figure 12-7: The Authentication Configuration tool

2. Click the User Information tab.

3. Click the Cache User Information check box. Setting this option causes the client to cache information retrieved from the server, making subsequent NIS lookups considerably faster.

4. Click the Enable NIS Support check box.

5. Click the Configure NIS button to open the NIS Settings dialog box, shown in Figure 12-8.

6. If the NIS Domain Name text box is not already filled in, type the NIS domain name.

7. Type the NIS server's IP address or name in the NIS Server text box. The NIS Settings dialog box should now resemble Figure 12-8.

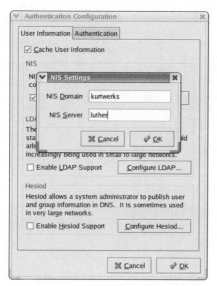

Figure 12–8: The completed NIS Settings dialog box

8. Click OK to close the NIS Settings dialog box.

9. Click OK to close the Authentication Configuration tool.

The following listing shows the edits made to /etc/yp.conf by the Authentication Configuration tool.

```
# /etc/yp.conf - ypbind configuration file
# Valid entries are
#
#domain NISDOMAIN server HOSTNAME
#       Use server HOSTNAME for the domain NISDOMAIN.
#
#domain NISDOMAIN broadcast
#       Use  broadcast  on  the local net for domain NISDOMAIN
#
#ypserver HOSTNAME
```

```
#       Use server HOSTNAME for the  local  domain.  The
#       IP-address of server must be listed in /etc/hosts.
#
domain kurtwerks server luther
```

 If you use the server's IP address instead of its name, the IP address will appear in place of the server name (luther, in this case).

NIS client programs, like the NIS servers, require RPC to function properly, so make sure the portmapper is running before starting the client daemon, ypbind. To start the client daemon, execute the following command, which invokes the ypbind initialization script:

```
# /sbin/service ypbind start
Binding to the NIS domain:                   [ OK ]
Listening for an NIS domain server.
```

After starting the NIS client daemon, use the command rpcinfo -u localhost ypbind to confirm that ypbind was able to register its service with the portmapper. The output should resemble the following:

```
# rpcinfo -u luther ypbind
program 100007 version 1 ready and waiting
program 100007 version 2 ready and waiting
```

 If you skip the test procedure outlined in this section, you must at least set the domain name and create the /var/yp directory. Without this directory, ypbind does not start.

Finally, use one of the NIS client commands discussed in the section titled "Key NIS Client Files and Commands" to test whether or not the client and server are communicating properly. For example, use the ypcat command to display the contents of the NIS shared password file:

```
# ypcat passwd.byname
```

In order for user lookups to work properly on the client, do not add users whose authentication information will be retrieved using NIS on the client system. Instead, add a + sign to the end of /etc/passwd on your NIS clients.

Now edit /etc/host.conf so that it uses NIS for hostname lookups. By default, the Red Hat host lookup configuration file looks like the following:

```
order hosts,bind
```

This configuration means that name service lookups first look in /etc/hosts, then use bind, the name server, to perform name look ups. Change this line so that it reads:

```
order hosts,nis,bind
```

This entry causes name lookups to query NIS after looking in /etc/hosts and before using the resolver library.

Lastly, look at /etc/nsswitch.conf. By default, Red Hat Enterprise Linux is configured to perform standard NIS (as opposed to NIS+) lookups when user authentication and related information is requested. Among other entries, you should see lines that look like the following:

```
passwd:     files nis
shadow:     files nis
group:      files nis
hosts:      files nis
```

Entries that begin with the hash sign (#) are commented out and can be ignored. If you don't see these entries, add them.

Configuring the Client Startup Files

As when configuring an NIS server, you must modify some system configuration files and make sure that the client daemon starts and stops when the system starts and stops. In addition to setting the NIS domain name in /etc/sysconfig/network and setting the server information in /etc/yp.conf, you must use the Service Configuration tool to make sure that the client daemon, ypbind, starts at boot time. To do so, start serviceconf as explained in the section on configuring an NIS server, scroll down to the bottom of the services list, and place a check mark beside the ypbind service (see Figure 12-9).

Select File → Save to save your changes, and then select File → Exit to close the Service Configuration tool. Finally, reboot the client system and watch the boot messages to ensure that ypbind actually starts. After rebooting the client system, NIS client services is up and running.

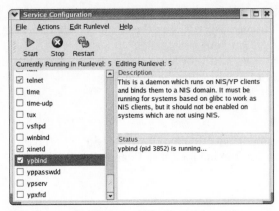

Figure 12-9: Enabling the NIS client at boot time

Key NIS Client Files and Commands

Table 12-2 lists the key NIS client configuration files and commands and briefly describes their purpose.

TABLE 12-2 NIS CLIENT CONFIGURATION FILES AND COMMANDS

File/Command	Description
ypwhich	Displays the name of the master NIS server
ypcat	Prints the entries in an NIS database
yppasswd	Changes user passwords and information on the NIS server
yppoll	Displays the server and version number of an NIS map
ypmatch	Prints the value of one or more entries in an NIS map
/etc/yp.conf	Configures the NIS client bindings
/etc/nsswitch.conf	Configures the system name database lookup
/etc/host.conf	Configures hostname resolution

ypwhich invoked with no arguments displays the name of the default NIS server. If invoked with the -d nisdomain option, it queries the master NIS server for the NIS domain named *nisdomain*. You can also specify use ypwhich hostname to query the NIS server, if any, on the machine named *hostname*. The -x option causes ypwhich to display the list of available maps.

The ypcat command allows you to view the contents of an NIS map. As with the ypwhich command, ypcat displays maps from the default server unless you request a specific NIS server using -d nisdomain. Similarly, to view the maps from a specific machine, use -h hostname, replacing *hostname* with the host in which you are interested. Suppose, for example, you want to know the list of hosts that the NIS server luther knows about. First, use ypwhich -x command to see a list of map nicknames available on luther:

```
$ ypcat -x
Use "ethers"    for map "ethers.byname"
Use "aliases"   for map "mail.aliases"
Use "services"  for map "services.byname"
Use "protocols" for map "protocols.bynumber"
Use "hosts"     for map "hosts.byname"
Use "networks"  for map "networks.byaddr"
Use "group"     for map "group.byname"
Use "passwd"    for map "passwd.byname"
```

This output means, for example, that the map hosts.byname can be accessed using the nickname or alias named host. So, let's try that with ypcat hosts:

```
$ ypcat hosts
192.168.0.3     advent
192.168.0.1     marta
192.168.0.5     martin
127.0.0.1       localhost.localdomain    localhost
127.0.0.1       localhost.localdomain    localhost
192.168.0.4     luther
```

The yppasswd command enables users to change their NIS passwords. What's wrong with using plain vanilla passwd? Simply put, the passwd command affects only the client machine. The yppasswd command updates the NIS maps on the NIS server, which means that the updated password will be effective across the network, not just on the client machine. In fact, if you use the passwd command for a user that is authenticated via NIS, the password change, if it succeeds, will be discarded the next time the NIS maps are updated.

Testing the NIS Configuration

If the preceding configuration steps work as they should, you can verify your NIS configuration with a few simple commands. For example, an NIS client configured as described in this chapter should retrieve its password information from the NIS server. So the following command, executed on an NIS client, should print the NIS server's password database:

```
# ypcat passwd
nfsnobody:!!:65534:65534:Anonymous NFS
User:/var/lib/nfs:/sbin/nologin
bubba:$1$F21EoTOW$32MNfbobZBidGOoSB9mks/:500:500:Bubba:/home/bubba:/
bin/bash
marysue:$1$Tn6MOck≡$VLfSEARlmgeRHzFHXuThr/:501:501:0. Mary
Sue:/home/marysue:/bin/bash
```

Notice that only the passwords printed maintained by the NIS maps are displayed. Local logins, that is, accounts present only on the client system, are not displayed. This separation is intentional – imagine the chaos that would ensue if the root account on client machine were controlled by an NIS server over which you had no control!

You can use the ypmatch command to print a specific piece of information. For example, to print an arbitrary user's NIS password entry, you can use a ypmatch command of the form ypmatch *username* passwd, where *username* is the name of the user in whom you are interested. So, to print bubba's password entry, the command is:

```
# ypmatch bubba passwd
bubba:$1$F21EoTOW$32MNfbobZBidGOoSB9mks/:500:500:Bubba:/home/bubba:/
bin/bash
```

To display marysue's group-file entry, likewise, the proper command is:

```
# ypmatch marysue group
marysue:!:501:
```

To display a list of the maps the NIS server is sharing, use the command ypcat -x, as shown in the following example:

```
# ypcat -x
Use "ethers"    for map "ethers.byname"
Use "aliases"   for map "mail.aliases"
Use "services"  for map "services.byname"
Use "protocols" for map "protocols.bynumber"
Use "hosts"     for map "hosts.byname"
Use "networks"  for map "networks.byaddr"
Use "group"     for map "group.byname"
Use "passwd"    for map "passwd.byname"
```

What About NIS+?

The Network Information Service Plus, NIS+, is a replacement for NIS that provides improved security, a more extensible naming model, and better support for large (okay, *enormous*) NIS installations. The security improvements include data encryption and secure RPC. The original NIS specification (often called *traditional NIS* to distinguish it from NIS+) transmitted information over the wire as clear text, making it an easy target for packet snoopers and ne'er-do-wells. Data encryption makes snoopers' job more difficult. The naming model in NIS+ is dramatically different. The new structure is very LDAP-like, organized around a tree of object nodes rather than a set of flat text files. Unfortunately, development of NIS+ for Linux has stopped. As a result, NIS+ for Linux is too immature to be considered for a production environment.

Configuring an Example NIS Client

This subsection illustrates configuring an NIS client to use the NIS services provided by the NIS server configured earlier in this chapter. As before, the NIS domain name is kurtwerks, running on the server `marta.kurtwerks.com`, which has an IP address 192.168.0.1.

1. Set the NIS domain name:

   ```
   # nisdomainname kurtwerks
   # nisdomainname
   kurtwerks
   ```

2. Edit `/etc/yp.conf` to identify the default NIS server. The completed configuration file is (without comments):

   ```
   ypserver 192.168.0.4
   ```

3. Make sure that the portmapper is running:

   ```
   # rpcinfo -p 192.168.0.4
      program vers proto   port
       100000    2   tcp    111  portmapper
       100000    2   udp    111  portmapper
   ```

4. Start the primary client daemon, `ypbind`:

   ```
   # /etc/rc.d/init.d/ypbind start
   Binding to the NIS domain:                    [ OK ]
   Listening for an NIS domain server.
   ```

5. Confirm that ypbind is running:

```
# rpcinfo -u 192.168.0.4 ypbind
program 100007 version 1 ready and waiting
program 100007 version 2 ready and waiting
```

6. Edit /etc/host.conf and add NIS to the services used for hostname lookups. The completed file looks like this:

```
order hosts,nis,bind
```

7. Use the Service Configuration tool, as explained earlier in this chapter, to configure ypbind to start at boot time (see Figure 12-9).

8. Reboot the server to make sure that the client daemon starts.

Strengthening NIS Security

In general, the same sorts of security issues that arise with NFS also pose a problem for NIS. Because NIS uses RPC, exploits based on the portmapper can lead to a system compromise. Moreover, because user passwords and other authentication information is transmitted as clear text, do not use NIS over the Internet unless you encrypt the transmission using SSH or another IP tunneling or encapsulation scheme. If possible and practical, your NIS domain name should not be a name associated with the server's DNS domain name, although this method is a common approach. The rationale for selecting different DNS and NIS domain names is that doing so makes it a little harder for crackers to retrieve the password database from your NIS server. On the server side, the primary security consideration is limiting access to NIS maps using the /var/yp/securenets configuration syntax described in the server configuration section of this chapter.

Summary

In this chapter, you saw how to configure NIS server and client services on Red Hat Enterprise Linux. You first learned how to set up and test an NIS server and how to ensure that the NIS server comes up after a system reboot. You also learned how to configure an NIS client to connect to an NIS server for user-authentication information.

Chapter 13

Connecting to Microsoft and Novell Networks

IN THIS CHAPTER

- ◆ Installing Samba
- ◆ Configuring the Samba server
- ◆ Starting the Samba server
- ◆ Connecting to a Samba client
- ◆ Connecting from a Windows PC to a Samba server
- ◆ Connecting to Novell networks
- ◆ Configuring the Novell client

USING A PROGRAM CALLED SAMBA, you can emulate the Windows file-sharing protocol and connect your Red Hat Network to a Windows network to share files and printers. Novell networks use a native protocol known as IPX, and with Red Hat Enterprise Linux you can emulate this protocol to enable file sharing and printing between Red Hat systems and Novel Netware systems. In this chapter, you learn how to connect a Red Hat network to a Microsoft network and a Novell network.

Connecting to Microsoft Networks

Computers running Windows 95 or greater use a protocol called Server Message Block (SMB) to communicate with each other and to share services such as file and print sharing. The Linux PC icon appears in the Windows Network Places window, and the files on the Linux PC can be browsed using Windows Explorer. The Windows filesystem can be mounted on your Linux system, and you can browse the Windows files from your Linux PC.

Installing Samba

Before you can use Samba to connect to the Windows computers, it must first be installed on the Linux PC. All current distributions of Red Hat Linux include three Samba packages: Samba, Samba-client, and Samba-common. They may not have been installed during the system installation. Even if they have been installed, you should always check for the latest versions to find out if any problems have been fixed by the latest release and to install it if necessary. To see if Samba is installed on your system, type the following at a terminal window:

```
rpm -q samba
```

If Samba is not installed, the command returns the output stating that Samba is not installed. If Samba is installed, the RPM query returns the version number of the Samba program installed on your system.

The latest version of Samba can be obtained at Samba's Web site: `http://www.samba.org`. Follow the instructions at the site for downloading the RPM file for your distribution. After downloading the Samba RPM file, install it as follows ("name of file" is the version number downloaded):

```
rpm -i samba(name of file)
```

Be sure to install the Samba-common RPM, and if you want to use the Samba-client, also install the Samba-client RPM. If you are unable to download the RPM version, or you want to compile the program yourself, download the file `samba-latest.tar.gz`. Extract the file using the following command:

```
tar -xfvz samba-latest.tar.gz
```

Change to the directory containing the extracted files (usually `/usr/src`) and type:

```
./configure
```

Press enter and wait for the command prompt to return. From the command prompt, type:

```
make
```

Press Enter and wait for the command prompt to return. Finally, type **make install** from the command prompt. If all goes well, Samba is installed when the command prompt returns. Now you need to configure it.

In order for Samba to provide its services, the Red Hat Linux PC needs to be configured.

 In this chapter, I refer to the Red Hat Linux PC as the Samba server and the Windows PC as the Samba client.

Configuring the Samba Server

Before you can use Samba to connect with your Windows PCs, it must be configured. While there are several graphical-based programs available for configuring Samba, these programs are just front ends that make changes to the Samba configuration file behind the scenes. It is much quicker and easier to just edit the Samba configuration file directly. The Samba configuration file is called smb.conf and is typically located in the /etc/samba directory by the installation program. A sample smb.conf file was created during the installation that can be used for reference and modification.

The smb.conf file is divided into several sections, called shares, the names of which I show as bracketed subsection titles in the following discussion. Shown next is the smb.conf file from one of the computers I use at school. Refer to this file to see what a section looks like as it is described.

```
# This is the main Samba configuration file. You should read the
# smb.conf(5) manual page in order to understand the options listed
# here. Samba has a huge number of configurable options (perhaps too
# many!) most of which are not shown in this example
# Any line which starts with a ; (semi-colon) or a # (hash)
# is a comment and is ignored. In this example we will use a #
# for commentry and a ; for parts of the config file that you
# may wish to enable
# NOTE: Whenever you modify this file you should run the command
"testparm"
# to check that you have not made any basic syntactic errors.
#======================= Global Settings
=====================================
[global]
        log file = /var/log/samba/%m.log
        smb passwd file = /etc/samba/smbpasswd
        load printers = yes
        passwd chat = *New*password* %n\n  *Retype*new*password* %n\n
*passwd:*all*authentication*tokens*updated*successfully*
        socket options = TCP_NODELAY SO_RCVBUF=8192 SO_SNDBUF=8192
        obey pam restrictions = yes
        encrypt passwords = yes
        passwd program = /usr/bin/passwd %u
        dns proxy = no
        netbios name = rhl
        writeable = yes
        server string = Samba Server
        printing = lprng
        path = /home
        default = homes
```

```
       unix password sync = Yes
       workgroup = Tardis
       printcap name = /etc/printcap
       security = user
       max log size = 50
       pam password change = yes

[homes]
       comment = Home Directories
       browseable = yes
       writeable = yes
       create mode = 0664
       directory mode = 0775
       max connections = 1

[printers]
       browseable = yes
       printable = yes
       path = /var/spool/samba
       comment = All Printers


[
```

[global]

The first section of the `smb.conf` file is the [global] section. The [global] section contains settings that apply to the entire server and default settings that may apply to the other shares. The [global] section contains a list of options and values in the format:

```
option = value
```

You have hundreds of options and values at your disposal, and you look at the most common ones here. For a complete listing of options, refer to the `smb.conf` man page. Some of the more significant options are discussed as follows.

- ◆ **workgroup = Tardis** is the name of the workgroup shown in the identification tab of the network properties box on the Windows computer.

- ◆ **smb passwd file = /etc/samba/smbpasswd** shows the path to the location of the Samba password file. Be sure that you include this option/value pair in your smb.conf file.

- ◆ **encryptpasswords = yes** beginning with Windows NT service pack 3 and later passwords are encrypted. If you are connecting to any systems running these versions of Windows, you should choose encrypted passwords.

- **netbios name = RHL** is the name by which the Samba server is known to the Windows computer.

- **server string = Samba Server** is shown as a comment on the Windows PC in the network browser.

- **security = user** is the level of security applied to server access. Other options are share, domain, and server. *Share* is used to make it easier to create anonymous shares that do not require authentication, and it is useful when the netbios names of the Windows computers are different from other names on the Linux computer. *Server* is used to specify the server to use if the password file is on another server in the network. *Domain* is used if the clients are added to a Windows NT domain using smbpasswd and login requests are executed by a Windows NT primary or backup domain controller.

- **log file = /var/log/samba/log** is the location of the log file.

- **max log size = 50** is the maximum size in kilobytes that the file can grow to.

- **socket options = TCP_NODELAY SO_RCVBUF=8192 SO_SNDBUF=8192** enables the server to be tuned for better performance. TCP_NODELAY is a default value; the BUF values set send and receive buffers.

- **dns proxy = No** indicates that the netbios name will not be treated like a DNS name and that there is no DNS lookup.

[homes]

The next section of the `smb.conf` file, [homes], is used to enable the server to give users quick access to their home directories. Refer to the `smb.conf` man page for a more complete description of how the [homes] section works.

- **comment = Home Directories** is a comment line.

- **browseable = yes** means that the directory will appear in the Windows file browser.

- **writeable = yes** means that users can write to their directories.

- **create mode = 0664** sets the default file permissions for files created in the directory.

- **directory mode = 0775** sets the default permissions for created directories.

- **max connections = 1** is the maximum number of simultaneous connections allowed. Setting this number to 1 prevents a user from logging in to the server from more than one location. Setting this number to 2 allows a user to log in from two locations and so on. Setting this number to 0 allows an unlimited number of connections.

[printers]

This section sets the options for printing.

◆ **path = /var/spool/samba** is the location of the printer spool directory.

◆ **printable = yes** enables clients to send print jobs to the specified directory. This option must be set, or printing does not work.

◆ **browseable = yes** means that the printer appears in the browse list.

 Be sure to have your printer properly configured for your Linux network before you attempt to set it up for use with Windows clients. You may need to enter the location of the path to the print spool for the printer you want to use in the smb.conf file.

The smb.conf file shown in the examples allows users who already have system accounts to access their home directories and to use printers. After modifying and saving the /etc/samba/smb.conf file, you should check the syntax of the file. To do this, you can use the testparm command as follows:

```
[root@terry terry]# testparm
Load smb config files from /etc/samba/smb.conf
Processing section "[printers]"
Processing section "[homes]"
Loaded services file OK.
Press enter to see a dump of your service definitions
```

Pressing Enter displays the contents of the configuration file. The smb.conf file is now ready to use.

Creating Samba Users

Next, you need to create a Samba users password file. You can convert all of your system users to Samba users by running the following command:

```
/etc/passwd | mksmbpasswd.sh > /etc/samba/smbpasswd
```

This utility creates only the users' accounts, not their passwords. You need to create passwords for your users by using the smbpasswd command and the user's name as shown in the following example:

```
[root@terry terry]# smbpasswd terry
New SMB password:
Retype new SMB password:
Password changed for user terry.
Password changed for user terry.
[root@terry terry]#
```

Starting the Samba Server

The last step is to start the Samba daemon. The command to start Samba is:

```
[root@terry terry]# /sbin/service smb start
Starting SMB services:                                    [  OK  ]
Starting NMB services:                                    [  OK  ]
[root@terry terry]#
```

At this point, you should have a functioning Samba server running on your system. It is configured to allow users who have accounts on your Red Hat Enterprise Linux system to access their home directories from a Windows PC. Logged-in users are also able to use the printers configured with the Red Hat system.

Connecting to a Samba Client

In this section, you learn how to connect your system to other systems running the smb protocol. Connecting a PC running Windows 2000 or XP is covered in the section "Connecting from a Windows PC to the Samba Server," later in this chapter. You can connect your system to any computer that is running the smb protocol, whether it is a Windows PC or another Linux system running Samba. The connection can be made from the command line using two methods. The first uses a utility called smbclient, and the command syntax is `smbclient //computer name/directory`, as shown in the following example. Be sure to replace the computer name in the example with the name of your computer.

```
[root@terry terry]# smbclient //terrycollings/c
added interface ip=192.168.9.93 bcast=192.168.9.255
nmask=255.255.255.0
Got a positive name query response from 192.168.9.102
(192.168.9.102)
Password:
Domain=[Tardis] OS=[Windows 5.0] Server=[Windows 2000 LAN Manager]
smb: \>
```

The preceding example shows me logging in to my Windows PC from my Red Hat system. I was prompted for a password to log in and was given some information about the Windows system and a command prompt. You can type **help** at the command prompt to get a list of possible commands. The commands at the smb prompt are very similar to command-line ftp commands. To exit the connection, type **exit**.

Another way to make the files on the Samba client accessible on your Red Hat system is to mount the client file system on your file system. You can do this using the smbmount command. The syntax for this command is smbmount //computer name/directory /mysystem/mount/point, as shown in the following example:

```
[root@terry terry]# smbmount //terrycollings/c /mnt/windows
Password:
[root@terry terry]# cd /mnt/windows
[root@terry windows]# ls
arcldr.exe              MSDOS.SYS             quicktime
arcsetup.exe            Muhlnet Setup         QuickTimeInstaller.zip
AUTOEXEC.BAT            My Download Files     Recycled
boot.ini                My Music              rhsa
camtasia                NALCache              W2K.CD
CONFIG.SYS              netplus               Windows Update Setup
Files
Documents and Settings  Novell                WINNT
Drivers                 NTDETECT.COM          WSREMOTE.ID
fgc                     ntldr                 WT61CE.UWL
hiberfil.sys            p2.pdf                WT61OZ.UWL
IO.SYS                  pagefile.sys          WT61UK.UWL
lconfig.aot             Program Files         WT61US.UWL
Local Muhlnet           PUTTY.RND
[root@terry windows]#
```

In this example, I am connecting to the same Windows PC to which I connected in the previous example. However, by using the smbmount command, I am mounting the Windows file system on my Red Hat file system. After entering the password for the Windows PC and returning to the command prompt, I change to the directory that I just mounted and run the ls command to obtain a directory listing of the Windows PC share I mounted. I can now easily move files between the two systems using regular file-system utilities.

You can put the mount command into a local startup script so that the directories are mounted at system boot, if you desire. Use the command as shown earlier and add an option to look for a file that contains the login username and password.

```
smbmount //terrycollings/c /mnt/windows -o credentials=/home/terry.sambacred
```

You need to create a file as shown in the following code. I created a hidden file called .sambacred and in the file I placed these two lines:

```
Username = terry
password = (password)
```

Be sure to put the information relevant to your system for the path to the file and the username and password. The reason for creating the hidden file and pointing to it from the `smbmount` command is to prevent someone from being able to find out the password that is in the file in plain text. Be sure to change the permissions on this file accordingly.

Using this method is preferable to placing the mount information in the `/etc/fstab` file. While it is possible to place the mount information in the `/etc/fstab` file, someone could find out the username and password by just looking at the `/etc/fstab` file.

To unmount the client file system, enter the following `smbumount` command and the path to the directory to unmount as follows:

```
# smbumount /mnt/windows
```

After you press enter, the file system will be unmounted.

Connecting from a Windows PC to the Samba Server

Now you are ready to test your connection on the Windows PC. For systems running Windows 2000 or XP, no configuration is required. On the Windows computer, double-click the My Network Places icon from the desktop. In the Network Places window, you should now see a listing for the Red Hat computer, which in this example should be rhl10. Double-click the rhl10 PC icon, and you will see the shares you made available.

When you double-click the directory share from the rhl10 PC, you are prompted for a username and password to enter the directories. That's all there is to it. Now you can share files between your Linux and Windows computers.

Why use Samba instead of NFS?

Earlier, you set up the Network File System to enable file sharing across your network. Why didn't you just use NFS to share the Windows files? Well, you could have, but it makes more sense to use Samba to communicate with Windows computers. The Server Message Block (SMB) protocol is how Windows computers communicate with each other. It is the Windows native protocol for sharing files and printers. By using the same protocol, you are ensuring that file and printer sharing operate with a minimum of difficulty.

You can use the Windows Map Network Drive command to set up a Windows system to always connect to your Samba share when you start the Windows PC.

To learn how to set up a printer to use under Samba, refer to Chapter 9.

Connecting to Novell Networks

With Red Hat Enterprise Linux, you can easily configure your system to connect to Novell Netware servers. In this section, you learn how to configure your Red Hat system to be a Novell client.

Configuring the Novell Client

Two packages need to be installed to enable communication between the Novell servers and your Red Hat system. The first package to load is ipxutils, which is Internetwork Packet Exchange, the Novell protocol for networking. The second package you need to load is ncpfs, the Novell filesystem package. If you do not have these packages installed on your system, the RPMs can be found on the Red Hat Installation CDs. Install the packages before continuing.

After the packages have been installed, two modules need to be loaded before you can configure the Novell client. From a terminal command prompt, enter the following command to load the modules.

```
#/sbin/modprobe ipx ncpfs
```

The ipx and ncpfs kernel modules are now in the kernel-unsupported package, which may not be installed. You may have to install this package to obtain the necessary modules.

After the modules are loaded, you need to configure your ipx connection by entering the following command, which attempts to automatically detect and configure your ipx connection.

```
#/sbin/ipx_configure -auto_interface=on -auto_primary=on
```

The previous command enables the automatic configuration of the interface and detects the primary connection. You can check if your configuration is successful by issuing the slist command from the terminal prompt. The output from the slist command is shown in Figure 13-1.

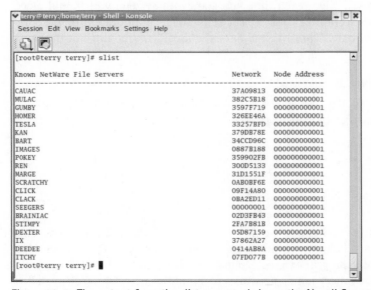

Figure 13-1: The output from the slist command shows the Novell Servers on the network.

If you receive a listing similar to that seen in Figure 13-1, your ipx configuration is correct and you can attempt to log in to a server and mount its filesystem on your system. To do this you will use the ncpmount command as follows:

```
ncpmount -S (fileserver name) (fileserver directory (optional)) -U (fileserver
login id (complete context)) -P (password) (directory mount point).
```

Be sure to replace the information in the parentheses with the information appropriate to your system.

Suppose I want to log in to the server BART, shown in Figure 13-1, and mount its filesystem on my system in the bart directory. I need to enter the following command:

```
# ncpmount -S BART -U terry.mediaservices.admin -P password
/home/terry/novell/bart
```

After logging in and mounting the Novell filesystem on my system, a directory listing shows the contents of the server Bart. Be sure to replace the information in the example with the information appropriate for your systems.

You can unmount an NCP filesystem by issuing the `ncpumount` command and specifying the mount point to unmount. During system shutdown, the ncp mounts are cleanly unmounted, so it is not necessary to unmount the filesystem before shutting down the system.

If you do not want to go through the manual configuration process to connect your system as a Novell client each time you start your system, you should place the commands in this section in your `rc.local` file. The configuration then occurs automatically at boot time. You can even have the filesystem mounted at the same time, if you desire.

 See the "Adding a Networked Novell (NCP) Printer" section in Chapter 9 to configure a Novell networked printer.

Summary

In this chapter, you learned about the Server Message Block (SMB) protocol. This protocol is used by Windows computers to communicate with each other. You learned about a Linux program called Samba, which emulates the SMB protocol and can be used to connect Linux networks to Windows networks. You installed and configured Samba on a Red Hat Enterprise Linux server and configured the Windows clients. You also learned how to configure your Red Hat system as a Novell client using the NCP filesystem.

Chapter 14

Connecting to Apple Networks

IN THIS CHAPTER

+ Understanding AppleTalk

+ Installing the AppleTalk software

+ Configuring the Appletalk daemons

+ Configuring Red Hat as an AppleTalk client

IN THIS CHAPTER, you learn how to connect a Red Hat machine to an Apple network. The Apple network uses a network routing and addressing suite called *AppleTalk* to communicate between Apple machines. Using a suite of Linux daemons known collectively as *Netatalk*, you can communicate with Apple machines using the various AppleTalk protocols. You can set up file and print sharing between Apple and Linux machines. You can even set up a Red Hat machine as an AppleTalk router.

Understanding AppleTalk

AppleTalk is the Apple standard for personal computer networking. Much as Linux uses NFS and LPR for file and printer sharing, Apple computers use AppleTalk. You need to install and configure AppleTalk for Red Hat Enterprise Linux in the event that you want to either access the files and printers of an Apple machine from the Red Hat machine, or vice versa. Luckily, AppleTalk is an intelligent set of protocols and is convenient to use. Almost all aspects of AppleTalk routing are worked out automatically by the AppleTalk routers. Therefore, AppleTalk networks require minimal configuration and maintenance.

AppleTalk Addressing

Each AppleTalk address is a network number combined with a node number. An AppleTalk *network number* is a 16-bit number and ranges from 0 to 65536. The range 1 to 65279 is open for arbitrary use, while the numbers 65280 to 65534 are reserved for networks that contain no AppleTalk routers. A *node number* is an 8-bit number (which means it ranges from 0 to 255) with two reserved addresses, allowing for 253 nodes per network number.

In the case of a stand-alone network that contains no AppleTalk routers, no configuration of addresses should be necessary. If the default configuration files are used, the clients and servers in the network resolve their various addresses automatically. If AppleTalk routers are already present in the network, the server can poll the existing routers in order to automatically configure itself. If the server is to be the first AppleTalk router in the network, network numbers must be assigned to the various network interfaces that communicate with the AppleTalk network. This auto-configuration function is controlled by the `atalkd` program file. Information on configuring this and other daemons can be found in the section "Configuring the Appletalk Daemons."

Apple Zones

AppleTalk zones exist for three reasons: organization of the network, descriptive naming, and access control. They are similar in this way to a hybrid of domain names and HTTP realms. In a small network, zones are not very useful. By default, all nodes are contained in the default zone, which is unnamed. In a larger network where organization and access control are issues, you can name zones and define which nodes are in which zones. Each zone can be assigned to multiple networks. Also, each network can be assigned to multiple zones. Flexibility in zone assignment allows for a very flexible system of network organization. However, zones can contain only addresses, not other zones. Since nesting zones is not possible, the namespace is more or less flat.

Zone naming is controlled by the AppleTalk routers. If the Red Hat machine is set up as an AppleTalk router, the zone-to-network-address mappings need to be defined in the `atalkd.conf` file. Otherwise, each machine simply needs to be configured to specify which zone it is in.

Installing the AppleTalk Software

This section discusses the AppleTalk DDP kernel module, installing Netatalk, and configuring Netatalk.

DDP is the AppleTalk datagram protocol (Datagram Delivery Protocol). It is similar to TCP, but uses AppleTalk addresses rather than IP addresses. DDP is the lowest level of the AppleTalk protocol suite. DDP is included as a kernel module in Red Hat Enterprise Linux.

You should first check to see if the DDP module is already running on your system. Execute the following command to see if the DDP module is loading:

```
# lsmod | grep -i apple
```

TIP You should use `lsmod` to see if a module is loaded rather than `dmesg`. The buffer that `dmesg` uses is small and circular, so when its buffer fills up, the first messages at the front of the buffer get overwritten, causing information loss.

If any lines are printed that look like this: "`AppleTalk 0.18a for Linux NET4.0`," the AppleTalk DDP module is already loaded. You can now progress to installing and configuring the Netatalk daemon.

If the DDP module is not already in the kernel, insert it with the command:

```
# modprobe appletalk
```

After inserting the kernel module, it is time to install and configure Netatalk.

Installing Netatalk

AppleTalk consists of a whole suite of protocols, such as RTMP, NBP, ZIP, AEP, ATP, PAP, ASP, and AFP. These are application-level protocols corresponding roughly to IP-based application-level protocols such as DHCP and DNS. Only DDP is in the kernel. The rest of the protocols are implemented in user-space daemons and are part of the Netatalk package. Netatalk runs on many variations of UNIX, including Linux. Two versions of Netatalk are available: the official version and a version extensively patched by Adrian Sun and known as *netatalk+asun*.

The Adrian Sun patches are primarily for supporting AFP 2.2 (AppleShare TCP/IP). The netatalk+asun version is generally preferable. However, the two versions merged in Netatalk 1.5.

If the most recent version of Netatalk is not installed, you can download it from `rpmfind.net`. The latest stable version of netatalk+asun at the time of this writing is 2.1.3-22. The latest development versions are available from the Netatalk project at `http://netatalk.sourceforge.net`.

You install the Netatalk package just like any other Red Hat package, as in the following command:

```
# rpm -ivh -install netatalk+asun-2.1.3-22.rpm
```

Once Netatalk is installed, you can configure all of the separate daemons that are included.

Some versions of Netatalk have PAM (Pluggable Authentication Module) support and others do not. The netatalk+asun package includes PAM support. If this is a desirable feature on your system, make sure that you have PAM correctly configured and that you install the netatalk+asun version of the package.

Configuring Netatalk

To use Netatalk under Linux, you need to have entries for the AppleTalk protocols in your /etc/services file. When you install the Netatalk RPM, it automatically appends these entries to your /etc/services file:

```
rtmp          1/ddp          # Routing Table Maintenance Protocol
nbp           2/ddp          # Name Binding Protocol
echo          4/ddp          # AppleTalk Echo Protocol
zip           6/ddp          # Zone Information Protocol
afpovertcp    548/tcp        # AFP over TCP
afpovertcp    548/udp
```

You should not have to modify these entries. However, you might want to check and make sure that they have been successfully added to your /etc/services file.

The Netatalk RPM package installs the /etc/rc.d/init.d/atalk script, which runs the various Netatalk daemons. The atalk script is run automatically during the boot process. You can configure several options that determine which daemons the atalk script launches and how it launches them. The atalk script reads its configuration information from the /etc/atalk/netatalk.conf script. This script sets the following options for how atalk should behave:

afpd_max_clients

This option determines the maximum number of clients that can connect to the AppleTalk filesharing daemon (afpd) at one time. The default value is 5, which is probably too small for most networks.

atalk_name

This option determines what the NBP name of the local AppleTalk host should be. The default for this option is to run the following shell script command:

```
# hostname | cut -d. -f1
```

This command takes the hostname of the machine and uses just the first part. So, for instance, if the hostname for the machine was blanu.net, the NBP name of the AppleTalk host would be set to blanu. This command may not set the NBP name to a desirable value if the hostname of the machine is not set correctly. You can type the command hostname to determine what the hostname of the machine is currently set to.

papd_run

This option determines whether the Printer Access Protocol Daemon (papd) should be run. The default is yes. You can change it to no if you want to prevent papd from running. You should disable papd if you do not want other computers to be able to access the machine's printers via the AppleTalk network.

afpd_run

This option determines whether the Apple File Protocol Daemon (afpd) should be run. The default is yes. You can change this to no if you want to prevent afpd from running. You should disable afpd if you do not want other computers to be able to access the machine's files via the AppleTalk network.

atalk_bground

This option determines whether the AppleTalk daemon (atalkd) should run in the background or take control of the executing process. The default value is yes, as the atalk script normally runs on boot, and it is customary to launch daemons in the background. The only reason to change this option to no is if you are going to run atalk manually from the command line.

After you have configured the settings in the /etc/atalk/config file, you can edit the configuration files for the various daemons: atalkd, papd, and afpd.

The atalkd program reads its configuration from /etc/atalk/atalkd.conf. A sample version of this file is automatically installed by the RPM. If for some reason this file is not present when atalkd is run, atalkd attempts to configure all interfaces automatically and then writes a configuration file.

Configuring the Appletalk Daemons

The primary daemon in the Netatalk suite is atalkd. The atalkd program is responsible for all AppleTalk network services other than DDP (which is, as you know, in the kernel). The atalkd daemon takes care of routing, name registration, name lookup, zone registration, zone lookup, and the AppleTalk Echo Protocol (similar to ping). The atalkd daemon is usually run at boot time. If you install the RPM package, it should automatically be set to run at boot time because the RPM installs the script /etc/rc.d/init.d/atalk. This is the script that should be run to start and stop atalkd and also to cause it to reload its configuration file.

Configuring atalkd

The atalkd configuration file, atalkd.conf, consists of one interface configuration command per line. Lines starting with # are comments and ignored. To configure atalkd, a number of steps need to be performed:

1. Configuring the AppleTalk interfaces

2. Configuring seed information

3. Configuring zone information

4. Configuring routing information

5. Configuring (optional) additional information

Each AppleTalk interface has a line in the `atalkd.conf` file specifying all of its configuration parameters. Each interface configuration entry has the following format:

```
interface [-seed] [-phase number] [-net net-range] [-addr address]
[-zone zonename]
```

All of the parameters except for the interface name are optional. The interface parameter is the name of the interface to configure. The default configuration file installed by the RPM is actually empty. This is fine because `atalkd` can automatically discover and configure all local interfaces without any configuration. The only reason to add interfaces to the `atalkd.conf` file is to specify the optional information about them or to exclude some local interfaces from configuration.

The simplest `atalkd.conf` file would have just a list of local interfaces, one on each line. You do not have to specify the loopback device interface as it is already configured automatically. Here is an example of a simple configuration file:

```
eth0
eth1
```

This file would have approximately the same effect as an empty configuration file. However, if you want to exclude some local interfaces from being configured by `atalkd`, excluding them from a nonempty configuration file should do the trick.

The primary use of the `atalkd.conf` file is to specify the seed options for your various interfaces. The `-seed` directive enables you to specify the seed information for an interface. Although all of the options for interface configuration are optional, if you specify a `-seed` option, all of the rest of the options are then mandatory. The `-seed` option does not take a parameter. It only specifies that the rest of the parameters should be considered as seed information and should be overridden by values obtained from the network's routers. If a router on the network disagrees with the seed information provided for an interface, `atalkd` exits when it is started. If `-seed` is not specified, all of the other specified parameters may be overridden automatically by `atalkd` when the interface is configured.

The first `-zone` directive in each interface configuration line specifies the default zone for that interface. Of course, each interface can be in multiple zones. The behavior of the default zone depends on the phase. Phase 1 has only one zone, so a different default zone cannot be specified. In Phase II, all routers on the AppleTalk network are configured to use the default zone and must all agree on what the default zone is. Specifying * for any `-zone` parameter is shorthand for specifying that the zone should be the same as the default zone on the first interface. The default zone for a machine is determined by the configuration of the local routers. If you want a service to appear in a zone other than the default zone for the machine, you must configure the service to tell it what zone to be in.

If you are connecting the Red Hat Netatalk router to an existing AppleTalk network, you must contact the administrators of the AppleTalk network to obtain appropriate network addresses for your network interfaces. The `atalkd` daemon automatically acts as an AppleTalk router if more than one local interface is configured.

Each interface must be assigned a unique net range. A net range is two network addresses separated by a `""`. The interface controls all network addresses in the net range. A network address is between 1 and 65279. The addresses 0 and 65535 are illegal. The addresses 65280 to 65534 are reserved. It is best to use the smallest net range that is still useful. When in doubt omit the `-net` option.

All of the optional parameters have default values. The default for `-phase` is 2. The phase can also be specified on the command line when running `atalkd` using the `-1` and `-2` command line options. If `-addr` is specified but `-net` is not, a net range of 1 is the default.

Additional configuration

One important issue to consider when configuring the Red Hat system is whether or not to disable `papd`, the AppleTalk printer daemon. By default, the system is configured to run `papd` with the default empty configuration file in `/etc/atalk.papd`. Since the configuration file is empty, `papd` attempts to make accessible to the network all local printers as configured in `/etc/printcap` to be accessible via AppleTalk and PAP (Printer Access Protocol). This procedure might be undesirable for several reasons:

◆ A printer on the Red Hat machine might not be meant for public access. For instance, it might require more expensive toner or paper. Also, it might be in an inaccessible location so that people would not be able to pick up their printouts.

◆ You might want to separate Linux printers and Apple printers for purposes of load balancing. You might not want everyone to be printing on the Linux printers when there are perfectly good Apple printers going unused.

◆ If the Red Hat machine is set up to be a client to remote AppleTalk printers, by default, these printers are exposed to AppleTalk as well as the local printers. This situation causes the AppleTalk printers to have two entries, which can be very confusing to users.

In the latter case you can put entries into the `papd.conf` file for any printers that you want to expose via AppleTalk, excluding remote AppleTalk printers. In the other cases, you can simply stop `papd` from running on boot. That way, no Red Hat printers are exposed via AppleTalk.

The `papd` program is executed on boot by the `/etc/rc.d/init.d/atalk` program. This program reads information about what daemons to run from the file `/etc/atalk/config`. If you want to disable `papd` from running, you can change the line `PAPD_RUN` from `yes` to `no`.

Configuring AppleTalk File Sharing

The `afpd` program provides an AppleTalk Filing Protocol (AFP) interface to the Linux file system. The `afpd` program is normally run at boot time by the `/etc/rc.d/init.d/atalk` script. The `afpd` program is useful if you want remote computers to be able to access the files on the Linux machine over the AppleTalk network. If this is not a desirable situation, `afpd` can be disabled. More information on disabling `afpd` is available in the section called "Configuring Netatalk." Note that it is not necessary to run `afpd` in order for the Red Hat machine to access remote file systems over AppleTalk, either on Macs or on other Linux machines, which are running `afpd`. The Red Hat machine needs only to run `afpd` to expose its own files to the network.

The `afpd` program has many command line arguments, all of which are optional. The syntax for calling `afpd` is as follows:

```
afpd [-d] [-f defaultvolumes] [-s systemvolumes] [-u] [-n nbpname]
[-c maxconnections] [-g guest] [-G] [-K] [-C] [-A]
```

Table 14-1 lists and briefly describes each argument to `afpd`.

TABLE 14-1 ARGUMENTS USED WHEN CALLING AFPD

Argument	Description
-d	Specifies that the daemon not fork, and that a trace of all AFP commands be written to `stdout`.
-f defaultvolumes	Specifies that `defaultvolumes` should be read for a list of default volumes to offer, instead of `/etc/atalk/AppleVolumes.default`.
-s systemvolumes	Specifies that `systemvolumes` should be read for a list of volumes that all users are offered, instead of `/etc/atalk/AppleVolumes.system`.
-u	Reads the user's `AppleVolumes` file first. This option causes volume names in the user's `AppleVolumes` file to override volume names in the system's `AppleVolumes` file. The default is to read the system `AppleVolumes` file first. Note that this option does not affect the precedence of filename extension mappings: the user's `AppleVolumes` file always has precedence.

Argument	Description
-n *nbpname*	Specifies that *nbpname* should be used for NBP registration, instead of the first component of the hostname in the local zone.
-c *maxconnections*	Specifies the maximum number of connections to allow for this afpd. The default is 5.
-g *guest*	Specifies the name of the guest account. The default is nobody.
-G	Causes the server to not offer NoUserAuthent logins. The default is to enable all available login methods.
-K	Causes the server to not offer Kerberos IV logins. The default is to enable all available login methods.
-C	Causes the server to not offer Cleartext Passwrd logins. The default is to enable all available login methods.
-A	Causes the server to not offer AFS Kerberos logins. The default is to enable all available login methods.

The afpd program reads several configuration files. The /etc/atalk/afpd.conf file configures options affecting the operation of the daemon. The volumes to share over the network are configured in several files. The /etc/atalk/AppleVolumes.system file is first read. Then, the /etc/atalk/AppleVolumes .default file is read, and the settings are combined with those from /etc/atalkAppleVolumes.system. If the /etc/atalk/AppleVolumes.default file is not found, the $HOME/AppleVolumes file is read instead. If $HOME/AppleVolumes is not found, the $HOME/.AppleVolumes file is read instead. Because afpd is normally run as root, it normally reads /root/AppleVolumes or /root/.AppleVolumes.

This automatic behavior can lead to confusing behavior if you try to test afpd manually as a user other than root and no /etc/atalk/AppleVolumes.default file is present. The settings are different when run as root or as another user. However, the /etc/atalk/AppleVolumes.system file is supplied by the RPM, so this is the file that is normally read when afpd is run.

You do not generally have to edit the /etc/atalk/AppleVolumes.default file. This file provides useful default file extension mappings. Changes should generally be made in the /etc/atalk/AppleVolumes.system file as the default version of this file is empty.

The `AppleVolumes` configuration files contain both volume and extension information. This information is formatted one item per line. The lines have the following syntax:

`pathname [volumename] .extension [type] [creator]`

If the `volumename` is omitted, the last portion of the `pathname` is used. If the `type` is omitted, the value `????` is used. If `creator` is omitted, the value `UNIX` is used.

Setting Up AFP Accounts

With Netatalk, AFP user accounts are the same as Linux user accounts. Therefore, you must add user accounts for each AFP user that you want to be able to log in. Authentication of these accounts is done using the standard Linux login authentication mechanism, which checks the password supplied by the user with the password stored in the `/etc/passwd` file. Note that `afpd` checks to see if the user has a valid login shell by checking the shell which the user is set to use against the list of shells in the `/etc/shells` file. If the user is using a shell that is not included in that file, authentication fails.

You can set up AppleTalk so that it works with AFS. First, of course, you must have the AFS server installed and configured properly. You also need Kerberos 4, patch level 10, properly installed and configured in order to do authentication.

Next, add an AFB principal name entry to enable Kerberos authentication. The entry takes the following form:

`afpserver.NBP_name@realm`

For example,

`afpserver.blanu@dnalounge`

The `NBP_name` must match the Kerberos principal name for authentication to occur. If `afpd`'s default NBP name does not match the site's method for generating principal names, you must use the `-n` option when running `afpd`.

Configuring AppleTalk Printer Sharing

You can configure AppleTalk printers in one of two ways. You can access a remote printer over AppleTalk from a Red Hat Enterprise Linux system or you can expose the printers accessible on the Red Hat system so that they are usable for remote computers via AppleTalk. In this section, I describe how to make printers on the Red Hat machine accessible over AppleTalk to remote machines. Setting up the Red Hat machine to act as a client to remote printers is presented in the section "Configuring Red Hat as an AppleTalk Client."

The program that exposes local printers over the AppleTalk network is named papd. It is a daemon that communicates over the network using the Printer Access Protocol (PAP). The papd daemon spools print jobs to lpd, the Linux printer daemon. After accepting a print job from the network, papd spools the job into the lpd spool directory and then wakes up the lpd daemon to examine and process the modified printing spool. The management of the spools and the actual process of printing are handled entirely by the lpd daemon.

The papd daemon is usually started at boot time just as atalkd and lpd are. It reads its configuration from the /etc/atalk/papd.conf file. /etc/atalk/papd .conf uses the same format as the /etc/printcap file used for configuring lpd. The name of the entry in the papd.conf file is registered via NBP, the AppleTalk Name Binding Protocol, so that the printer can be accessed remotely using AppleTalk and PAP.

The papd daemon has three optional parameters, described in Table 14-2.

TABLE 14-2 PAPD ARGUMENTS

Parameter	Description
-d	Do not fork or disassociate from the terminal. Write some debugging information to stderr.
-f configfile	Consult configfile instead of /etc/atalk/papd.conf for the configuration information.
-p printcap	Consult printcap instead of /etc/printcap for LPD configuration information.

The papd daemon is launched on boot by the /etc/rc.d/init.d/atalk script. This script is responsible for starting, stopping, and reloading all of the Netatalk daemons. You don't normally have to edit this script. However, because this is where papd is run, you might need to edit /etc/rc.d/init.d/atalk to add optional command line arguments. Generally you don't have to specify any of papd's optional command line arguments.

The printcap file format enables you to specify capabilities about a printer. Different printers support different capabilities. AppleTalk printers support the capabilities listed in Table 14-3.

The papd.conf file is only for exposing printers over the AppleTalk network. The printers must already be set up to work with lpd by having entries added to the printcap file.

TABLE 14-3 APPLETALK PRINTER CAPABILITIES

Name	Type	Default	Description
pd	str	".ppd"	Pathname to PPD file
pr	str	"lp"	LPD printer name
op	str	"operator"	Operator name for LPD spooling

If no configuration file is present, the hostname of the machine is used when the printers are registered with NBP and all other NBP options have default values. If no configuration file is present, papd attempts to expose all printers present in the lapd configuration file /etc/printcap to the network. This method works in most cases, and the configuration file installed by the RPM is in fact empty. The only reason to edit the papd.conf file is to exclude printers from being network accessible or to specify additional or nonstandard information about the printers.

Here is a sample /etc/atalk/papd.conf file:

```
Mac Printer Spooler::pr=ps:pd=/usr/share/lib/ppd/
HPLJ_4M.PPD:op=mcs:HP Printer::
```

This configuration file sets up two printers that are assumed to already be configured in /etc/printcap. The first printer is named ps in the printcap file and is exposed to the AppleTalk network via the NBP name Mac Printer Spooler. It uses the PPD file HPLJ_4M.PPD, located in /usr/share/lib/ppd. It specifies that all jobs run on this printer should be owned by the user named mcs. The second printer is exposed on the network by the NBP name HP Printer. As all capabilities are omitted from this entry, the defaults are assumed for all options. Since a configuration file exists, printers not included in the configuration file are not exposed to the network via AppleTalk even if they exist in the /etc/printcap file.

Configuring Red Hat as an AppleTalk Client

In addition to being an AppleTalk server and router, a Red Hat Enterprise Linux machine can be an AppleTalk client. This capability is useful if you're adding a Linux machine to an existing network of Apple machines or integrating a Linux network with an Apple one. The first order of business is of course to get Netatalk configured and to run atalkd. Once the Red Hat machine is connected to the AppleTalk network, it is time to choose an Apple Printer to connect to.

In order to print to an Apple printer, you need to know its zone. Use the nbplkup command to find this information. It is used to list all objects in the AppleTalk network along with zone, address, and type information. In order to find the zone for the specific printer you want, you must know its name. Of course, you can browse the available objects using nbplkup if you don't remember the printer's name.

The syntax for the nbplkup command is as follows:

```
nbplkup [-r maxresp] pattern
```

nbplkup uses NBP, the AppleTalk Name Binding Protocol, to find information about AppleTalk objects in the network. The *pattern* that you supply nbplkup with determines which objects it displays information about. The *maxresp* argument specified with -r is used to control how many entries are returned. The default number of entries to return is 1000.

The syntax for the nbplkup *pattern* is:

```
object:type@zone
```

The *object* and *type* field can have a literal value or =, which acts as a wildcard allowing for any values to match. The *zone* field can have a literal value or *, which matches the local zone. The fields can also be omitted individually. If they are omitted, the values for the omitted fields are taken from the $NBPLOOKUP environment variable. The format of the environment variable is the same as the command line pattern. Only fields not specified in the command line pattern are taken from $NBPLOOKUP. If the omitted fields are not supplied in $NBPLOOKUP (because it is not set or it also has omitted fields), they have hard-coded defaults. The default object name is the first component of the machine's hostname as supplied by gethostbyname(). The default type is AFPServer. The default zone is *, specifying the local zone.

Once the NBP name of the printer has been determined, you can configure the Red Hat machine to access the printer remotely via AppleTalk. First you should check on the status of the printer to make sure that it is connected and operational. The program to run this is called papstatus.

The papstatus command is used for reporting the status of a remote AppleTalk printer. It has one required argument, which specifies the NBP name of the remote printer. The papstatus program is executed as follows:

```
# papstatus [ -p nbpname ]
```

Here is an example of the papstatus command:

```
# papstatus -p "HP Writer"
```

After confirming that the printer is operational on the network, you may find it useful to print a test page using AppleTalk Printer Access Protocol (PAP). The program to do this is pap.

Using the pap Command

The pap command is used to connect to the AppleTalk printer daemon, papd, and to send it files to be printed. The pap program is not normally used directly to print files. Printing is normally done via the Red Hat printing mechanisms, which typically use lpd to print files. The lpd program needs to be configured to use pap behind the scenes for printing on remote AppleTalk printers. However, pap can be used directly to test the setup of the printers and the network before lpd has been configured. When the pap command is executed it attempts to make a connection with the remote printer using the AppleTalk Printer Access Protocol.

The syntax for pap is as follows:

```
pap [-c] [-e] [-p nbpname] [-s statusfile] [files]
```

All of the command line parameters are optional. If no *files* are specified on the command line, pap reads the file to print from standard input. If no printer is specified using -p *nbpname*, pap looks in its current working directory for a file named .paprc. If .paprc is present, pap parses it to find the NBP name of the printer to print to.

The format of the .paprc file is a list of NBP names. Lines beginning with # are treated as comments and ignored. If the type portion of the name is omitted, the printer type defaults to LaserWriter. If the zone portion of the name is omitted, the zone defaults to the default local zone of the host machine.

The -c option tells pap to inform the printer that it has been waiting forever. If this option is not specified, pap tells the printer how long it has actually been waiting. This option is useful for getting a print job printed immediately, cutting in front of other print jobs. Printers sometimes schedule print jobs so that the ones that have been waiting longer get printed sooner. Therefore, specifying that the print job has been waiting forever enables it to be printed sooner than it would have been otherwise.

The -e option specifies that any messages from the printer which pap might print should be sent to stderr instead of stdoiut. This option is useful when pap is invoked by another program. When pap is invoked by the psf program, for instance, pap is given this option.

The -s option specifies the file to which the printer status should be written. While pap is waiting for the printer to process the input that is sent to it, it receives messages detailing the status of the print operation. If this option is specified, the file is overwritten to contain the most recent status message received from the printer. If this option is not specified, status messages print to stdout unless the -e option has been specified, in which case they print to stderr. This option is useful when pap is invoked from another program. When pap is invoked by the psf program, for instance, pap is given this option.

Here is an example of pap:

```
# pap -c -p "HP Writer:LaserWriter@*" testfile.ps
```

This command prints the file testfile.ps on the printer named HP Writer, which is of type "LaserWriter" and is in the local zone, which is designated by the special name *. The printer is told that the print job has been waiting forever, so the print job is most likely scheduled immediately. Note that the default values were used in the NBP name sent to the pap command. Thus, this command is identical to the command:

```
# pap -c -p "HP Writer" testfile.ps
```

Summary

In this chapter, you learned about the AppleTalk protocol. This protocol is used by Apple computers to communicate with each other. You learned about a Linux protocol suite called Netatalk, which implements the AppleTalk protocols and can be used to connect Linux networks to Apple networks. You installed and configured Netatalk on a Red Hat Enterprise Linux server and then configured the various daemons that implement AppleTalk file and printer sharing on Linux.

Chapter 15

Optimizing Network Services

THIS CHAPTER EXPLAINS how to optimize Red Hat Enterprise Linux network services. For example, XFree86 desktops can be sped up by reducing the amount of eye candy, which results in less bandwidth consumption when applications run across a network. Similarly, print queues can be arranged such that large print jobs go to high-speed printers. NFS disk farms can be designed to spread the load across multiple disks. The information in this chapter helps you identify the best possible tradeoff among performance, usability, and security of the network services you provide. The point to bear in mind, though, is that you might often find yourself compelled to strike a balance. To apply the well-known programmer's axiom, "Good, cheap, fast. Pick any two," when it comes to server or application tuning, the pithy epigram might be, "Convenient, secure, fast. Pick any two."

Optimizing the X Window System

Optimizing the X Window System is not easy. The core X protocol, despite what its detractors say, is actually pretty well tuned. Of course, as Keith Packard and Jim Gettys point out in their Usenix paper, *X Window System Network Performance* (see `http://keithp.com/~keithp/talks/usenix2003/html/net.html`), protocol improvements are underway that should make X more efficient at the wire level. Nonetheless, the garden-variety system administrator usually lacks the time, not to mention the desire, to hack X at such a low level. There are, naturally, some steps you can take to improve the performance of X or, more specifically, the XFree86 system running on Red Hat Enterprise Linux.

◆ The biggest improvement comes from beefing up the hardware on which XFree86 is running. There is simply no way around the fact that a faster CPU, faster GPU (*graphics processing unit*) that supports hardware acceleration, more RAM, and more video RAM does more than anything else to speed up XFree86. Naturally, hardware upgrades are not always an option, but they are the best option you have.

◆ Use a lightweight window manager. The eye candy and functionality provided by desktop environments such as GNOME and KDE carry a heavy price tag in terms of overall system performance. If, like us, you use XFree86 mostly as a platform for running xterms, a Web browser, and other graphical applications, you might not even miss the integration between the applications and the window manager provided.

◆ Consider reducing the color depth at which you run XFree86. Obviously, if you need thousands of colors, such as for heavy-duty image processing or watching videos, 16-bit color will result in poor-quality images, but an awful lot of computing that takes place on a Red Hat system is text processing, programming, and e-mail. 24-bit and 32-bit color is computationally intensive; 16-bit color is much less demanding.

◆ Likewise, reduce the amount of eye candy on your desktop. A solid color background is much less memory-intensive than a full-color wallpaper image. Transparent backgrounds in terminal emulators are cool but usually impose overhead on the windowing system to keep the background properly rendered and up to date. Shaped windows and borders are aesthetically pleasing but somewhat expensive in terms of resources.

◆ Run a local font server. Doing so makes the fonts you want available locally, so they do not have to be sent across the network. Similarly, you can free up memory and speed up the server's font handling by getting rid of fonts (that is, not loading them in /etc/X11/XF86Config-4) that you do not use. For example, on my laptop computer, we disable the 100dpi fonts because we cannot run the X server at a high enough resolution to get any benefit from the better-quality fonts. We have also deleted the CID fonts and Cyrillic fonts because we never use them.

◆ Actively seek out XFree86-based lightweight applications. We no longer use Mozilla, for example, because we have found that Firebird, the browser-only replacement for Mozilla, provides everything we need in a Web browser.

◆ Make sure that the X server is up to date. The XFree86 project is working to separate drivers from the rest of the system, which will enable you to download and install an updated driver for your card without having to refresh the entire XFree86 installation. Drivers sometimes improve dramatically from release to release, so stay informed about the driver for you card.

◆ Unload modules you do not use. The standard XFree86 installation, for example, loads the RECORD and XTRAP extensions. Edit `/etc/X11/XF86Config-4` and comment out the lines that read:

```
Load "record"
Load "xtrap"
```

Granted, these are only two modules with negligible memory and CPU impacts, but every little bit helps.

◆ Run XFree86 at a lower, nice value. By increasing XFree86's priority over other processes, you get a more responsive system. One way to do this is to start XFree86 using the command `nice -n -10 X :0`. You need root access to use this command. If you run XFree86 from XDM, GDM, or KDM, modify the Xservers file (`/etc/X11/xdm/Xservers`). Find the line that resembles the following:

```
:0 local /usr/X11R6/bin/X
```

Change the line so that it looks like the following, and then exit and restart X:

```
:0 local nice -10 /usr/X11R6/bin/X
```

◆ Finally, if you run XFree86 for long periods of time, memory gets tied up as cache. Occasionally restarting X refreshes potentially stale caches and also frees up memory that might have been lost to leaks.

Optimizing NFS

The subject of performance tuning deserves its own book, and, indeed several books exist on the general topic of performance tuning. Nevertheless, we can provide some general guidelines for improving NFS's performance and offer a few tips for maintaining a responsive NFS environment. The suggestions are far from exhaustive, and you must also take into account the needs and requirements of your network. To make the point that we make throughout this chapter, test your assumptions and tuning methods against baseline performance metrics taken from an untuned system. Comparing pre- with post-tuning performance is the only way to ensure that your efforts have made a difference.

NFS is sensitive to network performance, more specifically to network congestion and bandwidth problems. As a general rule, if NFS performance starts to degrade, you can be reasonably certain that heavy network traffic is the culprit. However, NFS traffic, especially at the server, tends to be "bursty," characterized by periods of relative quiescence broken up with sharp upward spikes in activity. As a result, tuning efforts need to take into account such uneven access patterns to insure optimal performance under load *and* during less strenuous periods.

Here are a few general suggestions you can apply to improve a system's performance overall and the performance of an NFS server in particular. While most of these tips address a server system, they also have beneficial effects on a client system. Bear in mind that the impact of any changes will be more noticeable in large, heavily used NFS installations than in small installations where the total number of clients and servers is counted in single digits.

◆ Using a journaling file system offers two clear advantages for an NFS server. First, in the event of a crash, journaling file systems recover much more quickly than nonjournaling file systems. Ext3, JFS, and XFS all support version 3 NFS, so, if you value your data, use a journaling file system on an NFS server. Second, because journaling file systems need only update the journal to maintain data integrity, an NFS server running a journaling file system "completes" I/O much faster because only the journal needs to be updated. After updating the journal, the server can safely issue an I/O completed reply to the clients. Meanwhile, the actual file system update occurs when the server is less busy.

◆ Spread NFS exported file systems across multiple disks and, if possible, multiple disk controllers. The purpose of this strategy is to avoid disk *hot spots*, which occur when I/O operations concentrate on a single disk or a single area of a disk. Similarly, distribute disks containing NFS exported file systems across multiple disk controllers. This measure reduces the amount of I/O traffic on any single controller, which improves the overall performance of the I/O subsystem.

◆ Replace IDE disks with SCSI disks, and, if you have the budget for it, SCSI disks with FibreChannel disk arrays. FibreChannel, although markedly more expensive than SCSI, offers even faster performance. However, in small shops and for small servers, using FibreChannel is akin to killing gnats with a howitzer.

◆ If your NFS server is using RAID, use RAID 1/0 to maximize write speed and to provide redundancy in the event of a disk crash. RAID 5 seems compelling at first because it ensures good read speeds, which is important for NFS clients, but write performance is, well, lackluster, and good write speeds are important for NFS servers. Write performance is critical because NFS on Linux now (since about kernel version 2.4.7) defaults to synchronous mode, meaning that NFS operations do not complete until the data is actually synced to disk.

For more information about configuring NFS, particularly how to disable synchronous, see Chapter 11.

◆ Consider replacing 10Mbit Ethernet cards with 100Mbit Ethernet cards throughout the network. Although only slightly more expensive than their 10Mbit cousins, 100Mbit cards offer considerably more throughput per dollar. The faster cards result in better network performance across the board, not just for NFS. Of course, to reap the benefits of 100Mbit cards, they need to be used on both clients and servers, and the gateways, routers, and switches must be capable of handling 100MB speeds.

◆ In situations in which performance or availability is the paramount concern, Gigabit Ethernet (1000Mbit) is available, although expensive. Other high performance network options, such as Myrinet and SONET (Synchronous Optical Networking) exist as well but are typically used as cluster interconnect networks.

◆ Replace hubs with switches. Network hubs, while less expensive than switches, route all network traffic across the same data channel. During periods of heavy activity, this single-data channel can easily become saturated. Switches, on the other hand, transmit network packets across multiple data channels, reducing congestion and packet collisions and resulting in faster overall throughput.

◆ If necessary, dedicate one or more servers specifically to NFS work. CPU or memory-intensive processes, such as Web, database, or compute servers, can starve an NFS server for needed CPU cycles or memory pages.

◆ In extreme cases, resegmenting the network may be the answer to NFS performance problems. The goal with this tip is to isolate NFS traffic on its own segment again, reducing network saturation and congestion and allocating dedicated bandwidth to NFS traffic.

A good place to start evaluating NFS performance is to use the nfsstat command, which prints the NFS statistics maintained by the kernel. You can use nfsstat output to establish baseline performance metrics, to measure the effects, if any, of configuration changes, and to diagnose specific NFS performance problems. nfsstat's general syntax is:

```
nfsstat [-acnrsz] [-o facility]
```

Table 15-1 explains nfsstat's options.

TABLE 15-1 NFSSTAT COMMAND OPTIONS

Option	Description
-a	Prints all (NFS, RPC, and network) statistics for NFS clients and servers
-c	Prints NFS client statistics
-n	Prints only NFS statistics
-r	Prints only RPC statistics
-s	Prints only NFS server statistics
-z	Resets the kernel's NFS statistics counters to zero (not currently supported)
-o *facility*	Displays statistics for the specified *facility*

By default, nfsstat displays statistics for both NFS and the underlying RPC service. Use the -n option to display on NFS statistics or the -r option to print only RPC statistics. Likewise, nfsstat displays client and server statistics unless you specify -c for client statistics (which makes little sense because the client does not maintain statistics in the current implementation) or -s to for server statistics. The following listing displays NFS statistics only for an NFS server:

```
$ /usr/sbin/nfstat -n -s
Server nfs v2:
null        getattr     setattr     root        lookup      readlink
0      0%   0      0%   0      0%   0      0%   0      0%   0      0%
read        wrcache     write       create      remove      rename
0      0%   0      0%   0      0%   0      0%   0      0%   0      0%
link        symlink     mkdir       rmdir       readdir     fsstat
0      0%   0      0%   0      0%   0      0%   0      0%   0      0%

Server nfs v3:
null        getattr     setattr     lookup      access      readlink
0      0%   10861  43%  297    1%   6305   25%  95     0%   0      0%
read        write       create      mkdir       symlink     mknod
4151   16%  912    3%   621    2%   0      0%   0      0%   0      0%
remove      rmdir       rename      link        readdir     readdirplus
1236   4%   0      0%   0      0%   615    2%   0      0%   0      0%
fsstat      fsinfo      pathconf    commit
9      0%   9      0%   0      0%   91     0%
```

Notice that the statistics for NFS version 2 are all zeroes. This is because this particular server is running NFS version 3. The displayed information shows the type of operation performed (arranged by RPC call), such as `getattr`, `read`, or `write`, the number of such operations performed, and the distribution of each operation. For example, 10,861 `getattr` operations have been performed, which represents 43% of all NFS server operations.

The `facility` argument for the `-o` option enables you to fine-tune the type of information `nfsstat` displays. `facility` can have one of the following values:

- ◆ `fh` — Displays utilization data on the server's file handle cache, including the total number of lookups and the number of cache hits and misses.

  `net_` — Shows network layer statistics, such as the number of received packets or number of TCP connections.

- ◆ `nfs_` — Displays NFS protocol statistics categorized by RPC call.

- ◆ `rc` — Prints utilization data on the server's request reply cache, including the total number of lookups and the number of cache hits and misses.

- ◆ `rpc` — Prints general RPC information.

For additional information about improving the performance of NFS, see the Linux NFS-HOWTO on the NFS Web page at `http://nfs.sourceforge.net/ nfs-howto/`. The NFS-HOWTO dedicates an entire section to performance tuning the Linux NFS implementation. Another valuable source of general performance tuning information, not only for NFS but for all varieties of Linux issues, is the Linux Performance Tuning Web site at `http://linuxperf.nl.linux.org/`.

Optimizing NIS

Frankly, with NIS+ for Linux no longer in development, not much can be done to improve NIS' performance. That said, how do you know when you have an NIS performance problem? If you issue a command that touches NIS-maintained information (such as `yppasswd`) that takes longer than you expect to complete, NIS might have problems. Other symptoms of NIS stumbling include error messages with phrases like "Busy try again later" or "Not responding." Another sign of NIS problems is slow login times or apparent system hangs when you are logged in.

- ◆ Do not use recursive netgroups. A *recursive netgroup* is an NIS group defined in terms of other NIS groups. Recursive groups are quite convenient for administrators because they limit the maintenance burden, but resolving group names is time consuming and thus slows down the server.

◆ In large NIS installations, partition big NIS domains into smaller so-called *subdomains* that maintain authoritative maps for fewer systems. This reduces the overall load on any one NIS server and minimizes the size of NIS maps that have to be pushed around. Similarly, designating slave servers can reduce the load on a master server, provided the NIS maps are relatively static.

As awful as doing so may sound, the best way to optimize NIS' performance might be to replace it with something else, such as LDAP.

Optimizing Samba Networking

Probably the most important consideration for optimizing Samba performance is file-transfer speed between the Samba server and clients. There are options that can be set in the `smb.conf` file that will increase file-transfer performance between the client and server. You can try them to determine if your performance increases after implementing them.

◆ `socket options` — These are controls on the networking layer of the operating system that enable tuning of the connection. For a complete list of options, refer to the `smb.conf` man page. A good choice for tuning your local network is to use `socket options = IPTOS_LOWDELAY TCP_NODELAY`.

◆ `dns proxy` — This option should be set to *no* unless your Samba server is acting as a WINS server. Setting this option to *no* prevents the server from doing unnecessary name lookups and increases system performance.

◆ `debug level` — This option should be set to 2 or less. Setting the debug level higher than 2 causes the server to flush the log file after each operation, a time-consuming process indeed.

◆ `level2 oplocks` — This option provides for caching of downloaded files on the client machine. Setting this option to `true` can increase system performance.

Summary

This chapter gave you some hints for improving the performance of Red Hat networking services. Although this is not strictly necessary on a server system, you learned some steps to take to speed up the X Window System. We also highlighted the performance issues that can arise with NFS and the measures you can implement to solve some of these problems. NIS can also be fixed, although the best "fix" is often to replace NIS with LDAP. Finally, we offered some suggestions to get better speed out of Samba. Candidly, performance tuning requires a book all its own; we hope we have given you a good start.

Part III

Internet Services

Chapter 16

What Are Internet Services?

IN THIS CHAPTER

♦ Learning about secure services

♦ Learning how to avoid less secure Internet protocols

♦ Using your Linux machine as a server

♦ Configuring the inetd server

♦ Configuring the xinetd server

♦ Figuring out which services are started from xinetd and which are standalone

♦ Configuring Linux firewall packages

WHAT IS AN INTERNET SERVICE? An Internet Service can be defined as any service that can be accessed through TCP/IP based networks, whether an internal network (Intranet) or external network (Internet). Actually, TCP and IP are two of the protocols that are included in a group of protocols sometimes known as the *Internet protocols*. Since the two most frequently used or discussed protocols of the suite are TCP and IP, the entire suite is often referred to as just *TCP/IP*. Internet services can be provided through either secure or non-secure TCP/IP connections. Common services are Telnet, FTP, SMTP, HTTP, ICMP, ARP, DNS, ssh, scp, sftp, and others.

The significance of TCP/IP as the basis for these services cannot be overlooked. TCP/IP provides a platform- and operating system-independent protocol for these services. Any computer, running any operating system, can communicate with any other computer on the network if they both use TCP/IP protocols for establishing and maintaining the connection and formatting and transmitting the data.

The availability of a wide range of Internet services makes Linux machines versatile workhorses that can fulfill many different functions in a company's network. This chapter covers the wide range of common services that come standard with every Red Hat system.

XREF   Chapter 10 explains the TCP/IP suite of protocols. Chapter 19 discusses mail transfer and SMTP. Chapter 20 explains setting up and using FTP. Chapter 21 covers HTTP and setting up an HTTP server.

Secure Services

Common services such as Telnet and FTP were written in the days when everyone trusted everybody else on the Internet. These services send all of their traffic in plain text, including passwords. Plain-text traffic is extremely easy to eavesdrop on by anyone between the traffic's source and destination. Since the Internet has exploded in popularity, running insecure services such as these is not a good idea. That's why secure replacements have been developed. These replacements provide stronger authentication controls and encrypt all their traffic to keep your data safe. You should always run secure services instead of insecure services.

ssh

Secure Shell, also known as ssh, is a secure Telnet replacement that encrypts all traffic, including passwords, using a public/private encryption key exchange protocol. It provides the same functionality of Telnet, plus other useful functions, such as traffic tunneling.

This is what it looks like to ssh into a machine for the first time:

```
[vnavrat@buffy vnavrat$ ssh vnavrat@woolf.xena.edu
The authenticity of host 'woolf.xena.edu (123.456.789.65)'
can't be established.
RSA key fingerprint is
 b2:60:c8:31:b7:6b:e3:58:3d:53:b9:af:bc:75:31:63.
Are you sure you want to continue connecting (yes/no)? yes
Warning: Permanently added 'woolf.xena.edu,123.456.789.65'
(RSA) to the list of known hosts.
vnavrat@woolf.xena.edu's password:
 Welcome to woolf
Unauthorized usage prohibited.  Please check your quotas.
vnavrat:~>
```

ssh asks you if you want to accept and trust the host key being sent to you as being the real key. This question is asked only once, when you log in to a machine for the first time. After this first login, ssh behaves exactly like Telnet — you start ssh, it asks for your password, and then you have a regular terminal screen.

In addition to providing terminal access, ssh tunnels almost any other protocol through it. So it is possible to tunnel POP, rcp, and other protocols through ssh to turn them into encrypted, more secure protocols. With enough imagination and practice, you can make almost anything more secure with ssh.

Following is an example of how to tunnel your mail through ssh in order to keep your password and mail encrypted and secure during transit. In this example, you use POP3 to retrieve your mail from the remote machine buffy.xena.edu. Normally you would tell your POP3 software to connect from your localhost to port 110 (the POP port) of buffy.xena.edu.

But in this example the first step is to configure your POP mailer to connect to port 16510 of your own machine, and put in the password for your account on buffy.xena.edu. The second step is to set up the ssh tunnel, which encrypts and forwards the traffic over the network to buffy.xena.edu's POP port.

To set up the ssh tunnel, type the following at the command line:

```
ssh -N -L 16510:127.0.0.1:110 vnavrat@buffy.xena.edu
```

And voilà, you are now sending and receiving your mail through an encrypted ssh tunnel.

scp

Secure Copy, also known as scp, is part of the ssh package. It is a secure alternative to rcp and ftp, because, like ssh, the password is not sent over the network in plain text. You can scp files to any machine that has an ssh daemon running.

The syntax of scp is

```
scp user@host:file1 user@host:file2
```

To copy a file named swords-n-steaks.txt to remote host xena from local host buffy, type

```
[vnavrat@buffy vnavrat]$ scp swords-n-steaks.txt vnavrat@xena:weapons/
vnavrat@xena's password:
swords-n-steaks.txt          100% |*****************************|    54
00:00
```

And to copy a file named nixon-enemies-list.txt from remote host xena to your current directory on local host buffy, type

```
[vnavrat@buffy vnavrat]$ scp vnavrat@xena:nixon-enemieslist.txt .
vnavrat@buffy's password:
nixon-enemies-list.txt       100% |*****************************|    54
00:00
```

sftp

Secure File Transfer Program, also known as sftp, is an FTP client that performs all its functions over ssh.

The syntax for sftp is

```
sftp user@host:file file
```

Less Secure Services

These are insecure services that should not be used, since they trust that the network is absolutely secure. Their secure equivalents should be used instead.

Using these services should be discouraged, because all their traffic is sent over the network in plain text. This means that anyone with a common sniffer such as tcpdump can see every keystroke that is typed in the session, including your users' passwords.

Telnet

Telnet is a protocol and application that enables someone to have access to a virtual terminal on a remote host. It resembles text-based console access on a Unix machine.

Telnet is an application that's available almost everywhere. Because of this distribution, most beginning Unix users use Telnet exclusively to communicate with other Unix and NT machines. Since all Telnet traffic, including passwords, is sent in plain text, the Secure Shell (ssh) command should be used instead, if at all possible. ssh provides an equivalent interface to Telnet, with increased features, and most importantly, encrypted traffic and passwords.

This is what it looks like when you log into a machine with Telnet:

```
[vnavrat@buffy vnavrat]$ telnet xena
Trying 127.0.0.1...
Connected to xena.
Escape character is '^]'.
Welcome to null.xena.edu
login:
```

FTP

FTP is a ubiquitous file transfer protocol that runs over ports 20 and 21. For transferring software packages from anonymous ftp repositories, such as ftp.redhat.com, ftp is still the standard application to use. However, for personal file transfers, you should use scp. scp encrypts the traffic, including passwords. Once you have successfully logged on to an ftp server, you can type **help** for a list of available commands. Two important commands to remember are `put` to move a file from your machine to the remote machine, and `get` to pull a file from the remote server to your machine. To send multiple files you can use `mput`, and to retrieve multiple files you can use `mget`. `ls` or `dir` give you a listing of files available for download from the remote side.

To learn more about FTP commands, see Chapter 20.

rsync

`rsync` is an unencrypted file transfer program that is similar to `rcp`. It includes the added feature of allowing just the differences between two sets of files on two machines to be transferred across the network. Because it sends traffic unencrypted, it should be tunneled through `ssh`. Otherwise don't use it. The `rsync` server listens on port 873.

rsh

`rsh` is an unencrypted mechanism to execute commands on remote hosts. Normally you specify a command to be run on the remote host on `rsh`'s command line, but if no command is given, you are logged into the remote host using `rlogin`. `rsh`'s syntax is

```
rsh remotehostname remotecommand
```

rlogin

`rlogin` is a remote login program that connects your terminal to a remote machine's terminal. `rlogin` is an insecure protocol, because it sends all information, including passwords, in plain-text. It also enables an implicit trust relationship to exist between machines, so that you can use `rlogin` without a password.

finger

`finger` enables users on remote systems to look up information about users on another system. Generally `finger` displays a user's login name, real name, terminal name, idle time, login time, office location, and phone number. You should disable finger outside of your local network, because user information gathered from it could be used to compromise your system. The `finger` daemon listens on port 79.

talk and ntalk

`talk` and `ntalk` are real-time chat protocols. The `talk` server runs on port 517 and the ntalk server runs on port 518. To send someone else a talk request, type **talk** or **ntalk username@hostname**. If their server is running a talk or ntalk daemon and they are logged in, they will see a message inviting them to chat with you. `Talk` and `ntalk` aren't as popular as they once were, since instant messenger clients have become very popular.

Using Your Linux Machine as a Server

The following sections give you an overview of what common server protocols are available on Linux.

HTTP

The most common Web server used on Linux is Apache. Apache is started out of a system's `rc` scripts. Apache is easily configurable, and its configuration files live in `/etc/httpd/conf/`. While Apache can be set to listen to many different network ports, the most common port it listens on is port 80.

For more information on installing and configuring the Apache Web server, see Chapter 21.

sshd

The secure shell daemon (`sshd`) is started out of the system's `rc` scripts. Its global system configuration files are in `/etc/ssh`, and users' `ssh` configuration files are in `$HOME/.ssh/`. The `ssh` server listens on port 22.

`sshd` can be configured to run on an alternate port. Running `ssh` on a port other than 22 comes in handy if port 22 is being blocked by a firewall. Running `ssh` on a different port also adds a small measure of security through obscurity. Automatic scanners used by hackers will miss that `ssh` is running on your machine if they don't find it running on the standard port they expect.

ftpd

The FTP daemon uses ports 20 and 21 to listen for and initiate FTP requests. Its configuration files `ftpaccess`, `ftpconversions`, `ftpgroups`, `ftphosts`, and `ftpusers`, are located in the `/etc` directory.

You can find more information on setting up the FTP daemon in Chapter 20.

DNS

The Domain Name Service (DNS), which maps IP addresses to hostnames, is served by the named program on port 53. Its configuration file is `named.conf` in the `/etc` directory.

To read more about setting up DNS on your Linux machine, see Chapter 18.

xinetd

`xinetd` is a replacement for `inetd` that adds more security and functionality. `inetd` is the old workhorse of the Linux networking world, and `xinetd` is an improvement on an important program that has been around for several years. It incorporates new features that have been desired by system administrators for a few years now.

Another great reason to run `xinetd` is that it can run alongside `inetd`. You can set up secured and extensively logged services with `xinetd`, and still be able to run services such as RPC that don't run well with `xinetd` from `inetd`.

Essentially, `inetd` and `xinetd` behave the same way. They both start at system boot time, and they wait and listen for a connection to come in on the ports to which they are assigned in their `conf` files. Once a connection request is made, if the service requested requires that a new server be spawned, then both `inetd` and `xinetd` spawn a new server and keep listening for new connection requests on the service port.

One of the most notable improvements of `xinetd` over `inetd` is that anyone can start network services. With `inetd`, only root can start a network service, and that restriction leads to a host of security problems.

xinetd supports encrypting plain text services such as the ftp command channel by wrapping them in stunnel.

xinetd also enables you to do access control on all services based on different criteria, such as remote host address, access time, remote host name, and remote host domain. In the past this kind of access control could be accomplished only with tools like tcpwrappers, or firewall software. Even then, tcpwrappers could only reliably control tcp traffic.

xinetd also takes the extra security step of killing servers that aren't in the configuration file and those that violate the configuration's access criteria. It can help prevent Denial of Service (DOS) attacks by limiting normal functions that can cripple the machine if there are too many of them occurring at the same time.

For example, xinetd can limit the amount of incoming connections to the whole machine or from a single host to prevent network overflow attacks. It can limit the number of processes that are forked by a network service. xinetd can also stop a service if it is driving the machine's load up too high, to prevent the machine from being slowed to a crawl because of the incoming network traffic.

Log capabilities have also been improved in xinetd. For each service it runs, it can log the remote user and host address, how long the service has been running, and failed access control attempts.

xinetd is flexible enough to enable you to utilize increased security measures such as chrooted environments.

You may notice that the xinetd.conf file (Listing 16-1) is much shorter than inetd.conf, making it easier to read through and customize. The last line says that all the files in the /etc/xinetd.d directory are read into the xinetd.conf file as well. Each service started by xinetd gets its own dedicated file in the /etc/xinetd.d directory. This way you can tell, with a glance at the xinetd.d file listing, what services are being started by it.

Listing 16-1: The xinetd.conf file

```
#
# Simple configuration file for xinetd
#
# Some defaults, and include /etc/xinetd.d/
defaults
{
        instances              = 60
        log_type               = SYSLOG authpriv
        log_on_success         = HOST PID
        log_on_failure         = HOST
        cps                    = 25 30
}

includedir /etc/xinetd.d
```

The last line of the `xinetd.conf` file shown in Listing 16-1 shows the directory location of the individual configuration files for the services that use xinetd. Listing 16-2 shows the Telnet configuration file that is located in the `/etc/xinet.d` directory.

Listing 16-2: The xinetd config file entry required to set up a chrooted Telnet daemon

```
service telnet_chroot
{
        log_on_success  = HOST PID DURATION USERID
        log_on_failure  = HOST RECORD USERID
        no_access     147.125.11.93
        socket_type     = stream
        protocol        = tcp
        port            = 8000
        wait            = no
        user            = root
        server          = /usr/sbin/chroot
        server_args     = /var/public/servers
    /usr/libexec/telnetd
}
```

Note that, in this example, access is denied to the host whose IP address is 147.125.11.93. Other hosts can be added to this line by separating them by commas, and by using wildcard expressions such as *. `log_on_success` specifies what information is logged upon successful login, and `log_on_failure` specifies what's logged when someone attempts to Telnet into the machine and fails.

`xinetd` can read your `inetd.conf` file if it's run through a tool called `itox`. `itox` is included in the official `xinetd` package, which is available from `www.xinetd.org`. If you want to replace `inetd` with `xinetd` on your system, you can run `itox` by typing

```
itox < /etc/inetd.conf > /etc/xinetd.conf
```

In your `inetd.conf` file, if you don't have path names listed for each of your network daemons, that is, you have `in.telnetd` instead of `/usr/sbin/in.telnetd`, you should run the `itox` command with the `-daemon_dir` flag:

```
itox -daemon_dir=/usr/sbin < /etc/inetd.conf > /etc/xinetd.conf
```

If you still use a Telnet server on your system, you should be aware that by default `telnetd` does not start up with `xinetd`. In order to start a Telnet daemon in `xinetd`, you should use the `groups = yes` option within the `xinetd.conf` file.

xinetd vs. Stand-Alone

Which services are stand-alone, and which are started from xinetd? Sometimes it can get confusing keeping track of how to start a certain service, or keep it from running in the first place. In order to control a service, you need to know what spawns it. Here is a general listing of what services are spawned from superservers such as inetd and xinetd, and which are started on their own from rc scripts or root.

xinetd-started Services

The following services are started from xinetd. Each of these services should ideally have its own file in the /etc/xinetd.d directory, so you should look in that directory to enable or disable these services.

- chargen — Random character generator that sends its traffic over tcp
- daytime-udp — Gives you the time over udp
- finger — User information lookup program
- kshell — Restricts user access to the shell
- rlogin — Service similar to Telnet, but enables trust relationships between machines
- swat — Samba Web Administration Tool
- time — Gives you the time
- chargen-udp — Random character generator that sends its traffic over udp
- echo — Echoes back all characters sent to it over tcp
- gssftp — Kerberized FTP server
- rsh — Remote shell
- talk — A talk (real-time chat) server
- time-udp — Gives you the time over udp
- comsat — Notifies users if they have new mail
- echo-udp — Echoes back all characters sent to it over udp
- klogin — kerberos's answer to rlogin
- ntalk — A talk (real-time chat) server
- rsync — Remote file transfer protocol
- telnet — Telnet server
- wu-ftpd — An ftp server

- `daytime` — Gives you the time over `tcp`
- `eklogin` — Encrypting kerberized `rlogin` server
- `krb5-telnet` — Kerberized Telnet server
- `rexec` — Provides remote execution facilities
- `sgi_fam` — File monitoring daemon
- `tftp` — Trivial file transfer program

Stand-Alone Services

These services are started from the `rc` scripts specifically written for them in the `rc` directories. You can enable or disable these services from those directories.

- `apache` — Web server
- `sshd` — `ssh` server
- `sendmail` — Mail server
- `qmail` — Mail server
- `postfix` — Mail server
- `thttpd` — Semilightweight Web server
- `boa` — Lightweight Web server
- `named` — `dns` server
- `xfs` — X font server
- `xdm` — X display manager
- `portmap` — Maps RPC services to ports
- `rpc.quotad` — Serves quota information
- `knfsd` — Userspace portion of the NFS daemon
- `rpc.mountd` — NFS mount server
- `rpc.ypbind` — NIS server
- `squid` — Web proxy server
- `nessusd` — Penetration testing server
- `postgresql` — Database server
- `mysql` — Database server
- `oracle` — Database server

Linux Firewall Packages

Linux provides a few different mechanisms for system security. One of these mechanisms is Linux's firewall packages. Two of the firewall packages available are tcp-wrappers and iptables. tcp-wrappers is a minimalistic packet filtering application to protect certain network ports, and iptables is a packet filtering firewall.

To read more about iptables and Linux system security, see Chapter 31.

tcp-wrappers

The TCP Wrapper program is a network security tool whose main functions are to log connections made to inetd services and restrict certain computers or services from connecting to the tcp-wrapped computer.

Currently xinetd does many of the same things that tcp-wrappers does. But it's still worth running tcp-wrappers if you're also running inetd, or if you want to use the hosts.allow and hosts.deny configuration files to control access to your computer.

TCP wrappers works only on programs started from inetd. So services such as sshd, apache, and sendmail cannot be "wrapped" with tcp-wrappers. tcp-wrappers also cannot be used with udp or rcp services, because these services wait for a short time after a connection is closed to see whether another connection will be initiated soon. These daemons specify the "wait" option in inetd.conf, which is not recognized by the tcp-wrapper program.

You can see whether tcp-wrappers is running by checking to see if /usr/sbin/tcpd is in your process listing. You can see if it's installed on your system by looking at the inetd.conf.

An inetd.conf without tcp-wrappers would look like this:

```
telnet  stream  tcp    nowait  root    /usr/sbin/in.telnetd in.telnetd
```

An inetd.conf with tcp-wrappers looks like this:

```
telnet  stream  tcp    nowait  root    /usr/sbin/tcpd  in.telnetd
```

Once tcp-wrappers is installed on your system, you can specify the ruleset they follow in the config files /etc/hosts.allow and /etc/hosts.deny.

When inetd starts up, it looks through /etc/inetd.conf to see what network service connections it should start listening for. Then it checks /etc/services to discover what port it should listen to. On tcp-wrapped systems, `tcpd` is specified as the service to be started in `inetd.conf` instead of the regular service, as was shown in the second line of the example.

`tcpd` is then called and reads the `/etc/hosts.allow` file to see if the hostname of the computer that's trying to connect is listed there. If it is, the connection is allowed. If it is not, `tcpd` checks `/etc/hosts.deny` to see if there's an entry that matches the hostname. If the hostname is in `/etc/hosts.deny`, the connection is closed. If the hostname of the computer connecting is in neither `/etc/hosts.allow` nor `/etc/hosts.deny`, the connection is allowed to continue by default.

The syntax of an *allow* or *deny* rule follows this format:

```
service: hostname : options
```

So to enable all services from your own machine (localhost), use a rule like this in your `hosts.allow` file:

```
ALL: ALL@127.0.0.1 : ALLOW
```

To enable only machines from the `xena.edu` domain to Telnet into your machine, use this rule in your `hosts.allow` file:

```
in.telnetd: .xena.edu : ALLOW
```

To deny Telnet access to everyone on the Internet (who isn't explicitly mentioned in your `/etc/hosts.allow` file), and then e-mail a report to the root account on that machine that someone attempted a Telnet connection, use the following rule in your `hosts.deny` file:

```
in.telnetd:ALL : spawn (echo telnet connection tried from %h %a to %d at `date` | \
tee -a /var/log/tcp.deny.log |mail root@localhost )
```

iptables

`iptables` is Red Hat's built-in IP firewall administration tool. Using `iptables` enables you to run a personal firewall to protect your Linux machine. If the Linux machine is a routing gateway for other machines on your network, it can act as a packet filtering network firewall if more than one network interface is installed.

For more information on setting up a Linux firewall, see Chapter 31.

Summary

As a general rule, you should endeavor to use programs that encrypt their network traffic, instead of using those that use unencrypted protocols.

If you must use a plain-text protocol such as POP or rsync, wrapping it in ssh or ssl keeps your passwords and data safe from network listeners. ssh is versatile enough to wrap around almost anything.

In general, most services are started from inetd.conf or xinetd.conf. If a service you're looking into is not started from there, it is probably being started from the machine's rc scripts.

If you ever need to know on which port a network protocol operates, check the /etc/services file.

Linux's network capabilities have grown a great deal in the past couple of years. Currently, a properly configured Red Hat server can function as many different network devices — anything from an AppleTalk or Samba server to an LDAP server or firewall. Once you get a grasp of how the servers are started and configured in general, the possibilities of what you can do are nearly endless.

Chapter 17

Lightweight Directory Access Protocol (LDAP)

IN THIS CHAPTER

- ◆ Why use LDAP?

- ◆ LDAP daemons and utilities

- ◆ LDAP terminology

- ◆ Open LDAP configuration files

- ◆ Using elm

- ◆ Maintaining e-mail security

- ◆ Configuring the NNTP server

THE LIGHTWEIGHT DIRECTORY ACCESS PROTOCOL (LDAP) is a method for organizing information in a hierarchical manner using directories. It can be thought of as a very simple database. Once organized, the data can then be accessed over a network. LDAP is based on the X.500 standard for directory sharing but is not as resource-intensive as X.500. In fact, LDAP is sometimes referred to as "X.500-lite." LDAP directories can store a variety of information and can even be used to provide user authentication over a network in a manner similar to that of the Network Information System (NIS), allowing a user to access his or her account from any machine on an LDAP-enabled network.

In most cases, however, LDAP is used simply as a virtual phone directory, allowing users to easily access contact information about other users. But LDAP goes beyond a traditional phone directory, because it is capable of propagating its directories to other LDAP servers throughout the world, providing global access to information. Currently, however, LDAP is more commonly used within individual organizations, like universities, government departments, and private companies.

LDAP is a client-server system. The server can use a variety of databases to store a directory, each optimized for quick and copious read operations. When an LDAP client application connects to an LDAP server, it can either query a directory or upload information to it. In the event of a query, the server either answers the query or, if it cannot answer locally, refers the query upstream to a higher-level LDAP server that does have the answer. If the client application is attempting to upload information to an LDAP directory, the server verifies that the user has permission to make the change and then adds or updates the information.

This chapter discusses the configuration and use of OpenLDAP 2.0, an open-source implementation of the LDAPv2 and LDAPv3 protocols.

Why Use LDAP?

The main benefit of LDAP is that information for an entire organization can be consolidated into a central repository. For example, rather than managing user lists for each group within an organization, you can use LDAP as a central directory accessible from anywhere on the network. And since LDAP supports Secure Sockets Layer (SSL) and Transport Layer Security (TLS), sensitive data can be protected from prying eyes.

LDAP also supports a number of back-end databases in which to store directories. This allows administrators the flexibility to deploy the database best suited for the type of information the server is to supply. Also, because LDAP has a well-defined Application Programming Interface (API), the number of LDAP-enabled applications is numerous and increasing in quantity and quality. On the negative side, LDAP can require some work to configure properly.

OpenLDAP 2.0 Feature Enhancements

OpenLDAP 2.0 includes a number of important features:

- ◆ LDAPv3 Support – OpenLDAP 2.0 supports Simple Authentication and Security Layer (SASL), Transport Layer Security (TLS), and Secure Sockets Layer (SSL), among other improvements. Many of the changes in the protocol since LDAPv2 are designed to make LDAP more secure.

- ◆ IPv6 Support – OpenLDAP supports the next-generation Internet Protocol version 6.

- ◆ LDAP Over IPC – OpenLDAP can communicate within a system using interprocess communication (IPC). This enhances security by obviating the need to communicate over a network.

- ◆ Updated C API – Improves the way programmers can connect to and use the application.

- ◆ LDIFv1 Support – Full compliance with the LDAP Data Interchange Format (LDIF) version 1.

- ◆ Enhanced Stand-Alone LDAP Server – Includes an updated access control system, thread pooling, better tools, and much more.

OpenLDAP Daemons and Utilities

The suite of OpenLDAP libraries and tools is spread out over the following packages:

- openldap – Contains the libraries necessary to run the openldap server and client applications.

- openldap-clients – Contains command-line tools for viewing and modifying directories on an LDAP server.

- openldap-server – Contains the servers and other utilities necessary to configure and run an LDAP server.

There are two servers contained in the openldap-servers package: the Standalone LDAP Daemon (/usr/sbin/slapd) and the Standalone LDAP Update Replication Daemon (/usr/sbin/slurpd). The slapd daemon is the actual LDAP server, whereas the slurpd daemon is used to synchronize changes from one LDAP server to other LDAP servers on the network. The slurpd daemon is necessary only when dealing with multiple LDAP servers. To perform administrative tasks, the openldap-server package installs the following utilities into the /usr/sbin/ directory:

- slapadd – Adds entries from an LDIF file to an LDAP directory. For example, /usr/sbin/slapadd -l ldif-input will read in the LDIF file, ldif-input, containing the new entries.

- slapcat – Pulls entries out of an LDAP directory in the default format, Berkeley DB, and saves them in an LDIF file. For example, the command /usr/sbin/slapcat -l ldif-output will output an LDIF file called ldif-output containing the entries from the LDAP directory.

- slapindex – Re-indexes the slapd directory based on the current content.

- slappasswd – Generates an encrypted user password value for use with ldapmodify or the rootpw value in the slapd configuration file, /etc/openldap/slapd.conf. Execute /usr/sbin/slappasswd to create the password.

Be sure to stop slapd by issuing /usr/sbin/service slapd stop before using slapadd, slapcat, or slapindex. Otherwise, the consistency of the LDAP directory will be at risk.

See the man pages for each of these utilities for more information about how to use them.

The openldap-clients package installs tools used to add, modify, and delete entries in an LDAP directory into /usr/bin/. These tools include the following:

◆ ldapmodify – Modifies entries in an LDAP directory, accepting input via a file or standard input.

◆ ldapadd – Adds entries to your directory by accepting input via a file or standard input; ldapadd is actually a hard link to ldapmodify -a.

◆ ldapsearch – Searches for entries in the LDAP directory using a shell prompt.

◆ ldapdelete – Deletes entries from an LDAP directory by accepting input via user input at the terminal or via a file.

With the exception of ldapsearch, each of these utilities is more easily used by referencing a file containing the changes to be made rather than by typing a command for each entry you wish to change in an LDAP directory. The format of such a file is outlined in each application's man page.

NSS, PAM, and LDAP

In addition to the OpenLDAP packages, Red Hat Linux includes a package called nss_ldap that enhances LDAP's ability to integrate into both Linux and other UNIX environments. The nss_ldap package provides the following modules:

◆ /lib/libnss_ldap- glibc-version.so

◆ /lib/security/pam_ldap.so

The libnss_ldap- glibc-version.so module allows applications to look up users, groups, hosts, and other information using an LDAP directory via glibc's Nameservice Switch (NSS) interface. NSS allows applications to authenticate using LDAP in conjunction with Network Information Service (NIS) name service and flat authentication files.

The pam_ldap module allows PAM-aware applications to authenticate users using information stored in an LDAP directory. PAM-aware applications include console login, POP and IMAP mail servers, and Samba. By deploying an LDAP server on your network, all of these login situations can authenticate against one user ID and password combination, greatly simplifying administration.

PHP4, the Apache HTTP Server, and LDAP

Red Hat Linux includes a package containing LDAP modules for the PHP server-side scripting language. The php-ldap package adds LDAP support to the PHP4 HTML-embedded scripting language via the /usr/lib/php4/ldap.so module. This module allows PHP4 scripts to access information stored in an LDAP directory.

Red Hat Linux 8.0 and later no longer ships with the auth_ldap package, which provided LDAP support for versions 1.3 and earlier of the Apache HTTP server. See the Apache Software Foundation Web site at `http://www.apache.org/` for details on the status of this module.

LDAP Client Applications

Other graphical LDAP clients that support creating and modifying directories are available, but they do not ship with Red Hat Linux. One such application is LDAP Browser/Editor — a Java-based tool available at `http://www.iit.edu/~gawojar/ldap`. Most other LDAP clients access directories as read-only, using them to reference, but not alter, organization-wide information. Some examples of such applications are Mozilla-based Web browsers, Sendmail Balsa, Pine, Evolution, and Gnome Meeting.

LDAP Terminology

An entry is one unit in an LDAP directory. Each entry is identified by its unique Distinguished Name (DN). Each entry has attributes, which are pieces of information directly associated with the entry. For example, an organization could be an LDAP entry. Attributes associated with the organization might be its fax number, its street address, and so on. People can also be entries in the LDAP directory. Common attributes for people include their telephone numbers and email addresses.

Some attributes are required, while others are optional. An objectclass definition sets which attributes are required and which are not for each entry. Objectclass definitions are found in various schema files, located in the `/etc/openldap/schema/` directory. The LDAP Data Interchange Format (LDIF) is an ASCII text format for LDAP entries. Files that import or export data to and from LDAP servers must be in LDIF format. An LDIF entry looks similar to the following example:

```
[ id ]
dn:                        distinguished name
attrtype :                      attrvalue
attrtype :                      attrvalue
attrtype :                      attrvalue
```

An entry can contain as many *attrtype : attrvalue* pairs as needed. A blank line indicates the end of an entry.

All `attrtype` and `attrvalue` pairs must be defined in a corresponding schema file in order for LDAP to use this information.

Any value shown in italics is a variable and can be set whenever a new LDAP entry is created, except for `id`. The `id` is a number determined by the application you use to edit the entry.

You should never need to edit an LDIF entry manually. Instead, use an LDAP client application, such as the ones listed in the "Open LDAP Daemons and Utilities" section of this chapter.

OpenLDAP Configuration Files

OpenLDAP configuration files are installed into the `/etc/openldap/` directory. The following list briefly highlights the most important directories and files:

- `/etc/openldap/schema/` directory — This subdirectory contains the schema used by the slapd daemon. See the "/etc/openldap/schema Directory" section of this chapter for more information about this directory.

- `/etc/openldap/ldap.conf` — This is the configuration file for all client applications that use the OpenLDAP libraries. These include Sendmail, Pine, Balsa, Evolution, and Gnome Meeting.

- `/etc/openldap/slapd.conf` — This is the configuration file for the slapd daemon.

The nss_ldap package, if installed, will create a file named `/etc/ldap.conf`. This file is used by the PAM and NSS modules supplied by the nss_ldap package. See the section "Configuring Your System to Authenticate Using OpenLDAP" later in this chapter for more information about this configuration file.

slapd.conf

In order to use the slapd LDAP server, you need to modify its configuration file, `/etc/openldap/slapd.conf`, to make it specific to your domain and server. The `suffix` line names the domain for which the LDAP server will provide information. The `suffix` line should be changed from:

```
suffix                  "dc=your-domain,dc=com"
```

so that it reflects your domain name. For example:

```
suffix                  "dc=example,dc=com"
```

The `rootdn` entry is the Distinguished Name (DN) for a user who is unrestricted by access controls or administrative limit parameters set for operations on the LDAP directory. The `rootdn` user can be thought of as the root user for the LDAP directory. In the configuration file, change the `rootdn` line from its default value to something like the example below:

```
rootdn                  "cn=root,dc=example,dc=com"
```

Change the `rootpw` line to something like the example below:

```
rootpw                  {SSHA}vv2y+i6V6esazrIv7OxSSnNAJE18bb2u
```

In the `rootpw` example, you are using an encrypted root password, which is a much better idea than leaving a plaintext root password in the `slapd.conf` file. To make this encrypted string, type the following command:

```
slappasswd
```

You will be prompted to type and then retype a password. The program prints the resulting encrypted password to the terminal.

LDAP passwords, including the `rootpw` directive specified in `/etc/openldap/slapd.conf`, are sent over the network in plaintext unless you enable TLS encryption. For added security, the `rootpw` directive should be used only if the initial configuration and population of the LDAP directory occur over a network. After the task is completed, it is best to comment out the `rootpw` directive by preceding it with a hash mark (#).

If you are using the slapadd command-line tool locally to populate the LDAP directory, using the `rootpw` directive is not necessary.

The /etc/openldap/schema/ Directory

The `/etc/openldap/schema/` directory holds LDAP definitions, previously located in the `slapd.at.conf` and `slapd.oc.conf` files. All attribute syntax definitions and objectclass definitions are now located in the different schema files. The various schema files are referenced in `/etc/openldap/slapd.conf` using include lines, as shown in this example:

```
include         /etc/openldap/schema/core.schema
include         /etc/openldap/schema/cosine.schema
include         /etc/openldap/schema/inetorgperson.schema
include         /etc/openldap/schema/nis.schema
include         /etc/openldap/schema/rfc822-MailMember.schema
include         /etc/openldap/schema/autofs.schema
include         /etc/openldap/schema/kerberosobject.schema
```

You should not modify any of the schema items defined in the schema files installed by OpenLDAP.

You can extend the schema used by OpenLDAP to support additional attribute types and object classes using the default schema files as a guide. To do this, create a `local.schema` file in the `/etc/openldap/schema` directory. Reference this new schema within `slapd.conf` by adding the following line below your default `include` schema lines:

```
include                 /etc/openldap/schema/local.schema
```

Next, go about defining your new attribute types and object classes within the `local.schema` file. Many organizations use existing attribute types and object classes from the schema files installed by default and modify them for use in the `local.schema` file. This method can help you to learn the schema syntax while meeting the immediate needs of your organization.

Extending schema to match certain specialized requirements is quite involved and beyond the scope of this chapter. Visit `http://www.openldap.org/doc/admin/schema.html` for information on writing new schema files.

OpenLDAP Setup Overview

This section provides a quick overview for installing and configuring an OpenLDAP directory. For more details, refer to the following URLs:

- `http://www.openldap.org/doc/admin/quickstart.html` — The Quick-Start Guide on the OpenLDAP Web site.

- `http://www.redhat.com/mirrors/LDP/HOWTO/LDAP-HOWTO.html` — The LDAP Linux HOWTO from the Linux Documentation Project, mirrored on Red Hat's Web site.

The basic steps for creating an LDAP server are as follows:

1. Install the openldap, openldap-servers, and openldap-clients RPMs.

2. Edit the `/etc/openldap/slapd.conf` file to reference your LDAP domain and server.

3. Start slapd with the command:

   `/sbin/service/ldap start`

   After you have configured LDAP correctly, you can use chkconfig, ntsysv, or Services Configuration Tool to configure LDAP to start at boot time. For more information about configuring services, see Chapter 5.

4. Add entries to your LDAP directory with ldapadd. Refer to the ldapadd man page for a complete description and some examples of using this command.

5. Use ldapsearch to see if slapd is accessing the information correctly. Refer to the ldapsearch man page for a complete description and some examples of using this command.

6. At this point, your LDAP directory should be functioning properly and you can configure any LDAP-enabled applications to use the LDAP directory.

Configuring Your System to Authenticate Using OpenLDAP

This section provides a brief overview of how to configure a Red Hat system to authenticate using OpenLDAP. Unless you are an OpenLDAP expert, you will probably need more documentation than is provided here. Please see the references provided in the "Additional Resources" section for more information.

Install the Necessary LDAP Packages

First, you should make sure that the appropriate packages are installed on both the LDAP server and the LDAP client machines. The LDAP server needs the openldap-server package. The LDAP client machines need the following packages installed: openldap, openldap-clients, and nss_ldap.

Edit the Configuration Files

Use the directions in the following sections to edit each configuration file so that appropriate information is supplied to LDAP processes.

EDIT slapd.conf

Edit the /etc/openldap/slapd.conf file to make sure it matches the specifics of your organization.

EDIT /etc/ldap.conf AND /etc/openldap/ldap.conf

On all client machines, both /etc/ldap.conf and /etc/openldap/ldap.conf need to contain the proper server and search base information for your organization. The simplest way to do this is to run the authconfig application and select Use LDAP on the User Information Configuration screen. You can also edit these files manually.

EDIT /etc/nsswitch.conf

On all client machines, the /etc/nsswitch.conf file must be edited to use LDAP. The simplest way to do this is to run the authconfig application and select Use LDAP on the User Information Configuration screen. If editing /etc/nsswitch. conf manually, add ldap to the appropriate fields. For example:

```
passwd: files ldap
shadow: files ldap
group: files ldap
```

PAM AND LDAP

To have standard PAM-enabled applications use LDAP for authentication, run authconfig and select Use LDAP Authentication on the Authentication Configuration screen. For more on configuring PAM, consult Chapter 25 and the PAM man pages.

Migrating Old Authentication Information to LDAP Format

The /usr/share/openldap/migration/ directory contains a set of shell and Perl scripts for migrating authentication information into LDAP format.

You must have Perl installed on your system to use these scripts.

First, modify the `migrate_common.ph` file so that it reflects your domain. The default DNS domain should be changed from its default value to something like:

`$DEFAULT_MAIL_DOMAIN = "your_company";`

The default base should also be changed, to something like:

`$DEFAULT_BASE = "dc=your_company,dc=com";`

The job of migrating a user database into a format LDAP can read falls to a group of migration scripts installed with the `nss_ldap` package. Using Table 17-1, decide which script to run in order to migrate your user database.

TABLE 17-1 LDAP MIGRATION SCRIPTS

Existing name service	Is LDAP running?	Script to Use
/etc flat files	Yes	migrate_all_online.sh
/etc flat files	No	migrate_all_offline.sh
NetInfo	Yes	migrate_all_netinfo_online.sh
NetInfo	No	migrate_all_netinfo_offline.sh
NIS (YP)	Yes	migrate_all_nis_online.sh
NIS (YP)	No	migrate_all_nis_offline.sh

Run the appropriate script based on your existing name service. The README and the `migration-tools.txt` files in the `/usr/share/openldap/migration` directory provide more details on how to migrate the information.

Additional Resources

More information concerning LDAP is available. Please review these sources, especially the OpenLDAP Web site and the LDAP HOWTO, before configuring LDAP on your system.

◆ LDAP man pages — The ldap man page is a good place to get started for an introduction to LDAP. Man pages also exist for the various LDAP daemons and utilities.

◆ /usr/share/docs/openldap-versionnumber — Contains a general README document and miscellaneous information.

Summary

In this chapter, you took a brief look at the Lightweight Directory Access Protocol, or LDAP. LDAP is useful for maintaining directories containing information about authorized users of your network and even allowing them to authenticate to network services. You learned about the packages required for using LDAP and how to install them.

You examined the LDAP directory structure and looked at the LDAP configuration files. Then you learned how to setup and configure an LDAP server on your network. And finally, you learned about migrating existing authentication data into the format used by LDAP.

Chapter 18

BIND: The Domain Name System (DNS)

IN THIS CHAPTER

- ◆ Understanding DNS

- ◆ Installing the software

- ◆ Understanding types of domain servers

- ◆ Examining server configuration files

- ◆ Configuring a caching server

- ◆ Configuring a slave server

- ◆ Configuring a master server

- ◆ Using DNS tools

THIS CHAPTER PROVIDES INFORMATION about the Domain Name System (DNS), which is used for name address resolution. In this chapter, you learn how the Domain Name System works for finding hosts on TCP/IP networks. You also learn about different types of DNS servers and how to configure them for your own network. After configuring your servers, you'll learn about some diagnostic tools that can be used to check the configuration and performance of your DNS.

Understanding DNS

Name address resolution is, simply stated, the conversion of people friendly names into computer friendly numbers. Remember from Chapter 10 that each interface on the network has an IP address. This address is expressed as a dotted quad group. These groups of numbers present no problem to the computers in the network, but it is difficult for humans to remember many groups of numbers. So you need to be able to enter names and then have these names converted into numbers. Each time you type a Web site's address into your browser, the Domain Name System (DNS) goes to work. You enter names that are easy for you to remember, and the names are resolved into numbers that computers find easy to understand. Enabling efficient human/machine interaction is the function of name address resolution. In this chapter you learn how to install and configure the Domain Name System, which provides this name address resolution.

First, take a look at domain names and their organization using the domain name tactechnology.com. The first part of this domain name, tactechnology, is the name of the company, institution, or organization. The next part, after the period (dot in today's vernacular) is called the top-level domain. In addition to the com top-level domain, you will find a few others. Table 18-1 shows other top-level domains in the United States.

TABLE 18-1 UNITED STATES TOP-LEVEL DOMAINS

Top-Level Domain	Meaning
com	Typically, a business (for example, `www.tactechnology.com`)
edu	An educational institution (for example, `www.muhlenberg.edu`)
gov	A U.S. government agency (for example, `www.whitehouse.gov`)
mil	A branch of the U.S. military (for example, `www.army.mil`)
net	A network affiliated organization (for example, `www.tellurium.net`)
org	A noncommercial organization (for example, `www.lvcg.org`)
int	An international organization (for example, `www.wipo.int`)
us	The U.S. domain, with each listing as a lower level (for example, `www.state.pa.us`)

Top-level domains in other countries include a two-letter suffix, such as `fr` for France or `su` for Switzerland. Not all of the top-level domains are the same as the top-level U.S. domains, but a company in France could be `http://www.frenchcompany.com.fr`.

Large domains may be further broken down into subdomains. For example, the U.S. Department of Justice site is `www.usdoj.gov`. The Justice Department includes many agencies such as the Immigration and Naturalization Service. To find the INS, the usdoj domain contains the subdomain `www.ins.usdoj.gov`. An individual computer in the INS also has a host name, for example Mexico. The complete name for this computer is then `mexico.ins.usdoj.gov`, and you can find its IP address by using the DNS to look it up.

When you type in a host name, your system uses its resources to resolve names into IP addresses. One of these files is `/etc/nsswitch.conf` (nsswitch means name service switch), which contains a line telling the system where to look for host information. Figure 18-1 shows the /etc/nsswitch.conf file and the hosts line.

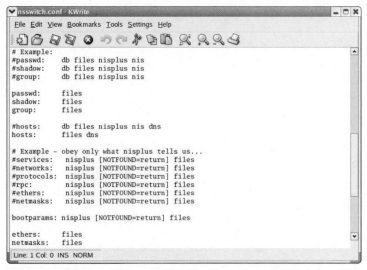

Figure 18-1: The nsswitch.conf file tells the resolver routines where to look for IP addresses.

The information following the word *host* tells the system to first look at the local files, and then to use the Domain Name Service (DNS) to resolve the names into IP numbers. One of the local files searched is the /etc/hosts file.

See Chapter 14 for more information about the /etc/hosts file.

The hosts file contains IP addresses and host names that you used on your sample network. So why couldn't you use this file for name resolution? Well, you could on a small internal network that you controlled and which did not have very many IP addresses. But, the hosts file is not a manageable solution on a large network, as it is an impossible task to keep it up to date. You could not have control over every IP address.

After the system looks in the hosts file and fails to find the address, the next file checked is /etc/resolv.conf. This file contains the IP addresses of computers that are known as Domain Name Servers, and these are listed in /etc/resolv.conf as just name servers. Figure 18-2 shows the /etc/resolv.conf file on one of the computers I use at work.

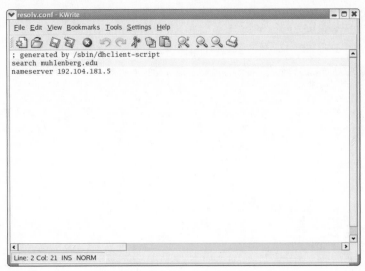

Figure 18-2: The /etc/resolv.conf file points to domain name servers used to resolve
IP addresses.

You could list up to three name servers, but one is all that is required. It is a good idea to list an additional name server, thus enabling a connection to one of the name servers in case the other name server is down or not reachable. Don't list more than three name servers, as any over three are ignored.

Installing the Software

So far you have learned about name address resolution and the structure of domains in the United States. Now you learn about the Domain Name System servers that resolve the name into IP numbers. The most common DNS server used in current Red Hat distributions is BIND, or the Berkeley Internet Name Daemon. The latest release of BIND can be obtained from the Internet Software Consortium at www.isc.org. A very convenient and easy way to install the latest version of BIND is to look for the distribution specific package. Check the Web site for your distribution to locate the RPM for BIND.

The RPM version of BIND is included with the Red Hat installation CD-ROMs. The RPM file can be installed at the command line by using the rpm command.

See Chapter 27 for instructions on installing and upgrading packages.

Understanding Types of Domain Servers

A top-level domain server, one that provides information about the domains shown in Table 18-1, is typically referred to as a Root Name Server. A search for www .muhlenberg.edu looks to the root name server for .edu for information. The root name server then directs the search to a lower-level domain name server until the information is found. You can see an example of this by using the dig command to search for the root name server for .edu, as shown in Figure 18-3.

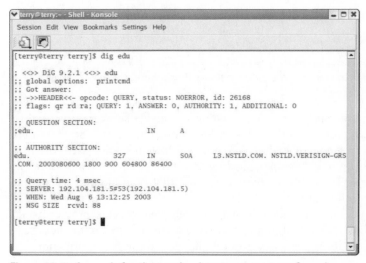

Figure 18-3: A search for the top-level root name servers for .edu

The figure shows the root name server that provides information for the .edu domain. You can continue the search for the second-level domain by adding the name of the domain you are looking for as shown in Figure 18-4.

After you have found the domain you are looking for, information about that domain is provided by its local domain name servers. The three types of local domain name servers are master, or primary, slave, or secondary, and caching-only servers. In the listing, two servers are shown; one is a master and the other is a slave.

The master contains all the information about the domain and supplies this information when requested. A master server is listed as an authoritative server when it contains the information you are seeking and it can provide that information.

The slave is intended as a backup in case the master server goes down or is not available. This server contains the same information as the master and provides it when requested if the master server cannot be contacted.

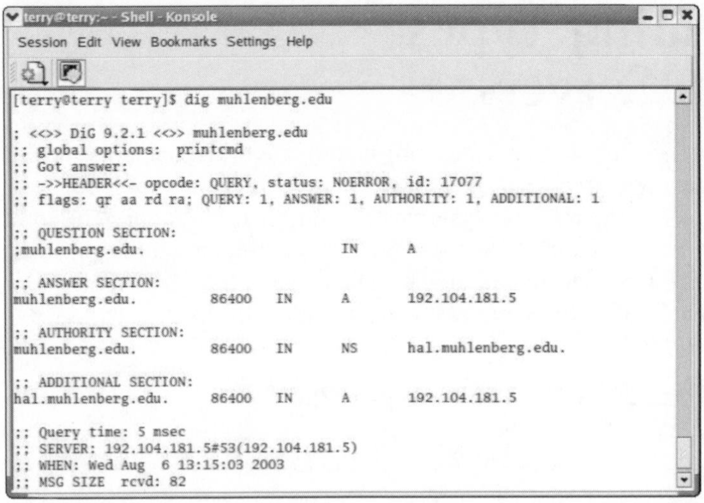

Figure 18-4: A search for the second-level domain shows the authoritative name server.

A caching server does not provide information to outside sources; it is used to provide domain information to other servers and workstations on the local network. The caching server remembers the domains that have been accessed. Use of a caching server speeds up searches since the domain information is already stored in memory, and the server knows exactly where to go rather than having to send out a request for domain information.

Where does the information that the master and slave servers provide come from? The server(s) have been configured to provide it when asked. In the next section, you learn how to configure a server to provide domain name information.

Examining Server Configuration Files

Before you begin to configure your servers, you need to take a closer look at the files you need to configure. The number of files you will use depends on the type of BIND server you want to use. There are six files that are used by the caching-only, slave and master servers. Five of the following files are configuration files, and one of them is the system initialization script that starts the process. A master and slave server require two additional files.

The six files used by all server types are:

♦ /etc/named.conf — This file contains global properties and sources of configuration files. A sample file is installed with the RPM from the Red Hat Installation CDs.

- `/var/named/localhost.zone` — This file contains the host names to IP address mapping information for the localhost. A sample file is installed with the RPM from the Red Hat Installation CDs.

- `/etc/sysconfig/named` — This is the BIND system configuration file. A sample file is installed with the RPM from the Red Hat Installation CDs.

- `/etc/rc.d/init.d/named` — This is the BIND server initialization file used to start BIND. A sample file is installed with the RPM from the Red Hat Installation CDs.

- `/var/named/named.ca` — This file contains the names and addresses of root servers. This file is typically known as the root server hints file. A sample file is installed with the RPM from the Red Hat Installation CDs.

- `/var/named/named.local` — This file provides reverse mapping information for the loopback address of your system. A sample file is installed with the RPM from the Red Hat Installation CDs.

The two additional files required for the master and slave servers are:

- `/var/named/named.(your ip information goes here)` — This file contains the host names to IP addresses mapping file.

- `/var/named/named.(your domain name goes here)` — This file provides information to map IP addresses to host names. This file is known as a reverse zone file.

You begin with the `/etc/named.conf` file. An example of this file is shown in Listing 18-1.

Listing 18-1: The /etc/named.conf file for a caching-only server installed by the default installation of BIND

```
// generated by named-bootconf.pl

options {
        directory "/var/named";
        forward only;
        /*
         * If there is a firewall between you and nameservers you
         * want
         * to talk to, you might need to uncomment the query-source
         * directive below.  Previous versions of BIND always asked
         * questions using port 53, but BIND 8.1 uses an unprivileged
         * port by default.
```

Continued

Listing 18-1 *(Continued)*

```
        */
        // query-source address * port 53;
};


//
// a caching only nameserver config
//
controls {
        inet 127.0.0.1 allow { localhost; } keys { rndckey; };
};
zone "." { type hint; file "named.ca"; };

zone "localhost" {
        type master;
        notify no;
        file "localhost.zone";
        allow-update { none; };
};

zone "0.0.127.in-addr.arpa" {
        type master;
        notify no;
        file "named.local";
        allow-update { none; };
};

logging {
        category lame-servers { null; };
        };

include "/etc/rndc.key";
```

The named.conf File

Look at this file in more detail beginning with the lines starting with //. These are comment lines and anything following them is ignored.

Commands are passed to the file in the form of statements. Several of these statements are shown in the sample file, but you actually can use seven configuration statements. These are listed here with a brief explanation of their function.

- ◆ **options** – Lists global configurations and defaults

- ◆ **include** – Gets information from another file and includes it

- ◆ **acl** – Specifies IP addresses used in an access control list

- **logging** – Specifies log file locations and contents

- **server** – Specifies properties of remote servers

- **zone** – Specifies information about zones

- **key** – Specifies security keys used for authentication

Information about the statement is contained within curly braces and terminated by a semicolon as shown here: {information about server};.

Options

The options statement is typically the first section of named.conf, and it contains information about the location of the files used by named. You can use only one options statement, but you can have more than one value for that statement. In the sample file shown in Listing 18-1, the options statement shows the path to where additional configuration files used by named are located. By specifying the directory where other files are located, it is not necessary to list the entire path to the file, just the name of the file for any files shown in the remainder of named.conf. Options statements use the following syntax:

```
options {
        value "property";
}
```

The list of values that can be used in the options statement is quite long. These values are shown, listed alphabetically, in Table 18-2.

TABLE 18-2 OPTIONS VALUES AND THEIR MEANINGS

Value	Meaning
allow-query	Accepts queries only from hosts in the address list (by default queries are accepted from any host). Usage: allow-query {"address-list"};.
allow-transfer	Zone transfers are accepted only by hosts in the address list (by default transfers are allowed to all hosts). Usage: allow-transfer {"address list"};.
auth-nxdomain	The server responds as an authoritative server (defaults to yes). Usage: auth-nxdomain "yes or no"; (choose one).

Continued

TABLE 18-2 OPTIONS VALUES AND THEIR MEANINGS *(Continued)*

Value	Meaning
check-names	Host names are checked for compliance with the RFC. Usage: check-names "master or slave or response warn or fail or ignore"; (choose one from each group).
cleaning-interval	Specifies the time period before expired resource records are removed by the server (defaults to 60 minutes). Usage: cleaning-interval "number"; (specify number in minutes).
coresize	Specifies largest size for core dump files. Usage: coresize "size"; (specify size in bytes).
datasize	Limits server memory usage. Usage: datasize "size"; (specify size in bytes).
deallocate-on-exit	Detects memory leaks (default is no). Usage: deallocate-on-exit "yes or no"; (choose one).
directory	Path of the directory where server configuration files are located. Usage: directory "path to directory"; (specify path).
dump-file	If named receives a SIGINT signal, it dumps the database to the file specified here (defaults to named_dump.db).
fake-iquery	If set to yes, the server sends a fake reply to inverse queries rather than an error (default is no). Usage: fake-iquery " yes or no"; (choose one).
fetch-glue	If set to yes, the server obtains the glue records for a response (default is yes). Usage: fetch-glue "yes or no"; (choose one).
files	Limits number of concurrently open files (default is unlimited). Usage: files "number"; (specify number).
forward	If set to first, the servers listed in the forwarders option are queried first, and then the server tries to find the answer itself. If set to only, just the servers in the forwarders list are queried. Usage: forward "first or only"; (choose one).
forwarders	Shows IP addresses of servers to forward queries (default is none). Usage: forwarders "IP addresses of servers"; (specify IP addresses).
host-statistics	If set to yes the server keeps statistics on hosts (default is no). Usage: host-statistics "yes or no"; (choose one).

Value	Meaning
interface-interval	Specifies interval for searching the network for new or removed interfaces (default is 60 minutes). Usage: interface-interval "time"; (specify time in minutes).
listen-on	Specifies port and interfaces on which server listens for queries (default is port 53). Usage: listen-on "port {address list}"; (specify port number and address list).
max-transfer-time-in	Specifies time server waits for completion of inbound transfer (default is 120 minutes). Usage: max-transfer-time-in "time"; (specify time in minutes).
memstatistics-file	When deallocate-on-exit is set, specifies the file where memory statistics are written (defaults to named.memstats). Usage: memstatistics-file "path to file"; (specify path and file name).
multiple-cnames	When set to yes, enables multiple CNAME usage (default is no). Usage: multiple-cnames "yes or no"; (choose one).
named-xfer	Specifies path to the named-xfer program. Usage: named-xfer "path to file"; (specify path).
notify	When zone files are updated, this option, when set to yes, sends DNS NOTIFY messages (default is yes). Usage: notify "yes or no"; (choose one).
pid-file	Name of file holding process ID. Usage: pid-file "path to file"; (specify path and file name).
query-source	Specifies port and IP address used to query other servers. Usage: query-source "address port"; (specify IP address and port).
recursion	The server recursively searches for query answers (default is yes). Usage: recursion " yes or no"; (choose one).
stacksize	The amount of stack memory the server can use. Usage: stacksize "number"; (specify the amount of memory).
statistics-interval	The time interval for logging statistics (default is 60 minutes). Usage: statistics-interval "time"; (specify the time in minutes).
topology	Sets server preference for remote servers. Usage: topology {"address list"};.

Continued

TABLE 18-2 OPTIONS VALUES AND THEIR MEANINGS *(Continued)*

Value	Meaning
transfer-format	When set to one-answer, only one resource record per message is sent. When set to many-answers, as many records as possible are transmitted in each message. (default is one). Usage: transfer-format "one-answer many-answers"; (choose one).
transfers-in	Maximum concurrent inbound zone transfers (default is 10). Usage: transfers-in "number"; (specify the number).
transfers-out	Maximum concurrent outbound transfers. Usage: transfers-out "number"; (specify the number).
transfers-per-ns	Limits inbound transfers from a single server (default is two). Usage: transfers-per-ns "number"; (specify the number).

include

The include statement lists the path and name of any files that you want to be included with the `named.conf` file. Use the same syntax as used in the options statement to specify the path.

acl

This option lets you specify a list of IP addresses in an access control list. Only hosts on this list have access to the server.

logging

The logging statement is where you specify your server's logging options. The logging statement contains two additional items, the channel and the category.

The channel is where you specify the location of the logged information. Logged information can be written to a file, sent to the syslog, or thrown away by specifying the appropriate command. Choosing to send the information to a file gives you several additional choices on how to handle the information. You can set the number of versions to keep, the size of the files, and whether the severity of the information and the time and category are included with the other information in the file.

The syntax for the logging statement is similar to the syntax for the option statement. The following commands send the information to a file. Items in italics indicate information you need to enter.

```
logging {
        channel channel_name {
        (file    path to file
        versions specify number or unlimited
        size specify size in bytes }If you want to send the
information to the syslog, the syntax is
```

```
logging {
        channel channel_name {
        syslog (choose where to send from following choices)
(kern,user,mail,daemon,auth,syslog,lpr,news,uucp,cron,\
        authpriv,ftp,local0 thru local7)
```

To discard the information, choose null as the destination.

```
logging {
        channel channel_name {
        null;)
```

Next you can set the severity level for the information written to the file or syslog. This section follows the sections shown previously for file or syslog. You also indicate here if you want the time, category, and severity included. If you are discarding the information, you don't need to set these parameters.

```
severity choose from critical,error,warning,notice,info,debug\
level,dynamic
print-time choose yes or no
print-severity choose yes or no
print-category choose yes or no
};
```

The category is where you specify the type of information to log. This value follows the severity and print parameters and takes the following syntax:

```
category    category name {
channel name; channel name;
};
```

You can choose from over 20 categories. These are shown, alphabetically, in Table 18-3.

TABLE 18-3 LOGGING CATEGORIES

Category	Type of Information Logged
cname	Information about CNAME references
config	Information about configuration files
db	Information about databases
default	The default if nothing is selected
eventlib	Information about event system debugging
insist	Details about failures from internal consistency checking
lame-servers	Information about lame servers
load	Information about zone loading
maintenance	Information about maintenance
ncache	Information about negative caching
notify	Information about tracing the NOTIFY protocol
os	Information about operating system problems
packet	Dumps of all sent and received packets
panic	Information about faults that shut down the server
parser	Information about processing configuration commands
queries	Information about all received DNS queries
response-checks	Information about response-checking results
security	Information about security status of server
statistics	Information about server statistics
update	Information about dynamic updates
xfer-in	Information about inbound zone transfers
xfer-out	Information about outbound zone transfers

Using the categories from the logging statement, you can obtain a large quantity of information about your server. This information can be useful if you are having problems with your DNS. You can enable logging for the area that you think is causing your problem and then read the appropriate log to find any messages that might indicate an error with your configuration.

server

In the server statement you can set the properties of a remote server. You can specify whether to send queries to the remote server from the local server, and you can set the method used for transferring information. The syntax for this statement is the same as for other statements. The valid values are:

- ◆ `bogus` – Specify yes or no (No is the default and indicates that queries are sent to the remote server.) Yes means that the remote server is not queried.

- ◆ `transfer` – Specify the number of transfers you want to allow.

- ◆ `transfer-format` – Specify whether you want one-answer or many-answers.

- ◆ `keys` – Specify key ID.

zones

Also included in the `/etc/named.conf` file are zone statements. These zone statements refer to files that are called zone files. Additional options for zone statements exist, of course. Each zone statement begins with the word `zone` followed by the domain name and the data class. The four data classes are `in`, `hs`, `hesiod`, and `chaos`. If no type is specified, the default is `in`, for Internet.

Next follows the type option which specifies whether the server is a master, a slave/stub, or is the hints file. A stub server loads only NS records, not the entire domain. The hints file is used to initialize the root cache and contains a list of root servers.

Next is the name of the zone file for the specified zone. This is a pointer to the file containing the data about the zone. You look at a zone file in detail a little later in this chapter.

The six other options for the zone statements are listed here, along with an explanation of their function.

- ◆ **allow-query** – Accepts queries only from hosts in the address list (by default queries are accepted from any host).

- ◆ **allow-transfer** – Zone transfers are accepted only by hosts in the address list (by default, transfers are allowed to all hosts).

- ◆ **allow-update** – Hosts in the address list are allowed to update the database.

- ◆ **also-notify** – Servers in the address list are sent a notify message when the zone is updated.

- ◆ **check-names** – Hostnames are checked for compliance with the RFC.

- ◆ **max-transfer-time-in** – Specifies the time the slave waits for a zone transfer.

- ◆ **notify** – When zone files are updated, this option, when set to yes, sends DNS NOTIFY messages (default is yes).

These options are the same as those shown in the options statement section and have the same function here. When listed in the options section, they apply to all zones, but if listed with a specific zone, they apply only to that zone. Settings listed in a specific zone section override those globally set in the options statement.

The /var/named/named.ca File

The first zone file is known as the cache file, and it references a file called /var/named/named.ca, which contains information about the world's root name servers. This information changes and needs to be updated periodically. Listing 18-2 shows the contents of this file.

Listing 18-2: The /var/named/named.ca file

```
;       This file holds the information on root name servers needed to
;       initialize cache of Internet domain name servers
;       (e.g. reference this file in the "cache  .  <file>"
;       configuration file of BIND domain name servers).
;
;       This file is made available by InterNIC
;       under anonymous FTP as
;           file                /domain/named.cache
;           on server           FTP.INTERNIC.NET
;
;        last update:   Nov 5, 2002
;        related version of root zone:   2002110501
;
;
; formerly NS.INTERNIC.NET
;
.                          3600000  IN  NS   A.ROOT-SERVERS.NET.
A.ROOT-SERVERS.NET.        3600000      A    198.41.0.4
;
; formerly NS1.ISI.EDU
;
.                          3600000      NS   B.ROOT-SERVERS.NET.
B.ROOT-SERVERS.NET.        3600000      A    128.9.0.107
;
; formerly C.PSI.NET
;
.                          3600000      NS   C.ROOT-SERVERS.NET.
C.ROOT-SERVERS.NET.        3600000      A    192.33.4.12
;
; formerly TERP.UMD.EDU
;
.                          3600000      NS   D.ROOT-SERVERS.NET.
D.ROOT-SERVERS.NET.        3600000      A    128.8.10.90
```

```
;
; formerly NS.NASA.GOV
;
.                        3600000      NS      E.ROOT-SERVERS.NET.
E.ROOT-SERVERS.NET.      3600000      A       192.203.230.10
;
; formerly NS.ISC.ORG
;
.                        3600000      NS      F.ROOT-SERVERS.NET.
F.ROOT-SERVERS.NET.      3600000      A       192.5.5.241
;
; formerly NS.NIC.DDN.MIL
;
.                        3600000      NS      G.ROOT-SERVERS.NET.
G.ROOT-SERVERS.NET.      3600000      A       192.112.36.4
;
; formerly AOS.ARL.ARMY.MIL
;
.                        3600000      NS      H.ROOT-SERVERS.NET.
H.ROOT-SERVERS.NET.      3600000      A       128.63.2.53
;
; formerly NIC.NORDU.NET
;
.                        3600000      NS      I.ROOT-SERVERS.NET.
I.ROOT-SERVERS.NET.      3600000      A       192.36.148.17
;
; operated by VeriSign, Inc.
;
.                        3600000      NS      J.ROOT-SERVERS.NET.
J.ROOT-SERVERS.NET.      3600000      A       192.58.128.30
;
; housed in LINX, operated by RIPE NCC
;
.                        3600000      NS      K.ROOT-SERVERS.NET.
K.ROOT-SERVERS.NET.      3600000      A       193.0.14.129
;
; operated by IANA
;
.                        3600000      NS      L.ROOT-SERVERS.NET.
L.ROOT-SERVERS.NET.      3600000      A       198.32.64.12
;
; housed in Japan, operated by WIDE
;
.                        3600000      NS      M.ROOT-SERVERS.NET.
M.ROOT-SERVERS.NET.      3600000      A       202.12.27.33
; End of File
```

The /var/named/localhost.zone File

The next zone file shown in /etc/named.conf is the host to IP address file for the localhost. Listing 18-3 shows this file.

Listing 18-3: The host to IP address file for the localhost

```
$TTL    86400
$ORIGIN localhost.
@                    1D IN SOA     @ root (
                                   42           ; serial
                                   3H           ; refresh
                                   15M          ; retry
                                   1W           ; expiry
                                   1D )         ; minimum

             1D IN NS     @
             1D IN A      127.0.0.1
```

The /var/named/named.local File

The last zone file contains the reverse lookup information for the localhost. The file referenced here is /var/named/named.local and is shown in Listing 18-4.

Listing 18-4: The /var/named/named.local file contains reverse lookup information about the internal network 127.0.0.1

```
$TTL    86400
@       IN      SOA     localhost. root.localhost. (
                                   1997022700 ; Serial
                                   28800      ; Refresh
                                   14400      ; Retry
                                   3600000    ; Expire
                                   86400 )    ; Minimum
        IN      NS      localhost.
1       IN      PTR     localhost.
```

Zone Files

Zone files contain resource records (RR) about IP addresses. A typical zone file is shown in Listing 18-5.

Listing 18-5: The host to address zone file for the tactechnology.com domain

```
;Start of Authority Record
;Last modified May 2000
$TTL    86400
@       IN      SOA     tactechnology.com. root.tactechnology.com (
```

```
                                    2000052101 ; Serial
                                    2880521    ; Refresh
                                    14400      ; Retry
                                    604800     ; Expire
                                    86400 )    ; Minimum

; Name Servers (NS)
@        IN    NS    main.tectechnology.com
@        IN    NS    p200.tactechnology.com.

; Mail Servers (MX)
@        IN    MX    10      main
@        IN    MX    20      p200.tactechnology.com.

;Address Records (A)
localhost IN   A     127.0.0.1
ns       IN    A     207.172.250.185
ns       IN    A     207.172.250.186
www      IN    A     207.172.250.185
ftp      IN    A     207.172.250.185

;PTR records
1        PTR           localhost
```

A zone file can contain many types of RRs, which are listed in the order in which they generally appear in the zone files, and explained next.

SOA: START OF AUTHORITY

The start of authority (SOA) is the first line in the zone file. The SOA identifies the name server as the authoritative source for information about this domain. Each zone file has only one SOA, and it contains the following data:

```
@  IN  SOA  main.tactechnology.com.    root.tactechnology.com. (
   200052101  ; Serial
   8h         ;Refresh
   2h         ;Retry
   1w         ;Expire
   1d)        ;Minimum TTL
```

The first character in the SOA line is a special symbol that means "to look at this domain." IN means Internet. SOA means Start Of Authority.

The authoritative server for this domain is main.tactechnology.com, and root.tactechnology.com is the e-mail address of the administrator. Note the trailing period after the domain names. If these are not included, the domain name is appended to the entry.

The opening parenthesis enables the first line to be extended so that anything between the opening and closing parenthesis is considered one line.

The information within the parenthesis is passed to other name servers, secondary masters, that use this information to update their records. The line containing `200052101 ; Serial` is the serial number of the file. Secondary servers compare this number with their stored information. If the numbers are the same, the information has not changed, and it is not necessary to download this file. If the serial numbers are different, the file is downloaded to update the information in the secondary server. The serial number can be any number desired as long as it can be incremented to indicate a revision to the file. The semicolon indicates that what follows to the end of the line is a comment.

TIP The recommended format for the serial field is YYYYMMDDNN for year, month, day, and revision number. Be sure to increment the revision number whenever you change the information in this file. Your DNS change will not appear if you forget to increment the revision number in the serial field.

Refresh is the amount of time the server should wait before refreshing its data.

Retry is the amount of time the server should wait before attempting to contact the primary server if the previous attempt failed.

Expire means that if the secondary master is unable to contact a primary master during the specified period, the data expires and should be purged.

Minimum specifies the Time to Live (TTL) for the data. This parameter is intended for caching name servers and tells them how long to hold the data in their cache.

All of the information contained by the SOA may be placed on one line, but it is usually written as shown previously. The order of the items is significant in the SOA header. Additional descriptive items about the servers are explained below.

NS: NAME SERVERS IN THIS DOMAIN
Shows the names of the name servers.

A: THE IP ADDRESS FOR THE NAME
Shows the IP address for the name servers.

MX RECORD: MAIL EXCHANGE RECORD
The MX record specifies the mail servers for the domain. In the tactech.com zone file, two MX addresses are listed, one followed by the number 10 and the other by the number 20. Any mail sent to tactechnology.com goes to main.tactechnology.com because it has a lower number. Priority is determined by the address with the lowest number receiving the highest priority. So, main is the primary mail server and p200 is the secondary mail server. If main is unable to receive mail, mail goes

to p200. p200 tries to send mail to main since it is also its primary mail server. When main is again able to receive mail, it receives all the mail that p200 has received.

PTR: POINTER FOR ADDRESS NAME MAPPING
Used to point to the name servers.

CNAME: CANONICAL NAME
Shows the real name of the host.

TXT: TEXT INFORMATION
Enables entry of descriptive information.

WKS: WELL-KNOWN SERVICE
Enables entry of descriptive information.

HINFO: HOST INFORMATION
Usually shows type of hardware and software.

The Reverse Zone File

The reverse zone file is used to provide information for reverse lookups. In the previous example you searched for tactechnology.com by using the domain name. This method is called forward address resolution since it uses a name to find an IP number and is the most common use of name resolution.

You can also find a name from an IP number, and this is called reverse address resolution. All you need to do is enter the IP address, and the server returns the domain name. Listing 18-6 shows the reverse lookup zone file for tactechnology.com.

Listing 18-6: The reverse zone file for the tactechnology.com domain

```
;Start of Authority Record
;Last modified May 2000
$TTL    86400
@       IN      SOA     tactechnology.com. root.tactechnology.com (
                                20000       ;Serial
                                2880521     ; Refresh
                                14400       ; Retry
                                604800      ; Expire
                                86400  )    ; Minimum


; Name Servers (NS)
@       IN      NS      main.tactechnology.com.
@       IN      NS      p200.tactechnology.com.
```

Configuring a Caching Server

Now you know which files need to be configured and you know the information that needs to be placed in them. You are ready to set up your own domain name servers. In this section you set up a caching server for the domain tactechnology.com. As stated earlier, six files are used in all three types of server configurations. Three of the six files are actual configuration files for the type of server, while the other three are used to pass global parameters, /etc/named.conf; start the named server /etc/rc.d/init.d/named; and control system logging, /etc/logrotate.d/named. In a caching-only server, the three files that make up the server configuration are /var/named/named.ca, /var/named/named.local, and /var/named/localhost.zone.

Begin by verifying the zone information in /etc/named.conf. When you installed the BIND package, the /etc/named.conf file was created, and it contained zone information for your localhost, but you need to check it to be sure. You are looking for three zone lines: one indicated by a ".", referencing the file named.ca, another shown as "localhost," referencing the file localhost.zone, and another shown as "0.0.127.in.addr.arpa", referencing named.local.

Next, you need to check the configuration of the /var/named/named.ca, /var/named/localhost.zone, and /var/named/named.local file. These files contain the root server hints file and the domain information for the localhost, and are typically created when BIND is installed. You usually don't have to make any changes to these files, but check that they are where they should be.

You should also check the /etc/nsswitch.conf file to be sure it includes the following line:

```
hosts:   files nisplusdns
```

Finally, you need to add your localhost to the list of nameservers in /etc/resolv.conf.

After you have completed all of the previous steps, it is time to start the named daemon and check your work.

Type service named start at a command prompt, wait for the prompt to return, and then type nslookup localhost. If you see a screen like that shown in Listing 18-7, you have successfully configured a caching server.

Listing 18-7: Using the nslookup command to test the configuration of the caching-only server

```
[root@laptop root]# nslookup localhost
Note:  nslookup is deprecated and may be removed from future releases.
Consider using the `dig' or `host' programs instead.  Run nslookup with
the `-sil[ent]' option to prevent this message from appearing.
Server:        127.0.0.1
```

```
Address:        127.0.0.1#53

Name:   localhost
Address: 127.0.0.1

[root@laptop root]#
```

Configuring a Slave Server

Next you set up a slave server for your domain. The procedure is similar to, and not much more difficult than, what you have already done. You already have three of the files in place and only need to slightly modify the /etc/named.conf file and add two more files to complete the slave configuration.

On the server you want to be the slave, go to the /etc/named.conf file and add two more zones, one for the forward lookup of your server, and one for the reverse lookup. For the forward lookup, you need to add the following. (For this example, the master server is called main.tactechnology.com, and the slave is p200 .tactechnology.com. Be sure to use your own domain name and IP addresses instead of the examples shown.)

```
zone "tactechnology.com" {
    notify no;
    type slave;
    file "tactech.com";
    masters { 192.168.1.1; };
};
```

For the reverse lookup, add this section:

```
zone "1.168.192.in-addr.arpa" {
    notify no;
    type slave;
    file "tac.rev";
    masters { 192.168.1.1; };
};
```

You do not need to create the two zone files that are referenced in /etc/ named.conf. These files will be created on the master server and are automatically transferred to the slave server. Start your server by issuing the command service named start.

Configuring a Master Server

The /etc/named.conf file on the master server also needs to be modified. Assuming that you already set up this server as a caching-only server, you just need to add the following lines to /etc/named.conf. (This example uses the names you defined earlier; be sure to use your own names and IP addresses.)

```
zone "tactechnology.com" {
    notify yes;
    type master;
    file "tactech.com";
};
```

For the reverse lookup, add this section:

```
zone "1.168.192.in-addr.arpa" {
    notify yes;
    type master;
    file "tac.rev";
};
```

Notice that you used the same names for the files on the master server as the slave server. This is because these files are downloaded by the slave in a zone file transfer and stored on the slave in the files shown by the file option. You did not create the files on the slave but created them on the master server.

You now need to create the zone files that are referenced by the /etc/named.conf file. First, create the host to IP address file /var/named/tactech.com by beginning with the Start of Authority section (SOA). For an explanation of the information contained in zone files, refer to the zone file section earlier in this chapter.

```
@   IN  SOA   main.tactechnology.com.mail.tactechnology.com. ( /
                  200005203; Serial
                  8h; Refresh
                  2h; Retry
                  1w; Expire
                  1d); Minimum TTL
```

Next, add name-server and mail-exchange information.

```
    NS  main.tactechnology.com.
    NS  terry.tactechnology.com.
    MX  10 main;Primary Mail Exchanger
    MX  20 p200;Secondary Mail Exchanger
```

Finally, you add information about your localhost, mail, FTP and Web server. You can also add information about every workstation on your network if you desire.

Next you set up the reverse lookup zone file, which is called `tac.rev` in this example. Again, you need to start with the SOA header as shown:

```
@  IN  SOA  main.tactechnology.com.  mail.tactechnology.com.(
                200005203;Serial
                      8h; Refresh
                      2h; Retry
                      1w; Expire
                      1d; Minimum TTL
```

Next, add the information about your name servers and their IP addresses.

```
        NS      main.tactechnology.com.
1       PTR     main.tactechnology.com.
2       PTR     p200.tactechnology.com.
```

If you have done everything as explained here, your name server should be working. Start your server by issuing the command `service named start`. You need to check your work again, but before you do, look at some of the tools available to you for checking name server information.

Using DNS Tools

The three very useful tools available for troubleshooting DNS problems that are included with BIND are nslookup, host, and dig. These utilities are briefly explained in this section. Please refer to the man pages for these commands for a listing of the options available.

nslookup

Earlier when you set up a caching name server, you checked your work using nslookup. Nslookup is one of several programs that can be used to obtain information about your name servers. This information helps you to fix problems that may have occurred. Notice that when you start nslookup, you see a message about it being deprecated and may not be available in future releases; however, it is still available and is quite useful.

`nslookup`, as its name implies, is a program that can be used either interactively, or noninteractively, to look up name servers. Entering `nslookup` at a command prompt starts the search for a name server by looking in the `/etc/resolv.conf` file. If you are running a name server on your system, your localhost (127.0.0.1) is searched, as this is the first listing for a name server in `/etc/resolv.conf`. You can also tell nslookup to search for a specific server by entering a hyphen and the name of the desired server after the command. After nslookup starts, the DNS server used for searches is shown, and a prompt is presented for entering commands.

The most common commands available for use with nslookup are

- ◆ ls—Used to list information about the domain in question

- ◆ set—Used to change search information for lookups

The set command also has many options, but the most commonly used option is to set the query type. The query type may be changed to any of the RR types you saw earlier in this chapter, plus a few other types. For example, if you want to see the mail servers on the tactechnology.com domain you could type the command as illustrated in Listing 18-8.

Listing 18-8: Output of the nslookup command querying for amil servers

```
[root@laptop root]# nslookup -sil -query=MX tactechnology.com
Server:          127.0.0.1
Address:         127.0.0.1#53

Non-authoritative answer:
tactechnology.com          mail exchanger = 10 mail.tactechnology.com.

Authoritative answers can be found from:
tactechnology.com          nameserver = ns2.ipowerweb.net.
tactechnology.com          nameserver = ns1.ipowerweb.net.
mail.tactechnology.com     internet address = 12.129.206.112
ns1.ipowerweb.net          internet address = 64.70.61.130
ns2.ipowerweb.net          internet address = 12.129.206.200

[root@laptop root]#
```

host

Another utility that is useful for obtaining information about a name server is host. Host enables you to find an IP address for the specified domain name. All that is required is the domain name of the remote host as shown here.

```
[root@laptop root]# host tactechnology.com
tactechnology.com has address 12.129.206.112
```

You can also search for resource record types by using the -t option and the type of resource record you want to search. For example, if you wanted to find information about the MX server for a domain, you would enter the following command:

```
[root@laptop root]# host -t MX ibm.com
ibm.com mail is handled by 0 ns.watson.ibm.com.
```

dig

The last utility you look at is dig. Dig can be used for debugging and obtaining other useful information. If nslookup does become unavailable in future versions, you can use dig to obtain the same information that nslookup provides. The basic syntax is:

```
dig (@server) domain name (type)
```

Items in parenthesis are optional. Listing 18-9 shows the output of a dig request to muhlenberg.edu.

Listing 18-9: A dig request to muhlenberg.edu

```
[root@laptop root]# dig muhlenberg.edu

; <<>> DiG 9.2.2 <<>> muhlenberg.edu
;; global options:  printcmd
;; Got answer:
;; ->>HEADER<<- opcode: QUERY, status: NOERROR, id: 3703
;; flags: qr rd ra; QUERY: 1, ANSWER: 1, AUTHORITY: 1, ADDITIONAL: 1

;; QUESTION SECTION:
;muhlenberg.edu.                    IN      A

;; ANSWER SECTION:
muhlenberg.edu.         7421    IN      A       192.104.181.5

;; AUTHORITY SECTION:
muhlenberg.edu.         7421    IN      NS      hal.muhlenberg.edu.

;; ADDITIONAL SECTION:
hal.muhlenberg.edu.     171450  IN      A       192.104.181.5

;; Query time: 52 msec
;; SERVER: 127.0.0.1#53(127.0.0.1)
;; WHEN: Sun Aug 10 10:59:18 2003
;; MSG SIZE  rcvd: 82

[root@laptop root]#
```

Dig can also be used to do reverse lookups by using the -x switch and specifying the IP address as seen in Listing 18-10.

Listing 18-10: Using dig to do a reverse address lookup

```
[root@laptop root]# dig -x 192.104.181.5

; <<>> DiG 9.2.2 <<>> -x 192.104.181.5
;; global options:  printcmd
;; Got answer:
;; ->>HEADER<<- opcode: QUERY, status: NOERROR, id: 28571
;; flags: qr rd ra; QUERY: 1, ANSWER: 1, AUTHORITY: 2, ADDITIONAL: 2

;; QUESTION SECTION:
;5.181.104.192.in-addr.arpa.      IN      PTR

;; ANSWER SECTION:
5.181.104.192.in-addr.arpa. 85913 IN     PTR      hal.muhlberg.edu.

;; AUTHORITY SECTION:
181.104.192.in-addr.arpa. 62567 IN       NS       hal.muhlberg.edu.
181.104.192.in-addr.arpa. 62567 IN       NS
stimpy.nwip.muhlberg.edu.

;; ADDITIONAL SECTION:
hal.muhlberg.edu.         18459   IN      A        192.104.181.5
stimpy.nwip.muhlberg.edu. 62567 IN       A        192.104.181.207

;; Query time: 9 msec
;; SERVER: 127.0.0.1#53(127.0.0.1)
;; WHEN: Sun Aug 10 11:11:08 2003
;; MSG SIZE  rcvd: 146
```

Summary

This chapter provided a brief but concise overview of the Domain Name System using a small, simple network as an example. You looked at name address resolution and found out how names that are easy for people to remember are converted to numbers that computers can understand. You obtained the BIND software package and installed it on your system and located the files that have to be configured for BIND to work. After configuring the files, you set up a caching name server and tested its operation. You then configured a slave and master name server and looked at some of the diagnostic utilities available for the BIND package.

Chapter 19

Configuring Mail Services

IN THIS CHAPTER

- ◆ E-mail explained
- ◆ Introducing SMTP
- ◆ Configuring Sendmail
- ◆ Configuring the e-mail client
- ◆ Using elm
- ◆ Maintaining e-mail security

USING ELECTRONIC MAIL, you can send messages to and receive messages from other computer users anywhere in the world. E-mail, as it is more commonly known, is a very powerful and useful tool. In this chapter, you learn how e-mail works and then configure your systems to put e-mail to work for you.

E-Mail Explained

An e-mail message, just like a letter sent through regular mail, begins with a sender and ends with a receiver. Between these two people are many postal workers who ensure that the letter is properly handled. Even though the sender and receiver never see these workers, their functions are essential in moving the mail. E-mail works in a similar fashion, and although there are not many people between the sender and receiver, programs perform the same function. These programs use network protocols to do the job of ensuring that the message goes from sender to receiver. In this chapter you configure e-mail to run across TCP/IP protocols.

Chapter 10 explains the TCP/IP protocol suite.

Before configuring an e-mail client or server, you need to understand how e-mail works and the programs to use or make available to your users. Several key components are essential for e-mail to work properly, and as a system administrator it is your responsibility to configure the following items. These items are explained in more detail later in this chapter.

- ◆ Programs:

    - A Mail User Agent (MUA) for users to be able to read and write e-mail

    - A Mail Transfer Agent (MTA) to deliver the e-mail messages between computers across a network

    - A Local Delivery Agent (LDA) to deliver messages to users' mailbox files

    - A mail-notification program to tell users that they have new mail

- ◆ The TCP/IP protocols for storing e-mail messages and transferring e-mail between MTAs

- ◆ Other communication and mail-storage components:

    - Ports

    - Mail queues

    - Mailbox files

In the next sections of this chapter, you track an e-mail message through the process from sending to delivery to learn how all the various components work to accomplish their jobs. After learning how the components work, you configure these components to build a fully functioning e-mail system for your server and clients.

Mail User Agent (MUA)

To be able to send mail, you, or your users, need a program called a Mail User Agent (MUA). The MUA, also called a mail client, enables users to write and read mail messages. Two types of MUAs are available: a graphical user interface (GUI), such as Mozilla Messenger, and a command-line interface, such as Mutt.

Whether your MUA is a GUI or command-line interface, after the message is composed, the MUA sends it to the mail transfer agent (MTA). The MTA is the program that sends the message out across the network and does its work without any intervention by the user. In fact, most users are unaware of the MTA; they just see their mail client.

Mail Transfer Agent (MTA)

Now that the MTA has received the message from the MUA, it can do its job. The MTA installed by default on your Red Hat system is called Sendmail. The MTA reads the information in the *To* section of the e-mail message and determines the IP address of the recipient's mail server. Then the MTA tries to open a connection to the recipient's server through a communication port, typically port 25. If the MTA on the sending machine can establish a connection, it sends the message to the MTA on the recipient's server using the Simple Message Transfer Protocol (SMTP).

The MTA on the receiving server adds header information to the message. The header contains information that is used for tracking the message and ensuring that it is delivered. Next the receiving MTA passes the message to another program to inform the receiver that new mail has arrived.

Local Delivery Agent (LDA)

After the LDA receives the message from the MTA, it places the message in the receiver's mailbox file that is identified by the username. On your Red Hat system this is a program called procmail. The location of the user's mailbox file is `/var/spool/mail/<user's name>`.

The final step in the process happens when the user who is the intended receiver of the message reads the message. The user does this using the MUA on his or her PC.

An optional program is a mail notifier that periodically checks your mailbox file for new mail. If you have such a program installed, it notifies you of the new mail.

The Red Hat Linux shell has a built-in mail notifier that looks at your mailbox file once a minute. If new mail has arrived, the shell displays a message just before it displays the next system prompt. It won't interrupt a program you're running. You can adjust how frequently the mail notifier checks and even which mailbox files to watch.

If you are using a GUI, mail notifiers are available that play sounds or display pictures to let you know that new mail has arrived.

Introducing SMTP

In the section describing the MTA, you learned that messages are sent between MTAs using SMTP. This section explains SMTP and two other protocols used to send mail, Post Office Protocol (POP3) and Internet Message Access Protocol (IMAP4). *SMTP* is the TCP/IP protocol for transferring e-mail messages between computers on a network. SMTP specifies message movement between MTAs, by the path the message takes. Messages may go directly from the sending to the receiving MTA or through other MTAs on other network computers. These other computers briefly store the message before they forward it to another MTA, if it is local to the MTA, or to a gateway that sends it to an MTA on another network.

The SMTP protocol can transfer only ASCII text. It can't handle fonts, colors, graphics, or attachments. If you want to be able to send these items, you need to add another protocol to SMTP.

The protocol you need is called Multipurpose Internet Mail Extensions, or MIME. MIME enables you to add colors, sounds, and graphics to your messages while still enabling them to be delivered by SMTP. In order for MIME to work, you must have a MIME-compliant MUA.

When E-mail Problems Happen

E-mail is very rarely lost in transport. This achievement is quite impressive when you consider the volume of e-mail sent each day. On occasion, e-mail messages get garbled or misrouted, just as a post office sometimes does with snail mail. E-mail can become garbled or lost due to lightning storms and other events that disrupt power supplies. Any network that is using unshielded 10Base-T cable is more susceptible to e-mail interruptions because the cabling is not protected against atmospheric power disturbances such as lightning. Luckily, this issue is becoming less important as cabling standards improve. However, it is always a good idea to install a surge protector on your system to protect yourself from damage caused by fluctuations in the power supply.

Most e-mail problems are the result of user or system administrator error. For example, the user may type an incorrect e-mail address. Misconfiguring an e-mail server causes e-mail problems. Make sure that mailboxes sit in the right directory for your distribution. If you add file system quotas to mailboxes, be aware that at some point, users may not be able to receive new messages until they (or you) clean up the mail files.

Understanding POP3

POP3 is the Post Office Protocol version 3. This protocol runs on a server that is connected to a network and continuously sends and receives mail. The POP3 server stores any messages it receives. POP3 was developed to solve the problem of what happens to messages when the recipient is not connected to the network.

Without POP3, the message could not be sent to the recipient if the recipient were offline. But with POP3, when you want to check your e-mail, you connect to the POP3 server to retrieve your messages that were stored by the server. After you retrieve your messages, you can use the MUA on your PC to read them. Of course, your MUA has to understand the POP3 to be able to communicate with the POP3 server.

The messages you retrieve to your PC are then typically removed from the server. This means that they are no longer available to you if you want to retrieve them to another PC.

Understanding IMAP4

The Internet Message Access Protocol version 4 (IMAP4) provides sophisticated client/server functionality for handling e-mail. IMAP4 has more features than POP3. IMAP4 enables you to store your e-mail on a networked mail server, just as POP3 does. The difference is that POP3 requires you to download your e-mail before your MUA reads it, whereas IMAP4 enables your e-mail to reside permanently on a remote server, from which you can access your mail. And you can do so from your office, your home, or anywhere else. Your MUA must understand IMAP4 to retrieve messages from an IMAP4 server.

 POP3 and IMAP4 don't interoperate. While there are e-mail clients and servers that speak both protocols, you can't use a POP3 client to communicate with an IMAP4 server or an IMAP4 client to communicate with a POP3 server. When you configure an e-mail server, you must decide whether your users need POP3 or IMAP4 functionality (or both). IMAP4 servers usually require much more disk space than POP3 servers because the e-mail remains on the mail server unless the users or system administrator deletes it.

Configuring Sendmail

A number of mail transport agents are available for Red Hat Enterprise Linux, including Qmail, Postfix, and Sendmail. The most widely used MTA is Sendmail, which is the default MTA for Red Hat Linux.

Checking that Sendmail Is Installed and Running

Before you start to configure Sendmail, be sure that it's installed on your computer. It probably is, because the installation program installs Sendmail. But just to be sure, check it out. The following example shows how to check, using the `rpm -q` command. The output shows not only that Sendmail is installed, but which version of Sendmail is installed:

```
root@main# rpm -q sendmail
sendmail-8.12.8-4
```

Next, make sure that Sendmail starts when your computers boot. You have several ways to check whether Sendmail is running. Pick your favorite. The next example uses `ps` to look for Sendmail. Notice that the terminal field is a "?" and that Sendmail is listening on port 25.

```
root@main# ps -auwx | grep sendmail
root  8977  0.0  0.3  1488  472  ?  S  12:16  0:00 sendmail:
accepting connections on port 25
```

You can also use telnet to check whether Sendmail is running. You telnet to yourself (localhost) and tell telnet specifically to use port 25.

Configuring Sendmail

Many system administrators think that Sendmail is difficult to configure. If you look at its configuration file, /etc/mail/sendmail.cf, this might seem to be the case. However, Red Hat Linux provides you with a default Sendmail configuration file that works for most sites. Your default Sendmail configuration file accepts mail deliveries to your computer, sends mail deliveries from your computer, and enables your computer to be used as a relay host.

If you need to edit the configuration file at all, you may need to make only a couple of minor changes. Here are the key lines a Red Hat system administrator might want to edit in /etc/mail/sendmail.cf. These are *not* in the order you find them in the file. In the following example, the tactechnology.com domain is set up to be a relay host.

```
# Copyright (c) 1998-2000 Sendmail, Inc. and its suppliers.
#       All rights reserved.
# Copyright (c) 1983, 1995 Eric P. Allman. All rights reserved.
# Copyright (c) 1988, 1993
#The Regents of the University of California. All rights #reserved.
#
# By using this file, you agree to the terms and conditions
# set forth in the LICENSE file which can be found at the top
# level of the sendmail distribution.
#################################################################
#####              SENDMAIL CONFIGURATION FILE
#####
#################################################################
            | File edited here |
==========
# "Smart" relay host (may be null)
DS

CHANGE THE LINE TO DEFINE THE NAME OF THE MAIL RELAY HOST (GATEWAY
COMPUTER THAT HAS THE RESPONSIBILITY FOR SENDING/RECEIVING INTERNET
MAIL). NOTE -- NO SPACES!

DSmailrelay.tactechnology.com
==========
# my official domain name
# ... define this only if sendmail cannot automatically          #
            determine your domain
#Dj$w.Foo.COM
```

Fortunately, you do not have to be a Sendmail expert in order to perform most configuration chores. In most cases, all you need is one of the predefined configuration files in /etc/mail. The basic process is to modify one of the predefined configuration files for your own needs, regenerate /etc/mail/sendmail.cf using the m4 macro processor, as explained in a moment; then test your configuration. This method enables you to make incremental changes, minimizing the risk of major problems. Red Hat Enterprise Linux comes with a generic Sendmail configuration file (/etc/mail/sendmail.cf).

Be sure to install the sendmail-cf package if it is not already installed. The m4 config portions of sendmail are in this package.

The m4 Macro Processor

What is a macro? A *macro* is a symbolic name for a long string of characters, much like a keyboard macro is a shorthand way to type a long series of keystrokes. Sendmail gets its rules from the entries in a Sendmail macro file. The location of the generic Sendmail macro file for Red Hat is /usr/share/sendmail-cf/.

The rules in the Sendmail macro file generate the default Sendmail configuration file, sendmail.cf. The m4 is a macro processor that reads the macro file and generates the configuration file. Unless you want Sendmail to use your own customized rules in a complex configuration, you can leave the macro file and macro processor alone.

An example of a macro in / is the OSTYPE macro that names the operating system. Remember that Sendmail runs on many different operating systems, not just UNIX and Linux. On a Linux system, if you look at Sendmail's macro file, you see the following line, which tells Sendmail which operating system it's running on so that Sendmail runs properly:

```
OSTYPE(`linux')
```

On Linux, the OSTYPE macro comes predefined so that you don't need to worry about it.

If you really want complete, technical information about the macro file and how it works, read the /usr/share/sendmail.cf/README file.

The default sendmail configuration does not listen to the network for incoming connections. Be sure to read the comment in /etc/mail/ sendmail.mc for a description of setting this parameter.

Understanding and Managing the Mail Queue

Sometimes e-mail messages can't go out immediately and the reasons for the delay are varied. Perhaps your network is down. Maybe your intranet's connection to the Internet is sporadic. Maybe the recipient's computer is unavailable. Whatever the reason, users can continue to compose e-mail with their MUAs. When they send the mail, Sendmail puts the message into the mail queue and keeps trying to send the message at intervals defined for the Sendmail daemon. You can find out what these intervals are by checking the initialization script that starts Sendmail. The following brief excerpt is from the file `/etc/sysconfig/sendmail`. The line beginning with `QUEUE` defines the interval to retry as one hour (1h). You can specify the interval in h (hours), m (minutes), or s (seconds). This Red Hat version defines the variable `QUEUE` and sets it to 1h. Some distributions hard-code the interval right into the Sendmail command (`sendmail -q1h`).

Setting Up Aliases to Make Life Easier

Mail aliases are useful for creating distribution lists and for making access to users more convenient. For example, if people have trouble spelling someone's name, you can create an alias with alternate spellings, so if someone misspells the name, the mail still reaches the intended recipient. You can also alias a nonexistent user to a real user. For example, you could set up an alias, bozo, which redirects all mail intended for bozo to user Wilson. The aliases file is usually `/etc/aliases`. The following example contains entries for

- ◆ System aliases for mailer-daemon and postmaster, which are required.

- ◆ Redirections for pseudo accounts such as lp, shutdown, and daemon. Most of these are all aliased to root by default, but you can change them.

- ◆ User aliases, such as bozo.

- ◆ Distribution lists, such as TCPAuthors.

```
# Basic system aliases -- these MUST be present.
mailer-daemon:  postmaster
postmaster:     root
# General redirections for pseudo accounts.
daemon:         root
lp:             root
sync:           root
shutdown:       root
usenet:         news
ftpadm:         ftp
ftpadmin:       ftp
ftp-adm:        ftp
```

```
ftp-admin:        ftp

# trap decode to catch security attacks
decode:           root

# Person who should get root's mail
root:             terry

#Users
wilson:           bozo


#Distribution lists
terry,wilson:                           clowns
```

To create an entry in the aliases file, use your favorite editor. Each entry consists of the username, a colon, space(s) or tab(s), and the alias. After you save the file, you must run the `newaliases` command to make the changes take effect. This step is necessary because Sendmail looks at the binary file /etc/mail/aliases.db to read alias information. The `newaliases` command reads your aliases text file and updates the binary file.

Using Other Files and Commands with Sendmail

Glancing through your Sendmail configuration file shows that Sendmail uses several files. The following list describes some of them.

- ◆ /usr/sbin/sendmail — The sendmail daemon executable image

- ◆ mailq — Shows the contents of the mail queue:

  ```
  root@main# mailq
  /var/spool/mqueue is empty
          Total requests: 0
  ```

- ◆ /var/spool/mqueue — The file that holds the mail queue

- ◆ /var/spool/mail — The file that holds a user's mail (the mailbox file), for example:

```
root@main# ls /var/spool/mail/*
-rw-rw----   1 terry  mail       0 Jun 21 23:53 /var/spool/mail/terry
-rw-rw----   1 wilson mail     554 Mar 14 21:48 /var/spool/mail/wilson
-rw-------   1 root    root    6416 Jan 26 04:02 /var/spool/mail/root
```

TIP For security, be sure that all mailbox files are readable and writable only by their owners.

- ◆ /etc/mail/access — List of addresses not permitted to send mail to your system

- ◆ /etc/mail/relay-domains — List of hosts that are permitted to relay e-mail through your system

- ◆ /etc/mail/local-host-names — Other names for your system

- ◆ /etc/mail/virtusertable — Maps e-mail addresses to usernames on the system

Configuring Postfix

This section describes how to build, install, and configure the Postfix mail transfer agent (*MTA*) on a system that does not have an existing MTA. The discussion makes two assumptions:

- ◆ You build as a mortal user. If you see a $ prompt, it means you're merely a mortal user.

- ◆ You install and configure as the root user. When you see a # prompt, it means you're the root user.

After building and installing Postfix, you might conclude that Sendmail is far too complex and baffling. While Sendmail might surpass Postfix in terms of configurability and features, Postfix provides all of the functionality *I* need without forcing me to learn arcane configuration hieroglyphics.

1. Download the latest Postfix release. I recommend using a mirror from the list at the Postfix Web site, http://www.postfix.org/download.html.

2. Unpack the tarball. I built it in my home directory, or, more precisely, $HOME/src:

```
$ gzip -cd postfix-2.0.6-20030305.tar.gz | tar -xf -
$ cd postfix-2.0.6-20030305
```

3. Build the Postfix distribution. There is no configuration step to perform before you compile it, and it should compile rather quickly (it took only 1 minute, 23 seconds on my Pentium III):

```
$ make
[...]
gcc -Wmissing-prototypes -Wformat -DHAS_PCRE  -g -O -I. -
I../../include
    -DLINUX2 -o proxymap proxymap.o ../../lib/libmaster.a
    ../../lib/libglobal.a ../../lib/libutil.a -L/usr/lib -
lpcre -ldb
    -lnsl -lresolv
cp proxymap ../../libexec
$
```

4. If you have an existing Sendmail installation, I recommend keeping the old Sendmail binaries around for a little while. Assuming the pathnames are correct, the following commands should do:

```
# mv /usr/sbin/sendmail /usr/sbin/sendmail.OFF
# mv /usr/bin/newaliases /usr/bin/newaliases.OFF
# mv /usr/bin/mailq /usr/bin/mailq.OFF
# chmod 755 /usr/sbin/{sendmail,newaliases,mailq}.OFF
```

The first three commands rename the binaries with innocuous names. The final command makes sure that the newly renamed binaries are executable. As the # prompt suggests, you need to execute these commands as the root user.

5. Create a user and group that *only* the Postfix system uses. The user account does not need a login shell or a home directory. For simplicity's sake, I used postfix for both the user and the group:

```
# /usr/sbin/groupadd postfix
# /usr/sbin/useradd -g postfix -d /dev/null -s /bin/false
postfix
```

Here are the resulting entries in /etc/group and /etc/passwd:

```
$ egrep postfix /etc/group /etc/passwd
/etc/group:postfix:x:102:
/etc/passwd:postfix:x:1001:102::/dev/null:/bin/false
```

6. Create a group named postdrop with a group ID (GID) not used by any other group. Not even the postfix user will use the postdrop group:

```
# /usr/sbin/groupadd postdrop
```

The resulting entry in /etc/group:

```
$ egrep postdrop /etc/group
postdrop:x:103:
```

7. Optionally, if you want to install stripped versions of the Postfix binaries, execute the following command:

```
$ strip bin/* libexec/*
```

If you don't understand what "stripped versions of the Postfix binaries" means, skip this step and go on to the next one.

8. Because this is your first installation of Postfix, use the make install command to perform an interactive installation. The interactive installation offers sane suggestions for pathnames (which you can override) and then stores these preferences in /etc/postfix/main.cf to make future upgrades easy (and, happily, noninteractive). The default values for each item appear between brackets (that is, [ ]) — press Enter to accept the defaults or type the input and then press Enter:

```
# make install
[...]
/bin/sh postfix-install

    Warning: if you use this script to install Postfix locally,
    this script will replace existing sendmail or Postfix programs.
    Make backups if you want to be able to recover.

    Before installing files, this script prompts you for some definitions.
    Most definitions will be remembered, so you have to specify them
    only once. All definitions should have a reasonable default value.

Please specify the prefix for installed file names. Specify this ONLY
if you are building ready-to-install packages for distribution to other
machines.
install_root: [/]

Please specify a directory for scratch files while installing Postfix. You
must have write permission in this directory.
tempdir: [/home/kwall/src/postfix-2.0.6-20030305]

Please specify the destination directory for installed Postfix
configuration files.
config_directory: [/etc/postfix]

Please specify the destination directory for installed Postfix daemon
programs. This directory should not be in the command search path of
any users.
```

```
daemon_directory: [/usr/libexec/postfix]

Please specify the destination directory for installed Postfix
administrative commands. This directory should be in the command search
path of administrative users.
command_directory: [/usr/sbin]

Please specify the destination directory for Postfix queues.
queue_directory: [/var/spool/postfix]

Please specify the full destination pathname for the installed Postfix
sendmail command. This is the Sendmail-compatible mail posting interface.
sendmail_path: [/usr/sbin/sendmail]

Please specify the full destination pathname for the installed Postfix
newaliases command. This is the Sendmail-compatible command to build
alias databases for the Postfix local delivery agent.
newaliases_path: [/usr/bin/newaliases]

Please specify the full destination pathname for the installed Postfix
mailq command. This is the Sendmail-compatible mail queue listing command.
mailq_path: [/usr/bin/mailq]

Please specify the owner of the Postfix queue. Specify an account with
numerical user ID and group ID values that are not used by any other
accounts on the system.
mail_owner: [postfix]

Please specify the group for mail submission and for queue management
commands. Specify a group name with a numerical group ID that is
not shared with other accounts, not even with the Postfix mail_owner
account. You can no longer specify "no" here.
setgid_group: [postdrop]

Please specify the destination directory for the Postfix on-line manual
pages. You can no longer specify "no" here.
manpage_directory: [/usr/local/man]

Please specify the destination directory for the Postfix sample
configuration files.
sample_directory: [/etc/postfix]

Please specify the destination directory for the Postfix README
files. Specify "no" if you do not want to install these files.
readme_directory: [no] /usr/local/doc/postfix
Updating /usr/libexec/postfix/bounce...
```

```
Updating /usr/libexec/postfix/cleanup...
[...]
Updating /usr/local/doc/postfix/VERP_README...
Updating /usr/local/doc/postfix/VIRTUAL_README...

    Warning: you still need to edit myorigin/mydestination/mynetworks
    parameter settings in /etc/postfix/main.cf.

    See also http://www.postfix.org/faq.html for information about dialup
    sites or about sites inside a firewalled network.

    BTW: Check your /etc/aliases file and be sure to set up aliases
    that send mail for root and postmaster to a real person, then run
    /usr/bin/newaliases.


#
```

9. We are replacing Sendmail altogether, even though the assumption noted at the beginning of this document was that we were installing Postfix on a machine with no MTA (Sendmail) installed. First, edit `/etc/postfix/main.cf` (or wherever you installed the Postfix configuration files if you did not accept the defaults when you executed `make install`). You need to edit or set the following variables in the configuration file:

- The `myorigin` variable identifies the domain name appended to unqualified addresses (that is, user names without the `@my.dom` goober attached):

  ```
  myorigin = $mydomain
  ```

  This causes all mail going out to have your domain name appended. Thus, if the value of `mydomain` (see below) is `possum_holler.com` and the username is `bubba`, then outgoing mail from bubba will appear to come from `bubba@possum_holler.com`.

- The `myhostname` variable identifies the local machine, that is, the one on which you've just installed Postfix.

  ```
  myhostname = luther.kurtwerks.com
  ```

- The `mydomain` variable specifies your domain name:

  ```
  mydomain = kurtwerks.com
  ```

- The `mydestination` variable tells Postfix what addresses it should deliver locally. For a standalone workstation, which is a system that is connected directly to the Internet and that has some sort of domain name resolver running, you want mail to that machine and to `localhost` (and/or `localhost.$mydomain`) delivered locally, so the following entry should suffice:

  ```
  mydestination = $myhostname, localhost, localhost.$mydomain
  ```

Postfix supports a larger number of configuration variables, but these are the mandatory changes you have to make.

10. Create or modify /etc/aliases. At the very least, you need aliases for postfix, postmaster, and root in order for mail sent to those addresses to get to a real person. Here are the contents of my initial /etc/aliases file:

```
postfix: root
postmaster: root
root: kwall
```

11. After creating/editing the aliases file, regenerate the alias database using the Postfix newaliases command:

```
# /usr/sbin/newaliases
```

12. Start Postfix:

```
# postfix start
postfix/postfix-script: starting the Postfix mail system
```

13. Make sure Postfix will start when you boot the system. The easy way to accomplish this is to edit /etc/rc.d/rc.local (which might be present as /etc/rc.d/init.d/rc.local on your system) and add the following command to that file:

```
/usr/sbin/postfix start
```

This assumes you installed the Postfix binaries in /usr/sbin, which appears to be the default location.

14. Finally, modify your syslog configuration to handle Postfix log messages appropriately. I prefer that mail log messages go to their own files to avoid cluttering up the primary system log. So, here at KurtWerks, I use the following entries in /etc/syslog.conf, which controls the system log:

```
*.info;*.!warn;authpriv.none;cron.none;mail.none;  -/var/log/messages
*.warn;authpriv.none;cron.none;mail.none;          -/var/log/syslog
mail.*;mail.!err                                   -/var/log/mail.log
mail.err                                           -/var/log/mail.err
```

The first two lines keep any mail related messages from being logged to /var/log/messages and /var/log/syslog. The third line logs everything but errors to /var/log/mail.log. The last line drops all error messages from Postfix into /var/log/mail.err. The - character before each file name tells the system logging daemon, syslogd, to use asynchronous writes, which means that the logging daemon does not force log messages out to the specified file before returning control to the system — this measure helps Postfix run somewhat faster, especially on a heavily loaded system.

15. Naturally, you have to restart syslogd to cause these changes to take effect.

```
# service syslog restart
```

At this point, you have a basic, functional Postfix installation. There is a great deal more customization that you *can* do and might *want* to do, but what has been covered here should get you started and offer some insight into the simplicity of Postfix installation and configuration.

If the system on which you install Postfix is behind a firewall or you have a dialup system without a direct or constant Internet connection, you probably want to define a relay host that handles your email. In this case, Postfix will simply hand locally-generated email off to the relay host, which must be configured to relay for you. For the internal network here at KurtWerks, I added the following entries to /etc/postfix/main.cf:

```
relayhost marta.$mydomain
disable_dns_lookups = yes
```

marta.$mydomain (marta.kurtwerks.com) handles actual mail delivery. Because I don't run DNS on the internal network, the second line disables SMTP client DNS lookups and causes Postfix to retrieve the IP address for my relay host from /etc/hosts. If you make these (or other) changes to the Postfix configuration file, you have to tell Postfix about them. Use the following command to do so:

```
# /usr/sbin/postfix reload
postfix/postfix-script: refreshing the Postfix mail system
```

Configuring the E-Mail Client

You need to configure an e-mail client (MUA) before you and your users can receive and send e-mail. The MUA(s) you decide to configure depend on user preferences and which user interfaces are available on your computer. If your Red Hat system has no GUI, you must choose a text-based e-mail client. The next sections show you how to configure one GUI MUA (Mozilla Mail) and a popular text-based MUA that is part of all Linux distributions, the mail program. Although the steps vary for other clients, the basic concepts are the same for configuring all MUAs.

Configuring Mozilla Mail

Most Red Hat users are familiar with Mozilla, the browser that comes with Red Hat Enterprise Linux. The Mozilla browser is just one program in the Mozilla suite. Another program in the Mozilla suite is the Mozilla Mail e-mail client program. You probably already have the package installed on your system. As usual with configuring software, you should use your favorite package manager query to be sure you have it installed. The following example uses rpm (piped through grep to search for all packages that include "mozilla" in their name) to query all installed packages to determine whether the Mozilla package is installed:

```
root@main# rpm -qa | grep mozilla
mozilla-1.4
mozilla-mail-1.4
mozilla-psm-1.4
mozilla-nspr-1.4
mozilla-nss-1.4
```

Chapter 27 describes how to install software packages.

Mozilla Mail has several advantages: it's easy to configure, it's easy to use, and it integrates well with the Mozilla browser. The major disadvantage of Mozilla Mail is that it runs somewhat slowly.

Setting up Mozilla Mail consists of filling in the forms that identify the user, and incoming and outgoing mail servers. The procedure is detailed in the following paragraphs.

Start the Mozilla browser and open Mail by clicking the envelope icon in the lower left corner of the browser window. The window seen in Figure 19-1 will appear.

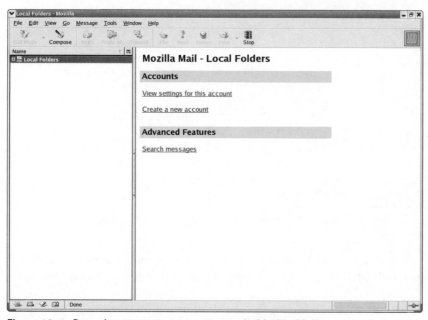

Figure 19-1: Preparing to create a new account in Mozilla Mail

Click Create a New Account to open the Identity form shown in Figure 19-2.

Figure 19-2: The Identity form is where you enter your name and e-mail address.

Add your name and e-mail address in the dialog box as shown in Figure 19-2 and then click Next to continue to the Server Information form as shown in Figure 19-3.

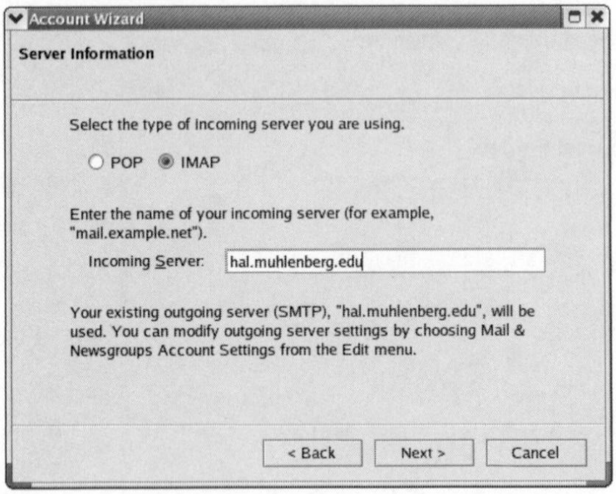

Figure 19-3: The Server Information form is where you enter your server type and name.

On this form you need to let Mail know the type of e-mail account you will be using, either POP or IMAP, and the name of your incoming and outgoing mail servers.

The way you set up the Outgoing Mail Server depends on whether you run your own MTA and SMTP server or whether the SMTP server belongs to your ISP. If you have your own SMTP server and MTA, you choose the hostname of the computer where your SMTP server runs.

If you want outgoing mail to go directly to your ISP, you type the hostname of your ISP's SMTP server. Some ISPs require that you enter your account name again. Enter the appropriate information into the proper field and click Next to continue to the User Name form shown in Figure 19-4.

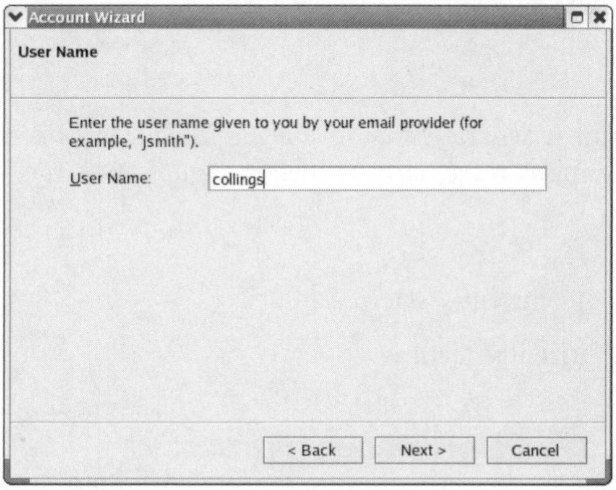

Figure 19-4: The User Name form is where you enter the user name your ISP gave you.

On this form you need to enter the user name that your e-mail provider gave to you. After entering the name, click Next to continue to the Account Name form as seen in Figure 19-5.

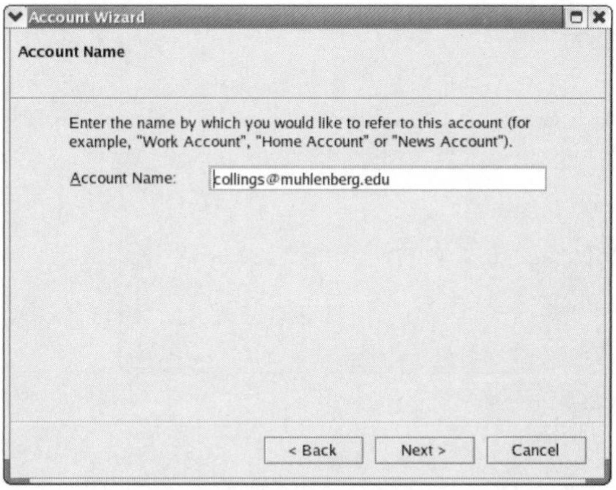

Figure 19-5: The Account Name form is where you enter the account name you use to identify this account in mail.

On the Account Name form you enter the name you will use to identify this account in the Mail program. Enter the information you desire in the appropriate field and click Next to continue. You will now see a page that lists all the information you entered. If you are satisfied with your choices, click Next to create the account.

You can always make changes to your account after you have created it. Click Edit from the menu bar and choose Mail and Newsgroup Account Settings to open the Account Settings dialog box to make any changes you desire.

Using Mozilla Mail

After Mail is configured, you can run it separately or inside the Mozilla browser window. The default Mail window contains three parts as seen in Figure 19-6.

- ◆ A list of your folders

- ◆ A list of e-mail messages in the currently selected folder

- ◆ The e-mail message you are currently reading

Figure 19-6: Looking inside the Mail window

Within Mail, you have two choices for retrieving your messages:

- ◆ From the File menu, select File → Get New Messages.
- ◆ Click Get Msg on the toolbar.

Reading messages, storing them in folders, and deleting them is easy, but when in doubt, use the Help menu in the far right corner of the window.

If your mail resides on a POP3 or IMAP4 server, Mail asks for your password before retrieving your messages to your inbox folder.

You have several choices for composing messages:

◆ From the Message menu, select Message → New Message.

◆ Click Compose on the toolbar.

Mail displays a form where you enter the message and the e-mail addresses of the recipients. Figure 19-7 shows the Compose window with a message in progress.

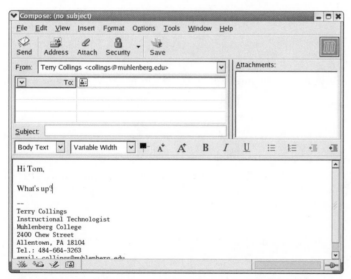

Figure 19-7: Composing an e-mail message using Mozilla Mail

When you're finished composing your message, you can either send it immediately or select Send Later from the File menu. If you want to send your message immediately, select Send Now from the File menu or click on the Send button on the toolbar. You must be connected to the network to be able to send messages immediately.

Sending E-mail from the Command Line

If you are not using a GUI-style desktop like GNOME or KDE, you are using one of the older text-based or console e-mail clients. Text-based e-mail clients perform an interesting balancing act between efficiency and user-friendliness. Older e-mail clients, such as mail and elm, were designed when computers ran more slowly. Their lack of a graphical interface let them send and retrieve e-mail quickly. Friendlier programs like Mutt are more popular these days as the cost of processor cycles has dramatically decreased. This section covers mail, one of the original text-based mail programs.

Reading Mail with Mail

Mail is the oldest, most primitive e-mail client. It has the advantage of being installed on every Linux system. It is also the most lightweight e-mail program, making it ideal for running on very old computers. It also doesn't require a GUI system such as the X Window system. In fact, mail works very well in shell scripts.

Sending e-mail using the mail program is simple.

1. At the command line, enter the command `mail`, followed by the recipient's e-mail address:

   ```
   mail <destination@recipient.com>
   ```

2. Press Enter. Mail responds with the `Subject:` prompt.

3. Type in the subject of your e-mail and press Enter a second time.

4. Now compose your message, just as you would a regular letter.

5. After you finish your message, press Enter.

6. Type a period on a line by itself, and then press Enter a second time. This step lets mail know that you are done composing the message. Mail displays the letters EOT (End Of Text) and sends your message on its way.

The screen should resemble the following listing (of course, the message you type would be different):

```
$ mail localhost
Subject: Type the Subject Here

Dear User,

I'm showing you how to use the mail e-mail
client. When you finish the message, press
Enter, and then type a period on a line by itself
```

to indicate the end of the message.

```
.
EOT
```

 On newer versions of the mail program, after typing a period and pressing Enter you get a `CC:` prompt. CC stands for *carbon copy,* and you can use this field to enter additional e-mail addresses.

To retrieve mail using the mail program, perform the following steps:

1. Type `mail` on the command line without any arguments. Mail lists information about itself, the location of your stored e-mails, and the e-mails you have received. It also gives you an ampersand (&) prompt, where you can enter commands to read, save, or delete mail.

2. Type any command you want to use at the ampersand sign prompt and press Enter.

Typing ? causes mail to display a short help screen listing the keystrokes it understands. They are listed in Table 19-1.

TABLE 19-1 COMMAND OPTIONS FOR THE MAIL PROGRAM

Command	Action
+	Move to the next e-mail.
-	Move back to the previous e-mail.
?	Show a list of mail commands.
R	Reply to sender.
d	Delete an e-mail.
h	Show the list of e-mails.
n	Go to the next e-mail and list it.
q	Quit, and save e-mail.
r	Reply to the sender and all the e-mail's original recipients.
t	List the current message.
x	Quit, and don't save e-mails.

Maintaining E-Mail Security

Do you think you have nothing to hide? Maybe you don't, but e-mail security is always a privacy issue even if you aren't mailing credit card numbers or corporate secrets. Using S/MIME for security is only a first step in protecting your users and yourself.

 This section briefly covers some of the most common vulnerabilities that affect e-mail security. E-mail security is a broad area and entire books have been written on this topic. It is well beyond the scope of this chapter to provide solutions for e-mail security problems. An excellent source for information about e-mail security is the sendmail Web site at `http://www .sendmail.org`.

Protecting Against Eavesdropping

Your mail message goes through more computers than just yours and your recipient's because of store and forward techniques. All a cracker has to do to snoop through your mail is use a packet sniffer program to intercept passing mail messages. A *packet sniffer* is intended to be a tool that a network administrator uses to record and analyze network traffic, but the bad guys use them too. Dozens of free packet sniffing programs are available on the Internet.

Using Encryption

Cryptography isn't just for secret agents. Many e-mail products enable your messages to be encrypted (coded in a secret pattern) so that only you and your recipient can read them. Lotus Notes provides e-mail encryption, for example.

Using a Firewall

If you receive mail from people outside your network, you should set up a firewall to protect your network. The *firewall* is a computer that prevents unauthorized data from reaching your network. For example, if you don't want anything from `ispy.com` to penetrate your net, put your net behind a firewall. The firewall blocks out all `ispy.com` messages. If you work on one computer dialed in to an ISP, you can still install a firewall. Several vendors provide personal firewalls, and some of them are free if you don't want a lot of bells and whistles.

Don't Get Bombed, Spammed, or Spoofed

Bombing happens when someone continually sends the same message to an e-mail address either accidentally or maliciously. If you reside in the U.S. and you receive 200 or more copies of the same message from the same person, you can report the bomber to the FBI. The U.S. Federal Bureau of Investigation has a National Computer Crimes Squad in Washington, DC, telephone +1-202-325-9164.

Spamming is a variation of bombing. A spammer sends junk mail to many users (hundreds and even thousands). You easily can be an accidental spammer. If you choose your e-mail's "Reply All" function, and you send a reply to a worldwide distribution list, you are a spammer.

Spoofing happens when someone sends you e-mail from a fake address. If spoofing doesn't seem like it could be a major problem for you, consider this: you get e-mail from a system administrator telling you to use a specific password for security reasons. Many people comply because the system administrator knows best. Imagine the consequences if a spoofer sends this e-mail faking the system administrator's e-mail address to all the users on a computer. All of a sudden, the spoofer knows everyone's passwords and has access to private and possibly sensitive or secret data. Spoofing is possible because plain SMTP does not have authentication capabilities. Without authentication features, SMTP can't be sure that incoming mail is really from the address it says it is. If your mail server enables connections to the SMTP port, anyone with a little knowledge of the internal workings of SMTP can connect to that port and send you e-mail from a spoofed address. Besides connecting to the SMTP port of a site, a user can send spoofed e-mail by modifying their Web browser interfaces.

TIP You can protect your data and configure your mail system to make mail fraud more difficult. If someone invades your mail system, you should report the intrusion to the Computer Emergency Response Team (CERT). You can find the reporting form on the Internet at `ftp://info.cert.org/pub/incident_reporting_form`.

Be Careful with SMTP

Use dedicated mail servers. First of all, keep the number of computers vulnerable to SMTP-based attacks to a minimum. Have only one or a few centralized e-mail servers, depending on the size of your organization.

Allow only SMTP connections that come from outside your firewall to go to those few central e-mail servers. This policy protects the other computers on your network. If your site gets spammed, you have to clean up the central e-mail servers, but the rest of your networked computers are okay.

If you use packet filtering, you need only configure your e-mail servers. Packet filtering analyzes packets based on the source and destination addresses. The analysis decides whether to accept the packets and pass them through to your networks or to reject them as being unsafe. Firewalls often use packet filtering techniques. The latest stable kernel, 2.4, has built-in packet filtering capabilities.

Summary

This chapter explained the steps a message takes through MUAs, MTAs (Sendmail and Postfix), TCP/IP protocols, LDAs, mail-notification programs, mail queues, and mailboxes. Along the way you learned how to configure both the client and server sides of an e-mail system.

Chapter 20

Configuring FTP Services

IN THIS CHAPTER

- Installing vsftp
- Configuring vsftp
- Advanced FTP server configuration

IN TODAY'S PECKING ORDER of Internet services, FTP, the File Transfer Protocol, arguably places third behind e-mail's enormous popularity and the Web's visual appeal. Despite its second-class status, FTP is a fundamental Internet service, one that almost every Internet user has used at one time or another. This chapter shows you how to install, configure, and maintain the Very Secure FTP daemon, vsftpd, the FTP server package that comes with Red Hat Enterprise Linux.

FTP itself is relatively straightforward and uncomplicated to install, configure, maintain, and monitor. For the lion's share of FTP installations, vsftpd and ProFTPD work with few modifications. Minimal tweaks are necessary to customize the FTP server for your site. When problems arise, though, they seem to be the result of unexpected interactions between the FTP server and measures intended to increase the overall security of a Red Hat system. After you've read this chapter, you should be able to configure an FTP server with your eyes closed.

vsftp

The default Red Hat Linux FTP server is vsftpd, the Very Secure FTP Daemon FTP daemon, which has a project Web site at http://vsftpd.beasts.org/. Red Hat feels confident enough about vsftpd, in fact, to use it to power their own FTP. vsftpd is extremely lightweight in that it makes sparing use of system resources and does not rely on system binaries for parts of its functionality. It can be tuned, to some degree, to use even fewer resources if need be. To the standard FTP services defined in RFC 959, the core RFC (Request for Comment) that defines the FTP protocol, vsftpd offers the additional security features and usability enhancements listed here:

- Support for virtual IP configurations
- Support for so-called virtual users

 ◆ Can run as a standalone daemon or from inetd or xinetd

 ◆ Configurable on a per-user or per-IP basis

 ◆ Bandwidth throttling

 ◆ IPv6-ready

Unlike with previous versions of Red Hat Linux, you no longer have to install a special RPM in order to provide anonymous FTP services. A couple of tweaks to the vsftpd configuration file and you are set to go. One of the reasons a special RPM is no longer required is that vsftpd is self-contained – that is, it doesn't need access to system binaries, such as a statically linked /bin/ls, in order to operate.

A complete Red Hat installation also installs in.mtftp, a server implementing the Trivial File Transfer Protocol (TFTP). However, TFTP is used almost exclusively for PXE boot services and for booting diskless workstations, such as X terminals and slave nodes in clusters, or transferring files to other diskless devices, such as network routers and bridges, so it is not mentioned again in this chapter.

Although Red Hat Linux prefers vsftpd, ProFTPD and NcFTPd deserve mention because they are widely used at busy FTP sites. ProFTPD (http://www.proftpd.org/) is a free FTP server licensed under the GPL. Roughly modeled on the Apache Web server, ProFTPD was designed to be more configurable and more secure than vsftpd. ProFTPD was written from scratch. Other Linux FTP servers, including vsftpd, evolved from the original BSD ftpd server. Key features that distinguish ProFTPD include:

 ◆ Per-directory access configuration using .ftpaccess files, much like Apache's .htaccess file

 ◆ An anonymous FTP root directory unencumbered by required directory structures and system binaries

 ◆ Support for hidden files and directories

 ◆ Self-contained and does not need to use system binaries or libraries, reducing the likelihood of exploits that take advantage of external programs

 ◆ Runs as an unprivileged user in standalone mode, decreasing exposure to security attacks that attempt to exploit its root privileges

NcFTPd (http://www.ncftp.com/) is a commercial FTP server that, like ProFTPD, was written from scratch, optimized for anonymous FTP service, and designed for high performance. Its primary architectural features are its self-described "no-forks" design – not spawning child processes to handle incoming connections and individual directory listings – and its independence from inetd and xinetd. It runs as a standalone server. It is *not* free software, but its features, security, and performance make it a popular FTP server.

Installing vsftpd

Depending on the type of installation you select when you install Red Hat Linux, anaconda, the Red Hat installation program, may or may not have installed vsftpd. To find out, execute the command `rpm -q vsftpd`. If the output resembles the following, vsftpd is installed:

```
# rpm -q vsftpd
vsftpd-1.1.3-8
```

If, on the other hand, you see this message:

```
# rpm -q vsftpd
package vsftpd is not installed
```

you must at least install the binary RPM before continuing with this chapter.

If vsftpd is installed, you can skip to the section titled "Configuring vsftpd." You might consider customizing vsftpd for your system by following the instructions in "Installing and Building the Source RPM" later in this section. Better still, you can install vsftpd's most recent version, which includes the latest security patches and bug fixes, by downloading, compiling, and installing it from the source distribution, as described in the section titled "Installing and Building the Source Distribution" later in this section.

Installing the Binary RPM

To install the vsftpd binary RPM from the Red Hat installation CD-ROM, follow these steps:

1. Log in as the root user or use `su` to become root.

2. Mount the Red Hat Linux installation CD-ROM (disk 1).

3. In an xterm session or at the console command prompt, type the following command to install vsftpd (replace `/mnt/cdrom` with the mount point of your CD-ROM drive if it is different):

   ```
   # rpm -ivh /mnt/cdrom/RedHat/RPMS/vsftpd*rpm
   ```

4. Continue with the section titled "Configuring vsftpd."

If you have not yet done so, you should import the Red Hat `security@redhat.com` public key to check package signatures. The command `rpm --import /usr/share/rhn/RPM-GPG-KEY` will do this for you. For more information about the Red Hat public keys, see `http://www.redhat.com/solutions/security/news/publickey.html`.

Installing and Building the Source RPM

If you choose to install and build the source RPM, follow these steps:

1. Log in as the root user or use `su` to become root.

2. Mount the Red Hat Linux Source RPM CD-ROM (disk 6).

3. Type the following command to install vsftpd (replace `/mnt/cdrom` with the mount point of your CD-ROM drive if it is different):

   ```
   # cd /mnt/cdrom/SRPMS
   # rpmbuild --rebuild vsftpd*src.rpm
   ```

4. Use the following command to install the newly built binary RPM:

   ```
   # rpm -ivh /usr/src/redhat/RPMS/i386/vsftpd*rpm
   ```

5. Continue with the section titled "Configuring vsftpd."

Installing and Building the Source Distribution

Installing and building any software package from the raw source code is the ultimate step in system customization because you can exercise almost complete control over the configuration and build process. Because Chapter 27 discusses building from source in detail, this section simply shows you the commands to execute to perform the build and installation. It does cover configuring the software in detail, however.

You can download the source code distribution from `ftp://vsftpd.beasts.org/users/cevans/`. At the time this chapter went to press, the latest released version of vsftpd was 1.2.0. After you have downloaded the source tarball or copied the tarball from this chapter's source code directory on the accompanying CD-ROM, the process consists of unpacking the source code, configuring it for your needs, building it, and installing it. The following steps walk you through the process (you must be the root user):

1. Unpack the archive using the following commands:

   ```
   $ tar xzf /tmp/vsftpd-1.2.0.tar.gz
   $ cd vsftpd-1.2.0
   ```

2. Compile vsftpd using the following command:

   ```
   $ make
   ```

3. Log in as root or become the root user using su.

4. Make sure the user nobody exists. It should be present on any Red Hat system because it is part of the default password file. You can use the following command. If it fails with the message useradd: user nobody exists, you can safely ignore the error message.

   ```
   # useradd nobody
   useradd: user nobody exists
   ```

5. Create the directory /usr/share/empty if it does not already exist. As with the user nobody, /usr/share/empty should always be present on a Red Hat system because it is part of the filesystem package installed on all systems. If you get the error message mkdir: cannot create directory `/usr/share/empty': File exists, you can safely ignore it.

   ```
   # mkdir -p /usr/share/empty
   ```

   The -p option causes mkdir to create any parent directories if they don't exist.

6. To enable anonymous FTP, the user ftp must exist, and it must have a home directory *not* owned and *not* writable by the user ftp:

   ```
   # mkdir /var/ftp/
   # useradd -d /var/ftp ftp
   # chown root:root /var/ftp
   # chmod go-w /var/ftp
   ```

   The first command creates the directory /var/ftp (if it already exists, the command will fail, but you can ignore the error message). The second command creates a user named ftp. The -d option designates /var/ftp as the ftp user's home directory. The chown command changes the user and group ownership of /var/ftp to root. The chmod command, finally, removes write privileges for /var/ftp from all users except the root user.

7. Install vsftpd using the following command:

   ```
   # make install
   # cp vsftpd.conf /etc
   ```

   The make install command does not copy the vsftpd.conf configuration file into place, so you have to do that manually.

8. Once the installation finishes, continue with the next section.

If you do not have physical access to the system on which you want to install vsftpd, you can always use up2date vsftpd to update or install the latest version of vsftpd from the Red Hat Network. For more information about the Red Hat Network and how to keep your Red Hat System up to date, see Chapter 23.

Configuring vsftpd

Installing vsftpd as described in the previous section creates a basic functioning FTP server that works for users with their own login accounts on the system and for anonymous FTP, using either the anonymous or ftp login names. Just to be sure everything is working, however, do a quick smoke test. Add the following line to the bottom of /etc/vsftpd.conf:

```
listen=YES
```

This configures vsftpd to run as a standalone daemon. The case is important, so add the line as shown.

If you build vsftpd from the source distribution, the daemon gets installed in /usr/local/sbin. If you install it from the RPM or if it was already installed, it is installed in /usr/sbin. The commands shown in this section assume an RPM-based installation. Start vsftpd:

```
# /usr/sbin/vsftpd &
```

Finally, try to log in as an anonymous user. You can use a login name of ftp or anonymous:

```
$ ftp localhost
Connected to localhost (127.0.0.1).
220 (vsFTPd 1.2.0)
Name (localhost:kurt): ftp
331 Please specify the password.
Password:
230 Login successful.
Remote system type is UNIX.
Using binary mode to transfer files.
ftp> ls -a
227 Entering Passive Mode (127,0,0,1,100,97)
150 Here comes the directory listing.
drwxr-xr-x    2 0        0            4096 Jun 16 06:00
drwxr-xr-x    2 0        0            4096 Jun 16 06:00
```

```
226 Directory send OK.
ftp> close
221 Goodbye.
ftp> bye
```

If all has gone well, and it should have, you will be able to log in as the anonymous user, as shown in the preceding example. Of course, we haven't populated the FTP directories yet, so there's not much to see. Go back and remove the listen=YES entry in /etc/vsftpd.conf, because you *really* want to run it from xinetd. How to do that is our next topic.

The stock configuration is only a start, a base that you should customize to enhance security and to fit your needs. In this section, you learn how to fine-tune the default FTP server configuration.

The ftp user name is a synonym for the user name *anonymous*.

The first step in FTP server configuration is to become familiar with the configuration files that control the server's behavior. Table 20-1 lists and briefly describes vsftpd's configuration files.

TABLE 20-1 VSFTPD CONFIGURATION FILES

File Name	Description
/etc/vsftpd/vsftpd.conf	Controls the operation of FTP daemon, vsftpd
/etc/vsftpd.ftpusers	Lists the users *not* allowed to login via FTP
/etc/vsftp.user_list	Defines user lists for FTP access

Configuring User Level FTP Access

The /etc/vsftpd.ftpusers file is the simplest to understand. It contains a list of user or account names, one per line, that are not allowed to log in using FTP. This file is used to increase security. For example, if a cracker somehow obtains the root password but (stupidly) tries to log in as root using FTP, the login attempt will fail. Note that the file name is counterintuitive: user accounts listed in this file are *not* permitted to log in to the system using FTP. In general, /etc/vsftpd.ftpusers is used to prevent privileged user accounts, such as root, from using FTP to obtain access to the system. The following list shows a typical Red Hat Linux /etc/vsftpd.ftpusers file.

- ◆ root
- ◆ bin
- ◆ daemon
- ◆ adm
- ◆ lp
- ◆ sync
- ◆ shutdown
- ◆ halt
- ◆ mail
- ◆ news
- ◆ uucp
- ◆ operator
- ◆ games
- ◆ nobody

So, to prevent a user named bubba from using FTP to log in, or, rather, to prevent user bubba from logging in to the system via FTP, add bubba to the end of /etc/vsftpd.ftpusers. In most cases, these default entries should be sufficient, but if you install a software package, such as a database package, that requires one or more special user accounts, consider adding such special accounts to /etc/vsftpd.ftpusers in order to maintain strict limits on how the FTP server can be accessed.

The default vsftpd configuration installed using the Red Hat RPM allows anonymous FTP access. If you choose *not* to enable anonymous FTP access, add the user ftp to /etc/vsftpd.ftpusers.

The /etc/vsftpd.user_list file serves a purpose similar to /etc/vsftpd .ftpusers, limiting FTP access, but it is more flexible. The users listed in /etc/vsftpd.user_list are the same ones listed in /etc/vsftpd.ftpusers, so what is the difference between the two files? /etc/vsftp.ftpusers unconditionally denies access to the system via FTP; /etc/vsftpd.user_list can be used to deny or permit access, depending on the value of the `userlist_deny` directive in `/etv/vsftpd/vsftpd.conf`. If `userlist_deny` is set to NO (that is, `userlist_deny=NO`), then vsftpd only allows FTP access to the users listed in `/etc/vsftpd.user_list`. If `userlist_deny` is set to `YES` (that is, `userlist_deny=YES`), any user listed in `/etc/vsftpd.user_list` will not be permitted to login via FTP. Such users will not even be prompted for a password.

Configuring vsftpd Features

By far, the most important (and potentially the longest) `vsftpd` configuration file is `/etc/vsftpd.conf`. The configuration directives in this file enable you to exercise finely grained control over `vsftpd`'s behavior. The configuration file itself has a pleasantly simple format. Each line is either a comment, which begins with #, or a directive. Directives have the form *option=value*. Most of the configuration options are Boolean, so they are either on or off, or, rather, `YES` or `NO`. Another large group of configuration options take numeric values, and a last, considerably smaller set of configuration options accept string values.

To organize the discussion of `/etc/vsftpd.conf`, we start with the default configuration file provided by Red Hat. It is shown in the following listing, with most of the comments removed to preserve space and to make it easier to read. Like most text configuration files, lines that begin with the hash sign (#) denote comments that are ignored by the program.

```
anonymous_enable=YES
local_enable=YES
write_enable=YES
local_umask=022
#anon_upload_enable=YES
#anon_mkdir_write_enable=YES
dirmessage_enable=YES
xferlog_enable=YES
connect_from_port_20=YES
#chown_uploads=YES
#chown_username=whoever
#xferlog_file=/var/log/vsftpd.log
xferlog_std_format=YES
#idle_session_timeout=600
#data_connection_timeout=120
#nopriv_user=ftpsecure
#async_abor_enable=YES
#ascii_upload_enable=YES
#ascii_download_enable=YES
#ftpd_banner=Welcome to blah FTP service.
#deny_email_enable=YES
# (default follows)
#banned_email_file=/etc/vsftpd.banned_emails
```

```
#chroot_list_enable=YES
# (default follows)
#chroot_list_file=/etc/vsftpd.chroot_list
#ls_recurse_enable=YES
pam_service_name=vsftpd
userlist_enable=YES
#enable for standalone mode
listen=YES
tcp_wrappers=YES
```

The first configuration option, `anonymous_enable=YES`, allows anonymous FTP access. You can set this to NO if you do not want to enable anonymous FTP. The directive `local_enable=YES` allows local users (users with accounts on the system on which vsftpd is running) to access the system via FTP. Similarly, `write_enable=YES` enables all variations of the FTP commands that allow FTP users to modify the file system, such as STOR (the FTP `put` and `mput` commands for uploading files) and DELE (the FTP `del` command for deleting files). As a rule, it is unwise to permit FTP users to modify the filesystem, so if security is a concern, you might consider disabling write commands by changing `write_enable` to `NO`.

At first glance, it might seem reasonable to allow local users to have write access, or at least to be able to log in. However, the reason local users should *not* be allowed to log in is that FTP is a clear text protocol; that is, user names and, more important, passwords, are transmitted in clear text. Anyone with a packet sniffer monitoring your FTP site (or, rather, IP traffic to and from your FTP server's address) can grab the authentication information and use it to compromise your system. Where FTP is concerned, one can argue that anonymous access is actually *less* of a security risk than normal, authenticated access because anonymous FTP does not require transmitting sensitive passwords over the wire. In fact, using `sftp`, part of the OpenSSH suite, is vastly superior because it encapsulates FTP inside a secure, encrypted communication session.

The directives `anon_upload_enable=YES` and `anon_mkdir_write_enable=YES` control whether or not anonymous FTP users can upload files and create directories, respectively. These two directives are commented out, so anonymous uploads are disabled. Hopefully, it is obvious that allowing anonymous uploads is fraught with danger. That said, should you decide to allow anonymous uploads, you will want to investigate additional vsftpd configuration directives that restrict this type of access. In particular, use the `chown_uploads=YES` directive to change the ownership of uploaded files to the username specified by the `chown_username` directive.

 For more secure FTP-like behavior, consider using the `sftp` (secure FTP) command or the very nice `lftp` FTP client. `sftp` is part of the OpenSSH suite of commands and implements a secure version of FTP. `lftp`, similarly, uses SSH of fish, a very handy feature.

In the configuration file shown, the `chown_username` is whoever. I recommend changing this to nobody (that is, `chown_username=nobody`) because the nobody user has special security semantics associated with it that reduce security risks. One of these semantics is that the nobody user is not allowed to login via FTP. Another feature of the nobody user is that it usually does not have a login shell.

The various `xferlog` directives `xferlog_enable`, `xferlog_file`, `xferlog_std_format`, control the location of the transfer log and the format of entries in this log file. If `xferlog_enable` is set to `YES`, file uploads (if permitted) and downloads are logged to a log file, which is specified with the `xferlog_file` directive. The default log file is `/var/log/vsftpd.log`, which should be suitable for most purposes. If you want to change the log entry format from the standard format, set `xferlog_std_format=NO` and add the directive `log_ftp_protocol=YES`, which will cause all FTP protocol requests to be dumped into the log file. Again, the standard format should be fine. Logging FTP at the protocol level is mostly valuable when trying to isolate server or network problems, or debugging vsftpd itself.

If you have ever wondered how FTP servers show you special messages when you cd into certain directories, the `dirmessage_enabled=YES` directive is how vsftpd, at least, accomplishes it. If this directive is set to `YES`, the first time a user enters a new directory, vsftpd displays the contents of a file named `.message`, if it exists. You can change the message file using the `message_file` directive. For example, `message_file=readme` sets the message file to `readme`. You can use the message file to display special notices specific to certain directories.

The `ftpd_banner` directive allows you to display a site-specific banner message when users connect to the server. For example, the directive `ftpd_banner=* * * * Welcome to the Possum Holler FTP Server * * * *` looks like the following when users first log in:

```
220 * * * * Welcome the Possum Holler FTP Server * * * *
User (192.168.0.3:(none)): ftp
331 Please specify the password.
Password:
230 Login successful. Have fun.
ftp>
```

Notice that the `ftpd_banner` directive is not embedded between double quotes (" "). This is because vsftpd would display the quotes as part of the banner.

If you want to deny access to your server based on the email address provided as part of an anonymous login, uncomment the `deny_email_enable=YES` and put the email addresses you want to deny access into a file named `/etc/vsftpd.banned_emails`. If you want to store the banned addresses in a separate file, uncomment the `banned_email_file=/etc/vsftpd.banned_emails` directive and change the file name. Although this measure can be used as a security feature, it is extremely weak because it is trivial to change an email address. Moreover, vsftpd, and Red Hat Linux in general, offer much stronger and more secure methods for limiting or denying access.

The two `chroot` entries, `chroot_list_enable=YES` and `chroot_list_file=/etc/vsftpd.chroot_list`, affect the behavior of vsftpd server when it runs in `chroot` mode. The first directive, if uncommented, causes vsftpd to execute a chroot to the home directory of local users when they log in. In order for this to work, however, the file `/etc/vsftpd.chroot_list` must contain a list of the users to whom this measure will be applied. `/etc/vsftpd.chroot_list` is the default. If you want to change it, uncomment `chroot_list_file=/etc/vsftpd.chroot_list` and change the file name appropriately. If you want to list users who should not be chrooted, set `chroot_local_user=YES` in `/etc/vsftpd/vsftpd.conf`. In this case, users listed in `chroot_list_file` will not be chrooted to their home directory.

Oh, what does *chroot* mean? *chroot* is short for *change root* and refers to changing a process's or a user's root directory so that it only sees a limited subset of the entire file system. For example, chrooting to `/home/bubba` turns `/home/bubba` into a process's root file system. Thereafter, `/home/bubba` is effectively the same as `/`, and the process or user can navigate no higher in the filesystem than `/home/bubba`. The only files and directories accessible are those in `/home/bubba` and its subdirectories. More practically, chrooting a user or process is an access restriction technique and a way to limit damage to a proscribed area should the user or process go awry.

As explained earlier, if you want to run vsftpd in standalone mode rather than from `xinetd`, set `listen=YES`. The default vsftpd configuration provided with Red Hat does not provide an `xinetd` configuration file in `/etc/xinetd.d`, so you need to make sure that `listen=YES` is set *and* that vsftpd starts at boot time (provided, of course, you intend to provide FTP services). To enable vsftpd at boot time when it is running as a standalone daemon not under xinetd's control, execute the following commands (as root):

```
# /usr/sbin/chkconfig --level 345 vsftpd on
# /usr/sbin/chkconfig --level 0126 vsftpd off
# /usr/sbin/chkconfig --list vsftpd
vsftpd          0:off 1:off 2:off 3:on 4:on 5:on 6:off
```

The first command sets vsftpd to start in run levels 3, 4, and 5. The second command disables vsftpd in all of the other run levels (0, 1, 2, and 6). The third command lists the configuration for vsftpd to double-check the settings.

The `ls_recurse` directive just enables the `-R` option to vsftpd's built-in `ls` command, so executing the command `ls -R` during an FTP session performs a recursive `ls` of all files and subdirectories of the current directory. The directive `pam_service_name=vsftpd` defines the name that vsftpd uses to interact with PAM. If you want to use TCP wrappers, finally, make sure that `tcp_wrapper=YES` is enabled, which causes vsftpd to use the access control features available with TCP wrappers and to check `/etc/hosts.allow` and `/etc/hosts.deny` to evaluate which remote systems to allow access.

Advanced FTP Server Configuration

The information in the previous sections should enable you to get a basic, fully functioning FTP server up and running in, if you type *really* slowly, 15 minutes. To be sure, there's nothing wrong with a plain vanilla FTP server. It will do what it is supposed to do, provide FTP access to designated files, reliably, quickly, and efficiently. Unfortunately, you will not be taking advantage of some of vsftpd's best features. For example, perhaps you do not want to run vsftpd as a standalone daemon but prefer to run it via xinetd.

The preferred Red Hat Linux method for starting vsftpd is as a service, using the command `service vsftp start`. It also works "out of the box" on any Red Hat system.

As remarked at the end of the previous section, the Red Hat Linux vsftpd installation does not install a configuration file for xinetd. However, all is not lost. vsftpd's author provides a sample configuration, which I have modified for Red Hat Linux. The modified file is listed as follows:

```
# default: on
# description:
#    The vsftpd FTP server serves FTP connections. It uses
#    normal, unencrypted usernames and passwords for authentication.
# vsftpd is designed to be secure.
service ftp
{
    socket_type         = stream
    wait                = no
    user                = root
    server              = /usr/sbin/vsftpd
    server_args         = /etc/vsftpd/vsftpd.conf
    log_on_success      += DURATION USERID
    log_on_failure      += USERID
    nice                = 10
    disable             = no
}
```

The modified file is available in this chapter's directory on the accompanying CD-ROM as `vsftpd.xinetd`. You can copy the file from the CD-ROM into `/etc/xinetd.d/vsftpd`, or you can create the file yourself.

Summary

This chapter discussed providing FTP services on your Red Hat system. You read how to install vsftpd. You also learned how to configure the vsftpd daemon and how to modify the default configuration. Finally, you learned how to start and stop the vsftpd FTP server using the traditional `xinetd` super-server.

Chapter 21

Configuring Web Services

IN THIS CHAPTER

- ◆ Introducing Apache

- ◆ How Web servers work

- ◆ Installing and configuring Apache

- ◆ Using the Apache Configuration Tool

- ◆ Implementing SSI

- ◆ Implementing CGI

- ◆ Creating a secure server with SSL

SIMPLY STATED, the Apache Web server is the most popular Web server in the world. Creating a low-cost and stable Web server is one of the most common reasons individuals and organizations use Linux. So, it should come as no surprise that Apache can often be found running on Linux servers. Indeed, some surveys indicate 30 percent of all Web servers run a combination of Linux and Apache. You can bet tomorrow's lunch money that a fair number of those Linux servers are running Red Hat Linux. In this chapter, you learn how to install, configure, and maintain the Apache Web server on your Red Hat system. You also learn how to install and configure Tux, a high performance, in-kernel Web server that excels at serving static Web pages. This chapter also shows you how to configure your Apache to support CGI and SSI so you can generate dynamic Web pages and how to create a secure Web server using SSL.

Introducing Apache

Before proceeding to the meat of this chapter, this section highlights the history of the Apache Web server, describes its key features, and provides pointers to additional Apache resources that you may find useful.

The Apache Web server began life as the NCSA (National Center for Supercomputing Applications) HTTP server (called *httpd* throughout the rest of this chapter). NCSA's server was the most popular of the early HTTP servers and its source code was in the public domain. After NCSA's active development of their httpd effectively stopped (late 1994 and early 1995), a small group of Web administrators who had modified the source code to address site-specific needs or to patch various bugs gathered together to coordinate their activities and merge their code changes into a single code tree.

In April 1995, this loosely organized group of Web masters, the original Apache Group, released the first official version of Apache intended for public consumption, Apache 0.6.2. Despite its known warts, the Apache server was instantly popular. However, even as the development team continued to stabilize the existing code base, add new features, and generate documentation, other members undertook a fundamental redesign that rather quickly (August 1995) resulted in Apache 0.8.8. This first (beta) release based on the redesigned architecture still bears a strong resemblance to the Apache available today. Another round of code base stabilization, bug fixes, feature enhancements, and documentation updates concluded on November 30, 1995. The next day, December 1, 1995, the Apache Group released Apache 1.0, the version that cemented Apache's status as the Internet's #1 HTTP server.

Although the actual numbers fluctuate, and overall growth of Apache's usage (and of the Web servers in general) has begun to flatten out, periodic Internet-wide surveys conducted by Netcraft (`http://www.netcraft.com/survey/`) consistently demonstrate that, seven years after its first releases, Apache continues to be the most widely used Web server, surpassing all other Web servers *combined*.

For more information about Apache's history, read "About Apache" at `http://httpd.apache.org/ABOUT_APACHE.html`.

Whence the Name "Apache"?

Here is the answer to *the* most frequently asked question about Apache, taken directly from the Apache FAQ (`http://httpd.apache.org/docs/misc/FAQ.html#name`):

3. Why the name "Apache"?

    A cute name which stuck. Apache is "A PAtCHy server." It was based on some existing code and a series of "patch files."

    For many developers it is also a reverent connotation to the Native American Indian tribe of Apache, well-known for their superior skills in warfare strategy and inexhaustible endurance. Online information about the Apache Nation is tough to locate; we suggest searching Google, Northernlight, or AllTheWeb.

In addition, `http://www.indian.org/welker/apache.htm` is an excellent resource for Native American information.

Apache Features

The complete list of Apache's features easily runs to three or four pages, far too many and far too tedious to recite here. In fact, many of its "features" are downright mundane because it performs the same function as any other Web server: sending some sort of data down the wire in response to a properly formatted request from a Web client. In another sense, these features, more properly called "functionality," are unremarkable because Apache is a standards-driven program providing mandated functionality. That is, many of its capabilities are the result of its full compliance with version 1.1 of the HTTP protocol. Apache implements all the required functionality described in RFC2616, the document that defines the current Web server protocol, HTTP/1.1 (Hyper Text Transfer Protocol version 1.1). Of course, the manner in which Apache implements mandated features is anything but mundane.

Apache's true standout qualities are its speed, configurability, stability, and rich feature set. Most benchmark studies have shown Apache to be faster than many other Web servers, including commercial servers. Apache is also both easy to configure and easy to reconfigure. Its configuration information resides in plain text files and uses simple English-language directives. Reconfiguring a running server is a simple matter of changing the appropriate configuration directive and restarting the server.

Few seriously question Apache's stability, even among its competitors. Sites receiving millions of hits each day report no problems. Moreover, while no software product of any complexity can be considered bug-free, Apache is beset with fewer (known) bugs than other Web servers, particularly closed source servers. Many factors contribute to Apache's stability, but the two most important are eyeballs and axle grease.

I hear you saying to yourself, "Huh? Eyeballs and axle grease? What *is* he talking about?" Read on for the answer:

◆ More eyeballs means fewer bugs. Apache's source code is freely available, so hundreds of developers have looked at it, found bugs, fixed them, and submitted their fixes for inclusion in the code base. Similarly, Apache's enormous user base means that virtually every segment of its code has been tested in real-world environments, uncovering most major bugs and many minor ones.

◆ The squeaky wheel gets the grease. Combine Apache's widespread usage with Web site administrators who quickly complain about server bugs and insist on the absolutely vital requirement to maintain a secure Web server, and you can easily understand why the Apache team consistently and frequently releases patches for confirmed bugs and security holes, often within just a few hours of their discovery.

The balance of Apache's features is the result of developer and user input. Apache is an open source software project (indeed, Apache is the poster child for the successful open source software project), so anyone can contribute code for inclusion in the server, although whether or not such code is accepted is up to members of the core Apache team. User feedback drives Apache's development and defines its feature set. A very short list of such features includes, in no particular order:

◆ Apache is easily extensible using Dynamic Shared Objects (DSOs), more commonly known as *modules*. Modules extend Apache's capabilities and new features without requiring recompilation because they can be loaded and unloaded at runtime, just as shared libraries are dynamically loaded and unloaded.

◆ Apache uses a binary database format for authenticating users' requests for password-protected Web pages. This format enables Apache to support very large numbers of users without becoming bogged down executing authentication requests.

◆ Apache supports virtual hosts, also known as *multi-homed servers*, which enables a single machine to provide Web services for multiple domains or IP addresses (or hostnames).

◆ Apache enables administrators to define multiple directory index files, the default page to display when a Web client requests a directory URL. So, for example, the server can return `index.html`, `index.htm`, `index.php`, or execute a script named `index.cgi` when a client requests a directory URL, depending on what Apache finds in the requested directory.

◆ Another boon for Web server administrators is Apache's rich support for server logging. You can define custom log file formats and control the level of detail contained in each log entry. Apache can send log file output to named pipes (FIFOs) on systems that support named pipes, primarily Linux, Unix, and similarly designed operating systems. This feature enables any arbitrary log manipulation that can be accomplished using a named pipe. In fact, Apache can be configured to generate a unique identifier that distinguishes one hit from every other hit, although there are some restrictions that apply.

◆ Within limits, Apache automatically adjusts to the capabilities of connected Web clients, a process called *content negotiation*. If a Web client is broken in a way that Apache can determine, incompletely or improperly implements HTTP standards, or does not support a given HTML specification (or, at least, the specification Apache supports), it sends Web pages modified to give the best representation of the requested information based on what the client can process. For more information about content negotiation, see the sidebar titled "What Is Content Negotiation?"

You learn more about these and many other Apache features as you read the chapter.

How Web Servers Work

To understand Apache, its configuration, and how to fine-tune it for your own environment, you should understand how Web servers work in general. Otherwise, lacking this context, Apache's behavior and configuration might seem arbitrary. Figure 21-1 shows the general process that takes place when a Web browser requests a page and the Apache Web server responds.

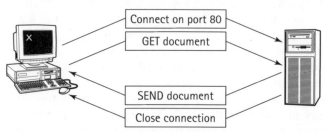

Connect on port 80

GET document

SEND document

Close connection

Figure 21-1: Apache transmits a document according to a client's request.

The Web client (a browser in this case) first performs a DNS lookup on the server name specified in the URL, obtains the IP address of the server, and then connects to port 80 at that IP address (or another port if the server is not using the default HTTP port). When the connection is established, the client sends an HTTP GET request for the document in the URL, which could be, among other possibilities, a specific HTML document, an image, or a script.

After the server receives the request, it translates the document URL into a filename on the local system. For example, the document URL `http://localhost/~kwall/news.html` might become `/home/kwall/public_html/news.html`. Next, Apache evaluates whether or not the requested document is subject to some sort of access control and requests a user name and password from the client or rejects the request outright, depending on the type of access control in place. If the requested URL specifies a directory (that is, the URL ends in /) rather than a specified document, Apache looks for the directory index page, index.html by default, and returns that document to the client. If the directory index page does not exist, Apache might send a directory listing in HTML format back to the client or send an error message, depending on how the server is configured. The document can also be a specially written script, a CGI (Common Gateway Interface) script. In this case, Apache executes the script, if permitted to do so, and sends the results back to the client. Finally, after Apache has transmitted the requested document and the client receives it, the client closes the connection and Apache writes an entry in one or more log files describing the request in varying levels of detail.

Depending on how the page is written and what it contains, additional processing takes place during the transfer. For example, embedded scripts or Java applets are transferred to and execute on the client side of the connection; server-side includes (discussed in the section titled "Implementing SSI"), however, are processed on the server side, as are CGI scripts, database access, and so forth.

Installing and Configuring Apache

If it has been awhile since you upgraded Red Hat Linux, you will probably want to know that Red Hat moved to Apache version 2.0 in Red Hat Linux 8.0. As a result of this update, some of Apache's configuration options have changed, some have been deleted, and new ones have been added. To migrate your existing configuration, refer to the migration guide in /usr/share/doc/httpd-*ver*/migration.html, where *ver* is the version number of Apache that is installed. You can find the version number by executing the command rpm -q httpd.

Depending on the installation profile you chose when you installed Red Hat Linux, Anaconda may or may not have installed Apache. To find out, execute the command rpm -q httpd. If the output resembles the following (the version numbers may be slightly different by the time you read this book), Apache is installed:

```
$ rpm -q httpd
httpd-2.0.45-14
```

If Apache is installed, you can skip ahead to the section titled "Additional Packages to Install." You might consider customizing Apache for your system by compiling it yourself using the instructions in "Installing and Building the Source RPMs" later in this section. Another alternative is downloading, compiling, and installing Apache's source distribution, as described in "Installing and Building the Source Distribution" later in the chapter.

Chapter 23 provides detailed information and step-by-step instructions for installing RPMs and compiling source RPMs. It also explains how to build and install programs from the original source code.

If, on the other hand, you see the message package apache is not installed, you must at least install the binary RPM before continuing with this chapter.

Installing the Binary RPMs

To install the Apache binary RPMs from the Red Hat installation CD-ROM, follow these steps:

1. Log in as the root user or use su to become root.

2. Mount the Red Hat Linux installation CD-ROM (disk 1).

3. Type the following command to install Apache and its supporting packages (replace /mnt/cdrom with the mount point of your CD-ROM drive if it is different):

```
# rpm -ivh /mnt/cdrom/RedHat/RPMS/apache*rpm
```

Continue with the section titled "Additional Packages to Install."

Installing and Building the Source RPMs

If you choose to install and build the source RPMs, follow these steps:

1. Log in as the root user or use su to become root.

2. Mount the Red Hat Linux installation CD-ROM (disk 2).

3. Type the following command to install Apache's source RPMs (replace /mnt/cdrom with the mount point of your CD-ROM drive if it is different):

```
# rpm --rebuild /mnt/cdrom/SRPMS/apache*src.rpm
# rpm -ivh /usr/src/redhat/RPMS/i386/apache*rpm
```

Continue with the section titled "Additional Packages to Install."

Installing and Building the Source Distribution

Installing and building Apache's source distribution enables you to select configuration defaults and compiled-in features that suit *your* needs, not someone else's. This section guides you through building Apache from scratch. To save download time, this chapter's source code directory includes the latest released version of the Apache Web server available at the time this book went to press. You might want to check Apache's home page (http://httpd.apache.org/) for updates, patches, or even a newer release, but the build process described here remains substantially unchanged.

1. Copy the tarball from the CD-ROM to /tmp.

2. Become the root user using su and then cd to /usr/local/src:

```
# cd /usr/local/src
```

3. Unpack the archive:

```
# gzip -cd < /tmp/httpd-2.0.45.tar.gz | tar xf -
```

4. cd into the base directory of the source code tree:

```
# cd httpd-2.0.45
```

5. Read the release documentation to familiarize yourself with changes, updates, new features, and known problems. At a bare minimum, read the files INSTALL, README, and README.configure.

6. If you are impatient, you can build and install Apache using its standard configuration, which installs the finished product into /usr/local/apache, by executing the following sequence of commands:

```
# ./configure
# make
# make install
```

For the time being, you can disregard the following error messages, if you receive them, displayed near the end of the build process (the addresses, shown in bold face, may be different on your system):

```
htpasswd.o: In function `main':
htpasswd.o(.text+0xa9a): the use of `tmpnam' is dangerous,
better use `mkstemp'
htdigest.o: In function `main':
htdigest.o(.text+0x462): the use of `tmpnam' is dangerous,
better use `mkstemp'
```

The linker generates these messages during the final link stage to remind programmers that the tmpnam() call, part of the standard C I/O library, has known security problems and should be replaced with the safer mkstemp() call.

7. If you are somewhat more patient, use the following command line to configure, build, and install Apache:

```
# OPTIM="-O2" CFLAGS="-march=CPU -mcpu=CPU" \
./configure \
--prefix=/usr/local/apache \
--enable-module=all \
--enable-shared=max
# make
# make install
```

OPTIM="-O2" is the optimization level passed to GCC. The CFLAGS argument uses CPU to generate code in the Apache binaries that takes advantage of your CPU's features. CPU can be one of i386, i486, i586 or pentium (for Pentium CPUs), i686 or pentiumpro (for Pentium Pro or better CPUs), or k6 for AMD's K6 CPU. --prefix=/usr/local/apache defines /usr/local/apache as Apache's base installation directory. --enable-module=all compiles and activates all of the modules shipped

in the standard Apache distribution. The `--enable-shared=max` statement, finally, enables the modules built with `--enable-module=all` to be
built as shared objects that Apache can load and unload at runtime on an
as-needed basis.

8. Regardless of the method you used to build Apache, make sure a previous
   installation of it is not running. If you had previously installed Red Hat's
   Apache binary, execute the following command:

   `# /sbin/service httpd stop`

9. If `ps -ax` still shows running `httpd` processes, use the following command to kill them:

   `# pkill httpd`

10. Start the new Apache installation as follows:

    `# /usr/local/apache/bin/apachectl start`

11. Finally, test the Web server by browsing its default home page. From any
    network accessible system, try `http://your.host.name/` or `http://`
    `web.server.ip.addr/` (replace `your.host.name` with your system's host-
    name or `web.server.ip.addr` with your system's IP address). If these
    options do not work, there is most likely some sort of network configura-
    tion problem. So, from the system in question, try `http://localhost/` or
    `http://127.0.0.1/`. If any of these methods work, you should see a page
    resembling Figure 21-2.

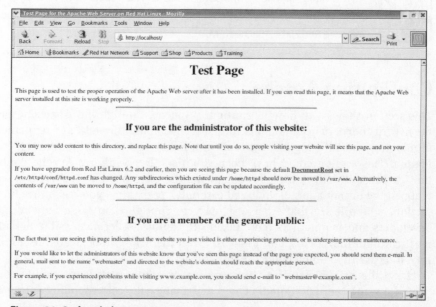

Figure 21-2: Apache's test page

12. If you do not want to continue running the newly installed server, shut it down with the following command:

```
# /usr/local/apache/bin/apachectl stop
```

Continue with the next section, "Additional Packages to Install."

Additional Packages to Install

The section titled "Creating a Secure Server with SSL" explains how to enable, configure, and use mod_ssl, a module giving Apache strong cryptography using the Secure Sockets Layer (SSL) and Transport Layer Security (TLS). Naturally, mod_ssl needs to be installed. If you built and installed Apache using the source RPMs as described earlier, mod_ssl is already installed. Otherwise, use the following procedure to install it:

1. Log in as the root user or use su to become root.

2. Mount the Red Hat Linux installation CD-ROM.

3. Type the following command to install Apache and its supporting packages (replace /mnt/cdrom with the mount point of your CD-ROM drive if it is different):

```
# rpm -ivh /mnt/cdrom/RedHat/RPMS/mod_ssl*rpm
```

 If you build Apache from a source tarball, you should remove the Apache RPM to prevent potential conflicts. Use the command rpm -e httpd to remove Red Hat's Apache RPM.

Configuring Apache

This section shows you how to configure Apache. Configuring Apache, especially for new or inexperienced administrators, seems a daunting task at first glance. The terminology is confusing, the concepts unfamiliar, and the configuration file intimidating. This section could have been subtitled "Demystifying Apache configuration" because it defines the terms, explains the concepts, and removes, or at least reduces, the intimidation. If you read carefully, by the time you reach the end of the section, you will see that Apache is easy to configure, in large part because its developers and maintainers have taken the trouble to define sensible defaults for most configuration items, and to create, with the help of a dedicated user community, a pleasantly complete documentation set.

Using the default Red Hat configuration as a base, you learn about groups of related Apache configuration directives and analyze the corresponding entries in Red

Hat's default Apache configuration. Finally, after evaluating a variety of changes and additions to the default configuration, you learn how to use Red Hat's new Apache configuration tool, `apacheconf` to maintain the Web server configuration.

APACHE'S STARTUP PROCESS

When Apache starts, either during system boot or when invoked after boot using the init script `/etc/rc.d/init.d/httpd` or the Apache-provided script `apachectl`, it reads and processes three files, in order: `/etc/httpd/conf/httpd.conf`, `/etc/httpd/conf/srm.conf`, and `/etc/httpd/access.conf`. The default location for each of these files is compiled into Apache but can be overridden using the -f option discussed later in the chapter. Apache also reads `/etc/mime.types`, which configures the MIME subsystem by mapping file name extensions to content types.

Using a single file simplifies maintaining the configuration file. `httpd.conf` is the primary configuration file. However, for backward compatibility with the original NCSA server conf and early versions of Apache, `srm.conf` and `access.conf` are also supported, but their use is deprecated. All configuration directives can and should be placed in `httpd.conf` or included from other files specified using the Include directive.

 A more complete and far more amusing explanation of the reason for three configuration files is available on the Web at Apache's home page: `http://httpd.apache.org/info/three-config-files.html`.

After processing these configuration files, Apache performs some other sanity checks and opens its log files. Next, this initial Apache process, often called the *master server*, which is owned by root in most cases, launches one or more child processes, as defined by the process creation directives discussed shortly, that are owned by a less privileged user and group (`apache`, on Red Hat Linux). These child processes do the actual work of listening for requests on the HTTP port (80, by default) and answering them.

Apache is highly configurable, a fact reflected in its configuration language, which contains, at the time this book was written, 210 distinct directives. Some directives are operating system specific, some provide backward-compatibility for deprecated features, and some are or should be used in only very specific situations. To keep the discussion manageable and to hold your attention, the configuration directives discussed in this chapter are limited to those that affect basic server configuration, those that reflect Red Hat configuration options, and those that permit you to implement common configuration customizations.

The following sections follow the basic layout of the primary Apache configuration file, `/etc/httpd/conf/httpd.conf`, which is organized into three sections. The first section configures Apache's global characteristics, the second section configures the primary or default server (the Web server that responds to all requests not handled by virtual hosts), and the third section configures virtual hosts.

CONFIGURING GLOBAL BEHAVIOR

The first group of configuration directives you examine, shown in Table 21-1, control the behavior of the server process as a whole. The default values set by the Apache Project or by Red Hat appear in bold face with those directives that have default values.

TABLE 21-1 GLOBAL CONFIGURATION DIRECTIVES

Directive	Description
ServerRoot /etc/httpd	Defines the top level directory for Apache's configuration files and log files (including error logs)
PidFile /var/run/httpd.pid	Defines the file containing the PID of the master server process
Timeout 300	Defines the maximum time in seconds Apache waits for packet send and receive operations to complete
KeepAlive On	Permits multiple requests on the same connection, speeding up delivery of HTML documents
MaxKeepAliveRequests 100	Sets the number of requests permitted per connection
KeepAliveTimeout 15	Sets the number of seconds permitted to elapse between requests from the same client on the same connection when KeepAlive is On
MinSpareServers 5	Defines the minimum number of spare (idle) child servers permitted
MaxSpareServers 20	Defines the maximum number of spare (idle) child servers the master server spawns
StartServers 8	Defines the number of child servers created when Apache starts
MaxClients 150	Sets the maximum number of simultaneous connections (child servers) supported
MaxRequestsPerChild 100	Sets the maximum number of requests each child server fills before terminating
Listen [ipaddress:]80	Determines the combination of IP address and port on which Apache listens for connections; multiple Listen directives may be used

Directive	Description
LoadModule *modname filename*	Links the module or library *filename* into the server and adds it to the list of active modules using the name *modname*
AddModuleInfo *module.c*	Activates the built-in but inactive module *module.c*

Some of the items in Table 21-1 bear additional discussion. When specifying the names of log files or additional configuration files, these names are appended to ServerRoot unless they begin with /. That is, if ServerRoot is /etc/httpd and a log file is specified as logs/mylog.log, the complete name is taken as /etc/httpd/logs/mylog.log, whereas /logs/mylog.log is interpreted as an absolute path name.

Specifying KeepAlive On results in significant performance improvements because it eliminates the overhead involved in initiating new HTTP connections between clients and the Web server. The MinSpareServers and MaxSpareServers directives enable Apache to self-regulate, adding and deleting child processes as Web server usage fluctuates. When more than MaxClients attempt to connect, each connection request is put onto a queue (in particular, a FIFO or *first-in-first-out* queue) and serviced in the order received as current connections close. For users, too long a wait, however, causes them either to send another request or to disconnect. Busy Web sites may need to adjust this value to accommodate heavy traffic.

For most sites, the default values for the configuration directives in Table 21-1 should be sufficient. In particular, do not modify the order in which modules are loaded and activated using the LoadModule and AddModuleInfo directives unless you know what you are doing. Some modules depend on other modules in order to function properly. Apache does not start if problems occur when loading modules.

Listing 21-1 shows the corresponding entries from Red Hat's default Apache configuration, except for the LoadModule and AddModuleInfo directives. Comments have been removed to save space and simplify the presentation.

Listing 21-1: Fedora Core's Global Configuration Directives

```
ServerRoot "/etc/httpd"
LockFile /var/lock/httpd.lock
PidFile /var/run/httpd.pid
ScoreBoardFile /var/run/httpd.scoreboard
Timeout 300
KeepAlive On
MaxKeepAliveRequests 100
```

Continued

Listing 21-1 *(Continued)*

```
KeepAliveTimeout 15
MinSpareServers 5
MaxSpareServers 20
StartServers 8
MaxClients 150
MaxRequestsPerChild 100
Listen 80
```

Nothing in Listing 21-1 *necessarily* needs to be changed. You might consider reducing the MaxSpareServers value to 10 and the StartServers value to 5, the default values given these directives by the Apache Group. Then, as you develop a usage profile for your Web server, adjust them if necessary.

CONFIGURING THE DEFAULT SERVER

As noted a moment ago, the *default* or *primary* server refers to the Web server that responds to all HTTP requests not handled by virtual hosts, also known as *virtual servers*. Without going into detail yet, a *virtual server* or *virtual host* is a Web server that runs on the same machine as the default server but that is distinguished from the main server by a different host name or IP address. Nonetheless, configuration directives defined for the primary server also apply to virtual servers unless specifically overridden. Conversely, directives used to configure the default server can also be used to configure virtual servers.

The next section,"Configuring virtual servers," discusses configuration directives specific to virtual servers and discusses virtual servers in general.

Table 21-2 lists directives used to configure the default server. Again, the default values for each configuration directive, whether assigned by the Apache Group or by Red Hat, are shown in bold face.

TABLE 21-2 DEFAULT SERVER CONFIGURATION DIRECTIVES

Directive	Description
User [#]apache	Specifies the user name or, if prefixed with #, the UID under which the child servers execute
Group [#]apache	Specifies the group name or, if prefixed with #, the GID under which the child servers execute

Directive	Description
`ServerAdmin root@localhost`	Defines the e-mail address included in error messages displayed to client connections
`ServerName`	Specifies an alternative name for the server, such as `www.mydomain.com`, that is different than the host's actual name (`webbeast.mydomain.com`)
`DocumentRoot "/var/www/html"`	Sets the base directory from which all requested documents will be served; document URLs (file names) are interpreted relative to `DocumentRoot`; see also `UserDir`
`UserDir public_html`	Defines the subdirectory in a user's home directory that is used when clients request documents belonging to a specific user
`DirectoryIndex filename`	Specifies one or more `filenames` that serve as a directory index when a request does not specify a particular file or document
`AccessFileName .htaccess`	Lists one or more file names in the complete path to the requested document that define and control access to documents in each directory or subdirectory at the same level as or below the topmost directory where the file(s) specified by `AccessFileName` (if any) is found
`TypesConfig /etc/mime.types`	Sets the file name of the MIME types configuration file (relative to `ServerRoot` if the file name does not begin with /), which maps file name extensions to content types (see also `AddType`)
`DefaultType text/plain`	Defines the default MIME type when a requested document's MIME type cannot be determined using the `TypesConfig` or `AddType` directives
`HostnameLookups Off`	Controls whether or not Apache performs DNS lookups on connecting hosts in order to log host names
`ErrorLog /var/log/httpd/error_log`	Defines the name of Apache's error log, relative to `ServerRoot` if the file name does not begin with /

Continued

TABLE 21-2 DEFAULT SERVER CONFIGURATION DIRECTIVES *(Continued)*

Directive	Description
LogLevel warn	Sets the amount and detail of information Apache records in its error log
LogFormat *formatstr*	Defines the format in *formatstr* Apache uses for messages it logs in the access log (see also TransferLog and CustomLog)
CustomLog /var/log/httpd/ access_log combined	Defines the name of Apache's access log and the log format used when logging requests to the server
ServerSignature On	Directs Apache to append the ServerName and version number as a footer to generated documents, such as error message, FTP file listings, and so forth
Alias *urlpath dirpath*	Links the directory *urlpath*, specified relative to DocumentRoot, to the file system directory *dirpath*, which is outside the server's file system
ScriptAlias *urlpath dirpath*	Functions exactly like the Alias directive and also indicates that *dirpath* contains executable CGI scripts
IndexOptions FancyIndexing	Specifies the behavior of Apache's directory indexing feature
AddIconByEncoding *icon mimeencoding*	Sets *icon* as the icon to display next to files with the MIME encoding of *mimeencoding*; used with the FancyIndexing directive
AddIconByType *icon mimetype*	Sets *icon* as the icon to display next to files with the MIME type of *mimetype*; used with the FancyIndexing directive
AddIcon *icon name*	Sets *icon* as the icon to display next to files ending with *name*; used with the FancyIndexing directive
DefaultIcon /icons/unknown.gif	Sets the default icon displayed next to files whose MIME or content type cannot be determined; used with the FancyIndexing directive

Directive	Description
AddDescription *str file*	Adds the string *str* as the description for one or more files named *file*; used with the FancyIndexing directive
ReadmeName README.html	Defines README.html as the file whose contents will be appended to the end of a directory listing
HeaderName HEADER.html	Defines HEADER.html as the file whose contents will be inserted at the top of a directory listing
AddEncoding *mimeencoding name*	Adds the MIME encoding specified by *mimeencoding* for files ending with *name*, overriding previous encodings for *name*
AddLanguage *mimelang name*	Maps the file name extension specified by *name* to the MIME language *mimelang*, overriding existing mappings for *name*
AddType *mimetype name*	Adds the specified *mimetype* for files ending in *name* to the list of MIME types read from the TypeConfig file

To facilitate further discussion of the directives in Table 21-2, Listing 21-2 shows the corresponding entries from Red Hat's default Apache configuration. We removed comments from the configuration file to shorten the listing and simplify the discussion.

Listing 21-2: Red Hat Linux's Default Server Configuration Directives

```
Port 80
User apache
Group apache
ServerAdmin root@localhost
DocumentRoot "/var/www/html"
<Directory />
    Options FollowSymLinks
    AllowOverride None
</Directory>
<Directory "/var/www/html">
```

Continued

Listing 21-2 *(Continued)*

```
    Options Indexes Includes FollowSymLinks
    AllowOverride None
    Order allow,deny
    Allow from all
</Directory>
UserDir public_html
DirectoryIndex index.html index.htm index.shtml index.php index.php4
index.php3 index.cgi
AccessFileName .htaccess
<Files ~ "^\.ht">
    Order allow,deny
    Deny from all
</Files>
UseCanonicalName On
TypesConfig /etc/mime.types
DefaultType text/plain
<IfModule mod_mime_magic.c>
    MIMEMagicFile conf/magic
</IfModule>
HostnameLookups Off
ErrorLog /var/log/httpd/error_log
LogLevel warn
LogFormat "%h %l %u %t \"%r\" %>s %b \"%{Referer}i\" \"%{User-
Agent}i\"" combine
d
LogFormat "%h %l %u %t \"%r\" %>s %b" common
LogFormat "%{Referer}i -> %U" referer
LogFormat "%{User-agent}i" agent
CustomLog /var/log/httpd/access_log combined
ServerSignature On
Alias /icons/ "/var/www/icons/"
<Directory "/var/www/icons">
    Options Indexes MultiViews
    AllowOverride None
    Order allow,deny
    Allow from all
</Directory>
ScriptAlias /cgi-bin/ "/var/www/cgi-bin/"
<Directory "/var/www/cgi-bin">
    AllowOverride None
    Options ExecCGI
    Order allow,deny
    Allow from all
</Directory>
```

```
IndexOptions FancyIndexing
AddIconByEncoding (CMP,/icons/compressed.gif) x-compress x-gzip
AddIconByType (TXT,/icons/text.gif) text/*
AddIconByType (IMG,/icons/image2.gif) image/*
AddIconByType (SND,/icons/sound2.gif) audio/*
AddIconByType (VID,/icons/movie.gif) video/*
AddIcon /icons/binary.gif .bin .exe
AddIcon /icons/binhex.gif .hqx
AddIcon /icons/tar.gif .tar
AddIcon /icons/world2.gif .wrl .wrl.gz .vrml .vrm .iv
AddIcon /icons/compressed.gif .Z .z .tgz .gz .zip
AddIcon /icons/a.gif .ps .ai .eps
AddIcon /icons/layout.gif .html .shtml .htm .pdf
AddIcon /icons/text.gif .txt
AddIcon /icons/c.gif .c
AddIcon /icons/p.gif .pl .py
AddIcon /icons/f.gif .for
AddIcon /icons/dvi.gif .dvi
AddIcon /icons/uuencoded.gif .uu
AddIcon /icons/script.gif .conf .sh .shar .csh .ksh .tcl
AddIcon /icons/tex.gif .tex
AddIcon /icons/bomb.gif core
AddIcon /icons/back.gif ..
AddIcon /icons/hand.right.gif README
AddIcon /icons/folder.gif ^^DIRECTORY^^
AddIcon /icons/blank.gif ^^BLANKICON^^
DefaultIcon /icons/unknown.gif
ReadmeName README.html
HeaderName HEADER.html
IndexIgnore .??* *~ *# HEADER* README* RCS CVS *,v *,t
AddEncoding x-compress Z
AddEncoding x-gzip gz tgz
AddLanguage en .en
AddLanguage fr .fr
AddLanguage de .de
AddLanguage da .da
AddLanguage el .el
AddLanguage it .it
LanguagePriority en fr de
<IfModule mod_php4.c>
  AddType application/x-httpd-php .php4 .php3 .phtml .php
  AddType application/x-httpd-php-source .phps
</IfModule>
```

Continued

Listing 21-2 *(Continued)*

```
<IfModule mod_php3.c>
  AddType application/x-httpd-php3 .php3
  AddType application/x-httpd-php3-source .phps
</IfModule>
<IfModule mod_php.c>
  AddType application/x-httpd-php .phtml
</IfModule>
AddType application/x-tar .tgz
AddType text/html .shtml
AddHandler server-parsed .shtml
AddHandler imap-file map
BrowserMatch "Mozilla/2" nokeepalive
BrowserMatch "MSIE 4\.0b2;" nokeepalive downgrade-1.0 force-
response-1.0
BrowserMatch "RealPlayer 4\.0" force-response-1.0
BrowserMatch "Java/1\.0" force-response-1.0
BrowserMatch "JDK/1\.0" force-response-1.0
<IfModule mod_perl.c>
  Alias /perl/ /var/www/perl/
  <Location /perl>
    SetHandler perl-script
    PerlHandler Apache::Registry
    Options +ExecCGI
  </Location>
</IfModule>
Alias /doc/ /usr/share/doc/
<Location /doc>
  order deny,allow
  deny from all
  allow from localhost .localdomain
  Options Indexes FollowSymLinks
</Location>
```

Because the default configuration file does not use `BindAddress` or `Listen` directives, the `Port 80` directive indicates that the server listens on port 80 for incoming requests. Because 80 is the default port, this does not need to be specified, but it does make the configuration slightly more transparent. When using a port below 1024, one of the privileged ports, the master server *must* be started by root. If you wish, you can configure Apache to listen on an unprivileged port (for example, with a `Port 8080` directive), in which case, the master server does not have to be run by the root user and group.

The `User` and `Group` directives indicate that the child servers are owned by the user and group `apache`, which are safer because they do not have the same privileges as the root user. In order to run the child servers under less privileged users in this fashion, the master server *must* be started by the root user. Why? Only processes running with root permissions can change their UID and GID at runtime in order to maintain the Linux security model.

The `ServerName` directive defines the name returned to clients if it is different from the host server's actual name. For example, if the server's DNS name is webbeast.mydomain.com, you can specify `ServerName www.mydomain.com` in order for the server to respond to requests sent to `http://www.mydomain.com/`.

The `DocumentRoot /var/www/html` directive sets the server's base document directory to `/var/www/html`, meaning that all URLs are served relative to this directory. For example, if the server is named www.mydomain.com, then given a client request for the URL `http://www.mydomain.com/index.html`, the server would return the file `/var/www/html/index.html` to the client.

Each `<Directory></Directory>` block configures access information for the named directory (or directories) and its subdirectories. The first block sets the default permissions for all directories:

```
<Directory />
    Options FollowSymLinks
    AllowOverride None
</Directory>
```

In this case the applicable directory is the server's root directory, `/`. Other `<Directory></Directory>` blocks apply to `/var/www/html`, `/var/www/icons`, and `/var/www/cgi-bin`.

The Options directive specifies the server features that apply to the named directory. Values for the Options directive can be a space-delimited list of one or more of the following:

◆ `All` — Enables all options except `MultiViews`. `All` is the default `Option`.

◆ `ExecCGI` — Enables execution of CGI scripts.

◆ `FollowSymLinks` — Enables the server to follow symbolic links in this directory.

◆ `Includes` — Enables SSI (server-side includes).

◆ `IncludesNOEXEC` — Enables SSI but disables the SSI #exec command and the use of #include for CGI scripts.

◆ `Indexes` — Instructs the server to return a formatted listing of a directory for which no directory index, such as `index.html`, exists.

◆ `MultiViews` — Enables `MultiView` searches. If the server receives a request for a resource that does not exist, for example, /docs/resource, the server scans the directory for all files named resource.*, if any, assigns them the same media types and content encodings they would have had if the client had asked for one of them by name, chooses the best match to the client's requirements, and returns that document.

◆ None — Disables all special directory features in this directory and its subdirectories.

◆ SymLinksIfOwnerMatch — Instructs the server to follow only those symbolic links for which the target file or directory has the same UID as the link.

Options preceded by a + are added to Options currently in force, and those preceded by a - are removed from Options currently in force. If multiple Options could apply to a directory, then the most specific one is applied. However, if *all* of the options in an Options directive are prefixed with + or -, the options are merged.

So the only option enabled for all of the directories under the server root (/) is the FollowSymLinks option. From this point forward, any divergence from this default must be specified, as in the following directory block:

```
<Directory "/var/www/html">
    Options Indexes Includes FollowSymLinks
    AllowOverride None
    Order allow,deny
    Allow from all
</Directory>
```

What Is Content Negotiation?

Content negotiation refers to the technique Web clients and servers use to select how to present a resource, such as a document, that is available in several different formats. For example, suppose a Web page is available in different languages. One way to select the proper language is to give the user an index page from which she chooses the desired language. Content negotiation enables the server to choose the preferred language automatically based on information a Web browser sends indicating what representations it prefers. For example, a browser could indicate that it would like to see information in French, if possible, or else in English if French is not available. Browsers indicate their preferences by transmitting specific data in each HTTP request's header. To request only French representations, the browser would send:

```
Accept-Language: fr
```

The next request shows a request that accepts both French and English, but prefers French:

```
Accept-Language: fr; q=1.0, en; q=0.5
```

Note that these preferences apply only when there is a choice of representations and when the choices vary by language.

The AllowOverride directive tells the server which directives declared in access files specified by the AccessFileName directive (AccessFileName .htaccess, in this case) it should honor. If set to None, the server ignores the access files. If set to All, any directive valid in the current context is enabled. For the server's root directory and its subdirectories, therefore, the server ignores access files unless AllowOverride All is specifically set for a given directory under the server root.

The Order directive controls the default access policy for various resources, such as files and directories, and the order in which the server evaluates Allow and Deny directives for those resources. Order can be one of the following:

♦ Order Deny,Allow — Evaluate Deny directives before Allow directives and enable access by default. Clients not matching a Deny directive or matching an Allow directive are allowed access.

♦ Order Allow,Deny — Evaluate Allow directives before Deny directives and deny access by default. Clients not matching an Allow directive or matching a Deny directive are denied access.

♦ Order Mutual-failure — Only clients appearing in the Allow list and not appearing in the Deny list are permitted to access the server. This ordering has the same effect as Order Allow,Deny. Apache's documentation states that Order Allow,Deny should be used instead of Mutual-failure.

For the server root directory, for example, all clients are permitted to access it, and Allow directives are evaluated before Deny directives. However, the <Files></Files> block specifies that access to all files beginning with .ht is denied to all clients, preventing clients from viewing their contents, an important measure considering that access files can contain security-sensitive information (a Files directive has the same effect for files that a Directory directive has for directories).

All directives inside an <IfModules></IfModule> block are evaluated only if the indicated module is loaded. The default configuration file has a number of such blocks. For example, consider the following IfModule directive:

```
<IfModule mod_mime_magic.c>

    MIMEMagicFile conf/magic
</IfModule>
```

If the mod_mime_magic module is loaded, the MIMEMagicFile directive causes Apache to read the contents of the configuration file named magic (/etc/httpd/conf/magic in this case), which is a file that gives Apache the ability to determine file types by reading the first few bytes of a file (mod_mime_magic works much like the Linux file command works and is, in fact, based on an older version of the file command). The MIMEMagicFile directive complements and extends the MIME typing provided by the TypesConfig /etc/mime.types directive.

The logging directives control the level and format of Apache's log output. The directive `ErrorLog /var/log/httpd/error_log` specifies the error log Apache uses. The four `LogFormat` directives define log formats named `combined`, `common`, `referer`, and `agent` (yes, `referer` *is* misspelled). These named formats can then be used in other log-related directives to identify the output format. For example, the `CustomLog` directive `CustomLog /var/log/httpd/access_log combined` uses the `combined` format defined previously to log entries. The `CustomLog` directive indicates the file used to log all requests sent to the server. Entries look like the following:

```
127.0.0.1 - - [21/Aug/2001:01:57:17 -0600] "GET /ssitest.html HTTP/1.1"
200 203 "-" "Mozilla/5.0 (X11; U; Linux 2.4.2-2 i686; en-US; 0.7)
Gecko/20010316"
127.0.0.1 - - [21/Aug/2001:01:57:32 -0600] "GET /ssitest.shtml HTTP/1.1"
404 296 "-" "Mozilla/5.0 (X11; U; Linux 2.4.2-2 i686; en-US; 0.7)
Gecko/20010316"
127.0.0.1 - - [21/Aug/2001:01:58:14 -0600] "GET /ssitest.shtml HTTP/1.1"
200 215 "-" "Mozilla/5.0 (X11; U; Linux 2.4.2-2 i686; en-US; 0.7)
Gecko/20010316"
```

These log entries from the access log record the requests the server processed when opening a Web page named ssitest.html (see Listing 21-3).

The long series of `AddIconByEncoding`, `AddIconByType`, and `AddIcon` directives define the various icons displayed next to files with a given icon. The directive `AddIcon /icons/tar.gif .tar`, for example, indicates that files ending with `.tar` should have the image `/icons/tar.gif` displayed next to them. Note that the directory /icons/ was aliased to `/var/www/icons/` using the Alias directive `Alias /icons/ "/var/www/icons/"` earlier in the `httpd.conf` file, so the file system path to `tar.gif` is expanded to `/var/www/icons/tar.gif`. As a fallback measure, the directive `DefaultIcon /icons/unknown.gif` defines the default icon Apache displays if it cannot determine the file type of a given file based on the definitions given by the `TypesConfig` and `MIMEModMagic` directives and additional types appended to the MIME type listing using `AddType` directives.

The `AddLanguage` directives map file names to language encodings. So, for example, files ending with `.en` are treated as English documents, and files ending with `.en.gz` or `.en.tgz` are treated as gzip compressed English documents. The `LanguagePriority` directive, similarly, determines which file the server returns if the browser does not indicate a preference. For example, if the files `index.en.html` and `index.fr.html` both exist and a client does not specify a preferred content language, the server returns `index.en.html`.

The `BrowserMatch` directives set environment variables that can be used in CGI scripts and SSI based on the information in the User-Agent HTTP request header field. The first argument is the text to match from the request header. The second and subsequent arguments name the variables to set, and, optionally, the values to which they should be set. The variable assignments can take one of the following forms:

- `varname` — Sets `varname` to 1

- `!varname` — Removes (unsets) `varname` if it was already set

- `varname=value` — Assigns `value` to `varname`

If a string matches multiple `BrowserMatch` strings, they merge. Entries are processed in the order in which they appear, and later entries can override earlier ones.

CONFIGURING VIRTUAL SERVERS

Table 21-3 shows the Apache configuration directives that control the configuration and behavior of virtual servers.

TABLE 21-3 VIRTUAL SERVER CONFIGURATION DIRECTIVES

Directive	Description
`<Virtual Host ipaddr[:port]>` `directives` `</VirtualHost>`	Defines a virtual host whose IP address is *addr* (listening on *port*, if specified); *directives* are one or more of the directives listed previously and override the directives listed for the default server
`NameVirtualHost ipaddr[:port]`	Defines the IP address *addr* (listening on *port*, if specified) for a name-based virtual host
`ServerName fqdn`	Sets the name of the virtual server to the FQDN *fqdn*
`ServerAlias altname`	Enables the virtual server to respond to one or more alternate host names *altname* when used with name-based virtual hosts

Virtual servers are primarily used to support multiple domains on a single system, but they can also be used to enable multiple workgroups or departments on the same network to maintain independent Web pages without burdening you with too much additional administrative responsibility or requiring dedicated departmental Web servers. A typical virtual server definition might resemble the following:

```
...
ServerName webbeast.domain.com
NameVirtualHost 192.168.0.1
<VirtualHost 192.168.0.1>
    DocumentRoot /var/www/thisdomain
    ServerName www.domain.com
</VirtualHost>
<VirtualHOst 192.168.0.1>
    DocumentRoot /var/www/thatdomain
    ServerName www.that.domain.com
</VirtualHost>
```

This example assumes that DNS lists www.domain.com and www.that.domain .com as aliases (that is, CNAME resource records) for the IP address 192.168.0.1, meaning that lookups for those two names and for webbeast.domain.com resolve to 192.168.0.1. The `NameVirtualHost` directive defines the server's IP address, 192.168.0.1, and `ServerName` identifies the machine running the server, webbeast.domain.com. A request to www.this.domain.com is served from the /var/www/thatdomain document root directory, but requests to `www.domain.com` are served from `/var/www/thisdomain`. The main or default server serves only requests sent to localhost (127.0.0.1) because requests to all other IP addresses about which Apache knows are served by the www.domain.com except those specifically sent to www.that.domain.com.

Using the Apache Configuration Tool

If you prefer graphical configuration tools, you can configure most of Apache's functionality using Red Hat's Apache Configuration Tool. The Apache Configuration Tool allows you to configure the `/etc/httpd/conf/httpd.conf` configuration file for the Apache HTTP server. Using the graphical interface, you can configure directives such as virtual hosts, logging attributes, and maximum number of connections. To start the application, click Red Hat → System Settings → Server Settings → HTTP Server, as shown in Figure 21-3.

Another way to start the Apache Configuration Tool is to type `redhat-config-httpd` at the command prompt in an xterm or GNOME terminal window. Regardless of how you start the tool, the initial screen you see will resemble Figure 21-4.

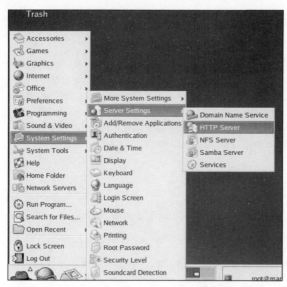

Figure 21-3: Starting the Apache Configuration Tool

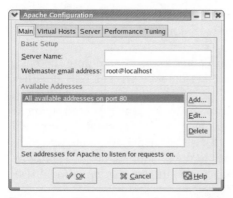

Figure 21-4: The Apache Configuration dialog box

As noted earlier in this chapter, some of Apache's configuration directives have changed in version 2.0. If you used previous versions of the Apache Configuration Tool to configure Apache, you might want to use the tool to migrate the Apache configuration file to the new version 2.0 format. To do so, start the tool, make your changes, and save the changes. When you do so, the Apache Configuration Tool updates the configuration file in a format compatible with Apache 2.0.

The downside of using the Apache Configuration Tool is that you can use it only to configure modules shipped with Red Hat Linux. If you install additional modules, you cannot configure them using this tool. Similarly, if you edit `/etc/httpd/conf/httpd.conf` configuration file manually, do not use the Apache Configuration Tool *after* you have made your manual edits. The graphical tool generates `/etc/httpd/conf/httpd.conf` after you save your changes and exit the program, so your custom changes might be lost. Finally, do not use the Apache Configuration Tool if you want to add modules or use configuration options not supported by the tool.

The general steps for configuring the httpd server using the Apache Configuration Tool are as follows:

1. Configure the basic settings under the Main tab.

2. Click the Virtual Hosts tab to configure the default settings.

3. Under the Virtual Hosts tab, configure the Default Virtual Host.

4. If you want to serve more than one host, add the virtual hosts.

5. Configure the server settings under the Server tab.

6. Configure the connections settings under the Performance Tuning tab.

7. Copy all necessary files to the `DocumentRoot` and `cgi-bin` directories and save your settings in the Apache Configuration Tool.

Basic Settings use the Main tab, shown in Figure 21-4, to configure the basic server settings. In the Server Name text area, enter the Web server's fully qualified domain name. This option corresponds to the `ServerName` directive in `httpd.conf`. The `ServerName` directive sets the Web server's hostname, which is used to create redirection URLs. If you do not define a server name, Apache attempts to resolve it based on the machine's IP address. However, the server name does not have to be the same as the domain name that corresponds to the IP address. For example, you can set `ServerName` to `www.possum-holler.com` even though the server's real DNS name is hound.possum-holler.com.

Enter the e-mail address of the person who maintains the Web server in the Webmaster email address text area. This option corresponds to the `ServerAdmin` directive in `httpd.conf`. If you configure the server's error pages to contain an e-mail address, the e-mail address provided here will be the one displayed. The default value is `root@localhost`.

The Available Addresses pane defines the ports on which the server listens for incoming requests. By default, Red Hat configures the Apache HTTP server to listen to port 80 for insecure (unencrypted) Web communication. To define additional ports, click the Edit button. A window resembling Figure 21-5 will appear.

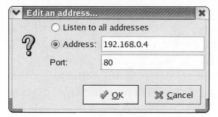

Figure 21-5: Available addresses

Choose the *Listen to all addresses* option to listen to all IP addresses on the defined port, or specify in the Address field a particular IP address over which the server will accept connections.

You should specify only one IP address per port number. If you want to specify more than one IP address with the same port number, create an entry for each IP address. If at all possible, use an IP address instead of a domain name to prevent a DNS lookup failure. Refer to `http://httpd.apache.org/docs-2.0/dns-caveats .html` for additional information regarding DNS and Apache.

> If you set the server to listen to a port under 1024, you must be root to start it. For port 1024 and above, `httpd` can be started as a regular user.

Entering an asterisk (*) in the Address field is the same as choosing Listen to all addresses. Clicking the Add button shows the same window as the Edit button, except that the fields are not yet populated. To delete an entry, select it and click the Delete button. After defining the Server Name, Webmaster e-mail address, and Available Addresses, click the Virtual Hosts tab. The resulting window is shown in Figure 21-6.

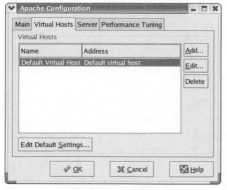

Figure 21-6: The Virtual Hosts tab

The Virtual Hosts tab is the entry point for configuring the httpd server's behavior. The settings you configure here apply to all hosts unless the configuration for a given virtual host specifically overrides settings for the default server. To express this differently, if you add a virtual host in addition to the default server, the settings you configure for that virtual host take precedence over the settings for the default host or server. Directives not defined for a given virtual host use the default values.

> **TIP**   The Apache Configuration Tool, and Apache itself, refers to the default server as the *default virtual host*. While this is technically true, the terminology is confusing. It might be a little clearer if you mentally map *default virtual host* to *default server*. I use the term *default server* unless I am specifically referring to virtual hosts (that is, nondefault servers).

Before you define any virtual hosts (if you define any at all), click the Edit Default Settings button to configure the default server. Figure 21-7 shows the resulting window.

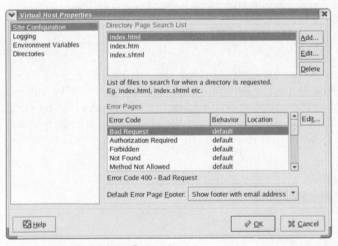

Figure 21-7: Virtual Host Properties

The entries listed in the Directory Page Search List define the DirectoryIndex directive. The DirectoryIndex is the default page served by the server when a user requests an index of a directory by specifying a forward slash (/) at the end of the directory name.

For example, users who request the page `http://your_domain/this_directory/` are going to get either the `DirectoryIndex` page if it exists, or a server-generated directory list. The server first tries to find one of the files listed in the `DirectoryIndex` directive, returning the first one it finds. If it does not find any of these files *and* if `OptionsIndexes` is set for that directory, the server generates and returns an HTML formatted list of the file and subdirectories in that directory.

Use the Error Code section to configure Apache HTTP server to redirect the client to a local or external URL in the event of a problem or error. This option corresponds to the `ErrorDocument` directive. If a problem or error occurs when a client tries to connect to the httpd server, the default action is to display the short-error message shown in the Error Code column. To override the default behavior, select the error code and click the Edit button.

Choose Default to display the default short-error message. Choose URL to redirect the client to an external URL and enter a complete URL, including the `http://`, in the Location field. Choose File to redirect the client to an internal URL and enter a file location under the document root for the Web server. The location must begin with a forward slash (/) and be relative to the `DocumentRoot`.

For example, to redirect a 404 Not Found error code to a Web page you created in a file called `404.html`, copy `404.html` to `DocumentRoot/errors/404.html`. In this case, `DocumentRoot` defaults to `/var/www/html`. Then choose File as the Behavior for 404, Not Found error code, and enter `/errors/404.html` as the Location.

From the Default Error Page Footer menu, you can choose one of the following options:

◆ `Show footer with email address` — Displays the default footer at the bottom of all error pages along with the email address of the website maintainer specified by the `ServerAdmin` directive (see Figure 21-5).

◆ `Show footer` — Displays just the default footer at the bottom of error pages.

◆ `No footer` — Does not display a footer at the bottom of error pages.

The default values for the Directory Page Search List and Error Pages will work for most servers. If you are unsure of these settings, do not modify them.

LOGGING

To modify the httpd server's logging behavior, click the Logging entry in the left-hand pane. By default, the server writes the transfer log to the file `/var/log/httpd/access_log` and the error log to the file `/var/log/httpd/error_log`. Figure 21-8 shows the logging configuration screen.

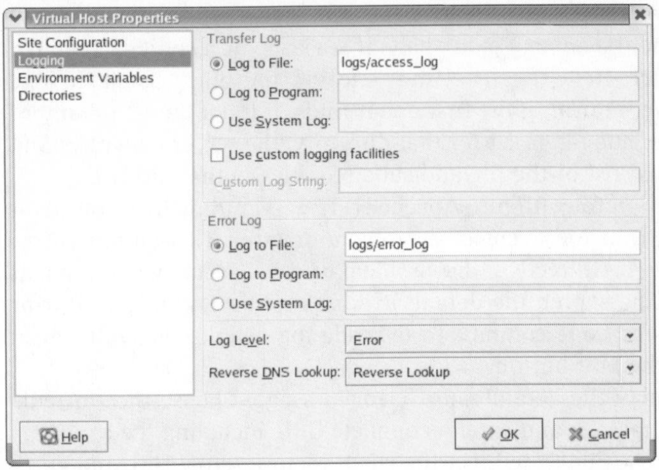

Figure 21-8: Logging

The *transfer log* contains a list of all attempts to access the server. The log records the IP address of the connecting client, the date and time of the attempt, and the file on the Web server that the client wants to retrieve. Enter the name of the path and file in which to store this information. If the path and file name do not start with a slash (/), the path is relative to the server root directory (`ServerRoot`) as configured. This option corresponds to the `TransferLog` directive.

You can configure a custom log format by checking Use custom logging facilities and entering a custom log string in the Custom Log String field. This configures Apache's `LogFormat` directive. Refer to `http://httpd.apache.org/docs-2.0/mod/mod_log_config.html#formats` for details on the format of this directive.

The *error log* records any server errors that occur. Enter the path and file name in which to store this information. If the path and file name do not start with a slash (/), the path is relative to the server root (`ServerRoot`) directory as configured. This option corresponds to the `ErrorLog` directive.

Use the Log Level menu to set how verbose the error messages in the error logs will be. It can be set (from least verbose to most verbose) to `emerg`, `alert`, `crit`, `error`, `warn`, `notice`, `info`, or `debug`. This option corresponds to the `LogLevel` directive.

The value chosen with the Reverse DNS Lookup menu defines the `HostnameLookups` directive. Choosing No Reverse Lookup sets `HostnameLookups` to `off`. Choosing Reverse Lookup sets `HostnameLookups` to `on`. Choosing Double Reverse Lookup sets `HostnameLookups` to `double`. If you choose Reverse Lookup, automatically looks up IP address for each incoming connection. If you choose Double Reverse Lookup, the server performs a reverse lookup, and then performs a forward lookup on the result of the reverse lookup. At least one of the IP addresses returned by the forward lookup must match the address returned by the reverse lookup.

Generally, you should leave this option set to No Reverse Lookup, because each DNS request adds load to the server. On a busy server, the impact of reverse lookups or double reverse lookups will be quite noticeable. Reverse lookups and double reverse lookups are also an issue for the Internet as a whole. All of the individual connections made to look up each hostname add up. Therefore, for your own Web server's benefit, as well as for the Internet's benefit, leave this option set to No Reverse Lookup.

ENVIRONMENT VARIABLES

The Apache HTTP server can use the mod_env module to configure the environment variables that are passed to CGI scripts and SSI pages. To modify or review the environment variables, click the Environment Variable item on the left hand side of the page. The Environment Variables page, shown in Figure 21-9, enables you to configure mod_env.

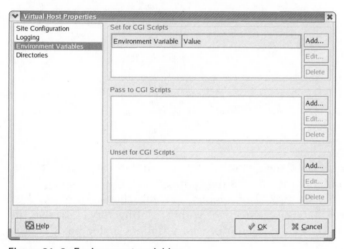

Figure 21–9: Environment variables

Use the Set for CGI Scripts section to set an environment variable passed to CGI scripts and SSI pages. For example, to set the environment variable MAXNUM to 50, click the Add button inside the Set for CGI Scripts section as shown below and type MAXNUM in the Environment Variable text field and 50 in the Value to set text field. Click OK. The Set for CGI Scripts section configures the SetEnv directive.

Use the Pass to CGI Scripts section to pass the value of an environment variable when the server was first started to CGI scripts. To see this environment variable, type **env** at a shell prompt. Click the Add button inside the Pass to CGI Scripts section and enter the name of the environment variable in the resulting dialog box. Click OK.

The Pass to CGI Scripts section configures the PassEnv directive. If you want to remove an environment variable so that the value is not passed to CGI scripts and SSI pages, use the Unset for CGI Scripts section. Click Add in the Unset for CGI Scripts section and enter the name of the environment variable to unset. This corresponds to the UnsetEnv directive.

DIRECTORIES

Use the Directories page, shown in Figure 21-10, to configure options for specific directories. The Directories page corresponds to the `Directories` configuration directive.

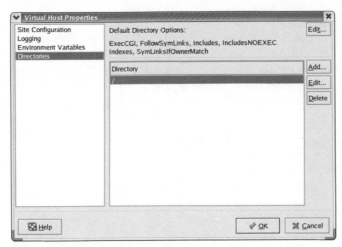

Figure 21–10: Directories

Click the Edit button next to the Default Directory Options label (in the top right-hand corner) to configure the options for all directories that are not specifically listed in the Directory list box. The options that you choose correspond to those specified with the `Options` directive within a Directory directive in `httpd.conf`. Figure 21-11 shows the Default Directory Options dialog box.

Figure 21–11: Directory Options

You can configure the following options:

◆ `ExecCGI` — Allows execution of CGI scripts (must be enabled to execute CGI scripts)

◆ `FollowSymLinks` — Allows following symbolic links

◆ `Includes` — Allows server-side includes (SSI)

◆ `IncludesNOEXEC` — Allows server-side includes but disables the #exec and #include commands in CGI scripts

◆ `Indexes` — Displays a formatted list of the directory's contents, if no `DirectoryIndex` (such as index.html) exists in the requested directory

◆ `Multiview` — Enables content-negotiated multiviews (disabled by default)

◆ `SymLinksIfOwnerMatch` — Follows symbolic links if the target file or directory and the link have the same owner

After you configure default directory options, click the OK button to close the dialog box and return to Directories page.

Click the Add button beside the Directory list box to specify directory options for specific directories, that is, directories other than or below `DocumentRoot` (see Figure 21-12).

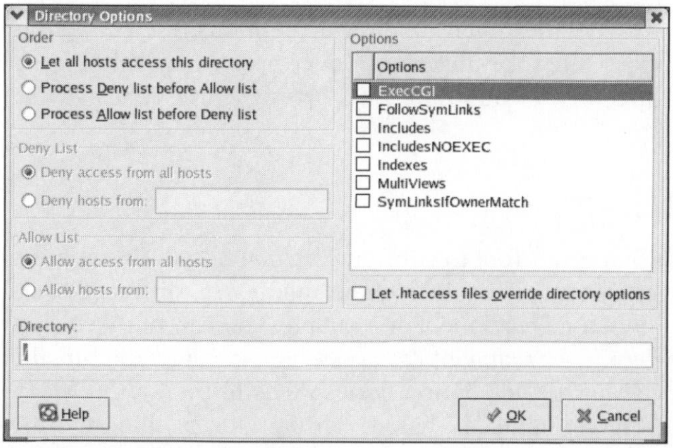

Figure 21-12: Directory options

Enter the directory to configure in the Directory text field at the bottom of the window. In the Options frame on the right-hand side of the window, you can set the direction options discussed in the previous section. The Order frame, which corresponds to the `Order` directive in `httpd.conf`, enables you to specify the order in which the httpd server evaluates server access. The Let all hosts access this directory radio button is the same as having no `Order` directive; the Process Deny list before Allow list radio button corresponds to the directive `Order allow,deny`; and the Process Allow list before Deny list radio button corresponds to the directive `Order deny,allow`.

In the Deny hosts from and Allow hosts from frames, you can control access on a per-host basis. The Deny access from all hosts radio button denies access to this directory from all hosts. Similarly, the Allow access from all hosts radio button allows access to this directory from all hosts. To exercise finer control over directory access, use the text boxes to specify one of the following:

- ◆ `all` — Denies/allows access to all hosts

- ◆ Partial domain name — Denies/allows all hosts whose names match or end with the specified string

- ◆ Full IP address — Denies/allows access to a specific IP address

- ◆ A subnet — Denies/allows access to hosts whose IP addresses match a range of IP addresses specified using network/netmask format, such as 192.168.1.0/255.255.255.0

- ◆ A network CIDR specification — Denies/allows access to hosts whose IP addresses match a range of IP addresses specified using a network/ bitmask format, such as 192.168.1.0/28

If you check the Let `.htaccess` files override directory options, the configuration directives in the `.htaccess` file take precedence over options specified in an `Options` directive for the directory in question. This setting corresponds to the `AllowOverride All` directive.

Virtual Hosts Settings

You can use the Apache Configuration Tool to configure virtual hosts. Virtual hosts are Apache servers or server instances for different IP addresses, different hostnames, or different ports on the same machine. For example, you can run Web sites for `http://www.possum-holler.com/` and `http://www.hound-dog.com/` on the same Web server using virtual hosts. This option corresponds to the `VirtualHost` directive for the default server and IP-based virtual hosts and to the `NameVirtualHost` directive for a name-based virtual host.

The directives set for a virtual host apply only to that particular virtual host. If a directive is set server-wide using the Edit Default Settings button and not defined within the virtual host settings, the default setting is used. For example, if you define a Webmaster e-mail address in the Main tab (see Figure 21-4) but do not define individual e-mail addresses for each virtual host, the Webmaster e-mail address defined for the default server will also be the Webmaster e-mail address for each virtual host.

TIP `http://httpd.apache.org/docs-2.0/vhosts/` and the Apache HTTP server documentation on your machine provide more information about virtual hosts.

To add a virtual host, click the Virtual Hosts tab; then click the Add button. The Virtual Host Properties Window, shown in Figure 21-13, enables you to configure a new virtual host. You can also edit an existing virtual host by selecting it in the list and clicking the Edit button.

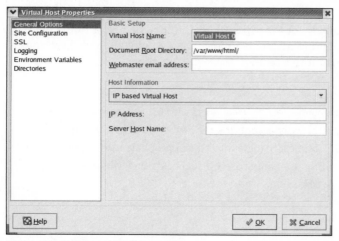

Figure 21-13: Virtual Host Properties

The General Options settings apply only to the virtual host that you are configuring. Set the name of the virtual host in the Virtual Host Name text area. The Apache Configuration Tool uses this name to distinguish between virtual hosts. Set the Document Root Directory value to the directory that contains the root document (such as `index.html`) for the virtual host. This option corresponds to the `DocumentRoot` directive within a `VirtualHost` directive. The default `DocumentRoot` is `/var/www/html`. The Webmaster email address corresponds to the `ServerAdmin` directive within a `VirtualHost` directive. This email address is used in the footer of error pages if you choose to show a footer with an e-mail address on the error pages.

In the Host Information section, choose Default Virtual Host, IP-based Virtual Host, or Name-based Virtual Host. You should configure only one default virtual host (one is set up by default). The default virtual host settings are used when the requested IP address is not explicitly listed in another virtual host. If no default virtual host is defined, the main server settings are used.

If you choose IP-based Virtual Host, a window appears in which you can con-figure the `VirtualHost` directive based on the IP address of the server. Specify this IP address in the IP address field. To specify more than one IP address, separate each IP address with spaces. To specify a port, use the syntax *ipaddr:port*, where *ipaddr* is the IP address and *port* is the port number. The special syntax, `:*`, con-figures the virtual host to listen on all ports for the IP address. Specify the host-name for the virtual host in the Server Host Name field.

If you choose Name-based Virtual Host, a window appears in which you can configure the `NameVirtualHost` directive based on the host name of the server. Specify the IP address in the IP address field. To specify more than one IP address, separate each IP address with spaces. To specify a port, use the syntax *ipaddr:port*, where *ipaddr* is the IP address and *port* is the port number. The special syntax, `:*`, configures the virtual host to listen on all ports for the IP address. Specify the hostname for the virtual host in the Server Host Name field. In the Aliases section, click Add to add a host name alias. Adding an alias here adds a `ServerAlias` directive within the `NameVirtualHost` directive.

You cannot use name-based virtual hosts with SSL, because the SSL hand-shake (when the browser accepts the secure Web server's certificate) occurs before the HTTP request that identifies the appropriate name-based virtual host. If you want to use name-based virtual hosts, they will work only with your nonsecure Web server.

Secure Socket Layer

If an Apache HTTP server is not configured with SSL support, communications between an Apache HTTP server and its clients are not encrypted. Unencrypted communication is appropriate for Web sites that do not use personal or confidential information. A Web site that distributes open source software and documentation, for example, has no need for secure communications. However, an e-commerce Web site that requires credit-card information should use the Apache SSL support to encrypt its communications.

Enabling Apache SSL support allows you to use the `mod_ssl` security module. To enable it through the Apache Configuration Tool, you must allow access to port 443 in the Available Addresses section of the Main tab. Refer to the "Basic Settings" sec-tion of this chapter for details. After you enable access to port 443,

1. Select the virtual host name in the Virtual Hosts tab.

2. Click the Edit button.

3. Choose SSL from the left-hand menu.

4. Check the Enable SSL Support option (see Figure 21-14).

The SSL Configuration section is preconfigured with the dummy digital certificate. A digital certificate provides authentication for your secure Web server and identifies the secure server to client Web browsers. You must purchase your own digital certificate. Do not use the dummy one provided in Red Hat Linux for your Web site.

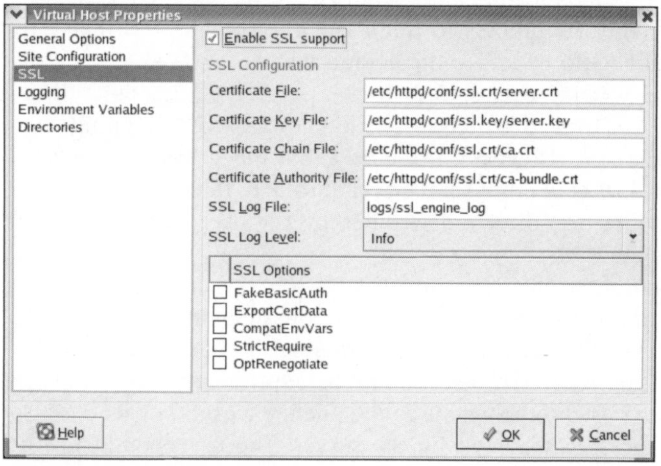

Figure 21-14: SSL support

Server Settings

The Server tab allows you to configure overall server settings, including the locations for the lock and PID file, the directory in which Apache should dump a core file (if it needs to, which it shouldn't), and the user and group names under which the child servers should run. As a rule, the default settings for these options are appropriate for most situations.

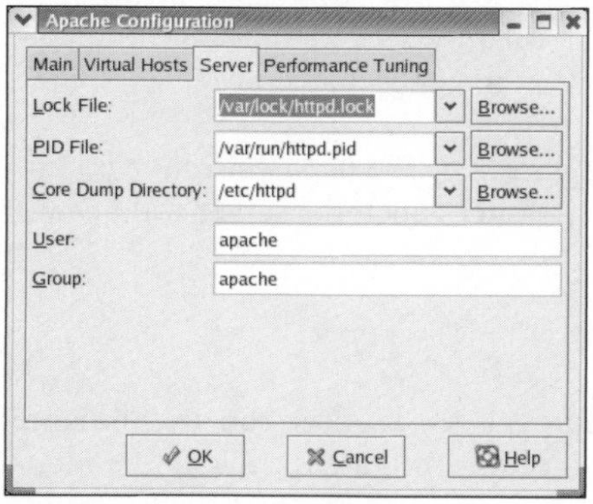

Figure 21-15: The Server tab

The Lock File value corresponds to the LockFile directive. This directive sets the path to the lockfile used when the server is compiled with either USE_FCNTL_ SERIALIZED_ACCEPT or USE_FLOCK_SERIALIZED_ACCEPT. It must be stored on the local disk. It should be left to the default value unless the logs directory is located on an NFS share. If this is the case, the default value should be changed to a location on the local disk and to a directory that is readable only by root.

The PID File value corresponds to the PidFile directive. This directive sets the file in which the server records its process ID (pid). This file should be readable by root only. In most cases, it should be left to the default value.

The Core Dump Directory value corresponds to the CoreDumpDirectory directive. The Apache HTTP server tries to switch to this directory before dumping core. The default value is ServerRoot. However, if the user that the server runs as cannot write to this directory, or if core dumps have been disabled, the core file will not be written. Change this value to a directory writable by the user name the server uses (which is apache, by default).

The User value corresponds to the User directive. It sets the user ID the server uses to answer requests and also controls Apache's permissions and access levels. Any files inaccessible to this user will also be inaccessible to your Web site's visitors. The default for User is apache. The user should have privileges only so that it can access files that are supposed to be visible to the outside world. The user is also the owner of any CGI processes spawned by the server. The user should not be allowed to execute any code that is not intended to be in response to HTTP requests.

 Unless you know exactly what you are doing, do *not* set the User directive to root. Using root as the User creates large security holes for your Web server.

The parent httpd process initially executes as root, but then hands off actual Web serving responsibilities to child processes running as the apache user. The server must start as root because it needs to bind to a port below 1024. Ports below 1024 are reserved for system use, so they cannot be used by anyone but root. Once the server has attached itself to the port, however, it hands the process off to the apache user before it accepts any connection requests.

The Group value corresponds to the Group directive. The Group directive is similar to the User directive. Group sets the group under which the server will answer requests. The default group is also apache.

Performance Tuning

The Performance Tuning tab, shown in Figure 21-16, enables you to configure Apache's performance profile. In particular, you can configure the maximum number of child server processes and client connection parameters. The default settings for these options are appropriate for most situations. Altering these settings may affect the overall performance of your Web server.

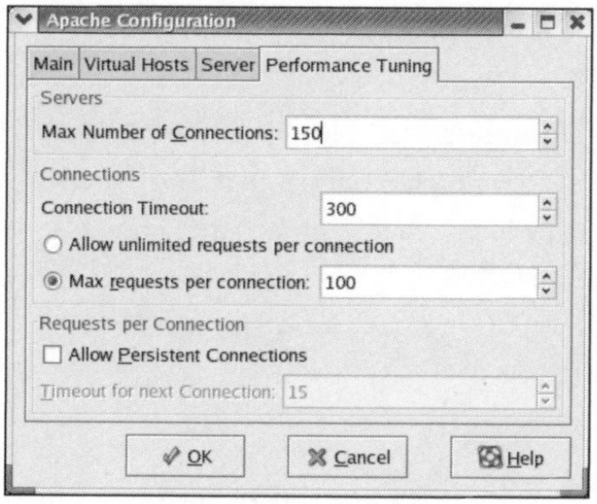

Figure 21-16: Performance tuning

Set Max Number of Connections to the maximum number of simultaneous client requests that the server will handle. Keep in mind that each connection to the httpd server spawns a child process — too many processes can slow the system to a crawl, resulting in the dreaded Server too busy error (you know, the Slashdot effect). After reaching the maximum number of connections, no one else will be able to connect to the Web server until a child server process is freed. You cannot set this value to higher than 256 without recompiling. This option corresponds to the `MaxClients` directive.

Connection Timeout defines, in seconds, the amount of time that your server will wait for receipts and transmissions during communications. Specifically, Connection Timeout defines how long the httpd server waits to receive a GET request after a connection, how long it waits to receive TCP packets on POST and PUT requests, and how long it waits between ACKs (acknowledgements) responding to TCP packets. By default, the Connection Timeout is 300 seconds, which is appropriate for most situations. This option corresponds to the `TimeOut` directive.

Set the Max requests per connection to the maximum number of requests allowed per persistent connection. There is a subtle interplay between the requests each connection can service, how many requests each child process can handle, and how long connections remain open before they timeout. The default number of Max requests per connection, which corresponds to the `MaxRequestsPerChild` directive, is 100. Enabling the Allow unlimited requests per connection option sets `MaxKeepAliveRequests` to 0, which permits an unlimited number of requests per connection.

If you disable the Allow Persistent Connections option, the `KeepAlive` directive is set to false. If enabled, the `KeepAlive` directive is set to true, and the `KeepAliveTimeout` directive is set to the number that is selected as the Timeout for next Connection value. This directive sets the number of seconds your server will wait for a subsequent request, after a request has been served, before it closes the connection. Once a request has been received, the Connection Timeout value applies instead.

 Setting Persistent Connections to a high value may cause a server to slow down, depending on how many users are trying to connect to it. The higher the number, the more server processes will be waiting for another connection from the previous client that connected to it.

Saving Your Settings

If you do not want to save your Apache HTTP server configuration settings, click the Cancel button in the bottom right corner of the Apache Configuration Tool window. The tool will prompt you to confirm this decision. If you click Yes to confirm this choice, your settings will not be saved.

If you do want to save your Apache HTTP server configuration settings, click the OK button in the bottom right corner of the Apache Configuration Tool window. A dialog box will appear. If you answer Yes, your settings will be saved in /etc/httpd/conf/httpd.conf. Remember that your original configuration file will be overwritten.

If this is the first time that you have used the Apache Configuration Tool, you will see a dialog box warning you that the configuration file has been manually modified. If the Apache Configuration Tool detects that the httpd.conf configuration file has been manually modified, it will save the manually modified file as /etc/httpd/conf/httpd.conf.bak.

Finally, after saving your settings, you must restart the httpd daemon using the command service httpd restart. You must be logged in as root to execute this command.

Implementing SSI

Server-side includes (SSI) are specially formatted statements placed in HTML documents and evaluated by the server before the server sends the document to a client. SSI lets you add dynamically generated content to an existing HTML page without needing to generate the entire page using CGI or another dynamic page generation technique. SSI is best used to add small amounts of dynamically generated content to otherwise static documents. SSI is a great way to add small pieces of information, such as the current time, to a Web page.

The default Red Hat Linux Apache configuration enables SSI for the document root (/var/www/html):

```
<Directory "/var/www/html">
    Options Indexes Includes FollowSymLinks
    AllowOverride None
    Order allow,deny
    Allow from all
</Directory>
```

The `Options Include` directive instructs Apache to process files it serves for SSI directives. The next step is to tell Apache which files to parse for SSI directives. Red Hat Linux uses Apache's `AddType` and `AddHandler` directives to identify SSI files:

```
AddType text/html .shtml
AddHandler server-parsed .shtml
```

The first line adds the file extension `.shtml` to the text/html MIME type. The `AddHandler` directive tells Apache that files with an `.shtml` extension should be processed using mod_include, the module that provides Apache's SSI support (the default Red Hat `httpd.conf` file should contain these directives).

TIP If, for some reason, you have to add the `AddType text/html .shtml` and `AddHandler server-parsed .shtml` directives to the `httpd.conf` file, the server must be restarted to make them take effect. You can use one of the following commands to force Apache to reread its configuration file:

```
# /sbin/service httpd restart
# /sbin/service httpd reload
```

The first command stops and restarts the server. The second one sends Apache the `SIGHUP` signal, which causes it to reread `httpd.conf`. The effect is the same regardless of which command you use.

To test the configuration, create the Web page shown in Listing 21-3, naming it ssitest.shtml and placing it in Apache's document root directory (the directory specified by the `DocumentRoot` directive):

Listing 21-3: SSI Test Document

```
<html>
<head>
 SSI Test Page
</head>

<body>
 <center>
  SSI Test Page Output
  <hr>
  <p>
   This file was last modified on:
  <p>
  <!--#echo var="LAST_MODIFIED" -->
  <p>
  <hr>
 </center>
</body>
</html>
```

SSI directives look like HTML comments. Their general form is:

```
<!--#element attribute=value ... -->
```

Because SSI directives look like comments, if SSI is improperly configured on the server, the browser ignores the contents. Otherwise, the server creates properly formatted HTML output that Web browsers render properly. In Listing 21-3, the SSI directive is `<!--#echo var="LAST_MODIFIED" -->`. It uses a built-in variable, `LAST_MODIFIED`, which contains the date the current file was last modified. Finally, open the document in your Web browser, using the URL `http://localhost/ssitest.shtml` if accessing the server locally or `http://your.server.name/ssitest.shtml` if accessing the server remotely (replace *your.server.name* with the name of your Web server). Figure 21-17 shows how the page appears in the Mozilla Web browser.

As you can see in Figure 21-17, the HTML shows that the file in question (`ssitest.shtml`) was last modified on November 28 at 8:43 p.m. After confirming that SSI is properly configured using the test page, your configuration is complete.

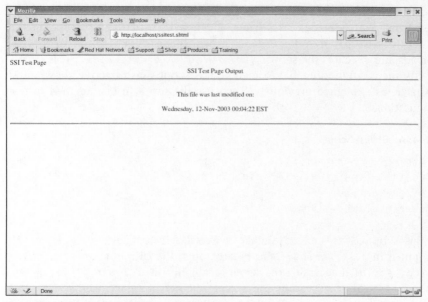

Figure 21-17: ssitest.html as seen in Mozilla

Implementing CGI

CGI, the Common Gateway Interface, is a protocol that defines a standard method enabling Apache (well, *any* Web server) to communicate with external programs. These programs are known as *CGI scripts* or *CGI programs*. CGI scripts are commonly used to create or update Web pages or parts of Web pages dynamically, much like SSI, but CGI scripts are more flexible than SSI and provide additional functionality that SSI cannot. For example, CGI scripts can be used for user authentication, to create a user interface on a Web page, and, within limits, in any situation in which a Web-based interface is used to execute programs and display the results in a near real-time environment. This section briefly explains Apache configuration directives and procedures that enable CGI.

As you might suspect by this point, your first task is to ensure that Apache's configuration permits CGI script execution. The ScriptAlias directive associates a directory name with a file system path, which means that Apache treats every file in that directory as a script. If not present, add the following directive to httpd.conf:

```
ScriptAlias /cgi-bin/ "/var/www/cgi-bin"
```

This directive tells Apache that any URL beginning with /cgi-bin/ should be served from /var/www/cgi-bin. Thus, given a URL of http://localhost/cgi-bin/cgiscript.pl or http://your.server.name/cgi-bin/cgiscript.pl, Apache reads and executes the script /var/www/cgi-bin/cgiscript.pl. If necessary, modify the configuration file to include the ScriptAlias directive shown, and restart Apache as explained previously. Then use the script in Listing 21-4 to test the configuration.

Listing 21-4: A CGI Test Script

```
#!/usr/bin/perl
print "Content-type: text/html\r\n\r\n";
$now_string = gmtime;
print "Current time is $now_string";
```

Save this script as cgitest.pl, make it executable (chmod a+x cgitest.pl), and then put it in /var/www/cgi-bin. Finally, open the URL http://localhost/cgi-bin/cgitest.pl if accessing the server locally or http://your.server.name/cgi-bin/cgitest.pl if accessing the server remotely (replace *your.server.name* with the name of your Web server). Figure 21-18 shows sample output from the CGI test script.

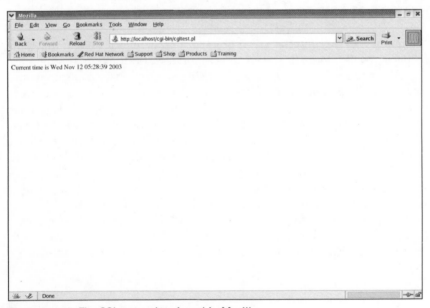

Figure 21-18: The CGI test script viewed in Mozilla

If you see similar output, your server's CGI configuration works. If you enable CGI execution for other directories, make sure to test those configuration options as well before putting the server into production.

Creating a Secure Server with SSL

This section provides basic information on the Apache HTTP server with the `mod_ssl` security module enabled to use the OpenSSL library and toolkit. The combination of these three components, provided with Red Hat Linux, will be referred to in this chapter as the secure Web server or just the secure server.

The `mod_ssl` module is a security module for the Apache HTTP server. The `mod_ssl` module uses the tools provided by the OpenSSL Project to add a very important feature to the Apache HTTP server – the ability to encrypt communications. In contrast, using regular HTTP, communications between a browser and a Web server are sent in plaintext, which could be intercepted and read by someone along the route between the browser and the server.

This section is not meant to be complete and exclusive documentation for any of these programs. When possible, we point you to appropriate places where you can find more in-depth documentation on particular subjects. This section shows you how to install these programs. You also learn the steps necessary to generate a private key and a certificate request, how to generate your own self-signed certificate, and how to install a certificate to use with your secure Web server.

The configuration for `mod_ssl` has moved from `/etc/httpd/conf/httpd.conf` to `/etc/httpd/conf.d/ssl.conf`. For this file to be loaded, and hence for `mod_ssl` to work, you must have the statement `Include conf.d/*.conf` in `/etc/httpd/conf/httpd.conf`.

An Overview of Security-Related Packages

To enable the secure server, you need to have the following packages installed, at a minimum.

◆ `httpd` – The httpd package contains the httpd daemon and related utilities, configuration files, icons, Apache HTTP server modules, man pages, and other files used by the Apache HTTP server.

◆ `mod_ssl` – The `mod_ssl` package includes the `mod_ssl` module, which provides strong cryptography for the Apache HTTP server via the Secure Sockets Layer (SSL) and Transport Layer Security (TLS) protocols.

◆ `openssl` – The `openssl` package contains the OpenSSL toolkit. The OpenSSL toolkit implements the SSL and TLS protocols and also includes a general-purpose cryptography library. Additionally, the following software packages included with Red Hat Linux can provide certain security functionalities (but are not required by the secure server to function).

◆ httpd-devel — The httpd-devel package contains the Apache HTTP server include files, header files, and the APXS utility. You will need all of these if you intend to load any extra modules, other than the modules provided with this product. If you do not intend to load other modules onto your Apache server, you do not need to install this package.

◆ httpd-manual — The httpd-manual package contains the Apache Project's Apache User's Guide in HTML format. This manual is also available on the Web at http://httpd.apache.org/docs-2.0/.

◆ openssl-devel — The openssl-devel package contains the static libraries and the header file needed to compile applications with support for various cryptographic algorithms and protocols. You need to install this package only if you are developing applications that include SSL support — you do not need this package to use SSL.

Table 21-4 displays the location of the secure server packages and additional security-related packages within the package groups provided by Red Hat Linux. This table also tells you whether or not each package is optional for the installation of a secure Web server.

TABLE 21-4 SECURITY PACKAGES

Package name	Located in group	Optional?
httpd	System Environment/Daemons	no
mod_ssl	System Environment/Daemons	no
openssl	System Environment/Libraries	no
httpd-devel	Development/Libraries	yes
httpd-manual	Documentation	yes
openssl-devel	Development/Libraries	yes

An Overview of Certificates and Security

Your secure Web server provides security and (in most cases) a digital certificate from a Certificate Authority (CA). SSL handles the encrypted communications and the mutual authentication between browsers and your secure Web server. The CA-approved digital certificate provides authentication for your secure Web server (the CA puts its reputation behind its certification of your organization's identity). When your browser is communicating using SSL encryption, you will see the `https://` prefix at the beginning of the Uniform Resource Locator (URL) in the navigation bar.

Encryption depends upon the use of keys (think of them as secret encoder/decoder rings in data format). In conventional or symmetric cryptography, both ends of the transaction have the same key, which they use to decode each other's transmissions. In public or asymmetric cryptography, two keys coexist: a public key and a private key. A person or an organization keeps their private key a secret, and publishes their public key. Data encoded with the public key can be decoded only with the private key; data encoded with the private key can be decoded only with the public key.

To set up your secure server, you will use public cryptography to create a public and private key pair. In most cases, you will send your certificate request (including your public key), proof of your company's identity, and payment to the CA. The CA will verify the certificate request and your identity and then send back a certificate for your secure Web server.

A secure server uses a certificate to identify itself to Web browsers. You can generate your own certificate (called a "self-signed" certificate) or you can get a certificate from a CA. A certificate from a reputable CA guarantees that a website is associated with a particular company or organization. Alternatively, you can create your own self-signed certificate. Note, however, that self-signed certificates should not be used in most production environments. Self-signed certificates will not be automatically accepted by a user's browser – the user will be asked by the browser if he or she wants to accept the certificate and create the secure connection. See the "Types of Certificates" section of this chapter for more information on the differences between self-signed and CA-signed certificates. Once you have a self-signed certificate or a signed certificate from the CA of your choice, you will need to install it on your secure Web server.

Using Preexisting Keys and Certificates

If you already have an existing key and certificate – for example, if you are installing the secure Web server to replace another company's secure Web server product – you will probably be able to use your existing key and certificate with the secure Web server. In the following two situations, you will *not* be able to use your existing key and certificate:

- ◆ If you are changing your IP address or domain name
- ◆ If you have a certificate from VeriSign and you are changing your server software

If you are changing your IP address or domain name, you cannot use your old key and certificate. Certificates are issued for a particular IP address and domain name pair. You will need to get a new certificate if you are changing your hostname.

VeriSign is a widely used CA. If you already have a VeriSign certificate for another purpose, you may have considered using your existing VeriSign certificate with your new secure Web server. However, you will not be allowed to, because VeriSign issues certificates for one particular server software and IP address/domain name combination. If you change either of those parameters (for example, if you previously used another secure Web server product and now you want to use the secure Web server), the VeriSign certificate you obtained to use with the previous configuration will not work with the new configuration. You will need to obtain a new certificate.

If you have an existing key and certificate you can use, you will not have to generate a new key and obtain a new certificate. However, you may need to move and rename the files that contain your key and certificate. Move your existing key file to:

```
/etc/httpd/conf/ssl.key/server.key
```

Move your existing certificate file to:

```
/etc/httpd/conf/ssl.crt/server.crt
```

After you have moved your key and certificate, skip to the section "Testing Your Certificate."

If you are upgrading from the Red Hat Secure Web Server versions 1.0 and 2.0, your old key (httpsd.key) and certificate (httpsd.crt) will be located in /etc/httpd/conf/. You will need to move and rename your key and certificate so that the secure Web server can use them. Use the following two commands to move and rename your key and certificate files:

```
# mv /etc/httpd/conf/httpsd.key /etc/httpd/conf/ssl.key/server.key
# mv /etc/httpd/conf/httpsd.crt /etc/httpd/conf/ssl.crt/server.crt
```

Then start your secure Web server with the command:

```
# /sbin/service httpd start
```

For a secure server, you will be prompted to enter your password. After you type it and press Enter, the server will start. You should not need to get a new certificate, if you are upgrading from a previous version of the secure Web server.

Types of Certificates

If you installed your secure Web server using the Red Hat installation program, a random key and a test certificate were generated and put into the appropriate directories. Before you begin using your secure server, however, you will need to generate your own key and obtain a certificate that correctly identifies your server.

You need a key and a certificate to operate your secure Web server – which means that you can either generate a self-signed certificate or purchase a CA-signed certificate from a CA. What are the differences between the two? A CA-signed certificate provides two important capabilities for your server:

◆ Browsers will (usually) automatically recognize the certificate and allow a secure connection to be made, without prompting the user.

◆ When a CA issues a signed certificate, it is guaranteeing the identity of the organization that is providing the Web pages to the browser.

If your secure server is being accessed by the public at large, your secure Web server needs a certificate signed by a CA, so that people who visit your website know that the website is owned by the organization that claims to own it. Before signing a certificate, a CA verifies that the organization requesting the certificate was actually what it claimed to be. Most Web browsers that support SSL have a list of CAs whose certificates they will automatically accept. If a browser encounters a certificate whose authorizing CA is not in the list, the browser will ask the user to choose whether to accept or decline the connection.

You can generate a self-signed certificate for your secure Web server, but be aware that a self-signed certificate will not provide the same functionality as a CA-signed certificate. A self-signed certificate will not be automatically recognized by users' browsers, and a self-signed certificate does not provide any guarantee concerning the identity of the organization that is providing the website. A CA-signed certificate provides both of these important capabilities for a secure server. If your secure server will be used in a production environment, you will probably need a CA-signed certificate.

The process of getting a certificate from a CA is fairly easy. A quick overview is as follows:

1. Create an encrypted private and public key pair.

2. Create a certificate request based on the public key. The certificate request contains information about your server and the company hosting it.

3. Send the certificate request, along with documents specified by the CA that prove your identity, to a CA. We cannot tell you which certificate authority to choose. Your decision may be based on your experiences, or on the experiences of your friends or colleagues, or purely on monetary factors. To see a list of CAs, click the Security button on your Web browser toolbar or on the padlock icon at the bottom left of the screen, then click on Signers to see a list of certificate signers from which your browser will accept certificates. You can also search the Web for CAs. Once you have decided upon a CA, you will need to follow the instructions it provides on how to obtain a certificate.

When the CA is satisfied that your organization is indeed what it claims to be, it sends you a digital certificate.

4. Install this certificate on your Web server and begin handling secure transactions.

Whether you are getting a certificate from a CA or generating your own self-signed certificate, the first step is to generate a key. See the section "Generating a Key" for instructions on how to generate a key.

Generating a Key

You must be root to generate a key. First, cd to the /etc/httpd/conf directory. Remove the fake key and certificate that were generated during the installation with the following commands:

```
rm ssl.key/server.key
rm ssl.crt/server.crt
```

Next, create your own random key. Change to the /usr/share/ssl/certs directory and type the following command:

```
make genkey
```

Your system will display a message similar to the following:

```
umask 77 ; \
/usr/bin/openssl genrsa -des3 1024 >
/etc/httpd/conf/ssl.key/server.key
Generating RSA private key, 1024 bit long modulus
.......++++++
..................................................++++++e is 65537
(0x10001)
Enter PEM pass phrase:
```

You now need to enter a password. For best security, your password should contain at least eight characters, include numbers and/or punctuation, and not be a word found in a common dictionary. Also, remember that your password is case-sensitive.

You will need to enter this password every time you start your secure Web server, so do not forget it.

You will be asked to retype the password, to verify that it is correct. Once you have done so, `/etc/httpd/conf/ssl.key/server.key`, containing your key, will be created.

Note that if you do not want to enter a password every time you start your secure Web server, you will need to use the following two commands instead of `make genkey` to create the key. Use this command:

```
# /usr/bin/openssl genrsa 1024 > /etc/httpd/conf/ssl.key/server.key
```

to create your key. Then use the command

```
# chmod go-rwx /etc/httpd/conf/ssl.key/server.key
```

to make sure that the permissions are set correctly on your key. After you use the preceding commands to create your key, you will not need to use a password to start your secure Web server.

 Disabling the password feature for your secure Web server is a security risk. We recommend *not* disabling the password feature for your secure Web server.

The problems associated with not using a password are directly related to the security maintained on the host machine. For example, an unscrupulous individual who compromises the regular UNIX security on the host machine could obtain your private key (the contents of your `server.key` file). The key could be used to serve Web pages that will appear to be from your Web server.

If UNIX security practices are rigorously maintained on the host computer (all operating system patches and updates are installed as soon as they are available, no unnecessary or risky services are operating, and so on), the secure Web server's password may seem unnecessary. However, since your secure Web server should not need to be rebooted very often, the extra security provided by entering a password is a worthwhile effort in most cases.

The `server.key` file should be owned by the root user on your system and should not be accessible to any other user. Make a backup copy of this file and keep the backup copy in a safe, secure place. You need the backup copy because if you ever lose the `server.key` file after using it to create your certificate request, your certificate will no longer work, and the CA will not be able to help you. Your only option will be to request (and pay for) a new certificate.

If you are going to purchase a certificate from a CA, continue to the next section. If you are generating your own self-signed certificate, continue to the section "Creating a Self-Signed Certificate."

Generating a Certificate Request to Send to a CA

Once you have created a key, the next step is to generate a certificate request that you will need to send to the CA of your choice. Make sure you are in the /usr/share/ssl/certs directory and type the following command:

```
make certreq
```

Your system will display the following output and will ask you for your password (unless you disabled the password option):

```
umask 77 ; \
/usr/bin/openssl req -new -key /etc/httpd/conf/ssl.key/server.key
-out /etc/httpd/conf/ssl.csr/server.csr
Using configuration from /usr/share/ssl/openssl.cnf
Enter PEM pass phrase:
```

Type the password that you chose when you were generating your key. Your system will display some instructions and then ask for a series of responses from you. Your inputs will be incorporated into the certificate request. The display, with example responses, will look like this:

```
You are about to be asked to enter information that will be incorporated into
your certificate request. What you are about to enter is what is called a
Distinguished Name or a DN. There are quite a few fields but you can leave some
blank.
For some fields there will be a default value,
If you enter '.', the field will be left blank.
-----
Country Name (2 letter code) [GB]:US
State or Province Name (full name) [Berkshire]:North Carolina
Locality Name (eg, city) [Newbury]:Raleigh
Organization Name (eg, company) [My Company Ltd]:Test Company
Organizational Unit Name (eg, section) []:Testing
Common Name (your name or server's hostname) []:test.example.com
Email Address []:admin@example.com
Please enter the following 'extra' attributes to be sent with your certificate
request
A challenge password []:
An optional company name []:
```

The default answers appear in brackets immediately after each request for input. For example, the first information required is the name of the country where the certificate will be used, shown like the following:

```
Country Name (2 letter code) [GB]:
```

The default input, in brackets, is GB. To accept the default, press Enter or fill in your country's two-letter code. You will have to enter the rest of the inputs (State or Province Name, Locality Name, Organization Name, Organizational Unit Name, Common Name, and Email address). All of these should be self-explanatory, but you need to follow these guidelines:

◆ Do not abbreviate the locality or state. Write them out (for example, St. Louis should be written as Saint Louis).

◆ If you are sending this CSR to a CA, be very careful to provide correct information for all of the fields, but especially for the Organization Name and the Common Name. CAs check the information provided in the CSR to determine whether your organization is responsible for what you provided as the Common Name. CAs will reject CSRs that include information perceived as invalid.

◆ For Common Name, make sure you enter the real name of your secure Web server (a valid DNS name), not any aliases the server may have.

◆ The Email Address should be the e-mail address for the Webmaster or system administrator.

◆ Avoid any special characters like @, #, &, !, and the like. Some CAs will reject a certificate request that contains a special character. So, if your company name includes an ampersand (&), spell it out as *and* instead of *&*.

◆ Do not use either of the extra attributes (A challenge password and An optional company name). To continue without entering these fields, just press Enter to accept the blank default for both inputs.

When you have finished entering your information, the file `/etc/httpd/conf/ssl.csr/server.csr` is created. This file is your certificate request, ready to send to your CA. After you have decided on a CA, follow the instructions provided on its Web site. The instructions will tell you how to send your certificate request, any other documentation required, and your payment. After you have fulfilled the CA's requirements, it will send a certificate to you (usually by e-mail). Save (or copy and paste) the certificate you receive as `/etc/httpd/conf/ssl.crt/server.crt`.

Creating a Self-Signed Certificate

You can create your own self-signed certificate. Note that a self-signed certificate will not provide the security guarantees provided by a CA-signed certificate. See the section "Types of Certificates" for more details about certificates.

If you would like to make your own self-signed certificate, you will first need to create a random key using the instructions provided in the "Generating a Key" section. Once you have a key, make sure you are in the /usr/share/ssl/certs directory and type the following command:

```
make testcert
```

You will see the following output and you will be prompted for your password (unless you generated a key without a password):

```
umask 77 ; \
/usr/bin/openssl req -new -key /etc/httpd/conf/ssl.key/server.key
-x509 -days 365 -out /etc/httpd/conf/ssl.crt/server.crt
Using configuration from /usr/share/ssl/openssl.cnf
Enter PEM pass phrase:
```

After you enter your password (if you created a key without a password, no prompt will be given), you will be asked for more information. The computer's output and a set of inputs will look like the following (you will need to provide the correct information for your organization and host):

```
You are about to be asked to enter information that will be incorporated into
your certificate request. What you are about to enter is what is called a
Distinguished Name or a DN. There are quite a few fields but you can leave some
blank
For some fields there will be a default value,
If you enter '.', the field will be left blank.
-----
Country Name (2 letter code) [GB]:US
State or Province Name (full name) [Berkshire]:North Carolina
Locality Name (eg, city) [Newbury]:Raleigh
Organization Name (eg, company) [My Company Ltd]:My Company, Inc.
Organizational Unit Name (eg, section) []:Documentation
Common Name (your name or server's hostname) []:myhost.example.com
Email Address []:myemail@example.com
```

After you provide the correct information, a self-signed certificate will be created in /etc/httpd/conf/ssl.crt/server.crt. You will need to restart your secure server with the following command after generating the certificate:

```
# /sbin/service httpd restart
```

Testing Your Certificate

When the secure server is installed by the Red Hat installation program, a random key and a generic certificate are installed, for testing purposes. You can connect to your secure server using this certificate. For any purposes other than testing, however, you need to get a certificate from a CA or generate a self-signed certificate.

See the "Types of Certificates" section of this chapter if you need more information on the different types of certificates available.

If you have purchased a certificate from a CA or generated a self-signed certificate, you should have a file named `/etc/httpd/conf/ssl.key/server.key`, containing your key, and a file named `/etc/httpd/conf/ssl.crt/server.crt`, containing your certificate. If your key and certificate are somewhere else, move them to these directories. If you changed any of the default locations or file names for the secure Web server in your Apache HTTP server configuration files, you should put these two files in the appropriate directory, based on your modifications.

Once these CA files have been moved, restart your server with the command

```
# /sbin/service httpd restart
```

If your key file is encrypted, you will be asked for the password. Enter your password to start your server. Point your Web browser to your server's home page. The URL to access your secure Web server will look like this:

```
https://your_domain
```

 The `https:` prefix is used for secure HTTP transactions.

If you are using a CA-signed certificate from a well-known CA, your browser will probably automatically accept the certificate (without prompting you for input) and create the secure connection. Your browser will not automatically recognize a test or a self-signed certificate, because the certificate is not signed by a CA. If you are not using a certificate from a CA, follow the instructions provided by your browser to accept the certificate. You can just accept the defaults by clicking Next until the dialogs are finished. Once your browser accepts the certificate, your secure Web server will show you a default home page.

Accessing Your Secure Server

To access your secure server, use a URL like this:

```
https://your_domain
```

Note that URLs intended to connect to your secure Web server should begin with the https: protocol designator instead of the more common http: protocol designator. Your nonsecure server can be accessed using an URL like this:

```
http://your_domain
```

The standard port for secure Web communications is port 443. The standard port for nonsecure Web communications is port 80. The secure Web server default configuration listens on both of the two standard ports. Therefore, you will not need to specify the port number in a URL (the port number is assumed). However, if you configure your server to listen on a nonstandard port (that is, anything besides 80 or 443), you will need to specify the port number in every URL intended to connect to the server on the nonstandard port.

For example, you may have configured your server so that you have a virtual host running nonsecured on port 12331. Any URLs intended to connect to that virtual host must specify the port number in the URL. The following URL example attempts to connect to a nonsecure Web server listening on port 12331:

```
http://your_domain:12331
```

 Some of the example URLs used in this book may need to be changed, depending upon whether you are accessing your secure Web server or your nonsecure Web server. Please view all URLs in this book as general examples, not as explicit instructions that will work under all circumstances.

Summary

This chapter introduced you to the Apache Web server configuration. You received an overview of the Apache project and a short history of the Apache server. After you learned how to download, build, and install Apache, you learned in detail how to configure Apache for your Red Hat system. In the last three sections, you saw how to use server-side includes and CGI scripts and how to configure a secure Apache server using SSL.

Chapter 22

Optimizing Internet Services

IN THIS CHAPTER

◆ Optimizing LDAP services

◆ Optimizing DNS services

◆ Optimizing mail services

◆ Optimizing FTP services

◆ Optimizing Web services

THIS CHAPTER DISCUSSES some of the optimizations available for the services we've called "Internet services." As always, there are no silver bullets or magic potions that can turn your system into, say, a mail-serving speed daemon. Server optimization requires analysis to narrow the problem domain, diagnosis to identify the performance problem, and experimentation in order to evaluate the effectiveness of your optimization. Naturally, though, it helps to know what kinds of tweaks and changes are most appropriate. In the case of LDAP, the directory layout can have a dramatic impact on overall LDAP performance. DNS can be optimized by having LAN clients run caching servers locally, by configuring multiple slave servers, by directing local lookups to internal servers first, by zone file tweaks, and so forth. Mail servers are sensitive to I/O binding, and Web servers respond especially well to additional memory. Each of the Internet services discussed in this part of the book really deserves an optimization chapter of its own, but we have only so much space within which to work.

Optimizing LDAP Services

Several items in the slapd configuration can be tweaked to give better server performance. The items shown here are all areas that can be modified.

◆ Indexing

◆ Logging

- ◆ Cache modification

- ◆ Write performance

- ◆ Database loading

- ◆ DNS name resolution

- ◆ System memory

- ◆ Disk subsystem

- ◆ Filesystem

The best source for tips on performance-tuning these items for your system can be found on the OpenLDAP Web site at http://www.openldap.org/faq/data/cache/190.html.

Optimizing DNS Services

Optimizing DNS services revolves around the notion of reducing the latency involved in making DNS queries. For client programs, that is, for applications requesting DNS services, the best all around performance enhancement is to maintain a local cache of DNS information. You get the most bang for your performance buck by reducing the number of DNS queries that have to go to a remote server, even if that server is inside the subnet to which you are connected. The typical approach is to run a caching-only name server on client machines. On the server side, you have a much wider range of options, as discussed in the section titled "Tweaking DNS Servers," later in this chapter.

Improving the Performance of DNS Clients

To increase the performance and security of your caching-only servers on the DNS clients, several options can be modified in the /etc/named.conf file created during the installation of BIND. The /etc/named.conf file is shown in Listing 22-1.

Listing 22-1: The /etc/named.conf file

```
// generated by named-bootconf.pl

options {
        directory "/var/named";
        /*
        * If there is a firewall between you and nameservers you
want
        * to talk to, you might need to uncomment the query-source
        * directive below.  Previous versions of BIND always asked
        * questions using port 53, but BIND 8.1 uses an unprivileged
```

```
        * port by default.
        */
        // query-source address * port 53;
};


//
// a caching only nameserver config
//
controls {
        inet 127.0.0.1 allow { localhost; } keys { rndckey; };
};
zone "." { type hint; file "named.ca"; };

zone "localhost" {
        type master;
        file "localhost.zone";
        allow-update { none; };
};

zone "0.0.127.in-addr.arpa" {
        type master;
        file "named.local";
        allow-update { none; };
};

include "/etc/rndc.key";
```

The section of the file in which you are interested is the options section. Since this is a caching-only server, you can safely disable functions that are not necessary for this type of server. You can also add options that do apply to a caching-only server.

By default, BIND allows zone transfers to all hosts. But zone transfers are necessary only for master and slave servers; you can disable this function by adding the following line:

```
allow-transfer { none; };
```

You can also configure you caching-only server to respond to regular queries only from specific hosts. The default setting in BIND is to allow queries from any host. Typically, you want to allow queries only from hosts inside your firewall. You can add the following line to the options section:

```
allow-query { your internal network number goes here; localhost; };
```

You can also configure you caching-only server to respond to recursive queries only from specific hosts. The default setting in BIND is to allow queries from any host. Typically, you want to allow queries only from hosts inside of your firewall. You can add the following line to the options section:

```
Allow-recursion { your internal network number goes here; localhost;
};
```

Typically, a caching-only server does not have direct access to the Internet, so it creates a cache file to hold dns information. This is the purpose of a caching-only server, and it boosts performance by not having to send queries to external servers. But if the server does not have the information it needs in its local cache, it needs to send a request to other servers. You can specify the IP address of the servers to which you want to forward requests. Add the following line to the options section of your file:

```
forwarders { ip address of servers; };
```

What happens if the servers you are forwarding to are down? Your server tries to forward the request to other servers. You can prevent this from happening by adding this line:

```
forward only;
```

Tweaking DNS Servers

To increase the performance and security of your master domain server on the DNS clients, several options can be modified in the /etc/named.conf file created during the installation of BIND. Make changes to the options section of /etc/named.conf.

By default, BIND allows zone transfers to all hosts. But since zone transfers are necessary only between the master and slave servers, you can specify the IP address of your slave server by adding the following line:

```
allow-transfer { IP address of slave DNS server goes here; };
```

You can also configure your master server to respond to regular queries only from specific hosts. The default setting in BIND is to allow queries from any host. Typically, you want to allow other types of queries only from hosts inside your firewall. You can add the following line to the options section:

```
allow-query { your internal network number goes here; localhost; };
```

You can also configure your caching-only server to respond to recursive queries only from specific hosts. The default setting in BIND is to allow queries from any host. Typically, you want to allow queries only from hosts inside of your firewall. You can add the following line to the options section:

```
Allow-recursion { your internal network number goes here; localhost;
};
```

LOGGING

You can configure your caching-only slave and master servers to automatically rotate your /var/log/named.log file to prevent your filesystem from filling up with old information. The file /etc/logrotate.d/named should have been created during the installation of BIND and should be similar to Listing 22-2.

Listing 22-2: The /etc/logrotate.d/named file controls log rotation

```
/var/log/named.log {
    missingok
    create 0644 named named
    postrotate
        /sbin/service named reload  2> /dev/null || true
    endscript
}
```

If you do not have this file on your system, create it by copying the file as shown above. Then make the following changes.

Remove this line:

```
create 0644 named named
```

Change the line:

```
/sbin/service named reload  2> /dev/null || true
```

to

```
/bin/kill -HUP `cat /var/run/named.pid 2> /dev/null` 2> /dev/null ||
true
```

Be sure to save your changes and restart the named server.

Another tweak you can do is disable logging for lame servers. These are servers that appear to be name servers for a domain but are not. This reduces system-resource use. Add the following line to your /etc/named.conf file:

```
Logging {
 category lame-servers { null; };
};
```

Optimizing Mail Services

To improve the speed of your mail services, you can take one of several approaches. Busy sites often use multiple mail servers in order to spread the mail processing load across a number of systems in order to reduce the demand on any single system. Another common performance enhancement is to replace Sendmail with another mail server, such as Postfix. If your mail server supports a number of mailing lists, you might consider handling list traffic on one server and regular (non-list) mail traffic on another server. If you are not in a position to buy a beefier mail server, to buy more mail servers, or to replace Sendmail with Postfix, the section titled "Getting More from Sendmail," later in this chapter, offers a number of tips and hints to help you squeeze more speed out of it. "Getting More from Postfix," also later in this chapter, gives you a number of methods you can try in order to get better performance from Postfix.

Getting More from Sendmail

The `/etc/mail/sendmail.cf` file contains many options that can be tweaked to give better performance and increase the efficiency of your mail server. A good source for some performance tuning tips can be found at the sendmail Web site at `http://www.sendmail.org/~ca/email/doc8.12/TUNING`.

Getting More from Postfix

If you have a lot of mail that just seems to sit in Postfix's outbound queue, you may be trying to deliver mail to a site that is quite busy. One way to work around this problem is to create a transport map entry for such a site that enables multiple parallel connections and then to give each connection to that site a shorter timeout. Suppose, for example, you know that `slowsite.com` and `reallyslowsite.net` are busy sites and you have trouble getting e-mail to them in a timely manner. First, create entries resembling the following in `/etc/postfix/transport`:

```
slowsite.com          deadbeats:
reallyslowsite.net    deadbeats:
```

These entries in `/etc/postfix/transport` add `slowsite.com` and `reallyslow site.net` to an alias named `deadbeats`. Next, create a corresponding entry in `/etc/postfix/main.cf` that increases the number of simultaneous connections to 50, which allows more mail to `slowsite.com` and `reallyslowsite.net` to be transmitted at once.

```
transport_maps = hash:/etc/postfix/transport
deadbeats_destination_concurrency_limit = 50
```

The key directive here is `deadbeats_destination_concurrency_limit = 50`, which increases the number of parallel connections to `slowsite.com` and `reallyslowsite.net` to 50.

```
deadbeats      unix    -    -    n    -    -    smtp
    -o smtp_connect_timeout=5 -o smtp_helo_timeout=5
```

These entries from `/etc/postfix/master.cf` tell Postfix that SMTP connections to sites in the `deadbeats` alias should timeout after 5 seconds and that, similarly, an SMTP transaction must commence within 5 seconds of the `HELO` command, or the connection will be closed.

If incoming mail seems to queue up while outbound mail gets delivered, then outgoing mail is crowding out incoming mail. Postfix can waste a great deal of time waiting for connections to time out, so, again, the solution is to reduce the connection timeout for incoming email, modifying `/etc/postfix/master.cf` as follows:

```
relay      unix     -    -    n    -    -    smtp
    -o smtp_connect_timeout=2 -o smtp_helo_timeout=2
```

If you see that Postfix pegs disk I/O when processing incoming mail, the *real* solution is to get faster disks or to allocate one disk for logging, one disk for the mail queue, and a third disk for user mailboxes. Postfix-caused disk saturation is especially a problem if you are serving multiple virtual hosts on a single system. One workaround is to configure multiple IP addresses for the machine and to run a Postfix instance for each IP address, where each Postfix instance writes to a different disk. It is easier to configure than it might seem at first glance. The key is starting each Postfix instance with a different configuration directory:

```
# postfix -c conf_dir start
```

Replace `conf_dir` with the name of the configuration directory assigned to each IP. Within each `conf_dir`, main.cf has a different $myhostname, $queue_directory, and $inet_interfaces setting, depending on the interface or IP it handles. For example, if you have two virtual hosts, `first.vhost.com` and `second.vhost.com`, you might arrange it like this. For `first.vhost.com`, suppose the Postfix's configuration directory is `/first/postfix`. Thus, the configuration file `/first/postfix/main.cf` might have the following entries:

```
queue_directory = /first/queue/dir
myhostname = first.vhost.com
inet_interfaces = $myhostname
```

Accordingly, start the Postfix instance for `first.vhost.com` this way:

```
postfix -c /first/postfix start
```

Make a similar arrangement for `second.vhost.com`. If the configuration directory is `/second/postfix`, the configuration file is `/second/postfix/main.cf`, which has the following entries for `second.vhost.com`:

```
queue_directory = /second/queue/dir
myhostname = second.vhost.com
inet_interfaces = $myhostname
```

The proper Postfix invocation is:

```
postfix -c /second/postfix start
```

If Postfix responds too slowly to incoming SMTP connections but POP or IMAP connections are acceptably fast, you need to run more SMTP server processes. Edit the `smtpd` entry in the `master.cf` file and increase the process limit. Alternatively, increase the `default_process_limit` setting in the `main.cf` file.

TIP Anytime you edit one of Postfix's configuration files, be sure to use the `postfix reload` command to activate the changes.

Optimizing FTP Services

Out of the box, vsftpd is pretty darn fast and makes lightweight demands on a system's memory and CPU resources. If its speed fails to suit you, the following tips, adapted from the vsftpd documentation, might help:

◆ If possible, disable the NIS and NIS+ (`nis` and `nisplus`) for `passwd`, `shadow`, and `group` lookups in `/etc/nsswitch.conf`. The idea with this tip is to avoid loading unnecessary runtime libraries into the vsftpd's memory space and to avoid using NIS for lookups that can be resolved more quickly by resorting to file-based lookups.

◆ Break directories with more than a few hundred entries into smaller directories. Many file systems, such as ext2 and ext3, do not handle such cases efficiently at all, and the process of creating listings of large directories (with, for example, the `ls` or `dir` commands) causes vsftpd to use moderate amounts of memory and CPU. If you are stuck with large directories, use a file system, such as XFS, JFS, or ReiserFS, designed to work with large directory structures.

◆ Limit the number of simultaneous connections to the FTP server.

◆ Take advantage of vsftpd's bandwidth throttling features to limit the net-work bandwidth consumed by any one connection or connection classes.

Optimizing Web Services

The section titled "Performance Tuning" in Chapter 21 briefly touches on Apache configuration settings you can modify that affect Apache's performance. The set-tings mentioned in that section are good starting points for fine-tuning Apache, but they do not exhaust the possibilities. To recap that discussion:

◆ Increasing the MaxClients setting (to a maximum of 256) increases the maximum number of simultaneous client connections to the httpd server before the server starts refusing additional connections. The default value is 150 (clients). One generally-accepted rule-of-thumb formula is:

$$\text{MaxClients} = \frac{\text{Physical RAM} - 128\text{MB} + \text{Size of Active Pages}}{\text{Non} - \text{Shared Memory per httpd process}}$$

The theory is that you should use physical RAM for system resources and caching active pages. Leftover RAM should be used by httpd process serv-ing up active pages. If you have more clients, you will end up swapping, which degrades performance. If you have fewer clients, you will not be maximizing the available system resources. In practice, you will have to decide what constitutes an active page. One way to go about this is to use the server logs to evaluate which pages are served more than once every TimeOut period, which defaults to 300 seconds (5 minutes).

◆ The TimeOut directive controls how long the server waits between proto-col messages before it closes a connection. The longer the TimeOut direc-tive, the longer a client connection will be tied up and, thus, unavailable to another client. The default value is 300 (seconds).

◆ The MaxRequestsPerChild setting controls how may HTTP requests an httpd child process will service before a new child process starts. The default value is 100, but setting it to 0, for unlimited requests, will work just fine on a Red Hat system.

◆ The KeepAlive directive controls whether or not HTTP clients are permitted to bundle multiple requests in a single connection. Setting KeepAlive to Off prevents multiple requests per connection. If KeepAlive is on, multiple client requests per connection are allowed, provided the time elapsed between requests is less than the value of KeepAliveTimeout (15 seconds by default).

◆ MaxKeepAliveRequests, 100 by default, sets the upper limit on the total number of requests from the same client on the same connection.

The following tips and suggestions appear in no particular order. As remarked at the beginning of this chapter, Terry and I are fresh out of Magic Performance Enhancing Potion. Some of the following might work better than others; others ideas might fail miserably. If your server is running a lot of CGI scripts or using PHP markup, you should look into resources that discuss Apache tuning in depth. The overhead requirements of PHP and CGI scripts involve creating new processes rather than merely additional RAM, network, or disk I/O.

◆ Set `HostnameLookups` to `Off`. Each resolver call impairs performance. If you need to resolve IP addresses to hostnames, you can use Apache's logresolve program or one of the resolver programs available in the the log reporting and analysis packages.

◆ Similarly, use IP addresses instead of host names in `Allow from` *domain* and `Deny from` *domain* directives — each such query, when *domain* is a name, performs a reverse DNS query followed by a forward query to make sure that the reverse query is not being spoofed. Using IP addresses avoids having to resolve names to IP numbers before performing the reverse and forward queries.

◆ If you do not use `Options FollowSymLinks`, or if you *do* use `Options SymLinksIfOwnerMatch`, Apache performs extra system calls to check symbolic links. For example, suppose you have the following configuration:

```
DocumentRoot /var/www/htdocs
<Directory />
    Options SymLinksIfOwnerMatch
</Directory>
```

If a client then requests `/index.html`, Apache performs an `lstat()` system call on `/var`, `/var/www`, `/var/www/htdocs`, and `/var/www/htdocs/index.html` to check the owner matching of the symbolic link. The overhead of these `lstat()` system calls occurs for *each* request, and Apache does not cache the results of the system calls. For the best performance (and, unfortunately, the least security against rogue symlinks), set `Options FollowSymLinks` for all directories and never set `Options SymLinksIfOwnerMatch`.

◆ A similar performance problem occurs when you use `.htaccess` files to override directory settings. In this case, Apache attempts to open `.htaccess` for each component of a requested filename. For the best performance use `AllowOverride None` everywhere in the Web space Apache is serving.

◆ Do not use NFS mounted file systems to store files that Apache serves. Not only is the read performance of NFS slower than the read performance of a local file, the file being served via NFS might disappear or change, causing NFS cache consistency problems. Moreover, if the Apache server is somehow compromised, the NFS mount will be vulnerable.

◆ The single most important system resource that Apache uses is RAM.
   As far as Apache is concerned, more RAM is better because it improves
   Apache's ability to store frequently requested pages in its cache. You can
   also help by limiting the non-Apache processes to the absolute minimum
   required to boot the system and enable Apache to run – that is, run a dedicated Web server that doesn't need to share the CPU or memory with
   other processes. Naturally, a faster CPU, a high-speed Ethernet connection,
   and SCSI disks are preferable.

Summary

Red Hat systems are most often deployed to provide Internet services, so this chapter mentioned some methods you can use to improve the performance of several
key Internet services: LDAP, DNS, e-mail, and Web services. We could list only
some of the areas to consider when tuning LDAP, because LDAP performance-
tuning is a complex subject best addressed by the LDAP authorities. DNS is more
easily tuned. A DNS client's performance can often be improved simply by running
a caching nameserver, while there are several methods available for getting better
query performance from a server. Mail servers are high-volume, heavy throughput
systems requiring careful tuning, but sometimes, simply replacing Sendmail with
Postfix can fix slow mail-processing times. We also mentioned a number of methods you can use to get faster, more consistent page-serving behavior from Apache.

Chapter 23 teaches you how to use the Red Hat Network to keep your Red Hat
system current and secure.

Part IV

System Maintenance

Chapter 23

Using the Red Hat Network

IN THIS CHAPTER

- ◆ Registering your system with Red Hat Network

- ◆ Configuring the Red Hat Update Agent

- ◆ Using the Update Agent

- ◆ Using the Red Hat Network Alert Icon

- ◆ Accessing the Red Hat Network via the Internet

THE RED HAT NETWORK is installed by default when you install the Red Hat Enterprise Linux operating system. The Red Hat Network software is used to register a profile with Red Hat that contains information about the software packages installed on your system. Whenever a package update is available, for whatever reason, you receive an e-mail notification from Red Hat.

This might not sound like much at first, but think about the many steps involved in keeping your system up-to-date with the latest versions of the hundreds of packages that are installed on your system. The Red Hat Network practically eliminates the need for you to search for these packages because you receive this information by e-mail. As a registered Red Hat Network user, you can also search for updates by using the Update Agent. With the introduction of the Red Hat Network, you can now easily keep your system running reliably and securely. A few steps are involved in setting up the Red Hat Network, but they are well worth the effort. In this chapter you learn how to register your system with Red Hat, configure the Update Agent, and then connect to look for updated files. The first step is registering, and this procedure is covered in the next section.

Registering Your System with the Red Hat Network

Before you can begin using the Red Hat Network, you must register your system with Red Hat by using the Red Hat Network registration client.

 You may also register for the Red Hat Network at the Red Hat Web site by using your Web browser to go to `http://rhn.redhat.com/newlogin`, choosing a personal or corporate account and filling in the online registration form.

You must be logged in as root to perform the registration, and you must have a connection to the Internet to be able to log on to the Red Hat Web site. If you are not connected to the Internet, you receive an error message and the program closes when you click OK.

Start the registration client by following the appropriate step for your system.

◆ From the KDE desktop, click the K on the Panel Main Menu → System Tools → Red Hat Network.

◆ From the GNOME desktop, click the Main Menu Icon → Programs → SystemTools → Red Hat Network.

◆ From a shell prompt, enter `rhn_register`.

You now see the Red Hat Network welcome screen that provides a description and lists the benefits of the Red Hat Network. If you choose not to use the Red Hat Network, you can click Cancel to end the process. Otherwise, click Next to continue to the Red Hat Privacy Statement screens, and then click Next to go to the User Account screen shown in Figure 23-1.

On this screen, you must fill in the user name and password that you want to use to access the Red Hat Network. The user name must be at least four characters and can not contain any spaces, tabs, line feeds, or reserved characters such as ', &, +, or %. You also enter your e-mail address here and can indicate that you want to receive e-mail notification of updates by checking the box. When you have entered the appropriate information, click Next to continue to another screen that enables you to enter additional information about yourself. All information on this page, shown in Figure 23-2, is optional, so you can fill in the information if you choose. Whether you enter additional information on this page or not, click Next to continue.

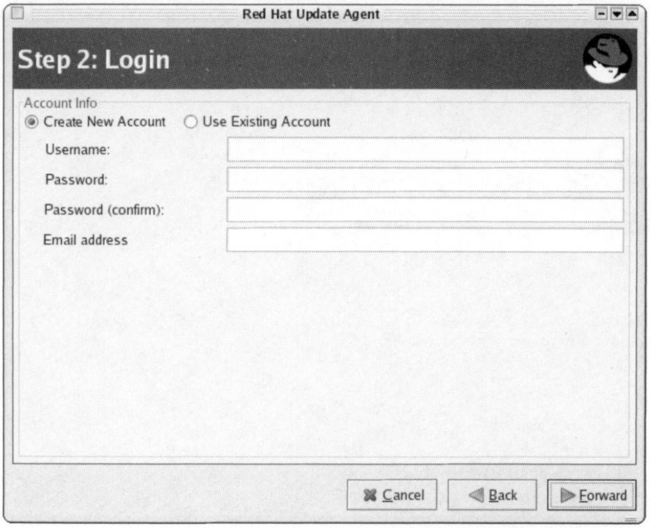

Figure 23-1: The Red Hat Network User Account screen is where you enter your personal information to create your account.

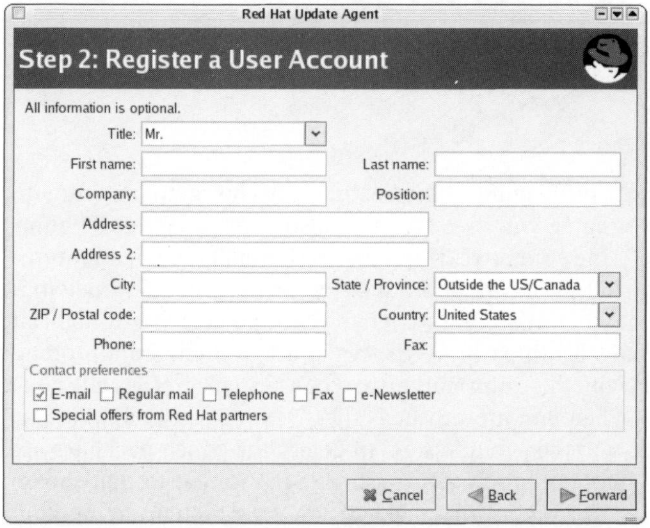

Figure 23-2: The Red Hat Network Register Account screen is where you enter more detailed personal information to create your account.

You now register a system profile for the hardware in your system. You do this by giving your system a profile name. Figure 23-3 shows the System Profile – Hardware registration form.

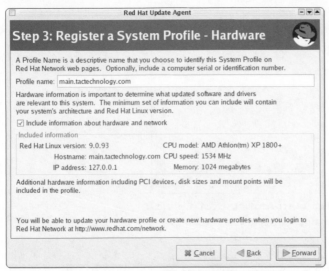

Figure 23-3: The System Profile – Hardware registration screen lists information about your system architecture and Red Hat version number.

On this screen, the default Profile name is the hostname of the computer, but you may change this to whatever name you like. You may also enter a Service ID number that helps you to identify the computer. The Service ID number is not a requirement. The check box for including information about your hardware and network is checked by default. Information about your computer's architecture and Red Hat version number are automatically filled in by the registration client from probing your system. If you don't want this information in your system profile, click the box to disable this feature. When you are finished, click Next to continue.

The registration client now probes your system to determine which packages are installed on your system. When the probing is finished, a list similar to that shown in Figure 23-4 is displayed, showing all the packages on your system; by default, they are selected to be included with your system profile.

If you do not want a package included, click the box next to the package name to remove it from the list. After making your selections, click Next to continue. Your system profile now is sent to the Red Hat Network. After the registration process is finished, you receive a confirmation message stating that you have successfully registered your system profile on the Red Hat Network. Now you are ready to configure the Update Agent.

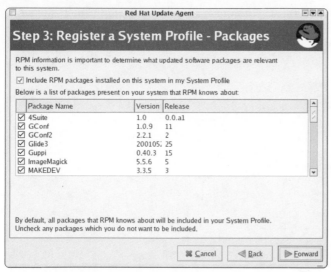

Figure 23-4: The Packages registration screen shows the packages installed on your system.

Configuring the Red Hat Update Agent

The Red Hat Update agent is configured automatically when the system is first started. You need to invoke it manually only if you make system-configuration changes, for example changing proxy settings. Start the Update Agent Configuration tool as follows:

◆ From the command line, type **up2date-config**.

◆ From the KDE desktop, click the K on the Panel → System Tools → Red Hat Network.

◆ From the GNOME desktop, click the Main Menu Icon → System Tools → Red Hat Network.

The Red Hat Network Configuration dialog box, shown in Figure 23-5, opens.
This dialog box has three tabs: General, Retrieval/Installation, and Package Exceptions. The General tab is shown by default when the dialog box opens. If you need to use a proxy server to connect to the Web, you can enter this information by first clicking the box labeled Enable HTTP Proxy and entering the name of your server in the field next to the check box. If you need to use authentication, you can

enable it by clicking the Use Authentication check box and filling in the fields with the Username and Password.

The next tab is the Retrieval/Installation settings tab shown in Figure 23-6.

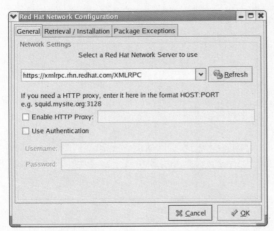

Figure 23-5: The Red Hat Network Configuration dialog box enables you to change the configuration of the Update Agent.

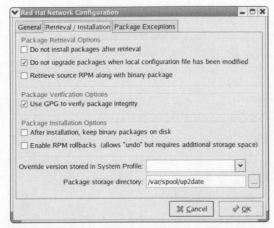

Figure 23-6: The Retrieval/Installation dialog box options control package retrieval and installation.

In this dialog box, you can choose options that affect how the packages are retrieved and subsequently installed. The package retrieval options are:

◆ Do not install packages after retrieval – By default, packages are automatically installed after they are retrieved. If you enable this option, packages are retrieved to the specified directory but not installed.

◆ Do not display packages when a local configuration file has been modified – If you have manually modified configuration files for packages on your system, these packages are not displayed by default. If you disable this option, the packages are displayed.

◆ Retrieve source RPM along with binary package – By default the source RPM is not downloaded with the binary version of the package. By enabling this option, you also retrieve the source of the RPM.

The package verification options are: Use GPG to verify package integrity – By default, for security purposes, the packages are verified to ensure they contain the Red Hat GPG signature. If you disable this option, the security check is not performed. The following are the package installation options:

◆ After installation, keep binary packages on disk – By default, the packages are removed from the local disk after they are installed. Enabling this option leaves a copy of the package in the specified directory.

The following are the last two options in this dialog box:

◆ Override version stored in System Profile – By filling in the field, you can override the version stored in your System Profile with the version in the field.

◆ Package storage directory – Here you can specify the storage location of the packages on your system.

The Package exceptions tab is last. Choosing this tab opens the Package Exception dialog box shown in Figure 23-7.

In this dialog box, you can choose to exclude packages by either the name of the package or the name of the file. To exclude a package by package name, type the name of the package in the Add new field in the Package Names to Skip section; then click the Add button. To exclude a package by file name, type the name of the file in the Add new field in the File Names to Skip section; then click the Add button.

After you have made any changes to the three tabbed dialog boxes, click OK. Your configuration changes are saved and you can now use the Update Agent.

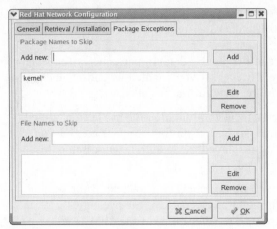

Figure 23-7: The Package Exceptions dialog box lets you choose to exclude packages.

Using the Red Hat Update Agent

The Update Agent is a valuable tool, as it helps you to keep your system running the most current versions of the packages installed on your system. Be sure you are logged in as root before running the Red Hat Update Agent.

The Red Hat Network is free for one system only. If you are installing the Red Hat Network on more than one system, you receive a message for each additional system telling you to go to the Red Hat Network site and enable the software for your system. You have to purchase additional licenses for each additional system.

The Update Agent can be started as follows:

◆ From the command line, type **up2date**.

◆ From the KDE desktop, click the K on the Panel → System Tools → Red Hat Network.

◆ From the GNOME desktop, click the Main Menu Icon → System Tools → Red Hat Network.

If you are running the Update Agent from the command line, you can use the options listed in Table 23-1 (obtained from Red Hat).

TABLE 23-1 COMMAND LINE OPTIONS

Argument	Description
`--configure`	Graphically configure Red Hat Update Agent options through the Red Hat Update Agent Configuration Tool.
`-d, --download`	Download packages only; do not install them. This argument overrides the configuration option Do not install packages after retrieval.
`-f, --force`	Force package installation. This option overrides the file, package, and configuration skip lists.
`-i, --install`	Install packages after they are downloaded. This argument overrides the configuration option Do not install packages after retrieval.
`-k, --packagedir`	Specify a colon-separated path of directories to look for packages before trying to download them.
`-l, --list`	List packages available for retrieval/installation.
`--nosig`	Do not use GPG to check package signatures.
`--tmpdir=directory`	Override the configured package directory. The default location is `/var/spool/up2date`.
`--justdb`	Only add packages to the database and do not install them.
`--dbpath`	Specify a path where an alternate RPM database to use is found.

When the Update Agent starts, you are prompted to install the Red Hat GPG key used to verify the Red Hat security signature on the downloaded packages. Click Yes to install the key. You now see the Red Hat Update Agent Welcome screen as shown in Figure 23-8.

If you are running the Update Agent from the command line and do not have X Window system enabled, you have to install the GPG key manually. Go to the Red Hat Web site at `http://www.redhat.com/support/resources/faqs/ecommerce/top10_faq.html#public_key` for more information.

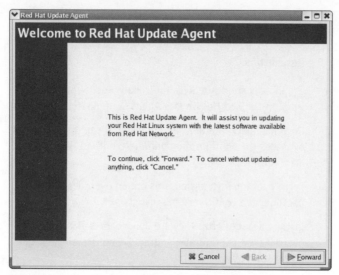

Figure 23-8: The Red Hat Update Agent Welcome screen

To begin updating your system, click Next and the Update Agent displays the channels screen as shown in Figure 23-9. This screen should show the source from where you will obtain your updates and the current version of Red Hat Linux that your system is using.

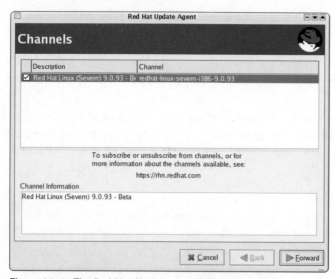

Figure 23-9: The Red Hat Update Agent Channels screen

Click *forward* and your system connects to the Red Hat Network to obtain a list of updates for your system. If your system is already current, you see a dialog box, shown in Figure 23-10, telling you that no additional packages are needed. If you are running the Update Agent for the first time immediately after a new system installation, this is typically the result.

Figure 23-10: The Red Hat Update Agent informs you that your system is not in need of any updates.

If you chose to exclude any packages by unchecking them when you registered your system profile earlier in this chapter, you will see a screen listing the excluded packages.

If your system is in need of updating, you see a list of packages that can be retrieved. You must choose the packages you want to download by clicking the box to the left of the package name. To select all packages, click the button to the left of Select all packages. After you've finished selecting packages, click Next. You see the status of the download as each package is retrieved and an All Finished when all packages have been retrieved. If you didn't change the default setting in the Update Configuration Retrieval/Installation settings to automatically install packages, the packages that were retrieved are immediately installed after download. You see a progress indicator as they are being installed followed by an All Finished message. The All Finished screen lists the packages that have been updated. Click Finish to end the Update Agent session.

As long as you install the latest packages automatically, your system always synchronizes with the System Profile stored on the Red Hat Network. If you download and install the packages yourself, you must update the RPM package list in your System Profile manually by running the command:

```
up2date -p
```

Using the Red Hat Network Alert Icon

If you desire, you can run the Red Hat Network Alert Icon program that will place an icon into the panel on your desktop. The icon will give you an immediate visual notification of the state of your system regarding updates. The alert icon is placed on the right side of the panel near the system clock as shown in Figure 23-11.

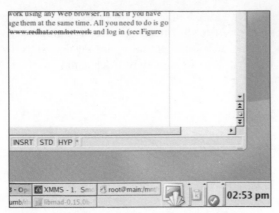

Figure 23-11: The Red Hat Network Alert Icon indicates
system-update status.

Figure 23-11 shows a round icon with a checkmark that signifies that the system is fully updated. The following are other icons that can be used:

◆ Gray with a question mark means an error connecting to the Red Hat Network.

◆ Green with arrows facing each way shows that the system is checking for updates.

◆ Red with an exclamation point shows that the system needs to be updated.

To start the Red Hat Network Alert Icon, from the main menu choose System Tools → Red Hat Network Alert Icon. The Welcome page will appear, and you can click Forward to continue to the Terms of Service page shown in Figure 23-12.

You should read through the information to be sure you understand the terms. Click Forward to continue to the next page. If you have already run the program, you can click on the Remove From Panel button to remove the icon from your panel.

The next page to appear is the Proxy Configuration page as shown in Figure 23-13. If you use a proxy server, enter the appropriate information on this page.

Click on forward to continue to the last page. Finally click on Apply and the Network Alert Icon will be placed into your panel. If you want to change the configuration, or manually start the update process on demand, left-click the icon and choose the appropriate choice from the pop-up menu.

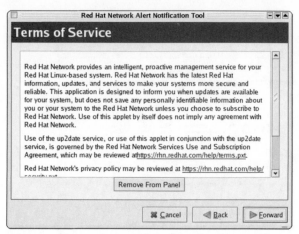

Figure 23-12: The Red Hat Network Alert Icon Terms of Service page

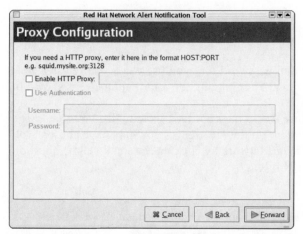

Figure 23-13: You can enter information about your proxy server on the Proxy Configuration page.

Using the Red Hat Network via the Internet

You can access the Red Hat Network using any Web browser. In fact, if you have multiple machines, you can manage them at the same time. Go to the Red Hat Web site at `http://rhn.redhat.com` and log in (see Figure 23-14).

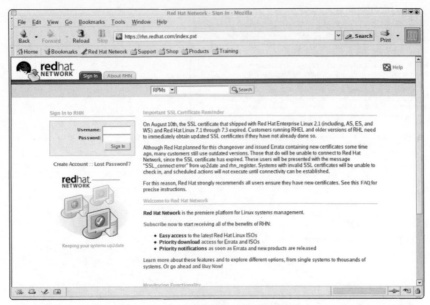

Figure 23-14: Logging in to the Red Hat Network Web site

You use the same user name and password that you use when you register your System Profile earlier in this chapter. After logging in, your main page, as shown in Figure 23-15, displays.

The Main page shown in Figure 23-15 may not look exactly like your page. The information shown here is dependent on the preferences you may have chosen. You can get help about using the Red Hat Network by clicking the small yellow question mark to the right of the Your RHN title.

You can get context-based help about using the Red Hat Network by click-ing the small yellow question mark to the right of the item for which you want help.

Immediately after logging in, you are on the Your RHN page. On the left side of the page are several links of interest. The Your Account link will open the Account Details page as shown in Figure 23-16. On this page you can enter and change some of the details about your account, such as your name, street address, and e-mail address. You can also deactivate your account from this page.

Figure 23-15: The Red Hat Network Main page for your System Profile

Figure 23-16: The Red Hat Network Account Details page shows your personal information.

Clicking the Your Preferences link on the left side of the page opens the Preferences page as shown in Figure 23-17. On the Preferences page, you can set you choices for receiving e-mail notifications, number of listing per page, your time zone, and contact information.

Figure 23-17: The Red Hat Network Preferences page shows your preference information.

At the top of the Your RHN page are tab links for choosing other pages presenting different information. Clicking the Systems tab on the top of the page opens the Systems Page shown in Figure 23-18.

The Systems page lists all the systems you have registered with Red Hat Network. The current status of the listed systems is shown. On the left side of the page is a legend explaining the meaning of the icons shown in the status column. Also shown on the left of the page are links to other systems that you may have that are out of date, unentitled, or inactive. You can click these links to obtain information relevant to the link you chose. You also have the ability to change the status of the systems indicated by these links.

The next tab is Errata. Click this tab to open the Errata page to view any errata that pertains to your system. Any errata will be shown in a list on the page. If there are no errata, the page will so indicate. Figure 23-19 shows the errata page for one of my systems. There are additional links on the left side of the page as well as a legend explaining the meanings of the icons on the page.

Figure 23-18: The Red Hat Network Systems page shows your registered systems.

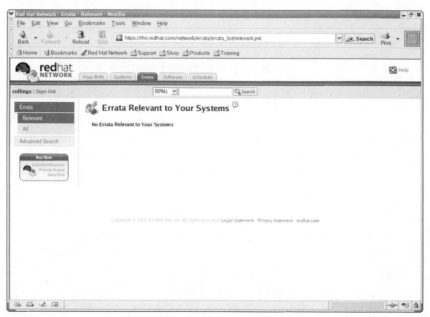

Figure 23-19: The Red Hat Network Errata page shows you errata for your registered system.

The next tab at the top of the page is Software. Clicking this tab opens the Software page that lists the software available for download. You can click on the links for the software you want to download. Figure 23-20 shows the Software page. In most cases, you need to have purchased a subscription to the Red Hat Network to be able to take advantage of the download feature.

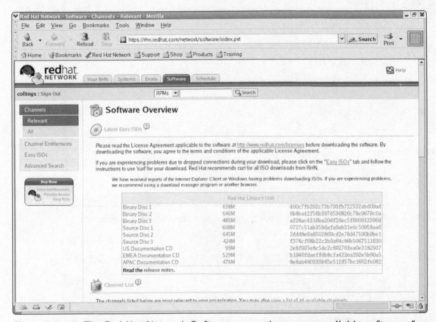

Figure 23-20: The Red Hat Network Software page shows you available software for your registered system.

The last tab shown on the top of the Red Hat Network page is Schedule. This page lists any actions scheduled to be performed. On the left side of the Schedule page are additional links that show failed, completed, and archived actions. Figure 23-21 shows the Schedule page.

You should not routinely install the latest update of a software package without considering the implications of such an action. You should research the update and decide whether installing the updated package would benefit your system. In many cases, updating one package can affect the operation of other programs running on your system, perhaps even making them unrunnable.

Figure 23-21: The Red Hat Network Schedule page shows you pending, failed, completed, and archived actions for your system.

TIP Running `up2date` from the command line is an easy way to install packages. Simply run the command with the name of the package you want to install. For example, if you want to install `php`, typing `up2date php` and `up2date` will solve dependencies, download the packages, and install them. You can obtain a complete listing of all available software by typing `up2date -showall` at the command line.

Summary

In this chapter, you learned about the Red Hat Network, which is used for updating your system. The Red Hat Network continuously monitors your system based on the profile you registered. Whenever an updated version of a package is available, the Red Hat Network notifies you of the type of update so you can take immediate action. Using the Red Hat Network ensures that you are running the latest and most secure versions of the packages installed on your system. This means that you work more efficiently and that your system is more secure and productive.

Chapter 24

Upgrading and Customizing the Kernel

BECAUSE THE LINUX KERNEL is available in source-code form, you can customize it to fit precisely your needs. This chapter shows you how to rebuild the Red Hat Linux kernel. In particular, it covers whether and when to upgrade the kernel, where to obtain the source code, how to download and install it, how to configure the source code specifically for your system, how to compile it, how to install a new kernel, and how to configure your system to boot the new kernel while retaining the ability to boot a known good kernel should something go awry.

As you know, the kernel is the core of the operating system, and runs the CPU, manages system memory, controls access to disk drives, and contains device drivers that enable you to interact with the system and use the hardware and peripherals attached to the computer. As perverse as it might seem at first glance, the ability to update and customize the Linux kernel is one of the things that many like best about Linux. Naturally, this feature appeals most to incorrigible tweakers and tinkerers, but it also appeals to system administrators who are responsible for wringing the most performance and benefit out of their existing hardware and software. In some cases, rebuilding the kernel is required in order to support new hardware that is not supported, or that is poorly supported, by your system's existing kernel.

Should You Upgrade to a New Kernel?

Should you upgrade to a new kernel? Strictly speaking, no, it is rarely *necessary* to do so. The kernel provided with Red Hat Linux is deliberately configured to support the widest possible array of existing PC hardware. Moreover, practically all of the functionality that most users need (both in hobbyist and home environments and in business and professional settings) is already available in the current kernel (version 2.4.21 at the time this paragraph was written). Many users, especially those coming from a predominantly Windows environment, are conditioned to downloading and installing the latest and greatest version of application X, regardless of whether or not they need the features and bug fixes it provides. The fact is that most users do not need to do this because they use perhaps 20 percent of the feature sets of existing software. Adding still more unused features contributes to software bloat and, potentially, to system instability.

In other cases, however, you *will* find it necessary to rebuild the kernel. Often as not, you rebuild the kernel usually to provide better support for the odd hardware device, to add support for new hardware you have added to an existing system, to add a driver for a device not supported by the existing kernel, to fix the occasional bug, or to close a security hole. Red Hat releases a steady stream of patches to address kernel security issues, and these errata should be applied as quickly as possible, especially on systems exposed to the Internet. We personally consider a kernel customized for your specific hardware, usage profile, and personal preferences superior to the stock Red Hat kernel, although you will not go wrong using the standard Red Hat Linux kernel.

Okay, that takes care of the practical reasons for and against upgrading to a new kernel. A significant portion of the Linux community, particularly home users, hobbyists, and developers, constantly upgrade and rebuild their kernels simply because they can or for the sheer satisfaction of the undertaking. "Because I can," "because it's there," or "because I want to" are not therefore less valid because they are not immediately practical. Knowing how to roll your own kernel racks up serious geek points.

For many, including the authors of this book, Linux is a hobby, just as is stamp collecting or flying model airplanes – few people question the value of these more traditional hobbies or ask why people pursue them, so this new hobby should not be considered any different.

Chances are, however, that if you are reading this book, the previous paragraph amounts to preaching to the choir. If not, the following list summarizes the most common reasons you might want or need to upgrade or customize the kernel on your Red Hat Linux system:

- ◆ You can recompile the kernel to support your specific CPU, especially features that improve performance. The default Red Hat Linux installation installs a kernel configured to run on the widest possible variety of Intel CPUs. As a result, it does not take advantage of all of the features and improvements available in the newest CPUs or motherboard chipsets.

- ◆ Similarly, the default kernel often includes system features that you do not need or does not include features that you do need or want. Customizing and recompiling the kernel enables you to remove unnecessary or unwanted features and to add needful and desired features.

◆ The default kernel supports an enormous variety of the most common hardware, but no single system needs all of that support. You might want to create a new kernel that includes support for only the hardware actually installed on your system.

◆ If you have a system with hardware not supported when you installed Red Hat Linux or for which only experimental support was available, you can rebuild the kernel to include that support once it becomes available or to improve existing support.

Why should you not build a custom kernel? The best reason is that when you diverge from the Red Hat–blessed kernel or kernel sources, you lose official Red Hat support — if Red Hat support is important to you, stick with official Red Hat kernels. Another common problem with custom kernels is that a newly-installed piece of hardware will not work because you failed to compile a driver. Conversely, a newly-compiled kernel might accidentally omit support for a vital piece of hardware. Finally, one of the virtues of "official" Red Hat Linux kernels is that they reduce the likelihood of subtle compatibility problems that can develop when you roll your own.

Upgrading versus Customizing

As used in this chapter, *customizing the kernel* and *upgrading the kernel* refer to two different procedures. *Customizing the kernel* refers to reconfiguring an existing kernel source code tree, recompiling it, installing the new kernel, and booting it. *Upgrading the kernel*, likewise, has two meanings. One way to upgrade the kernel is to obtain binary kernel RPMs from Red Hat and install a new, precompiled kernel as modified by Red Hat. Indeed, the most common method of performing a kernel upgrade on Red Hat Linux systems is to download prebuilt kernels from the Red Hat Network.

You can download either a complete source tree (now over 30MB even when compressed) or one or more patches (described later in the section titled "Patching the Kernel"). Of the two options, downloading a series of patch files is faster than downloading an entire kernel source tree.

To put it another way, *upgrading* the kernel means obtaining new source code and customizing it. Whether you customize or upgrade, though, the end result is the same: a new kernel configured to your liking.

Checking the Current Kernel Version

Before building a new kernel, you need to know which version you are running. You can use one of several ways to check the current version. The canonical method that works on any running Linux system is to use the `uname` command, which displays a single line of output containing a variety of system information, depending on the command line option used. Its syntax is:

```
uname [-amnrspv]
```

Invoked with no options, `uname` prints `Linux`. To obtain the kernel version that is currently running, use the `-r` option, which prints the operating system release level. For example:

```
$ uname -r
2.4.18-7.95
```

The first three numbers are the kernel version, so the system in question is running kernel version 2.4.18. The last two numbers, 7.95, are Red Hat specific, but have no concrete meaning outside of Red Hat's offices. The build instructions provided later in the chapter build a kernel from pristine source code downloaded from one of the dozens of kernel archive sites. The downloaded kernel source does not include the last two Red Hat-specific kernel version numbers.

Table 24-1 lists the meanings of `uname`'s other options.

TABLE 24-1 UNAME COMMAND LINE OPTIONS

Option	Description
-a	Displays all information
-m	Displays the hardware (CPU) type
-n	Displays the system's host name
-s	Displays the operating system name (equivalent to `uname`)
-p	Displays the system's processor type
-v	Prints the Linux version — that is, when it was compiled

The `-v` option consists of a sequence number followed by a date and time stamp, useful information if you build several kernels in a single day:

```
$ uname -v
#1 Tue Jul 30 14:54:56 EDT 2003
```

Another way to check which version of the kernel you are running is to query the RPM database. You can use either of the following commands. The first command shows only the version of the kernel binary that is installed.

```
$ rpm -q kernel
kernel-2.4.18-7.95
```

The next command shows all of the kernel-related RPMs installed.

```
$ rpm -qa | grep kernel
kernel-headers-2.4.18-7.95
kernel-doc-2.4.18-7.95
kernel-source-2.4.18-7.95
kernel-2.4.18-7.95
kernel-pcmcia-cs-3.1.27-12
kernel-debug-2.4.18-7.95
kernel-smp-2.4.18-7.95
```

Using RPM to install, upgrade, and query RPM packages is covered in detail in Chapter 27. The next section of this chapter, "Building a New Kernel," shows the bare bones command to install the kernel related RPMs if they are not installed.

The second command queries the entire RPM database and uses the `grep` command to show only the output lines that contain the word "kernel." If you are considering rebuilding your kernel, the second command is probably more useful to you because it lets you know which kernel related packages you have installed. The following list briefly describes each package.

◆ **glibc-kernheaders:** Contains the C header files for the Linux kernel. The header files define structures and constants that are needed for building most standard programs, and are also needed for rebuilding the kernel.

◆ **kernel-doc:** Contains documentation files from the kernel source. Various portions of the Linux kernel and the device drivers shipped with it are documented in these files. Install this package if you need a reference to the options that can be passed to Linux kernel modules at load time.

◆ **kernel-source:** Contains the source code files for the Linux kernel with Red Hat's custom patches applied.

- **kernel:** Contains the Linux kernel, the core of the Red Hat Linux operating system.

- **kernel-pcmcia-cs:** Contains a set of loadable kernel modules that implement PCMCIA (also known as *CardBus*) support for laptop computers.

- **kernel-smp:** Contains a kernel compiled for SMP (*Symmetric Multi Processor*) systems, that is, systems with more than one CPU.

- **kernel-unsupported:** Contains all of the drivers included with Red Hat Linux and the kernel but which Red Hat does not support.

The Red Hat Linux kernel is custom built by the Red Hat kernel team to ensure its integrity and compatibility with supported hardware. Before Red Hat releases a kernel, the kernel must pass a rigorous set of quality assurance tests. Official Red Hat Linux kernels are packaged in RPM format so that they are easy to upgrade and verify.

For example, the kernel RPM package creates the `initrd` image; it is not necessary to use the `mkinitrd` command after installing a different kernel if you install the kernel from the Red Hat RPM package. The RPM package also modifies the boot loader configuration file to include the new kernel if either GRUB or LILO is installed. You do need to set the new kernel as the default kernel to boot.

Red Hat Linux ships with a custom 2.4 kernel, which offers the following features:

- Kernel source directory is `/usr/src/linux-2.4` instead of `/usr/src/linux`

- Support for the ext3 file system

- Multi-processor (SMP) support

- USB support

- Preliminary support for IEEE 1394, more popularly know as *FireWire*, devices

Preparing to Upgrade

Before you upgrade your kernel, you must take a few precautionary steps. The first step is to make sure you have a working boot diskette for your system in case a problem occurs. If the boot loader is not configured properly to boot the new kernel, you will not be able to boot your system unless you have a boot diskette.

To create a boot diskette for your system, you need to determine which version of the kernel you are currently running. Execute the following command:

```
# uname -r
```

You must be root to create a boot diskette for your system. Log in as root at a shell prompt, and type the following command:

```
# /sbin/mkbootdisk kernelversion
```

Replace *kernelversion* with the output of the `uname -r` command. In fact, if you want to be a *real* gearhead, you can combine these two commands this way:

```
# /sbin/mkbootdisk $(uname -r)
```

 Refer to the `mkbootdisk` man page for more options.

After you create the boot disk, perform a quick sanity check: Reboot your machine with the boot diskette to verify that the diskette works before continuing. You will probably not have to use the diskette, but you should store it in a safe place just in case.

From the output of the `rpm -qa | grep kernel` command you executed earlier, you can determine which packages you need to download for the kernel upgrade. For a single-processor system, the only required package is the kernel package. If you have a computer with more than one processor, you need the `kernel-smp` package, which contains support for multiple processors. It is recommended that you also install the kernel package in case the multi-processor kernel does not work properly for your system. If you have a computer with more than 4GB of memory, you need the `kernel-bigmem` package. Again, it is recommended that you also install the kernel package for debugging purposes. The `kernel-bigmem` package is built for the i686 architecture only.

If you are upgrading the kernel on a laptop or are using PCMCIA, the `kernel-pcmcia-cs` package is also required. You do not need the `kernel-source` package unless you plan to recompile the kernel yourself or plan to perform kernel development. The `kernel-doc` package contains kernel development documentation and is not required. The `kernel-util` package includes utilities that can be used to control the kernel or the system's hardware and is not required.

Red Hat builds kernels that are optimized for different x86 versions. The options are listed below:

◆ **Athlon:** The corresponding kernel is optimized for AMD Athlon and AMD Duron systems.

◆ **i686:** The corresponding kernel is optimized for Intel Pentium II, Pentium III, and Pentium 4 systems.

◆ **i586:** The corresponding kernel is optimized for Intel Pentium and AMD K6 systems.

◆ **i386:** The corresponding kernel will run on any x86 or x86-compatible CPU.

If you do not know the version of your x86 system, use the kernel built for the i386 version because it will run, albeit less than optimally, on any x86 or x86-compatible system.

The CPU type of the RPM package is included in the file name. For example, `kernel-2.4.22-1.2061.nptl.athlon.rpm` is optimized for AMD Athlon or Duron systems, `kernel-2.4.22.1-1.2061.nptl.i686.rpm` is optimized for Intel Pentium II, Pentium III, and Pentium 4 systems, and so forth. When you have determined which packages you need in order to upgrade your kernel, select the proper versions of the kernel, `kernel-smp`, and `kernel-bigmem` packages to match the architecture of your machine. Use the i386 versions of the other packages.

Obtaining Upgraded Kernel RPMs

There are several ways to determine if there is an updated kernel available for your system.

◆ Go to `http://www.redhat.com/apps/support/errata/`, choose the version of Red Hat Linux you are using, and view the errata for it. Kernel errata are usually under the Security Advisories section. From the list of errata, click the kernel errata to view the detailed errata report for it. In the errata report, there is a list of required RPM packages and a link to download them from the Red Hat FTP site. You can also download them from a Red Hat FTP mirror site. A list of mirror sites is available at `http://www.redhat.com/download/mirror.html`.

◆ Use Red Hat Network to download the kernel RPM packages and then manually upgrade to the latest kernel. Or, if you have elected to let the Red Hat Update Agent upgrade packages for you, Red Hat Network can upload the latest kernel, upgrade the kernel on your system, create an initial RAM disk if needed, and configure the boot loader to boot the new kernel. All you have to do is reboot into the new kernel. For more information, refer to the Red Hat Network User Reference Guide available at `http://www.redhat.com/docs/manuals/RHNetwork/`.

If there is an updated kernel for the version of Red Hat Linux you are running, obtain the appropriate packages using one of these methods. If you used Red Hat Network to upgrade your kernel automatically, you are finished — just reboot your system to use the new kernel. If you downloaded only the RPM packages from the Red Hat Linux errata page or from Red Hat Network, proceed to the next section.

Installing the Upgraded RPMs

Now that you have the necessary kernel RPM packages, you can upgrade your existing kernel. At a shell prompt as root, change to the directory that contains the kernel RPM packages and follow these instructions.

It is strongly recommended that you keep the old kernel in case you have problems with the new kernel.

Use the `-i` argument with the `rpm` command if you want to keep the old kernel, as shown in the following command. If you use the `-U` option to upgrade the kernel package, the installation process will overwrite the currently installed kernel:

```
# rpm -ivh kernel-2.4.22-1.2061.nptl.i386.rpm
```

The kernel version and CPU version you use might be different than versions shown in the example. For a multi-processor system, install the `kernel-smp` packages as well:

```
# rpm -ivh kernel-smp-2.4.22-1.2061.nptl.i386.rpm
```

If the system is i686-based and contains more than 4GB of RAM, install the `kernel-bigmem` package built for the i686 architecture as well (again, the exact version number might vary):

```
# rpm -ivh kernel-bigmem-2.4.22-1.2061.nptl.i686.rpm
```

If you plan to upgrade the `kernel-source`, `kernel-docs`, or `kernel-utils` packages, you probably do not need to keep the older versions. Use the following commands to upgrade these packages:

```
# rpm -Uvh kernel-source-2.4.22-1.2061.nptl.i386.rpm
# rpm -Uvh kernel-docs-2.4.22-1.2061.nptl.i386.rpm
# rpm -Uvh kernel-utils-2.4.22-1.2061.nptl.i386.rpm
```

If you are using PCMCIA (for example, on a laptop), you also need to install the `kernel-pcmcia-cs` package and keep the old version. If you use the `-i` switch, the installation process will probably return a conflict because the older kernel needs this package in order to boot with PCMCIA support. To work around this, use the `--force` switch, as shown in the following example:

```
# rpm -ivh --force kernel-pcmcia-cs-3.1.31-13.i386.rpm
```

If you are using the ext3 file system or a SCSI controller, you need an initial RAM disk. The purpose of the initial RAM disk is to allow a modular kernel to have access to modules that it might need to boot from before the kernel has access to the device where the modules normally reside.

The initial RAM disk is created with the `mkinitrd` command. However, the Red Hat kernel RPM package performs this step for you. To verify that it was created, use the command `ls --l /boot`. You should see the file `initrd-2.4.22-1.2061-nptl.img` (the version should match the version of the kernel you just installed).

Now that you have installed the new kernel, you need to configure the boot loader to boot the new kernel. See the section titled "Configuring the Boot Loader" at the end of this chapter to configure the boot loader.

Installing Kernel Source Code from the Internet

The method we prefer to use for upgrading and customizing the kernel is to work with the pristine source code as distributed from the various kernel archive sites scattered around the Internet. Why? Each major Linux vendor, including Red Hat, applies patches to the kernel source code that support the hardware of their strategic partners. There is nothing wrong with this practice because Linux is open source software, but it *does* have the unfortunate side effect of causing the source code distributed by Red Hat to diverge from the source code Linux maintains. As a result, applying patches becomes a hit-or-miss affair (see the section titled "Patching the kernel" to learn how and why to use kernel patches to upgrade the source code).

The primary site for the kernel source code is `http://www.kernel.org/` (see Figure 24-1).

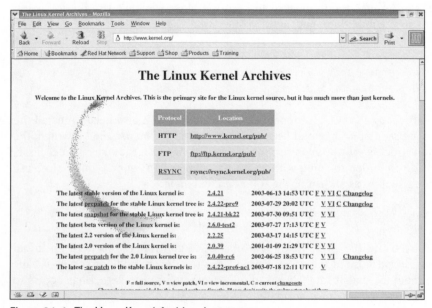

Figure 24-1: The Linux Kernel Archives home page

However, because kernel.org is heavily loaded, especially after a new release, you are better off using one of its many mirrors throughout the world. Often, you can find one close to you – most countries have at least one mirror and some, like the United States and the United Kingdom, have many. In fact, the Linux Kernel Archives Mirror System, described following Figure 24-2, currently consists of 138 sites in 51 countries or territories. Another 74 countries or territories are supported by download sites situated in other countries. To locate a mirror near you, point your Web browser at `http://www.kernel.org/mirrors/`, scroll down the alphabetically-ordered list of countries, and click your country name to view a list of mirror sites in your country. Figure 24-2, for example, shows part of the list of HTTP mirror sites in the United States:

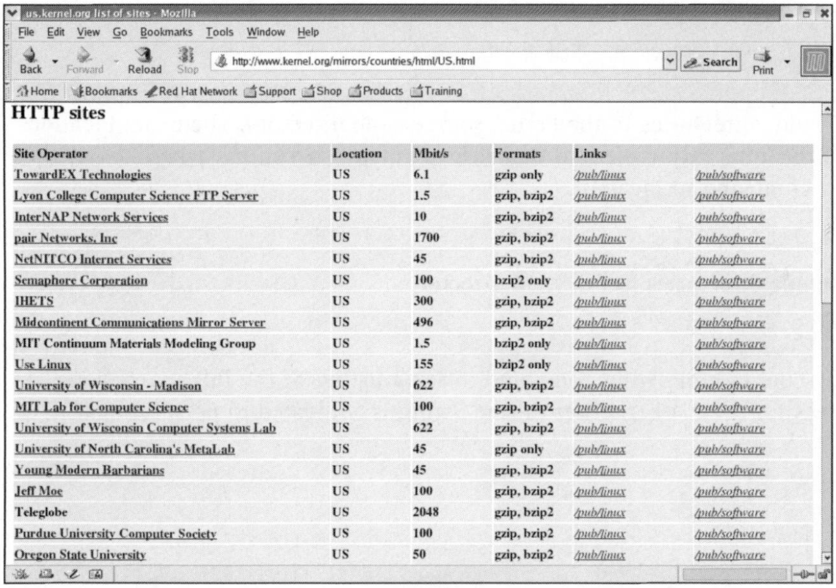

Site Operator	Location	Mbit/s	Formats	Links	
TowardEX Technologies	US	6.1	gzip only	/pub/linux	/pub/software
Lyon College Computer Science FTP Server	US	1.5	gzip, bzip2	/pub/linux	/pub/software
InterNAP Network Services	US	10	gzip, bzip2	/pub/linux	/pub/software
pair Networks, Inc	US	1700	gzip, bzip2	/pub/linux	/pub/software
NetNITCO Internet Services	US	45	gzip, bzip2	/pub/linux	/pub/software
Semaphore Corporation	US	100	bzip2 only	/pub/linux	/pub/software
IHETS	US	300	gzip, bzip2	/pub/linux	/pub/software
Midcontinent Communications Mirror Server	US	496	gzip, bzip2	/pub/linux	/pub/software
MIT Continuum Materials Modeling Group	US	1.5	bzip2 only	/pub/linux	/pub/software
Use Linux	US	155	bzip2 only	/pub/linux	/pub/software
University of Wisconsin - Madison	US	622	gzip, bzip2	/pub/linux	/pub/software
MIT Lab for Computer Science	US	100	gzip, bzip2	/pub/linux	/pub/software
University of Wisconsin Computer Systems Lab	US	622	gzip, bzip2	/pub/linux	/pub/software
University of North Carolina's MetaLab	US	45	gzip only	/pub/linux	/pub/software
Young Modern Barbarians	US	45	gzip, bzip2	/pub/linux	/pub/software
Jeff Moe	US	100	gzip, bzip2	/pub/linux	/pub/software
Teleglobe	US	2048	gzip, bzip2	/pub/linux	/pub/software
Purdue University Computer Society	US	100	gzip, bzip2	/pub/linux	/pub/software
Oregon State University	US	50	gzip, bzip2	/pub/linux	/pub/software

Figure 24-2: Linux kernel archives mirror sites in the United States

The kernel's archive mirror system is set up so that for each two-letter country code you can simply use the host names `http://www.`*`country`*`.kernel.org/` or `ftp.`*`country`*`.kernel.org` to reach a mirror supporting that specific country. For example, in the United States, you would use the URL `http://www.us.kernel.org/` in your Web browser. Each mirror has a full archive of `/pub/linux`, the top-level kernel source directory, but it may not carry the source code in both gzip and bzip2 compression formats – the bzip2 format takes less time to download than gzip format, but also takes longer than gzip format to decompress.

After locating an archive that is near you, in network terms, download the desired file. The instructions that follow assume you use the standard FTP client in a terminal window, such as an xterm.

1. Change directories to a directory to which you have write permission, for example, your home directory:

   ```
   $ cd ~
   ```

2. Open an FTP session to the archive site you selected and log in as the anonymous user using your e-mail address as the password:

   ```
   $ ftp ftp.us.kernel.org
   Connected to ftp.us.kernel.org.
   220 mirror.services.wisc.edu FTP server ready.
   User (ftp.us.kernel.org:(none)): ftp
   331 Anonymous login ok, send your complete email address as
   your password.
   Password:
   230 Anonymous access granted, restrictions apply.
   ftp>
   ```

3. Change directories to the kernel source code directory. The exact location of this directory varies from mirror to mirror, so you may have to use the `ls` command to locate it.

   ```
   ftp> cd /pub/linux/kernel
   ```

4. Change directories to the `v2.4` directory:

   ```
   ftp> cd v2.4
   ```

5. Execute the following command to see a listing of the full source code trees for the 2.4 kernel series (the listing is truncated to preserve space):

```
ftp> ls linux-2.4*
...
-rw-r--r--   1 kernel   kernel   22192379 Aug 11 04:13 linux-2.4.8.tar.bz2
-rw-r--r--   1 kernel   kernel        248 Aug 11 04:13 linux-2.4.8.tar.bz2.sign
-rw-r--r--   1 kernel   kernel   27402470 Aug 11 04:13 linux-2.4.8.tar.gz
-rw-r--r--   1 kernel   kernel        248 Aug 11 04:13 linux-2.4.8.tar.gz.sign
-rw-r--r--   1 root     kernel   22232256 Aug 16 18:32 linux-2.4.9.tar.bz2
-rw-r--r--   1 root     kernel        248 Aug 16 18:32 linux-2.4.9.tar.bz2.sign
-rw-r--r--   1 root     kernel   27474071 Aug 16 18:32 linux-2.4.9.tar.gz
-rw-r--r--   1 root     kernel        248 Aug 16 18:32 linux-2.4.9.tar.gz.sign
```

6. Identify the file to download. In this case, I chose to download the 2.4.22 archive file in bzip2 format, that is, `linux-2.4.22.tar.bz2`.

7. Make sure you are in binary download format:

   ```
   ftp> binary
   ```

8. Use the following commands to download the archive file and its MD5 checksum file (`linux-2.4.22.tar.bz2.sign`):

```
ftp> get linux-2.4.22.tar.bz2
ftp> get linux-2.4.22.tar.bz2.sign
```

9. Close the FTP session:

```
ftp> bye
```

After you have the archive file, verify the file's integrity and unpack it as described in the next section.

Verifying and unpacking the archive

Before you unpack the archive, you should check its signature to make sure that it has not been tampered with. Files placed in the Linux Kernel Archives are OpenPGP-signed, and you can use these digital signatures to prove that files you have downloaded from the kernel archive site really originated at the Linux Kernel Archives. The current Linux Kernel Archives OpenPGP key is always available from `http://www.kernel.org/signature.html`.

The first step is to import the Linux Kernel Archive key. With an active Internet connection, execute the following command:

```
# gpg --keyserver wwwkeys.pgp.net --recv-keys 0x517D0F0E
gpg: /home/kwall/.gnupg: directory created
gpg: new configuration file `/ home/kwall /.gnupg/gpg.conf' created
gpg: keyring `/ home/kwall /.gnupg/secring.gpg' created
gpg: keyring `/ home/kwall /.gnupg/pubring.gpg' created
gpg: / home/kwall /.gnupg/trustdb.gpg: trustdb created
gpg: key 517D0F0E: public key "Linux Kernel Archives Verification
Key <ftpadmin@kernel.org>" imported
gpg: Total number processed: 1
gpg:               imported: 1
```

This step adds the Linux Kernel Archive key to root's public key ring. Next, change directories to the directory in which you downloaded the source files and execute the following commands, again as the root user, to verify the file signature:

```
$ gpg --verify linux-2.4.22.tar.bz2.sign linux-2.4.21.tar.bz2
gpg: Signature made Fri 13 Jun 2003 10:58:13 AM EDT using DSA key ID 517D0F0E
gpg: Good signature from "Linux Kernel Archives Verification Key
<ftpadmin@kernel.org>"
```

As long as you see the two lines of output shown in the example (beginning with `gpg:`), the file is authentic. Replace the file names used in the preceding command with file names that reflect the files you downloaded. Because you probably have not added a trusted path to the archive verification key, this command probably also generates the following error message, which you can safely disregard:

```
gpg: checking the trustdb
gpg: no ultimately trusted keys found
gpg: WARNING: This key is not certified with a trusted signature!
gpg:          There is no indication that the signature belongs to the owner.
Primary key fingerprint: C75D C40A 11D7 AF88 9981  ED5B C86B A06A 517D 0F0E
```

Now you are ready to unpack the archive. If you downloaded a bzip2 format archive file, execute the following command:

```
$ bunzip2 -c linux-2.4.22.tar.bz2 | tar -xf -
```

This command decompresses the archive file using `bunzip2` and pipes the output to the `tar` command, which extracts the archive. The operation might take some time to complete because bzip2 compression and decompression takes longer than the more familiar and faster gzip compression. If you downloaded the gzip formatted archive, the proper command to use is:

```
$ gunzip -c linux-2.4.22.tar.gz | tar -xf -
```

The end result of either command is a new directory named `linux-2.4.21` in the directory in which you decompressed and extracted the archive that contains version 2.4.22 of the Linux kernel source code.

Patching the Kernel

If you have already downloaded the main source code tree, you can save both bandwidth and time by downloading and applying patches. Patches contain only changes to the underlying files from one kernel version to the next. For example, if you downloaded the 2.4.8 kernel source code tree, you do not need to download the 2.4.9 source code, only the patch, which is named, in this case, `patch-2.4.9.tar.bz2`. If, alternatively, you have the source code for version 2.4.5, you need to download four patches (`patch-2.4.9.tar.bz2`, `patch-2.4.9.tar.bz2`, `patch-2.4.9.tar.bz2`, `patch-2.4.9.tar.bz2`) and apply them in sequential order. The following procedure illustrates the process:

1. Change directories to a directory to which you have write permission, for example, your home directory:

   ```
   $ cd ~
   ```

2. Open an FTP session to the archive site you selected and log in as the `anonymous` user using your e-mail address as the password:

```
# ftp ftp.us.kernel.org
220 ProFTPD 1.2.0pre10 Server (Global NAPs) [kernel.gnaps.com]
Name (ftp.us.kernel.org:root): anonymous
331 Anonymous login ok, send your complete e-mail address as password.
Password:
230 Anonymous access granted, restrictions apply.
Remote system type is UNIX.
Using binary mode to transfer files.
ftp>
```

3. Change directories to the kernel source code directory. The exact location of this directory varies from mirror to mirror, so you might have to use the `ls` command to locate it.

   ```
   ftp> cd /pub/linux/kernel
   ```

4. Change directories to the `v2.4` directory:

   ```
   ftp> cd v2.4
   ```

5. Execute the following command to see a listing of the full source code trees for the 2.4 kernel series (the listing is truncated to preserve space):

```
ftp> ls patch-2.4*
...
-rw-r--r--   1 root      kernel       785040 Aug 11 04:13 patch-2.4.8.bz2
-rw-r--r--   1 root      kernel          248 Aug 11 04:13 patch-2.4.8.bz2.sign
-rw-r--r--   1 root      kernel      1008692 Aug 11 04:13 patch-2.4.8.gz
-rw-r--r--   1 root      kernel          248 Aug 11 04:13 patch-2.4.8.gz.sign
-rw-r--r--   1 root      kernel       607194 Aug 16 18:32 patch-2.4.9.bz2
-rw-r--r--   1 root      kernel          248 Aug 16 18:32 patch-2.4.9.bz2.sign
-rw-r--r--   1 root      kernel       722077 Aug 16 18:32 patch-2.4.9.gz
-rw-r--r--   1 root      kernel          248 Aug 16 18:32 patch-2.4.9.gz.sign
```

6. Identify the file or files to download. In this case, we download the 2.4.22 patch file in bzip2 format, that is, `patch-2.4.9.tar.bz2`.

7. Make sure you are in binary download format:

   ```
   ftp> binary
   ```

8. Use the following commands to download the archive file and its MD5 checksum file (`patch-2.4.21.tar.bz2.sign`):

   ```
   ftp> get patch-2.4.22.bz2
   ftp> get patch-2.4.22.bz2.sign
   ```

9. Close the FTP session:

```
ftp> bye
```

10. Use the procedure described earlier to verify the downloaded file, substituting the appropriate file names.

The next step is to apply the patch. To do so, change directories to the directory in which you unpacked the kernel source code. So, for example, if you unpacked the kernel source code in your home directory, change to that directory. Next, execute the following command for each patch file, in sequential order:

```
$ bunzip2 -c patch-2.4.NN.bz2 | patch -p0
```

Replace *NN* with the patch number of each patch you want to apply. For this example, suppose we are patching from the kernel version 2.4.21 to 2.4.22. So we need to apply the patch that takes us to version 2.4.22. So, the command to execute is:

```
$ bunzip2 -c patch-2.4.22.bz2 | patch -d linux-2.4.21 -p1
patching file linux-2.4.21/CREDITS
patching file linux-2.4.21/Documentation/Configure.help
patching file linux-2.4.21/Documentation/DMA-mapping.txt
patching file linux-2.4.21/Documentation/SubmittingDrivers
...
patching file linux-2.4.21/net/unix/af_unix.c
patching file linux-2.4.21/net/wanrouter/wanmain.c
patching file linux-2.4.21/net/wanrouter/wanproc.c
patching file linux-2.4.21/net/x25/af_x25.c
```

The exact list of file names varies from patch to patch, and some patches change more files than others. The end result, however, is a kernel source tree updated to the latest version.

Finally, execute the following two commands to ensure you are working with a unblemished source code tree:

```
$ cd linux-2.4.21
$ make mrproper
make[1]: Entering directory `/home/kwall/linux-2.4.21/arch/i386/boot'
rm -f tools/build
rm -f setup bootsect zImage compressed/vmlinux.out
rm -f bsetup bbootsect bzImage compressed/bvmlinux.out
make[2]: Entering directory `/home/kwall/linux-2.4.21/arch/i386/boot/compressed'
rm -f vmlinux bvmlinux _tmp_*
make[2]: Leaving directory `/home/kwall/linux-2.4.21/arch/i386/boot/compressed'
...
```

```
rm -f .depend
rm -f /home/kwall/linux-2.4.20/scripts/mkdep-docbook
make[1]: Leaving directory `/home/kwall/linux-2.4.21/Documentation/DocBook'
$ cd ..
$ mv linux-2.4.21 linux-2.4.22
```

The `make mrproper` command removes any detritus remaining from previous kernel compiles — if you are starting from scratch, you can skip this step, but it does no harm to include it, either. After cleaning the source tree, we renamed the directory from `linux-2.4.21` to `linux-2.4.22`. At this point, you are ready, at length, to configure the kernel.

Building a Customized Kernel

Customizing the kernel involves two steps, choosing between building a modular or monolithic kernel, and then performing the actual kernel configuration. When configuring the kernel, you have two options for the device drivers needed to support various hardware devices in Linux:

◆ **Build device support directly into the kernel.** You can build the drivers for all hardware on your system into the kernel. As you can imagine, the size of the kernel grows as device driver code is incorporated into the kernel. A kernel that includes all necessary device driver support is called a *monolithic kernel.*

◆ **Use modules to provide device support.** You can create the necessary device drivers in the form of modules. A *module* is a block of code that the kernel loads and unloads on an as-needed basis while it is running. Modules enable you to add support for a device without having to rebuild the kernel for each new device you add to your system. Modules do not have to be device drivers; you can use them to add any sort of new functionality to the kernel. A kernel that uses modules is called a *modular kernel.*

As it happens, you do not have to choose between a fully monolithic or a fully modular kernel. Creating a hybrid kernel is a common practice. A *hybrid kernel* links some device support directly into the kernel while building other, infrequently used device drivers in the form of modules.

For distribution builders such as Red Hat, it makes sense to distribute a fully modular kernel. Red Hat provides a generic kernel along with a large number of modules to support many different types of hardware. The installation program configures the system to load only those modules needed to support the hardware installed in a user's system. The example shown in this chapter builds a hybrid kernel.

After choosing between a modular or monolithic kernel, you begin the configuration process proper. You can use one of three options for the configuration interface: an X Window System-based configuration tool, a text based GUI, or an interactive, command-line based tool. If you are running the X Window system, the recommended method is to use the command make xconfig. Components are listed in different levels of menus and are selected using a mouse. You can select Y (yes), N (no), or M (module). After choosing your components, click the Save and Exit button to create the configuration file, .config, in the top level kernel source code directory and exit the Linux Kernel Configuration program.

If you want to use the settings of a default Red Hat Linux kernel, copy a configuration file from the directory /usr/src/linux-2.4/configs to the directory in which you build the kernel. The copied file must be saved with the name .config. Next, run the make xconfig command and make only the desired changes. Be sure to save your changes to the configuration file. Other available methods for kernel configuration are listed below:

- make config — This configuration method presents kernel configuration options one at a time in a linear format and you answer them one at a time. This method does not require the X Window System and does not allow you to change your answers to previous questions.

- make menuconfig — This method uses a text-mode, menu-driven program to present kernel configuration components a menu of categories; you select the desired components in the same manner used in the text-mode Red Hat Linux installation program. Toggle the tag corresponding to the item you want included: [*] (built-in), [ ] (exclude), M (module or module capable). This method does not require the X Window system.

- make oldconfig — This is a noninteractive script that sets up your configuration file using the default settings from your current kernel configuration (if one exists). If there is a new setting that you have not previously configured, make oldconfig prompts you to configure that item. If you are using the default Red Hat Linux kernel, the script will create a configuration file for the kernel that shipped with Red Hat Linux for your architecture. This is useful for setting up your kernel with default values known to work — you can then turn off features that you do not want.

The end result is the same, so choose the interface with which you feel most comfortable. The example configuration that follows concentrates on the X-based configuration, but the overall process is the same for all three methods. Regardless of which method you choose, you must be in the linux directory created when you unpacked the source code archive before beginning:

```
$ cd ~/linux-2.4.22
```

Configuring a Custom Kernel

Type make xconfig to use an X Window system–based configuration program to configure the kernel. After a short pause, during which the GUI tool builds itself, you see a dialog box resembling Figure 24-3.

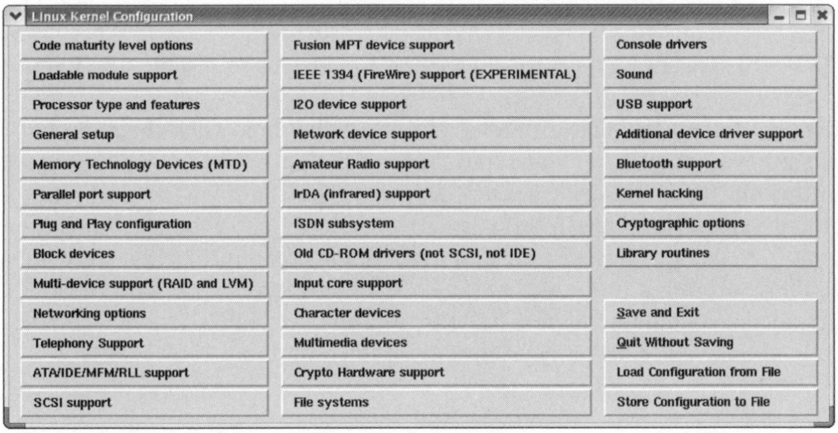

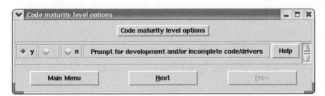

Figure 24–3: The Linux Kernel Configuration dialog box

To configure the kernel, click each button in the main dialog box and select the configuration options that suit your needs or liking. You will find it easiest to start with the Code maturity level options (see Figure 24-4).

Figure 24–4: The Code maturity level options dialog box

Some of the various things that Linux supports (such as network drivers, new hardware devices, network protocols, and so on) have not been adequately tested. Clicking Y in the Code maturity level options dialog box enables you to select and configure such options during the configuration process. Clicking N disables these features, and you will not be prompted for them. This option also makes obsolete drivers available, that is, old drivers that have been replaced by something else or that are scheduled to be removed in a future kernel release. You should probably click N here unless you enjoy living on the edge or running the risk of crashing your system.

As you configure the kernel, you have to select how to include support for specific devices. For many configuration options, you must choose one of the following:

- Click *y* to build support for a given option into the kernel or to accept a configuration option.

- Click *m* to use a module for the indicated device or option (not available for all configuration items).

- Click *n* to skip the support for that specific device or to disable that item.

For example, in the Code maturity level options dialog box, click the radio button next to *y* if you want to enable configuration dialog boxes for experimental features or incomplete device drivers. Click the n radio button if you do not want to see such dialog boxes. Note that in this case, if you select *y* and then click the Main Menu button to return to the main configuration dialog box, buttons that were previously disabled (or *greyed out*), such as the IEEE 1394 (FireWire) support (EXPERIMENTAL) and the Bluetooth support buttons, are now available. If a device does not have a modular device driver, you do not see the m option.

The kernel configuration discussed in this chapter does not illustrate configuring experimental kernel options.

For almost every option in a configuration dialog box, you can click the Help button to get detailed or additional information about the option in question. Figure 24-5 shows the configuration help for the sole option in the Code maturity level options dialog box. When you are done reading the help text, click the OK button to close the help screen.

After you have completed selecting the configuration options in a dialog box, click the Next button to proceed to the next dialog box. All dialog boxes except the first one enable you to click the Prev button to return to the previous dialog box, and all dialog boxes have a Main Menu button that returns you to the main Linux Kernel Configuration dialog.

The next few pages illustrate most of the main configuration dialogs and describe their purpose and the effect the options have on the compiled kernel. Due to space restrictions, all of the possible dialog boxes are not covered, nor are all of the possible configuration options. If you need additional information, use the Help button in the configuration dialogs.

Figure 24-6 shows the Loadable module support dialog box. As explained earlier in the chapter, kernel modules are small pieces of compiled code which can be inserted in or removed from a running kernel to add and remove support for infrequently used hardware devices and to enable and disable support for other types of functionality. If you want to use modules, click *y* for all three options. If you are unsure, you should still click *y* for all three options. Later in the configuration process, you need to identify which drivers and kernel functionality to build as modules, which to include in the kernel, and which to disregard completely.

If you click *y* for the third item, Kernel module loader, the kernel is able to load modules without requiring your intervention. Be sure to read the file `Documentation/kmod.txt` to learn how to configure `kmod`, the kernel module autoloader. Click Next to continue with the configuration.

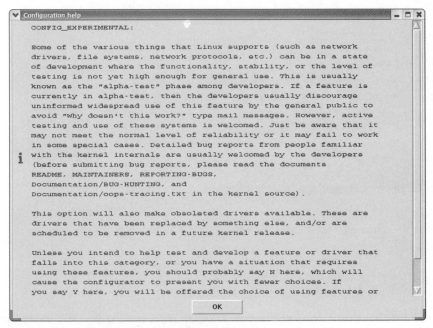

Figure 24-5: A Configuration help dialog box

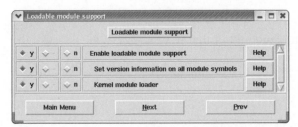

Figure 24-6: The Loadable module support dialog box

In the next dialog box, shown in Figure 24-7, you can customize the kernel for your particular CPU. Proceed cautiously here because you can easily create a kernel that doesn't boot. This information is used to configure the build process to optimize code generation to take advantage of specific CPU features. In order to compile a kernel that can run on any Intel x86 or x86-compatible CPU, click the 386 option.

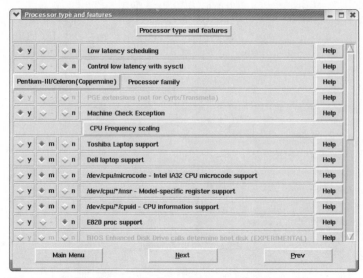

Figure 24–7: The Processor type and features dialog box

Here are the settings, taken from the help text, recommended for the best speed on a given CPU:

◆ 386 for the AMD/Cyrix/Intel 386DX/DXL/SL/SLC/SX, Cyrix/TI86DLC/ DLC2, UMC 486SX-S and NexGen Nx586 CPUs

◆ 486 for the AMD/Cyrix/IBM/Intel 486DX/DX2/DX4 or SL/SLC/SLC2/ SLC3/SX/SX2 and UMC U5D or U5S CPUs

◆ 586/K5/5x86/6x86/6x86MX for generic Pentium CPUs

◆ Pentium-Classic for the original Intel Pentium processors

◆ Pentium-MMX for the Intel Pentium MMX

◆ Pentium-Pro/Celeron/Pentium-II for the Intel Pentium Pro/Celeron/ Pentium II

◆ Pentium-III/Celeron(Coppermine) for the Intel Pentium III and Celerons based on the Coppermine core

◆ Pentium-4 for the Intel Pentium 4

◆ K6/K6-II/K6-III for the AMD K6, K6-II and K6-III (also known as K6-3D)

◆ Athlon/Duron/K7 for the AMD K7 family (Athlon/Duron/Thunderbird)

◆ Opteron/Athlon64/Hammer/K8

◆ Elan

◆ Crusoe for the Transmeta Crusoe series

◆ Winchip-C6 for original IDT Winchip

◆ Winchip-2 for IDT Winchip 2

◆ Winchip-2A/Winchip-3 for IDT Winchips with 3dNow! capabilities

◆ CyrixIII/C3 for VIA Cyrix III or VIA C3

◆ VIA-C3-2

Unless you have more than 1GB of physical RAM installed in your system, leave High Memory Support set to *off*. Similarly, if you have a uniprocessor system, then select *n* for Symmetric multiprocessing support. You can safely leave the other options at their default values as shown in Figure 24-7. Click Next to continue.

Figure 24-8 shows the CPU Frequency scaling dialog box. If you are configuring a kernel for a laptop computer, you can use this dialog to configure the CPU to reduce, or scale down, its power consumption when the system is idle. Frequency scaling saves battery life on laptop computers.

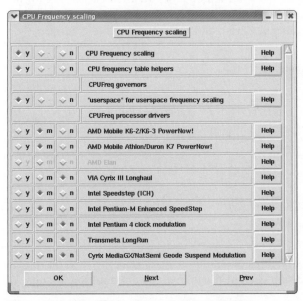

Figure 24-8: The CPU Frequency scaling dialog box

The General setup dialog box, shown in Figure 24-9, enables you to enable and disable a variety of miscellaneous kernel features. Again, the default values are reasonable for most systems. Click Next to continue.

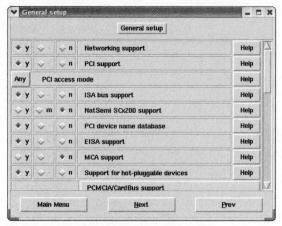

Figure 24-9: The General setup dialog box

If you are not configuring a kernel for a laptop, click Next when you get to the PCMCIA/CardBus support dialog (see Figure 24-10). Otherwise, configure support for your system's PCMCIA/CardBus device(s), and then click Next to continue.

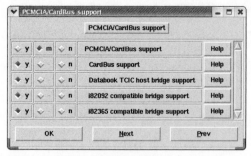

Figure 24-10: The PCMCIA/CardBus dialog box

If you do not use flash memory chips or similar devices, click the Next button in the appropriate dialog boxes to skip each of the following configuration dialogs:

◆ Memory Technology Devices (MTD)

◆ RAM/ROM/Flash chip drivers

◆ Mapping drivers for chip access

◆ Self-contained MTD device drivers

◆ NAND Flash Device Drivers

Eventually, you see the Parallel port support configuration dialog box, shown in Figure 24-11. You should click *y* or *m* for both the Parallel port support and PC-style hardware options if you want to use a printer, ZIP drive, or other device attached to your system's parallel port. Click Next to continue.

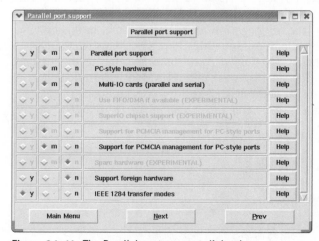

Figure 24–11: The Parallel port support dialog box

Figure 24-12 shows the Plug and Play configuration dialog box. Most modern PCs and PC BIOSes support the Plug and Play protocol, so click *y* or *m* for the Plug and Play support, and if you have any legacy ISA bus devices, click *y* or *m* for the ISA Plug and Play option. If you do not have ISA devices in your system, leave this option disabled (click *n*) and then click Next to continue.

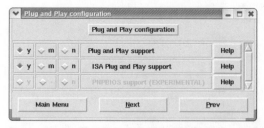

Figure 24–12: The Plug and Play configuration dialog box

The Block devices dialog box (see Figure 24-13) enables you to configure support for block devices such as disk drives, drives attached to the parallel port, a few RAID controllers (such as the Compaq SMART2 and Mylex RAID cards), and RAM disks, which are important if you need initrd (*Initial RAM Disk*) support, such as for booting from a SCSI disk. A *block device* is so-named because I/O to such a device occurs in groups, or blocks, of bytes, rather than one byte at a time as occurs with character devices, which read and write one character at a time.

At a bare minimum, click *y* or *m* for Normal PC floppy disk support (unless, for some reason, your system does not have a standard 3.5-inch floppy drive). If you have one of the parallel port IDE devices, click *m* for Parallel port IDE device support, and then click *m* next to the device you want to use. Be sure, in this case, to read the help text and note any conditions, qualifications, or caveats related to driver support for the selected device. Scroll down to the bottom of the dialog box and click *y* for RAM disk support, followed by *y* for Initial RAM disk (initrd) support if you know that you need an initial RAM disk (initrd) in order to boot — the easiest way to make this determination is to execute the command `ls -l /boot`. If you see a file name that begins with `initrd`, such as `initrd-2.4.2.img`, then you need initrd and RAM disk support. Click Next to continue.

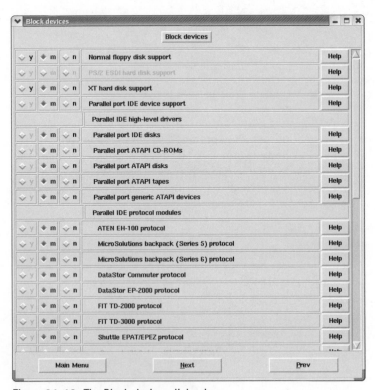

Figure 24–13: The Block devices dialog box

Figure 24-14 shows the configuration dialog for enabling kernel support for software RAID (Redundant Array of Inexpensive Disks) and for LVM (Logical Volume Management). Software RAID enables you to combine multiple hard disk partitions to create a single logical block device. It is called Software RAID because the kernel, rather than special hardware, implements the RAID functionality. LVM combines multiple devices in a volume group. A *volume group* is roughly analogous to a virtual disk. You can resize volume groups after creating them as your disk space capacity requirements change. For more information, read `Documentation/LVM-HOWTO`. Most people do not need this support, which is disabled by default.

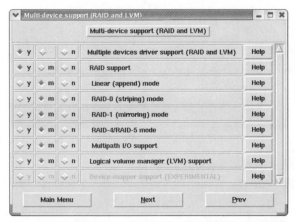

Figure 24-14: The Multi-device support (RAID and LVM) dialog box

The Networking options dialog box (see Figure 24-15) enables you to configure a wide array of networking options for your system. If you want to use programs like tcpdump, a packet sniffer that facilitates troubleshooting opaque network problems, click *y* or *m* for the Packet socket option. If you connect this system to the Internet and want to use a packet filter (firewall), click *y* to enable Network packet filtering, which enables you to use the Netfilter firewall feature, which replaces ipchains (the 2.2 kernel packet filter). Netfilter also enables you to use your Red Hat Linux system for IP masquerading. *IP masquerading*, also known as *NAT* or Network Address Translation, enables you to route all Internet traffic through a single system without requiring all systems to have valid Internet addresses (IPs) and without making the systems on the internal network visible to the Internet. Make sure, too that the following three options are enabled, because they provide standard networking functionality:

- ◆ Unix domain sockets

- ◆ TCP/IP networking

- ◆ IP: multicasting

Scroll down in the Networking options dialog box. Click *y* for IP: TCP syncookie support, which enables legitimate users to continue to use systems that are experiencing a SYN flood, a type of denial of service attack. If you do enable this option, you also need to enable `sysctl` and `/proc` file system support later in the configuration process (which you should do anyway) and add the following command to `/etc/rc.d/rc.local` or another initialization script:

```
echo 1 > /proc/sys/net/ipv4/tcp_syncookies
```

 Chapter 31 explains how to use iptables to create and maintain firewalls.

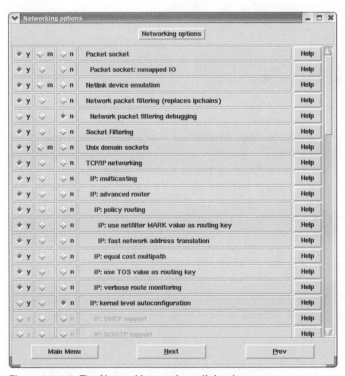

Figure 24–15: The Networking options dialog box

If you need support for IPX or the Appletalk protocols, enable those options as well, and then click Next to view the IP: Netfilter Configuration dialog box. If you intend to use IP masquerading, click *m* or *y* to enable the Connection tracking and IP tables support options. If you are building a modular kernel, click *m* for the following options:

◆ Packet filtering

◆ REJECT target support

◆ Full NAT

◆ MASQUERADE target support

◆ REDIRECT target support

◆ Packet mangling

◆ LOG target support

◆ ipchains (2.2-style) support

Click Next to bypass the IPv6: Netfilter Configuration, QoS and/or fair queuing, and the Telephony support dialog boxes.

When you get to the ATA/IDE/MFM/RLL dialog box, you should almost certainly click *y* here unless you have a *SCSI only* system, and then click Next to display the IDE, ATA and ATAPI Block devices dialog box, shown in Figure 24-16. Click *y* or *m* for Enhanced IDE/MFM/RLL disk/cdrom/tape/floppy support if you have any IDE devices that you want to use — if you want to boot from such a device, like an IDE disk drive, click *y* to build support into the kernel. You might want to enable PCM-CIA IDE support if your laptop uses PCMCIA devices. Scrolling down, you can disable and enable support for specific devices such as IDE CD-ROM and floppy drives, for bug fixes and workarounds for specific IDE chipsets that have known problems, such as the CMD640 or RZ1000 chipsets, and for a large number of specific chipsets and controllers. If you do not need such support, click *n*. The other values are fine at their defaults, so click Next to continue.

Figure 24-17 shows the SCSI support dialog box. This dialog box has a number of child dialog boxes that permit you to configure the low-level drivers pertaining to specific SCSI devices and controllers (see Figure 24-18), so take some time to review the information carefully, resorting to the help text if necessary. In particular, older SCSI controllers often need to have their I/O addresses and IRQ numbers specified in the kernel configuration dialog. Drivers for new controllers can usually autodetect the I/O addresses and IRQ numbers.

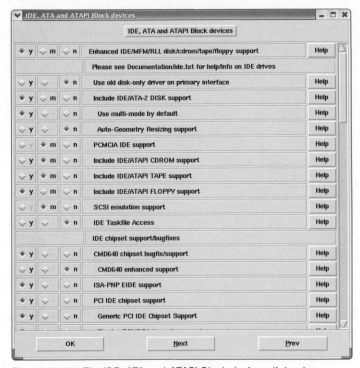

Figure 24-16: The IDE, ATA and ATAPI Block devices dialog box

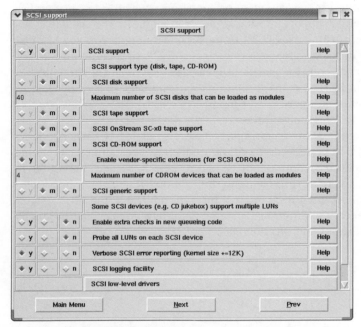

Figure 24-17: The SCSI dialog box

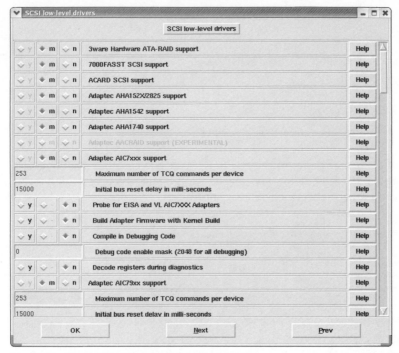

∨ y	◆ m	∨ n	3ware Hardware ATA-RAID support		Help	
∨ y	◆ m	∨ n	7000FASST SCSI support		Help	
∨ y	◆ m	∨ n	ACARD SCSI support		Help	
∨ y	◆ m	∨ n	Adaptec AHA152X/2825 support		Help	
∨ y	◆ m	∨ n	Adaptec AHA1542 support		Help	
∨ y	◆ m	∨ n	Adaptec AHA1740 support		Help	
∨ y	∨ m	∨ n	Adaptec AACRAID support (EXPERIMENTAL)		Help	
∨ y	◆ m	∨ n	Adaptec AIC7xxx support		Help	
253			Maximum number of TCQ commands per device		Help	
15000			Initial bus reset delay in milli-seconds		Help	
∨ y	∨	◆ n	Probe for EISA and VL AIC7XXX Adapters		Help	
∨ y	∨	◆ n	Build Adapter Firmware with Kernel Build		Help	
∨ y	∨	◆ n	Compile in Debugging Code		Help	
0			Debug code enable mask (2048 for all debugging)		Help	
∨ y	∨	◆ n	Decode registers during diagnostics		Help	
∨ y	◆ m	∨ n	Adaptec AIC79xx support		Help	
253			Maximum number of TCQ commands per device		Help	
15000			Initial bus reset delay in milli-seconds		Help	

OK   Next   Prev

Figure 24-18: The SCSI low-level drivers dialog box

Note that if you want to use an Iomega Zip drive that attaches to a parallel port, you should click *y* or *m* for SCSI support and SCSI disk support, and then enable support for either IOMEGA parallel port (ppa – older drives) or IOMEGA parallel port (imm – newer drives) depending on the type of Zip drive. Briefly, if your Zip drive came with a cable labeled "AutoDetect," click *n* to disable the ppa module and *m* to use the imm module). The good news is that both the ppa and imm drivers enable you to use both the Zip drive and a printer while running Red Hat Linux, just as you can with Windows.

Additional information on configuring and using Zip drives under Red Hat Linux is available in the README file for the ppa module, which is part of the kernel source code distribution (see *kerneldir*/drivers/scsi/ README.ppa, where *kerneldir* is the top-level directory of the kernel source tree) and also The Linux 2.4 SCSI subsystem HOWTO, which is available online at http://www.tldp.org/HOWTO/SCSI-2.4-HOWTO/ index.html.

The next few dialog boxes probably don't apply to you. They allow you to configure:

◆ PCMCIA SCSI adapters

◆ Fusion MPT SCSI adapters

◆ IEEE 1394 (FireWire) devices

◆ I2O (pronounced "eye square oh") devices

Keep clicking Next until you get the to the Network device support dialog box shown in Figure 24-19. This dialog box and its child dialog boxes enable you to configure NICs and other networking-related hardware.

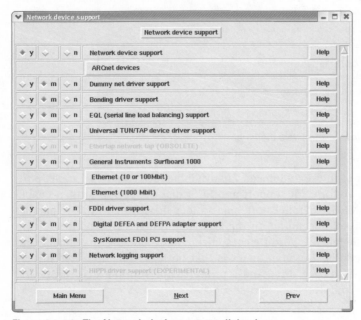

Figure 24-19: The Network device support dialog box

If you have a network card of any sort, click *y* for Network device support. The Dummy net driver support is not strictly required, but it does enable you to assign a configurable IP address to otherwise inactive PPP addresses, which can make programs requiring an Internet connection work properly. Because it does not increase the size of the kernel, click *m* or *y*. Enable FDDI support if you need support for fiber optic networking. PLIP (parallel port) support builds a module that enables you to create a network connection using the parallel port, but most people do not need this. If you are building a kernel on a system that connects to the Internet using a PPP (point-to-point protocol) connection, click *m* or *y* for PPP support and click *m* for the following options:

♦ PPP support for async serial ports

♦ PPP support for sync tty ports

♦ PPP Deflate compression

♦ PPP BSD-Compress compression

Leave SLIP (serial line) support disabled unless you use SLIP instead of PPP. Enable Fibre Channel driver support only if you need it. The dialog boxes for specific classes of network devices, such as ARCnet, Ethernet (10 or 100Mbit), Ethernet (1000Mbit), Token Ring devices, PCMCIA network device support, and so on, enable you to configure support for these devices if you need it. Although you can probably skip or ignore the dialog boxes for devices you do not use, it does not hurt anything to look at each one and make sure that support *is* in fact disabled for unnecessary devices. Each dialog box has an option at the top for disabling that category of device. Figure 24-20, for example, shows the Wireless LAN (non-hamradio) dialog box – notice that all wireless support is disabled (the configuration items are greyed out) because *n* is clicked for Wireless LAN (non-hamradio) support. Each class of networking devices can be similarly disabled. Use the Next button in each dialog to proceed sequentially through each class of devices.

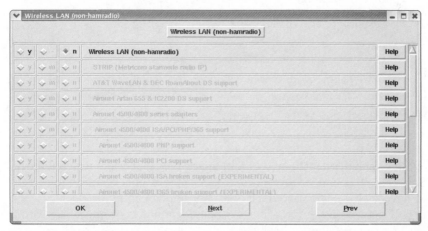

Figure 24-20: The Wireless LAN (non-hamradio) configuration dialog box

Figure 24-21 shows the configuration dialog box for 10 or 100MB Ethernet devices. Devices are organized by manufacturer, and then by make or model (and, in some cases, submodels). For instance, the system used for this chapter's example (see Figure 24-21) has an Intel EtherExpress Pro 100 NIC, so support for this particular card is being built as modules.

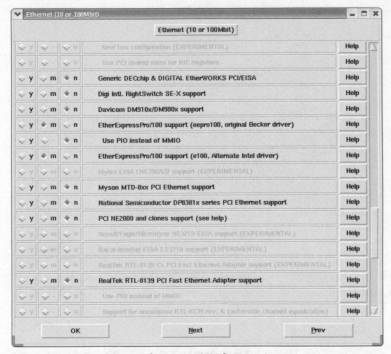

Figure 24-21: The Ethernet (10 or 100Mbit) dialog box

 You also might need specifically to disable PCMCIA network device support — for some reason, the kernel configuration enables this support on some systems, even if they do not have PCMCIA devices.

Before exiting the Ethernet (10 or 100Mbit) dialog box, make sure to scroll down to the EISA, VLB, PCI, and on board controllers option and click *n* (unless, of course, you have such a device, in which case, you should configure it).

The range of networking devices Linux supports continues to grow. The list of dialog boxes you can usually skip includes the following:

◆ Ethernet (1000 Mbit) – also known as Gigabit Ethernet

◆ Wireless

◆ Token Ring devices

◆ WAN (Wide Area Network) interfaces

- ◆ PCMCIA networking devices

- ◆ ATM (Asynchronous Transfer Mode) drivers

- ◆ Amateur Radio support

- ◆ IrDA (Infra Red networking)

- ◆ ISDN

If you need support for proprietary CD-ROM interfaces, such as the old Panasonic or Sound Blaster CD-ROMs, configure them appropriately using the Old CD-ROM drivers dialog box. *Do not use this box to configure SCSI or IDE CD-ROM drives!* You need this support only if you have one of the drives listed in the dialog box, and only older systems should need this support. Click the Next button to continue.

If you need support for USB (Universal Serial Bus) input devices, such as mice, keyboards, or joysticks, click *m* or *y* for the Input core support option when you see the Input core support dialog box (see Figure 24-22), and then click *m* for the device you want to use. If you need support for a USB digitizer or graphic tablet, click *m* for Mouse support and then provide the horizontal and vertical screen resolution values in the corresponding check boxes. Click the Next button to continue.

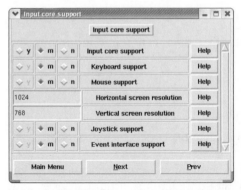

Figure 24-22: The Input core support dialog box

Figure 24-23 shows part of the configuration dialog box for character devices, which includes serial ports, keyboards (strictly speaking, TTYs), printers, mice, joysticks, tape drives, special purpose chips and devices such as watchdog cards and clock chips, and a selection of video adapters. You can also configure such devices that are provided by PCMCIA cards. Only the top of the dialog is shown because it is rather long – character devices are the primary means of interacting with a Linux system, so the array of supported devices is mind-numbingly long.

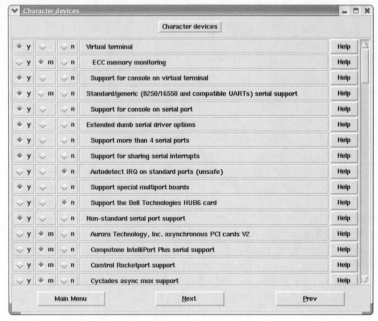

Figure 24-23: The Character devices dialog box

At a bare minimum, make sure that the first three configuration options are enabled:

◆ Virtual terminal

◆ Support for console on virtual terminal

◆ Standard/generic (8250/16550 and compatible UARTs) serial support

If you have a special serial card, such as a multiport serial device, click *y* for Non-standard serial port support to enable the configuration of those devices, and then select your devices from the long list of support hardware and configure it appropriately. The defaults for Unix98 PTY support should be sufficient. If you intend to use a printer attached to this system, click *m* or *y* for Parallel printer support. Support for special-purpose devices, such as the enhanced real-time clock or the hardware random number generator, is optional. Read the help text if you want to experiment with these features.

Continuing further down the character devices dialog box, the next set of options, for motherboard and graphics chipsets, is also optional. AGP (Accelerated Graphics Support) GART (Graphics Aperture Relocation Tables) support enables XFree86 to use AGP graphics acceleration for 3D display, a nice feature if your video hardware supports it. If you enable this support and have one of the support graphics chipsets, enable support for the graphics chipset and edit your XFRee86 configuration file to load the GLX module. You must also have a supported graphics chipset if you want to enable the Direct Rendering Manager, which provides kernel support for XFree86 4.1's DRI (Direct Rendering Infrastructure), which permits direct access to video hardware and results in significant performance increases for OpenGL 3D graphics. When you have completed configuring the primary character device support options, click the Next button to continue.

The next series of dialog boxes enable you to configure character devices subsets. Unless you know you need I2C support, click Next to skip the dialog box. If you use a mouse (most users do), especially PS/2 mouse support, enable this support by clicking *y* or *m* in the Mice dialog box, and then click Next. Similarly, configure joystick support and support for various watchdog cards if you need it. The Ftape configuration dialog box enables you to configure support for a wide variety of floppy tape devices. Click Next to proceed. Finally, if you need to support PCMCIA character devices, use the PCMCIA character devices configuration to configure support for PCMCIA serial devices, and then click Next to continue.

Figure 24-24 shows the first of the series of Multimedia devices configuration dialog boxes. As usual, only enable support and configure devices you have or use, clicking Next to skip unnecessary devices.

If you have cryptographic hardware, then you will likely want to enable kernel support for it, if possible, in the Crypto Hardware dialog box (see Figure 24-25). If you *do* have cryptographic acceleration hardware, you know who you are (and *They* know who you are, too!). Otherwise, click the Next button to continue.

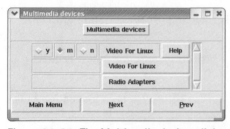

Figure 24-24: The Multimedia devices dialog box

Figure 24-25: The Crypto Hardware dialog box

The primary File systems configuration dialog box, shown in Figure 24-26, enables you to configure support for the file systems you expect to use or access from your system. New in Red Hat Linux is support for the ext3 file system, which includes journaling and other high-end features. Read Chapter 4 to find out how to work with the ext3 file system and take advantage of its features and benefits, and how to avoid potential problems and known pitfalls.

If you intend to use file system quotas, as described in Chapter 21, click *y* to enable Quota support. Click *m* or *y* for Kernel automounter version 4 support (also supports v3) if you want to mount and unmount file systems on the fly. Similarly, if you need to access various DOS or Windows file systems, click *m* or *y* for DOS FAT fs support and for MS-DOS and VFAT file systems. As a general rule, build non-Linux file system support as modules to minimize the size of the kernel. Other file systems you may want to enable include:

◆ Virtual memory file system support – enables the kernel to utilize swap disks and swap files

◆ ISO 9660 CD-ROMs – enables kernel support for the standard CD-ROM file system

◆ Microsoft's Joliet extensions – enables the kernel to support Microsoft Windows long file name extensions for CD-ROMs

◆ /proc file systems support – enables applications to utilize the proc interface to kernel tuning and information

◆ /dev/pts for Unix98 PTYs – enables kernel support for the standard Unix-style terminal interface

◆ ext2 – enables kernel support of the ext2 file system, the current native Linux file system

◆ ext3 – enables the kernel to support the ext3 file system, a journaling version of the ext2 file system

Click Next to continue, which brings up the Network File Systems configuration dialog box, shown in Figure 24-27. I recommend enabling support for NFS (Network File System) version 3, which has considerable improvements and better kernel support for NFS, so click *y* for Provide NFSv3 client support and Provide NFSv3 server support.

Chapter 11 discusses NFS server and client configuration in detail. Chapter 13 explains how to use Samba to access Windows file systems.

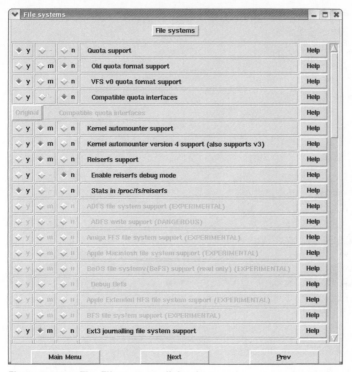

Figure 24-26: The File systems dialog box

If you want to use Samba to access Windows file systems, click *m* or *y* for SMB file system support (to mount Windows shares, and so forth). Similarly, click *m* or *y* for NCP file system support if you need to mount Netware file systems, and then select the specific options for Netware file systems as fits your situation. When you are done, click Next to continue.

In addition to support for foreign (non-Linux) file systems, you will find it advantageous to configure the kernel to provide support for foreign partition types. After clicking *y* for Advanced partition selection on the Partition Types dialog, select the specific partition types you want to use by clicking *y* next to the appropriate partition types listed in the dialog box. When you have finished, click Next to continue, which brings up the Native Language Support configuration dialog box. Here, click *m* or *y* to load the code page for your particular locale or language, and then click Next to continue, which opens the Console drivers configuration dialog box, shown in Figure 24-28.

Click *y* to enable both VGA text console and Video mode selection support. The latter option enables you to use the `vga=` kernel option to select the high resolution text modes your video adapter most likely supports. The file `Documentation/svga.txt` in the kernel source code tree explains how to use this feature in greater detail. Click Next to continue the configuration process.

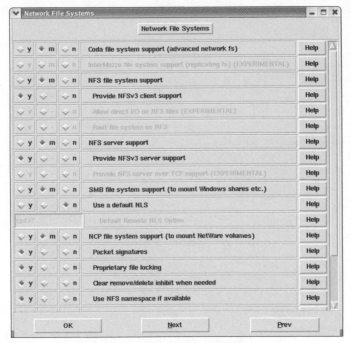

Figure 24-27: The Network File Systems dialog box

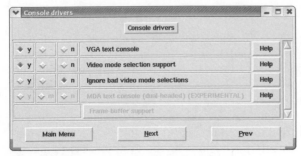

Figure 24-28: The Console drivers dialog box

Use the Sound configuration dialog box (see Figure 24-29) to configure support for your sound card, if any. Because the kernel now supports an amazingly wide array of sound cards, it simply is not possible to describe each option in this space. Locate the device or chipset for which you need support, enable it, and be sure to read and understand the help text and any supporting documentation to ensure that you can take full advantage of your sound card. If the list does not include a driver for your particular card, you might be able to use the OSS (Open Sound System) modules to run your sound card. To do so, click *m* or *y* for OSS sound modules (scroll down the dialog box to find this option), and then click *m* or *y* to build the module or modules for your card. Click Next to continue.

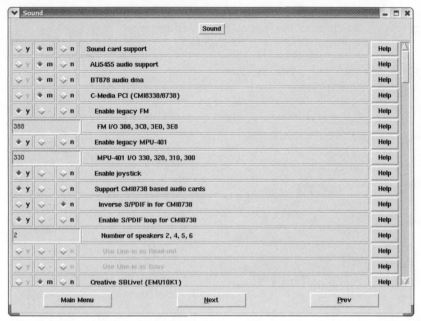

Figure 24-29: The Sound dialog box

Figure 24-30 shows the USB support dialog box. Select the devices you need to support, and then click Next to continue.

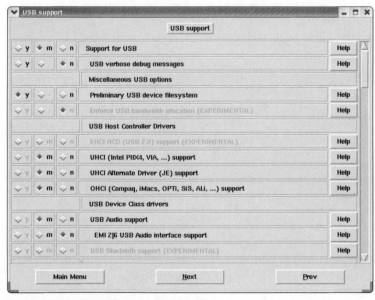

Figure 24-30: The USB support dialog box

Figure 24-31 shows the final configuration option, the Kernel hacking dialog box. Unless you will be hacking the kernel, leave this option set to *n*.

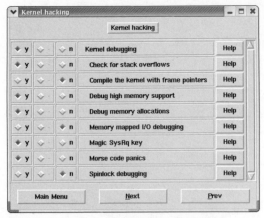

Figure 24-31: The Kernel hacking dialog box

Click Main Menu to return to the primary Linux Kernel Configuration dialog box (see Figure 24-3). At this point, you are ready to save the configuration and proceed with compiling the kernel. To do so, use the following procedure, which includes a precautionary step, saving a backup copy of the configuration options you have just spent some time selecting:

1. Click Store Configuration to File to save a backup copy of the configuration file to a file *outside* of the kernel source code tree. In Figure 24-32, for example, the file is being saved to `/home/kwall/config-2.4.9`.

Figure 24-32: Saving the kernel configuration to a backup file

2. Click Save and Exit to save the configuration file where the build process can find it.

3. After reading the Kernel build instructions dialog box (see Figure 24-33), click OK to close it and exit the kernel configuration.

Figure 24–33: The Kernel build instructions dialog box

4. Unless you are interested in using other kernel configuration interfaces, continue with the section titled "Compiling and Installing the New Kernel."

CONFIGURING THE KERNEL USING make menuconfig

Type make menuconfig to configure the kernel configuration using a text mode menu interface. The configuration options are the same as those provided by the make xconfig X interface, but the interface itself is slightly different. The initial screen resembles Figure 24-34.

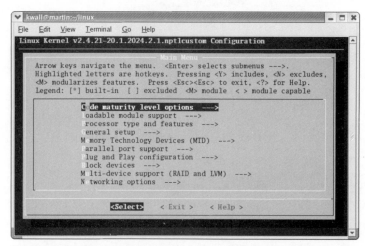

Figure 24–34: The initial text mode kernel configuration menu

The following list shows the keystrokes you can use:

- ◆ Use the arrow keys to move the blue highlight cursor up and down the menu.

- ◆ Highlighted letters are hotkeys.

- ◆ To select an item, press Enter.

- ◆ Submenus are indicated by `--->`.

◆ To enable a configuration option, press *y* or ***.

◆ To disable a configuration option, press *n*.

◆ Configuration items preceded by angle brackets (<>) can be built as modules.

◆ Press *m* to build options as modules.

◆ Press *?* or use the Help button to view the help text for a given option.

◆ Press the Tab key to move the cursor from the menu to the buttons at the bottom and to move between the buttons.

For example, use the arrow key to move the cursor down to the `Networking options ---> selection`. Then press Enter to open the submenu, which is shown in Figure 24-35.

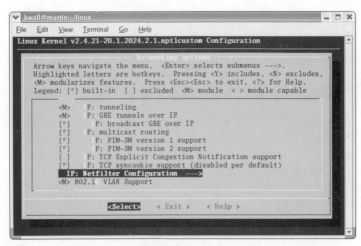

Figure 24-35: The Networking options configuration menu

The `TCP syncookie support (disabled per default)` option has an `*` next to it, meaning it has been enabled. The other options have not been included or enabled. The `IP: tunneling` and `IP: GRE tunnels over IP` options have (empty) <>, meaning that they can be built as modules by pressing *m* or built into the kernel by typing *y* or *** (see Figure 24-36). Many of the so-called submenus have submenus of their own. In Figure 24-35, for example, the `IP: Netfilter Configuration --->` option indicates the existence of a subsubmenu, as it were. Pressing Enter results in Figure 24-36, the IP: Netfilter Configuration menu. Note that all of the options on this menu are being built as modules, as indicated by the M in the angle brackets next to each option.

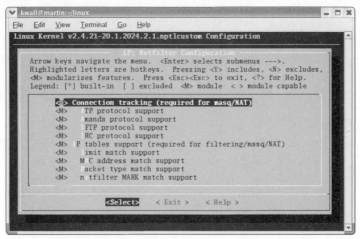

Figure 24-36: The IP: Netfilter Configuration submenu

When you have completed the configuration process, use the Exit button to exit the configuration menus – you may have to press it several times. Before it exits, the configuration tool gives you the option to save the changes, as shown in Figure 24-37. Highlight the Yes button, and press Enter to save the new configuration (or No to abandon it) and exit the utility. At this point, you are ready to build and install the kernel as explained in the section titled "Compiling and Installing the New Kernel."

Figure 24-37: Save the kernel configuration before exiting the configuration tool.

CONFIGURING THE KERNEL USING make config

Type make config to use a text-based program that prompts you for each configuration option one by one. When you use this option, you undergo a long question-and-answer process to specify the configuration process. As with the other kernel configuration methods, you have to select how to include support for specific devices and features. For most configuration options, you must type one of the following choices:

- ◆ *y* to build support into the kernel

- ◆ *m* to use a module

- ◆ *n* to skip the support for that specific device

- ◆ *?* to get help on that kernel configuration option

If a device does not have a modular device driver, you do not see the m option. For some configuration options, you may have to type a specific answer. For example, when responding to the processor type, you type Pentium to indicate that you have a Pentium PC. When you complete the configuration process, use the instructions in the next section to compile and install the kernel.

Compiling and Installing the New Kernel

Regardless of the configuration interface you used, the next step is to execute make dep to recompute the kernel's dependencies properly, and then to build the kernel, the modules, and to install the kernel and modules. Here are the steps to follow:

1. In the top-level directory of the kernel source tree ($HOME/linux in this example), execute the following commands:

```
$ make dep
$ make bzImage
```

TIP When we build the kernel, we prefer to see only the error messages in order to make it easier to track down build errors, so we redirect stdout to a file and use tee to copy stderr to a file while displaying on the screen, too. For example, to build the kernel image, the command we use is:

```
make bzImage > bzImage.log 2>| tee bzImage.err
```

If you want to save both stdout and stderr to the same file, which places errors in the context of standard kernel compilation output, use the following command line:

```
make bzImage > bzimage.log 2>&1
```

2. If you opted to build a modular or hybrid kernel as described earlier, execute the following command in order to build the modules:

```
$ make modules
```

Assuming nothing has gone awry, the kernel built successfully and you are ready to install the new kernel and, if necessary, the modules.

3. The next few commands require root privileges, so use su to become the root user:

```
$ su
Password:
#
```

4. Make a backup copy of your existing kernel in case the new kernel does not boot properly.

5. Copy the new kernel into place:

```
# cp linux/arch/i386/boot/bzImage /boot/vmlinuz-2.4.22
```

6. If you opted to build a modular or hybrid kernel, install the modules:

```
# make modules_install
```

7. If you need an initial RAM disk (usually because your boot device is a SCSI disk), create it using mkinitrd:

```
# mkinitrd -v /boot/initrd-2.4.22.img 2.4.22
```

The next step is to configure your bootloader, GRUB or LILO, to boot the new kernel, as described in the next section.

Configuring the Boot Loader

The kernel RPM package configures the GRUB or LILO boot loader to boot the newly installed kernel if either boot loader is installed. However, it does not configure the boot loader to boot the new kernel by default. It is always a good idea to confirm that the boot loader has been configured correctly. This is a crucial step. If the boot loader has been configured incorrectly, you will not be able to boot your system. If this happens, boot your system with the boot diskette you created earlier and try configuring the boot loader again.

GRUB

If you selected GRUB as your boot loader, confirm that the file /boot/grub/grub.conf contains a title section with the same version as the kernel package you just installed (if you installed the kernel-smp and/or kernel-bigmem packages, you will have a title section for that package as well):

```
# NOTICE:    You have a /boot partition.    This means that
#            all kernel paths are relative to /boot/
default=0
timeout=30
splashimage=(hd0,0)/grub/splash.xpm.gz
title Red Hat Linux (2.4.22)
        root (hd0,0)
        kernel /vmlinuz-2.4.22 ro root=/dev/hda3
        initrd /initrd-2.4.22.img
```

If you created a separate /boot partition, the paths to the kernel and initrd image are relative to the /boot partition.

To configure GRUB to boot the new kernel by default, change the value of the default variable to the title section number for the title section that contains the new kernel. The count starts with 0. For example, if the new kernel is the second title section, set the default to 1. You can begin testing your new kernel by rebooting your computer and watching the messages to ensure that your hardware has been detected properly.

LILO

If you selected LILO as your boot loader, confirm that the file /etc/lilo.conf contains an image section with the same version as the kernel package you just installed:

```
boot=/dev/had
map=/boot/map
install=/boot/boot.b
prompt
timeout=50
message=/boot/message
linear
default=linux

image=/boot/vmlinuz-2.4.22
        label=linux
        initrd=initrd-2.4.22.img
        read-only
        root=/dev/hda5
```

The kernel RPM package activates the changes by running the command /sbin/lilo. To configure LILO to boot the new kernel by default, set the default variable to the value of label in the image section for the new kernel. You must run the /sbin/lilo command as root in order to enable the changes. After running it, you will see output similar to the following:

```
Added linux *
```

The * character after the word `linux` means that the section labeled `linux` is the default kernel that LILO will boot. You can begin testing your new kernel by rebooting your computer and watching the messages to ensure your hardware has been detected properly.

Summary

Access to the source code and the ability to rebuild the kernel or upgrade the kernel is one of Linux's biggest points of popularity. This chapter discussed why you might want to build a new kernel and why you might *not* want to build a new kernel. You learned how to install new binary kernel RPMs and how to download pristine kernel source code. Finally, the chapter walked you through the kernel configuration process, compiling a kernel, creating a new initial RAM disk image, and configuring the new kernel to boot. Chapter 25 describes how to configure your system using command line tools.

Chapter 25

Configuring the System at the Command Line

IN THIS CHAPTER

♦ Administering your system from the command line

♦ Administering users and groups

♦ Managing processes

♦ Maintaining the file system

♦ Tracking and controlling system usage

♦ Maintaining the date and time

♦ Automating system maintenance

THIS CHAPTER EXPLAINS how to use command line programs to perform system and network administration tasks. Using GUI tools for system administration is convenient when such tools are available, but they are not always available and often fail to offer a complete interface to subsystem administration. In fact, many GUI administration tools are little more than graphical wrappers around the command line programs you learn to use in this chapter.

System Administration at the Command Line

Why should you learn how to administer your Red Hat Enterprise Linux system from the command line? First, although the range of GUI system and network administration tools available for Red Hat systems continues to grow in both number and sophistication, not all administrative tasks have a matching GUI tool, and the available tools are often incomplete, out-of-date, or as unintuitive and awkward to use as the command line programs they attempt to replace.

Secondly, GUI tools are not always available. Red Hat systems installed strictly as server machines, rather than desktop or end user workstations, rarely run the X Window System, much less have it installed. They are not only *headless*, that is, lack an attached monitor, they usually lack an attached keyboard or mouse. Running the X Window System on a server uses CPU cycles, RAM, disk space, process table entries, and file descriptors, better used to provide another service. Moreover, underpowered systems may lack the horsepower to run the X Window System, and thus GUI tools.

Another shortcoming of graphical tools is, ironically, the very user friendliness that makes them so popular. That is, graphical administration tools *require* user interaction – they do not readily, if at all, lend themselves to automated, unattended execution. They are rarely scriptable or support the capability for making bulk changes, such as adding 25 user accounts in a single operation. On the other hand, you rarely find a command line tool that *cannot* be scripted in order to facilitate bulk system changes or that *cannot* be automated using cron or another scheduling utility.

 To be fair, in cases in which GUI tools are available, they can usually be used via X tunneling in ssh (ssh's -X option), which makes it possible to use GUI tools to administer a remote system.

Automating and simplifying system administration cannot be underestimated. In a small environment with few users, workstations, and servers, the inability to script GUI configuration and administration tools may not be an issue. However, system maintenance becomes a challenge even at the top end of the SOHO (*Small Office/Home Office*) sector, say 25 users and workstations, 2 or 3 servers, and half a dozen printers. At large installations with multiple servers, dozens or hundreds of users and workstations, plus all of the associated administrative overhead, administrators, and there are usually several, *must* be able to make bulk changes and perform system maintenance and administration unattended and automatically. To do otherwise is inefficient and impractical.

 The second half of this chapter shows you how to write Bash shell scripts and use scripts to automate system administration tasks.

Finally, graphical administration tools, by their very nature, encourage uninformed or ill-informed system administration habits. GUI tools deliberately hide complex, often unintuitive configuration files and commands behind an attractive, convenient interface. Hiding the complexity does not make it disappear, though. In fact, it may make it worse because you never learn how a service really works, how to troubleshoot a misbehaving daemon, or how to customize a program's behavior using command line options the GUI tool does not support. In some cases, thankfully less common, GUI tools interfere with system administration tasks because, for example, the modifications they make to a configuration file overwrite your own changes.

Should you use graphical system administration tools? Absolutely. They are helpful, convenient, and timesaving additions to every system administrator's toolbox. Not every problem is a nail, so you need more tools than a hammer. GUI tools are only *one* of many tools at your disposal. You do yourself, your employer, your colleagues, and your users a valuable service if you take the time to understand the details of system administration. Think of it this way: if the graphical utility for configuring a mission-critical service stops working for some reason, do you *really* want to tell your boss you do not know how to fix it? You need to know how to use the perfectly serviceable command line utility.

The following sections discuss user and group administration, working with processes, file system management, monitoring and controlling system performance, configuring the system logs, keeping the system's date and time accurate, and writing and using scripts to perform maintenance tasks. Because many commands can be used by both normal users and the root user, discussion focuses on usage and options pertinent to administrative needs.

Administering Users and Groups

The commands covered in this section concern user and group management. Commands used for working with users and groups fall into three broadly defined categories: creating, modifying, and deleting user accounts; creating, modifying, and deleting group accounts; and displaying current and historical login and usage information.

 Chapter 26 discusses user and group management in detail. Please refer to that chapter for examples of using the commands discussed in this section.

Working with User Accounts

One of the most common administrative tasks is working with user and group accounts. The commands you use most often are:

- `useradd` – Create user login accounts
- `userdel` – Delete user login accounts
- `usermod` – Modify user login accounts
- `passwd` – Set or change account passwords

◆ `chsh` — Set or change a user's default shell

◆ `chage` — Modify password expiration information

The `useradd` command creates new user accounts and, when invoked with the `-D` option, modifies the default values applied to new accounts. As a result, it can be invoked in two ways. The syntax of the first form is:

```
useradd [-c comment] [-d home_dir] [-e expire_date]
        [-f inactive_time] [-g initial_group]
        [-G group[,...]] [-m [-k skeleton_dir] | -M]
        [-p passwd] [-s shell] [-u uid [-o]]
        [-n] [-r] username
```

The first form creates a new user account named *username*. Optional values not specified using options are assigned default values drawn from `/etc/login.defs` and `/etc/default/useradd`. Table 25-1 lists the options `useradd` accepts.

TABLE **25-1** USERADD OPTIONS AND ARGUMENTS

Option	Description
-c *comment*	Uses *comment* for the name field
-d *home_dir*	Names the new user's home directory *home_dir*
-e *expire_date*	Sets the account's expiration date to *expire_date*
-f *inactive_time*	Disables the account *inactive_time* days after the password expires
-g *initial_group*	Sets the user's primary group membership, or *login group*, to *initial_group*
-G [*group*[,...]]	Makes the user a member of each supplemental group *group*
-m	Creates the home directory if it does not exist and copies the files and directory structure in /etc/skel to the new directory
-k *skeleton_dir*	Copies the files and directory structure in *skeleton_dir*, not /etc/skel, to the new home directory; must be specified with -m
-M	Disables creation of the home directory; cannot specify -m and -M
-p *passwd*	Sets the account password to the encrypted password *passwd*

Option	Description
-s *shell*	Sets the user's default shell to *shell*
-u *uid*	Sets the user's UID (User ID) to *uid*, which must be a unique number
-o	Allows the UID specified with -u *uid* not to be unique; must be specified with -u
-n	Disables use of Red Hat's user private groups
-r	Creates a system account (an account with a UID less than 100) but does not create a home directory
username	Sets the login name to *username*

The adduser program is a symbolic link to useradd.

The second way to invoke useradd uses the -D option. Invoked with only -D, useradd displays its current default settings. Using -D with any of the options listed in Table 25-2 modifies the default value for the corresponding field. Here is the syntax for the second form:

```
useradd -D [-g default_group] [-b default_home_dir]
        [-f default_inactive_time] [-e default_expire_date]
        [-s default_shell]
```

useradd's default values are stored in /etc/default/useradd.

TABLE 25-2 OPTIONS FOR CHANGING USERADD DEFAULTS

Option	Description
-g *default_group*	Sets the default group to *default_group*
-b *default_home_dir*	Sets the default home directory to *default_home_dir*

Continued

<small>TABLE</small> **25-2 OPTIONS FOR CHANGING USERADD DEFAULTS** *(Continued)*

Option	Description
-f *default_inactive_time*	Sets the default account disable time to *default_inactive_time* days
-e *default_expire_date*	Sets the default account expiration date to *default_expire_date*
-s *default_shell*	Sets the default login shell to *default_shell*

The `userdel` command deletes a user account and, optionally, related files. Its syntax is:

```
userdel [-r] username
```

username identifies the user account to delete. Using -r deletes the corresponding home directory and mail spool. Without -r, `userdel` removes only the account references in the user and group database files. You cannot delete the account of a logged in user, so `userdel` fails if *username* is logged in.

The `usermod` command modifies an existing user account. Its syntax is:

```
usermod [-c comment] [-d home_dir [-m]] [-e expire_date]
        [-f inactive] [-g initial_group]
        [-G group[,...]] [-l new_username] [-p passwd]
        [-s shell] [-u uid [-o]] [-L|-U] username
```

`usermod` accepts the options and arguments listed in Table 25-1 for `useradd` and adds three new ones, -l *new_username*, -L and -U. -l *new_username* changes the account name from *username* to *new_username*. -L disables (locks) *username*'s account by placing a ! in front of the user's encrypted password in /etc/shadow. -U enables (unlocks) the account by removing the !. At least one option must be specified, but -p, -U, and -L may not be used together in any combination. If *username* is logged in, `usermod` fails because you cannot change the login name of a logged in user.

The `passwd` command, generally regarded as "the password changing utility," actually has more capabilities than merely changing passwords. In general, it updates all of a user's authentication tokens, of which the login password is only one. Its syntax is:

```
passwd [-dkluf] [-S] username
```

-d removes the password for *username*, disabling the account. -k causes passwd to update only expired authentication tokens (passwords, in this case). -l or -u lock or unlock, respectively, *username*'s password by placing and removing a ! in front of *username*'s password in /etc/shadow. The -S option, finally, displays a short status message about *username*, indicating whether the account is locked or unlocked, the kind of encryption used, and so forth.

Another very handy method to set or change a password is to use the passwd option with the openssl command. The openssl command provides a command line interface to the cryptography functions made available in the OpenSSL libraries. One of the options the openssl command supports is passwd, which you can use to generate hashed passwords. The command to use is openssl passwd -1, which prompts you for a password, prompts you again to verify it, and then displays a hashed version of the password suitable for use in the /etc/shadow password file. For example:

```
$ openssl passwd -1
Password:
Verifying - Password:
$1$vhr1Mh7u$a1FJTM3UrHGz31bWh18Ppl
```

You can use the displayed password as the input to the passwd command to change a user's password:

```
# echo '$1$vhr1Mh7u$a1FJTM3UrHGz31bWh18Ppl' | passwd --stdin bubba
Changing password for user bubba
Passwd: all authentication tokens updated successfully.
#
```

This command pipes the password through the passwd command. When used with the --stdin option, passwd reads its input from stdin rather than interactively at the keyboard. Notice that the echo command embeds the password in single quotes because the password contains shell metacharacters that must be protected from expansion (metacharacters and other shell arcana are discussed later in this chapter).

The chsh command changes a user's login shell. Its syntax is:

```
chsh [-s shell ] [-l] [username]
```

-s *shell* sets *username*'s login shell to *shell*. Unless configured otherwise, *shell* can be the full pathname of any executable file on the system. One common way to take advantage of this feature is to disable an account by setting shell to /bin/false or another command that does not give the user a login prompt. Using the -l option displays the shells listed in /etc/shells.

The chage command changes the expiration policy for a user's password. Its syntax is:

```
chage [-1] [-m mindays] [-M maxdays] [-d lastday] [-I inactive]
      [-E expiredate] [-W warndays] username
```

Table 25-3 lists the valid options that chage accepts.

TABLE 25-3 OPTIONS FOR THE CHAGE COMMAND

Option   Description

Option	Description
username	Specifies *username* as the account name to query or modify
-1	Displays expiration information for *username*
-m *mindays*	Sets *mindays* days as the minimum amount of time permitted between password changes
-M *maxdays*	Sets *maxdays* days as the maximum number of days a password is valid
-d *lastday*	Sets *lastday* as the date on which the password was last changed, expressed as the number of days elapsed since 1 January 1970. *lastday* can be set using a more convenient date format, such as June 21, 2003, or 2003-0621
-I *inactive*	Sets *inactive* days as the number of days *username*'s account may be inactive *after* the password has expired before the account is locked
-E *expiredate*	Sets *expiredate* as the date on which *username*'s account expires
-W *warndays*	Sets *warndays* as the number of days before the password expires that a warning message is issued

---

If no options are used, chage goes into interactive mode, prompting the user for each item of information.

Working with Group Accounts

The commands for working with group accounts are:

- ◆ groupadd – Creates a group account
- ◆ groupdel – Deletes a group account
- ◆ groupmod – Modifies a group account

In large part, the group account administration commands parallel the interface of user administration commands with similar names, except that the group commands have fewer command line options.

To create a new group, call groupadd, passing it at least the name of the new group. Its syntax is:

```
groupadd [-g gid [-o]] [-rf] group
```

group is the name of the group to create. -g gid sets the GID of the new group to gid, which must be unique. If -o is specified with -g, gid does *not* have to be unique. The -r option creates a system group account, one with a GID below 100. If the group named group already exists, groupadd refuses to create the account and exits with an error. The (poorly chosen) -f option suppresses this error message (the duplicate group is not created).

To delete a group, use the command groupdel group, where group is the name of the group you want to delete. You cannot delete a user's primary group, however, which poses a problem in isolated cases because Red Hat Linux uses a user private groups permissions scheme.

Chapter 26 describes Red Hat's user private group convention in detail.

groupmod changes a group's GID or its name. Its syntax is:

```
groupmod [-g gid [-o]] [-n new_group_name ] group
```

group indicates the group to modify, -g gid sets the group's GID to gid, and -n group_name renames group to new_group_name. -o permits gid to be nonunique.

Modifying Multiple Accounts Simultaneously

As remarked at the beginning of the chapter, one of the advantages of command line tools is that they can be used to perform bulk or mass changes. Two commands, chpasswd and newusers, make multiple changes to the user password database in a single operation.

The newusers command creates new user accounts and updates existing ones in a batch operation. It takes a single argument, the name of a file listing the accounts to create or modify, one per line. Each line has the same format as the entries in /etc/passwd:

```
username:password:uid:gid:gecos:homedir:shell
```

If *username* already exists, newusers ignores *uid*. *password* must be plain text (newusers encrypts it at run time). Similarly, for new and existing users, *newusers* creates *homedir* if it does not exist.

The chpasswd command updates existing user passwords *en masse*. It reads a file consisting of colon-separated *username:password* pairs. *password* must be plain text, which will be encrypted at run time, unless chpasswd is invoked with the -e option, in which case *password* must already be encrypted using a crypt(3)-compatible encryption algorithm.

Type man 3 crypt to learn more about how the password is encrypted.

Viewing Login and Process Information

To view current and past login information and to determine what processes users are running, you can use one of the following commands:

◆ last – Displays historical login information

◆ who – Displays information about currently logged in users

◆ w – Displays a user's currently running process

last prints the username, tty, date, time, elapsed time, and the hostname or IP address of the remote host, if applicable, from which the login originated of all user logins, starting with the most recent login. Its syntax is:

last [-R | [-ai]] [-*num* |-n *num*] [*username*] [*tty*]

By default, last lists all the entries in /var/log/wtmp, so you can use -*num* and -n *num* to specify the number of output lines to display. Ordinarily, last displays the hostname in the third column, but using -a places the hostname in the rightmost column, -i shows the hostname's IP address, and -R completely suppresses display of the hostname. To view the login activity of a specific user, use the *username* argument. *tty* enables you to view logins per TTY. Multiple *username*s and *tty*s can be listed.

The who command displays information about currently logged in users. Its default output includes the username, login TTY, and the date and time each user logged in. who's syntax is:

who [-Hil] | [-q]

Using the -H option adds column headings to who's output. Specifying -i adds each user's idle time to the display. Use -l to force who to show complete FQDNs (Fully Qualified Domain Names). To obtain the total number of logged in users, use the -q option by itself.

The w command is very similar to who, except that it also displays the command line of each user's currently running process and a summary of each user's CPU usage. w's syntax is:

```
w [-husf] [username]
```

By default, w prints header information when it starts; -h disables the header. -s generates a short output format that omits the login time and the CPU usage. -f disables displaying the host from which users are logged in. Specifying *username* lists only *username*'s login session and process information.

Managing Processes

Administering processes includes identifying, monitoring, controlling, modifying, and obtaining a variety of information about them. The ps, top, and kill commands are the most familiar commands used for working with processes, but there are others that are more focused and, especially in the case of the ps command, probably easier to use. This section looks at three categories of commands:

◆ Commands used to obtain process information

◆ Commands used to send signals, usually the kill signal (SIGKILL), to processes

◆ Commands used to modify running processes

Obtaining Process Information

Process information is easy to obtain, if you know how to get it. The commands discussed in this section include the following:

◆ ps – Displays process status

◆ pgrep – Lists the PIDs of processes matching a given pattern

◆ pidof – Displays the PID of the process running a specified program

◆ pstree – Displays processes in a hierarchical format

◆ top – Displays process information and status on an ongoing basis

◆ tload – Displays a text mode load average graph

Tables 25-4 through 25-7 borrow the layout of ps's syntax description from its manual page and organize each group of options into tables based on the options' purpose. However, the following tables omit all GNU long options (those preceded with --) and options related to defining custom output formats. ps supports both Unix98 options, which are preceded by a hyphen (-), and BSD options, which lack the initial -. Where the functionality is identical or very similar, the BSD options have been omitted. In some cases, apparently identical Unix98 and BSD are listed because the BSD option shows different output from the similarly invoked Unix98 option.

TABLE 25-4 BASIC PROCESS SELECTION

Option	Description
-N	Negates the selection criteria specified with other options
-a	Selects all processes with a TTY except session leaders
-d	Selects all except session leaders
-e	Selects all processes
T	Selects all processes on the invoking terminal
r	Selects only running processes
x	Selects processes without controlling TTYs

TABLE 25-5 PROCESS SELECTION BY CATEGORY

Option	Description
-C *command*	Selects by command name matching pattern *command*
-G *rgid* | *name*	Selects by RGID (Real Group ID) *rgid* or group *name*
-U *ruid* | *name*	Selects by RUID (Real User ID) *ruid* or user *name*
-p *pid*	Selects by PID *pid*
-u *euid* | *name*	Selects by EUID (Effective User ID) *euid* or user *name*
p *pid*	Selects by PID *pid* and displays command line
U *name*	Selects processes for user *name* and displays command line

TABLE 25-6 STANDARD OUTPUT FORMATS

Option	Description
-f	Displays full listing
-j	Displays output in jobs format
-l	Displays output in long format
j	Displays output in job control format
l	Display long output format
s	Displays output in signal format
v	Displays output in virtual memory format

TABLE 25-7 MODIFYING OUTPUT FORMAT

Option	Description
-H	Show process hierarchy (forest)
-w	Wide output
C	Use raw CPU time for %CPU instead of decaying average
S	Include some dead child process data (as a sum with the parent)
c	True command name
e	Show environment after the command
f	ASCII-art process hierarchy (forest)
h	Do not print header lines (repeat header lines in BSD personality)
w	Wide output

If ps's plethora of options and arguments seems daunting, the pgrep command provides relief because it provides a simpler interface, enabling you to select processes using simple pattern matching. It lists the PIDs (Process IDs) of processes matching the specified pattern. You can then use those PIDs with ps's p or -p options to obtain more information, if you wish. pgrep's syntax is:

pgrep [-flnvx] [-P ppid] [-u euid] [-U uid] [-G gid] [pattern]

If you specify multiple criteria, the selected processes match *all* criteria, so keep the selection criteria as simple as possible. *pattern* contains the expression to match against process names or command lines. -f matches *pattern* against the process name (the default if -f is not specified) or the full command line. -l causes pgrep to list both the PID and the process name. If multiple processes match *pattern* and other criteria, -n limits the output to the most recently started process. -v reverses the matching, showing all processes not matching the specified criteria. -x forces an exact match of *pattern*. -P *ppid* restricts the output to matches with a parent PID of *ppid*. Similarly, -u *euid*, -U *uid*, and -G *gid*, limit the output to processes whose EUIDs, UIDs, and/or GIDs, respectively, match *euid*, *uid*, and/or *gid*, respectively. Multiple *ppid*s, *euid*s, *uid*s, and *gid*s may be specified by separating each with commas.

pidof enables you to locate the PID of a process by name. Its syntax is:

pidof [-s] [-x] [-o *pid*] *program*

program is the base name of the program whose PID(s) you want to find. You can specify multiple *program*s by separating their names with whitespace. -s returns only the first PID located, additional PIDs are ignored. -x causes pidof to return the PID(s) of shell scripts running *program*. -o *pid* lists one or more PIDs that pidof should ignore (omit).

pstree displays all running processes as a tree, making clear the parent/child relationships between processes. Its syntax is:

pstree [-a] [-c] [-H *pid*] [-n] [-p] [-G] [*basepid* | *baseuser*]

Called with no arguments, pstree shows all processes, with init as the root. Specifying *basepid* or *baseuser* begins the display from the PID specified by the PID *basepid* or the user name *baseuser*, respectively. -a includes the command line for each process. -c expands identically named child processes (such as the mingetty instance spawned for each terminal). -H *pid* highlights the PID *pid* and its ancestor (parent) processes. If *pid* does not exist, pstree exits with an error. -n sorts the output by PID (the default is by ancestry). -p causes each process's PID to display and implies -c. -G, finally, draws the tree using the VT100 drawing characters rather than the default ASCII characters |, +, -, and `.

top displays real time CPU and memory usage and current system uptime information. Although it is an interactive command, top is a vital tool in every system administrator's toolbox, so its command line interface (not its interactive use) is covered here.

top [-bcisqS] [-d *delay*] [-p *pid*] [-n *iter*]

-d *delay* specifies the number of seconds between screen updates (default is 5), and -q specifies constant updates, which run at the highest priority if used by the root user. -p *pid* identifies up to twenty PIDs in whitespace delimited *pid*s to monitor. `top` continues to run unless `-n` *iter* is specified, *iter* defining the number of iterations `top` refreshes its display before exiting (0 is interpreted as 1). `-S` enables cumulative mode, in which each process's CPU time is shown as a sum and includes the CPU time of any dead child processes. Of course, for a child process's time to count, it must have died. `-s` runs `top` in secure mode and disables potentially dangerous commands in the interactive interface, such as k, which can kill processes. `-i` instructs `top` to omit idle or zombie processes from its display. `-b`, finally, runs `top` in batch mode and runs until specifically killed or until the number of iterations specified with `-n` have elapsed (all other command line input ignored).

`tload` displays a real-time text mode graph of the system's *load average*, which is the number of processes waiting to run during the last minute, the last five minutes, and the last fifteen minutes. Its syntax is:

```
tload [-s scale] [ -d delay ] [tty]
```

`tload` displays its graph to the current terminal, unless *tty* is specified, when it then becomes `tload`'s output target. `-d` *delay* sets the delay between graph updates to *delay* seconds (if *delay* is 0, the graph never updates). `-s` *scale* sets the vertical height of the graph in *scale* characters. Thus, the smaller the value of *scale*, the larger the scale.

Terminating Processes

"Signaling processes" might be a better title for this section, because the commands it discusses (see the following list), can be used to send any signal, not just one of the kill signals, to a running process. Kill signals are the most common, of course, but the complete list of *possible* signals is significantly longer. The commands this section covers include

- ◆ `kill` — Sends a signal to a process
- ◆ `pkill` — Kill or send another signal to a process matching a given pattern
- ◆ `killall` — Kill processes by name

Most Linux users are familiar with the `kill` command. Note, however, that most shells, including Bash, have a built-in `kill` command. The shell's `kill` is executed before `/bin/kill` in most shells because they execute built-in commands, aliases, and functions, where applicable, before using a command in the PATH. The discussion here covers the `kill` command `/bin/kill`, not the shell command. `kill`'s syntax is:

```
kill [-s signal | -p] [-a] [--] pid
kill -l
```

pid is one or more whitespace delimited tokens specifying the processes to kill. Each token can be a PID (where *pid* > 0); a process name; -1, which kills all processes with PIDs between 2 and 35,767; or -*pid*, which kills all processes in the process group whose PGID (Process Group ID) is *pid*. If you specify -a, all processes matching *pid* are killed (only root may use -a). -p lists only the PID; no processes are killed. -s *signal* indicates the signal to send; *signal* can be either a numeric or symbolic name, as shown with kill -1.

pkill, which has a comparable call interface to pgrep, sends a signal to one or more processes matching a given pattern. Its syntax is:

```
pkill [-signal] [-fnvx] [-P ppid] [-u euid] [-U uid] [-G gid]
[pattern]
```

If you specify multiple criteria, the selected processes match *all* criteria, so keep the selection criteria as simple as possible. *pattern* contains the expression to match against process names or command lines. -*signal* specifies the numeric or symbolic signal to send (SIGTERM is the default). -f matches *pattern* against the process name (the default if -f is not specified) or the full command line. If multiple processes match *pattern* and other criteria, -n sends the signal to the most recently started process. -v reverses the matching, showing all processes not matching the specified criteria. -x forces an exact match of *pattern*. -P *ppid* sends the signal to processes whose parent process has a PID of *ppid*. Similarly, -u *euid*, -U *uid*, and -G *gid* send the signal to processes whose EUIDs, UIDs, and/or GIDs, respectively, match *euid*, *uid*, and/or *gid*, respectively. Multiple *ppid*s, *euid*s, *uid*s, and *gid*s may be specified by separating each with commas.

killall kills all processes matching a name. Its syntax is:

```
killall [-1] | [-giqvw] [-signal] name
```

Specifying -1 lists the numeric value and symbolic names of all recognized signals, and it cannot be used with any other options or arguments. *name* lists the command whose process should be signaled. Multiple *name*s may be specified if separated by whitespace. -*signal* specifies the signal to send; SIGTERM is the default. -g kills the process group to which *name* belongs. -i runs killall in interactive mode and requests confirmation for each *name* signaled. -q suppresses error messages if no processes match *name*. -v displays a short message if the signal was sent successfully. -w instructs killall to wait for each *name* to die.

Modifying Process Priorities

In some cases, it is not necessary to terminate a process, but simply to modify the priority at which it runs. The following two commands accomplish this goal.

- ♦ nice — Starts a program with a given scheduling priority
- ♦ renice — Alters the scheduling priority of one or more running processes

The `nice` command enables you to start a program with a higher or lower nice number, which controls how much CPU time the kernel gives a program relative to other programs with the same priority. The `nice` command's syntax is:

`nice [-n value | -value] [prog [arg]]`

prog is the program to run. *arg* lists the arguments to *prog*, and is specified using the format *prog* understands. *value* expresses the modified nice number at which to run *prog*. Valid values for *value* are -20 to 19, smaller values representing a higher priority relative to other programs.

Use the `renice` command to modify the CPU scheduling priority of a running process. Its syntax is:

`renice priority [[-p] pid] [[-g] pgrp] [[-u] user]`

priority expresses the new nice number at which to run the specified process(es). `-p` *pid* identifies the processes to modify by PID. `-g` *pgrp* modifies all processes in the process group *pgrp*. `-u` *user* causes all processes owned by *user* to run at the new *priority*.

Part II of this book is entirely devoted to network configuration, so we have omitted discussion of network configuration commands in this chapter and cover the material in the relevant chapters of Part II.

Maintaining the File System

A significant portion of administrative time and effort involves file system maintenance. These tasks include modifying existing file systems, creating new ones, fixing broken ones, monitoring all of them, and ensuring that users do not monopolize any of them. The file system maintenance commands this section covers have been divided into three categories: commands for creating and maintaining file systems, commands for working with files and directories, and commands for managing disk space usage.

Creating and Maintaining File Systems

Unless you have an extremely active system, creating and formatting a file system is an infrequent necessity. Actively *maintaining* a file system, however, is an ongoing process. The commands for creating, formatting, and checking the integrity of Red Hat Linux file systems discussed in this section are:

- ◆ fdisk — Creates, deletes, and modifies hard disk partitions

- ◆ me2kfs — Creates a file system on a device

- ◆ e2fsck — Checks, and optionally repairs, a Linux file system

- ◆ symlinks — Validates, and optionally repairs, symbolic links

- ◆ mount — Mounts a file system

- ◆ umount — Unmounts a file system

- ◆ mkswap — Creates a swap partition or file

- ◆ swapoff — Disables a swap partition or file

- ◆ swapon — Enables a swap partition or file

The fdisk program prepares hard disks to hold Linux file systems. It is an inter-active program and accepts few command line options. You can invoke it using one of the following forms:

```
fdisk -s partition
fdisk [-lu] device
```

The first form uses the -s option to display the size in (blocks) of the disk parti-tion specified by *partition* and then exits. The second form operates on the disk specified by device. The -l option, lists the disk geometry of *device*, followed by a columnar list of each partition on *device* that shows each partition's boot status, starting and ending cylinders, total size (in 512 byte blocks), and the partition type. If device is omitted, fdisk lists the same information based on the contents of the file /proc/partitions. The -u option instructs fdisk to show disk and partition sizes in terms sectors instead of cylinders. Omitting -l (second form) starts an interactive fdisk session on *device*.

mke2fs creates a Linux ext2 file system on a disk. Its syntax is:

```
mke2fs [-c | -l list] [-b size] [-i bytes-per-inode] [-n]
       [-m reserve] [-F] [-q] [-v] [-L label] [-S] device
```

device indicates the disk partition or other device on which to create the file system. Specifying -n results in a test run; mke2fs goes through the entire creation process but does not actually create the file system. Use -q to suppress output, for example, when mke2fs is used in a script. Conversely, use -v to generate verbose output.

To check the disk for bad blocks while creating the file system, specify -c, or use -l *list* to read a list of known bad blocks from the file named *list*. By default, mke2fs calculates file system block sizes based on the size of the underlying parti-tion, but you can specify -b *size* to force a block size of 1024, 2048, or 4096 bytes.

Similarly, to override the default inode size, use `-i bytes-per-inode` (*bytes-per-inode* should be no smaller than the block size defined with `-b size`). `-m reserve` instructs mke2fs to make *reserve* percent of the file system for the root user. If `-m reserve` is omitted, the default reserve space is 5%. `-L label` sets the file system's volume label, or name, to *label*.

Normally, mke2fs refuses to run if *device* is not a block device (a disk of some sort) or if it is mounted; `-F` overrides this default. `-F` is most commonly used to create a file that can be mounted as a loopback file system. `-S`, finally, causes mke2fs to write only the superblocks and the group descriptors and to ignore the block and inode information. In essence, it attempts to rebuild the high level file system structure without affecting the file system contents. It should be used only as a final attempt to salvage a badly corrupted file system, and may not work. The manual page recommends running e2fsck immediately after using `-S`.

e2fsck checks a file system for possible corruption and repairs any damage found. Its syntax is:

```
e2fsck [-pcnyfvt] [-b sblock] [-B size] [-l list] device
```

device is the partition (/dev/hda1, for example) to test. `-b sblock` tells e2fsck to use the backup superblock located on block number *sblock*. `-B size` specifies block sizes of *size* bytes. `-l list` instructs e2fsck to add the block numbers listed in the file name *list* to the list of known bad blocks. Using `-c` causes e2fsck to identify bad blocks on the disk. Ordinarily, e2fsck asks for confirmation before repairing file system errors; specifying `-p` disables any confirmation prompts, `-n` automatically answers "No" to all questions and sets the file system read-only, and `-y` automatically answers "Yes" to all questions. e2fsck's default behavior is not to check a file system that is marked clean, but using `-f` forces it to do so. `-v` enables verbose output. `-t` generates a timing report at the end of e2fsck's operation.

The symlinks command scans directories for symbolic links, displays them on the screen, and repairs broken or otherwise malformed symbolic links. Its syntax is:

```
symlinks [-cdrstv] dirlist
```

dirlist is a list of one or more directories to scan for symbolic links. `-r` causes symlinks to recurse through subdirectories. `-d` deletes dangling links, symbolic links whose target no longer exists. `-c` converts *absolute links*, links defined as an absolute path from /, to *relative links*, links defined relative to the directory in which the link is located. `-c` also removes superfluous / and . elements in link definitions. `-s` identifies links with extra ../ in their definition and, if `-c` is also specified, repairs them. To see what symlinks would do without actually changing the file system, specify `-t`. By default, symlinks does not show relative links; `-v` overrides this default.

To make an existing file system available, it has to be mounted using the mount command. mount's syntax is:

```
mount -a [-fFnrsvw] [-t fstype]
mount [-fnrsvw] [-o fsoptions] device | dir
mount [-fnrsvw] [-t fstype] [-o fsoptions] device dir
```

The first two forms use the information in /etc/fstab when mounting file systems. Invoked with no options, mount lists all mounted file systems, and specifying only -t fstype lists all mounted file systems of type fstype. fstype will be one of devpts, ext2, iso9660, or vfat, but many other file system types are supported – the complete list of valid types is available in mount's manual page.

The -a option mounts all the file systems listed in /etc/fstab (subject to restriction using the -t option as explained in the previous paragraph) that are configured using the auto mount option (see Table 25-6). The second form is most commonly used to override the mount options, using -o fsoptions, listed in /etc/fstab. Note that you only have to specify device, the device containing the file system, or dir, where in the directory hierarchy the file system should be attached.

Use the third form to mount file systems not listed in /etc/fstab or to override information it contains. The third form is also the most widely used. In general, it attaches the file system on device to the system's directory hierarchy at the mount point dir, using a file system type of fstype and the file system options fsoptions. Table 25-8 lists mount's global options. fsoptions is a comma-delimited list of one or more of the options listed in Table 25-9.

Because Linux supports so many file systems, this chapter discusses only a few of the many file systems and file system options. mount's manual page contains a complete list of the file systems and their corresponding mount options that Linux currently supports.

TABLE 25-8 GLOBAL OPTIONS FOR THE MOUNT COMMAND

Option	Description
-a	Mounts all file systems, subject to restrictions specified using -t
-F	Mounts all file systems (used only with -a) in parallel by creating new processes for each file system to mount
-f	Fakes the mount operation, doing everything but actually mounting the file system
-h	Displays a short usage message

Option	Description
-n	Mounts the file system without creating an entry in the mount table (/etc/mtab)
-o fsoptions	Mounts the file system using the file system-specific options fsoptions
-r	Mounts the file system in read-only mode
-s	Ignores options specified with -o that are invalid for the given file system type (the default is to abort the mount operation)
-t fstype	Restricts mount's operation to file system types of type fstype (first and second forms) or specifies the file system type of the file system being mounted (third form)
-v	Prints informational messages while executing (verbose mode)
-w	Mounts the file system in read-write mode

TABLE 25-9 COMMON FILE SYSTEM OPTIONS FOR THE MOUNT COMMAND

Option	Type*	Description
async	1	Enables asynchronous system I/O on the file system
auto	1	Enables mounting using the -a option
defaults	1	Enables the default options (rw, suid, dev, exec, auto, nouser, async) for the file system
dev	1	Enables I/O for device files on the file system
exec	1	Enables execution of binaries on the file system
gid=gid	2,3	Assigns the GID gid to all files on the file system
mode=mode	3	Sets the permissions of all files to mode
noauto	1	Disables mounting using the -a option
nodev	1	Disables I/O for device files on the file system
noexec	1	Disables execution of binaries on the file system

Continued

TABLE 25-9 COMMON FILE SYSTEM OPTIONS FOR THE MOUNT COMMAND
        (Continued)

Option	Type*	Description
nosuid	1	Disables set-UID and set-GID bits on the file system
nouser	1	Permits only root user to mount the file system
ro	1	Mounts the file system in read-only mode
remount	1	Attempts to remount a mounted file system
rw	1	Mounts the file system in read-write mode
suid	1	Enables set-UID and set-GID bits on the file system
sync	1	Enables synchronous file system I/O on the file system
user	1	Permits nonroot users to mount the file system
uid=*uid*	2,3	Assigns the UID *uid* to all files on the file system

1=All file systems, 2=devpts, 3=iso9660

To unmount a file system, use the command umount. Its syntax is much simpler, thankfully, than mount's:

```
umount -a [-nrv] [-t fstype]
umount [-nrv] device | dir
```

All of umount's options and arguments have the same meaning as they do for mount, except for -r. Of course, the options must be understood in the context of unmounting a file system. If -r is specified and unmounting a file system fails for some reason, umount attempts to mount it in read-only mode.

To create and manipulate swap space, use the mkswap, swapon, and swapoff commands. mkswap initializes a swap area on a device (the usual method) or a file. swapon enables the swap area for use, and swapoff disables the swap space. mkswap's syntax is:

```
mkswap [-c] device [size]
```

device identifies the partition or file on which to create the swap area and *size* specifies the size, in blocks, of the swap area to create. *size* is necessary only if you want a swap area smaller than the available space. If *device* is a file, it must already exist and be sized appropriately. -c performs a check for bad blocks and displays a list of any bad blocks found.

TIP   To create a swap file before using `mkswap`, use the following command:

`dd if=/dev/zero of=/some/swap/file bs=1M count=128`

Replace `/some/swap/file` with the file you want to create as a swap file.

To enable the kernel to use swap devices and files, use the `swapon` command. Its syntax takes three forms:

```
swapon -s
swapon -a [-ev]
swapon [-p priority] [-v] device
```

The first form displays a summary of swap space usage for each active swap device. The second form, normally used in system startup scripts, uses `-a` to activate all swap devices listed in `/etc/fstab`. If `-e` is also specified, `swapon` ignores devices listed in `/etc/fstab` that do not exist. The third form activates the swap area on `device`, and, if `-p priority` is also specified, gives `device` a higher priority in the swap system than other swap areas. `priority` can be any value between 0 and 32,767 (specified as 32767), where higher values represent higher priorities. `-v` prints short status messages.

To deactivate a swap area, use the `swapoff` command. Its syntax is simple:

```
swapoff -a | device
```

Use `-a` to deactivate all active swap areas, or use `device` to deactivate a specific swap area. Multiple swap areas may be specified using whitespace between `device` identifiers.

Working with Files and Directories

This section reviews the basic call syntax of the following commands:

- ◆ `chmod` — Modifies file and directory permission settings
- ◆ `chown` — Modifies file and directory user ownership
- ◆ `chgrp` — Modifies file and directory group ownership
- ◆ `lsattr` — Lists special file attributes on `ext2` files
- ◆ `chattr` — Modifies special file attributes on `ext2` files
- ◆ `stat` — Shows detailed file information
- ◆ `fuser` — Displays a list of process IDs using a file
- ◆ `lsof` — Identifies files opened by a process

Here are the syntax summaries for chmod, chown, and chgrp:

```
chmod [-cfRv] symbolic-mode file
chmod [-cfRv] octal-mode file
chown [-cfhRv] owner[:[group]] file
chown [-cfhRv] :group file
chgrp [-cfhRv] group file
```

chmod, chown, and chgrp accept the common options -c, -v, -f, -R, and *file*. *file* is the file or directory to modify and multiple *file* arguments can be specified. -R invokes recursive operation on the subdirectories and of *file*; -v generates a diagnostic for each file or directory examined; while -c generates a diagnostic message only when it changes a file. -f cancels all but fatal error messages.

chmod has two forms because it understands both symbolic and octal notation for file permissions. For both forms, *file* is one or more files on which permissions are being changed. *symbolic-mode* uses the symbolic permissions notation, while *octal-mode* expresses the permissions being set using the standard octal notation.

For a quick refresher on using octal and symbolic permissions notation, refer to the chmod manual page.

With the chown and chgrp commands, *group* is the new group being assigned to *file*. For the chown command, *owner* identifies the new user being assigned as *file*'s owner. The colon (:) enables chmod to change *file*'s group ownership. The format *owner:group* changes *file*'s user and group owners to *owner* and *group*, respectively. The format *owner:* changes only *file*'s owner and is equivalent to chown *owner file*. The format *:group* leaves the owner untouched but changes *file*'s group owner to *group* (equivalent to chgrp *group file*).

The lsattr and chattr commands are Linux-specific, providing an interface to special file attributes available only on the ext2 file system. lsattr lists these attributes, and chattr sets or changes them. lsattr's syntax is:

```
lsattr [-adRVv] file
```

file is the file or directory whose attributes you want to display; multiple whitespace separated *file* arguments may be specified. -a causes the attributes of all files, such as hidden files, to be listed. -d lists the attributes on directories, rather than listing the contents of the directories, and -R causes lsattr to recurse through subdirectories if *file* names a subdirectory.

chattr's syntax is:

```
chattr [-RV] [-v version] +|-|=mode file
```

file is the file or directory whose attributes you want to display; multiple whitespace separated *file* arguments may be specified. -R causes lsattr to recurse through subdirectories if *file* names a subdirectory. -v *version* sets a version or generation number for *file*. +*mode* adds *mode* to *file*'s attributes; -*mode* removes *mode* from *file*'s attributes; =*mode* sets *file*'s attributes to *mode*, removing all other special attributes. *mode* can be one or more of the following:

- ◆ A — Do not change file's time (last access time)

- ◆ S — Update *file* synchronously

- ◆ a — *file* is append-only

- ◆ c — Kernel automatically compresses/decompresses *file*

- ◆ d — *file* cannot be dumped with the dump command

- ◆ I — *file* is immutable (cannot be changed)

- ◆ s — *file* will be deleted securely using a special secure deletion algorithm

- ◆ u — *file* cannot be deleted

The stat command displays detailed file or file system status information. Its syntax is:

stat [-l] [-f] [-t] *file*

file specifies the file or directory about which you want information. Use multiple whitespace delimited *file* arguments to specify multiple files. If -l is used and *file* is a link, stat operates on the link's target (the file that is linked) rather than the link itself. Using -f causes stat to display information about *file*'s file system, not *file*. Specifying -t results in a shorter (terse) output format suitable for use in scripts.

Often, an administrator needs to identify the user or process that is using a file or socket. fuser provides this functionality. Its syntax is:

fuser [-a | -s] [-n *namespace*] [-*signal*] [-kimuv] *name*

name specifies the file, file system, or socket to query. By default, fuser assumes that *name* is a file name. To query TCP or UDP sockets, use -n *namespace*, where *namespace* is udp for UDP sockets and tcp for TCP sockets (file is the default *namespace*). -a results in a report for all *name*s specified on the command line, even if they are not being accessed by any process. -s, on the other hand, causes fuser to run silently (do not use -s with -a, -u, or -v). -k kills processes using *name* with the signal SIGKILL; use -*signal* to specify an alternate signal to send. Use -i (interactive) to be prompted for confirmation before killing a process. Only use -i with -k. -m indicates that *name* specifies a file system or block device, so fuser lists all processes using files on that file system or block device. -u adds the user name of a process's owner to its output when listing processes. -v, finally, generates a verbose, ps-like listing of processes using the specified *name*.

lsof performs the reverse function from fuser, showing the files open by a given process or group of processes. A simplified version of its syntax is:

```
lsof [-L1NRst] [-c c] [+f | -f] [+r | -r [t]] [-S [t]] [file]
```

file specifies the file or file systems (multiple *file* arguments are permitted) to scan. Specifying -c *c* selects processes executing a command that begins with the letter *c*. -f causes *file* to be interpreted as a file or pathname, +f as a file system name. -L suppresses displaying the count of files linked to *file*. -1 displays UIDs rather than converting them to login names. Specifying -N includes a list of NFS files in lsof's output. +r causes lsof to repeat the display every 15 seconds (or *t* seconds if *t* is specified) until none of the selected files remain open; -r repeats the display indefinitely. -R lists the parent process ID of displayed processes. -S enables lsof to time out after 15 seconds, or after *t* seconds if *t* is specified.

Managing Disk Space Usage

Monitoring and controlling disk space usage is another important part of a system administrator's tasks. The commands covered in this section for managing disk space usage include the following:

- ◆ df — Shows available (free) disk space on mounted file systems
- ◆ du — Shows disk space usage for files, directories, and file systems
- ◆ edquota — Modifies user disk space quota limits
- ◆ quota — Displays current disk usage and disk usage limits
- ◆ quotaoff — Disables disk quotas on file systems
- ◆ quotaon — Enables disk quotas on file systems
- ◆ quotactl — Manages the quota system
- ◆ quotastats — Prints statistics about the quota system
- ◆ repquota — Displays a report summarizing disk quota usage
- ◆ setquota — Sets disk quotas
- ◆ quotacheck — Compares disk usage to limits set using the quota system

Implementing and using the quota subsystem is discussed in detail in Chapter 26. Please refer to that chapter for examples and illustrations of the quota commands introduced in this section.

The df and du commands perform complementary functions, listing detail and summary information about the amount of disk space free and used, respectively. df's syntax is:

```
df [-ahklTmx] [-t type] [--sync|--nosync] [name]
```

name, which can contain multiple whitespace delimited values) is the name of a file whose file system should be checked, or the file system itself (the default is all mounted file systems). -a includes empty file systems in the display, which would ordinarily be omitted. -h uses more familiar display units, such as GB, MB, or KB, rather than default, blocks. -k causes df to use block sizes of 1024 bytes, and -m block sizes of 1,048,576 bytes. -l limits df's report to local file systems, ignoring, for example, NFS mounted file systems. -x limits df's report to the current file system or the file system to which *name* refers. -t type limits the report to file systems of *type*, and --nosync prevents df from syncing file systems before generating its report (the default is to sync the disks to obtain the most accurate report).

du displays information about the disk space used. Its syntax is:

```
du [-abcDhklmSsx] [-X file] [--exclude=path] [--max-depth=n] [name]
```

name, which can contain multiple whitespace delimited values) is the name of a file whose file system should be checked, or the file system itself (the default is all mounted file systems). -a displays counts for all files, not just directories. -b prints all sizes in bytes. -c displays a grand total for *names*. -h uses more familiar display units, such as GB, MB, or KB, rather than default, blocks. -k causes df to use block sizes of 1024 bytes, and -m block sizes of 1,048,576 bytes. -l limits df's report to local file systems, ignoring, for example, NFS mounted file systems. If a file or directory in *name* includes a symbolic link, -L causes it to be dereferenced to obtain the target's disk usage, rather than the link's usage. -S ignores subdirectories, which are recursed by default. -s results in a summary total for each *name* rather than a detailed report for each file in *name*. -x limits du's report to the current file system or the file system to which *name* refers. -X *file* causes du to ignore any file matching a pattern contained in file. Similarly, use --exclude=*pattern* to specify a single pattern to ignore. --max-depth=*n*, finally, limits the displayed report to directories (or files, if --all specified) within *n* levels of a path specified by *name* (all directories and files are evaluated, but the granularity of the report is limited to *n* levels).

As you learn in Chapter 26, the quota package is valuable for establishing and enforcing disk space usage policies. The discussion here summarizes its syntax.

edquota edits established quotas for users and groups. Its syntax is:

```
edquota [-p model] [-ug] name
edquota [-ug] -t
```

The first form edits the quota for the user named *name* (equivalent to -*u name*), or, if -g is specified, the group named *name*. Using -*p model* applies the quotas established for the prototype user or group *model* to the user or group *name*. The second form uses the -t option to edit the soft time limits for each file system on which quotas are enforced. Add -u or -g to restrict the edits to users or groups.

repquota displays a report summarizing the quota policy in place and actual quota usage for a given file system. Its syntax is:

```
repquota [-vugs] -a | filesystem
```

-a displays a report for all mounted file systems (the default). *filesystem* limits the report to the specified file system (multiple file systems may be specified using whitespace to separate the names). -v forces a verbose report that includes file systems on which there is no usage. Use -u to restrict the report to users, or -g to limit it to groups. -s includes summary statistics in the report.

setquota sets disk quotas and the time limits permitted for exceeding the soft quotas. It is ideally suited for use in scripts. Its syntax is:

```
setquota [-u | -g] filesys softb hardb softi hardi name
setquota [-u | -g] filesys -p model name
setquota -t  [-u | -g] filesys timeb timei
```

In all forms of the command, -g interprets *name* as a group name rather than a user name, which is the default (equivalent to specifying -u), *filesys* as the file system to which the quota should be applied, and *name* as the user or group name to which the quotas or limits apply. In the first form, *softb* and *softi* represent the soft limits for numbers of blocks and inodes, respectively, used. *hardb* and *hardi* represent the hard (absolute) usage limits in terms of numbers of blocks and inodes, respectively. The second form duplicates the limits set for the user or group *model* for the user or group *name*. The third form sets *timeb* and *timei*, in numbers of seconds, during which the soft limits on block and inode usage, respectively, may be exceeded on *filesys*.

quota prints current disk usage and limits. Its syntax is:

```
quota -q [-gv]
quota [-v | -q] user
quota [-gv] group
```

The first form, intended for use by users, prints a short usage report identifying file systems where usage exceeds the quota. If -g is also specified, quotas for groups of which the user is a member are also displayed. -v includes in the report file systems on which no space is used or for which no quota has been set. The second form enables root to see the quota usage report for the specified *user* (-v and -q function as described). The third form displays the report for the specified *group*, subject to modification by -v and -q.

To enable and disable quotas, use the `quotaon` command. Its syntax is:

```
quotaon [-e | -d] [-vug] -a | filesys
```

filesys identifies the file system on which to enable or disable quotas (do not use with `-a`). Use `-a` to affect all mounted file systems to which quotas have been applied. `-e` enables quotas (the default); `-d` disables quotas. `-v` displays a short message for each file system as quotas are enabled or disabled. `-u` affects only user quotas; `-g` affects only group quotas.

The `quotaoff` command, not covered here, makes `-d` the default behavior and, in fact, is merely a symbolic link to `quotaon`.

Tracking and Controlling System Usage

Administrators must know how to monitor memory and CPU usage at a finely-grained level. The commands discussed in this section make such close monitoring possible. They include:

- ◆ `vmstat` — Displays virtual memory usage information
- ◆ `sar` — Collects, saves, and reports a broad range of system usage statistics

`vmstat` provides a detailed report covering process activity, paging, memory usage, disk I/O, and CPU usage. Its syntax is:

```
vmstat [-n] [delay [count]]
```

delay specifies the number of seconds between `vmstat`'s updates. *count* expresses the number of iterations `vmstat` executes. `-n` prints `vmstat`'s report header once, rather than repeatedly.

For many years, the `sar` (an acronym for System Activity Report) command, well known and widely used in the Unix world, was not available as a native Linux command. Fortunately, it is now available (at least on Red Hat systems), and it provides a wealth of information allowing system administrators a very detailed view of system activity. A slightly shortened version of its syntax is:

```
sar [-b] [-B] [-c] [-r] [-R] [-t] [-u] [-v] [-w] [-y]
    [-n {DEV | EDEV | SOCK | FULL}]
    [-x {pid | SELF | SUM | ALL}]
```

```
[-X {pid | SELF | ALL}]
[-I {irq | SUM | ALL | XALL}]
[-o [ofile] | -f [ifile]] [-s [hh:mm:ss]]
[-e [hh:mm:ss]] [interval [count]]
```

interval specifies in seconds how often sar displays its statistics. If *count* is also specified, it states the number of samples to be taken. -o *ofile* names the output file in which sar should save its reports, and -f *ifile* instructs sar to display a report using the data (saved in a binary format) read from *ifile*. If -f is specified, -s and -e define the starting and ending times, respectively, in military format, sar uses to create its report. The default values for -s and -e are 08:00:00 and 18:00:00, respectively, but these can be overridden using *hh:mm:ss* arguments to either or both options.

Use -b to report disk I/O and data transfer statistics. -B produces data on the system paging activity. -c includes data on process creation. -r reports memory and swap usage statistics, and -R reports raw memory usage data. -u provides data on the CPU utilization for user, kernel, idle, and niced processes. -v reports the usage of the kernel's file-related structures. -w produces the number of CPU context switches, and -y displays the number of receive and transmit interrupts detected on each serial line (usually, a TTY device).

Depending on the argument provided, -n reports a variety of network performance and traffic statistics. The DEV keyword specifies normal traffic statistics, EDEV specifies error reports, SOCK requests a report on sockets currently in use, and FULL requests DEV, EDEV, and SOCK.

The -x option requests detailed process information for the process whose PID is *pid*. If SELF is specified, sar reports on itself, while ALL includes the sar process along with all other processes. The SUM directive, ignored if -o is specified, lists the system's total major and minor page faults. To report on child processes, use -X, which has the same restrictions as -x and does not report the summary data produced with -x's SUM directive.

The -I option reports system interrupt activity for a specific IRQ if *irq* is specified, all IRQ's if ALL is used, or total interrupts per second if SUM is asserted. The XALL directive includes APIC interrupts in the report.

Timekeeping

In most situations, maintaining the system date and time is a secondary concern. In larger networks, however, particularly those with multiple servers, synchronizing the time across the network is considerably more important. This is especially true for file and database servers, which use finely-grained time values to govern disk writes, reads, and to maintain logs of their activity should one or more operations need to be rolled back. This section discusses key commands for showing, setting, and maintaining the date and time on a Red Hat system, specifically:

- ◆ hwclock — Displays and sets the hardware clock
- ◆ date — Displays and sets the system time and date
- ◆ rdate — Displays and sets the system clock from a network time server
- ◆ ntpd — Keeps system time synced to one or more time servers

Unlike most of the sections in this chapter, this section includes examples and illustrations because the material they cover is not discussed elsewhere in the book.

Single Use Commands

The hwclock, date, and rdate commands are *single use commands* for setting the system date and time. That is, hwclock, date, and rdate have no inherent ability to *keep* a system's clock synced. Rather, you run one of them, the time gets set, and you are done. Unless executed from cron or another periodic command scheduling service, none of these commands work to keep system time accurate on an ongoing basis.

The hwclock command displays and sets the hardware clock. Its syntax is:

hwclock [-a | -r | -s | -u | -w | --set --date=*newdate*]

hwclock invoked by itself or with the -r option displays the current time, converted to local time, as maintained by the computer's hardware clock (often called the RTC, or Real Time Clock). Specifying -w updates the hardware clock with the system time, while -s updates the system time based on the hardware time. The following examples first show the current system and hardware time, then updates the hardware clock to the system time using the -w option:

```
# date
Sun Jul  8 19:15:50 EDT 2003
# hwclock
Sun 08 Jul 2003 07:15:49 PM EDT  0.067607 seconds
# hwclock -w
# hwclock
Sun 08 Jul 2003 07:16:03 PM EDT  0.899255 seconds
```

Note that after syncing the hardware clock to the system clock, the hardware clock gained approximately 14 seconds (of course, some time elapsed while the commands were typed). Using hwclock -w or hwclock -s in a system initialization script (or, as you will see shortly, using rdate to sync the system and hardware time to an external time source), enables you to maintain accurate and consistent time on your Red Hat system.

Updating the system time after the system has booted could cause unpredictable behavior. Do not use the -s option except early in the system initialization process.

Use the -u option to tell hwclock that the time stored in the hardware clock is
maintained in UTC (Coordinated Universal Time) format, rather than in the local
time (the default). The -a option enables you to adjust the hardware clock's time to
account for systematic drift in its time. --set, finally, sets the hardware clock to
the date and time specified by the *newdate* argument to the --date option. *newdate*
can be any date in a format accepted by the date command. The next example shows
how to use the --set argument to update the system time.

Yes, you read that correctly. The acronym almost always appears as UTC,
even though it refers to Coordinated Universal Time or Universal Coordinate
Time — just another one of the curious Linux/Unix idiosyncrasies.

```
# hwclock --set --date="July 8, 2003 7:24 PM"
# hwclock
Sun 08 Jul 2003 07:24:05 PM EDT  0.429153 seconds
```

As you will see in the discussion of the date command, you can use practically any common date and time specification to set the date using
hwclock and date.

The date command displays the current time in a specified format or sets the system time to the specified value. Its syntax comes in two forms:

```
date [-d datestr] [-f datefile] [-r reffile] [+format]
date [-u] [MMDDhhmm[[CC]YY][.ss]] | -s datespec
```

The first form displays the time in the format specified by *format* subject to
modification by one of the -d, -f, -r, or -u options. By default, date prints the current date and time, but specifying -d *datestr* prints the date and time in *datestr*;
-f *datefile* prints the date and time of the date strings contained in the file *datefile* (one per line); and -f *reffile* prints the date and time that *reffile* was last
modified. The next three examples show date's output using these first three
options.

```
$ date -d "July 6, 2004 11:48 AM"
Tue Jul  6 11:48:00 EDT 2004
$ cat datefile
January 1, 2010 00:01:01
December 31, 2010 11:59:59 PM
[root@luther /root]# date -f datefile
Fri Jan  1 00:01:01 MST 2010
Fri Dec 31 23:59:59 MST 2010
$ date -r /boot/vmlinuz
Sun Apr  8 18:57:28 EDT 2003
```

Note that regardless of how the source or input date is formatted, date's output always has the same format. To modify the output format, use the +*format* argument. Specify *format* using one or more of the tokens listed in Table 25-10.

TABLE 25-10 OUTPUT FORMAT TOKENS FOR THE DATE COMMAND

Token	Description
%a	Prints the locale's three-letter abbreviated weekday name (Sun–Sat)
%A	Prints the locale's full weekday name (Sunday–Saturday)
%w	Prints the day of the week (0–6, 0 represents Sunday)
%d	Prints the day of the month (01–31)
%e	Prints the blank padded day of the month (1–31)
%j	Prints the day of the year (001–366)
%U	Prints the week number of the year, with Sunday as the first day of the week (00–53)
%V	Prints the week number of the year, with Monday as the first day of the week (01–52)
%W	Prints the week number of the year, with Monday as the first day of the week (00–53)
%b	Prints the locale's three-letter abbreviated month name (Jan–Dec)
%B	Prints the locale's full month name (January–December)
%m	Prints the two-digit month (01–12)
%y	Prints the last two digits of the year (00–99)
%Y	Prints the four-digit year (1970)

Continued

TABLE **25-10** OUTPUT FORMAT TOKENS FOR THE DATE COMMAND *(Continued)*

Token	Description
%D	Prints the date (mm/dd/yy)
%x	Prints the locale's date representation (mm/dd/yy)
%S	Prints the two-digit second (00–60)
%M	Prints the two-digit minute (00–59)
%H	Prints the two-digit hour in 24-hour format (00–23)
%I	Prints the two-digit hour in 12-hour format (01–12)
%p	Prints the locale's AM or PM
%Z	Prints the time zone (for example, EDT) or nothing if no time zone is determinable
%T	Prints the 24-hour time (hh:mm:ss)
%r	Prints the 12-hour time (hh:mm:ss AM|PM)
%X	Prints the locale's time representation (same as %H:%M:%S)
%c	Prints the locale's date and time (Sat Nov 04 12:02:33 EST 1989)
%s	Prints the seconds elapsed since 00:00:00, Jan 1, 1970
%%	Prints a literal %
%n	Prints a newline
%t	Prints a horizontal tab

Here are some examples using *+format*. The first example prints the 4-digit year, the Julian day, the hour in 24-hour format, the minute, and the second, separating each element with a hyphen (-). Note that characters, such as the hyphen, that are not part of a formatting token (prefixed with %) are interpreted literally as part of the output.

```
$ date +%Y-%j-%H-%M-%S
2003-189-20-44-05
```

The next example mimics date's standard output for US locales. Note that because the *format* string contains spaces, you have to use strong (') or weak quotes (") to prevent the shell from interpreting the spaces:

```
$ date +'%a %b %e %H:%M:%S %Z %Y'
Sun Jul  8 20:49:24 EDT 2003
```

The final example shows the current date and time using full names for the month and day using the standard 12-hour time format:

```
$ date +"%A, %B %d, %Y%n%-I:%M %p"
Sunday, July 08, 2003
8:59 PM
```

The example also used the %n to insert a newline and the - modifier between % and I to remove the default padding GNU date inserts into numeric fields. Again, because the *format* string used spaces, the string had to be surrounded with quotes.

Use the second form of the date command to set the system date and time. Use -u to indicate that the specified date and time are relative to Coordinated Universal Time. The string *MMDDhhmmCCYY.ss* defines the time to set. The pairs of characters, in order, mean:

- ◆ *MM* – The month
- ◆ *DD* – The day
- ◆ *hh* – The hour
- ◆ *mm* – The minute
- ◆ *CC* – The century (optional)
- ◆ *YY* – The year (optional)
- ◆ *ss* – The second (optional)

So, for example, to set the current system date and time to 11:59 p.m. on December 31, 2002, you would execute the command (as root):

```
# date 123123592002
Tue Dec 31 23:59:00 MST 2002
```

Fortunately, you can also use more familiar date and time specifications. In fact, GNU date can interpret most commonly used date and time formats. To use this type of syntax, use the -s option and place the date in quotes if it contains embedded whitespace. For example, the following command sets the current date and time to 5:55:55 a.m. on May 5, 1955:

```
# date -s "May 5, 1955 5:55:55 am"
Thu May  5 05:55:55 MST 1955
```

The next command just sets the time, leaving the date untouched:

```
# date -s "9:33 PM"
Thu May  5 21:33:00 MST 1955
```

The last example, finally, corrects the date, but, unfortunately, has the side effect of resetting the time:

```
# date -s "07/08/2003"
Sun Jul  8 00:00:00 EDT 2003
```

The rdate command is a simple, effective way to maintain accurate system and hardware clock time on your system. Its syntax is:

```
rdate [-sp] host
```

host indicates the name of the network time server to contact. If -p is specified, rdate prints the time *host* returns and, if -s is also specified, the system time is set to the time *host* returns. rdate, like hwclock, is best used during system initialization.

Of course, because it needs network connectivity, rdate must be executed after network has started, perhaps during one of the scripts executed when starting run level 3.

Using the Network Time Protocol

The Network Time Protocol, or NTP, is a standardized way to keep system time synchronized across a network. NTP consists of a daemon, ntpd, a configuration file, /etc/ntp.conf, and a set of supporting utilities (ntpdate, ntpdc, ntpd, ntptime, and so forth) that, working together, keep your Red Hat system's clock set. NTP is also quite simple to use on Red Hat systems because Red Hat configured it to sync against their NTP servers, clock.redhat.com. All you have to do is start it (if it is not already started):

```
# /sbin/service ntpd start
```

To make sure NTP starts at each boot, use chkconfig:

```
# chkconfig --levels 345 ntpd on
```

Automating System Maintenance

System administration is frequently performed on a repetitive or ongoing basis. As a result, such duties are prime candidates for automation because repeatedly typing the same commands is tedious, error-prone, and time-consuming. This section teaches you to use Bash's programming language to automate standard system administration tasks. After you read an overview of the fundamentals of Bash programming, you will learn how to use some very useful shell utility programs that ease the task of shell scripting. You will also receive some guidance in selecting an alternative scripting language if you do not like Bash or find its abilities insufficient for your needs.

 The discussion assumes that you are comfortable using Bash as an end user and concentrates on Bash features from a shell programmer's perspective.

As a programming language, Bash has all the features one would expect: wildcards, variables, operators, functions, and input and output capabilities. Although Bash's programming support is not as complete, fully featured, or powerful as traditional programming languages such as C or Python, it is nevertheless surprisingly capable and well-suited to the task. In this section you will learn about wildcards, command line expansion, variables, operators, flow control, shell functions, input and output processes, and command line arguments in scripts.

Wildcards and Special Characters

Wildcards are single characters that stand for or substitute for one or more values. Bash uses the familiar * and ? as wildcards. * stands for one or more characters and ? represents any single character. For example, the command ls d* executed in /bin on a Red Hat system should result in output resembling the following:

```
$ ls d*
date  dd  df  dmesg  dnsdomainname  doexec  domainname
```

The command ls d?, however, shows only the commands beginning with d followed by any single alphanumeric value:

```
$ ls d?
dd  df
```

The command `ls ??` shows all files with names consisting of any two alphanumeric characters:

```
$ ls ??
cp  dd  df  ed  ex  ln  ls  mv  ps  rm  sh  su  vi
```

The * and ? characters are useful, but somewhat blunt tools. Bash also supports set operators or set wildcards. *Set operators* allow you to define a range or set of characters to use as wildcards. The notation for defining a set is [*set*], where [and] delimit the range and *set* lists the alphanumeric characters making up the range. The range can be inclusive, disjoint, discrete, or a combination of all three. An *inclusive set* includes all the characters in the set, and is defined using a hyphen, for example, [b-f]. A *disjoint set* is at least two inclusive ranges separated by a comma (,), such as [1-4,7-0]. A *discrete set* refers to a simple list of characters, such as [13579]. Table 25-11 lists some examples of the kinds of sets you can create using the [] set operator.

TABLE 25-11 EXAMPLES OF SETS

Set	Explanation
[b-f]	Denotes any characters in the set b, c, d, e, f
[1-4,7-9]	Denotes any two numbers, the first of which must be 1, 2, 3, or 4 and the second of which must be 7, 8, or 9
[aeiou]	Denotes any character that is a vowel
[b,aeiou]	Denotes any character that is either b or a vowel
[aeiou][a-z]	Denotes any vowel followed by any lowercase character between and including a and z

For the second set in Table 25-10, possible matches include 17, 38, and 49, but 57 and 94 do not match. The next few commands show a few examples of using this set notation in the /bin directory on a Red Hat system.

```
$ ls [b-c]*
basename  bash2  cat    chmod   consolechars  cpio  cut
bash      bsh    chgrp  chown   cp            csh
```

The resulting set consists of any file name beginning with b or c.

```
$ ls [b-d,f]?
cp  dd  df
```

The resulting display consists of any file name beginning with b, c, d, or f followed by any single alphanumeric character.

```
$ ls [a-z][a-z][a-z]
ash  awk  bsh  cat  csh  cut  pwd  red  rpm  rvi  sed  tar
```

The resulting display consists of files whose name is made up of any combination of three lowercase characters between a and z, inclusive.

Bash also has a way to reverse the meaning of the set notation. That is, the notation [!set] refers to all characters not in the set defined by set. So, for example, an easy way to look for all file names not beginning with a consonant is to use [!aeiou]*, that is:

```
$ ls [!aeiou]*
basename    cut       gettext  mkdir    red     stty
bash        date      grep     mknod    rm      su
bash2       dd        gtar     mktemp   rmdir   sync
bsh         df        gunzip   more     rpm     tar
cat         dmesg     gzip     mount    rvi     tcsh
...
```

Bash's wildcard and set operators are a subset of its special characters, also called metacharacters. *Metacharacters* are characters to which Bash assigns a special meaning or interpretation. Table 25-12 lists all of Bash's special characters.

TABLE 25-12 BASH SPECIAL CHARACTERS

Character	Description
*	Multicharacter wildcard
?	Single-character wildcard
<	Redirect input
>	Redirect output
>>	Append output
|	Pipe
{	Start command block
}	End command block
(	Start subshell

Continued

T<small>ABLE</small> 25-12 BASH SPECIAL CHARACTERS *(Continued)*

Character	Description
)	End subshell
`	Command substitution
$	Variable expression
'	Strong quote
"	Weak quote
\	Interpret the next character literally
&	Execute command in background
;	Command separator
~	Home directory
#	Comment

You should already be familiar with redirecting input and output and using pipes, but you will see examples of all three operations later in the chapter. Input and output redirection should be familiar to you. Commands in a block, that is, delimited by { and } elicit different behavior from Bash than commands executed in a subshell, that is, commands delimited by (and).

You will read about subshells in the section titled "Shell functions" later in the chapter.

The commands between two ` characters cause command substitution (that is, their output or result replaces the expression itself). Consider the command ls `which tar`. Before ls executes, `which tar` will be replaced by its result (/bin/tar, in this case). So, for example the two commands

```
$ which tar
/bin/tar
$ ls -l /bin/tar
-rwxr-xr-x    2 root      root          150908 Mar  6 11:34 /bin/tar
```

produce the same result as the single command

```
$ ls -l `which tar`
-rwxr-xr-x    2 root      root        150908 Mar  6 11:34 /bin/tar
```

Command substitution is very commonly used in shell scripts, and you will see it used throughout this chapter. Another commonly used metacharacter is $, used to obtain the value of a variable, as in the command echo $PATH.

A more readable syntax for command substitution is $(...). This syntax works just like back quotes, with the interesting exception that $(...), unlike `...`, can be nested. So, for example, the following commands are exactly equivalent:

```
$ ls -l `which tar`
-rwxr-xr-x    2 root      root        150908 Mar  6 11:34 /bin/tar
$ ls -l $(which tar)
-rwxr-xr-x    2 root      root        150908 Mar  6 11:34 /bin/tar
```

Why are ' and " called strong quote and weak quote characters, respectively? In short, because ' is stronger than ". That is, ' forces Bash to interpret *all* special characters literally, while " protects only *some* of Bash's special characters from interpretation as special characters. To illustrate, compare the effect of ' and " on the output of the command echo $PATH:

```
$ echo $PATH
/usr/local/bin:/bin:/usr/bin:/usr/X11R6/bin:/home/kwall/bin
$ echo "$PATH"
/usr/local/bin:/bin:/usr/bin:/usr/X11R6/bin:/home/kwall/bin
$ echo '$PATH'
$PATH
```

Note how using ' around the PATH variable caused it to be echoed literally, rather than producing the path listing displayed by the other two commands. You will see the implication of this difference throughout the scripts used in this chapter.

Using Variables

Like any programming language, Bash has *variables*, named entities that store values. Bash supports both string or character variables and numeric (integer) variables. By convention, variables are named using upper case characters, but this is only a convention, and one not universally followed. For purposes of discussion, this section examines user-defined variables, predefined variables, and positional variables.

If you read the Bash manual page, it might seem that my discussion of variables contradicts the manual page, which treats variables as "parameters that have names." I avoided the manual page's approach because it was potentially confusing, especially for nonprogrammers. The information I present is correct, I just don't use the same terminology as the author of the manual page.

A *user-defined* variable is just that, a variable created by the shell programmer or end user, rather than one of the many predefined variables intrinsic to Bash. To assign a value to a variable, use the following syntax:

```
varname=value
```

To obtain a variable's value, you can use one of the following two formats:

```
$varname
${varname}
```

Of the two formats, `$varname` is more commonly used, but `${varname}` is more general. You *must* use the second form in order to distinguish variable names from trailing letters, digits, or underscore characters. Consider a variable named STRVAR with the value See Rock City!. Suppose you want to display STRVAR's value followed by an underscore character. The following command fails because Bash attempts to print the value of the variable STRVAR_, not STRVAR.

```
$ echo $STRVAR_
```

In this situation, you must use the more general form, illustrated in the following:

```
$ echo ${STRVAR}_
```

Listing 25-1 shows the code for `refvar.sh`, a script illustrating this distinction.

Listing 25-1: Referencing variables

```
#!/bin/sh
# refvar.sh - Referencing a variable

STRVAR='See Rock City!'
echo '${STRVAR}_ yields: ' ${STRVAR}_
echo '$STRVAR_ yields  : ' $STRVAR_
```

The output from the script, shown in the following example, makes it clear that $STRVAR_ prints nothing, but ${STRVAR}_ produces the expected output:

```
$ ./refvar.sh
${STRVAR}_ yields:  See Rock City!_
$STRVAR_ yields  :
```

Many of Bash's *predefined* or built-in variables are environment variables, such as BASH_VERSION or PWD. The complete list is available from the Bash man page. Table 25-13 lists commonly used Bash predefined variables:

TABLE 25-13 BASH 2.X PREDEFINED VARIABLES

Variable Name	Description
PPID	Stores the process ID of the Bash's parent process.
PWD	Contains the current working directory (as set by the cd command).
OLDPWD	Stores the most previous working directory (as set by the next most recent cd command).
UID	Contains the user ID of the current user as set when the shell started.
BASH_VERSION	Stores the version string of the current Bash instance.
RANDOM	Returns a random number between 0 and 32,767 each time it is referenced.
OPTARG	Contains the last command line argument read using the getopts built-in command.
OPTIND	Points to the array index of the next argument to be processed using the getopts built-in command.
HOSTNAME	Stores the name of the current host system.
SHELLOPTS	Contains a colon-separated string of the currently enabled shell options (as set using the set -o shell built-in command).
IFS	Stores the value of the Internal Field Separator, used to define word boundaries. The default value is a space, a tab, or a new line.
HOME	The home directory of the current user.

Continued

TABLE 25-13 BASH 2.X PREDEFINED VARIABLES *(Continued)*

Variable Name	Description
PS1	Defines the primary command prompt. The default value is "\s-\v\$ ".
PS2	Defines the secondary command prompt, used to indicate that additional input is required to complete a command.
HISTSIZE	The number of commands retained in Bash's command history. The default value is 500.
HISTFILE	The name of the file in which Bash stores the command history. The default value is $HOME/.bash_history.

Listing 25-2 shows the code for predef.sh that displays the names and values of a select subset of Bash's predefined variables.

Listing 25-2: Referencing predefined Bash variables

```
#!/bin/sh
# predef.sh - Show the values of a select predefined
#             Bash variables

echo "       PPID = $PPID"
echo "BASH_VERSION = $BASH_VERSION"
echo "     RANDOM = $RANDOM"
echo "   SHELLOPTS = $SHELLOPTS"
echo "        IFS = $IFS"
echo "   HISTSIZE = $HISTSIZE"
```

The output from this script should resemble the following:

```
$ ./predef.sh
       PPID = 663
BASH_VERSION = 2.04.21(1)-release
     RANDOM = 19869
   SHELLOPTS = braceexpand:hashall:interactive-comments
        IFS =

   HISTSIZE = 1000
```

The value of PPID and RANDOM will surely vary on your system.

Bash has another group of predefined variables, positional parameters. *Positional parameters* are variables that contain the arguments, if any, passed to a script on its command line. The parameter 0 contains the name of the script; the actual parameters begin at 1. If there are more than nine such parameters, you must use the ${} syntax, such as ${10}, to obtain their values. Positional parameters passed to a script are read-only, that is, you cannot change their values.

In addition to the numerically named positional parameters, Bash recognizes three special ones, #, @, and *. # is the number of positional parameters passed to the script, not counting 0. * contains a list of all the positional parameters passed to a script, except 0, formatted as a string. Each parameter is separated from the others by the first character of IFS, the internal field separator. @, finally, is a list of all of the positional parameters stored as separate strings delimited by weak quotes.

Bash Operators

In a programming context, *operators* are tokens that perform some sort of operation or manipulation. For example, many programming languages use the plus sign, +, to indicate addition and the asterisk, *, to indicate multiplication. Bash operators behave similarly. They fall into several categories, including comparison operators, file test operators, substitution operators, and pattern matching operators. This section looks at each class of operators and shows examples of how to use them.

COMPARISON OPERATORS

Comparison operators, the simplest to use and understand, compare one variable or value to another, returning 0 if the comparison is true or 1 if the comparison is false. There are two sets of comparison operators, one for string or character data and one for numeric (integer) data. Tables 25-14 and 25-15 list Bash's string and numeric operators.

TABLE 25-14 BASH STRING COMPARISON OPERATORS

Operator	Expression	True if...
=	*str1* = *str2*	*str1* matches *str2*
==	*str1* == *str2*	*str1* matches *str2*
!=	*str1* != *str2*	*str1* does not match *str2*
<	*str1* < *str2*	*str1* is less than *str2*
>	*str1* > *str2*	*str1* is greater than *str2*
-n	-n *str*	*str*'s length is nonzero
-z	-z *str*	*str*'s length is zero

Table 25-15 BASH NUMERIC COMPARISON OPERATORS

Operator	Expression	True if...
-eq	*val1* -eq *val2*	*val1* equals *val2*
-ne	*val1* -ne *val2*	*val1* is not equal *val2*
-ge	*val1* -ge *val2*	*val1* is greater than or equal to *val2*
-gt	*val1* -gt *val2*	*val1* is greater than *val2*
-le	*val1* -le *val2*	*val1* is less than or equal to *val2*
-lt	*val1* -lt *val2*	*val1* is less than *val2*

When comparing strings, keep in mind that A–Z come before a–z in the ASCII character set, so A is "less than" a and foo is "greater than" bar.

 TIP   If you are not familiar with the ASCII sort order, Red Hat Linux includes a manual page (man ascii) that lists the ASCII character set.

Listings 25-3 and 25-4, strcmp.sh and numcmp.sh, respectively, illustrate the use of the string and comparison operators.

Listing 25-3: Using Bash string comparison operators

```sh
#!/bin/sh
# strcmp.sh - Using Bash string comparison operators

C1="b"
C2="F"
S1="STRING"
S2="string"
S3="some darn string"

if [[ $C1 > $C2 ]]; then
        echo "$C1 is greater than $C2"
else
        echo "$C1 is less than $C2"
fi
```

```
if [[ $S1 > $S2 ]]; then
        echo "$S1 is greater than $S2"
else
        echo "$S1 is less then $S2"
fi

if [[ -n $S3 ]]; then
        echo "S3 is $S3"
else
        echo "S3 is empty"
fi

if [[ -z $S4 ]]; then
        echo "S4 is empty"
else
        echo "S4 is $S4"
fi
```

`strcmp.sh`'s output looks like this:

```
$ ./strcmp.sh
b is greater than F
STRING is less then string
S3 is some darn string
S4 is empty
```

A few notes are in order. First, do not worry about understanding the syntax of the `if...then...else` construct right now. The section titled "Flow control" later in the chapter discusses it, so just accept that it works for the time being. Secondly, the `[` operator must be terminated with a `]`. Finally, as noted earlier, F precedes b in the ASCII character set, so b is greater than F lexicographically. Similarly, STRING is less than string. The last two tests use the `-z` and `-n` operators to test for empty and nonempty strings.

Listing 25-4 presents `numcmp.sh`, a script that illustrates how to use some of Bash's numeric comparison operators.

Listing 25-4: Using Bash numeric comparison operators

```
#!/bin/sh
# numcmp.sh - Using Bash numeric comparison operators

W=7
X=10
```

Continued

Listing 25-4: Using Bash numeric comparison operators *(Continued)*

```
Y=-5
Z=10

if [ $W -gt $X ]; then
        echo "W is greater than X ($W > $X)"
else
        echo "W is less than X ($W < $X)"
fi

if [ $X -lt $Y ]; then
        echo "X is less than Y ($X < $Y)"
else
        echo "X is greater then Y ($X > $Y)"
fi

if [ $X -eq $Z ]; then
        echo "X equals Z ($X = $Z)"
fi

if [ $Y -le $Z ]; then
        echo "Y is less than or equal to Z ($Y <= $Z)"
else
        echo "Y is greater than or equal to Z ($Y >= $Z)"
fi
```

`numcmp.sh`'s output should be

```
$ ./numcmp.sh
W is less than X (7 < 10)
X is greater then Y (10 > -5)
X equals Z (10 = 10)
Y is less than or equal to Z (-5 <= 10)
```

The next section extends your ability to work with numeric values in shell scripts, showing you how to use arithmetic operators to perform basic arithmetic operations in Bash shell scripts.

ARITHMETIC OPERATORS

If Bash allows you to compare numeric values and variables, it follows that Bash allows you to perform arithmetic on numeric values and variables. In addition to the comparison operators discussed in the previous section, Bash uses the operators listed in Table 25-16 to perform arithmetic operations in shell scripts.

TABLE 25-16 BASH ARITHMETIC OPERATORS

Operator	Expression	Description
++	*var*++	Increments *var* after obtaining its value
++	++*var*	Increments *var* before obtaining its value
- -	*var*- -	Decrements *var* after obtaining its value
- -	- -*var*	Decrements *var* before obtaining its value
+	*var1* + *var2*	Adds *var1* and *var2*
-	*var1* - *var2*	Subtracts *var2* from *var1*
*	*var1* * *var2*	Multiplies *var1* by *var2*
/	*var1* / *var2*	Divides *var1* by *var2*
%	*var1* % *var2*	Calculates the remainder of dividing *var1* by *var2*
=	*var* = *op*	Assigns result of an arithmetic operation *op* to *var*

The complete list of Bash's arithmetic operators also includes bitwise and logical functions, a conditional evaluation operator, C-style assignment operators, and a comma operator. Refer to Bash's excellent manual page for complete details.

FILE TEST OPERATORS

Many common administrative tasks involve working with files and directories. Bash makes it easy to perform these tasks because it has a rich set of operators that perform a variety of tests. You can, for example, determine if a file exists at all or if it exists but is empty, if a file is a directory, and what the file's permissions are. Table 25-17 lists commonly used file test operators.

TABLE 25-17 BASH FILE TEST OPERATORS

Operator	Description
-d *file*	*file* exists and is a directory.
-e *file*	*file* exists.
-f *file*	*file* exists and is a regular file (not a directory or special file).

Continued

TABLE 25-17 BASH FILE TEST OPERATORS *(Continued)*

Operator	Description
-g *file*	*file* exists and is SGID (set group ID).
-r *file*	You have read permission on *file*.
-s *file*	*file* exists and is not empty.
-u *file*	*file* exists and is SUID (set user ID).
-w *file*	You have write permission on *file*.
-x *file*	You have execute permission on *file* or, if *file* is a directory, you have search permission on it.
-O *file*	You own *file*.
-G *file*	*file*'s group ownership matches one of your group memberships.
file1 -nt *file2*	*file1* is newer than *file2*.
file1 -ot file2	file1 is older than *file2*.

The script in Listing 25-5 illustrates how to use the file test operators. It applies several file test operators to each file in the top level of a directory name provided as an argument.

Listing 25-5: File test operators

```
#!/bin/sh
# filetest.sh - Illustrate file test operators
# Arguments: Name of directory to scan

# Have to provide the argument
if [[ $# != 1 ]]; then
    echo "usage: filetest.sh DIR"
    exit 1
fi

# Only accept directory arguments
if [ ! -d $1 ]; then
    echo "$1 is not a directory"
    exit 1
fi
```

```
# Process each file in the directory
for FILE in $1/*
do
    # Ignore directories and special files
    if [ -f $FILE ]; then
        echo $FILE
        if [ -r $FILE ]; then
            echo -e "\tReadable by $USER"
        fi
        if [ -w $FILE ]; then
            echo -e "\tWritable by $USER"
        fi
        if [ -x $FILE ]; then
            echo -e "\t/Executable by $USER"
        fi
        if [ -O $FILE ]; then
            echo -e "\tOwned by $USER"
        fi
    fi
done
```

The first `if` statement ensures that the script was called with one argument, using the $# positional parameter discussed earlier in the chapter. If not, it displays a usage message and exits; otherwise, execution continues with the next if statement. The second if statement makes sure that the argument passed to `filetest.sh` (the $1 parameter) is a directory name. If it is not, the script exits after displaying an error message. Otherwise, processing continues with the `for` loop.

The section titled "Determinate loops using `for`" explains the syntax of the `for` statement.

The `for` loop processes each file in the directory. For each file, the script first tests whether or not it is a regular file using the `-f` operator. If it is not, it skips to the next file. Otherwise, `filetest.sh` tests whether or not the user executing the script has read, write, and execute permission on the file (using the `-r`, `-w`, and `-x` operators, respectively), whether or not the user owns the file (using the `-O` operator), displays the results of each test on `stdout`, and then repeats these tests for the next file. After evaluating the last file, the script exits.

The output of this script will vary, of course, but it should resemble the following:

```
$ ./filetest.sh $HOME
```

```
/home/kwall/CliffHanger_1.pps
        Readable by kwall
        Writable by kwall
        Owned by kwall
/home/kwall/important.txt.gz
        Readable by kwall
        Writable by kwall
        Owned by kwall
/home/kwall/newapt.bmp
        Readable by kwall
        Writable by kwall
        Owned by kwall
/home/kwall/Plaid2.jpg
        Readable by kwall
        Writable by kwall
        Owned by kwall
/home/kwall/vmstat.out
        Readable by kwall
        Writable by kwall
        Owned by kwall
```

Flow Control

Any programming language worth the name must support *flow control*, the ability to control the order in which code executes. Flow control allows code to loop, branch, or execute conditionally. To *loop* means to execute the same block of code multiple times. To *branch* means to execute a block of code specific to the value of a condition. *Conditional execution* means to execute or not to execute code, depending on the value of some variable. Bash supports flow control, and this section explains the syntax and use of all its flow control structures, listed in Table 25-18.

TABLE 25-18 BASH FLOW CONTROL STATEMENTS

Statement	Type	Description
if	Conditional	Executes code if a condition is true
for	Looping	Executes code a fixed number of times
while	Looping	Executes code as long as a condition is true
until	Looping	Executes code as long as a condition is false
case	Branching	Executes code specific to the value of a variable
select	Branching	Executes code based on a selection made by a user

CONDITIONAL EXECUTION USING if

The syntax of Bash's if statement is shown in the following:

```
if condition then
        statements
[elif condition then
        statements]
[else
        statements]
fi
```

condition is the control variable that determines which statements execute. elif is Bash's equivalent to else if in other programming languages. fi signals the end of the if structure. Be careful when creating condition because if checks the exit status of the *last* statement in condition. That is, if condition consists of multiple tests, only the last one (unless grouping using () is applied) affects the control flow. Most Linux programs return 0 if they complete successfully or normally and nonzero if an error occurs, so this peculiarity of Bash's if statement usually does not pose a problem.

Bash's if statement works just like the if structures in most other programming languages. If the exit status is 0 (true), then statements will be executed. If it is nonzero (false), the statements following an elif or else clause, if present, will be executed, after which control jumps to the first line of code following fi. The else clause executes only if all other conditions in elif clauses are false. The else and elif clauses are optional and you can use multiple elif clauses if you wish.

While *most* Linux programs return 0 if they complete successfully and nonzero otherwise, this is not universally true. The diff program, for example, returns 0 if it does not find differences, 1 if it does, or 2 if a problem occurred. Nonstandard exit values such as these can alter the way a shell script works, so double-check return codes in a program's or command's documentation.

Evaluating exit codes, and the order in which you evaluate them, is important because Bash allows you to use the && and || operators to combine exit codes in condition. && is known as a *logical AND*, which means that a condition is true if and only if the expressions on both sides of the && operator are true. So, given the condition *expression1* && *expression2*, the condition is true if and only if *expression1* and *expression2* are true. If *expression1* is false (nonzero), Bash will not evaluate *expression2*. The ||, called a *logical OR*, requires only that either one or the other of the expressions on either side of the operator be true. Thus, the condition *expresison1* || *expression2* is true if either *expression1* or

expression2 is true. The condition follows the general form *expression1 ||*
expression2.

How do these operators work? Suppose that you have to change the current
working directory and copy a file before executing a certain code block. One way to
accomplish this is to use nested `if` statements, as in the following snippet:

```
if cd $DATADIR then
    if cp datafile datafile.bak then
        #
        # Code here
        #
    fi
fi
```

Using the `&&` operator, you can write this much more concisely, as the following
code snippet illustrates:

```
if cd $DATADIR && cp datafile datafile.bak then
    #
    # Code here
    #
fi
```

Both code snippets accomplish the same thing, but the second example is shorter
and, in my opinion, easier to read and understand because you do not get bogged
down sorting out the nested `if`s. If, for some reason, the `cd` command fails, Bash
will not attempt the copy operation.

Several shell scripts in this chapter have used the `if` structure, so refer to the
previous examples to see various ways to use `if`.

DETERMINATE LOOPS USING for

The `for` structure allows you to execute a section of code a fixed number of times,
so the loops it creates are called *determinate*. The `for` loop is a frequently used loop
tool because it operates neatly on lists of data, such as Bash's positional parameters
($1-$9) or lists of files in a directory. The general format of the `for` statement is
shown here:

```
for value in list
do
    command
    [...]
done
```

list is a whitespace separated list of values, such as file names. *value* is a single list item; for each iteration through the loop, Bash sets *value* to the next element in *list*. *command* can be any valid Bash expression, and, naturally, you can

execute multiple *command*s. *command* typically uses or manipulates *value*, but it does not have to.

 The `for` statement is a Bash built-in command, so you can type `help for` at the command prompt to get a quick syntax summary.

Suppose you want to copy a number of files in the same directory, adding the extension `.bak` to the copies. DOS users accustomed to the way DOS copies multiple files are dismayed when they discover that the same approach does not work in Linux. To illustrate, the following DOS command uses the `COPY` command to copy every file with a `.dat` extension, replacing `.dat` with `.bak`:

```
C:\> copy *.dat *.bak
data1.dat
data2.dat
data3.dat
        3 file(s) copied
```

The same method does not work for Linux's `cp` command because if you specify multiple files to copy, `cp` expects the final argument to be a directory. One way around this inconvenience is to use Bash's `for` loop. The following example illustrates using `for` at the command line to emulate the DOS `COPY` command's behavior:

```
$ for FILE in *.dat
> do
>           cp -v $FILE ${FILE%.dat}.bak
> done
`data1.dat' -> `data1.bak'
`data2.dat' -> `data2.bak'
`data3.dat' -> `data3.bak'
```

The `cp` command's `-v` (verbose) option causes it to display what it is doing. Note the use of the `%` pattern matching operator to replace `.dat` with `.bak` for each file copied. Notice also how the Bash command prompt changes to the secondary prompt (`PS2`), `>`, indicating that Bash needs more input to complete the command. The previous listing showed a slightly more complex usage of the `for` loop.

INDETERMINATE LOOPS USING while AND until

The `for` loop is ideal when you know in advance, or can determine before entering the loop, how many times a given section of code must execute. If you do not know in advance or cannot determine at runtime how many times to execute a code block, you need to use one of Bash's indeterminate loop structures, `while` and `until`.

while and until constructs cause continued code execution as long as or until a particular condition is met. The key here is that your code must ensure that the condition in question is eventually met, or you will get stuck in an infinite loop.

The general form of a while loop is:

```
while condition
do
    command
    [...]
done
```

In a while loop, as long as condition remains true, execute each command until condition becomes false. If condition is initially false, execution jumps to the first statement following done.

The general form of the until loop is:

```
until condition
do
    command
    [...]
done
```

until's structure and meaning is the opposite of while's because an until loop executes as long as condition is false; a while loop executes as long as condition is true.

Listing 25-6 illustrates the use of Bash's while loop. It makes 150 copies of a file named junk in the current directory.

Listing 25-6: Bash while loops

```
#!/bin/sh
# while.sh - Illustrate using Bash while loops

declare -i CNT
CNT=1

if [ ! -r junk ]
then
    touch ./junk
fi

while [ $CNT -le 150 ]
do
    cp junk junk.$CNT
    CNT=$CNT+1
done
```

`while.sh` illustrates several Bash programming features. Of course, you see the `while` loop in action. It also uses the `-e` file test operator to test for the existence of the file named `junk` and, if it does not exist, uses the `touch` command to create it. The `declare` statement creates an integer variable, `CNT`, to server as the loop control variable. Each iteration of the loop increments `CNT`, making sure that the loop condition eventually becomes false. Do not forget to delete the files the script creates!

The following code snippet shows how to use an `until` loop to accomplish the same thing as the `while` loop in Listing 25-6.

```
until [ $CNT -gt 150 ]
do
    cp junk junk.$CNT
    CNT=$CNT+1
done
```

The logic of the condition is different, but the end result is the same. In this case, using a `while` loop is the appropriate way to handle the problem.

SELECTION STRUCTURES USING case AND select

This section discusses the `case` and `select` selection structures, which allow a shell script to execute a specific section of code depending on the value of a variable or expression or in response to user input. You will learn about the case statement first and then about the select statement.

THE case STATEMENT The `case` structure, approximately comparable to C's `switch` keyword, is best suited for situations in which a variable or expression can have numerous values and as a replacement for long if blocks. The complete syntax for `case` is as follows:

```
case expr in
    pattern )
        commands ;;
    pattern )
        commands ;;
    ...
esac
```

The space between *pattern* and `)` is required, as is the space between *commands* and `;;`. *expr* can be any valid Bash expression. *expr* is compared to each *pattern* until a match is found, at which point the commands associated with the first match are executed. `;;`, equivalent to C's `break`, signals the end of the code block and causes control to jump to the first line of code past `esac` (`case` in reverse), which marks the end of the `case` structure. If no pattern matches, execution resumes at the first line of code after `esac`. Listing 25-7 shows the `case` statement at work.

Listing 25-7: Using the case statement

```
#!/bin/sh
# case.sh - Using the case selection structure

clear
echo -n "Type a single letter, number, or punctuation character: "
read -n 1 OPT
echo

case $OPT in
    [[:upper:]] ) echo "$OPT is an upper case letter" ;;
    [[:lower:]] ) echo "$OPT is a lower case letter" ;;
    [[:digit:]] ) echo "$OPT is a digit" ;;
    [[:punct:]] ) echo "$OPT is punctuation" ;;
esac
```

After clearing the screen with the `clear` command, the script prompts for a single character of input and uses the `read` built-in to read a single character from `stdin` and store it in `OPT`. The case statement uses a special notation, explained shortly, to represent sets of characters. If the character typed at the prompt matches one of the four patterns ([:upper:], [:lower:], [:digit:], or [:punct:]), `case.sh` displays the appropriate message. If no match is found, the script silently exits.

In addition to illustrating the case selection structure, `case.sh` introduces two new Bash programming elements, `read` and character classes. You will learn about the `read` built-in command in the section "Processing input and output" later in the chapter. A *character class* is a symbolic name embedded between [: and :] that represents a group of characters. In fact, character classes are special cases of the [ ] set notation described in the section titled "Wildcards and special characters" near the beginning of the chapter. For example, the set [a-z] is equivalent to the character class [:lower:]. The most common character classes are listed in Table 25-19.

TABLE 25-19 COMMON BASH CHARACTER CLASSES

Class	Description
alnum	All alphabetic and numeric characters
alpha	All alphabetic characters
Digit	All numerals
lower	All lowercase letters
punct	All punctuation symbols
upper	All uppercase letters

THE select STATEMENT   The select control structure makes it easy to create menus. Indeed, it seems almost to have been designed specifically for that purpose. Its syntax is

```
select value [in list]
do
     commands
done
```

The `select` statement creates a numbered menu for each `value` in `list`. Selecting the number corresponding to a `value` causes `commands` to execute. Listing 25-8, `dircnt.sh`, illustrates how `select` works. It counts the number of files in a user-specified directory, using the `select` statement to identify the directory to analyze.

Listing 25-8: Creating menus with select

```
#!/bin/sh
# dircnt.sh - Using the select statement

PS3="[Number]: "
IFS=:

clear

select ITEM in $PATH Quit
do
    [ "$ITEM" = "Quit" ] && exit 0
    if [ "$ITEM" ]; then
        CNT=$(ls -Al $ITEM | wc -l)
        echo "$CNT files in $ITEM"
    else
        echo "Invalid selection"
    fi
    echo
done
```

The script first sets the PS3 environment variable, which is the prompt that `select` displays to request user input. Next, it sets the IFS (internal field separator) variable to : to enable `select` properly to parse the PATH environment variable. After clearing the screen, it enters a loop, presenting a numbered menu of options derived from the PATH variable and the literal string Quit. Then it prompts the user to make a choice, as shown in the following (the exact appearance depends on the value of the PATH variable):

```
1) /usr/kerberos/bin   4) /usr/bin          7) Quit
2) /usr/local/bin      5) /usr/X11R6/bin
3) /bin                6) /home/kwall/bin
[Number]:
```

If the user selects the numeral corresponding to the Quit option (7 in this example), dircnt.sh exits. Selecting a valid choice (1–6 in this case) stores the corresponding directory name in ITEM, which is then used in the statement CNT=$(ls -Al $ITEM | wc -l). This command counts the number of files (not including . and ..) in the directory specified by ITEM. The file count is displayed to stdout, and the menu redrawn. If the user makes an invalid selection, dircnt.sh displays an error message and then redraws the menu.

Bash has a fully capable range of flow control structures. Although they behave in ways slightly differently from their counterparts in traditional programming languages such as C, C++, or Pascal, they enable you to create powerful, flexible shell scripts.

Shell Functions

Shell functions offer two important advantages over aliases. First, shell functions accept command line arguments that can be processed within the body of the function. Aliases do not accept arguments in this way. Secondly, shell functions increase the modularity of your scripts. If you store frequently used shell functions in a separate file, you can use the source built-in to read that file into your scripts. Then, if you change a function, you have to change only one file rather than edit each file that uses the script.

TIP   Aliases, do not work in shell scripts unless the shell option expand_aliases is set (shopt expand_aliases).

Define shell functions using one of the following two forms:

```
function fname
{
    commands
}
```

or

```
fname()
{
    commands
}
```

fname is the name of the function and *commands* are the statements and expressions that define its behavior. Both forms are widely used and there is no difference between them. You must define functions before they are used, such as at the beginning of a script or in another file that is sourced before the functions are called. The following example defines a function (at the command prompt) named mydate that displays the output of the date command in a custom format.

```
$ function mydate
> {
> date '+%A, %B %d, %Y'
> }
$
```

To use a function, simply invoke it using its name followed by any arguments it needs. Once a function has been defined, you can use it on the command line or in a script. For example, to use the mydate shell function just defined on the command line, type its name at the Bash prompt:

```
$ mydate
Wednesday, June 27, 2003
```

Alternatively, place the definition in a script and then execute the script. The Red Hat startup scripts use precisely this strategy. The file /etc/rc.d/init.d/functions defines at least 15 shell functions used throughout the initialization scripts. Near the top of every init script in /etc/rc.d/init.d you will find these two lines:

```
# Source function library.
. /etc/rc.d/init.d/functions
```

The key command is ./etc/rc.d/init.d/functions, which allows the init script to use the functions defined in the file. In fact, studying the contents of /etc/rc.d/ init.d/functions gives you great insight into using Bash functions and into the larger subject of shell programming in general.

Processing Input and Output

Bash sports a surprisingly rich collection of input and output features. Many of them, such as manipulating file descriptors or reading and writing to device files, are esoteric and most useful to low-level system programmers and will not be covered in this section. Rather, it covers I/O redirection, using the echo command for output, and using the read command for input.

REDIRECTING I/O
The basic I/O redirectors, > and <, redirect output from stdout and input from stdin, respectively. Most often, > is used to save the output from a command to a file. For example, the command cat /etc/passwd > out captures the output of the cat

command and sends it to a file named `out` in the current directory. To capture stderr output to a file, put a 2 immediately in front of `>`. For example, if you invoke `tar` with no options or arguments, it displays an error message to stderr (usually the display). The following command sends the error message to `/dev/null` (the bit bucket):

```
$ tar 2> /dev/null
```

Of course, you can also redirect stdout to `/dev/null`. In fact, it is common practice in shell scripts to redirect both stdout and stderr to `/dev/null`. Why? In many cases, a command's output is less important than whether or not it succeeded or failed. Because most programs return an exit code indicating success (usually 0) or failure (usually any nonzero value), from a programmatic standpoint it is sufficient to use the predefined Bash variable ? to check a program's exit status. In other cases, hiding output gives a script a more polished, professional appearance and lets *you* control how your script appears to users.

TIP

To redirect stdout and stderr to the same file, such as `/dev/null`, use a command of the form

`mycommand > /dev/null 2>&1`

Replace *mycommand* with the command and any arguments the command requires. The notation 2>&1 redirects stderr to stdout, which was previously redirected to `/dev/null`. A less familiar but functionally identical form and more concise version of this command is

`mycommand &> /dev/null`

The section titled "Redirecting Standard Output and Standard Error" in the Bash man page explains how and why this syntax works.

If you use `>` to redirect stdout to an existing file, you will lose the file's original contents. To avoid this circumstance, use Bash's append operator, `>>`, which adds data to the end of a file, thus protecting the file's original contents.

To redirect stdin, which is ordinarily the keyboard, use the input redirector, `<`. For example, the command `cat < /etc/passwd > out` redirects both input and output.

So-called here-documents, which use the `<<` operator, are an interesting case of input redirection. The term *here-document* derives from the fact that Bash reads its input from the current source, "here," if you will, rather than from stdin or a separate file. A here-document stores the input to a command in the script. The syntax, which looks somewhat odd, is:

```
command << label
    commandinput
label
```

label demarcates the beginning and end of the command's input. *commandinput* is the input itself and *command* is the program or utility or command to execute. This syntax says that *command* should read *commandinput* until it encounters *label* on a line by itself.

A typical use of here-documents is for scripting programs that lack a convenient scripting interface. The familiar `ftp` client program is a fine example of this. Listing 25-9, ftp.sh, illustrates how to script the `ftp` client using a here-document.

Listing 25-9: Scripting ftp using a here-document

```
#!/bin/sh
# ftp.sh - Scripting ftp using a here-document

USER=anonymous
PASS=kwall@kurtwerks.com

ftp -i -n << END
open localhost
user $USER $PASS
cd pub
ls
close
bye
END
```

`ftp -i -n` uses `-i` to start in noninteractive mode and `-n` to suppress the automatic login. The script uses `END` as the label to signal the end of input. Using various `ftp` commands, the script first opens an ftp session to localhost. Then it sends the login sequence using the `USER` and `PASS` variables defined at the beginning of the script. Once logged in, it changes to the standard public ftp directory, `pub`, and then executes an `ls` command to demonstrate that the script worked. Finally, it closes the connection and exits the program. When Bash encounters the second `END` label, the script exits.

Actually, the last sentence is not quite true. Scripts containing a here-document do not begin executing until *after* the here document is closed. Similarly, scripts containing a here document do not terminate when they encounter the ending marker of the here document (which signifies the end of stdin). Rather, scripts terminate after the execute the last executable statement in the flow of control. It just happens that many Linux utilities terminate when stdout is closed, so it appears that many scripts using here documents terminate after the here document ends.

The output shown in the following illustrates `ftp.sh` in action:

```
$ ./ftp.sh
total 0
-rw-r--r--   1 root       50            0 Jun 28 04:18 herfile
-rw-r--r--   1 root       50            0 Jun 28 04:18 hisfile
-rw-r--r--   1 root       50            0 Jun 28 04:18 myfile
-rw-r--r--   1 root       50            0 Jun 28 04:18 ourfile
-rw-r--r--   1 root       50            0 Jun 28 04:18 yourfile
```

Another typical use for here-documents is to include documentation, such as online help, in scripts.

STRING I/O

Many of the scripts that you have seen in this chapter use the echo command to display information. It supports a number of useful options. You have already seen -e, which enables the interpretation of escaped characters, such as \n (newline) and \t (tab). echo's -n option omits appending the final newline to its output. Table 25-20 lists escape sequences that echo interprets when called with the -e option.

TABLE 25-20   ECHO ESCAPE SEQUENCES

Sequence	Description
\a	Alert
\b	Backspace
\c	Omits the final newline appended to output
\f	Formfeed
\r	Return
\v	Vertical tab
\n	Newline
\\	A single \

To work with string input, use the read command. Its syntax is

```
read var1 var2 ...
```

Although ideal for getting input in an interactive mode from a user, read also works with files. In interactive mode, read is simple to use, as the following code fragment illustrates:

```
echo -n 'Name: '
read NAME
echo "Name is $NAME"
```

Using read to process text files is somewhat more complicated. The easiest way is to create a script and then redirect its input from the file you want to process. Listing 25-10 processes the contents of /etc/passwd.

Listing 25-10: Using read to process a text file

```
#!/bin/sh
# read.sh - Using read to process a text file

IFS=:
while read name pass uid gid gecos home shell
do
    echo "*********************"
    echo "name   : $name"
    echo "pass   : $pass"
    echo "uid    : $uid"
    echo "gid    : $gid"
    echo "gecos  : $gecos"
    echo "home   : $home"
    echo "shell  : $shell"
done
```

Setting IFS enables the script to parse the /etc/passwd entries properly. The while read statement reads each line of input, assigns the value of each field to the appropriate variable, and then uses the echo command to display the password information on stdout. You can execute this script with (at least) one of the following two commands:

```
$ ./read.sh < /etc/passwd
```

or

```
$ cat /etc/passwd | ./read.sh
```

The output should be identical regardless of which command you use.

Table 25-21 lists useful options the read command accepts.

TABLE 25-21 USEFUL READ OPTIONS

Option	Description
-n *num*	Reads *num* characters from stdin
-p *prompt*	Displays *prompt* followed by a space to solicit user input
-s	Disables echoing input read from stdin
-t *secs*	Cancels the read operation after *secs* seconds elapse without reading an input line

---

Using read's -p option allows user input code to be more concise. For example, the statement read -p "User Name: " NAME is identical to the following fragment:

```
echo "User Name: "
read NAME
```

Listing 25-7, case.sh, uses read -n 1 to read a single character from standard input. The -s (presumably, a mnemonic for silent), is ideal for reading a user password or other sensitive information. The following commands define a shell function, getpass, that uses all four of the options listed in Table 25-7 to read a user's password, and then invokes the function.

```
$ getpass()
> {
> read -s -p "Password: " -n 8 -t 5 PWORD
> echo -e "\nYou entered: $PWORD";
> }
$ getpass
Password: [At the prompt, type your password and press Enter.]
You entered: secret
```

-t 5 causes the read command to time out if the user does not press Enter in 5 seconds (the echo command still executes, though). -n 8 causes read to read no more than 8 characters from stdin. As you can see in the output, -s suppressed displaying what the user typed.

Working with Command Line Arguments

Most nontrivial shell scripts need to handle arguments passed to them on the command line. In order to maintain consistency with Linux's command line environment, options should be preceded with a - (for example, foo -v). Bash's getopts built-in command makes meeting both of these requirements simple. getopts' basic syntax is quite simple:

getopts *optionstring varname*

   optionstring consists of a string of letters and colons. Letters define the valid option characters; if an option requires an argument, it must be followed by a colon (:). *varname* stores the option character being evaluated. Listing 25-11, getopts.sh, illustrates the use of getopts and simplifies the subsequent explanation of how it works.

Listing 25-11: Using Bash's getopts command

```
#!/bin/sh
# getopts.sh - Using Bash's getopts command to
#              process command line arguments

while getopts "xy:z:" OPT;
do
    case $OPT in
        x ) XOPT='You used -x' ;;
        y ) YOPT="You used -y with $OPTARG" ;;
        z ) ZOPT="You used -z with $OPTARG" ;;
        ? ) echo 'USAGE: getopts.sh [-x] [-y arg] [-z arg]'
            exit 1 ;;
    esac
done

echo ${XOPT:-'did not use -x'}
echo ${YOPT:-'did not use -y'}
echo ${ZOPT:-'did not use -z'}

exit 0
```

   getopts processes each character in *optionstring*, picking options off one at a time and assigning them to *varname*. An option character followed by a : indicates that the option requires an argument, which getopts assigns to OPTARG, one of Bash's predefined variables. As long as options remain to be processed, getopts returns 0, but after it has processed all options and arguments, it returns 1, making getopts suitable for use in a while loop.

   As you can see in Listing 25-10, the valid options are x, y, and z. Because y and z are each followed by a :, they require arguments. The case statement handles each of the valid options and also includes a default case, indicated by ?, that prints a usage message and exits the script if it is invoked with invalid options (options not listed in *optionstring*). The arguments passed with the y and z options are stored in OPTARG. The echo statements at the end of the script report the option used and, if applicable, the value of its corresponding argument.

This ends your whirlwind survey of the fundamentals of Bash programming. The next two sections, "Processes and Job Control" and "Creating Backups," present sample scripts for monitoring and managing processes and creating backups, using many of the concepts and features discussed in this section.

Using Processes and Job Control

This section presents a few Bash shell scripts that automate process monitoring and management. They use both Bash built-in commands and standard Linux commands and utilities available on any Red Hat system. As is often the case in Linux, there are many ways to accomplish most administrative tasks, so consider the scripts in this section starting points rather than the only valid ways to perform a certain task.

Listing 25-12, kujob.sh, kills all processes owned by the user whose login name is passed as an argument to the script.

Listing 25-12: Killing a selected user's jobs

```
#!/bin/sh
# kujob.sh - Kill all processes owned by a user
# Arguments - User's login name

# Must be root
[ $UID -eq 0 ] || usage root

# Were we called properly?
getopts ":u:" OPT || usage syntax
[ "$OPT" = ":" ] && usage arg

# Does the user exist?
UNAME=$OPTARG

id $UNAME &> /dev/null || usage user

# Kill the user's processes
for SIG in TERM INT HUP QUIT KILL
do
    echo "Trying SIG$SIG"
    pkill -$SIG -u $UNAME &> /dev/null
    sleep 1
    pgrep -u $UNAME &> /dev/null || exit 0
done
```

```
# Display a short usage message
function usage
{
    ERR=$1
    case $ERR in
        "root" ) echo "Only root can run this script" ;;
        "syntax" ) echo "USAGE: kujob.sh -u UNAME" ;;
        "arg" ) echo "-u requires user name" ;;
        "user" ) echo "No such user" ;;
    esac
    exit 1
}


/et
```

The usage function is a crude but convenient error handler. It always terminates the script after displaying the error message associated with the argument it is passed. It is convenient because it centralizes all of the script's error handling; it is crude because it makes no attempt to recover from errors.

The first block of code uses Bash's built-in UID variable to see if root, whose user ID (UID) is 0, is invoking the script. If the test returns false, meaning the user running the script is not root, kujob.sh calls usage with an argument of root. Otherwise, execution continues.

The second block of code uses getopts to process its command line arguments. The only valid option, as you can see in the option string, is -u. The first : (in front of u) turns off Bash's default error messages, allowing the script to provide its own error messages. The trailing :, as you recall, means that -u requires an argument. If an invalid option was used, kujob.sh calls usage with an argument of syntax. The following line makes sure the required login name argument was provided. getopts stores a : in the OPT variable if a required argument was omitted, so if the test returns true, it calls usage with the arg argument.

Once kujob.sh determines it was invoked properly, the next code block performs a sanity check: making sure the named user actually exists. The rest of the script relies on this information. After copying the user name passed to the UNAME variable, the grep command searches for that name in the /etc/passwd file. If it is present, grep returns 0 (true) and execution continues with the for statement. If the name is not present, grep returns 1 (false) and kujob.sh calls usage with an argument of user. Note how both stderr and stdout from the grep command are redirected to /dev/null, resulting in a more polished runtime appearance for the script.

Finally, kujob.sh attempts to kill all of the user's processes. The signals it uses are listed in order of increasing severity and prejudice (see the signal(7) man page for more information). If one signal fails to kill a process, the next strongest one is tried until all processes associated with the user have been killed. The sleep 1 statement gives the kernel time to complete the housekeeping associated with process termination before the script continues. After all the user's processes have been terminated, the script exits (pgrep returns 1, or false, if it finds no processes that match the specified search criteria).

 In addition to terminating the user's processes, kujob.sh kills the user's login shell, too. Be careful when using this script.

The pkill and pgrep commands are part of the procps package, a suite of process management and monitoring tools. pkill and pgrep, in particular, provide a simpler interface to the ps command and its bewildering array of command line options. In short, the pkill statement sends the signal specified by SIG to all processes owned by the user in UNAME, specified by the -u $UNAME construct. pgrep, using the same -u option, lists the process IDs (PIDs) of all processes that match (you do not see them, however, because pgrep's stdout and stderr are redirected to /dev/null). See the pkill and pgrep man pages for further information.

The script in Listing 25-13, dskusg.sh, prints a report of disk usage for each mounted file system, sorting the output from the largest to the smallest directory.

Listing 25-13: Displaying disk usage sorted by top-level directory size

```
#!/bin/sh
# dskusg.sh - Print disk usage on each file system for top level
#             directories in descending order

[ $UID -eq 0 ] || usage
for FS in $(grep  ^\/ /etc/mtab | cut -f2 -d" ")
do
    echo -e "$FS\n--------"
    du -x --max-depth=1 --exclude=/dev* $FS | sort -rg
    echo
done
function usage
{
        echo "You must be root to get an accurate report"
        exit 1
}
```

The first statement makes sure the user executing the script is the root user, printing an error message and exiting if the user is not root or root equivalent. Normal users do not have access to many directory trees on a Red Hat Linux system (such as /root and parts of /var/log, so this statement makes sure the report is accurate and, in the process, eliminates the necessity to redirect stderr to /dev/null. The script selects mounted file systems as listed in /etc/mtab, which contains the list of currently mounted file systems. It uses /etc/mtab rather than mount's output or the contents of /proc/mounts because /etc/mtab is easier to parse. For each file system, the script prints the file system name, followed by the disk usage (in blocks) of the file system itself, followed by the top level directories on each file system in descending order of disk usage, accomplished using the --maxdepth=1 argument. Using the -x option limits du to analyzing the given file system. This prevents the script from analyzing /proc, for example. --exclude=/dev* keeps the /dev special files out of the analysis. By piping the output to sort, the script can sort its output, using -g to sort based on numeric values and -r to reverse the sorting order. The output from this script might resemble the following:

```
# ./dskusg.sh
/
--------
172552  /
106636  /var
39720   /lib
10892   /etc
9252    /sbin
5376    /bin
268     /root
48      /tmp
48      /tftpboot
16      /lost+found
12      /mnt
4       /opt
4       /misc
4       /.automount

/boot
--------
3485    /boot
12      /boot/lost+found

/home
--------
297920  /home
270828  /home/kwall
27048   /home/bubba
24      /home/mysql
16      /home/lost+found

/usr
--------
2113504 /usr
853948  /usr/share
```

```
746872   /usr/lib
167220   /usr/bin
126072   /usr/X11R6
102200   /usr/src
59948    /usr/include
30428    /usr/sbin
12236    /usr/i386-glibc21-linux
6228     /usr/libexec
5512     /usr/kerberos
2612     /usr/games
120      /usr/html
80       /usr/local
16       /usr/lost+found
4        /usr/etc
4        /usr/dict
```

Listing 25-14, vmstat.sh, runs the vmstat command, redirecting its output to a file for later analysis using a spreadsheet or other analysis tool. vmstat.sh is intended to run as a cron job. The section titled "Automating Scripts" later in this chapter discusses cron and the at facility to run scripts automatically.

Listing 25-14: Collecting vmstat statistics for offline analysis

```
#!/bin/sh
# vmstat.sh - Collect vmstat reports for later analysis

LOG=/var/log/vmstat.log.$$
[ $UID -eq 0 ] || LOG=$HOME/vmstat.log.$$

DELAY=${1:-60}

vmstat -n $DELAY >> $LOG
```

The first statement sets the default log file to which vmstat's output will be saved. The next statement changes this default if the invoking user is not root, because normal users do not have write permission in the /var/log directory tree. The $$ operator returns the script's PID and is used in this case to distinguish one log file from another. The next statement uses one of Bash's substitution operators to set a default value for number of seconds between vmstat's updates. As you recall, the :- operator sets DELAY to the value of the positional parameter 1 (referenced using $1), or assigns a default value of 60 if 1 is null or not set. Note that the script has to use the :- operator rather than :=, because the positional parameters are read only at run time and the "natural" substitution operator to use in this case, :=, would cause an error because it attempts to set the 1's value. Finally, the script calls vmstat, using -n to print the header only once, with a delay as specified, and redirecting the output to the file specified by LOG.

`vmstat.sh`'s output should resemble the following after running a few minutes:

procs				memory		swap		io		system		cpu		
r	b	w	swpd	free	buff	cache	si	so	bi	bo	in	cs	us	sy	id
0	1	0	4548	6936	47624	10528	0	0	7	3	104	12	0	0	99
0	0	0	4548	5252	47640	11920	0	0	6	1	103	13	0	0	100

In this case, the output was stored in the file /home/kwall/vmstat.log.1933. Of course, on your system, the file would have a different PID at the end.

Automating Scripts

Admittedly, scripts enable a greater degree of customization, flexibility, and convenience in performing system administration tasks, but repeatedly typing script names soon becomes just as tedious and impractical as complete command line invocations. You can use at and cron to run commands automatically and unattended, enabling you to realize the full power and benefit of the scripting administrative tasks.

Use the at command to schedule scripts you want to run later and that you want to run only once. Use the cron facility for programs and scripts that need to run on some sort of regular schedule.

USING at FOR ONE-SHOT JOBS

The at command provides an interface to the atd daemon's scheduler. It is the atd daemon that executes the scripts. Scheduling a job with at is surprisingly simple to do: just type at followed by the time at which you want the script to run, and then press Enter. For example, the following sequence of commands schedules the /home/kwall/bin/incrback.sh script to run at 1:05 a.m. tomorrow.

```
$ at 1:05
warning: commands will be executed using (in order) a) $SHELL b)
login shell c) /bin/sh
at> /home/kwall/bin/incrback.sh
at> <EOT>
job 11 at 2003-07-10 01:05
$
```

The at> prompt is a small interactive shell for scheduling commands. The initial command, at 1:05, used the simplest possible format for specifying the time. Table 25-22 shows additional options for indicating time to at. Once you have the at> prompt, enter scripts and other commands just as you would at the shell prompt. To specify multiple commands, press Enter after each command, type the next one, press Enter, and so on. Press Ctrl+D after you have entered all the commands you want. at responds with the <EOT> sign and then displays a job number (11, in the example) for your commands and the date and time (July 10 at 1:05 a.m.) the job will execute.

TABLE 25-22 SPECIFYING TIME WITH THE AT COMMAND

Command	When the Job Runs
at now	Executes the job immediately.
at now + 15 minutes	Executes the job 15 minutes from now.
at now + 2 hours	Executes the job 2 hours from now.
at now + 10 days	Executes the job 10 days from now.
at noon	Executes the job at noon today. If it is past noon, the job executes tomorrow at noon.
at now next hour	Executes the job 60 minutes from now.
at 15:00 tomorrow	Executes the job at 3:00 p.m. tomorrow.
at 1:05am	Executes the job at 1:05 a.m. today (if it is past 1:05 a.m., the job executes tomorrow at 1:05 a.m.
at 3:00 Aug 16, 03	At 3:00 a.m. on August 16, 2003.

To view the current list of jobs in the at queue, use the atq command. To remove a job from the queue, use the atrm command. The following commands show the current list of jobs using atq, and then removing them using atrm.

```
$ atq
10      2003-07-10 01:05 a kwall
11      2003-07-11 01:05 a kwall
$ atrm 10 11
```

The first field of atq's output shows its job number, the same one displayed when you submitted the job. The rest of the fields are, in order, date and time the job will execute, the queue (a, in this case), and the user who submitted the job. Only the root user can see all of the jobs submitted; normal users can see only their own. Removing a job from the queue is a simple matter of typing atrm followed by the job number of the job you want to remove, as shown in the example.

USING cron FOR REGULARLY SCHEDULED JOBS

To run a script automatically at regular intervals, use the cron service. You schedule repeating jobs using the crontab command, either by placing the script name and scheduling information in a specially formatted file that crontab reads, or using crontab interactively. The cron daemon, crond, takes care of running the job and, as with at, e-mails its output to you.

To use `cron`, you need to understand the format of its job file, also called a *crontab* (which should not be confused with the `crontab` command, although the two are related). Each job in a crontab file is specified on a single line and each line contains at least six fields. The first five define when the job executes, and the sixth and subsequent fields name the script or program to run, along with any arguments the script or program takes. For example, this line executes the `incrback.sh` shell script in 1:05 a.m. each day:

```
05 01 * * * incrback.sh
```

Table 25-23 lists the meaning of the first five fields.

TABLE 25-23 CRONTAB FIELD VALUES

Field	Description	Valid Values
1	Minute	0–59
2	Hour	0–23
3	Day of month	0–31
4	Month	1–12 (1 is January)
		Three letter month abbreviations (Jan, Feb, Mar, Apr, May, Jun, Jul, Aug, Sep, Oct, Nov, Dec)
5	Day of week	0–7 (0 and 7 both mean Sunday, 1 is Monday)
		Three letter day abbreviations (Sun, Mon, Tue, Wed, Thu, Fri, Sat)

Entries may be single values, a comma-delimited set of values to specify multiple days, a range of values separated by a hyphen (-), or any combination of these three options. An asterisk (*) represents all possible values for that field. So, an asterisk in the hour field means a job would execute every hour of the day.

For example, to run `incrback.sh` at 4:55 p.m. on the 1st and 15th of January, March, June, and September, the crontab entry would look like one of the following:

```
55 16 1,15 1,3,6,9 * incrback.sh
55 16 1,15 Jan,Mar,Jun,Sep * incrback.sh
```

In this case, the * in the day of the week field is ignored because it is overridden by the other date and time specifications.

The easiest way to schedule a job with cron is to place the crontab entry in a file, and then invoke the `crontab` command with the file name as an argument. So, if one of the crontab entries shown previously was stored in a file named `kwall.crontab`, you would submit the job using the following command:

```
$ crontab kwall.crontab
```

To verify that the job is indeed scheduled, type `crontab -l` to list your crontab entries:

```
$ crontab -l
# DO NOT EDIT THIS FILE - edit the master and reinstall.
# (/tmp/crontab.2433 installed on Mon Jul  9 17:48:30 2003)
# (Cron version -- $Id: crontab.c,v 2.13 1994/01/17 03:20:37 vixie
Exp $)
55 16 1,15 1,4,6,9 * incrback.sh
```

To remove all of your cron jobs, type `crontab -r`. Once you become comfortable with the crontab format, you might find it most convenient to use crontab's interactive mode. To do so, type `crontab -e`. The interactive mode uses the `vi` editor, so use `vi` keystrokes to enter, edit, save your changes, and, of course, to exit the interactive mode.

Summary

In this chapter, you learned the basic commands that every system administrator must know how to use in a command line environment. You explored a number of commands for working with users and groups, including adding and deleting users and groups and how to modify multiple accounts simultaneously. You also learned how to obtain useful information about who is logged in and what they are doing. Managing file systems is also important, and this chapter discussed commands for creating and checking file systems and managing disk space usage using quotas. The process administration commands discussed include commands for identifying what processes are active, killing processes, and modifying running processes.

This chapter also discussed shell programs and scripts as tools to ease the burden of system administration by handling certain tasks programmatically. First, you received a thorough introduction to the basics of Bash shell programming, including wildcards, shell variables, operators, Bash's flow control structures, shell functions, input and output processes, and command line arguments. The chapter presented a number of scripts that showed many of these shell programming features in action. You reviewed scripts for working with running processes, killing processes, reporting disk usage, and creating backups. You also learned how to use `at` and `cron` to run scripts automatically, and got some final tips and hints on writing, testing, and debugging shell scripts.

Chapter 26

Administering Users and Groups

IN THIS CHAPTER

- ◆ Understanding the root account

- ◆ Implementing Sudo

- ◆ Creating and maintaining users and groups

- ◆ Managing disk usage with user and group quotas

THIS CHAPTER DISCUSSES the details of user and group maintenance on Red Hat Enterprise systems. In addition to learning how to add, modify, and delete user accounts, you will learn about the capabilities of the root account, how to use `sudo` to give normal users root capabilities on a limited and monitored basis, the Red Hat user private group scheme, and how to implement user and group file system quotas to control and monitor disk space usage.

Understanding the Root Account

With very few and limited exceptions, the root account has unlimited power on any Linux or Unix system, and, in this respect, Red Hat Linux is no exception. The root account, or, to use the expression you see throughout this chapter, root, can access any file and modify any process. Indeed, it is for this reason that root is often called the *superuser* – root is effectively omnipotent.

The exceptions to root's capabilities are few. As explained in Chapter 11, root on an NFS client (that is, a system mounting an NFS exported file system from an NFS server) typically *cannot* exercise root privileges on the exported file system because the NFS server exports the file system using the `root_squash` option. As you should recall, the `root_squash` option maps root's UID and GID to the UID and GID of the anonymous user on the client system. Keep in mind that this is the default behavior of the NFS server daemon (`exportfs`) and can be overridden using `no_root_squash` on the NFS server. This is one limit on root's power.

The ext2 and ext3 file systems also restrict root's power, although only slightly. The ext2 and ext3 file systems support a number of special file attributes, including immutability. Using the `chattr` utility, root can set a file's immutable attribute, which prevents *all* users, including root, from modifying the file — it cannot be deleted, renamed, or written to, and hard links cannot be created to it until the immutable attribute is cleared. You guessed it — only root can set or clear a file's immutable attribute.

Finally, so-called Linux capabilities and Linux ACLs (Access Control Lists) are being developed that enable root's power with respect to process management and file access to be subdivided into more finely grained capabilities. Based on the IEEE's POSIX capabilities and first appearing in the 2.2 kernel, *Linux capabilities* (and, for that matter, POSIX capabilities) work by splitting root's traditional privileges into smaller sets of more specific privileges that can be enabled and disabled. Eventually, POSIX capabilities will also be applied to files in the file system.

The most immediately useful application is what is referred to as a *capability bounding set*, which defines a list of capabilities any process running on a Linux system can hold. If a capability does not appear in the bounding set, no process, regardless of how privileged it is, can exercise it. For example, you can disable kernel module loading by removing this capability from the bounding set. Although manipulating kernel capabilities is an advanced topic beyond this book's scope, you might find it interesting or useful, depending on your environment, to examine the Linux Kernel Capability Bounding Set Editor (LCAP), a tool that takes advantage of and manipulates POSIX capabilities. Additional information about POSIX capabilities is available via FTP from the kernel source code repository at `ftp://ftp .kernel.org/pub/linux/libs/security/linux-privs/`.

The LCAP editor's old Web page, `http://pweb.netcom.com/~spoon/ lcap/`, no longer works. Nevertheless, you can still download the editor from the kernel.org FTP site or from the Security Focus Web site, `http:// www.securityfocus.com/tools/lcap-0.0.2.tar`.

Implementing Sudo

Considering root's privileges, you can easily understand why root access on a Red Hat system is carefully protected and the root password tightly guarded. Nevertheless, it is often desirable to grant privileges to a nonroot user that have traditionally been solely root's domain, such as printer management, user account administration, system backups, or maintaining a particular Internet service. Indeed, in many environments, subdividing system administration responsibilities is a necessity because the responsibilities of maintaining an active server in a large IT shop or a series of servers in an ISP can quickly overwhelm a single individual.

The problem in such a situation is clear: How do you grant administrative privileges to nonroot users *without* providing unfettered root access? In many situations, Sudo, a mnemonic for *superuser do*, is the solution. Sudo enables you to give specific users or groups of users the ability to run some (or all) commands requiring root privileges. Sudo also logs all commands executed, which allows you to maintain an audit trail of the commands executed. As the README in the source distribution states, Sudo's "basic philosophy is to give as few privileges as possible but still allow people to get their work done." Sudo's features include:

◆ Enabling the ability to restrict the commands a given user may run on a per host basis.

◆ Maintaining a clear audit trail of who did what using the system logger or Sudo's own log file. In fact, you can use Sudo in lieu of a root shell to take advantage of this logging.

◆ Limiting root-equivalent activity to a short period of time using timestamp based "tickets," thus avoiding the potential of leaving an active root shell open in environments where others can physically get to your keyboard.

◆ Allowing a single configuration file, /etc/sudoers, to be used on many machines, permitting both centralized Sudo administration and the flexibility to define a user's privileges on a per host basis.

After the configuration file has been created, a typical Sudo session proceeds as follows:

1. An authorized user prefixes the root command she wants to execute with sudo followed by a space, for example:

   ```
   $ sudo shutdown -h +5 "System halting for disk replacement"
   ```

2. Sudo prompts the user for her personal password (*not* the root password) and then checks the configuration file (/etc/sudoers) to make sure she has permission to run the given command on a given machine.

3. If the user is permitted to use that command, Sudo runs the command as root (or another user if specified), logs the details, and timestamps the Sudo session ticket.

4. If the user is *not* permitted to use that command, Sudo logs the attempt and exits. Sudo also logs problems and other invalid sudo uses.

5. After executing the first command, the user can use multiple sudo commands without being prompted for her password again. The session ticket expires five minutes after the last sudo command is issued, after which the user is again prompted for a password.

By default, sudo logs to /var/log/messages using the system logger (syslogd), but you can configure the system logger to log sudo-related messages to a different file. Sudo can even bypass the system logger completely and maintain its own log file. If Sudo is invoked by an invalid user, is invoked with an invalid command, or if other abnormal situations arise, Sudo notifies the root user (by default) via e-mail.

Sudo's configuration file is `/etc/sudoers`, which must be edited using `visudo`, part of the Sudo distribution. Using `visudo` is vital because it locks the `/etc/sudoers` to prevent simultaneous edits and validates the grammar and syntax in the configuration file, cowardly refusing to save changes if it believes it has detected an error.

Deciphering Sudo's Configuration File

Sudo's configuration file, `/etc/sudoers`, is the key file. It contains three types of entries — alias definitions, privilege specifications, and global configuration defaults. *Alias definitions* are variables or placeholders that you can reuse throughout the configuration file. They come in four flavors: user aliases, command aliases, so-called runas aliases, and host aliases. The rationale for aliases is to simplify maintaining the configuration file — rather than editing multiple user or command lists when you update `/etc/sudoers`, you simply modify the appropriate alias and let `sudo` substitute the alias definition each place it is used. *Privilege specifications* define which users may execute what commands. *Global configuration defaults* are general settings that control `sudo`'s overall behavior.

Instead of trying to understand `sudoer`'s configuration syntax in the abstract, consider the following example that illustrates typical Sudo usage. Suppose you want to enable the users `marysue` and `bubba` to reset passwords for all users except root, which means that `marysue` and `bubba` need to be able to use the `passwd` command to set passwords for users other than themselves. Somehow, though, they must be prevented from changing the root password. As you know, the command for changing passwords is

```
passwd username
```

The general procedure is to use `visudo` to edit `/etc/sudoers` and create a *user alias* defining the users to whom you are granting access to one or more commands, a *command alias* that represents the command or commands to execute, a *host alias* to identify the host or hosts on which the named users are permitted to execute the named command (if necessary) a *runas alias* (again, if necessary) that identifies the user a command should run as, and a *user privilege specification* to connect the necessary aliases together to form a Sudo rule. The following procedure shows the specific steps to follow.

1. As the root user, start the edit session by executing `visudo`. Initially, the file should resemble the following:

```
# sudoers file.
#
# This file MUST be edited with the 'visudo' command as root.
#
```

```
# See the sudoers man page for the details on how to write a
sudoers file.
#

# Host alias specification

# User alias specification

# Cmnd alias specification

# User privilege specification
root    ALL=(ALL) ALL
```

The hash sign, #, prefixes a comment unless it is used in the context of a user name and is followed by one or more digits, for example, #502, in which case sudo interprets it as a UID.

2. Add the following line in the user alias section:

```
User_Alias PWADMIN=marysue,bubba
```

This statement defines a user alias named PWADMIN consisting of the accounts marysue and bubba.

3. Add the following line in the command alias section:

```
Cmnd_Alias PW=/usr/bin/passwd [A-z]*,!/usr/bin/passwd root
```

This statement defines a command alias named PW that has two components separated by a comma. Command aliases must include a full path specification and any arguments that you wish to permit to be invoked using sudo. The first component, /usr/bin/passwd [A-z]*, indicates that /usr/bin/passwd may be used with any argument that begins with the letters A–Z or a–z followed by zero or more characters. The second element uses the ! character to prevent /usr/bin/passwd from being used with an argument of root.

The character used as wildcards, permitted in both path name specifications and command arguments, are:

- *: Matches any set of zero or more characters, but not a / in a path specification. That is, /usr/bin/* matches /usr/bin/bc, but not /usr/bin/filter/filter_innd.pl

- ?: Matches any single character

- [...]: Matches any character in the specified range

- [!...]: Matches any character *not* in the specified range

- \x: Escapes the character x, including *, ?, [,], (,), @, !, =, :, ,, and \

4. Add the following line in the user specification section:

```
PWADMIN ALL = PW
```

This statement says that the PWADMIN users can use the PW command on all hosts (the ALL keyword). More generally, a user privilege specification takes the form

```
user_alias host_alias=[(runas_alias)] cmnd_alias[,...]
```

Note that the runas alias is not required and that you can specify multiple command aliases in the same entry if each is separated by a comma. In fact, it was not strictly necessary to create the user and command aliases, as the user privilege specification could have been written as follows:

```
marysue,bubba ALL=/usr/bin/passwd [A-z]*,!/usr/bin/passwd root
```

After these edits, /etc/sudoers should resemble the following:

```
# sudoers file.
#
# This file MUST be edited with the 'visudo' command as root.
#
# See the sudoers man page for the details on how to write a
sudoers file.
#

# Host alias specification

# User alias specification
User_Alias PWADMIN=marysue,bubba

# Cmnd alias specification
Cmnd_Alias PW=/usr/bin/passwd [A-z]*,!/usr/bin/passwd root

# User privilege specification
root     ALL=(ALL) ALL
PWADMIN ALL=PW
```

5. Save the changes and exit visudo.

6. As marysue or bubba, test the configuration to make sure that everything works as intended. The first test confirms that bubba can use passwd:

```
$ sudo passwd gnuuser

We trust you have received the usual lecture from the local
System
```

```
Administrator. It usually boils down to these two things:

        #1) Respect the privacy of others.
        #2) Think before you type.

Password:
Changing password for user gnuuser
New password:
Retype new password:
passwd: all authentication tokens updated successfully
```

The next test demonstrates that members of the PWADMIN alias *cannot* change the root password:

```
[marysue@localhost]$ sudo passwd root
Sorry, user marysue is not allowed to execute
'/usr/bin/passwd root' as root on luther.
```

Sudo rules can be fine-tuned using flags and keywords in the configuration file. The source code directory for this chapter contains the sample.sudoers file shipped in Sudo's source code configuration. The file sample.sudoers contains many examples (with informative comments) that you can adapt to suit your own needs. In addition, the manual pages for sudo, visudo, and sudoers (man sudo, man visudo, and man sudoers) have complete information on the syntax and useful examples of configuring sudoers and using visudo.

Sudo Configuration and Usage Tips

You should plan ahead for security, because sudo can be used to gain further power by obtaining root access. For example, if you enable users to run less as root, they could use its shell command, !, to run other commands as root or to view sensitive files, such as /etc/shadow. Indeed, the sudoers manual page cautions: "There is no easy way to prevent a user from gaining a root shell if that user has access to commands allowing shell escapes." In general, when configuring root command access using Sudo, adhere to the least-access principle, granting the minimum necessary privileges to accomplish a given task. You should also exercise caution when using Sudo in such a way that lets users edit files because a malicious user can set the $EDITOR environment variable to almost any command or program, which creates a serious security risk.

When using visudo, consider using its -s option, which enables a more rigorous level of syntax and grammar checking. In addition, do *not* give users permission to use visudo for two reasons: first, they can use vi's :! command to obtain a root shell, and, more important, it enables them to edit /etc/sudoers and alter its contents to give themselves unfettered root access and to disable logging.

Working with Users and Groups

Administering users and groups, or, more precisely, administering user and group *accounts*, is a fundamental Red Hat system administration activity. Ordinarily, most people understand user accounts as accounts tied to a particular physical user. However, as you will see later in this chapter, Red Hat systems also have *logical user accounts*, user accounts that can exist for particular applications, such as PostgreSQL, or system functions, such as the mail and bin user accounts.

Other than this distinction between real and logical user accounts, there are few substantive differences between actual and logical users. In particular, both actual and logical have user identification numbers (UIDs), numeric values that the kernel and many applications use instead of the account name. Ordinarily, each user account has a unique UID (on a given system), but this is not strictly required.

Unlike user accounts, group accounts always represent some sort of logical organization of users. Like user accounts, groups have group identification numbers, or GIDs, and it is common for users to be members of several groups. Groups are used to tie one or more users together in order to simplify administrative tasks. For example, an administrator can assign to a group permission to execute a certain application, and then add and delete users from that group, rather than giving individual users permissions, clearly a simpler, less labor-intensive way to handle access control. Similarly, file access can be controlled at the group level because files are assigned user and group owners when files are created and also carry separate read, write, and execute permissions for the file's owner, the group assigned to the file, and any other users on that host.

Because properly managing user and group accounts and assigning and revoking user and group permissions is so important on any Red Hat system, this chapter spends a good deal of time examining the command line and GUI tools for doing so.

Understanding User Private Groups

Before delving into user and group administration tools, however, you need to understand the Red Hat user private group (UPG) scheme, which makes Linux groups much easier to use. Although the UPG scheme does not add or change the normal Linux way of handling groups, it *does* introduce a new convention that is different from traditional Linux user and group idioms: when you create a new user, Red Hat Linux creates a unique group for that user. After you become accustomed to the user private group scheme, you will find that it is very natural to use and makes good sense.

The UPG scheme has the following salient characteristics:

◆ Each user has a primary group with the same name as the user account.

◆ Each user is the only member of her primary group.

♦ Each user's umask defaults to 002 — because every user has her own private group in the UPG scheme, the group protection afforded by the traditional Linux umask of 022 is unnecessary.

♦ Group-specific directories, such as project directories, have the set-GID (set group ID) bit enabled. If you set the set-GID bit on a directory, all files created in that directory have their group set to the directory's group.

TIP The default umask is set in `/etc/profile`.

For example, suppose the finance department maintains a large number of files in the `/opt/finance` directory and that many people work with these files on a daily basis. Using the UPG scheme, you would first create a group named, say, `finance`, use the `chgrp` command to change the group ownership on `/opt/finance` to the `finance` group, use the `chmod` command to enable the set-GID bit on `/opt/finance`, and then add the appropriate users to the `finance` group. As a result, all `finance` users can edit existing files in the `/opt/finance` directory. Similarly, when new files are created in the `/opt/finance` directory, the files are automatically assigned ownership by the `finance` group and all users who are members of the `finance` group can edit them without taking any special steps. Another benefit of the UPG scheme is that if you have users who work on multiple projects, they do not have to change their umask or group as they move from project to project (that is, directory to directory) because each main project directory's set-GID bit automatically sets the proper group for all files created in that directory and its subdirectories.

NOTE Because each user's home directory is owned by that user and her private group, it is safe to set the set-GID bit on the home directory, but unnecessary. Why? By default, files are created with the primary group of the user; the set-GID bit is redundant with respect to a user's home directory and its subdirectories.

The following steps illustrate the scenario and process just described. The point of this exercise is to provide a concrete illustration of Red Hat's UPG scheme, so I defer discussing the commands and their options until later in the chapter.

1. Create the `finance` group:

```
# /usr/sbin/groupadd finance
```

2. Change the group ownership of /opt/finance to the finance group to associate the directory contents with the finance group:

```
# /bin/chgrp -R finance /opt/finance
```

3. Add the proper users to the group (add the user bubba in this case):

```
# /usr/bin/gpasswd -a bubba finance
Adding user bubba to group finance
```

4. To enable the finance group's members to create, make the directory writeable by the group:

```
# /bin/chmod g+w /opt/finance
```

5. Set the set-GID bit on /opt/finance to cause newly created files in the /opt/finance tree to have finance group ownership:

```
# /bin/chmod g+s /opt/finance
```

After this command, the letter s appears where the group execute bit (denoted by the letter x) would ordinarily appear when you generate a long listing of /opt/finance's attributes:

```
ls -ld /opt/finance
drwxrwsr-x   4 root      finance      4096 Sep 23 21:49 /opt/finance/
```

With the default umask set to 002, files that bubba creates in /opt/finance are owned by the user bubba and the group finance, enabling other finance users to modify the file:

```
$ [bubba@localhost]$ touch /opt/finance/20010923
$ [bubba@localhost]$ ls -l /opt/finance/20010923
-rw-rw-r--   1 bubba     finance      0 Sep 23 22:15 /opt/finance/20010923
```

To summarize, the Red Hat UPG scheme makes it trivial to create project groups that permit members of those groups to write files in the groups' common directory without unduly burdening users.

Adding, Modifying, and Deleting Users

Although some administrators find the traditional command line tools for managing users and groups tedious or inconvenient to use, this chapter examines them in detail. For those readers who prefer GUI tools, the section titled "Using the Red Hat User Manager" covers Red Hat's User Manager tool, a GUI application for creating, modifying, and deleting both users and groups.

Table 26-1 lists the commands for adding, modifying, and deleting user accounts. They are discussed in detail in the following subsections.

TABLE 26-1 USER ACCOUNT ADMINISTRATIVE COMMANDS

Command	Description
chage	Changes password aging information
chsh	Changes the user's shell
passwd	Sets or changes user account passwords
newusers	Adds user accounts in batch
useradd	Adds new user accounts
userdel	Deletes user accounts
usermod	Modifies existing user accounts

Readers who may have used one version or another of an adduser script in earlier versions of Red Hat Linux, other Linux distributions, or various Unix versions should note that Red Hat has replaced adduser with a symlink to /usr/sbin/adduser.

THE USER DATABASE FILES

In order to understand the following discussion, you need to know the format of the user database files, /etc/passwd and /etc/shadow. Each line in both files consists of colon-separated fields, one line per user. The format of the password file, /etc/passwd, is

username:password:uid:gid:gecos:directory:shell

Table 26-2 describes the fields in /etc/passwd.

TABLE 26-2 FIELDS IN THE PASSWORD FILE

Field	Description
username	The user's account name on the system
password	username's encrypted password or an x
uid	username's numeric UID (user ID)
gid	username's numeric primary group ID (group ID)

Continued

TABLE 26-2 FIELDS IN THE PASSWORD FILE *(Continued)*

Field	Description
gecos	An optional field used for informational purposes that usually contains *username*'s full name
home	*username*'s home directory
shell	*username*'s login shell

On Red Hat systems (and most Linux systems these days), the actual password is stored in /etc/shadow, indicated by an x in the *password* field. Because /etc/passwd is readable by all users, storing even encrypted passwords in it makes password guessing easier. However, /etc/shadow is more secure because it is readable only by programs that run with root privileges, such as login and passwd. The sidebar "The Shadow Password System" discusses shadow passwords in greater detail.

The Shadow Password System

Red Hat Linux, like most, if not all, Linux and Unix systems, uses shadow passwords because they offer enhanced protection for your system's authentication files. During the installation of Red Hat, shadow password protection for your system is enabled by default, as are MD5 passwords. MD5 passwords are an alternative and far more secure method of encrypting passwords because they are longer and use a stronger encryption method than the standard DES encryption used by the standard authentication utilities.

Shadow passwords offer a number of distinct advantages over the traditional password system, including:

- ◆ Improved system security by moving the encrypted passwords (normally found in /etc/passwd) to /etc/shadow, which is readable only by root

- ◆ Information concerning *password aging*, how long it has been since a password was last changed

- ◆ Control over how long a password can remain unchanged before the user is required to change it

- ◆ The ability to set and enforce a security policy using settings in /etc/login.defs, particularly concerning password aging

The shadow password suite contains a number of utilities that simplify working with shadow passwords and, if you wish, reverting to traditional password management. These utilities include:

- `pwconv` and `pwunconv` for switching from normal to shadow passwords and back, respectively

- `pwck` and `grpck` for verifying the contents and consistency of the password and group files, respectively, against their shadowed counterparts

- `useradd`, `usermod`, and `userdel`, the standard commands for adding, deleting and modifying user accounts

- `groupadd`, `groupmod`, and `groupdel`, the standard commands for adding, deleting, and modifying group accounts

- `gpasswd`, the standard command for administering the groups file, `/etc/group`

Strictly speaking *shell* identifies the program to run when a user logs in. If it is empty, `/bin/sh` is used. If it is set to a nonexistent executable or `/bin/false`, the user is unable to log in. An entry in `/etc/passwd` would resemble the following:

```
marysue:x:502:502:Mary Sue:/home/marysue:/bin/bash
```

In this entry, *username* is marysue; *password* is x, meaning it is stored in `/etc/shadow`; *uid* is 502; *gid* is 502; *gecos* is Mary Sue; *home* is `/home/marysue`; and *shell* is `/bin/bash`.

The *gecos* field is primarily of historical interest. *GECOS* is an acronym meaning General Electric Comprehensive Operating System and was renamed to GCOS when Honeywell purchased General Electric's large systems division. Dennis Ritchie, one of the creators of Unix, writes of it: "Sometimes we sent printer output or batch jobs to the GCOS machine. The gcos field in the password file was a place to stash the information for the $IDENT card. Not elegant."

In addition to storing the encrypted password, `/etc/shadow` stores password expiration information. Like `/etc/passwd`, fields are separated by colons. It contains the following fields, listed in the order in which they appear in `/etc/shadow`:

◆ The account name

◆ The account's encrypted password

◆ The number of days since 1 January 1970 that the password was last changed

◆ The number of days permitted before the password can be changed

◆ The number of days after which the password must be changed

◆ The number of days before the password expires that the user is warned

◆ The number of days after the password expires before the account is disabled

◆ The number of days since 1 January 1970 after which the account is disabled

◆ Reserved for future use

The entry from /etc/shadow that corresponds to the entry from /etc/passwd shown earlier is:

```
marysue:$1$EmRh1cmZ$gkXY3OH43D7NtpQXjm9F01:11589:0:99999:7:::
```

Notice that the last three fields are empty. Rather than interpret these fields manually, you can use the chage command's -l option to obtain a friendlier display:

```
# chage -l marysue
Minimum:           0
Maximum:           99999
Warning:           7
Inactive:          -1
Last Change:                Sep 24, 2003
Password Expires:           Never
Password Inactive:          Never
Account Expires:            Never
```

chage does not display the fields in the order in which they appear in /etc/shadow.

ADDING USERS

The useradd command creates a new user account or, when invoked with the -D option, updates the default values applied to all new user accounts. useradd's syntax is shown in the following listing:

```
useradd [-c comment] [-d home] [-e expire_date] [-f n]
        [-g initial_group] [-G group[,...]]
```

```
          [-m [-k skel_dir] | -M] [-p passwd] [-s shell]
          [-u uid [ -o]] [-n] [-r] login
useradd -D [-g group] [-b home] [-f n] [-e expire_date]
          [-s shell]
```

As you can see in the syntax listing, useradd's only required argument is *login*, which identifies the user account to create. If no other command line options are specified, useradd uses built-in values and default values listed in /etc/login. defs (or, optionally, /etc/default/useradd if it exists). To view the current default values, invoke useradd with -D and no other arguments. The following short listing shows the defaults on a stock Red Hat installation:

```
# useradd -D
GROUP=100
HOME=/home
INACTIVE=-1
EXPIRE=
SHELL=/bin/bash
SKEL=/etc/skel
```

Table 26-3 lists and briefly describes useradd's options.

TABLE 26-3 USERADD COMMAND LINE OPTIONS

Option	Description
-c comment	Sets the comment (GECOS) field to *comment* (usually used for the full name associated with the account)
-d home	Sets the home directory to *home* (the default is to append *login* to /home)
-D	Displays or updates the default values used for the -d, -e -f, -g, and -s options
-e expire_date	Sets the account expiration date to *expire_date* in YYYY-MM-DD format (the default is no expiration)
-f n	Disables the account *n* days after the account password expires (the default value is -1, which disables this feature)
-g initial_group	Sets the primary login group name or GID (group ID) to *initial_group* (defaults to 100)
-G group	Adds the user to one or more *group*s (no default)

Continued

TABLE 26-3 USERADD COMMAND LINE OPTIONS *(Continued)*

Option	Description
-m	Creates the home directory if it does not exist and copies any files in /etc/skel (see -k) to the newly created directory (by default, Red Hat Linux creates the home directory)
-M	Disables creation of the home directory even if the default behavior specified in /etc/login.defs requires creation of the home directory
-k *skel_dir*	Causes the file and directory structure in *skel_dir* to be created in the home directory (only valid with -m)
-p *passwd*	Specifies *passwd* as the encrypted password associated with the account
-s *shell*	Specifies the account's default shell
-u *uid*	Sets the account's UID (user ID) to *uid* (the default value is the next unused UID)
-o	Disables the requirement for unique UIDs (only used with -u)
-n	Disables use of the Red Hat UPG scheme (a user private group will not be created)
-r	Creates a system account
login	Specifies the name of the account to create

To create the user joebob using useradd's default settings, execute the following command:

```
# useradd joebob
```

In addition to creating the home directory, /home/joebob in this case, useradd copies the file and directory structure of /etc/skel to the user's home directory. If -p *passwd* is omitted, the account is disabled, so be sure to use the passwd command (discussed shortly) to set the password for the new account. The command just shown adds the following entries to /etc/passwd, /etc/group, and /etc/shadow (the grep command is used to isolate the entries for joebob and adds the file names to the output):

```
# grep joebob /etc/passwd /etc/shadow /etc/group
/etc/passwd:joebob:x:503:503::/home/joebob:/bin/bash
```

```
/etc/shadow:joebob:!!:11589:0:99999:7:::
/etc/group:joebob:x:503:
```

Refer to the earlier discussion of the format of the password and shadow files to understand the meaning of the fields displayed from those files. Notice that the account has been disabled (the first ! in the password field) and that no password has been set, as indicated by the second ! in the password field. Bear in mind, too, that the entry in the group file represents the user private group created for joebob.

 Red Hat has modified the standard useradd command to support its UPG scheme.

The next command uses some of useradd's command line options to override the default values:

```
# useradd -c "Mary Sue" -e 2001-09-30 -f 3 -n  marysue
```

-c "Mary Sue" sets the comment (or GECOS) field to Mary Sue; -e 2001-09-30 sets the account's expiration date; -f 3 disables the account three days after the password expires (if it is not changed); and -n disables the UPG scheme. Here are the entries created for marysue in /etc/passwd, /etc/shadow, and /etc/group:

```
# grep marysue /etc/passwd /etc/shadow /etc/group
/etc/passwd:marysue:x:503:100:Mary Sue:/home/marysue:/bin/bash
/etc/shadow:marysue:!!:11589:0:99999:7:3:11595:
```

First, note that no entry appeared for /etc/group because -n prevented the creation of marysue's user private group. Instead, useradd used the default GID, 100, which corresponds to the users group. Also notice that the comment, Mary Sue, appears in the record added to /etc/passwd instead of the blank field (indicated by ::) for joebob. Finally, notice the slightly different entry added to /etc/shadow, reflecting the use of account expiration information.

To set or change an account password, use the passwd command. After creating a new account, you need to use passwd to set the account's password, unless you specified the encrypted password using useradd's -p option. passwd's syntax is quite simple:

```
passwd [-l] [-u [-f]] [-d] [-S] [username]
```

username indicates the user account on which to operate. If not specified, passwd operates on the current user's account. -l locks a user account by prefixing the password in /etc/shadow with !. -u, conversely, unlocks a user account. If the account password is *only* !, that is, it has no password, you must use the -f option to enable the account. -d disables a user account by removing the password, and -S shows the status of a user account (whether it is locked or not). Only the root user can use these options. In fact, normal users can only invoke passwd to change their own passwords. Only root can use any of passwd's command line options.

ADDING MULTIPLE USERS SIMULTANEOUSLY

In busy or large IT environments, system administrators often find themselves faced with the necessity of creating multiple user accounts. Using useradd to add one or two accounts is relatively simple, but it quickly becomes tedious if ten or twenty accounts need to be created. Fortunately, the shadow password suite includes the newusers utility, which can be used to create and update multiple user accounts. Its syntax is:

```
newusers userfile
```

userfile is the name of a text file consisting of lines in the same format as the standard password file, subject to the following exceptions:

◆ The password field appears as clear text — newusers encrypts it before adding the account

◆ pw_age: This field is ignored for shadow passwords if the user already exists.

◆ The GID can be the name of an existing group or a nonexistent GID. If the GID is the name of an existing group, the named user is added to that group, but if it is a nonexistent numeric value, a new group with the specified GID is created.

◆ If the specified home directory refers to a nonexistent directory, newusers creates the specified directory. Otherwise, ownership of the directory is set to that of the named user.

The following code shows the contents of newusers.txt, which is passed to newusers to create three new user accounts, bubba, joebob, and marysue:

```
bubba:mypass:901:901:Bubba User:/home/bubba:/bin/bash
joebob:yourpass:902:902:Joe Bob:/home/joebob:/bin/bash
marysue:somepass:903:903:Mary Sue:/home/marysue:/bin/bash
```

After executing the command newusers newusers.txt, you will see the entries in /etc/passwd, /etc/group, and /etc/ shadow, as shown in Listing 26-1.

Listing 26-1: Entries in user database files after using newusers

```
# tail -3 passwd
bubba:x:901:901:Bubba User:/home/bubba:/bin/bash
joebob:x:902:902:Joe Bob:/home/joebob:/bin/bash
marysue:x:903:903:Mary Sue:/home/marysue:/bin/bash
# tail -3 group
901:x:901:bubba
902:x:902:joebob
903:x:903:marysue
# tail -3 shadow
bubba:1Uv9E9KXbhuLY:11591:0:99999:7:::
joebob:1WFbzZpUa1z5g:11591:0:99999:7:::
marysue:1WrZ2DoIcmafo:11591:0:99999:7:::
```

MODIFYING AND DELETING USER ACOUNTS

To modify the account information set by useradd, use the usermod command. usermod accepts most of the same options as useradd plus two more, -L and -U. -L locks an account and -U unlocks an account. These options are comparable to the passwd command's -l and -u options. usermod's -l *login_name* option, not available with useradd, enables you to change an account name. usermod does not enable you to change the name of a user who is logged in.

Keep in mind some additional subtleties when you're using usermod. In particular, if you use -G to modify the list of supplementary or additional groups to which the user account belongs, if the user is currently a member of a group which is not listed, the user is removed from the unlisted group(s). If you use -l to change an account name, you need to update the name of the user's home directory manually to reflect the new login name. When you use usermod's -u option to change a user's UID, all files and directories rooted in the user's home directory are updated automatically to the new UID, but any files outside of the user's home directory must be altered manually. In addition, crontab files or at jobs must be updated manually; changes involving NIS must be made on the NIS server. If you do change the UID, ensure that no processes belonging to the named users are executing when the UID is changed. Similar caveats apply to changing the user account's GID (using -g).

To change user account expiry information, use the chage command. In general form, its syntax is

chage [*options*] *username*

chage supports the command line options shown in Table 26-4 in addition to the -l option mentioned previously. Normal (nonroot) users are permitted to use only the -l option and only for their own accounts.

TABLE 26-4 CHAGE COMMAND LINE OPTIONS

Option	Description
username	Identifies the account on which to operate
-d *lastday*	Sets *lastday* as the number of days elapsed since 1 January 1970 that the account password was last changed (*lastday* may be specified in YYYY-MM-DD format)
-E *expireday*	Sets *expireday* as the number of days permitted to elapse after 1 January 1970 before the user account is disabled (*expireday* may be specified in YYYY-MM-DD format); a value of 0 disables account expiration
-I *inactivedays*	Sets *inactivedays* as the number of days permitted to elapse after the account password has expired before the account is disabled
-m *mindays*	Sets *mindays* as the number of days required to elapse before a user can change her password (a value of 0 permits changing the password at any time)
-M *maxdays*	Sets *maxdays* as the number of days permitted to elapse before a password must be changed
-W *warndays*	Sets *warndays* as the number of days before password expiration during which the user is warned that her password is due to expire

Using the marysue account created previously, the following listing shows marysue's account expiration information:

```
# chage -l marysue
Minimum:           0
Maximum:           99999
Warning:           7
Inactive:          3
Last Change:              Sep 24, 2003
Password Expires:         Never
Password Inactive:        Never
Account Expires:          Sep 30, 2003
```

The next command uses some of the options Table 26-4 listed to modify marysue's expiry information, specifically, the minimum number of days between password changes (-m), the maximum number of days permitted to elapse before the password *must* be changed (-M), and the account's expiration date (-E):

```
# chage -m 5 -M 30 -E 0 marysue
# chage -l marysue
Minimum:           5
Maximum:           30
Warning:           7
Inactive:          3
Last Change:               Sep 24, 2003
Password Expires:          Oct 24, 2003
Password Inactive:         Oct 27, 2003
Account Expires:           Never
```

As you can see from the output of chage -l, marysue must wait 5 days between password changes, she must change her password every 30 days, and her account will never expire. Notice that changing the minimum and maximum values caused chage to display the dates on which the password expires and (oddly, because the inactivity date was not modified) the date on which the account becomes inactive if marysue fails to change her password.

To change a user's login shell, use the chsh command. Its syntax is:

```
chsh [-l] | [-s shell] username
```

shell is the shell to use and must be specified as a full path. *username* specifies the user account name to modify. To list the full path names of the available shells (from /etc/shells), specify -l.

TIP You can also view the available shells by executing the command cat /etc/shells.

For example, to change the shell for marysue to the C shell, execute the following commands:

```
# chsh -l
/bin/bash2
/bin/bash
/bin/sh
/bin/ash
/bin/bsh
/bin/tcsh
/bin/csh
```

```
# chsh marysue
Changing shell for marysue.
New shell [/bin/bash]: /bin/csh
Shell changed.
```

The first command lists the available command so you can see the full path names. The second command changes marysue's shell. chsh prompts for the new shell after displaying the current shell in square brackets. If you do not specify a new shell, the shell remains unchanged. chsh fails if you do not provide an absolute path. You can also specify an arbitrary command name, which must be a full path, for the new shell, but if the command is not listed in /etc/shells, chsh displays a warning message before changing the shell, as shown in the following listing:

```
# chsh marysue
Changing shell for marysue.
New shell [/bin/csh]: /bin/false
Warning: "/bin/false" is not listed in /etc/shells
Shell changed.
```

Using chsh this way can disable a user's account because specifying a command that does not invoke a login shell prevents the login process from completing.

Finally, to delete a user account, use the userdel command. Its syntax is the simplest of all the user account administration commands you have seen so far:

```
userdel [-r] username
```

username indicates the user account to delete. The -r option causes userdel to delete the user's home directory, mail spool (/var/mail/*username*). If -r is omitted, only the account information is deleted from /etc/passwd, /etc/shadow, and /etc/group. Even if -r is used, any files owned by *username* not in /home/*username* must be searched for and deleted manually. One of the following commands can be used to accomplish this:

```
find / -user username -exec rm -rf -- {} \;
find / -user username | xargs rm -rf
```

The first command finds all files owned by *username*, beginning from the root (/) file system, and executes the rm -rf command for each file found. The second command pipes the output of the find command to xargs, which builds a command line using rm -rf and the file names generated by the find command. The second command may prove faster if *username* owns many files because the rm command is executed after the file name list has been generated, instead of iteratively, which is how the -exec argument find works. For more information about find and xargs, see their texinfo documentation (info find and info xargs) or their manual pages (man find and man xargs).

Adding, Modifying, and Deleting Groups

As the section "Understanding User Private Groups" earlier in the chapter suggests, Red Hat Linux makes greater use of group accounts than other Linux distributions. So knowing how to add, modify, and delete group accounts is more important on Red Hat systems than it is with other Linux distributions. Table 26-5 lists the commands used to add, modify, and delete group accounts. They are discussed in greater detail in the following subsections.

TABLE 26-5 GROUP ACCOUNT ADMINISTRATIVE COMMANDS

Command	Description
gpasswd	Sets group passwords and modifies group accounts
groupadd	Creates a new group account
groupdel	Deletes an existing group account
groupmod	Modifies existing group accounts

As with the discussion of the password file in the previous section, you will find the following discussion of working with group accounts less confusing if you understand the format of the group file, /etc/group. It has one entry per line, and each line has the format:

groupname:*password*:*gid*:*userlist*

- ◆ *groupname* is the name of the group

- ◆ *password* is an optional field containing the encrypted group password

- ◆ *gid* is the numeric group ID number

- ◆ *userlist* is a comma-separated list of the user account names that comprise the group

If x appears in the password field, nonmembers of the group cannot join it using the newgrp command. A typical entry in the group file might resemble the following:

admins:x:507:joebob,marysue,bubba

groupname is admins; *password* is empty, meaning no group password has been set; *gid* is 503; and *userlist* is joebob,marysue,bubba.

CREATING GROUPS

To create a new group, use the `groupadd` command. Its syntax is:

```
groupadd [[-g gid [-o]] [-r] [-f] groupname
```

groupname is the only required argument and must be the name of a nonexistent group. When invoked with only the name of the new group, `groupadd` creates the group and assigns it the first unused GID that is both greater than 500 and not already in use. Specify `-f` to force `groupadd` to accept an existing *groupname*. Use the `-g gid` option if you want to specify the new group's GID, replacing *gid* with a unique GID (use the `-o` option to force `groupadd` to accept a nonunique GID). To create system group, one that has special privileges, use the `-r` option.

The following command creates a new group named `admins`:

```
# groupadd admins
```

Here is the resulting entry created in `/etc/group`:

```
admins:x:507:
```

As this point, `admins` has no members and the password field has an `x` in it, meaning that no nonmembers (which is everyone at this point) except root can join the group using `newgrp`.

MODIFYING AND DELETING GROUPS

After creating a new group, you will likely want to add user accounts to it. Two commands modify group accounts, each serving different purposes. `groupmod` enables you to change a group's GID or name, and `gpasswd` enables you to set and modify a group's authentication and membership information. You should rarely need to change a group's name or GID, so I leave it to you to read the short manual page for `groupmod`. Here, I concentrate on `gpasswd`, which enables the root user to administer all aspects of a group account and to delegate some administrative responsibilities to a group administrator. To simplify the following discussion, I first explain the uses of `gpasswd`, *only* available to root, and then cover the `gpasswd` calls a group administrator can perform. As a result, keep in mind that root can administer all aspects of a group account.

From root's perspective, `gpasswd`'s syntax is:

```
gpasswd [-A username] [-M username] groupname
```

Root can use `-A username` to assign *username* as *groupname*'s group administrator. `-M username` adds *username* to *groupname*'s membership roster. Assigning a group administrator using `-A` does not make the administrator a member of the group — you have to use `-M` to add the administrator as a member of the group. Multiple *username*'s can be specified with `-A` and `-M`. The following command shows how to add `marysue` and `joebob` to the `admins` group:

In order to use the -A option, the shadow group file, /etc/gshadow must exist. Read the subsection titled "Using a Shadowed Group File" to understand the implications of using shadowed group files.

```
# gpasswd -M marysue,joebob admins
```

After this change, the admins entries in /etc/group should resemble the following:

```
admins:!:507:marysue,joebob
```

Notice that adding users to the admins group account replaced x with ! in the password field, meaning that password-based access to the group (using newgrp) is disabled.

For group administrators, gpasswd's syntax is:

```
gpasswd [-R] [-r] [-a username] [-d username] groupname
```

gpasswd called with only *groupname* changes the group password. Once a group password is set, group members can still use newgrp to join the group without a password, but nonmembers of the group must supply the password. For example, the following commands show what happens when the user bubba uses newgrp to join the admins group after root sets a group password, which, for the record, is secret:

newgrp *groupname* changes the group identification of the calling user to *groupname*. After calling newgrp successfully, file access permissions are calculated based on the new GID. If *groupname* is omitted, the GID is changed to the calling user's primary (login) GID.

```
$ newgrp admins
Password:
$ groups
admins bubba
```

By contrast, here is what happens when joebob, who *is* a member of admins, uses newgrp to join the admins group. Notice that joebob is not prompted for a password as bubba was:

```
$ newgrp admins
$ groups
admins joebob
```

Conversely, if no group password is set, *only* group members can use `newgrp` to join the group. To remove a group password, use the `-r` option. The next snippet shows what happens when bubba tries to join `admins` after the group password is removed. Keep in mind that the password field in the group file will be empty after the password is removed using `-r`:

```
$ newgrp admins
newgrp: Permission denied.
```

This time, `bubba` was not even prompted for a password. `joebob`, however, has no problem:

```
$ newgrp admins
$ groups
admins joebob
```

Calling `gpasswd` with the `-R` option disables access to a group using the `newgrp` command. Oddly, if you use this option, `gpasswd` places a `!` in the password field in the group file, so nonmembers of the group get a password prompt but no password works.

To add a user to the group, a group administrator must use the `-a username` option. The `-d username` option removes a user from a group. The next example shows how to add and remove `bubba` using `gpasswd`'s `-a` and `-d` options:

```
# gpasswd -a bubba admins
Adding user bubba to group admins
# grep admins /etc/group
admins:!:507:marysue,joebob,bubba
# gpasswd -d bubba admins
Removing user bubba from group admins
# grep admins /etc/group
admins:!:507:marysue,joebob
```

USING A SHADOWED GROUP FILE

Much of the behavior described in the previous subsection does not apply if the shadow group file, `/etc/gshadow`, is present. In particular, if the shadow group file is in use:

◆ Adding a group creates an entry for that group in the shadow group file that resembles the following:

```
admins:x:507:
admins:!::
```

◆ Adding a user to a group adds that user to both the standard group file and the shadow group file:

```
# gpasswd -M marysue admins
# grep admins /etc/group /etc/gshadow
group:admins:x:507:marysue
gshadow:admins:!::marysue
```

◆ The third field in the shadow group file holds the name of the group administrator, not the GID, if an administrator is added using gpasswd's -A username option:

```
# gpasswd -A marysue admins
# grep admins /etc/gshadow
admins:!:marysue:marysue
```

◆ A group administrator cannot join the group unless the administrator's account is also a member of the group. Similarly, a group administrator can add and delete her user account from the group without affecting her administrative function.

◆ Only group members can use newgrp to join the group. To put it another way, nonmembers of a group cannot use newgrp to join groups of which they are not members, even if they know the group password. In fact, passwords are irrelevant because they do not work for nonmembers and members do not need to use them.

Deleting a group is quite simple. Use the groupdel command, which takes no options except the name of the group to delete. For example, the following command deletes the admins group:

```
# groupdel admins
```

Those of you who find typing commands tedious, the next section shows you how to use User Manager, Red Hat's new GUI tool for administering user and group accounts.

Using the Red Hat User Manager

The Red Hat User Manager is a graphical tool for managing user and group accounts that replaces Linuxconf user and group management modules. To use it, you need to be logged in as root or know the root password. To start User Manager, click Main Menu → Programs → System → User Manager on the GNOME desktop, K → Red Hat → System → User Manager on the KDE desktop, or execute the command redhat-config-users in a terminal window. The initial screen resembles Figure 26-1.

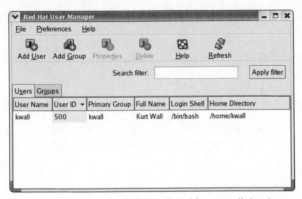

Figure 26-1: The main Red Hat User Manager dialog box

From this screen you can view, modify, and delete existing user and group accounts or create new ones. To reduce the list of displayed accounts or to search for a specific account, type the first few letters of an account name in the Filter by text box and click the Apply filter button. You can update most windows by clicking the Refresh button on the toolbar. To get context sensitive help, click the toolbar's Help button or, to view the entire User Manager manual, select Help → Manual from the toolbar.

CREATING USER ACCOUNTS
To add a new user:

1. Click the New User button. The Create New User dialog box, as shown in Figure 26-2, appears.

Figure 26-2: Adding a new user

2. Type the new account name in the User Name text box.

3. Type the user's full name in the Full Name text box.

4. Type the user's password in the Password and Confirm Password fields. The password must be at least six characters.

5. Select a login shell. If you choose not to accept the default shell, select an alternative shell from the Login Shell drop-down box.

6. As noted earlier in this chapter, the default home directory is `/home/username`. You can change the home directory by editing the Home Directory text box or not create a home directory at all by unchecking the Create home directory check box.

7. To prevent creation of a user private group, remove the check from the Create new group for this user check box. A completed Create New User dialog box might resemble Figure 26-3.

Figure 26-3: A newly configured user account

8. Click OK to create the user.

MODIFYING AND DELETING USER ACCOUNTS

After you have created a user account, you can configure additional properties by clicking User Manager's User tab, selecting the user, and clicking the Properties button to open the User Properties dialog box. To add the user to additional groups, click the Groups tab (see Figure 26-4). Click the check box next to the groups of which the user should be a member; then click the Apply button.

Other account data you can modify from the User Properties window includes the basic user information you supplied when you created the user (the User Data tab), account information (the Account Info tab), and password expiration information (the Password Info tab). On the Password Info tab, click the Enable account expiration check box to set the user account's expiration date if you want the account to expire on a certain date. To prevent this user account from logging in, place a check mark in the User account is locked check box.

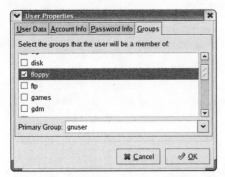

Figure 26-4: Adding a user to additional groups

Click the Password Info tab to view and change the account password expiration information (see Figure 26-5). The date that the user last changed her password appears across the top of the tab. Click Enable password expiration to force a password change after a certain number of days, and then enter the number of days between required password changes in the Days before change required text box. You can also set the number of days before the user can change her password, the number of days before the user is warned to change her password, and the number of days before the account becomes inactive. When you have finished modifying the user account properties, click OK to apply the changes and close the User Properties dialog box.

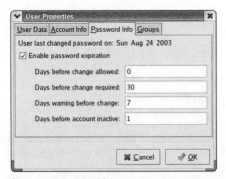

Figure 26-5: Modifying user account password expiration information

Finally, to delete a user account, click the account to delete on User Manager's Users tab and then click the Delete button.

CREATING GROUP ACCOUNTS

To add a new user group, click the New Group button. In the Create New Group dialog box (see Figure 26-6), type the name of the new group, and then click OK to create the group.

Figure 26-6: Adding a new group

MODIFYING AND DELETING GROUP ACCOUNTS

To view or modify the properties of an existing group, select the group to modify from the group list on the Groups tab and click the Properties button. The Group Properties dialog box, as shown in Figure 26-7, appears.

Figure 26-7: Modifying group properties

The Group Users tab (see Figure 26-8) displays the users that are members of the group. To add other users to the group, place a check mark next to the user account names in the list, and deselect account names to remove them from the group. Click OK to apply the changes and close the Group Properties box.

After you have finished adding or modifying user and group accounts, click Action → Exit to close the Red Hat User Manager.

Figure 26-8: Modifying group properties

Using File System Quotas

The aphorism "Disk space is cheap" has never been more true than it is today, when 20GB disk drives are standard equipment on new PCs and a 40GB disk drive can be purchased for $150. Unfortunately, just as the heralded paperless office has been answered by skyrocketing paper consumption, the proliferation of massive disk drives has been answered by ever-increasing pressures on disk space. For system administrators, one of the perennial challenges is managing disk space and making sure that no single user takes more than her fair share. The final section of this chapter shows you how to use the quota utilities to set, monitor, and enforce file system usage quotas for individual users and for groups of users. After you have performed the initial setup, managing file system usage with the quota suite is a largely automated task that leaves you free to concentrate on more pressing matters.

The programs you use to set and enforce disk usage quotas include the following:

♦ `edquota` – Sets, edits, and removes user and group file system quotas

♦ `quota` – Displays defined quotas and current file system usage

♦ `quotacheck` – Creates, checks, and repairs file system quota files

♦ `quotaoff` – Disables file system quotas

♦ `quotaon` – Enables file system quotas

♦ `repquota` – Summarizes and reports on quota utilization

♦ `warnquota` – Checks file system usage and sends email to users exceeding their assigned quotas

Note that quotas are set on a per file system basis, rather than per disk. You also must use disk blocks or disk inodes to set quotas, not the more familiar and more easily understood units of megabytes. Despite these inconveniences, however, the procedure for initializing quotas on file systems is straightforward. Briefly, the steps to follow are:

1. Edit /etc/fstab to enable quotas on the desired file systems.

2. Create the quota accounting files on the root directory of each file system for which quotas are enforced.

3. Turn on quotas.

4. Set the desired file system quotas.

5. Review quota utilization regularly and frequently.

In the following subsections, you look at each of these steps and the commands to accomplish them.

Preparing the System for Quotas

To prepare the system for quotas, the first step is to drop the system to single user mode. To do so, press Ctrl+Alt+F1 to flip over to the first virtual console and then log in as root. After you have logged in, execute the following command to bring the system down to single user mode:

```
# /sbin/telinit 1
```

The reason you should put the system into single user mode is to prevent logged in users from altering files and possibly losing data while you are setting up the quotas. Next, edit /etc/fstab and add the mount option usrquota to enable quotas for users, the mount option grpquota to enable quotas for groups, or both if you want to enable quotas for both users and groups. For example, the following line from /etc/fstab enables user quotas on the /home file system:

```
LABEL=/home    /home    ext3    defaults,usrquota    1 2
```

Note that mount ignores the usrquota keyword but that programs in the quota suite expect to see it in /etc/fstab.

Finally, execute the mount command using the remount option to update the kernel's mount table (/etc/mtab) with the quota option. For example, to activate quotas on the /home file system shown in the example, execute the following command:

```
# mount /home -o remount,rw
```

Creating the Quota Files

Now that the system is prepared, the next phase of the procedure for setting up quotas is to create the accounting files quota uses to monitor file system usage. There are two such files for each file system on which quotas are used, aquota.user if user quotas are enforced and aquota.group if group quotas are enforced. The quota accounting files are stored in the root directory of each file system. To create these accounting files, execute the quotacheck command, as shown in the following example:

```
# quotacheck -uv /home
quotacheck: Scanning /dev/hdc1 [/home] done
quotacheck: Checked 1158 directories and 24352 files
```

quotacheck scans the specified file system to determine its current usage and then writes this information into the quota accounting files. In the example shown, I have enabled only user quotas, so only the user quota file, /home/aquota.user, is created. quotacheck's -u option causes quotacheck to create (or check) only user quotas, and the -v option specifies verbose operation. /home, as you might guess, tells quotacheck which file system to scan. quotacheck's most commonly used syntax is:

```
quotacheck [-bcgRuv] -a | filesys
```

filesys specifies the file system to check. If specified, -a instructs quotacheck to scan all mount file systems listed in /etc/mtab that are not NFS mounts. If -a is *not* specified, then filesys must be specified. Table 26-6 explains the other options.

TABLE 26-6 QUOTACHECK OPTIONS

Option	Description
-b	Make backup copies of quota files before overwriting old ones
-c	Ignore existing quota files
-g	Only check file system group quotas
-R	Used with -a, tells quotacheck not to check the root file system
-u	Only check file system user quotas, the default behavior if neither -g nor -u is specified
-v	Operate in verbose mode

Enabling Quotas

After creating the quota accounting files, use the `quotaon` command to turn on quotas. `quotaon`'s invocation is simple

```
quotaon [-guv] -a | filesys
```

`quotaon`'s options have the same meaning as the corresponding options for `quotacheck` listed in Table 26-6. So, to turn on quotas for the `/home` file system used in this section, execute the following command:

```
# quotaon /home
```

Pretty easy, eh?

Setting and Modifying Quotas

At this point, you are finally ready to configure file system quotas because all of the preliminary setup is now complete. To set quotas, use the quota editor, `edquota`, which has the following syntax:

```
edquota [-ug] -t
edquota [-ug] account
```

The `-u` and `-g` options have the meaning listed in Table 26-6. The `-t` option in the first form of the command enables you to edit the time limits during which file system usage is permitted to be over quota, that is, to exceed the defined limits. Red Hat configures the default time limit, called a grace period, to seven days. To change this default value, execute the following command:

```
# edquota -u -t
```

By default, `edquota` uses the vi editor, so the resulting screen should resemble the following:

```
Grace period before enforcing soft limits for users:
Time units may be: days, hours, minutes, or seconds
  Filesystem              Block grace period      Inode grace period
  /dev/hdc1                     7days                   7days
```

To change the time limit, change the text that reads `7days` to another value. You can use time units of seconds, minutes, hours, days, weeks, and months. So, for example, to set a time limit of three weeks, change the line that reads

```
  /dev/hdc1                     7days                   7days
```

so that it reads

```
/dev/hdc1                3weeks              3weeks
```

After making the changes, save your changes and exit `edquota` using the standard vi keystrokes (`:wq`).

The second form of the `edquota` command enables you to set the actual file system usage limits. *account* must be the name of a user or group for which you are setting quotas. The following listing shows the `edquota` session for editing the user `bubba`'s quotas. It was invoked using the command `edquota -u bubba` (the display may wrap on your system).

```
Disk quotas for user bubba (uid 500):
  Filesystem          blocks     soft     hard     inodes     soft     hard
  /dev/hdc1           950051        0        0      25020        0        0
```

The first column shows the file system(s) for which `bubba` has quotas; the second column shows the number of blocks `bubba` has used, followed by the soft and hard limits for block usage. The fifth column shows the number of inodes, or file system entries, `bubba` is currently using, followed by the soft and hard limits for inode usage. A *hard limit* is the absolute value beyond which file system usage is forbidden to go—once `bubba` reaches the hard limit, he will not be permitted to create any more files until he deletes enough files on the specified file system to go below his quota. A *soft limit*, on the other hand, is less restrictive than a hard limit—users (or groups) are permitted to exceed their soft limits for the grace period mentioned previously. After the grace period expires, however, no more files can be created until the user (or group) takes steps to reduce file system utilization below the soft limit.

How big is a block? It varies from system to system depending on the size of the underlying disk. On this system, a block is 1024K. To set `bubba`'s quota, set the soft and hard limits for block usage to a nonzero value. For example, the following entry shows `bubba`'s soft limit set to 960,000 blocks and his hard limit set to 975,000 blocks:

```
/dev/hdc1           950051   960000   975000      25020        0        0
```

After setting the limit, save your changes and exit `edquota` using the standard vi keystrokes (`:wq`).

 TIP I strongly recommend not using inode limits. Each file a user creates requires *at least* one inode, so it is much easier to limit overall disk space usage than it is to limit the number of files a user can create.

Reviewing Quota Utilization

Reviewing and monitoring quota utilization is an ongoing process, but also easy to accomplish if you automate the process using a couple of cron jobs. One cron job should run the `warnquota` utility on a daily basis. The other cron job should run the `repquota` program, again on a daily basis. `warnquota` is a script that sends users a short e-mail message resembling that shown in Listing 26-2 if they are over quota.

Listing 26-2: Quota exceeded warning message from warnquota

```
From: root@localhost
Reply-To:
Subject: Disk Quota usage on system
To: bubba@localhost.localdomain
Cc: root@localhost.localdomain

Hi,

We noticed that you are in violation with the quota system
used on this system. We have found the following violations:

                    Block limits          File limits
Filesystem       used    soft   hard  grace   used  soft  hard  grace
/dev/hdc1    +  960051  960000 975000 6days  25920    0    0

We hope that you will cleanup before your grace period expires.

Basically, this means that the system thinks you are using more disk space
on the above partition(s) than you are allowed.  If you do not delete files
and get below your quota before the grace period expires, the system will
prevent you from creating new files.

For additional assistance, please contact us at 800-GET-HELP
or via phone at 800-WHO-AREU.
```

The contact phone numbers, the subject line, and the CC list in `warnquota`'s message can be customized by editing `/etc/warnquota.conf`, an example of which is shown in Listing 26-3. As shipped, the `sendmail` invocation defined by the `MAIL_CMD` line is incorrect, reading `MAIL_CMD = "/usr/sbin/sendmail/.sendmail -t"`. Change it to read `MAIL_CMD = "/usr/sbin/sendmail -t"` instead, or `warnquota` will fail with an error message and the warning message will not be sent.

Listing 26-3: A customized /etc/warnquota.conf file

```
MAIL_CMD = "/usr/sbin/sendmail -t"
FROM     = "root@localhost"
```

Continued

Listing 26-3 *(Continued)*

```
SUBJECT  = Disk Quota usage on system
CC_TO    = "root@localhost"
SUPPORT  = "800-GET-HELP"
PHONE    = "800-WHO-AREU"
```

warnquota generates its report by calling the quota program to check user quotas. You can use quota to check file system quota usage manually. quota's syntax is:

quota [-gus] *user*

The -g and -u options have the meaning shown in Table 26-6. Specifying -s tells quota to use more understandable units for displaying disk usage and limits. For example, the following command shows bubba's quota statistics:

```
# quota -s bubba
Disk quotas for user bubba (uid 500):
    Filesystem blocks   quota   limit   grace   files   quota   limit   grace
    /dev/hdc1    928M*   928M    939M   6days   25020       0       0
```

To see a complete list of quota statistics for all users and groups for a file system, use the repquota program, which accepts the same options as quota but requires a file system argument rather than a user argument. You can use the -a option to see a report for all file systems on which quotas are being used. The following command shows a repquota report for /dev/hdc1, using the -s option to display the output in units of megabytes:

```
# repquota -s /dev/hdc1
*** Report for user quotas on device /dev/hdc1
Block grace time: 7days; Inode grace time: 7days
                        Block limits                File limits
User            used    soft    hard  grace    used  soft  hard  grace
----------------------------------------------------------------------
root      --    579M       0       0            489     0     0
bubba     +     928M    928M    939M  6days   25020     0     0

Statistics:
Total blocks: 7
Data blocks: 1
Entries: 2
Used average: 2.000000
```

Summary

This chapter briefly recapped the power of the root account on a Red Hat Enterprise Linux system and showed you how to delegate some of that power to nonroot users using Sudo. You also learned to create and manage user and group accounts using a variety of command line utilities and the new Red Hat User Manager graphical administration tool. Finally, you read about how to prevent users and groups from monopolizing disk space and how to monitor system disk space utilization using the quota suite of programs.

Chapter 27

Installing and Upgrading Software Packages

IN THIS CHAPTER

- ◆ Using the Red Hat Package Manager
- ◆ Checking software versions
- ◆ Obtaining newer software
- ◆ Installing software

ONE OF LINUX'S MOST ENJOYABLE QUALITIES is the variety and number of software packages available for it. Even novice Linux users can download and install new or updated software with little or no difficulty using RPM, the Red Hat Package Manager. Blindly installing software, even on an RPM-based system, may cause problems, though, and in general the more you understand about software installation and maintenance, the more comfortable you will be with the process. This chapter provides detailed information and instructions for locating, downloading, building, and installing new and updated software. First, however, the chapter explains how to use RPM because it is the preferred tool for software management on Red Hat systems.

Using the Red Hat Package Manager

RPM is a powerful software configuration manager and the dominant tool for installing, removing, verifying, and updating software packages on Red Hat systems. Red Hat Enterprise Linux installs tools for using RPM at the command line and using a GUI. Although RPM is not the only software management option available, as you will see later in the chapter, it is the one most people use. This section describes how to use most RPM features. We cover some topics in greater detail in later sections of the chapter, though, so they are mentioned only briefly in this one. Most examples illustrate command line usage, but some show how to use Gnome-RPM, a GUI front end to RPM.

RPM consists of two components: a set of databases that store information about installed software and the programs that interface with the databases. RPM can work with binary and source packages. *Binary packages,* generally referred to simply as RPMs, contain compiled software ready for installation. They use the file extension .rpm. *Source packages*, more often called source RPMs, are uncompiled packages used to create binary RPMs and have a .src.rpm file extension. Because RPM offers a rich feature set that makes it seem complex and difficult to learn to use, the following sections each explore one of RPM's modes, in order to simplify the discussion:

- ◆ General options
- ◆ Querying
- ◆ Package maintenance
- ◆ Package verification
- ◆ Package building
- ◆ Administrative options
- ◆ Miscellaneous options

The query functions can be used to obtain a considerable amount of information about installed software. Package maintenance enables package installation, removal, and upgrading. Package verification gives system administrators the ability to compare the present state of files installed by an rpm against information taken from the original package. The package building mode is used to build or rebuild RPMs from source code. The administration and miscellaneous modes, finally, affect RPM itself, rather than software packages. They are used to fix possible database corruption and to determine RPM's general configuration.

General Options

At the command line, the primary RPM command is rpm. In addition to the mode-specific command line options discussed in the following sections, rpm accepts the general command line options listed in Table 27-1.

TABLE 27-1 GENERAL RPM COMMAND LINE OPTIONS

Option	Description
-v	Displays basic information about the RPM operation's status.
-vv	Displays debugging information. Most useful to software packagers and RPM developers.

Option	Description
--quiet	Displays only error information.
--help	Shows a usage summary.
--version	Shows the RPM version number.
--justdb	Updates only the database, not the file system.

The -vv option may prove useful when troubleshooting package installation or removal that fails, but be prepared to sort through voluminous and frequently cryptic-looking output to find the information you need. --justdb is used to help repair the database. The results of any operation, such as installing or removing an RPM, affect only RPM's databases; no files are added or removed from the file system. For example, the following command uses --justdb to delete the whois package from RPM's database without actually deleting the files:

```
# rpm --justdb -e whois
# rpm -q whois
package whois is not installed
# ls -l /usr/bin/whois
-rwxr-xr-x   1 root     root         7996 Feb 16 08:47 /usr/bin/whois
```

The second command uses the -q (query) option to see if the whois RPM is installed. As the output indicates, it is not in the database. But, the ls command shows that whois *is*, in fact, still installed. Only the RPM database changed, not the file system.

The rpm command supports more options than those listed in Table 27-1. To simplify the discussion, this chapter examines only the most common and helpful options.

One common use of --justdb is to remove an RPM's entry from the database after the package has been upgraded using a non-RPM source, such as a tarball. In such cases, the RPM entry is invalid and needs to be removed without deleting the installed files. The most common use of --justdb is to repair the RPM database if it becomes corrupted.

Query Mode

RPM's query mode is one of its most powerful and useful features. The general form of an RPM query is

```
rpm -q [query_opts]
```

-q (or --query, if you prefer) specifies a query operation and *query_opts* specifies what to query, the type of query, how the query should run, or the format of its output. Most commonly, however, queries use the following general syntax:

```
rpm -q [query_opts] package [...]
```

package names the RPM to query. Query multiple RPMs using a space-separated list of package names. Query mode's power comes at the cost of a long list of options for the *query_opts* argument. The options fall into two broad categories. One group controls which package or packages to query, and the other defines what information to display. Table 27-2 lists many but not all of the options available in query mode. The Type column uses S to mark a package selection option and I to mark an information selection option. Unless mentioned otherwise, all options require at least one package name as an argument.

TABLE 27-2 RPM QUERY MODE OPTIONS

Option	Type	Description
-a	S	Query all installed RPMs. Does not require a package specification.
--whatrequires *capability*	S	Query all RPMs that need *capability* in order to function properly.
--whatprovides *capability*	S	Query all RPMs that provide *capability*.
-f *file*	S	Query the RPM that owns *file*. Does not require a package specification.
-g *group*	S	List the packages in the RPM group named *group*. Does not require a package specification.
-p *package [...]*	S	Query the *uninstalled* RPM named *package*.
-i	I	Display complete information about the queried RPM(s).

Option	Type	Description
`--requires`	I	List all RPMs on which the package depends.
`--provides`	I	List all of the capabilities the queried RPM(s) provides.
`--changelog`	I	Display change information about the queried RPM(s).
`-l`	I	List all of the files stored in the RPM.
`-s`	I	For each file in the original RPM, display its state, which is one of `normal`, `not installed`, or `replaced`.
`-d`	I	List only the documentation files stored in the RPM.
`-c`	I	List only the configuration files stored in the queried RPM(s).
`--dump`	I	For each file stored in the queried RPM(s), display its path, size, modification time, MD5 checksum, permissions, owner, group, and whether it is a configuration file, documentation file, a device, or a symlink (must be used with `-l`, `-c`, or `-d`).
`--last`	I	Display the installation date and time of each RPM queried, starting with the most recently installed RPM.
`--querytags`	I	Print all known tags for use with the `--qf` option. Does not require a package specification.
`--qf 'format_str'`	I	Create a customized output format for displayed information, using `format_str` as the model.

As you can see in Table 27-2, RPM's query mode is extensive and flexible, allowing you to obtain any type of information the RPM databases store. Using the `--qf` option, in fact, you can create customized query output for use in reports and scripts. The next few sections demonstrate how to use many of these options. First, however, some of the option descriptions need additional elaboration. When using the -f, option, the *file* argument must be to a full path. That is, the command rpm -qf /usr/bin/xmms will show the name of the RPM that contains xmms; rpm -qf xmms will not. Finally, when specifying a package name with the -p option, you must use the complete RPM file name.

QUERYING PACKAGE DEPENDENCIES

The --provides, --requires, --whatrequires, and --whatprovides options allow you to identify dependencies between packages. The *capability* argument represents the dependency itself, which is often the name of another RPM or the name of a particular file. RPM uses dependencies to maintain system integrity, so, for example, if one RPM requires something a second RPM provides, you cannot, in normal usage, delete the second RPM. To illustrate, to determine on what capabilities the RPM package depends, use the --requires option as shown in the following command:

```
$ rpm -q --requires rpm
/bin/sh
config(rpm) = 4.2.1-0.11
fileutils
libbeecrypt.so.6
libbz2.so.1
libc.so.6
[...]
```

The example output is truncated to preserve space. As the output shows, the RPM package requires, in part, the /bin/sh capability and a config(rpm) capability greater than or equal to version 4.1.2. In this case, the /bin/sh capability refers to the existence of default shell, /bin/sh, and the config(rpm) capability identifies the minimum acceptable version of rpm.

To identify what capabilities a package provides, use the --provides option:

```
$ rpm -q --provides rpm
config(rpm) = 4.2.1-0.11
librpm-4.2.so
librpmbuild-4.2.so
librpmdb-4.2.so
librpmio-4.2.so
rpm = 4.2.1-0.11
```

The first three lines state that RPM provides the capabilities (most of which are file names, in this case) librpm.4.2.so, librpmbuild.4.2.so, and librpmio.4.2.so. The last line shows both the version number of the rpm package itself and indicates that RPM is a capability of its own.

To determine what RPMs depend on a given capability, use `--whatrequires` *capability* to list all packages requiring *capability*. For example, the following command shows all the packages that require the RPM capability the RPM package provides. Although potentially confusing, keep in mind that the name of the package can be used as a capability.

```
$ rpm -q --whatrequires rpm
rpm-python-4.2.1-0.11
rpm-build-4.2.1-0.11
rpm-devel-4.2.1-0.11
up2date-3.9.14-2
```

The command output shows six packages requiring the rpm capability, including two packages that you might not suspect require it, `rhn_register` and `up2date`. Before you could remove the RPM package, therefore, you would have to remove the six packages that depend on it.

The options for querying RPM dependency information offer system administrators valuable information about the relationships between the many RPMs that constitute an installed Red Hat system.

WHAT'S IN THAT RPM?

Naturally, it is often useful or necessary to determine the contents of an RPM, whether it is installed or not. A number of the options listed in Table 27-2 make this possible. The possibilities range from simply displaying the package name and version numbers all the way to detailed information about each file an RPM installs. In fact, you can list all installed RPMs using the `-a` option. Most queries, though, fall somewhere between these extremes and query a limited subset of packages or a limited selection of package characteristics or files.

The simplest query option, `-q`, shows only an RPM's name and version number, as the following command illustrates.

```
$ rpm -q jwhois
jwhois-3.2.2-1.1
```

If you want more — and more descriptive — information, add `-i`:

```
$ rpm -qi jwhois
Name        : jwhois              Relocations: (not relocateable)
Version     : 3.2.2                    Vendor: Red Hat, Inc.
Release     : 1.1                  Build Date: Fri 04 Jul 2003 04:38:33
AM EDT
Install Date: Sun 20 Jul 2003 02:15:50 AM EDT    Build Host:
daffy.perf.redhat.com
```

```
Group      : Applications/Internet     Source RPM: jwhois-3.2.2-1.1.src.rpm
Size       : 198144                             License: GPL
Signature  : DSA/SHA1, Wed 16 Jul 2003 06:33:49 PM EDT, Key ID fd372689897da07a
Packager   : Red Hat, Inc. <http://bugzilla.redhat.com/bugzilla>
URL        : http://www.gnu.org/software/jwhois/
Summary    : Internet whois/nicname client.
Description :
A whois client that accepts both traditional and finger-style queries.
```

The `-i` option results in a more comprehensive listing describing the RPM. Two of the entries may require additional explanation. The Group label organizes RPM packages by function. Descriptors, Applications, and Internet in the example, are separated by / and become increasingly specific moving from left to right. Unfortunately, the values in the Group field are not standardized, and vary from vendor to vendor and even among RPM packagers. Browse the file `/usr/share/doc/rpm-4.2.1/GROUPS` to see the current list of groups that Red Hat uses (as of the most recent version of Red Hat Linux available when this chapter was written).

To list all of the files in an installed RPM, use the `-l` option:

```
$ rpm -ql jwhois
/etc/jwhois.conf
/usr/bin/jwhois
/usr/bin/whois
/usr/share/doc/jwhois-3.2.2
/usr/share/doc/jwhois-3.2.2/COPYING
/usr/share/doc/jwhois-3.2.2/NEWS
/usr/share/doc/jwhois-3.2.2/README
/usr/share/doc/jwhois-3.2.2/TODO
/usr/share/info/jwhois.info.gz
[...]
```

The `-f file` option approaches package listing from another direction. For any given file, you can find out which RPM installed it using `-f file`, where `file` contains the full path specification. The following command illustrates one way to use this option.

```
$ rpm -qf /usr/bin/find
findutils-4.1.7-9
```

Not much to it, right? Well, suppose you do not know the path to an application binary, just its name. In such a case, take advantage of shell commands and standard Linux utility programs. For example, the next command uses the `which` command and the Bash shell's command substitution to resolve a binary's name to a full path before invoking `rpm`:

```
$ rpm -qf $(which emacs)
emacs-21.3-6
```

As you should recall from Chapter 25, the shell substitutes the value of $(which emacs) with /usr/bin/emacs before passing it to rpm -qf. The result is the same as the output of rpm -qf /usr/bin/emacs.

TIP By default, the which command works only with executable files available in the directories listed in the $PATH environment variable.

So far, every RPM query option discussed applies to installed packages. As it happens, many of them can be used on uninstalled packages, but only if the query specifies -p, which tells RPM to query an uninstalled package. Suppose, for example, you just downloaded the fortune-mod-1.2.1-1.i386.rpm package. To list its files, use -l, as explained earlier, and -p:

```
$ rpm -qpl fortune-mod-1.2.1-1.i386.rpm
/etc/profile.d/fortune.sh
/usr/bin/randstr
/usr/bin/rot
/usr/bin/strfile
/usr/bin/unstr
...
```

The output, truncated to conserve space, is identical to that of an installed package.

FORMATTING QUERY OUTPUT

Inveterate tweakers and hard-core tinkerers appreciate the --qf option because it allows custom formatting of query output. On the downside, it may not work with all query options, and RPMs rarely contain all of the information that can *potentially* be displayed. The general form of a query using query format strings is:

```
$ rpm --qf 'format_str' -q [query_opts]
```

format_str is the workhorse of custom query formatting. A *format_str* must contain at least one tag; all other components are optional. Optional elements include literal text, directives to control the output's width and justification, control character sequences, output modifiers, and array iterators. A *tag* is a predefined token or symbol representing a piece of information. Examples include SUMMARY, DESCRIPTION, NAME, and VERSION, but there are many more; as of version 4.2.1,

RPM understood 139 tags! Each tag must be embedded in a %{} construct, for example: %{SUMMARY} or %{NAME}.

TIP   Type rpm --querytags to view the entire list of tags RPM understands.

There are a couple of details to bear in mind. First, *format_str* should be delimited by single quotes ('), also called apostrophes or strong quotes, or by regular double quotes ("), often called *weak quotes*. Format strings used in shell scripts should be embedded between strong quotes to protect them from effects of shell expansion, described in Chapter 25. Secondly, make sure to type --qf (note the double dash); -qf means something else entirely, as you just read. To avoid confusion or the possibility of a typing error, consider using the long option --queryformat, a synonym of --qf.

To keep this chapter from turning into a book about RPM, we only discuss a few format string elements. The most important are directives to control the minimum width and justification of the displayed fields and escape sequences. To specify the width of a field, place a number between a tag's percent sign and its opening brace. By default, output is right justified, so to force left justification, prefix the field width with -. The escape sequences are the same as discussed in Chapter 25, such as \n for a newline and \t for a tab.

To illustrate, try the following examples and compare their output. The first example is the output of an unmodified query:

```
$ rpm -q setup db1 hdparm popt
setup-2.4.7-1
db1-1.85-5
hdparm-3.9-6
popt-1.6.2-8
```

You have seen this sort of query output already. It is simple and informative but not terribly attractive. The next command uses two tags, NAME and VERSION, to specify the output fields:

```
$ rpm -q --qf '%{NAME}%{VERSION}' setup db1 hdparm popt
setup2.4.7db11.85hdparm3.9popt1.6.2$
```

Blech! This looks worse than the first example because all of the output runs together, including the command prompt. But it serves as a starting point. First, separate the fields using field-width specifications:

```
$ rpm -q --qf '%-20{NAME}%10{VERSION}' setup db1 hdparm popt
setup       2.4.7db1        1.85hdparm       3.9popt      1.6.2$
```

Each NAME field has a width of 20 characters and is left justified. The VERSION column is 10 characters wide and is right justified (the default). Judicious use of the \t and \n escape sequences solves the jumbled output problem:

```
$ rpm -q --qf '%-20{NAME}\t%10{VERSION}\n' setup db1 hdparm popt
setup                    2.4.7
db1                       1.85
hdparm                     3.9
popt                     1.6.2
```

\t, the tab character, separates the name and version number fields; \n, the newline, puts the command prompt back on its own line, where it belongs.

This short discussion is only a taste of the capabilities of query formatting. Nevertheless, it provides a solid foundation for creating richer, more visually appealing query output. It is also worth pointing out that the query format capability lets you create custom queries that simply are not possible using any other query option available. So, if you need RPM information you cannot obtain using the standard query options, use --qf to create a custom query that displays the information you need, and *only* that information.

Package Installation and Removal

Although RPM's query feature is one of its most powerful features, it earns its keep because of its package-management features. This section summarizes how to install, remove, and upgrade software packages using RPM.

INSTALLING RPMs

The basic syntax for installing an RPM is:

```
# rpm -i [options] package [...]
```

package is the complete name of the RPM to install and *options* refines the installation process. Table 27-3 lists commonly used *options* values. See the rpm man page for a comprehensive listing.

TABLE 27-3 COMMON RPM INSTALLATION OPTIONS

Option	Description
--force	Install the package even if it is already installed, install an older package version, and replace files already installed. --force also ignores dependencies.
--h	Print up to 50 hash marks (#) to illustrate the progress of the installation.
--nodeps	Do not perform a dependency check before installing or upgrading a package.
--test	Do not install the package or update the database, just identify and display possible conflicts or dependency errors.
-v	Be slightly verbose and show some useful information during the installation.

Although they appear similar, --force and --nodeps serve different purposes. --nodeps only disables dependency checks. Use it only if you are certain that a dependency conflict will not cause problems later on. --force forces a package's installation regardless of all potential problems. As a result, some situations may require using --force and --nodeps together. Common uses of --force include installing a package when one or more of its files conflict with files installed by another package or when any other severe installation failure would occur. Do *not* use --force to install older packages over new packages – use the --oldpackage option for that. To overwrite dependencies, similarly, you should use --nodeps whenever possible. --force is a blunt instrument that might not have the results you want, expect, or intend.

The following command demonstrates installing an RPM:

```
# rpm -ivh fortune-mod-1.2.1-1.i386.rpm
Preparing...               ######################################### [100%]
   1:fortune-mod            ######################################### [100%]
```

The next example shows the error generated by trying to install a package already installed and how to use --force to ignore the error.

```
# rpm -ivh fortune-mod-1.2.1-1.i386.rpm
Preparing...               ######################################### [100%]
package fortune-mod-1.2.1-1 is already installed
```

```
# rpm -ivh --force fortune-mod-1.2.1-1.i386.rpm
Preparing...                     ########################################### [100%]
   1:fortune-mod                 ########################################### [100%]
```

--force caused RPM to ignore the conflict and perform the installation. To avoid encountering such conflicts, use the --test option, as shown in the next command, to perform a "dry run" installation to catch any problems:

```
# rpm -ivh --test fortune-mod-1.2.1-1.i386.rpm
Preparing...                     ########################################### [100%]
package fortune-mod-1.2.1-1 is already installed
```

As you can see in the preceding example, adding --test to the command line generated an error message. What you cannot see is that neither RPM's databases nor any files changed. Testing a package installation using --test is great protection against the heartburn caused by installing incompatible software.

UPGRADING RPMs

The options for upgrading existing RPMs come in two flavors, -U, for upgrade, and -F, for freshen. What is the difference between upgrading a package and freshening it? Upgrading a package, using -U, installs it even if an earlier version is not currently installed, but freshening a package, using -F, installs it only if an earlier version is currently installed. Other than this subtle but important difference, -U and -F are identical to -i, even down to the options they accept (see Table 27-3).

The upgrade (-U) option is almost always the method to use because it simply *does the right thing.* The only exception is installing multiple versions of the kernel, in which case you *do* want to have several versions of the same package(s) installed.

The following sequence of commands illustrates how to upgrade an RPM and the difference between the -U and -F options:

```
# rpm -Fvh fortune-mod-1.0-13.i386.rpm
# rpm -q fortune-mod
package fortune-mod is not installed
```

Hmm. Nothing happened. The rpm command line used -F, so it did not install the fortune-mod package because an earlier version did not exist.

```
# rpm -Uvh fortune-mod-1.0-13.i386.rpm
Preparing...                  ######################################### [100%]
   1:fortune-mod               ######################################### [100%]
```

With -U, RPM "upgraded" the fortune-mod package, even though an earlier version was not installed.

```
# rpm -Fvh fortune-mod-1.2.1-1.i386.rpm
Preparing...                  ######################################### [100%]
   1:fortune-mod               ######################################### [100%]
```

This time, the freshen operation succeeded.

REMOVING RPMs

Removing or deleting RPMs and their contents is easy, perhaps frightfully so. The general form of the command is:

```
rpm -e package [...]
```

package is the name, only, of the RPM to remove. Multiple packages can be removed simultaneously by listing each package on the command line. For example, the following command removes the fortune-mod and whois RPMs:

```
# rpm -e fortune-mod whois
```

Note that successful removal generates no additional output.

Verifying RPMs

Verifying an RPM compares the current status of files installed by an RPM to the file information recorded at the time the RPM was installed, such as file sizes and MD5 checksum values, and reports any discrepancies. The general form of the verify command is:

```
rpm -V package [...]
```

The -V option requests RPM to verify the status of files in *package*, the name of the RPM to verify. As with many other RPM operations, multiple packages can be verified simultaneously. Table 27-4 explains the file characteristics RPM evaluates when verifying an RPM.

TABLE 27-4 FILE INFORMATION EVALUATED DURING RPM VERIFICATION

Characteristic	Description
MD5 checksum	The file's MD5 checksum (calculated using the md5sum command)
File size	The file's size, in bytes
Modification time	The date and time the file was last modified
Device	The device file or files in the case of drivers and hardware devices
User	The file's owner, such as root or bin
Group	The file's group
Mode	The file's permissions and type

If none of the characteristics listed in Table 27-4 have changed for any of the RPM's files since they were installed, RPM displays no information, as the following example shows.

```
$ rpm -V whois
```

In this example, the rpm command generates no output save for the shell command prompt, so the whois package's files remain unchanged from their initial state at installation.

If, on the other hand, any of the tracked file characteristics have changed, the output will resemble the following:

```
$ rpm -V fortune-mod
S.5....T    /usr/bin/rot
.......T    /usr/bin/strfile
.....UG.    /usr/bin/unstr
.M......    /usr/man/man1/randstr.1
missing     /usr/man/man1/unstr.1
```

At the very least, it should be clear that something is up with the fortune-mod package. Each line out of the output consists of eight fields and a file name, separated by whitespace to format the output. Table 27-5 shows the keys for interpreting verification output.

TABLE **27-5 RPM VERIFICATION KEYS**

Column	Value	Description
1	5	The MD5 checksum has changed
2	S	The file size has changed
3	L	A symbolic link has changed (points to a different file)
4	T	The file's modification time has changed
5	D	The device designation has changed
6	U	The file's user (owner) has changed
7	G	The file's group has changed
8	M	The files mode (permissions or type) has changed
ANY	.	No change detected in the corresponding characteristic
ANY	?	This characteristic's current status could not be determined (usually because file permissions prevent reading the file)
N/A	missing	The corresponding file does not exist in its default location

Translating the admittedly cryptic output from the `rpm -V fortune-mod` command, you know the following:

◆ `/usr/bin/rot`'s file size, MD5 checksum, and modification time has changed

◆ `/usr/bin/strfile`'s modification time has changed

◆ `/usr/bin/unstr`'s user and group ownership has changed

◆ `/usr/man/man1/randstr.1`'s mode (either its permission bits, type, or both) has changed

◆ `/usr/man/man1/unstr.1` has been deleted, moved, or renamed

Depending on the file and the local environment, some changes indicate a potential problem, but others do not. If a binary file's size, checksum, modification time, or user or group ownership has changed and you have not manually upgraded the package, this is cause for alarm because under normal circumstances, these characteristics do not change. That is, it is highly likely that the original file has been replaced or modified, perhaps by a cracker, and you should take steps to address this problem immediately. Exercise similar caution if a file is listed as missing. On the other hand, application and system configuration files, for example, files in the `/etc` directory and its subdirectories, change due to edits by administrators and system configuration tools.

TIP Maintaining a log that tracks changes to your system, such as installing, upgrading, and removing RPMs, is a very useful habit to acquire because it records each modification made to the system. Although we used to recommend handwritten logs, it is probably more sensible to use some sort of soft format, such as a Web page on an intranet or another type of document that can be shared, the idea being that multiple administrators might need to access it.

In some situations, such as RPM verification reports, maintenance and administrative logs become an invaluable resource because you can compare log entries to the verification report to evaluate whether or not a reported discrepancy poses a security threat or is just the result of a long-forgotten file edit or package installation.

Unfortunately, it is impossible to define a general rule that distinguishes a legitimate change from a pernicious one. The best policy to follow is to know your system and to keep careful track of updates and changes so you can identify and respond quickly and appropriately to anomalous and potentially malicious modifications.

Checking Software Versions

Before downloading and installing SuperWidget version 1.3.2-5, you may want to know what version is currently installed in order to avoid "upgrading" to an old, unstable, development, or possibly buggy version. Unfortunately, no single command for obtaining version information works for all software packages. Rather, a variety of methods exist. This section covers the most common methods for locating software version information.

On a Red Hat system, the easiest way to identify software versions is to use RPM. Suppose, for example, you want to find out which version of Emacs, a popular editor, is installed on your system. As explained earlier in the chapter, use `rpm`'s query option, `-q`. For example:

```
$ rpm -q emacs
emacs-21.3-6
```

The output indicates that the Emacs version is 21.3-6. What exactly does emacs-21.3-6 mean, though? RPM uses a standardized naming and version numbering scheme mirroring a very common approach used in the Linux development community. Its general format is *name-major_num.minor_num[.patch_num]-build_num*. Table 27-6 explains the meaning of each element in the format.

TABLE 27-6 COMMON VERSION NUMBERING ELEMENTS

Element	Interpretation
name	The name of the package (balsa, emacs, mozilla).
major_num	The primary version number; changes between major updates to the package.
minor_num	The secondary version number; increments to reflect updates less dramatic than those indicated by *major_num*.
patch_num	The patch number; usually reflects only the application of bug fixes to a given version. Not all applications use *patch_num*.
build_num	The build number; an RPM-specific feature indicating the packager's version.

So, the package name emacs-21.3-6 breaks down to the *name* emacs, the *major_num* 21, the *minor_num* 3, no *patch_num*, and the *build_num* 6. The build number means that it is the 6th version of Red Hat's Emacs 21.3 RPM.

 Non-RPM software packages frequently use the same naming scheme as RPM.

If you do not want to use RPM, or for packages not installed using RPM, other options exist. Many applications accept command line options that cause them to display their version numbers. The most common such options are -v, -V, -version, and --version. Programs from the GNU project, in particular, almost always accept --version. For example, the next two examples pass -v and --version to mutt (a popular text-based e-mail client) and emacs, respectively, to obtain their version numbers:

```
$ mutt -v
Mutt 1.4.1i (2003-03-19)
Copyright (C) 1996-2002 Michael R. Elkins and others.
Mutt comes with ABSOLUTELY NO WARRANTY; for details type `mutt -vv'.
Mutt is free software, and you are welcome to redistribute it
under certain conditions; type `mutt -vv' for details.

System: Linux 2.4.21-20.1.2024.2.1.nptl (i686) [using slang 10405]
Compile options:
-DOMAIN
-DEBUG
-HOMESPOOL  -USE_SETGID  -USE_DOTLOCK  -DL_STANDALONE
+USE_FCNTL  -USE_FLOCK
+USE_POP  +USE_IMAP  +USE_GSS  +USE_SSL  +USE_SASL
+HAVE_REGCOMP  -USE_GNU_REGEX
+HAVE_COLOR  -HAVE_START_COLOR  -HAVE_TYPEAHEAD  -HAVE_BKGDSET
-HAVE_CURS_SET  -HAVE_META  -HAVE_RESIZETERM
+HAVE_PGP  -BUFFY_SIZE -EXACT_ADDRESS  -SUN_ATTACHMENT
+ENABLE_NLS  -LOCALES_HACK  +HAVE_WC_FUNCS  +HAVE_LANGINFO_CODESET
+HAVE_LANGINFO_YESEXPR
+HAVE_ICONV  -ICONV_NONTRANS  +HAVE_GETSID  +HAVE_GETADDRINFO
ISPELL="/usr/bin/ispell"
SENDMAIL="/usr/sbin/sendmail"
MAILPATH="/var/mail"
PKGDATADIR="/usr/share/mutt"
SYSCONFDIR="/etc"
EXECSHELL="/bin/sh"
-MIXMASTER
To contact the developers, please mail to <mutt-dev@mutt.org>.
To report a bug, please use the flea(1) utility.

$ emacs --version
GNU Emacs 21.3.1
Copyright (C) 2002 Free Software Foundation, Inc.
GNU Emacs comes with ABSOLUTELY NO WARRANTY.
You may redistribute copies of Emacs
under the terms of the GNU General Public License.
For more information about these matters, see the file named
COPYING.
```

For better or worse, many applications display more information than simple version numbers, as the example demonstrates, but at least you get the information you sought.

When invoked as discussed in this section, most applications display their version information and then exit (that is, they do not start).

Many X Window System applications use `-version` to show their version numbers. Similarly, almost every X application provides a dialog box (commonly accessible by selecting Help → About) that displays a version number. Figure 27-1, for example, shows GNOME Calendar's About dialog box, which includes version information.

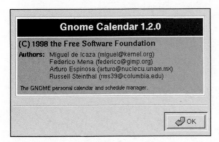

Figure 27-1: GNOME Calendar's About dialog box displays its version number.

If none of these suggestions work, try using `-help` or `--help` to generate a short usage summary that lists a program's options. If all else fails, read the package's documentation or manual page to find out how to access its version information, because it is very rare for an application, whether text mode or GUI, not to display version information.

Obtaining Newer Software

How and from where do you obtain newer software? There are many more options than can be covered here, so this section discusses the most common methods. The first step is to locate the software package you want. Then, of course, you have to download it.

The most popular sites for locating and downloading Linux software are the RPM repository at the Fedora Project, the repository at `rpmfind.net`, and the Ibiblio Web and FTP site.

Using the Fedora Project

The Fedora Project is the community-maintained complement to the official Red Hat Enterprise Linux releases. Its home page on the Web is `http://fedora .redhat.com/` .In addition to the Fedora Core, a general release of the Red Hat Linux operating system targeting desktop Linux users, Fedora also offers an interface to Red Hat Rawhide, Rawhide contains existing Red Hat Linux packages with additional bug fixes and patches applied since the last Fedora Core release. Rawhide also provides early access to new packages (and old packages with new features) to RPMs that might be rolled into Fedora Core. To access Rawhide, point your Web browser at `ftp://ftp.redhat.com/pub/redhat/linux/rawhide/` or, better, use one of the Rawhide mirrors listed on the Mirrors page at `http://www.redhat.com/ download/mirror.html`.

For more information about Red Hat's exciting new community development model, the Fedora Project, see the project information pages and the FAQs at `http://fedora.redhat.com/about/`.

Using rpmfind.net

The `rpmfind.org` Web site is a huge repository of RPM-based software packages covering all the major distributions and many of the minor ones and spanning the entire range of application categories. It also lists RPMs by platform, such as Intel x86, SPARC, and Macintosh. Its finely tuned search engine makes it easy to find the RPM you want, or at least to reduce the possibilities from some 100,000+ to a more manageable figure.

To get started, point your Web browser at `http://www.rpmfind.net/` and then click the Go directly to the RPM database link at the top of the page. Click the Search link in the upper right-hand corner of the page, type **fortune-mod** in the text box, and then click the Search button to perform the search. The resulting page should resemble Figure 27-2.

As you can see in Figure 27-2, there are a number of fortune-mod RPMs available, so you could go back to the previous screen, refine the search criteria, and redo the search to reduce the number of results shown.

Selecting one of the listed RPMs takes you to its information page (see Figure 27-3). The information page includes a link to the package's home page, information about the listed RPM, and, most importantly, a download link.

	A program which will display a fortune.	Kondara Jirai DOS	fortune-mod-1.0-13k DOS.rpm
	A program which will display a fortune.	Kondara Jirai Sources	fortune-mod-1.0-13k.src.rpm
fortune-mod-1.0-13cl.src.html	fortune cookie program with bug fixes	Conectiva Linux	fortune-mod-1.0-13cl.src.rpm
fortune-mod-1.0-13cl.i386.html	fortune cookie program with bug fixes	Conectiva Linux	fortune-mod-1.0-13cl.i386.rpm
fortune-mod-1.0-13.src.html	A program which will display a fortune.	ASPLinux	fortune-mod-1.0-13.src.rpm
fortune-mod-1.0-13.i386.html	A program which will display a fortune.	ASPLinux	fortune-mod-1.0-13.i386.rpm
fortune-mod-1.0-13.i386.html	A program which will display a fortune.	RedHat-7.0 for i386	fortune-mod-1.0-13.i386.rpm
fortune-mod-1.0-13.alpha.html	A program which will display a fortune.	RawHide 1.0 for Alpha	fortune-mod-1.0-13.alpha.rpm
fortune-mod-1.0-13.i386.html	A program which will display a fortune.	ASPLinux	fortune-mod-1.0-13.i386.rpm
fortune-mod-1.0-13.i386.html	A program which will display a fortune.	RedHat-7.1 for i386	fortune-mod-1.0-13.i386.rpm
	A program which will display a fortune.	RawHide 1.0 Sources	fortune-mod-1.0-13.src.rpm
fortune-mod-1.0-13.Sparc.html	A program which will display a fortune.	RawHide 1.0 for Sparc	fortune-mod-1.0-13.sparc.rpm
fortune-mod-1.0-13.i386.html	A program which will display a fortune.	RawHide 1.0 for i386	fortune-mod-1.0-13.i386.rpm
fortune-mod-1.0-13.src.html	A program which will display a fortune.	ASPLinux	fortune-mod-1.0-13.src.rpm
	A program which will display a fortune.	RedHat-7.1 Sources	fortune-mod-1.0-13.src.rpm
fortune-mod-1.0-13.src.html	A program which will display a fortune.	ASPLinux	fortune-mod-1.0-13.src.rpm
fortune-mod-1.0-13.i386.html	A program which will display a fortune.	ASPLinux	fortune-mod-1.0-13.i386.rpm
fortune-mod-1.0-13.i386.html	A program which will display a fortune.	ASPLinux	fortune-mod-1.0-13.i386.rpm
	A program which will display a fortune.	RedHat-7.0 Sources	fortune-mod-1.0-13.src.rpm
fortune-mod-1.0-12k.alpha.html	A program which will display a fortune.	Kondara Jirai alpha	fortune-mod-1.0-12k.alpha.rpm
fortune-mod-1.0-12k.i586.html	A program which will display a fortune.	Kondara Jirai i586	fortune-mod-1.0-12k.i586.rpm
	A program which will display a fortune.	Kondara Jirai Sources	fortune-mod-1.0-12k.src.rpm
fortune-mod-1.0-11kl.sparc.html	A program which will display a fortune.	Kondara 1.2 sparc	fortune-mod-1.0-11kl.sparc.rpm

Figure 27-2: rpmfind.net lists many fortune-mod RPMs.

Figure 27-3: The information page for fortune-mod-1.0.13 at rpmfind.net

Click the RPM file name at the top of the page (fortune-mod-1.0.13.ii386.rpm, in this case) to download the RPM to your system.

Using FreshRPMS

FreshRPM, at http://www.freshrpms.net/, is a (mostly) Red Hat Linux-specific RPM download site. It contains a large and actively-updated index of RPM-based open source software. Although Freshrpm's database is newer than rpmfind.net's, and it currently (as of this writing) lacks a search interface, we have found the quality of its offerings to exceed the quality of rpmfind.net's.

Using Ibiblio.org

Ibiblio.org is arguably the sire of all of the Linux and open source software repositories currently available. It began life as Sunsite (strictly speaking, `ftp://sunsite.unc.edu/` and, after the World Wide Web became popular, `http://sunsite.unc.edu/`), one of a number of information repositories scattered throughout the world, hosted on hardware donated by Sun Microsystems (hence, the name) and provided as a public service by both Sun and the sites' administrators. In the late 1990s, the University of North Carolina renamed Sunsite to Metalab, and the URLs changed to `ftp://metalab.unc.edu/` and `http://metalab.unc.edu/`). In 1999, Metalab became Ibiblio.org, reflecting its phenomenal growth in size and popularity and its focus on providing the computing public at large access to a comprehensive store of information (and software) on a variety of topics.

Ibiblio.org (and its predecessors, Metalab and Sunsite) is a public repository for information of all sorts, not just downloadable software. For example, at the time this chapter was written, it featured an exhibit commemorating America's World War II veterans in honor of Memorial Day, including articles, photographs, and multimedia items. At the same time, Ibiblio.org hosted a stunning *55GB* of downloadable Linux software, and Linux software is only *one* of Ibiblio.org's software collections!

To access Ibiblio.org's Linux archive, point your Web browser at `ftp://www.ibiblio.org/pub/Linux/`. Browse through the archives at your leisure to locate the package that interests you. As usual, to download one to your system, click the corresponding link. If you are using the Netscape browser, it may be necessary to hold down the left Shift key and left click to download the archive file.

Ibiblio.org does not store RPM files in its standard Linux software archive. Rather, the preferred format is compressed tarballs. However, distribution-specific directories (stored under the `/pub/Linux/distributions` directory tree) do contain RPMs if the distribution in question is RPM-based (such as Red Hat Linux, Caldera OpenLinux, and Linux-Mandrake).

If you are uncertain about the contents of a particular directory or its subdirectories, the files `!INDEX`, `!INDEX.html`, `!INDEX.short.html`, and `README` in each directory describe, in varying levels of detail, the contents of each directory and, if applicable, its subdirectories. If you prefer not to browse Ibiblio.org's Linux archive directly, you can use its Linsearch interface, based on the Linux Software Map described in the next section, by pointing your browser at `http://www.ibiblio.org/pub/Linux` and selecting the Linsearch link.

 TIP   The Linux Software Map, less actively maintained than other sites discussed in this chapter, is a database of Linux software. It supports searches by keywords and titles and also lets you browse the entire database by application title.

Additional Software Repositories

In addition to the sites just described, the following Web sites offer Linux or open source software for download:

◆ **The Fedora Project** — `http://fedora.redhat.com/`

◆ **Sourceforge** — `http://sourceforge.net/`

◆ **FreshRPMS** — `http://www.freshrpms.net/`

◆ **GNU** — `http://www.gnu.org/`

The Fedora Project is a Red Hat–sponsored, community-driven open source project that serves as the proving ground for software and technology that Red Hat might incorporate into their official releases. Although it is relatively new, Fedora is sure to become the premier source for Red Hat Linux software. Sourceforge is the most popular open source development project on the Web today, hosting thousands of software projects. If you cannot find what you are looking for at Sourceforge, it might not exist. FreshRPMS is another very popular RPM-centric site with hundreds of high-quality RPMs ready to download, install, and run on your Red Hat system. Linux.com is a popular news and information site, hosted by VA Software, which also contains some downloadable software, and links to much more. Linuxberg is part of the Tucows software repository dedicated to Linux software.

A final source for locating new or upgraded software is software developers. Many Linux developers maintain either entire Web sites or individual Web pages from which you can download their software packages and patches, report bugs, track package development, and subscribe or unsubscribe to package-related mailing lists.

Installing Software

After downloading either an RPM, SRPM, or a source archive such as a tarball, naturally, you will want to install it. The section titled "Using the Red Hat Package Manager" explained in detail how to install binary RPMs using the commands `rpm -i`, `rpm -U`, and `rpm -F`, so refer to that section if you need a refresher. This section shows you how to install software from source code, that is, to unpack, configure, build, and install a software package you download as uncompiled source code. Next, you will learn how to use RPM to build and install SRPMs, source RPMS, and how to use RPM to build software from tarballs.

Installing Software from Source

Before package management suites such as RPM became popular, you upgraded and installed software by downloading a *gzipped tarball* (a tar archive compressed using the `gzip` utility), unpacking it, configuring it by manually editing one or more header files or using a `configure` script that automatically customized the package to your system, executing `make` to build it, and then, more often than not, executing `make install` to install it. Despite RPM's popularity, a considerable amount of software still uses this approach, so this section walks you through the process to familiarize you with it. The method is much simpler than it might seem at first blush. The example used in this section configures, builds, and installs `bc`, an arithmetic processing language used in the text mode `dc` calculator.

CONFIGURING THE BUILD ENVIRONMENT

Implicit in the previous paragraph is the assumption that your system has a development environment installed. For end users and system administrators, a *build environment* consists of the compiler, gcc, and its supporting libraries, the `make` utility for automating compiler invocations, a few key development libraries (mostly consisting of header files), and the install utility for handling the details of copying files and assigning the proper ownership and setting file permissions appropriately.

During installation, select the development workstation option to install a complete development environment. Otherwise, make sure at least the following RPMs are installed on your system:

- gcc (for C programs)

- g++ (for C++ programs)

- make

- glibc-devel

- fileutils

- ◆ kernel-headers
- ◆ kernel-source
- ◆ gzip
- ◆ bzip2
- ◆ ncompress
- ◆ tar

Packages that have additional requirements usually state what they are, so read the package documentation to ensure your system has the required software.

UNPACKING THE SOFTWARE

After downloading the bc package (`bc-1.0.6.tar.gz` in this chapter's source code directory), move it to a location where it will not interfere with the system. For this example, I moved it to `/tmp`. After `cd`ing to `/tmp`, you can use one of two commands to decompress and unpack the archive. The first command combines decompression and unpacking the tar archive in a single command:

```
$ tar zxf bc-1.0.6.tar.gz
```

The z option uses `tar`'s built-in `gunzip` routine to decompress the file, x extracts the archive files, and f specifies the name of the file on which to operate. The second command you can use sends `gunzip`'s output to `tar`'s input using a pipe (|), that is:

```
$ gunzip -c bc-1.0.6.tar.gz | tar xf -
```

 TIP If you want more feedback from either of these commands, use `tar`'s v option to cause it to display the files it is extracting from the archive.

`gunzip`'s -c option sends the result of the decompression to standard output; using -f - with `tar` tells it to read its standard input; the pipe connects the two commands. In either case, you wind up with a directory named `bc-1.0.6` in the current directory (`/tmp`, in this case). So, `cd` into `bc-1.0.6` to proceed with configuring `bc`.

CONFIGURING THE SOFTWARE

Now that the `bc` package has been unpacked, the next step is to configure it for your system. In most cases, customizing a package for your system boils down to specifying the installation directory; but many packages, including bc, allow you to request additional customizations. Happily, this is an easy step.

bc, like numerous other software packages, uses a configure script to automate configuration and customization. A configure script is a shell script that makes educated guesses about the correct values of a variety of system-specific values used during the compilation process. In addition, configure allows you to specify the values of these same values, and others, by invoking configure with command line options and arguments. Values that configure "guesses" and that you pass to configure on its command line are normally written to one or more *Makefiles*, files that the make program uses to control the build process, or to one or more header (.h) files that define the characteristics of the program that gets built.

To see the items you can customize, execute ./configure --help in the base directory of the package you are building, as shown in Listing 27-1 (which has been edited to conserve space).

Listing 27-1: configure's Command Line Options

```
$ ./configure --help
Usage: configure [options] [host]
Options: [defaults in brackets after descriptions]
Configuration:
...
Directory and file names:
  --prefix=PREFIX         install architecture-independent files in PREFIX
                          [/usr/local]
  --exec-prefix=EPREFIX   install architecture-dependent files in EPREFIX
                          [same as prefix]
...
Host type:
  --build=BUILD           configure for building on BUILD [BUILD=HOST]
  --host=HOST             configure for HOST [guessed]
  --target=TARGET         configure for TARGET [TARGET=HOST]
Features and packages:
  --disable-FEATURE       do not include FEATURE (same as --enable-FEATURE=no)
  --enable-FEATURE[=ARG]  include FEATURE [ARG=yes]
  --with-PACKAGE[=ARG]    use PACKAGE [ARG=yes]
  --without-PACKAGE       do not use PACKAGE (same as --with-PACKAGE=no)
  --x-includes=DIR        X include files are in DIR
  --x-libraries=DIR       X library files are in DIR
--enable and --with options recognized:
  --with-pkg              use software installed in /usr/pkg tree
  --with-libedit          support fancy BSD command input
editing
  --with-readline         support fancy command input editing
```

The key options in Listing 27-1 are `--prefix` and the three under the heading `--enable and --with` options recognized, `--with-pkg`, `--with-libedit`, and `--with-readline`. `--prefix` enables you to specify an installation directory other than the default (indicated in brackets, `[]`), `/usr/local/`. For this example, the root installation directory is `/tmp/bctest`, specified as `--prefix=/tmp/bctest` on `configure`'s command line. The second group of command line options enables other features. This example uses `--with-readline`, which turns on support for the GNU readline library. The readline library enables command line editing inside the `bc` program, just as the Bash shell permits editing the shell command line.

After selecting the desired options, run `configure` with the appropriate options, as shown in the following example (again, the output has been edited to conserve space).

```
$ ./configure --prefix=/tmp/bctest --with-readline
creating cache ./config.cache
checking for a BSD compatible install... /usr/bin/install -c
checking whether build environment is sane... yes
checking whether make sets ${MAKE}... yes
checking for working aclocal... found
checking for working autoconf... found
checking for working automake... found
checking for working autoheader... found
checking for working makeinfo... found
checking for gcc... gcc
checking whether the C compiler (gcc  ) works... yes
...
checking for readline in -lreadline... yes
checking for readline/readline.h... yes
Using the readline library.
updating cache ./config.cache
creating ./config.status
creating Makefile
creating bc/Makefile
creating dc/Makefile
creating doc/Makefile
creating lib/Makefile
creating config.h
```

The lines beginning with `checking` indicate that `configure` is testing for the presence of a certain feature such as `gcc`. Because the command line specified `--with-readline`, the last two checking lines make sure the readline library is installed (`checking for readline in -lreadline... yes`) and that the appropriate header file, `readline.h`, is installed. Once all of the tests are completed, `configure` uses the test results to create a number of Makefiles and a header file.

TIP If you are in the habit of building software as the root user, *stop!* It is extremely rare to require root access to build software. The only step that needs root access is the `make install` step, which requires write permissions to the installation directories. We routinely build the kernel and major system applications as mortal users, only using `su` when we are ready to install.

At this point, you are ready to build `bc`.

BUILDING THE SOFTWARE

To build `bc`, type `make` and press Enter. The following example shows the end of the build process's output:

```
$ make
...
gcc -DHAVE_CONFIG_H -I. -I. -I.. -I./.. -I./../h    -g -O2 -Wall -funsigned-char
-c dc.c
gcc -DHAVE_CONFIG_H -I. -I. -I.. -I./.. -I./../h    -g -O2 -Wall -funsigned-char
-c misc.c
gcc -DHAVE_CONFIG_H -I. -I. -I.. -I./.. -I./../h    -g -O2 -Wall -funsigned-char
-c eval.c
gcc -DHAVE_CONFIG_H -I. -I. -I.. -I./.. -I./../h    -g -O2 -Wall -funsigned-char
-c stack.c
gcc -DHAVE_CONFIG_H -I. -I. -I.. -I./.. -I./../h    -g -O2 -Wall -funsigned-char
-c array.c
gcc -DHAVE_CONFIG_H -I. -I. -I.. -I./.. -I./../h    -g -O2 -Wall -funsigned-char
-c numeric.c
gcc -DHAVE_CONFIG_H -I. -I. -I.. -I./.. -I./../h    -g -O2 -Wall -funsigned-char
-c string.c
gcc  -g -O2 -Wall -funsigned-char  -o dc  dc.o misc.o eval.o stack.o array.o
numeric.o string.o ../lib/libbc.a
make[2]: Leaving directory `/tmp/bc-1.06/dc'
Making all in doc
make[2]: Entering directory `/tmp/bc-1.06/doc'
make[2]: Nothing to be done for `all'.
make[2]: Leaving directory `/tmp/bc-1.06/doc'
make[2]: Entering directory `/tmp/bc-1.06'
make[2]: Leaving directory `/tmp/bc-1.06'
make[1]: Leaving directory `/tmp/bc-1.06'
```

Depending on the size and complexity of the program you are building, make's output might be extensive. In the example shown, you see the final compiler invocations and, most importantly, no errors. Accordingly, the next step is to test the build.

TESTING THE BUILD

Many programs, especially those from the GNU projects, include some sort of test suite to validate the program. The idea is to make sure the program works properly *before* installing it. In some cases, you execute the command make test to run the test suite. In other cases, as with bc, a special subdirectory of the build tree, conveniently named test or Test, contains the test suite. Each package handles testing slightly differently, so read the package documentation. In the case of bc, the test suite lives in a subdirectory named Test, and a shell script named timetest performs the actual test. In this case, timetest evaluates how long it takes bc to perform certain mathematical calculations, but it also serves to ensure that bc built properly. The following commands invoke bc's test suite:

```
$ cd Test
$ ./timetest
```

timetest takes at least ten minutes to run, so have a cup of coffee or whatever your favorite beverage is while the test runs. If no errors occur during the test, you are ready to install it.

INSTALLING THE SOFTWARE

In the case of bc, as with many, many other programs installed from source, installing the built and tested program is simply a matter of executing the command make install in the build tree's base directory (/tmp/bc-1.0.6, in this case). More complex programs might have additional commands, such as make install-docs to install only documentation, that break up the installation into more steps or that perform only part of the installation. Still, other packages might use scripts to perform the installation. Regardless of the process, however, the goal is the same: Install program executables and documentation in the proper directories, create any needed subdirectories, and set the appropriate file ownership and permissions on the installed files.

In the case of the bc package, the installation command is a simple make install, as shown in the following code:

```
$ make install
...
/bin/sh ../mkinstalldirs /tmp/bctest/bin
mkdir /tmp/bctest
mkdir /tmp/bctest/bin
```

```
 /usr/bin/install -c  bc /tmp/bctest/bin/bc
...
make  install-man1
make[3]: Entering directory `/tmp/bc-1.06/doc'
/bin/sh ../mkinstalldirs /tmp/bctest/man/man1
mkdir /tmp/bctest/man
mkdir /tmp/bctest/man/man1
 /usr/bin/install -c -m 644 ./bc.1 /tmp/bctest/man/man1/bc.1
 /usr/bin/install -c -m 644 ./dc.1 /tmp/bctest/man/man1/dc.1
...
```

The output, edited to conserve space, shows the creation of the installation directory, /tmp/bctest (recall the --prefix=/tmp/bctest command line option passed
to configure), a subdirectory for the binary (/tmp/bctest/bin) and the subdirectory
for the manual pages, /tmp/bctest/man/man1. The output also shows the invocation of the install program that actually performs the installation. The -c option is
ignored because it is used for compatibility with install programs used on proprietary Unix systems. The -m option sets the file permissions using the octal permission notation. So, -m 644 makes the files bc.1 and dc.1 (which are manual pages)
read/write for the file owner and read-only for the file group and all other users.

For more information about the install program, read the manual page
(man install) or the TeX-info page (info install).

At this point, package installation is complete. Although this example of building and installing a package from a source tarball is simple, the basic procedure is
the same for all packages: unpack the source archive, configure it as necessary,
build it, test the program, and then install it. One final exhortation before proceeding to the next section: *Read the documentation!* Most software you obtain in
source code form includes one or more files explaining how to build and install the
software – we strongly encourage you to read these files to make sure your system
meets all the prerequisites, such as having the proper library versions or other software components. The documentation is there to help you, so take advantage of it
and save yourself some frustration-induced hair loss!

Building and Installing Source RPMs

In the simplest case, building and installing software from SRPMs requires one or possibly two commands. The same unpack/configure/build/install procedure described in

the previous section takes place, but RPM handles each of these steps for you. In this section, you will learn how to use the two command cases (building and installing an RPM), and how to invoke each step of the RPM build process.

As you learn in the section titled "Building RPMs," the general form of the command to build a binary RPM from a source RPM is:

```
rpm -b[stage] spec_file [...]
```

Any of the values listed in Table 27-7 is a valid value of *stage*.

TABLE 27-7 VALID BUILD STAGES FOR RPM'S –B MODE

Stage	Mnemonic	Meaning
p	Prep	Unpacks the source code and applies any patches
l	List	Makes sure all the package files exist
c	Compile	Compiles the source code
i	Install	Installs the files
b	Binary	Builds only a binary RPM
s	Source	Builds only a source RPM
a	All	Builds both binary and source RPMs

Stages are executed in the order listed, and later stages require preceding ones, with one exception. That is, the l (list) step, for example, cannot be performed before the p (prep) stage, and the b (binary) stage happens after the p, l, c, and i (prep, list, compile, and install) stages have been completed. The exception is that building a source RPM (the s stage) does not require first building a binary RPM.

Note that the install stage of the RPM build process does not mean that files are moved into the working file system. Rather, files are "installed" in their proper paths underneath RPM's build directory. For example, if RPM's build directory is /var/tmp/myrpm, the files /usr/bin/foo and /usr/man/man1/foo.1 would be installed underneath /var/tmp/myrpm, so their complete paths would be /var/tmp/myrpm/usr/bin/foo and /var/tmp/myrpm/usr/man/man1/foo.1. This step is necessary because of the way binary RPMs are built and how RPM installs them.

The following two commands illustrate building the mount-2.10 binary RPM from its corresponding SRPM (and assume that the SRPM is already installed using the instructions in "Installing RPMs" earlier in the chapter).

```
# cd /usr/src/redhat/SPECS
# rpm -bb mount.spec
Executing(%prep): /bin/sh -e /var/tmp/rpm-tmp.59234
+ umask 022
+ cd /usr/src/redhat/BUILD
+ cd /usr/src/redhat/BUILD
+ rm -rf mount-2.10r
+ /bin/mkdir -p mount-2.10r
+ cd mount-2.10r
+ /usr/bin/bzip2 -dc /usr/src/redhat/SOURCES/util-linux-
2.10r.tar.bz2
+ tar -xf -
...
Wrote: /usr/src/redhat/RPMS/i386/mount-2.10r-5.i386.rpm
Wrote: /usr/src/redhat/RPMS/i386/losetup-2.10r-5.i386.rpm
Executing(%clean): /bin/sh -e /var/tmp/rpm-tmp.86539
+ umask 022
+ cd /usr/src/redhat/BUILD
+ cd mount-2.10r
+ rm -rf /var/tmp/mount-root
+ exit 0
```

The build process generates quite a bit of output, most of which was deleted in the output listing. The SPECS directory contains the spec (presumably, short for *specification*) files that control RPM's build process. The rpm command shown uses -bb to build a binary RPM using the instructions in the mount.spec file. As the initial few lines of output shows, RPM first decompresses the archive file, using bzip2 (which uses a more efficient compression algorithm than gzip), and unpacks the archived files using tar. Additional steps apply any necessary patches, configure the package as necessary, invoke the build process, and then "install" the files as explained previously. The following two lines appear near the end of the output listing:

```
Wrote: /usr/src/redhat/RPMS/i386/mount-2.10r-5.i386.rpm
Wrote: /usr/src/redhat/RPMS/i386/losetup-2.10r-5.i386.rpm
```

They indicate that RPM created two binary RPMs, mount-2.10r-5.i386.rpm and losetup-2.10r-5.i386.rpm, in the /usr/src/redhat/RPMS/i386 directory. First, how can one SRPM produce two binary RPMs? This is simply one of RPMs features. More importantly, *why* would it do so? Typically, one SRPM results in multiple binary RPMs because the binary RPMs are related, but not closely enough to put all of the programs into a single RPM. In this case, losetup and mount are related so the packager put them in the same SRPM. However, someone installing mount may not need or want losetup, so it was put in its own RPM.

> **TIP** You do not have to cd into the directory to build an RPM. You could just as well use a full path name in the command, for example, rpm -bb /usr/src/redhat/SPECS/mount.spec.

Once the packages are built, you can install them as you would any other binary RPM, as the following command illustrates:

```
# cd ../RPMS/i386
# rpm -ivh mount-2.10r-5.i386.rpm losetup-2.10r-5.i386.rpm
Preparing...                   ######################################### [100%]
   1:losetup                   ######################################### [ 50%]
   2:mount                     ######################################### [100%]
```

You can also build an RPM in stages by specifying one of the earlier stages. Although this is typically an exercise that package builders perform when debugging a binary RPM, you can do the same. For example, the following command executes only the prep (p) stage against the mount SRPM:

```
# rpm -bp mount.spec
```

The next command stops the process after the compile (c) stage:

```
# rpm -bc mount.spec
```

Again, using the build stages in this manner is not something end users usually need to do, but the capability is there. Note also that the results of one incomplete build invocation overwrite the results of a previous one. Thus, if you execute rpm -bp foo.spec, somehow change the unpacked files, and then execute another rpm -bp foo.spec, you will lose your changes.

Using RPM with Source tarballs

As it happens, you can also use RPM to build binary RPMs from source tarballs. The key requirement is that the tarball *must* contain a spec file in order for RPM to know how to build the binary RPM. Software developers who are not familiar with RPM often provide a spec file in their source packages for the benefit of users who prefer to use RPM to build and install software. Indeed, this is a considerable benefit for users of RPM-based systems because building and installing source tarballs bypasses RPM completely – RPM does not track dependencies or requirements of packages installed from source tarballs, so using a spec file embedded in a tarball offers a very handy way to avoid this possibility.

To use this feature specify `-t[`*`stage`*`]` instead of `-b[`*`stage`*`]`, where stage is one of the options listed in Table 27-7. So, for example, to build a binary RPM from `util-linux-2.10r-5.tar.gz` using an embedded spec file named `util-linux .spec`, use the following command line:

```
# rpm -ta util-linux-2.10r-5.tar.gz
```

This technique is especially useful if you would like to create an SRPM from a tarball for later reuse and, as noted, is an invaluable tool for maintaining an accurate an up-to-date RPM database.

Summary

This chapter covered a lot of territory. You learned how to use each of RPM's major operating modes, including querying the RPM database, installing, upgrading, and removing RPMs, and performing RPM maintenance. You also learn a variety of methods for obtaining the version information of installed software. The chapter also lists some popular software repositories and how to use them, and discussed a variety of methods for downloading software. Finally, you learned how to build and install software from source using both the traditional tools (`tar`, `gcc`, `make`, `install`) and RPM's higher level interface to these tools.

Chapter 28

Backing Up and Restoring the File System

IN THIS CHAPTER

- ◆ Creating a backup plan
- ◆ Choosing media for backups
- ◆ Understanding backup methods
- ◆ Using backup and restore tools

IN THIS CHAPTER, you learn how to make backups of your files and restore damaged file systems from backups. It is important to make backups of the file system in order to avoid the loss of important information in the case of catastrophic hardware or software failure. An efficient backup and restoration process can minimize downtime and avoid the need to recreate lost work. In this chapter you learn how to choose a backup medium and how to use backup tools. Red Hat Enterprise Linux provides several packages for dealing with backup and restoration of the file system. The `tar` and `dump` commands provide low-level interfaces to system backups. In addition, sophisticated backup tools such as Amanda can do automatic backups of multiple machines.

Creating a Backup Plan

Determining what to back up on a particular machine depends largely on what data the machine contains and how the machine is used. However, there are some general guidelines that can be useful in determining what to back up.

Generally, temporary and cached files need not be backed up. The contents of the `/tmp` directory, for instance, are usually deleted when the machine is rebooted. Therefore, it is alright to not back up these files. Also, the cache directory used by Netscape and found in users' `.netscape` directory is automatically regenerated by Netscape if it is deleted. You may find it worthwhile to investigate whether any other packages installed on the machine generate significant amounts of ignorable temporary data.

Depending on the situation, it may or may not be advisable to back up the machine's system files. If the machine is a standard installation of Red Hat Enterprise Linux without any customizations or extra packages installed, the system files can be restored by reinstalling Red Hat Linux. The tradeoff is that reinstalling and reconfiguring a system probably takes more time and attention than restoring the file system from backup. However, this tradeoff may be worthwhile because of the amount of backup media that can be saved. In the particular case that a single Red Hat installation is copied verbatim onto many machines, it may be appropriate to back up the system files of just one of the machines. If the system files are identical across machines, a single backup should restore all of them. In any case it is probably wise to back up at least the /etc directory of each machine. Probably the machines have at least some differing configuration information, such as network and hostname settings.

One other thing needs to be backed up and indeed needs to be backed up via a special method: database files. Doing a straight tar from database files won't save you from a database crash, because the database files will all be in different states, having been written to backup when open. Oracle, Informix, Sybase, and so forth all allow the administrator to put the database tablespaces in backup mode. In backup mode, the data to be written goes to a memory cache rather than the file and transaction logs are updated only when the cache is flushed. This procedure slows things down but makes certain that the database will survive a crash.

The other aspect of the file system, other than the system files that need to be backed up, is the user files. Generally, all user files are stored in subdirectories of the /home directory. You should find it easy, therefore, to back up all user files at once. Even when the entire file system – both system and user files – is being backed up, you should still back them up separately. System and user files can have different relative priority depending on the situation. The user files are important because they may be irreplaceable, whereas many of the system files generally can be replaced by reinstalling Red Hat Linux. On the other hand, restoration of the system files is necessary for the machine to function and provide services, whereas the machine can be totally functional without restoration of the user files. Such priority considerations must be made when designing a backup strategy.

Give special thought to resources that do not easily fall into the system and user categories. Information stored in SQL databases, for instance, is often technically owned by root or by a special system user, but also often contains irreplaceable content entered by users. This kind of data can often be the most important to back up. You may find it beneficial to investigate which of the installed packages use this kind of data. Other examples besides databases are Web servers and mailing list archivers.

Choosing Media for Backups

A variety of backup media are available on the market today. Which backup media you use depends on a number of factors and the particular needs of the situation. You should consider how often files are backed up, how long the backups need to last, how redundant the backups need to be, and how much money can be allocated to purchasing backup media. Table 28-1 provides a comparison of backup media.

TABLE 28-1 COMPARISON OF BACKUP MEDIA

Medium	Capacity	Reliability	Cost	Speed
Magnetic tape	High	High	Cheap	Slow
Writable CDs	Medium	Medium	Cheap	Fast
Hard drive	High	High	Expensive	Fast
Floppy disks	Low	Low	Cheap	Slow
DVD	High	High	Medium	Slow
Zip disks	Medium	Low	Medium	Slow
Flash ROM	Medium	High	Expensive	Fast
Removable hard drive (FireWire)	High	High	Expensive	Fast
Removable hard drive (USB)	High	High	Expensive	Medium

Understanding Backup Methods

In order to save time and money in creating backups and restoring corrupted file systems and in purchasing backup media, it is important to institute a methodology for creating scheduled backups. The number of different backup methodologies is unlimited. How you should perform backups depends on the particular needs of your institution and computing infrastructure. The scheduling and type of backups depends on the type of backup media being used, the importance of the data, and the amount of downtime you can tolerate.

The simplest backup methodology is creating a full backup. A full backup copies the entire file system to the backup medium. This methodology can be good for small systems in which there is not much data to back up or systems in which the data is very important, is changing rapidly, and where historical snapshots of the system at different points in time are useful.

Performing frequent full backups has several disadvantages. Full backups take a long time to perform if there is a lot of data to back up or if the backup medium is slow. In order to get a clear snapshot of the system you may need to suspend the execution of processes that modify the file system while the backup process takes place. If backups take a long time, the downtime might be prohibitive. Full backups have no disadvantages when it comes to restoring an entire file system from backup. However, there is a disadvantage when restoring a partial file system from backup. If a sequential media such as magnetic tape is used, it must be searched sequentially in order to find the files that need to be restored. This process can cause a partial restoration to take as long as a full file system restoration in the worst case. Full backups also take significantly more space to archive than incremental backups. This situation is not too much of a disadvantage if you reuse the same backup media – you can just overwrite the old backup with the new one. However, it is often advisable to keep multiple generations of backups. Sometimes problems with the file system, such as corrupted or erased files, are not detected or reported immediately. If the file system is backed up once a day on the same backup tapes and an accidentally erased file is not found for two days, it cannot be recovered. On the other hand, if the file system is backed up once a week, any files lost between backups cannot be recovered. Keeping multiple full backups also has a disadvantage. If a full backup is made every day, the amount of archive media necessary to store it quickly becomes prohibitive.

The alternative to doing full backups is to do incremental backups. An incremental backup archives only the files that have changed or been added since the last backup. Incremental backups solve all of the disadvantages of full backups. Incremental backups are fast. In fact, the more often you do them, the faster they are because there is less to back up. Since the backups are smaller, searching from a given backup for a particular file is faster, thus making partial restorations faster if you need to restore from a particular known incremental backup archive. Because less is backed up each time, less media is used, so either less backup media needs to be bought or a longer history can be kept in the same amount of backup media. In the latter case, backups are more robust against lost or damaged files that are not discovered for a while.

Using incremental backups has disadvantages as well. While incremental backups are faster for retrieving individual files, they are slower for restoring entire file systems. To explain this problem, imagine that you have a week-long backup cycle. On the first day of the week you make a full backup. The rest of the week, you make an incremental backup. If a file system is erased accidentally on the last day of the week (right before a new full backup is to be made), you have to start at the last full backup and then load in a whole week of tapes in order to entirely restore the file system. If you made a full backup every day, you would have to load only the full backup; then you would be done restoring the file system.

When to use full backups and when to use incremental backups depends on the particular data stored on the machines, the way the machines are used, and how much money can be allocated to buying backup media. After you have decided on a backup methodology, you must configure your tools to use this methodology. Full and incremental backups can be implemented in scripts on top of the primitive backup tools such as tar. More advanced tools such as dump and Amanda have built-in support for backup levels and scheduling of various kinds of backups. Amanda even has a complex configuration language that lets you specify all kinds of details about the various types of backups you might want to do, the length of your backup cycle, and what files should be excluded from backup (such as private or temporary files).

Another thing to consider is the criticality of the system. If the system must be up at all times and downtime is a critical situation, then full backups are necessary in order to minimize downtime. One strategy for backing up critical machines is to create a separate volume group on mirrored disks solely for backups and use it as an intermediate area to copy files to prior to writing them to tape. A compressed tar file can be created on disk and then be written to tape faster than a normal tar file. Also, since a backup exists on disk, the tape archive is only used as a last resort if the disk archive fails. This strategy is similar to the one that the Amanda automated backup utility uses to take into account faulty backup devices or media. Even if the tape drive fails, the backup on disk can be written to tape when the problem has been solved.

Tape Rotation

Another consideration after you select a backup method is a proper tape rotation schedule. A well thought out schedule can lower your media costs and increase the life of your tapes while ensuring that every file is protected. There are several popular tape rotation methods currently in use.

Grandfather-father-son (GFS) is probably the most common tape rotation scheme. The grandfather backup is a monthly full backup, the father is a weekly full backup, and the son is a daily incremental backup. It is usually a good idea, and more secure, to store at least the full monthly backups off-site. In the event of a catastrophe at your location, a fire that damaged or destroyed your on-site backups, for example, you would be able to restore your data from tapes stored off-site.

For a detailed explanation of tape rotation methods, a good place to look is the Seagate Web site: http://www.seagate.com/products/ tapesales/backup/A2g1.html.

Using Backup Tools

Red Hat Linux provides numerous tools for doing file system backups. There are tools for interacting with backup media, such as ftape for manipulating tapes drives, cdrecord for writing to CD drives, and mirrordir for making backups to hard drives. Command line tools such as tar and dump allow for low-level control of file system backups and also easy automation through scripting. Using only shell scripts and periodic scheduling through cron jobs, you can develop a robust automated backup solution for many situations. Graphical tools also exist to create a more user-friendly interface to performing manual backups. Advanced backup tools exist which can be configured to fully automate the process of backing up multiple machines.

Command Line Tools

Red Hat Linux provides a number of command line tools for performing backups and restoring from backups. The tools for interacting directly with backup media are ftape, cdrecord, and mirror. The standard tools for creating archives are tar and dump for tape archives and mkisofs for CD archives. Each command provides a different interface and a number of options.

USING ftape
The ftape package is a collection of command line tools for accessing and managing magnetic tape drives. These utilities are useful if you are using tape drives to store your backups.

The mt command is used to scan, rewind, and eject magnetic tapes if you have an IDE drive. If you have a SCSI tape drive, the st command performs the same functions.

TESTING
You must be root in order to access the tape drives. As root, you can test a new magnetic tape by inserting it into the tape drive and then using the following command:

```
mt -f /dev/rft0 rewind
```

This command should rewind the magnetic tape. You can also format the magnetic tape with the command:

```
ftformat -f /dev/rft0
```

However, many tapes come preformatted, so it is usually unnecessary to format new tapes.

USING THE cdrecord PACKAGE
In order to make backups on CDs under Red Hat Enterprise Linux, you need the cdrecord package installed. It contains several commands such as cdrecord, devdump, isodump, isoinfo, isovfy, and readcd. These commands are useful utilities for creating and managing writable CDs.

The cdrecord package requires that you have a SCSI CD drive. If you have an IDE CD drive, you must configure it to use SCSI emulation in order to use the cdrecord package.

The disadvantage to making backups on CD is that you must first create a CD image on the file system and then copy the CD image to the actual CD all in one step. This process requires that you have empty space on a single file system partition which is large enough to hold a CD image (up to 650MB). You create a CD image with the `mkisofs` command:

```
mkisofs -o /tmp/cd.image /home/terry
```

You can also use `mkisofs` to send content to stdout and then fed directly into `cdrecord`. Using this method does run the risk of the output being larger than the CD capacity and possibly buffer underruns on slow systems that don't use burnproof or a similar technology.

This command makes a CD image file in the `/tmp` directory called `cd.image`. The CD image file contains all the files in the `/home/terry` directory. You must have enough space to make the image file on the partition holding the `/tmp` directory. You can determine how much is free with the `df` command. You can determine how much space the image file is going to take up using the command `du /home/terry`. By default, `mkisofs` preserves the ownership and permissions from the file system in the CD image.

In order to burn the image file to an actual CD, you must determine which SCSI device has the CD drive. If you don't actually have any SCSI drives and are using SCSI emulation with an IDE drive, the drive is probably on device `scsi0`. You can see what drives are on what SCSI devices with the following command:

```
dmesg | grep scsi
```

Next, you must determine which SCSI device ID the drive is using. You can find this with the following command:

```
cdrecord -scanbus
```

Next, you must determine the Logical Unit Number. If the device ID is zero, the Logical Unit Number should always be zero. You supply the SCSI device number, the device ID, and the logical unit number to the `cdrecord` command, in that order, as part of the `dev` option. A sample `cdrecord` command is as follows:

```
cdrecord -v dev=0,0,0 -data /tmp/cd.image
```

This command does not generally produce a bootable CD. In order for a CD to be bootable, the image file being recorded onto the CD needs to follow a specific format. Also, your BIOS must support booting from your particular CD-ROM. In order to produce a bootable image file, you need to follow several steps. First, you need to obtain a boot image. If you have a bootable CD-ROM in the disk drive, the boot image can be written to a file with the following command:

```
dd if=/dev/fd0 of=boot.img bs=10k count=144
```

 TIP One handy boot image is the `bootnet.img` that ships with Red Hat. It's available via ftp and can be used instead of a custom bootdisk.

This command puts the boot image in the file `boot.img`. You must put this somewhere in the directory which you are going to put on the CD. In the example provided, you could create a directory `/home/terry/boot` and place the file there. You also need to give `mkisofs` some extra parameters in order to have it create a bootable image.

```
mkisofs -r -b /home/terry/boot/boot.img -c
/home/terry/boot/boot.catalog -o /tmp/cd.image /home/terry
```

The `boot.catalog` file need not already exist. It is generated by `mkisofs`. The command line option just tells `mkisofs` where in the image to store the generated file.

USING mirrordir

The `mirrordir` command (in the mirrordir package) is a tool that enables you to easily back up a file system to an additional hard drive. In order to use `mirrordir`, you must first mount the additional hard drive.

```
mount /dev/hdb1 /mnt/backup (Be sure to use the correct path for
your system.)
```

Then you can back up a given directory to the mounted hard drive using the `mirrordir` command.

```
mirrordir /home /mnt/backup
```

The command backs up the /home directory, which contains all of the users' personal files, to the backup hard drive. You must get the order of the arguments correct. If the arguments were reversed, the /home directory would be overwritten with the contents of the backup hard drive, erasing valuable data. When executed, the mirrordir command makes the contents of the hard drive mounted on /mnt exactly identical to the contents of /home. All of the files are copied, and any files not present in /home are deleted. Subdirectories and their files are also copied.

To recover lost files if the partition containing /home crashes, the arguments to the mirrordir command are simply reversed. The following command overwrites the contents of /home with the contents of /mnt.

```
mirrordir /mnt /home
```

Note that any files extant in /home that are not also in /mnt are erased. Therefore, mirrordir is not useful for recovering individual files, but only in the situation where the entire directory, partition, or drive has been corrupted or erased.

If /home happens to be alone on a separate partition from the rest of the file system, you don't even need to restore the directory using mirrordir. The partition mounted on /mnt (in the example, /dev/hdb1) is an exact copy of the /home directory and so, in this case, an exact copy of that partition. So you can simply modify the /etc/fstab file and change the partition mounted under /home to be the partition where it is mirrored.

USING dump

The dump package consists of several commands for doing backup and restoration of the file system. The dump command is used to do backups of either entire partitions or individual directories. The restore command is used to restore an entire partition, individual directories, or individual files.

SYNTAX OF THE dump COMMAND   The first argument to the dump command is a list of options. Following that are all of the arguments required by the various options in the same order as the options were specified. The last argument is the file system to back up. Table 28-2 lists the available dump options.

TABLE 28-2 DUMP OPTIONS

Option	Meaning	Type
B	The number of records per volume.	Number
b	The number of kilobytes per dump record.	Number
h	The dump level at which to use nodump flags.	Number

Continued

TABLE **28-2** DUMP OPTIONS *(Continued)*

Option	Meaning	Type
f	Name of file or device to write to.	Filename
d	Tape density.	Number
n	Tell dump to send a message when done.	None
s	Length of dump tape.	Number in feet
u	Record the date of this dump in /etc/dumpdates.	None
T	Add only files older than the given time.	Time (ctime)
W	List the file systems that need to be backed up.	None
w	List individual files that need to be backed up.	None
0-9	Specify a dump level of 0 through 9.	None

Using `dump` on a live file system can be dangerous and unreliable. For more information on this topic, see `https://www.redhat.com/archives/ext3-users/2003-January/msg00034.html`.

SAMPLE dump COMMAND   If you want to see a sample of the output from the `dump` command, try entering the command shown here:

```
dump 0uf /dev/rft0 /dev/hda3
```

This command specifies that the file system on /dev/hda3 should be backed up on the magnetic tape on device /dev/rft0. It specifies that the backup should use backup level 0 (full backup) and write the time of the backup to the /etc/dumpdates file.

USING restore

The `restore` command is used to retrieve files from the backups created with dump. You can use `restore` to restore an entire file system or you can use it to interactively select which files you want to restore.

The syntax for the `restore` command is the same as for the `dump` command, although it has different options. Table 28-3 lists the options.

TABLE 28-3 RESTORE OPTIONS

Option	Meaning	Type
r	Restore the entire dump archive	None
C	Compare the files on the file system to those in the dump archive	None
R	Start the restore from a particular tape in a multivolume sequence	None
x	Extract only specified files	List of files
t	List the contents of the dump archive	List of files
I	Restore files in interactive mode	None
b	Block size of the dump in kilobytes	Number
D	Name of the file system to be compared against	File system
f	Name of the dump archive to restore from	Filename
h	Recreate directories but do not restore their contents	None
m	Extract files by inode number instead of name	None
N	Print file names rather than extracting them	None
s	Specify the tape number to start on when using the R option	Number
T	Specify where to write temporary files	Directory
v	Verbose mode	None
y	Do not prompt when bad blocks are encountered	None

RESTORING THE FILE SYSTEM   In order to restore a damaged or erased file system, you must first recreate the directory or partition that has been lost. If, for instance, you want to recreate the /home directory, which existed by itself on the /dev/hdb1 partition, you could use the following commands:

```
mkfs /dev/hdb1
mount /dev/hdb1 /home
```

Note that this command erases all of the data on the /dev/hdb1 partition. This method of restoration is useful only for restoring all of the files previously archived with dump. If any files have been added, modified, or deleted since the last backup, those changes are lost. Restoring individual files is covered in the section "Using Restore Interactively." Also, if mkfs is accidentally run on a different partition than the one meant to be restored, all of the data on the partition on which it is mistakenly run are irrevocably erased.

The restore command must be run inside the directory that is going to be restored. So, restore can restore the /home directory with the following commands:

```
cd /home
restore rf /dev/rft0
```

The r flag tells restore to restore the entire archive rather than just some files. The f flag tells restore that the archive is located on the device /dev/rft0.

USING restore INTERACTIVELY   The restore command, in addition to being used to restore an entire file system, can also be used in an interactive mode, which enables you to restore individual files. The interactive mode is invoked as follows:

```
restore if /dev/rft0
```

This command runs restore in interactive mode and specifies that it should restore from the archive on the device /dev/rft0. The interactive mode enables you to type options to restore in order to control its behavior. It includes the options shown in Table 28-4.

TABLE **28-4 RESTORE COMMANDS**

Command	Meaning
add	Add a file or directory to the list of files to be extracted. If a directory is specified, all contained files, subdirectories, and files contained in subdirectories are extracted. File paths are relative to the current directory being viewed in the dump archive.
cd	Change which directory within the dump archive is being viewed.
delete	Remove a file or directory from the list of files to be extracted. If a directory is specified, all files in that directory, subdirectories, and files in subdirectories are removed from the list as well. Note that this does not affect what is stored in the dump archive, but rather which files are extracted during the restore.

Command	Meaning
extract	Extract all of the files and directories currently in the list of files to extract and restore them in the file system.
help	List available commands.
ls	List the contents of the directory currently being viewed in the dump archive. If a directory is specified, the contents of the specified directory are listed rather than the contents of the current directory. Files and directories marked with * in the file listing are currently marked for extraction.
pwd	Print the path within the dump archive of the directory currently being viewed.
quit	Exit the restore program. No other actions are taken by restore.
setmodes	Rather than extract the files, set the permissions on the files in the file system so that they match the permissions of the files in the dump archive that are marked for extraction.
verbose	Switch verbose mode on or off.

USING tar

Red Hat Linux includes the GNU version of tar. It includes some extensions to the older standard versions of tar, including multivolume archiving. Multi-volume archiving is an automated process in which tar prompts for new media to be inserted whenever it runs out of space. The tar program is a utility originally designed for making magnetic tape backups, but is useful for any kind of archiving purpose. When making archives, it is important to specify a leading ./ for files. That creates a relative path, which will be necessary when restoring the files later.

The tar command requires one command option followed by any number of optional options. Table 28-5 lists the command options.

TABLE 28-5 TAR OPTIONS

Command	Explanation
A	Append the contents of the given tar files to the specified tar archive.
d	Find differences between what's in the tar archive and what's in the file system.

Continued

TABLE 28-5 TAR OPTIONS *(Continued)*

Command	Explanation
r	Append the given files to the specified tar archive.
t	List the contents of the specified tar archive.
u	Append the given files to the specified tar archive, but only if they are newer than the files in the tar archive.
x	Extract the given files from the specified tar archive.

In addition to specifying a command, you must specify a device or file to act as the destination of the tar archive.

CREATING A tar ARCHIVE   To create a tar file use the following command syntax.

```
tar -cf (name of tar file to create) (list of files to add)
```

If you wanted to create a tar file of the files testing1.txt, testing2.txt, and testing3.txt and place them into a tar archive called testing.tar, you would issue this command:

```
tar -cf testing.tar testing1.txt testing2.txt testing3.txt
```

In this example, you could use wildcards to make your job easier by using testing*.txt instead of typing the file names individually.

You can also use tar to backup entire directories by issuing the directory name you want to tar instead of file names. For example, if you wanted to tar a directory called ch4, you would issue this command:

```
tar -cf ch4.tar ch4/
```

This command would create a tar file called ch4.tar and would contain the contents of ch4, including all files as well as any subdirectories.

EXTRACTING A tar ARCHIVE   To extract a tar archive, use the following syntax:

```
tar -x (name of tar file)
```

To extract the tar file created in the previous section, issue this command:

```
tar -x testing.tar
```

This would extract the files from the tar file and place them in the current directory. If you extract a tar file containing a directory and subdirectories, if any, the directory and its subdirectories will be extracted into their original directory structure at the location from where the `tar` command was issued.

Advanced Tools

This section discusses a number of advanced backup tools including AMANDA, the `amdump` test, pax, and taper.

USING AMANDA

The AMANDA (Advanced Maryland Automatic Network Disk Archiver) package is a set of tools for doing backups of multiple machines over the network. Using Amanda, you can configure your Red Hat Linux machine to be a backup server for the other machines in the network, including Windows systems. Amanda is included with Red Hat Linux. To use Amanda, install the following packages:

- `Amanda`
- `Amanda-client`
- `Amanda-server`
- `Gnuplot`

You need to install the Amanda-server and gnuplot packages only on the machine that is going to be the backup server. However, you must install Amanda-client on any machine that you want to back up using Amanda. You must install the base Amanda package on both the client and server machines. The Amanda package contains several commands, shown in Table 28-6.

TABLE **28-6 AMANDA COMMANDS**

Command	Use
amdump	Normally executed periodically by a cron job, this utility is run on the Amanda server. It requests backups from the various Amanda clients.
amflush	If amdump has trouble writing backups to tape, they are kept in temporary storage space on disk until the problem is corrected. After the problem is fixed, this command is run to write the data in the temporary storage space to the tapes.

Continued

TABLE **28-6** AMANDA COMMANDS *(Continued)*

Command	Use
amcleanup	If the Amanda server crashes during the running of amdump, this utility should be run to cleanup after the interrupted amdump.
amrecover	This utility provides a way to select which tapes should be used to recover files.
amrestore	This utility is used to restore individual files or directories or entire partitions from Amanda backups.
amlabel	This utility is used to write an Amanda label onto a tape. You must use this command to label tapes before they can be written to with amdump.
amcheck	This utility should be run before amdump to verify that the correct tape is in the drive.
amadmin	This utility does various administrative tasks.
amtape	This utility is used for low-level tape control, such as loading and ejecting disks.
amverify	This utility checks Amanda tapes for errors.
amrmtape	This utility deletes a tape with a particular label from the Amanda tape database.
amstatus	This utility reports on the current status of a running amdump program.

INSTALLING AMANDA   After installing the necessary RPMs, some additional installation is required to get Amanda running. You must create subdirectories in the /etc/Amanda and /usr/admn/Amanda directories for each backup schedule you are going to run. For instance, if you plan to run a backup schedule called test, you must execute the following commands:

```
mkdir -p /etc/Amanda/test
mkdir -p /usr/admn/Amanda/normal
```

You also need to create some temporary space for Amanda to keep files, which it is in the process of backing up. So if, for instance, you want to create this space as a directory on your root partition, you can use the following command to make an Amanda directory:

```
mkdir /Amanda
```

CONFIGURING AMANDA   To configure Amanda, you must create an `Amanda.conf` file and put it in the subdirectory in `/etc/Amanda` that you created. So in the example, for instance, it would be called `/etc/Amanda/Amanda.conf`. The `Amanda.conf` file has many options, shown in Table 28-7, but has defaults for most of them.

TABLE 28-7 AMANDA.CONF OPTIONS

Option	Example	Meaning
org "name"	org "Tristero"	This option specifies the name used in reports generated by Amanda.
mailto "accounts"	mailto "root example"	This option specifies account names that Amanda should put in charge of the backup process.
dumpuser "account"	dumpuser "Amanda"	This option specifies the user account that the Amanda dump process should run as.
inparallel number	inparallel 5	This entry specifies the number of amdump processes that can run simultaneously.
netusage num unit	netusage 1000 Kpbs	This entry indicates the bandwidth that Amanda is allowed to consume while doing backups. It should be set such that even if all of the allocated bandwidth is consumed there is still enough bandwidth for other tasks that might operate at the same time as the Amanda backup process.
dumpcycle num unit	dumpcycle 1 week	This option specifies the length of the backup cycle.
runspercycle num	runspercycle 7	This option specifies the number of backups that should be done during a single dump cycle. So with a dump cycle of 1 week and 7 runs per cycle, Amanda makes one full backup and 6 incremental backups every week.
tapespercycle num unit	tapespercycle 7 tapes	This option specifies how many tapes are available for use in a single backup cycle.

Continued

TABLE 28-7 AMANDA.CONF OPTIONS *(Continued)*

Option	Example	Meaning
runtapes num	runtapes 1	This option specifies how many tapes are available for use in each backup.
tapedev "device"	tapedev "/dev/ rft0"	This option specifies the device name of the tape device.

The `Amanda.conf` file also has some complex options, which consist of blocks with multiple subfields. The holdingdisk block defines a temporary storage space for holding data that is being backed up. You can define multiple holdingdisk blocks in a single file. The definition has the following format:

```
Holdingdisk name
{
      directory "name"
      use num unit
}
```

Example holdingdisk block:

```
Holdingdisk example
{
      directory "/example"
      use 4 Gb
}
```

The tapetype block defines a particular kind of magnetic tape that might be used in backups. It defines properties about the tape such as length and speed. The tapetype definition has the following format:

```
Define tapetype name
{
comment "freeform string"
length num unit
filemark num unit
speed num unit
}
```

Example tapetype definition:

```
Define tapetype EXAMPLE
{
comment "These are fictional numbers."
Length 5000 mbytes
Filemark 100 kbytes
Speed 500 kbytes
}
```

The interface block defines a particular network interface that can be used for communication between an Amanda server and client. The interface definition specifies how much bandwidth can be used on that particular network interface. The syntax of the definition is as follows:

```
Define interface name
{
comment "Freeform string"
use num unit
}
```

Example interface definition:

```
Define interface eth0
{
comment "This sets the bandwidth usage of the Ethernet network
interface"
use 500 kbps
}
```

The dumptype block defines a particular kind of dump. The entries in the disklist file refer to these definitions. A corresponding dumptype block must exist in the `Amanda.conf` file for it to be referenced in the disklist file. The dumptype block specifies certain properties of the kind of dump, such as which program to use for dumping, whether or not to compress backups, and files that should not be backed up.

The dumptype block has many options, shown in Table 28-8, which define how the dump works.

TABLE 28-8 DUMPTYPE OPTIONS

Option	Explanation
auth	This option specifies which authorization method should be used between the client and the server. This option can be set to either "bsd" or "krb4" and defaults to "bsd."
comment	This option is a freeform string and is ignored.
comprate	This option specifies the compression rates for backed up files in terms of how the size of the compressed file should compare to the size of the uncompressed file. This option can either be a single value or two values separated by a comma. The first value specifies the compression rate for full backups. The second value specifies the compression rate for incremental backups and is assumed to be the same as the first value if omitted.
compress	This option specifies the method to be used for compressing the data. The options are presented in the separate Table 28-9. The default compression type is "client fast."
dumpcycle	This option specifies the number of days in the backup cycle. A full backup is performed at the beginning of each backup cycle.
exclude	This option specifies which files should not be included in the backup. This option works only when the backup program being used is tar. When used with dump or samba it is ignored. The possible values for exclude are either a quote wildcard pattern or else the list keyword followed by a quoted filename. If the list keyword is used, the filename should refer to a file on the client machine, which contains a list of wildcard patterns to match. Wildcard patterns are listed one per line. Any files matched by either the quoted patterns or any of the patterns in the specified file are excluded from the Amanda backups.
holdingdisk	This option specifies whether or not the holding disk should be used for temporarily storing files that are going to be dumped. The default is "yes."
ignore	This option specifies that this dump type should not actually be backed up even if the disklist file specifies that it should.
index	This option specifies whether or not to keep an index of files that have been backed up. The default is "no."

Option	Explanation
kencrypt	This option specifies whether or not the connection between the client and the server should be encrypted. The default is "no."
maxdumps	This option specifies how many simultaneous instances of the amdump process can be run. The default is 1.
priority	This option specifies the priority of the dump. When Amanda runs out of tape or is otherwise unable to write backups for some reason, all the data, which can be kept on the holding disk is put there in order of highest priority dump type to lowest priority. The possible values for the priority of a dump are "high," "medium," and "low." The default is "medium."
program	This option specifies which program should be used for making the backup dump. The possible values are "DUMP" and "GNUTAR." The default is "DUMP." You must change this to "GNUTAR" if you wish to use the "exclude" option.
record	This option specifies whether or not the date of the dump should be written to the /etc/dumpdates file. The default is "yes."
skip-full	This option specifies that when Amanda is scheduled to do a full backup it should refrain from doing so. This option is useful if you want to use Amanda for incremental backups or to use some other method for full backups.
skip-incr	This option specifies that when Amanda is scheduled to do an incremental backup it should refrain from doing so. This option is useful if you want to use Amanda for full backups but to use some other method for incremental backups or if you do not want to do incremental backups at all.
starttime	This option specifies that the starting time of the dump should be delayed.
strategy	This option specifies the dumping strategy that should be used for this kind of dump. The various available dump strategies are listed in Table 28-10. The default strategy is "Standard."

TABLE 28-9 AMANDA COMPRESSION TYPES

Type	Explanation
none	This option specifies that no compression should be used on Amanda backups.
client best	This option specifies that the client should use the compression algorithm that results in the highest compression levels.
client fast	This option specifies that the client should use the fastest compression algorithm.
server best	This option specifies that the server should use the compression algorithm that results in the highest compression levels.
server fast	This option specifies that the server should use the fastest compression algorithm.

TABLE 28-10 AMANDA DUMPING STRATEGIES

Strategy	Explanation
standard	This option specifies that Amanda should use the standard dumping strategy, which includes both full and incremental backups.
nofull	This option specifies that Amanda should use level 1 incremental backups always and never do full backups. This is useful when a set of machines all have the same base installation and setup with only minor differences that do not change rapidly. Amanda then saves space by backing up only the changes that occur over time.
noinc	This option specifies that incremental backups should never occur and that Amanda should always do full backups. This is useful if it is important to make the restoration of a machine as swift and easy as possible. However, it makes backups much slower and requires much more storage space for the backups.
skip	This option specifies that the dump type should never be backed up either with full backups or incremental backups. The dump type is ignored even if it occurs in the disklist file.

You need to adapt the `Amanda.conf` file to your system. Most important, you need to correctly specify the paths to the tape drive devices, the type of tape drives, and the path to the directory that Amanda can use as temporary space.

You must also create a disklist file that specifies which partitions to back up. In the example setup this file would be stored as `/etc/Amanda/test/disklist`.

The format of the disklist file is a series of entries, one per line, in the following format:

```
Hostname device dumptype
```

The disklist file has the arguments shown in Table 28-11.

TABLE 28-11 DISKLIST ARGUMENTS

Argument	Explanation
hostname	This argument specifies the hostname of the Amanda client to be backed up. For the Amanda client to enable a connection from the Amanda server, the hostname of the Amanda server must be in that client's `.amandahosts` file.
device	This argument specifies the name of the directory to be backed up.
dumptype	This argument specifies the name of the dumptype definition in the `Amanda.conf` file, which defines the properties associated with this type of dump.

The following is an example disklist file:

```
Blanu.net /home/blanu/public_html normal
Tristero.sourceforge.net /cvsroot/tristero incremental
Baldwinpage.com /var/www/htdocs/bruno/ normal
```

AMANDA CLIENT CONFIGURATION In order to enable the Amanda backup servers to connect to the clients to request backups, you must create on each client an `.amandahosts` file in the `/root` directory of the machine. The file consists simply of the names of the server machines that are allowed to connect to the client in order to request backups.

Here is an example `.amandahosts` file:

```
Blanu.net
Thalassocracy.org
Tristero.sourceforge.net
Baldwinpage.com
```

You are wise to set the permissions of this file to 600 using `chmod`. That ensures that only root can modify the file and other users cannot add hosts to the file, thus bypassing the permission system and gaining access to the full file system.

PERFORMING BACKUPS WITH AMANDA   In order to perform a backup, you simply run `amdump` with the name of the backup that you want to run. The configuration information and list of partitions to back up are read from the configuration files in the particular subdirectory in `/etc/Amanda` that you created for this particular backup type.

amdump TEST

The `amdump` commands then go through the list of the partitions specified in `amdump` and back up each of them, in order, to the tape drives specified in the associated `Amanda.conf` file. The partitions in the disklist file should be specified in order of importance so that in case of problems the most important files are more likely to have already been backed up. The results of the `amdump` operation, including any errors, are written to the `/usr/adm/Amanda/test` directory.

USING pax

The pax tool is useful for converting between different archive formats. This capability is especially important in an environment where there may be different operating systems and distributions running in conjunction. Incompatibilities between the various tools and various versions of tools can be quite a hassle. Pax solves this problem by knowing how to read many versions of several different archiving formats. Table 28-12 lists the options you can use with pax.

TABLE **28-12** PAX OPTIONS

Option	Meaning
-r	Read files from archive.
-w	Write files to archive.
-a	Append files to an existing archive.
-b blocksize	Specify the size of a block of data in the archive. Block sizes must be a multiple of 512.

Option	Meaning
-c	Match all files except those with the specified pattern.
-d	Match wildcards against the file names only, rather than the complete path.
-f	Specifies the name of the archive file.
-I	Prompt to rename files when archiving.
-k	Do not overwrite existing files.
-l	Link files with hard links when in copying mode.
-n	Match only the first file that matches the supplied pattern.
-o options	Specifies a list of additional options that are specific to the archiving format.
-p string	Specifies file characteristics that should be retained on the archived versions of the files.
-s string	Specifies that the names of the files should be modified using the regular expression given in the argument string before the files are archived.
-t	Specifies that the access time information associated with the files that are being archived should be retained in the archived copies of the files.
-u	Specifies that pax should not overwrite files in the archive even if the files in the archive are older than the files specified to be archived.
-v	Specifies that pax should produce verbose output.
-x format	Specifies which format the archive should be in. The possible values for the format are cpio, bcpio, sv4cpio, sv4rc, tar, and ustar. The default format is ustar. When reading an archive instead of writing one, pax automatically determines the type of the archive, so this option is needed only when writing an archive.
-B number	Specifies the number of bytes in each volume of the archive. It is useful for creating multivolume archives on volumes with a known size such as CD-ROMs or floppy disks.
-D	Specifies that pax should not overwrite files in the tar archive with files supplied to be archived if the supplied files are older than the files already in the archive.

Continued

Table 28-12 PAX OPTIONS *(Continued)*

Option	Meaning
-E number	Specifies the number of times that pax should attempt to retry reading or writing an archive in the case of an error.
-G group	Specifies that only files in the given group should be written or read. The given group string is assumed to be a group name unless it starts with the "#" character, in which case it is assumed to be a group ID number.
-H	Specifies that only command-line symbolic links should be followed.
-L	Specifies that all symbolic links should be followed.
-P	Specifies that no symbolic links should be followed.
-T time	Specifies that only files with the given modification time should be read or written.
-U user	Specifies that only files owned by the given user should be written or read. The given user string is assumed to be a user name unless it starts with a "#" character, in which case it is assumed to be a user ID number.
-X	Specifies that directories should not be entered if the directory is on a different partition or device than the parent directory.

Summary

In this chapter, you learned how to back up and restore your file system. You learned how to choose which files are important to back up and to choose a backup medium, a backup method, and a tape rotation schedule appropriate for the needs of your situation. You also learned how to use low-level archiving tools such as tar and dump to produce archives and file-system data and to restore corrupted file-system data from archives. In addition, you learned how to configure and use Amanda, an advanced archiving tool.

Part V

System Security and Problem Solving

Chapter 29

Security Basics

IN THIS CHAPTER

- ◆ Introducing basic security concepts
- ◆ Developing a security policy
- ◆ Creating a recovery plan

SECURITY isn't a tangible thing, it is applied psychology" (Alec Muffett, author of the crack password cracking program).

Before digging into the hands-on elements of system security, you need to understand the underlying principles of system security. Although the popular perception of security rightly focuses on fending off and recovering from deliberate, malevolent attempts to compromise a Linux system, security also involves protecting against accidents and establishing a recovery plan that restores an exploited or otherwise damaged system as quickly and as safely as possible. Moreover, the better you understand how crackers think and operate, the better you are able to protect your systems and your data from ne'er-do-wells. This chapter attempts to survey the basic principles that should inform any attempt to secure a Linux system and to describe the methods crackers use to defeat security measures.

Introducing Basic Security Principles

The general subject of computer and network security is usually subdivided into two basic categories: host-based security and network-based security. *Host-based security* refers to security measures taken at the server or workstation in order to secure the machine against tampering or being compromised. We use the term *local security* to refer to host-based security. Examples of local security measures include login passwords and keyboard locks. *Network-based security* refers to security measures implemented to enhance the security of a local area network (*LAN*) as a whole. One example of a network security feature would be a firewall between the Internet and the LAN.

Most of the high-profile media attention of late has focused on network security, where *blackhats* (the bad guys) and *whitehats* (the good guys) contend with each other for the public's attention. As a result, local security often gets short-shrift, a circumstance that Chapter 30 aims to rectify. Any given host can benefit from a number of measures that leave it far less likely to be the scene or source of a future compromise. Most local security measures are surprisingly simple — there is no excuse for not implementing at least some of them on practically every system in use within the organization

Local and network security is often a series of judgment calls and a matter of layering incremental defensive measures. The quality of these judgments can never exceed the importance an organization assigns to security matters. Ultimately, success or failure hinges on a series of value judgments of the worth of the organization's assets. System administrators are rarely qualified to make such judgments because such decisions are properly the purview of management staff. Nevertheless, as a system administrator, you *can* help — clarify exactly what assets are at stake, what threats they are under, what defenses are available, and how much various defensive efforts might cost. A great deal can be accomplished through effective marshalling of evidence, provided you are willing to spend time massaging your data into a form useful to your managers. With good information in hand, responsible managers will be all the more likely to heed your opinions as to what is important and what isn't.

Network security is a huge topic, and only a few essentials can be covered here. Keeping in the house what should not leave might turn out to be a greater challenge than keeping out what should not get in — we make the reasons for this clear in Chapter 31.

We finish the discussion of security topics with Chapter 32. Intrusion detection spans both local and network security, with different kinds of tools and different aims coming to the fore in each case. The question of how to respond once an intrusion has taken place is never an easy one, so we offer a few pointers in that area also.

What is the appropriate frame of mind for approaching the task of securing a computer network site? Paranoia is counter-productive because it wastes resources on inessentials. Panicked anxiety is not helpful either because it produces paralysis, a fearful inability to act. Rather, the proper mindset to adopt combines native curiosity about everything, compounded with *a degree* of suspicion and *a degree* of being somewhat on edge. To the mix, you might add a smidgen of pessimism, a tad of skepticism, and a large helping of acceptance when Murphy makes his inevitable appearance and the worst *possible* outcome indeed becomes *the* outcome. Then the balancing act becomes how to avoid slipping backwards into general cynicism, which unfortunately lives just next door to paranoia. A passion for learning can carry you a long way because there is never a shortage of new things to learn in this neighborhood.

Security as Loss Prevention

Unfortunately, two dangerous misconceptions pervade the popular view of computer security. The first of these is that the only really secure computer is one not connected to any network. Nothing could be farther from the truth, as you learn when you read Chapter 30. The other mistaken belief is that computer security is primarily a matter of holding at bay legions of blackhats, properly referred to as *crackers* rather than *hackers*. Although crackers have captured popular imagination, and some, such as Kevin Mitnick, have been romanticized as inequitably victimized antiheroes, please do not be misled or deceived: the dollar losses attributable to cracker exploits are anything but romantic.

Data can be lost and services interrupted as a result of malicious action brought about by many others besides the cracker. At the top of the list might be the disgruntled former employee who, when discharged, carried several passwords out the door. Of course, it is not only former employees who can become disgruntled. Personnel still on the payroll can disseminate company data to the competition or simply post it for the entire world to see. Indeed, keeping what belongs in-house actually *in the house* is much more likely to be more of a concern on an ongoing day-in, day-out basis than keeping the crackers and script kiddies out.

As for keeping the wrong people out, do not be misled by popular media to think that only mad scientists and rambunctious adolescents want to get in for the sake of the thrill or for subculture status that accrues to those who succeed with notorious *sploits*, as they are called in that subculture. Depending on the nature and value of the data and services comprising a given site's assets, attacks may be forthcoming from rather serious individuals, perhaps in the service of industrial or political espionage, and also to satisfy motives that remain unknown.

Loss prevention goes beyond protecting against deliberate acts. Accidents and mistakes account for a huge proportion of costs due to data loss and service interruptions. While some accidents or similar events appear to be outright negligence, more are simple mistakes born of ignorance, and even more still are outright mistakes. Attributing to malice what can instead be attributed to stupidity is often unwise. From the standpoint of a security administrator, or a system administrator charged with maintaining system security, the point is that the more randomness in an event, as opposed to deliberate intention on the part of a human being, the more difficult it is to defend against the given threat.

Consider, for example, mechanical failures. They cannot be predicted with any degree of reliability and frequently you can defend against them only by building redundancy into the hardware where feasible and desirable. Human error is another matter, in that it can be mitigated through training and anticipated to some degree. Beyond a certain point, however, human error is as unpredictable as any machine's. We discussing how to anticipate and defend against both hardware failure and human fallibility in the next chapter.

What of floods, earthquakes, civil insurrection, war, and the like? How many threats found under the rubric "act of God" ought to fall into the purview of a computer security policy and security analysis? The answer here, as in many other places throughout this chapter, is, "It depends." On *what* does it depend? Until we arrive at a better understanding of exactly what the term "secure" means, it is difficult to say. The fundamental notion underlying all four security-related chapters in this book is that the definition of "secure" is not amenable to technical considerations only, but involves a number of factors any one of which at certain times can be assessed only via an act of *judgment*.

For now, though, the following definition should serve as a solid starting point. *Secure* should always be taken to mean *"strengthened with regard to a given installation, configured in a given manner, against a defined list of possible threats, as far as these data, operations, or services are concerned, as long as these specific measures and practices are adopted and maintained, according to the best of our knowledge of current realities, and in light of all sorts of unforeseen and unforeseeable contingencies."* You are correct if you observe that there are a lot of qualifications in this definition, but the temptation to oversimplify security concerns is widespread and, potentially, catastrophically costly.

As if to underline the second misconception mentioned earlier, that the task of the computer security analyst is mostly to fend off exotic hacker cult members, the Sans Institute recently compiled a list of "The Seven Worst Security Mistakes Senior Executives Make." The Sans Institute ranked relying primarily or solely on a firewall as number four on the list of seven. Computer security is much more than network security, and installing a given piece of firewall software never finishes the job of hardening a site, regardless of the claims made by the software vendor.

The last section of this chapter, "Finding Security-Related Resources," includes a link to the Sans Institute Web site.

Security: A Distributed Venture

Having just claimed that there is much more to computer security than network security, we readily acknowledge that the Internet's phenomenal growth has put a whole new face on things. Using one compromised computer as a remote launch site for attacks on yet other computers is not a new technique — all self-respecting crackers leave back doors in all the machines they have compromised so that they can carry out further depredations from those machines rather than their own. The advent of distributed denial of service (*DDoS*) tools, which can trigger hundreds of these remote back doors simultaneously, has upped the ante so dramatically that it is no longer an overstatement to say that going online with an insecure machine makes one, at the very least, rather an irresponsible netizen. Even if, for the sake of argument, you could care less about the data you store or the operations you perform on your own system, if you connect to the Internet and pay no attention at all to what passes in and especially out of that system, then you increase the risk for everyone connected to the Internet.

Showing due regard for *everyone else* when *you* go online is rather a new twist on netizenship — it signals the beginning of the end of rugged individualism on the Internet. Indeed, as broadband Internet access for individuals becomes the norm rather than the exception thanks to DSL and cable modems, some ISPs, bowing to consumer pressure, have rewritten their EUAs (End User Agreements) so that there is no longer explicit language forbidding the use of servers, such as Web and e-mail servers, on residential accounts. Instead, they contain vague mutterings about "excessive traffic" or "interfering" with others' use of the network.

One consequence of this more relaxed attitude combined with the notion of irresponsible Internet citizenship was evident during the Blaster and SoBig infestations of July and August 2003. Hundreds if not thousands of home users of cable networks, especially those with routable Internet addresses (as opposed to masqueraded or translated ones), provided an enormously fertile ground for Blaster traffic.

The interested reader might appreciate this note. In the first edition of this book, the first sentence of the preceding paragraph read, "One consequence of this more relaxed attitude combined with the notion of irresponsible Internet citizenship was evident during the Code Red infestations of July and August 2001."

The news here is not good, amounting to "ask not for whom the bell tolls; it tolls for thee." The mixture of elements is highly volatile: the Internet's future rests on increased security awareness in the face of the proliferation of insecure servers in the hands of everyday consumers hard wired to routable IP addresses in the presence of increasingly sophisticated worms, viruses, and trojans. In particular, one wonders how the implementation of the next generation Internet addressing scheme, IPv6, will fare under these increasingly bizarre conditions.

The Fundamental Mindset: Shades of Grey

The previous section suggests that security assessments, or the lack thereof, are fundamentally acts of judgment, rather than evaluations based on the application of a discrete set of black and white rules. One might say that estimating the degree of a site's security is an analog, not a digital, process. That is, a site is not simply secure or insecure, but exists along a continuum ranging from less secure to more secure. This chapter dwells on a notion of security as an iterative process or a journey because security is radically different in kind from almost all the other parameters that a network operator might have to consider. You can quantify the traditional considerations of a system or network administrator, such as bandwidth, storage capacity, power requirements, CPU utilization, and you can evaluate in unambiguous terms the needs and capacities of a given system. Further, such evaluations can be the subject of comparisons from one system to another, or to a group of systems. Where security is concerned, though, you have no such luxury.

Secure and *insecure* are designations that have meaning *only* in a particular setting, under particular conditions, and, most importantly, only in light of specific decisions, usually made beforehand, about what constitutes acceptable levels of risk and acceptable tradeoffs between the cost of security measures and their anticipated benefits. Typically, managers make risk tolerance and cost/benefit analyses about the worth of assets, not engineers or consultants. The more deeply the system administrator comes to understand and embrace the conditions relevant to her site's security needs, the better she will be prepared to navigate the difficult, irksome, but all-important battleground where management and technical administration go head to head.

As a system administrator, particularly in a business or professional setting, your managers will likely put a lot of accountability but little responsibility in your hands. Being able to articulate clearly and convincingly that intangible quality Alec Muffett mentioned in the quote that opened this chapter, the nature of security matters, to your managers in terms that even they can grasp is your ace in the hole. Not that there are any guarantees in these affairs, but if *you* are clear about the nature of the beast, you will be that much more likely to communicate that nature to those in authority, and communicate you must. Conversely, if you fail to comprehend the nature of the threat and how to meet it, you will not be able to convey this to your managers.

Understanding the Enemy

One way to appreciate the psychological nature of the security game is to consider an imaginary attacker. Suppose this malevolent character possesses infinite technical skill; there is no firewall, no cryptography, and no operating system bag of tricks that such a criminal cannot defeat *given enough time*. Being human, after all, our hypothetical attacker can only tolerate so much frustration. Sooner or later one of two possible outcomes prevails: either the attacker succeeds, or the attacker moves on in search of easier, less troublesome prey. When this moment is reached in any given case is beyond anyone's guess, but one thing is certain: Any attacker, delayed long enough, will move on.

For some would-be assailants, this moment could come very early in the chase. It may arrive, for instance, when the blackhat determines that a given network's operating system is of a certain kind or that a network supports only encrypted traffic and none other. Because many of the most dangerous attacks do not come over the network wire, some intruders might be discouraged when they learn, for instance, that they cannot sweet-talk any receptionist, secretary, or telephone operator into giving them information about the network when they pose as a consultant. Well-trained staff members are easy to spot; they always refer *all* questions or requests about the firm's computing systems to a full-time system administrator.

Visitors to a facility who are up to no good might lose interest when they notice that not one single monitor has a yellow sticky attached to it bearing a password. Perhaps they will notice that no computer in clear view seems to have a floppy drive installed. Maybe they have gone through the trash out back long enough to learn that only shredded paperwork (and no old computer manuals) winds up there. You simply cannot predict what measure, when followed consistently, will prove to be the last straw that convinces a given marauder to move on. This is the point. As a system administrator charged with maintaining security on your systems, you are dealing with countless shades of grey. What might be appropriate $24 \times 7 \times 365$ in one department would be ridiculous overkill in another.

Developing a Security Policy

An effective security policy does several things, all related to the meaning of the term *secure* as used in this chapter. Recalling that definition, a security policy reflects decisions made relative to factors that include:

◆ The value of the organization's data, processes, and services to the organization, its customers, and to unknown others, such as potential customers, competitors, and business or strategic partners

◆ The degree, intensity, and skillfulness of attacks that might be directed against that data, the business processes, and services

◆ The costs of securing systems to various degrees of hardness commensurate with points 1 and 2, plus the costs of maintaining security at those levels

To begin, a security policy should state in concrete terms each of the items enumerated. This is a large task, even for a small organization, because smaller organizations generally have fewer resources that can be allocated to what might seem a non-productive and labor-intensive task. The tendency is to call in a consultant, and consultants can be a valuable supplement to in-house efforts and expertise.

Consultant-bashing is a popular sport, and there are undoubtedly outside consultants who do little more than repackage what you already know and give you an invoice for their trouble. Nevertheless, we believe the shyster consultant or third-party vendor is the exception rather than the rule. Security consultants and outside vendors bring a valuable, outside perspective to the task of information security. Just as authors need a fresh set of eyes for copy edits, bringing in an outside firm that has no previous involvement with or preconceptions about your company's security needs can give you a fresh perspective on your situation that you might otherwise never develop using native or in-house expertise.

Of course, do not toss your own skills, knowledge, and experiences out the door when and if you do bring in an outside party. Working together, your own competencies and those brought to bear by impartial outsiders can dramatically improve the overall security at your site. As always, there is a proper middle ground wherein one is always a bit on edge, a bit skeptical about things, and always curious about the unusual.

Process, not Policy

Even if you avoid the canned solution approach, you ought to view other products in the security marketplace with extreme skepticism. Often the very term *security policy* suffers a supposed upgrade to security assertions. *Security assertions* are typically impressive-looking documents, presented in designer three-ring binders emblazoned with rather attractive logos that contain little more than customized versions of the canned solution. The one-size-fits-all approach of the canned solution is not the problem here. Rather, the problem is that even though the specific operations of your organization have been worked into the contents, and some basic measures and practices spelled out, the net result remains a dead document that could very well migrate to the nether reaches of that bookcase behind you that holds catalogs and manuals from the past five years.

These security assertions are little more than expensive exercises in collective deniability. If security planning begins and ends with the three-ring binder, the result is fairly predictable. When trouble strikes and losses occur, the claim will be, "Well, we followed the security policy! It must be defective." Moreover, the consultants who authored the document will be well prepared to demonstrate how, within the terms of their consulting contract, they exercised due diligence preparing the security assertions, and could not possibly be held liable for what transpired. We have finally arrived at the crux of the matter, where management frequently draws the line and says, in so many words, "You've got to be kidding. There's no way we can budget any time or money for security planning as an ongoing continuous process. Either we have a plan, or we don't."

If this is management's mindset towards security, you would do well to learn so early in the game, for a couple of reasons. First, this is precisely the attitude that purveyors of canned solutions and fancy security assertions look for and hope to find as often as possible. It is their gravy train. Neither will they want to tell you up front that, where security policies are concerned, there is more to review and revise than an item on the agenda of a meeting that may or may not be held every month, if that often.

The bitter pill here, at least for those responsible for keeping costs in check, is this: *a security policy is not an object, but a process.* The three-ring binder ideally should be dog-eared and coffee-stain-ridden. It should always be open on someone's desk. Indeed, periodically it ought to be reprinted so that all the notes placed in the margins can be made readable for everyone. *Antistasis*, or constant change, needs to be the spirit of a security policy. The good news is that you can thank the recent high-profile exploits, typified by Blaster, you will not find it difficult to make the case that someone needs to constantly monitor not only the current state of threats and reported incidents, but also the latest information regarding newly discovered vulnerabilities and whatever fixes or patches that may have been released for them. With all these caveats in mind, you are ready to begin the initial how-to for security policies.

Creating the Policy: A First Iteration

The first task is to make lists, lots of lists. Make lists of assets, processes, services, threats, and costs. Why? So that you know what you have to protect and, therefore, how stringent a security policy to create.

ASSETS

What assets need to be secured? This list should contain both objects (physical and virtual), and processes, that is, operations, services, tasks and the like. Examples of objects to include on this list are:

◆ Computer hardware

◆ Stored data and system backups

◆ Technical manuals

◆ Security documents, audit reports, and the security policy itself

◆ Equipment configuration records

◆ Original software media

◆ Power backup equipment

◆ Network cabling

◆ Keys

Some examples of processes and services are:

◆ Data processing and a statement of desired uptime

◆ E-mail communications (privacy, authenticity)

◆ Periodic data and system backups and the intervals at which they are performed

◆ Communication channels, such as telephone, fax, radio, or satellite, and a statement of desired uptime

◆ Software updates (upgrades, patches)

◆ Security reviews/audits

When you've completed your list, try to prioritize each item according to worth or value. You might consider an item's cost-of-replacement, including ancillary losses; that is, what will the loss of this item bring down with it? Also make a first *estimate* at ranking assets according to degree of exposure to loss; how at risk is each item currently (to the best of your knowledge)?

THREATS

Listing potential threats is an endless affair, especially for one endowed with the degree of pessimism and fatalism (or paranoia) needed to make a good security officer. Examples of what might be on this list are:

◆ Loss of Internet connection

◆ Loss of power

◆ Computer failure (drives, power supply, boards, connectors, and so on)

◆ Network cable failure

- Theft of passwords — sure, you do not allow yellow stickies on monitors, but what about the 3×5 index cards taped to the underside of desk drawers?

- Script kiddies running a probe or attack script

- Skillful attacker attempting to gain root privilege

- Unauthorized person wandering into server room and trying Ctrl+Alt+Delete at the database server's system console

- Use of a system for unauthorized activity

- Personnel changes, especially key personnel — what and where *are* their passwords?

- Burglaries, fires, floods, tornadoes, hurricanes, earthquakes

- E-mail viruses/macros

- Release of confidential company information to a Usenet group

- Industrial espionage compromises proprietary company data

- Your site is targeted for a DDoS attack

- Social engineering

- Bugs or other defects in mission critical proprietary or open source software

- Use of unauthorized — or worse, unknown — software, servers, and workstations

This list is never complete. As with the asset list, the list of possible threats should be ranked according to several different factors. What does the list look like ranked according to the worth, such as the replacement or repair cost, of the asset threatened? Next, try to rank the threats in order of their likelihood of occurrence. Essentially, one needs to wonder, "How realistic is this particular threat?"

Cataloging potential threats and assessing the value of the organization's assets can be a daunting task, so consider spreading the work of creating these lists over several weeks, during which you can invite different staff members to take a try at it. Your maintenance staff may be able to give you a best grasp of the reliability of the power supply from the pole in the street, as well as the physical security of the plant. On the other hand, third-shift system administrators can tell you whether or not the night cleaning staff props the back door open with a broom for hours at a time. Ask some of the administrative assistants in private and off the record exactly what kind of paperwork is shredded before being discarded. A security policy needs to reflect a rather complete picture of everything that transpires within the organization.

Trust Whom? Trust What?

One way to grasp the essentially incommensurable nature of risk in computer security considerations is to read Ken Thompson's classic paper "Reflections on Trusting Trust" in *Communications of the ACM,* vol. 27, No. 8, August 1984, pp. 761–63, online at `http://www.acm.org/classics/sep95/`. Thompson describes the construction of a compiler that, when used to build a new compiler, produces one that will, according to whether a given pattern is or is not matched in a piece of source code, introduce a given bug into the resultant binary. The bug could be a bug in the `login` command that enables a user named `dilbert` to login, for example. This evil compiler will always build a bona fide — but tainted — C compiler binary from pristine, unaltered compiler source code, and that build will not throw errors when the bug-introduction feature is compiled in.

The point? What source code and which binaries should you trust? Thompson offers this:

> "The moral is obvious. You can't trust code that you did not totally create yourself. (Especially code from companies that employ people like me.) No amount of source-level verification or scrutiny will protect you from using untrusted code. In demonstrating the possibility of this kind of attack, I picked on the C compiler. I could have picked on any program-handling program such as an assembler, a loader, or even hardware microcode. As the level of program gets lower, these bugs will be harder and harder to detect. A well installed microcode bug will be almost impossible to detect."

The idea here is not to instill panic, but to encourage a realistic grasp of the big picture. Here again, you are confronted with this fundamental truth: a skilled attacker will *always* succeed if given enough time. There is no such thing as a site that has been secured, as if that is the end of it. One needs to be comfortable working with all those shades of grey. Only then will the method of building incremental layers of security, *some quite small in and of themselves,* make sense.

COSTS

Listing and prioritizing assets and threats and then comparing the lists will, over time, produce a cross tabulation of the most valuable assets that are at the greatest risk. At this point one can begin to assess the cost of implementing preventive *and* recovery measures. Also, getting the big picture into perspective should be near to hand, since now it ought to be evident that fire or the loss of key personnel can be far more damaging than a denial of service attack, the spread of a virulent virus, or a successful root compromise.

The goal of cost analysis is a set of data that can be presented to management so that *they* will be able to account for the expenditures you want them to authorize. The essential determination, for each threat and its target asset, is simplicity itself:

Which is larger, the value of a lost asset or the cost of avoiding that threat? The value of the asset should be prorated according to the probability that it will be in fact lost during a given time period plus the cost to replace it. After the most crucial threats – the ones most likely to occur and do the most damage – have been identified, cost/benefit figures can be produced for defending against them. Management needs to know they are getting the best value for each dollar they allot to security measures.

The Policy Itself

Thankfully, there is no universal recipe for creating the security policy itself. Some are quite short, laying out in essence the company's philosophy with regard to security, the orientation, and the fundamental working assumptions that ground all security decisions and initiatives. Policies cast in this format are frequently published with extensive addenda that lay out standards and procedures on a more detailed level. Do not bury the principal security assertions in a maze of technical details.

We need to address one final essential ingredient of a good security policy. Such a policy must leave no doubt as to who is responsible for the safety of a given asset. This element ought to be carefully worded, and the language of blame *must* be avoided. Every asset addressed in the policy needs to have an owner or a responsible party identified. Indeed, depending on the nature of the asset, there might be need for a chain of command. Simply indicating where the buck finally stops may not be sufficient; some of the intermediate stops might have to be enumerated. These types of questions merge imperceptibly into the domain usually covered by operations manuals, but there is no avoiding certain sorts of questions that arise regarding any asset or threat:

◆ In the absence of an asset's primary responsible party, who covers? Have the owners of the most valuable assets left documents or instructions indicating who should carry on and what must be done in their absence or incapacity?

◆ If a given threat appears to escalate, is there a clear point in that escalation when the asset's owner must be notified?

◆ Is there fuzziness about responsibility and authority? Is it clear who *must* do what, and who *can* do what?

◆ Documentation: of what, by whom, how often, reviewed by whom? Are we saving logs? Which ones? For how long?

◆ Periodic Security Audits: of what, how often, performed by whom, with what documentation, reported to whom?

Obviously this sort of thing can go on pretty much forever; there is no end to the questions that can be raised in a hypothetical vein. I have been stressing that security decisions are exercises of judgment rather than, say, logical conclusions derived from indubitable presuppositions. One such judgment will be about when the sort of questioning I have just indulged in should grind to a halt, at least as far as the preparation of the security policy is concerned. Of course, highly valued assets and credible threats merit answers carved in granite, as the saying goes. For instance, if only for purely academic reasons, you might want to ensure that the logs or databases produced by intrusion detection system (*IDS*) programs are saved for some considerable period of time. It is very early in the game of defending against DDoS attacks, and it is easily within the realm of the feasible that IDS logs will prove valuable in learning more about the detection and analysis of such attacks. Similarly, some workstations ought to have their `syslog` facility configured to save considerably more `wtmp` files than is the default, with provision for backing up these files before they are rotated and/or deleted. A lot of common sense is called for: the system administrator certainly has enough tasks on any given day to make tweaking system logging settings on run-of-the-mill workstations a very low priority task indeed — which of course assumes you are clear on *which* workstations *are* run-of-the-mill!

Chapters 30 and 31 discuss IDS programs and DDoS attacks and how to defend against them.

Recovery Plans

Many aspects of computer security get taken for granted, and recovery planning is one of them. Disaster recovery seems almost self-evident, but all too often the actual scenario is not thought through beyond, for example, a simplistic "reformat the drive and reinstall the system from the backup tape." Moreover, recovery plans often do not form part of the security policy *per se*, but rather belong in a standards and practices or policies and procedures manual. The owner of each asset ought to be responsible for seeing that an up-to-date and workable recovery plan is in place, and that the plan is available on-site to personnel faced with the job of implementing the plan should it become necessary.

Again, the emphasis on this facet of planning might appear unwarranted. Perhaps it seems obvious that plans need to be kept up to date. One or two imaginary scenarios can help flesh out the possibilities here, and the need for attention to details. As the old saying goes, the devil is in the details, and that is perhaps nowhere more true than in the formulation of plans for recovering from disasters.

A hard drive on a key server crashes, rendering data irretrievable in the short term and the server useless until the disk is replaced. The plan might seem simple: replace the drive and get on with things. Simple, that is, to all except the weekend staff responsible for implementation! Some idle reflection easily turns up pitfalls, any one of which can delay the successful outcome of the plan:

- Is the make, model and part number of the drive documented anywhere, or will the box have to be opened and the drive pulled to find these things out?

- Is there a record of which vendor should be contacted for the replacement drive? Will the weekend staff know where this record is kept?

- Has anyone thought to check periodically whether the drive is still manufactured and still stocked by the vendor?

- Are the accounts with those vendors active? If not, who is going to pony up a company credit card? And can *that* person be reached on the weekend, and if not, who can?

Such problems arise with deadening regularity. In and of themselves, they are not insurmountable, but in the context of getting uptime back for a system that may be losing thousands of dollars for every hour of downtime, they become incredibly irksome hassles, to put it mildly. Ask the weekend staff.

Consider another all-too-common scenario: that hundred-year blizzard hits this year. A city plow takes out the pole in front of your building, and the power goes. For the sake of argument, assume your connectivity to the Internet backbone is still up, having been safely secreted underground, that you were generous in spending on UPS equipment, and that you even went the extra mile and bought enough on-site generator capacity to keep your primary server farm up and running. Here are some questions:

- Who owns a four-wheel drive vehicle? Since telephone poles are down all over the place, who has the cell phone numbers of those who *do* own four-wheel drive vehicles?

- Has a "phone tree" been set up to get news of the storm to the staff due in Monday morning? What about that office manager you fired last month? Is she still on the phone list?

- Is anyone charged with the job of testing that generator? Is there more than one person available who knows anything at all about it? Will you have the means to get that person to the job, if the need arises?

- As for the UPSes — is there provision for monitoring their condition? If so, have you followed up to ensure that monitoring has been documented?

- How much fuel for the generator have you planned on? How is it stored? Has the fire department been in for an inspection lately, or don't they know about that fuel storage? Have you wondered what your insurance carrier might have to say about that?

Yes, you are supposed to think these things through; that's why you get paid the big bucks, right?

You can easily see how at some point a bit of comic relief is needed. Once again, as a system or network administrator, you will find yourself confronted with problematic situations over which you had no authority, and over which in all likelihood you do not *want* any authority. Ideally, your expertise here will be, again, to communicate to management the nature of the problem, and if possible, quantify the cost/benefit picture for them. Thus, expending a lot of resources creating recovery plans for those assets already protected by elaborate defenses may not make as much sense as working on plans to recover those assets where the cost/benefit outcome went against a lot of protection.

Of course there will be key assets that merit both extensive recovery planning and defensive measures. The trick here is to realize that, *in general*, assets left unprotected because it would not be cost-effective to protect them will *probably* need more thorough recovery plans than those which have the benefit of expensive defensive measures. If this chapter has a moral, if you take nothing else away from it after reading it, this is it: the weightiest decisions are going to have to be judgment calls.

A Disaster Recovery Case Study

Perhaps an illustration of the impact of a disaster recovery plan, or its absence, might illustrate its importance.

Social Engineering

The cracker community sometimes refers to social engineering as *wetware hacking*, where wetware is cynical shorthand for human being. Unfortunately, the easiest point of entry in an organization that may budget tens or hundreds of thousands of dollars a year on the technical pursuit of computer security may be through an employee who has not been adequately educated in the ways of the digital confidence artist. Further, the really sly cracker knows that vulnerable employees are not found only in the word processing pool or answering the 800-number phone lines. A carefully crafted approach to middle or senior management can, if successful, reap huge rewards for the intruder.

WETWARE TECHNIQUES 101

At its simplest, social engineering could be nothing more profound than simply phoning someone with a question or two. Quite a few companies list employee's full names on their Web sites, so that even if confronted by one of those dreadful "If you know your party's extension you may dial it at any time; press the pound key for the company directory" recordings, a caller can get all sorts of people on the phone. Social engineers know that most people want to be helpful and want you to like them; this human characteristic is their stock-in-trade. Traditionally, confidence tricksters played on another human motive, greed; that is rarely helpful now to the social engineer because social engineering plays upon more contemporary anxieties: needing to be accepted and having self-esteem.

After you are on the phone talking to them, it can be all downhill: "Hello, Shania, my name is Archibald, and I'm the new system administrator here at WidgetsGalore Inc. I'm having a lot of trouble getting oriented, so I need to check with everyone whether or not they're using the correct password for their accounts. So, if you don't mind, may I ask you what your password is? According to my records it's 'clooney'; is that right? Ok, thanks; and you're spelling that c-l-o-o-n-e-y, all lowercase? Thanks again. One last thing, your username is shaniat; is that correct? Thank you so very much; you've been very helpful. What's that? Oh, you're *more* than welcome. You sound like a very interesting person too. Let's do coffee sometime. Have a nice day."

A variation on this scenario might be for the social engineer to send an e-mail to anyone at your organization whose e-mail address falls into the wrong hands — and make no mistake, e-mail addresses are splattered all over the Web, as the proliferation of spam flooding your e-mail inbox should confirm. The e-mail could say something like: "Hello, I'm Archibald, the system administrator here at WidgetsGalore. We recently had a hacker break into our computer system, so we need to ask everyone to change their password. In the interest of increasing our network security, you have been assigned a new, special, randomly generated password. Your new password is: r578yw3r. Please open the settings menu on your workstation and change your password to this new one. Thank you so very much, and we are sorry for this disruption of your work day!"

Yes, both of these tactics have in fact worked, many times!

What's wrong with this picture? You cannot expect Shania to understand that Red Hat system administrators never need to ask anyone for their password. Nor can you expect Shania to know that Red Hat system administrators cannot (for the most part, there are exceptions) determine what password is currently being used on any account. More than likely these subtleties about Red Hat system administration are lost on quite a few middle managers. Create an education campaign, and build refresher courses into it. Mounting this campaign can be a tricky business because few people consider themselves stupid and react poorly if made to feel so. Indeed, arguably the most frequent complaint lodged against "techie" system administrator types is that they do just that: talk down to staff members.

One approach is to focus the primary subject matter *on the network and system administrators themselves.* That is, educate staff as to just what the administrators do, what they are there for, in so many words. This approach keeps the focus off of the staff members; they feel less under the gun. Fewer sentences should begin with "You" and more should begin with "I" and "We." You can easily underestimate what effects can issue from such a shift in emphasis. People are, as a rule, sufficiently intelligent to draw conclusions if the data is presented clearly in a unthreatening fashion. Your presentation might go something like this:

"WidgetsGalore wants warm and helpful people representing the company on the front lines of the 800 number phones. That's why you are here, because you are that kind of person. It will not be news to you that not everyone who calls is in fact a good person. All you need to do is page us if you feel that a caller is asking just a few too many questions of too inquisitive a nature about the internal workings of the company, especially the company's computer and network facilities. Such a caller could seem to be an employee or even part of management; they might know that employee's name and quite a bit about the personal life of that employee. Remember, no employee or manager should ever call your number asking about computer accounts; every employee was given the phone numbers of the system administrator's office to use in the event there is a problem such as a lost password. Also, remember that *we* will never under any circumstances call you and ask you for your password or username."

ADVANCED WETWARE TECHNIQUES

The previous examples depicted the basic paradigms of social engineering. The possible variations are, obviously, endless. For instance, some crackers will go to extraordinary lengths to learn as much as possible about an employee, in order to pose either as that employee or as someone in that employee's life. Many companies post far too much information about their personnel on the Web. Usually this is an effort to impress potential clients with the quality of people working for the company.

For example, it is now trivial in many cases to gain in a very short time an astounding amount of information about someone's personal life: where they went to school, including graduate school, undergraduate, and high school. Given the ubiquity of Web sites and the astonishing amount of information available on the Web, alumni records can be searched for home addresses, maybe even home phone numbers. Depending on how illustrious a given employee is in her local community, a search of hometown newspaper articles can yield all sorts of personal goodies.

Remember that office paper shredder? Is it used? Some security policies require shredding anything from the office on paper that gets thrown into the trash. Why? Consider all those pink telephone message slips. Only one or two of those could give a bad person all the entrée they need to get a social engineering foot in the door.

When a cracker has enough information in hand, crafting a scenario around which to build a telephone calling campaign is trivial. Such a campaign might involve several calls to all sorts of places. It is not all that hard; use your imagination! Scenarios can be built around any sort of everyday "bump in the road" event: My car broke down, I missed the flight, the babysitter cancelled, my wife went to the ER, the police called, and I have to meet them at the office, the school nurse called, and I have to pick up my kid – right now, I forgot to pick up the laundry, my house burned down (probably too dramatic), my dog died, and so on ad infinitum. Given a talented, motivated social engineer, one who has done some homework, any one of these seemingly preposterous premises can be parlayed into a system compromise. It happens all too often. And it keeps happening. The end result is usually the same: someone is manipulated into being helpful, and information is given out over the phone that enables the cracker to gain the desired access.

Finding Security-Related Resources

Here are some organizations every security-minded person should know about, along with a brief list of readings.

Web Sites

The following Web sites are some of the premier sources of security-related information on the World Wide Web.

- ◆ **CERT** (http://www.cert.org/): The CERT Coordination Center is the single most authoritative body that disseminates information concerning computer and network security. CERT engages in training and publishing, and maintains an important e-mail list for the circulation of security advisories and summaries. CERT advisories are issued as new vulnerabilities surface, but usually only when patches and/or workarounds have been made available for all effected systems. CERT does some of its most important work behind the scenes, gathering and collating incident reports, and analyzing vulnerabilities and exploits. CERT strives to maintain the highest possible standards of reliability in the information it releases.

- ◆ **BugTraq** (http://www.securityfocus.com/): To quote their Web site: "BugTraq is a full disclosure moderated mailing list for the *detailed* discussion and announcement of computer security vulnerabilities: what they are, how to exploit them, and how to fix them." Bugtraq thus has a different, but complementary, mission than CERT. Security items frequently first see the light of day on bugtraq. In general however the information found there is not as reliable as that issued by CERT. It comes in sooner, and as a consequence it is likely to be a tad shaky at times.

- ◆ **Sans** (http://www.sans.org/): The Sans Institute's primary business is training and certification of security professionals, but they offer a large assortment of resources, including e-mail lists of various sorts. They also produce http://www.incidents.org, a site noteworthy for its Internet Storm Center. Sans is required reading for anyone charged with responsibility for security matters. They offer information of extremely high reliability, and are always abreast of the current security scene.

Recommended Reading

Here are a few book-length studies of computer and network security:

- ◆ *Red Hat Linux Security and Optimization* (Wiley, 2002), Mohammed J. Kabir

- ◆ *Security Engineering: A Guide to Building Dependable Distributed Systems* (Wiley, 2001), Ross Anderson

- ◆ *Linux Security Toolkit* (Wiley, 2000), David A. Bandel

Links

Just a sprinkling of various and sundry pages. All good stuff. Not necessarily Linux-specific. Not in any particular order. Check 'em all out!

- **RobertGraham.com** (http://robertgraham.com/): All kinds of really good security information.

- **Gibson Research Corporation** (http://grc.com/): Steve Gibson's site contains a wealth of threat analyses and measures you can take to mitigate them.

- **Security Archive** (http://security-archive.merton.ox.ac.uk/: This archive combines postings to security-related mailing lists, including the Bugtraq, CERT, linux-security, linux-alert, rootshell, and security-discuss and security-audit mailing lists.

- **2600** (http://www.2600.com/): Crackers stuff, but provides valuable information into the way that crackers think and operate.

- **Whitehats** (http://www.whitehats.com/): Whitehats.com is an online community resource for those — including network and security administrators — who are interested in network security.

Summary

This chapter staked out the basic lay of the land of computer security, delineating its fundamental nature. Social engineering exemplifies the nature of the subject matter. Computer and network security is not primarily a technological challenge, but a managerial one. This fact can be either good news or bad news for the system administrator. The good news is that if one learns how to communicate effectively with management, there is at least the possibility that a really effective cooperation can be brought to bear on security issues. The bad news is that some organizations seem unable to come to terms with reality, regardless of how effectively that reality is conveyed to them. Any given system's degree of security will always lie on a continuum that ranges from less secure to more secure. Estimating the position of a given system on this continuum is an exercise in judgment, not the outcome of the application of a set of technical metrics.

Chapter 30

Implementing Local Security

IN THIS CHAPTER

◆ Exploring the nature of physical security

◆ Working with boot security

◆ Maintaining user and password security

◆ Securing file integrity

◆ Securing services

THIS CHAPTER ADDRESSES the security questions that fall into the *host-based security* category. The measures suggested here are not as flashy as their network-based cousins, but, in their own prosaic fashion they are no less necessary to the task of hardening a network installation.

Host-based security refers to two related activities:

◆ Defending against threats to a given individual computer that do not come in over the wire, but arise from how that particular host is used or misused, quite apart from any network connection it might have.

◆ Detecting at the level of that particular host's operation any evidence of compromise from any source, either local (host-based) or remote (network-based).

Network-based security, on the other hand, covered in Chapter 31, refers to defending against any threat a given computer is exposed to as a result of being connected to a network, particularly those threats that might come in *via* a network (primarily the Internet). Network-based security also refers to protecting a connected group of hosts from threats that arise out of system-wide factors, such as the network's topology or layout, the design of its firewalls, proxies, and so-called demilitarized zones (DMZs), and the network's use of certain protocols, encryption, and so forth.

A *DMZ* refers to one or more publicly accessible hosts that are outside the protected or private network and thus more exposed to attack by crackers and other Internet ne'er-do-wells.

As suggested in Chapter 29, on a dollar-for-dollar basis, losses due to incursions from remote sources on the Internet for the most part pale in comparison to the losses that issue from other, mostly internal or local sources. You can have the finest firewall or virtual private network technology money can buy, but your efforts are for naught if, for instance, password handling becomes sloppy. More than one high-profile commercial Web site co-location facility has suffered serious compromise because an administrator was less than scrupulous in safeguarding a password.

It is also worth repeating that, considered individually, some of the measures described in this chapter may seem, perhaps not trivial, but of very little consequence. Recall, however the point made repeatedly in the previous chapter: *There is no predicting at what point an intruder navigating a series of defensive measures grows weary of the chase and moves on to new targets.* An observant eye can quickly pick up many of the telltale signs that announce, "Here is an installation that suffers from careless site security." Conversely, a well-run site ought to broadcast to all comers: "Don't even *think* about playing games here; you're wasting your time." The gestalt you want to accomplish can be created only by attending to one detail after another. In host-based security, vigilant monitoring is the nature of the beast.

Exploring the Nature of Physical Security

Physical security involves protecting a system, as much as possible, against the different sorts of loss that might come about as a result of someone having physical access to your computer. Such losses come not only from the black hats, but also from others who might have a right to be in the building but who do not have any business touching a server or workstation. In a similar vein, physical security includes protecting against certain undesirable behaviors, whether mistaken or intentional, on the part of those who should be working at those machines.

Physical security ranks very near the top of any list of "Most Neglected Security Issues." It is potentially a huge subject because, depending on the value of the assets under consideration, it can extend from alterations of the power supply wiring inside a computer case to fundamental building construction considerations. Disabling the power and reset buttons on the front of a computer case can, in some situations, be thought of as part of physical security. At the other extreme, physical security might involve hiring a building inspector to survey the condition of a party, or shared, wall inside your building. Most of this spectrum is outside the scope of this chapter. The goal here is to raise consciousness regarding the potential scope of physical security concerns and to address a few selected measures that hopefully have wide applicability.

Building Construction

Buildings new and old each have their own native pitfalls for a truly secure computer installation. Here are some examples of problem areas:

◆ The expensive new Halon fire extinguisher system is just great: it will not drown any electronic components. But what about the plumbing in the bathroom down the hall? How high off the floor should your servers be to stay above the high-water mark should a pipe burst?

◆ You have renovated a loft in an old mill building to house your new dot-com. What about the suspended ceilings? Do the new office-partition walls extend only up to them, or do the walls connect to the old original ceiling? What about those raised floors beneath your feet? About those shared walls: you may be fairly certain they are intact in the floors you are occupying, where there is no evidence of alterations to the original wall, but has anyone gone into the basement and looked at them? From *both* sides? It is truly amazing how small a hole a dedicated person can pass through!

◆ You have refused to accept any temporary network cabling, right? Take the cost hit now and be certain all cables are at the very least in ordinary conduit. Do you have any really "fat pipes" (very high bandwidth) running out of the place? Consider the cost/benefit picture of putting them in pressurized double-walled conduit or some other type of armored protection.

◆ You have no control over your backbone connection once it hits the street, but what about that manhole in your company parking lot or the one in the corner behind the Dumpster, where it cannot be visually checked from the street, or from the building? Odds are better than average that it is not locked and can be popped open with an ordinary pry bar.

◆ The salesman says the safe you bought to house your backup tapes is fireproof. What does "fireproof" mean in the safe business? If this seems counterintuitive, consider this bit of high school physics: the temperature at which paper ignites is higher than the temperature at which backup tapes, CD-ROMs, and DVD-ROMs melt. Or, to put it another way, your plastic backup media will melt before your money burns. Even in a safe.

◆ As noted in Chapter 29, what about the night cleaning crew and the back door they use?

The list is of course endless. Your site must undergo its own examination of conscience, so to speak, to determine whether or not it has kept faith with the organization's decisions about assets and their value. Clearly at some point, as the value of these assets rises, further costs have to be incurred because few technology-based companies have the requisite in-house civil, mechanical, and electrical engineering capabilities to see to it that faith is kept with those assets. If there is company data on a piece of tape that could do hundreds of thousands, if not millions of dollars, of damage should it fall into the wrong hands, how sane is it to keep that tape under conditions that have not had the best loss-protection engineering that money can buy?

Boot Security

Perhaps "Reboot Security" would be a more apt title for this section. Alas, there are many ways to coax a computer into rebooting itself when only one is really wanted: a system administrator with the proper permissions or privileges, traditionally the superuser, who enters the command to do so. `shutdown`, `halt`, or `reboot` should not be commands available to every user with an account on the system. Nor should anyone strolling by the keyboard or computer case be able to easily accomplish these tasks. From the standpoint of the security administrator, it is prudent to assume that anyone with physical access to a computer will sooner or later, or, perhaps, sooner *rather than* later, gain root access to the machine. The aim here is to push that event towards the "later" end of that scale.

Some of the vulnerability to unauthorized shutdown or reboot can be remedied only by changing the wiring of the power and reset switches inside the computer case, unless it happens to be a rack mounted unit, where the design has in all likelihood taken care of these vulnerabilities. Rack mounts are of course easier to secure physically because their design permits building them into enclosures with no exposed power or data connectors.

THOSE OTHER DRIVES

Most PCs can boot from their floppy and CD-ROM drives, so you should think about how this vulnerability ought to be handled. For some machines it makes sense to simply remove the drives and replace them with blank panels. Many networked machines can do without a CD-ROM drive. As for the floppy drive, although it is useful for rebooting during a troubleshooting session, for some systems the tradeoff of the loss of this convenience is a good one. Nothing says, "Go away. You cannot get anywhere on this system." quite as persuasively as a computer case with no visible drive doors.

Frequently, though, the easiest, although not the best, approach is to simply disable removable media drives from the system BIOS, and, depending on the particulars of the computer under consideration, install a BIOS password. The latter step might depend, for example, on the location of the computer, the kind of foot traffic common in that area, the value of the machine's contents or purpose, and the potential usefulness of its network connection to an intruder. Hot-swappable SCSI drives are a similar invitation to intrusion or theft. Left in an unlocked room or on an unsecured server rack, hot-swap disks are just as vulnerable as any other removable media.

The real point is simple: *If someone has physical access to a machine, the machine can be compromised, destroyed, or stolen regardless of what you do.* The corresponding lesson is equally uncomplicated: server racks and machine rooms should be locked with secure locks and access limited to those personnel whose business it is to maintain those systems. Even in locked server rooms, lock the server units into their racks. Physical and network access should be recorded and logged. The more valuable the data and services, the stronger the measures should be that secure that data and services.

TIGHTENING UP FEDORA CORE RED HAT ENTERPRISE LINUX

Unfortunately, Fedora Core and Red Hat Enterprise Linux ship in a default condition that gives `poweroff`, `halt`, and `reboot` ability to any logged-in user. Happily, this condition is easily reversed with the following three commands:

```
# rm /etc/security/console.apps/poweroff
# rm /etc/security/console.apps/halt
# rm /etc/security/console.apps/reboot
```

You may prefer renaming these files to deleting them, so you have a reminder of taking them out of action. While you are at it, take a look at the other files in `/etc/security/console.apps`, keeping in mind their purpose: giving ordinary console users access to the commands with the same name as the files. You might want to think about removing more of these. Some of these do require the root password, but it is also worth finding out which ones, if only as an exercise in increasing your overall security consciousness.

The next thing to eliminate is the Ctrl+Alt+Delete method of rebooting. This procedure requires editing `/etc/inittab`. To eliminate *all* use of this keystroke combination, simply comment out the line that begins with `ca`:

```
# Trap CTRL-ALT-DELETE
#ca::ctrlaltdel:/sbin/shutdown -t3 -r now
```

This change does not take effect until you execute the following command:

```
# telinit q
```

You don't need to reboot. `telinit` can be thought of as "tell init" because it acts as a communication link to `init`. Notice the unusual syntax; there is no hyphen preceding q. Executed like this, with just the q, `telinit` prompts `init` to reread its `/etc/inittab` file.

If you are in the mood to be helpful, consider substituting another command for Ctrl+Alt+Delete, such as the following:

```
#Trap CTRL-ALT-DELETE
ca::ctrlaltdel:/usr/bin/logger -isp kern.notice "Ctrl-Alt-Del has
been disabled. Sorry."
```

This inittab entry can be fine-tuned so that only select users (and root, of course) can use the three-fingered salute. First, add the -a option to the command line in /etc/inittab:

```
# Trap CTRL-ALT-DELETE
ca::ctrlaltdel:/sbin/shutdown -a -t3 -r now
```

Next, create the file /etc/shutdown.allow containing the name of the user authorized to activate Ctrl+Alt+Delete. For instance:

```
# echo bubba > /etc/shutdown.allow
```

The behavior now is: If bubba or root is logged in on any console, then anyone currently logged in can use Ctrl+Alt+Delete. If you try this use of the -a option, be sure to test your results, because the logic is quirky and a bit counterintuitive. A safe bet is to make root the only user listed in /etc/shutdown.allow. Then, Ctrl+Alt+Delete is enabled only if root is logged in, a condition not satisfied by a merely mortal user employing su to become the root user.

X DISPLAY MANAGERS

If you opted for a graphical login screen, that is, one of the X display managers, xdm, gdm, or kdm (the choice depends on which desktop you selected when you installed Red Hat Linux), then you have to make some adjustments, or, perhaps better yet, back out of that login mode and revert to an ordinary virtual console login process. To back out, try simply changing the default runlevel in /etc/inittab from 5 to 3 and rebooting:

```
id:3:initdefault:
```

Why disable the graphical login? X display managers typically exhibit two kinds of security problems. In some configurations, a menu of usernames (or faces) is presented, but this offers the whole wide world information it just does not need to have. There is simply no reason to offer a list of valid usernames to anyone, particularly the intrepid social engineer discussed in the previous chapter, who might happen by and do a bit of *shoulder surfing*, that is, look over someone's shoulder as they log in. Indeed, early in the development of the Unix password system, observant people noted that the login procedure inadvertently revealed to any user whether or not a given username was a valid user on the system. It did so because only the passwords of valid users would be compared via encryption to the contents of the /etc/passwd file. Checking passwords of only valid users produced a noticeable difference in the time required, say, for the login prompt to return after a valid user entered an incorrect password, compared to the time needed when an invalid username was followed by any password. The fix was obvious and it has stayed with us: the passwords entered for all usernames, valid and invalid, are sent through the same encryption and comparison process so no time differential appears between the two cases.

The thoughtful reader with experience on Unix and Linux systems rightfully and immediately asks, though, "What is the gain when any user on the system can simply execute the following command and get a listing of every directory under /home, and, hence of every valid user name on the system?"

```
$ cd
$ ls ../
```

The answer has two parts. First, it matters quite a bit less if user names are revealed to another user, who has a valid account and a password and is *already known to the system* than it does to reveal that information to someone who has no access at all (yet!). There are always users who insist on creating what are called *joeys*, users who use their user name, or simple-minded variations thereof, as their password. Here are a few of the common twists on this theme, taken from some of the rules used by crack, a password-guessing program discussed in greater detail later in the chapter.

◆ Reverse: "Fred" becomes "derF"

◆ Duplicate: "Fred" becomes "FredFred"

◆ Reflect: "Fred" becomes "FredderF"

◆ Reverse and then capitalize: "Fred" becomes "Derf"

Even a system with only a few user accounts is vulnerable to this sort of lapse. You are prudent to assume that sooner or later all that is needed to gain some kind of access to the system is a valid user name.

The other problem with the graphical login screen is that some X display managers offer reboot and shutdown as options to ordinary users. If you are confronted with a user who is really attached to the X-based login arrangement, then you ought to disable the provisions for halting or rebooting the system that are available in, for example, the gdm login screen under the System drop-down menu. To disable this misfeature, use the following procedure:

1. Start the GDM Configurator by clicking Main Menu → System Settings → Login Screen. You need to enter the root password to get in if you are not already logged in as root. Figure 30-1 shows the initial screen.

2. Click the Security tab (see Figure 30-2) and uncheck the check box labeled Show system menu.

3. Click Close.

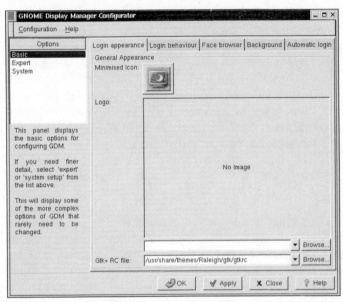

Figure 30-1: The GNOME Display Manager (GDM) Setup dialog box

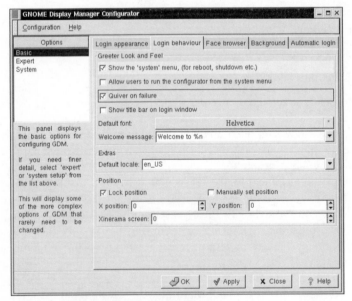

Figure 30-2: The GDM Setup Security tab

Another method here is to use xdm instead of gdm or kdm. The simplest way to change the display manager is to edit /etc/X11/prefdm. If, for example, GNOME is the default desktop, look for the lines (about line 23) that resemble

```
if [ "$DESKTOP" = GNOME ]; then
    preferred=gdm
```

Change gdm to xdm, save the change, and end the edit session. Why use xdm? Because xdm's login screen is a simple, no-nonsense affair with edit boxes for only a user name and password.

Clicking the GNOME main menu button and selecting Logout brings up a dialog box with Reboot and Shutdown options; however, if the preceding steps have been taken, those two options should not have their intended effect, but instead bring back just one to the X display manager login screen. Be sure to test that this is *in fact* the case.

AUTOLOGOUT THE SUPERUSER

Here is a security measure that perfectly exemplifies the strategy of layering incremental levels of protection discussed in Chapter 29. As the system administrator you most likely find yourself using su to obtain root privileges on a fairly regular basis. Also on a fairly regular basis you probably get paged or otherwise called away from your desk for all manner of exigencies. Since it is never possible to predict how long your workstation will remain unattended, it is prudent to arrange for superuser console sessions to automatically log out after a certain period of inactivity.

In the Bash shell, the environmental variable TMOUT sets this feature. In $HOME/.bash_profile, put a line such as:

```
export TMOUT=300
```

This command sets a timeout of 300 seconds. It is helpful to add a reminder about the setting:

```
echo "Autologout set to 5 minutes!"
```

Users of the C shell (tcsh or csh) can put set autologout=5 in their $HOME/.cshrc file to achieve the same result. Unless otherwise set, tcsh's autologout defaults to sixty minutes, unless the shell detects that it is running in a windowed environment by testing whether or not environment variable DISPLAY is set.

While you have your $HOME/.bash_profile file open in an editor, turn off the $HOME/.bash_history file:

```
export HISTFILESIZE=0
```

Then delete the file ($HOME/.bash_history), if it exists, in your home directory.

wheel, sudo, OR BOTH?

One handy security measure found on most Unix systems is not usually present or, if present, rarely used, on Linux computers: the wheel group. The theory is that making certain crucial system binaries only owner- and wheel group–executable and then adding only certain users to the `wheel` group allows the administrator to exercise greater control over the use of superuser privileges. Red Hat Enterprise Linux ships with a `wheel` group already created, so all that is needed is to change the ownership and permissions of whatever binaries you desire to place under the control of the `wheel` group. The following procedure illustrates the process using the `su` command:

```
# chgrp wheel /bin/su
# chmod 4750 /bin/su
# ls -l /bin/su
-rwsr-x--- 1 root wheel       18452 Jul 23 12:23 /bin/su
```

Next, add the users you trust with the root password to the `wheel` group by using `usermod -G` to modify the user's group membership:

```
# usermod -G wheel bubba
# usermod -G wheel marysue
# usermod -G wheel joebob
```

The resulting entry in /etc/group is:

```
root:x:0:root
[...]
wheel:x:10:root,bubba,marysue,joebob
```

The `sudo` facility is quite a bit newer than the `wheel` group, and many administrators prefer it because of its greater flexibility and logging facilities. In its basic operation, `sudo` first prompts for the user's password (not the root password), and then grants that user superuser privileges for a default period of time, usually five minutes. `sudo` consults its configuration file, `/etc/sudoers`, to determine what privileges to grant which users when they invoke `sudo`.

`/etc/sudoers` must be edited with its own editor, `visudo`, which utilizes file locking during the edit and performs some syntax checking to minimize errors introduced during the editing session. `sudo` has a powerful configuration syntax and vocabulary, so you can probably create the necessary set or combination of users, groups of users, commands, groups of commands, and logging options to suit your needs very precisely with a properly constructed `/etc/sudoers` file. Here is a very simple example:

```
# Host alias specification
# User alias specification
User_Alias GOODGUYS = bubba, suzyque

# Command alias specification
# User privilege specification
```

```
root          ALL=(ALL) ALL
GOODGUYS      ALL=(ALL) ALL
%wheel        ALL=(ALL) ALL
```

This example grants `root`, `bubba`, `suzyque`, and all members of the `wheel` group complete root privileges. The possibilities are vastly more powerful than this example, and virtually every aspect of `sudo`'s operation, and every compiled-in default, can be altered at run time by editing `/etc/sudoers`. Time spent with the man pages for `sudo` and `/etc/sudoers` is richly rewarded.

A one-size-fits-all solution for controlling access to superuser privileges does not exist. For many installations the relatively simple expedient of a `wheel` group suffices. Indeed, some will argue that, all other things being equal, simplicity should always carry the day. However some situations call for the increased flexibility of `sudo`. One example frequently cited is of a group of administrators charged with managing user accounts. These users do not need full superuser privileges but do need access to a subset of superuser commands, such as `useradd`, `passwd`, and others needed to manage accounts.

The discussion of `sudo` in the context of controlling access to commands such as `halt`, `reboot`, and `shutdown` brings you squarely into the territory of this chapter's next section, which delves further into the management of user accounts and passwords.

Maintaining User and Password Security

The Sans Institute (`http://www.sans.org/topten.htm`) rates "User IDs, especially root/administrator with no passwords or weak passwords" eighth on its list of "The Ten Most Critical Internet Security Threats." Their trenchant one-paragraph summary cannot be improved upon:

> Some systems come with "demo" or "guest" accounts with no passwords or with widely-known default passwords. Service workers often leave maintenance accounts with no passwords, and some database management systems install administration accounts with default passwords. In addition, busy system administrators often select system passwords that are easily guessable ("love," "money," "wizard" are common) or just use a blank password. Default passwords provide effortless access for attackers. Many attackers try default passwords and then try to guess passwords before resorting to more sophisticated methods. Compromised user accounts get the attackers inside the firewall and inside the target machine. Once inside, most attackers can use widely-accessible exploits to gain root or administrator access.

Two points in the preceding paragraph deserve reinforcement, because many computer users, including even very experienced ones, have never had reason or opportunity to encounter them.

◆ The ease of guessing passwords is truly astounding. Especially impressive are password *cracking* (guessing) programs such as crack or John the Ripper. While these programs basically do no more than guess passwords; they are *very* good at it.

◆ The use of administration or maintenance accounts, along with their default passwords, is truly ubiquitous in proprietary software, especially in database software. Anyone familiar with one installation finds easy entrée to other similar installations that have not been altered from the installation defaults.

After discussing password policy, I offer a few hints for managing user accounts in a security-conscious and conscientious fashion.

Passwords: Theory and Practice

Nostalgic, quaint, even quixotic, sentiments die hard. Only recently the operator of a rather substantial Unix site had to pull all of his public shell accounts off line due to a rather vicious compromise that mangled quite a few of those accounts. However, reading his commentary on the episode revealed that he clearly was taken aback by the fact that there are people who abuse the privilege of a free, public shell account, even to the extent of tampering with other folks' accounts.

The problem? The administrator had evidently clung to his origins in the early days of Unix, and part of that early Unix culture was a warm, collegial atmosphere in which trust, community, and mutual respect were assumed to be values shared by all users of the system. In those days, the likelihood of incurring community censure and opprobrium were (rightfully, at the time) thought to be adequate disincentives for keeping misbehavior in check. The possibility of deliberate malice was barely glimpsed, so much so that the first Unix implementations had no password facility at all! It was, in so many words, an add-on.

To set a good password policy you need to make several decisions. First, will users be allowed to choose their own passwords? If so, what limits will you put on their freedom of choice? If not, how will you communicate passwords to users? Will they be able to select from a list of randomly generated passwords, and if so, is there such a thing as a random password generator? What are the pros and cons of randomly generated passwords?

Before you proceed any farther we *highly* recommended that you obtain, install, and take a few practice spins on one of the password crackers available for the Linux platform. Both crack and John the Ripper install fairly easily on any Linux system. These programs take advantage of a couple of linguistic and computing facts of life. First, there is nary a word in any dictionary of any language that has not been scanned into a digitally readable format. Both of these password cracking programs can utilize a huge array of these dictionary files. Second, some very clever programmers have taken it upon themselves to eat, sleep, and drink password guessing for many years now, so there are probably very few methods of permuting dictionary words that they have not thought of and programmed into their password guessing algorithms. If you thought it was pretty slick to spell your dog's name backwards with every other letter made uppercase, and every o transformed into a 0, think again! Such transformations are easy pickings for crack or John the Ripper.

 John the Ripper can be downloaded from the Openwall Project's Web site at `http://www.openwall.com/john/`. crack is available via anonymous FTP from `ftp://ftp.cerias.purdue.edu/pub/tools/unix/pwdutils/crack/`.

The advent of shadow passwords, and improvements on the old DES encryption standard used by most Linux systems, made the work of password crackers more difficult. However, these enhancements have been paralleled by increases in computing horsepower and storage capacity. The point of trying out some of the password cracking programs is to drive home just how easy it is to guess passwords, especially short ones. The single greatest benefit of using the MD5 encryption algorithm now installed by default in Red Hat Enterprise Linux is that passwords up to 255 characters long are now permitted; the old limit was eight. Given this fact it makes sense to think about imposing a minimum password length of greater than the typical six characters found on most systems. Required reading in this regard is the PAM documentation found on your Red Hat installation in `/usr/share/doc/pam-0.77`. Be sure to look at the description of the cracklib module, which uses the same password guessing algorithms as the crack password guesser.

If you are confronted with an unfamiliar computer, you can easily determine if the standard Unix DES password encryption has been updated with MD5, Blowfish, or one of the other more advanced ciphers used for passwords. Look at the `/etc/shadow` file and count the number of characters in the encrypted password field, the first field following the user name. If there are thirteen characters, then you are dealing with the old DES encryption. DES-based passwords are limited to eight characters. Longer passwords are accepted by the system, but only the first eight characters are used. Consider upgrading such a system to MD5 as soon as possible. See Lance Spitzner's excellent paper "Armoring Linux" at his Web site, `http://enteract.com/~lspitz/linux.html`. Fedora and Red Hat Enterprise Linux systems can be upgraded via the command line utility `setup`, which runs Red Hat's Text Mode Setup Utility. The following procedure illustrates the process.

1. Log in or use `su` to become the root user.

2. Type **setup**, and press Enter. Figure 30-3 shows the initial screen.

3. Use the arrow keys to highlight Authentication configuration, press Tab to highlight the Run Tool button, and then press Enter.

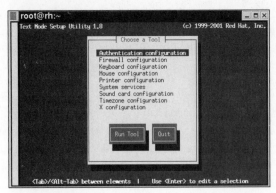

Figure 30-3: The Text Mode Setup Utility dialog box

4. Skip the User Information Configuration dialog box, pressing Tab until the Next button is highlighted, and then press Enter.

5. Figure 30-4 shows the Authentication Configuration dialog box. The Use Shadow Passwords option should be enabled. If not, press Space to place an asterisk (also called a *splat*) next to Use Shadow Passwords.

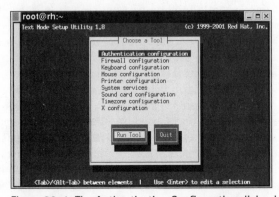

Figure 30-4: The Authentication Configuration dialog box

6. Press Tab to move the cursor to the Use MD5 Passwords option. Make sure it is enabled— if not, press Space to place a splat in the check box next to Use MD5 Passwords.

7. Press Tab until the OK button is highlighted and press Enter.

8. Highlight the Quit button, and press Enter again to exit the Text Mode Setup Utility.

Here is a fairly complete set of dos and don'ts for picking passwords. You can pass them on to your users, and then from time to time run crack or John on your own `/etc/shadow` file to detect any serious lapses in password selection. Only one moronic password puts the entire system at risk. Some of these rules are based on the rudiments of social engineering, described in the last chapter. Human nature being what it is, you can predict with a great deal of probability that left to their own devices your users gravitate towards passwords related to the eternal themes of sex, love, and money. Try to discourage this tendency if you can!

Now for *The Rules*. Do *not* use any of the following as a password:

◆ Your computer's host name or domain

◆ Your real name according to the computer, or any other such information kept in the password file

◆ The name of your pet or any family member's pet

◆ Your name or nickname, or any family member's name or nickname

◆ The name or nickname of a close friend, or anyone with whom or for whom you work

◆ The name of any fantasy, fictional, historical, mythological, or biblical character, book, or author

◆ The name of your operating system

◆ Anybody's name: first, middle or last or any proper name

◆ Any phone number or license plate

◆ Any part of your Social Security number

◆ Any username on the computer in any form (reversed, capitalized, doubled, and so on)

◆ Any place name

◆ Anybody's birthday

◆ Any part of your address, the name of your alma mater, or any other easily accessible information about you

◆ A password of all the same letters or numbers or a pattern of them

◆ Patterns of letters on the keyboard, such as `qwerty`

◆ Any word found in any dictionary of any language

◆ Any of the previous spelled backwards

◆ Any of the previous followed or prepended by a single digit

◆ Any of the previous modified by simplistic substitutions, such as certain numerals for letters, for example, 0 for O, 1 for l, 2 for Z, 3 for E, 5 for s or S, or 7 for L or T

Do try to:

- Create a password easy for you to memorize

- Use numbers, spaces, and punctuation marks

- Use both upper and lowercase letters

- Use special characters, avoiding @, #, and ?

- Never use less than seven characters

- Invent acronyms based on sayings familiar to you, for instance, "a fool and his money are soon parted" becomes, first, afahmasp, or afah$asp, or 1fAh$Asp.

One of the methods in the previous list, particularly the last one, results in a fairly easy to remember password that would give crack a run for its money.

ABOUT PASSWORD GENERATORS

The very notion of a password generator is problematic. Alec Muffett, crack's author, explains it like this in the documentation in the crack distribution (`doc/appendix.v4.1.txt`, to be precise):

> You can't say that a certain method provides secure, random passwords, because, in defining an algorithm to create these passwords, you use only a subset of all the possible passwords that could ever exist. You have shrunk the "search space" for the passwords.

Simply put, using a password generator makes the work of password cracking programs simpler. With Muffett's caveat in mind, you should proceed very carefully if you decide to require users to choose from a set of generated passwords. A number of password generators are available for Linux, but some of them have had problems, and some of them are quite old. Unless you are an accomplished programmer and grasp the difficulties of random number generation, it is more than likely that the best solution is to enable users to create their own passwords, but aggressively restrict the parameters of that choice by using the PAM password modules, and follow that up with routine and frequent scans of your /etc/shadow file with crack or John the Ripper. Perhaps the single most important variable is the length of the password. Consider enforcing a minimum length of up to fourteen characters if you have followed the suggestion made a moment ago to use MD5 password authentication.

USING AN ANALOG PASSWORD GENERATOR

Enticing a machine to behave in a truly random fashion is bound to be a challenge, since it goes completely against how we want machines to behave, that is, in a totally predictable manner. At least one method has been developed for using old-fashioned nonmechanical means of producing random events for generating random passwords. Actually, the Diceware (`http://www.diceware.com/`) method was designed for producing random passphrases for PGP, SSH, Tripwire, and related software, but it can be adapted to turn out passphrases of one word, that is, passwords. A *passphrase* is just that, a phrase used as a password, or, rather, *in place of* a password. All that is needed is a 6 × 6 matrix filled in like this:

```
  1  2  3  4  5  6
1 A  B  C  D  E  F
2 G  H  I  J  K  L
3 M  N  O  P  Q  R
4 S  T  U  V  W  X
5 Y  Z  0  1  2  3
6 4  5  6  7  8  9
```

Suppose your security policy requires ten-character passwords. Put fifteen pair of dice (thirty pieces) in a can, and, after closing the door and pulling the shades on the windows, roll the dice out onto your desk. Group the dice into ten groups of three each, and arrange each group of three in a row. Establish a convention for counting across each row, either right to left, or the reverse. Then simply use the first two dice in each group to identify a row/column pair in the matrix, and use the third die to modify the character found at that matrix location.

For instance, if the third die is even, then for a letter, make it uppercase; if odd, lowercase. If the row/column specifies a numeral, then if the third die is even use the numeral, if odd use a special character. A rule for picking the special character might be: use the character's position in the password to count across the row of number keys on your keyboard and use the special character at that location, skipping the @, #, and ? keys. For the next special character start counting at the next position on the keyboard. You can use endless variations on this example. This method is, admittedly, time consuming, and of course, cannot (or should not) be automated, but it produces highly random passwords that prove very difficult for any password cracker program to solve in a timely manner, that is, before the attacker gives up and moves on to other, arguably more fruitful targets.

The Diceware site also argues persuasively for moving away from passwords altogether. With modern cryptographic algorithms, such as MD5, Blowfish, and others (for instance, one derived from the John the Ripper password cracker), password length now accommodates passphrases. The rationale is that a good passphrase of several words is easier to remember and considerably harder to guess than the typical randomly generated password. Thus, passphrases answer one of the most frequent criticisms of the latter, that it is more likely to be written down, possibly even in a file kept on the computer. And, passphrases are useful in quite a few contexts other than just system access authentication. Symmetric (private key) encryption of files is available in the form of Phil Zimmerman's PGP (Pretty Good Privacy) and GNU's PGP cognate, GPG (GNU Privacy Guard). A good passphrase goes a long way toward ensuring the safety of files encrypted in this fashion.

Those Pesky Users

Administrative headaches seem to rise in direct, exponential proportion to the number of users on a system. Linux, taking its cue from its Unix forebears, has evolved an impressive array of tools and strategies for keeping track of users. This section can address only a few of the more important of these. The following list identifies a few simple commands for tracking user logins:

◆ `users` – prints a simple list of the usernames of everyone currently logged on. By default the list is derived from `/var/run/utmp`. For additional information, see the GNU texinfo pages for the shell-utils package (`info shell`).

◆ `who` – prints more data about currently logged-on users (also part of the GNU shell-utils package).

◆ `last` – prints data about current and recent logins. This data is also derived from `/var/log/wtmp`. Execute the command `last reboot`, for example, to view information about the last system reboots. See the `last` manual page for more information, as this command takes a number of useful options.

◆ `lastlog` – prints data from `/var/log/lastlog` about past and current logins. A good deal of system history is available via this command. `man lastlog` contains useful reference information.

Checking Logs

Red Hat Linux routinely, and quietly, logs a huge amount of data during its ordinary operations. Because of the volume of information, the busy system administrator soon confronts the job of filtering the wheat from the chaff, that is, of finding ways to identify and focus on those logged events that deserve attention. Two utilities to a certain degree automate the job of scanning log files for unusual events, `logwatch`, and `logcheck`. `logwatch` is installed by default on Red Hat systems, at least in its router/firewall flavor.

Key to using either of these utilities is setting a proper mail alias for root so that the utility mails its reports to a system administrator (you), not to root's mail spool. Edit the file `/etc/aliases`, paying particular attention to the following line at the bottom of the file:

```
# Person who should get root's mail
root:            bubba
```

After editing the file, execute `newaliases` to rebuild the alias database and update the running `sendmail` daemon with the new alias:

```
# newaliases
/etc/aliases: 41 aliases, longest 10 bytes, 404 bytes total
```

The exact output may vary somewhat on your system. Once this step is done, e-mail sent to the root user is redirected to the named user, bubba in this case.

logcheck and logwatch are similar in some respects but produce, at least in their default settings, fairly different reports. logcheck's configuration is simplicity itself, but, as usual with Linux and Unix software, the more complicated configuration of logwatch permits greater variation and finer control over the reports it generates. Red Hat's binary rpms install logwatch to run once daily; logcheck runs once every hour. Given the nature of each report, these are reasonable defaults, but they can be changed in the system cron settings. Listing 30-1 illustrates a typical logcheck report.

Listing 30-1: An example logcheck report

```
Security Violations
=-=-=-=-=-=-=-=-=-=
Sep  2 18:47:23 rh login(pam_unix)[11196]: authentication failure;
logname=LOGIN uid=0 euid=0 tty=tty3 ruser= rhost=  user=bubba
Sep  2 18:47:25 rh login[11196]: FAILED LOGIN 1 FROM (null) FOR
bubba, Authentication failure


Unusual System Events
=-=-=-=-=-=-=-=-=-=
Sep  2 04:02:08 rh syslogd 1.4.1: restart.
Sep  2 11:52:58 rh mc: /dev/gpmctl: No such file or directory
Sep  2 11:52:58 rh mc: /dev/gpmctl: No such file or directory
Sep  2 13:00:42 rh login(pam_unix)[2914]: session closed for user
 bubba
Sep  2 16:58:44 rh login(pam_unix)[867]: session closed for user
 root
Sep  2 18:44:58 rh su(pam_unix)[11519]: session opened for user
 root by wingnut(uid=502)
Sep  2 18:45:02 rh mc: /dev/gpmctl: No such file or directory
Sep  2 18:45:02 rh mc: /dev/gpmctl: No such file or directory
Sep  2 18:47:23 rh login(pam_unix)[11196]: authentication failure;
 logname=LOGIN uid=0 euid=0 tty=tty3 ruser= rhost=  user=bubba
Sep  2 18:47:25 rh login[11196]: FAILED LOGIN 1 FROM (null) FOR
 bubba, Authentication failure
Sep  2 18:47:32 rh login(pam_unix)[11196]: session opened for user
 bubba by LOGIN(uid=0)
Sep  2 18:47:32 rh  -- bubba[11196]: LOGIN ON tty3 BY bubba
Sep  2 18:50:46 clio login(pam_unix)[11439]: session opened for
 user bubba by LOGIN(uid=0)
Sep  2 18:50:46 rh  -- bubba[11439]: LOGIN ON tty4 BY bubba
Sep  2 18:59:16 rh mc: /dev/gpmctl: No such file or directory
```

Continued

Listing 30-1 *(Continued)*

```
Sep  2 18:59:55 rh last message repeated 2 times
Sep  2 18:52:13 rh sudo: ruptured : TTY=tty4 ; PWD=/home/bubba ;
 USER=root ; COMMAND=/bin/rpm -ivh logcheck-1.1.1-4.i386.rpm

From root  Sun Sep  2 19:07:50 2001
```

Several items of information can be gleaned from this report. First, bubba may be having some personal problems, or working too much overtime, since he seems a tad shaky when it comes to remembering his password. Then, Midnight Commander seems to want to find a particular device file for gpm; that might bear a little investigation, especially because gpm is not running on this system. Finally, you can see that bubba *could* recall his password long enough to use sudo to install the logcheck RPM.

Both logwatch and logcheck can be customized to widen or narrow the focus of their reporting. Typically, you want to narrow the focus in order to look at real or potential problems, not administrative noise. The needs of different systems dictate different emphases in what is included, and excluded, from a report. The logs on a server with few ordinary users other than its administrators does not need the same sort of vigilance as the logs on, say, a dial-up server host across the room that provides PPP connections to modem users dialing in from all over the place. Each of these log monitoring programs has its own strengths and weaknesses. One option very much worth trying is simply to run them both. After you review their reports for a week or so, you can make an informed decision about how they ought to be used on a production system.

Summary

In this chapter, you learned about host-based security, including securing your system against unauthorized reboots, configuring X display managers for better security, and making the building that houses a system secure. You also saw how to implement sturdier user and password security, including using password generators. After examining log checking tools, you learned to configure and fine-tune Tripwire, a host-based intrusion detection system.

Chapter 31

Implementing Network Security

IN THIS CHAPTER

◆ Understanding network security

◆ Limiting network services

◆ Implementing a firewall

CHAPTER 30 STARTS THE DISCUSSION of securing Red Hat Enterprise Linux systems, focusing on the measures most appropriate to securing workstations. This chapter continues that discussion by focusing on security measures that you should apply at the network level (that is, security measures that can protect entire networks of systems using a Red Hat system as the barrier or fence between a protected internal network and the black hats that intend to compromise it).

Limiting Network Services

The first thing to do when securing a Red Hat system is to identify what services are running, what services you need, and what services you do not need. Then you should disable the unneeded services. The term *services*, in this context, refers to the traditional server daemons and programs, such as Apache (the Web server), Sendmail (the mail server), TELNET, or the FTP server, and to lesser known access points, such as open ports for chargen, daytime, finger, and so forth. To express it slightly differently, a *service* refers to any process that listens on a network port or socket for requests for data.

From the point of view of the administrator trying to implement network security, limiting network services also means determining who is doing what on the system, particularly via a network connection of some sort. This section and the next review some of the configuration files and tools that control running services, that enable you to turn services on and off at your discretion, and that empower you to find out what kind of system activity is taking place on your system, who is doing it, and from where the activity originates.

What Services Are Running?

Like most Linux distributions, Red Hat's default installation procedure leaves too many network services available. Of course, some services were enabled as a result of choices made during the installation process itself. Other services, however, seem simply to be enabled by default, that is, for no apparent reason. "For no apparent reason?" What do we mean by that? Many installations literally have *no* need to make *any* network services available. The typical workstation is probably in this category; it is a *consumer* of services, not a *provider* of them. For example, workstations ordinarily do not need to provide Web, e-mail, TELNET, or FTP services. In the course of this chapter, you see how the effort to disable unneeded services works out in practice.

The first step toward limiting the availability of these services is finding out which ones are actively listening. This task is actually twofold, because a service running on a given host might be available to respond to requests originating from the host itself but not to requests from other systems that are connected to it. The potential for security weakness here arises from the fact that the service is on in the first place.

Even though you keep a service from responding to other hosts on the network using packet filtering or TCP wrappers, these methods of access control can be circumvented and thus become possible points of entry into the system. Therefore, the availability of services ought to be examined both internally and externally, that is, from inside the host itself, from inside the host's trusted network, and from outside the host's trusted network. Part, but not all, of the process of securing a network involves running a port scan from outside your network. The next few subsections explore a few utilities that come into play when performing these port scans — netstat, lsof, and nmap.

USING netstat

netstat is a powerful utility for monitoring and reporting almost every aspect of the kernel's networking functionality and behavior. Most users are familiar with netstat's use to display the current routing table, as shown in the following command:

```
$ netstat -r
Kernel IP routing table
Destination     Gateway         Genmask         Flags   MSS Window  irtt Iface
192.168.1.0     *               255.255.255.0   U       40  0          0 eth0
127.0.0.0       *               255.0.0.0       U       40  0          0 lo
default         possum.holler   0.0.0.0         UG      40  0          0 eth0
```

A glimpse at netstat's man page conveys some idea of this command's many different uses, but for current purposes only one or two command line options are required, as listed in Table 31-1.

TABLE 31-1 NETSTAT COMMAND LINE OPTIONS

Option	Description
-r	Displays the kernel routing table
-p	Displays the PID and process name of processes listening on each port
-l	Displays only listening sockets

For instance, to display only listening sockets:

```
$ netstat -l
Active Internet connections (only servers)
Proto Recv-Q Send-Q Local Address          Foreign Address      State
tcp     0      0 *:http                    *:*                  LISTEN
tcp     0      0 *:ftp                     *:*                  LISTEN
tcp     0      0 *:ssh                     *:*                  LISTEN
tcp     0      0 *:https                   *:*                  LISTEN
Active UNIX domain sockets (only servers)
Proto RefCnt Flags      Type      State       I-Node Path
unix  2      [ ACC ]    STREAM    LISTENING   1139   /tmp/.font-unix/fs7100
```

The output from this command indicates that five servers are listening for requests on this host: http, a Web server, ftp, an FTP server, ssh, a secure shell server, https, a secure Web server, and the X font server. This display can be fine-tuned by protocol, showing, for instance, only Unix domain sockets (using the --unix argument with -l), or only Internet (TCP) sockets (using the --inet argument with -l):

```
$ netstat --unix -l
Active UNIX domain sockets (only servers)
Proto RefCnt Flags      Type      State       I-Node Path

unix  2      [ ACC ]    STREAM    LISTENING   1139   /tmp/.font-unix/fs7100

$ netstat --inet -l
Active Internet connections (only servers)
Proto Recv-Q Send-Q Local Address          Foreign Address      State
tcp     0      0 *:http                    *:*                  LISTEN
tcp     0      0 *:ftp                     *:*                  LISTEN
tcp     0      0 *:ssh                     *:*                  LISTEN
tcp     0      0 *:https                   *:*                  LISTEN
```

USING lsof

This utility's name is an acronym for *list open files*. On Red Hat systems, this means "list just about everything." Part of what distinguishes Linux and Unix-like operating systems from almost all other operating sytstems is that many diverse entities are handled as if they were files. The lsof man page lists a few of these. An open file might be a regular file, a directory, a block special file, a character special file, an executing text reference, a library, a stream, or a network file (Internet socket, NFS file, or UNIX domain socket).

The syntax for lsof is at least as arcane as netstat's, but as with that command only a small subset of lsof's options are needed to keep tabs on what services are running. With no options, lsof churns out an impressive amount of data (over sixteen hundred lines):

```
# lsof | wc -l
   1617
```

Again, as with netstat, the trick is to limit this output to what interests you, and the -i option starts you on this path; with it, lsof lists all Internet and x.25 network files:

```
# lsof -i
COMMAND   PID USER    FD    TYPE DEVICE SIZE NODE NAME
sshd      677 root     3u   IPv4    980       TCP *:ssh (LISTEN)
xinetd    696 root     3u   IPv4    999       TCP *:ftp (LISTEN)
httpd     750 root    16u   IPv4   1116       TCP *:https (LISTEN)
httpd     750 root    17u   IPv4   1117       TCP *:http (LISTEN)
X        9551 root     1u   IPv4  26045       TCP *:x11 (LISTEN)
httpd    9892 root    16u   IPv4   1116       TCP *:https (LISTEN)
httpd    9892 root    17u   IPv4   1117       TCP *:http (LISTEN)
httpd    9893 root    16u   IPv4   1116       TCP *:https (LISTEN)
httpd    9893 root    17u   IPv4   1117       TCP *:http (LISTEN)
httpd    9894 root    16u   IPv4   1116       TCP *:https (LISTEN)
httpd    9894 root    17u   IPv4   1117       TCP *:http (LISTEN)
httpd    9895 root    16u   IPv4   1116       TCP *:https (LISTEN)
httpd    9895 root    17u   IPv4   1117       TCP *:http (LISTEN)
httpd    9896 root    16u   IPv4   1116       TCP *:https (LISTEN)
httpd    9896 root    17u   IPv4   1117       TCP *:http (LISTEN)
httpd    9897 root    16u   IPv4   1116       TCP *:https (LISTEN)
httpd    9897 root    17u   IPv4   1117       TCP *:http (LISTEN)
httpd    9898 root    16u   IPv4   1116       TCP *:https (LISTEN)
httpd    9898 root    17u   IPv4   1117       TCP *:http (LISTEN)
httpd    9899 root    16u   IPv4   1116       TCP *:https (LISTEN)
httpd    9899 root    17u   IPv4   1117       TCP *:http (LISTEN)
```

This output can be filtered by host, service port or name, or protocol (TCP or UDP), for example:

```
# lsof -i:x11
COMMAND   PID USER     FD    TYPE DEVICE SIZE NODE NAME
X        9551 root     1u    IPv4  26045      TCP *:x11 (LISTEN)
# lsof -i:https
COMMAND   PID USER     FD    TYPE DEVICE SIZE NODE NAME
httpd     750 root     16u   IPv4  1116       TCP *:https (LISTEN)
httpd    9892 root     16u   IPv4  1116       TCP *:https (LISTEN)
httpd    9893 root     16u   IPv4  1116       TCP *:https (LISTEN)
httpd    9894 root     16u   IPv4  1116       TCP *:https (LISTEN)
httpd    9895 root     16u   IPv4  1116       TCP *:https (LISTEN)
httpd    9896 root     16u   IPv4  1116       TCP *:https (LISTEN)
httpd    9897 root     16u   IPv4  1116       TCP *:https (LISTEN)
httpd    9898 root     16u   IPv4  1116       TCP *:https (LISTEN)
httpd    9899 root     16u   IPv4  1116       TCP *:https (LISTEN)
```

netstat and lsof together form a powerful team for examining the workings of the kernel from many different angles. See, for instance, the discussion of using them together in lsof's documentation: /usr/share/doc//lsof-4.51/00QUICKSTART.

USING nmap

No discussion of detecting network services would be complete without including nmap. Although usually mentioned in the context of probing remote hosts to determine their open ports, nmap can also port scan its own host. A simple port scan looks like this:

```
$ nmap -sT 127.0.0.1

Starting nmap V. 2.54BETA22 ( www.insecure.org/nmap/ )
Interesting ports on possum.holler.org (127.0.0.1):
(The 1537 ports scanned but not shown below are in state: closed)
Port       State        Service
21/tcp     open         ftp
22/tcp     open         ssh
80/tcp     open         http
443/tcp    open         https
6000/tcp   open         X11
Nmap run completed -- 1 IP address (1 host up) scanned in 2 seconds
```

Regardless of the picture of a host's open services one gets from inside that host, the old attitude of "I'm from Missouri; show me!" applies where security is at stake. After all of the commands just described, sooner or later one needs to assume a vantage point on a remote host and examine from there the state of your network's hosts and services. For that nmap is the ideal tool. Depending on how you configure your firewall, the simple ping scan just described may not be adequate to the task, but nmap is equipped to deal with those situations, which I discuss later in this chapter.

Stopping Running Services

You should be aware of two general issues regarding services, and, to carry forward a theme to which we continually return in this part of the book, neither issue can be resolved via solely technical considerations:

◆ What services should be running?

◆ What access should be allowed to services that are running?

Each question can be broken down further. The first question, what services should be running, also involves the more practical issue of *how* to control a given service, that is, how to turn it off and on. The basic answer is that services are controlled either through xinetd, with an initialization script in /etc/init.d/, or both.

The follow-up question for the second issue, allowing access to running services, is how to control access to a given service. In this case, the answer is similar: access control is usually applied through xinetd, the access control files used by TCP Wrappers (/etc/hosts.allow and /etc/hosts.deny), or using a service's own access control facilities.

Red Hat Linux uses xinetd, an enhanced version of inetd, which adds a great deal of flexibility and that might include features that are unfamiliar to users who have grown comfortable over the years with plain vanilla inetd and TCP Wrappers. Fortunately, the installation defaults selected for the various services and daemons that xinetd runs are such that the transition from inetd to xinetd need not be traumatic. Some services are started out of xinetd, and some are not. For the latter, chkconfig and its companion, redhat-config-services, form a dynamic duo for managing network services and other system daemons. chkconfig and edhat-config-services are *run level editors*, tools that provide an interface to the slightly convoluted SystemV initialization script setup. chkconfig, a command line tool, is arguably the more powerful of the two programs, whereas edhat-config-services presents a simpler, more pleasant menu-driven console interface.

USING chkconfig

chkconfig, in its basic use (chkconfig --list), lists each service named in /etc/init.d and whether that service is enabled (on or off) for each of the seven run-levels (0–6). It also lists each service handled by xinetd and whether that service is on or off. Here is a sample showing the current state of the host I have been using as an example. On this system, only sshd, httpd, and ftpd are available to other hosts:

```
# chkconfig --list
ntpd        0:off    1:off    2:off    3:off    4:off    5:off    6:off
atd         0:off    1:off    2:off    3:off    4:on     5:on     6:off
```

```
keytable    0:off    1:on     2:on     3:on     4:on     5:on     6:off
rwhod       0:off    1:off    2:off    3:off    4:off    5:off    6:off
kdcrotate   0:off    1:off    2:off    3:off    4:off    5:off    6:off
syslog      0:off    1:off    2:on     3:on     4:on     5:on     6:off
gpm         0:off    1:off    2:on     3:off    4:on     5:on     6:off
kudzu       0:off    1:off    2:off    3:off    4:on     5:on     6:off
nscd        0:off    1:off    2:off    3:off    4:off    5:off    6:off
lpd         0:off    1:off    2:on     3:off    4:on     5:on     6:off
sendmail    0:off    1:off    2:on     3:on     4:on     5:on     6:off
autofs      0:off    1:off    2:off    3:off    4:on     5:on     6:off
snmpd       0:off    1:off    2:off    3:off    4:off    5:off    6:off
rhnsd       0:off    1:off    2:off    3:off    4:off    5:off    6:off
rawdevices  0:off    1:off    2:off    3:off    4:on     5:on     6:off
netfs       0:off    1:off    2:off    3:off    4:on     5:on     6:off
network     0:off    1:off    2:on     3:on     4:on     5:on     6:off
random      0:off    1:off    2:on     3:on     4:on     5:on     6:off
ipchains    0:off    1:off    2:on     3:on     4:on     5:on     6:off
apmd        0:off    1:off    2:on     3:off    4:on     5:on     6:off
iptables    0:off    1:off    2:on     3:off    4:on     5:on     6:off
isdn        0:off    1:off    2:on     3:off    4:on     5:on     6:off
identd      0:off    1:off    2:off    3:off    4:off    5:off    6:off
portmap     0:off    1:off    2:off    3:off    4:on     5:on     6:off
nfs         0:off    1:off    2:off    3:off    4:off    5:off    6:off
nfslock     0:off    1:off    2:off    3:off    4:on     5:on     6:off
radvd       0:off    1:off    2:off    3:off    4:off    5:off    6:off
crond       0:off    1:off    2:on     3:on     4:on     5:on     6:off
anacron     0:off    1:off    2:on     3:on     4:on     5:on     6:off
xfs         0:off    1:off    2:on     3:on     4:on     5:on     6:off
xinetd      0:off    1:off    2:off    3:on     4:on     5:on     6:off
ypbind      0:off    1:off    2:off    3:off    4:off    5:off    6:off
sshd        0:off    1:off    2:on     3:on     4:on     5:on     6:off
rstatd      0:off    1:off    2:off    3:off    4:off    5:off    6:off
rusersd     0:off    1:off    2:off    3:off    4:off    5:off    6:off
rwalld      0:off    1:off    2:off    3:off    4:off    5:off    6:off
vncserver   0:off    1:off    2:off    3:off    4:off    5:off    6:off
yppasswdd   0:off    1:off    2:off    3:off    4:off    5:off    6:off
ypserv      0:off    1:off    2:off    3:off    4:off    5:off    6:off
ypxfrd      0:off    1:off    2:off    3:off    4:off    5:off    6:off
httpd       0:off    1:off    2:off    3:on     4:off    5:off    6:off
squid       0:off    1:off    2:off    3:off    4:off    5:off    6:off
tux         0:off    1:off    2:off    3:off    4:off    5:off    6:off
rarpd       0:off    1:off    2:off    3:off    4:off    5:off    6:off
linuxconf   0:off    1:off    2:on     3:on     4:on     5:on     6:off
```

```
xinetd based services:
    chargen-udp:    off
    chargen:        off
    daytime-udp:    off
    daytime:        off
    echo-udp:       off
    echo:           off
    time-udp:       off
    time:           off
    sgi_fam:        off
    rsh:            off
    talk:           off
    finger:         off
    rexec:          off
    rlogin:         off
    ntalk:          off
    telnet:         off
    wu-ftpd:        on
    rsync:          off
```

That is an awful lot of information for one gulp, so it is handy to pipe the output through `grep`, looking for `on`. On a server not running X, you can make that `3:on`. The following command illustrates the fine tuning of the command (note that this does not display the `xinetd` entries):

```
# chkconfig --list |grep 3:on
keytable    0:off    1:on     2:on     3:on     4:on     5:on     6:off
syslog      0:off    1:off    2:on     3:on     4:on     5:on     6:off
sendmail    0:off    1:off    2:on     3:on     4:on     5:on     6:off
network     0:off    1:off    2:on     3:on     4:on     5:on     6:off
random      0:off    1:off    2:on     3:on     4:on     5:on     6:off
ipchains    0:off    1:off    2:on     3:on     4:on     5:on     6:off
crond       0:off    1:off    2:on     3:on     4:on     5:on     6:off
anacron     0:off    1:off    2:on     3:on     4:on     5:on     6:off
xfs         0:off    1:off    2:on     3:on     4:on     5:on     6:off
xinetd      0:off    1:off    2:off    3:on     4:on     5:on     6:off
sshd        0:off    1:off    2:on     3:on     4:on     5:on     6:off
httpd       0:off    1:off    2:off    3:on     4:off    5:off    6:off
```

How can you determine the current run level? It might be 3, but if an X display manager is in use, it very well could be 5. Use the run level command as shown in the following example:

```
$ runlevel
N 3
```

runlevel returns the previous and current run levels. In cases in which there is no previous run level, run level displays an N, as shown in the preceding example.

---

chkconfig has several modes of operation; the listing mode demonstrated just now is only one of them. Other modes enable chkconfig to add or delete services to the /etc/init.d startup hierarchy or to turn a given service on or off in any of the runlevels. This is a lot of control, most of which is not needed in the ordinary course of events. Only rarely is it necessary to alter the arrangement of symlinks in /etc/init.d — the installation defaults are perfectly adequate for all normal use. To start a service at boot time, or to prevent a service from starting at boot time, use the ntsysv utility, discussed in the next subsection.

USING redhat-config-services

redhat-config-services provides an interface that permits any of the services listed by chkconfig to be turned on or off in the current run level, the run level in effect when redhat-config-services was launched. Other run levels can be similarly edited by passing their number(s) on the command line, but great care ought to be exercised in using this feature. As noted, it is the rare situation indeed that calls for altering the default run levels that the various services and daemons install for themselves.

The short answer to the question raised previously, "What services *should* be running?" is "None." If this seems to be an unduly harsh generalization, take another look at the question asked from the standpoint of understanding clearly what a host's role is. That is, "What services should be running?" arises only when there is fuzziness as to the role of a given host. Certainly, when setting up a Web server, one would never ask, "Should this host run httpd?" The point? *There is almost no need whatever to run a network service that the host is not designed to provide to other hosts.* For many computers (that is, workstations on a network), then, one can simply run redhat-config-services and click off everything except syslog, crond, sshd, and xinetd, which are almost always needed for proper functioning of the system as a whole.

This is hardly the end of the story, though. Rather, it is the starting point for adding any further services. For instance, Sendmail is not needed to get or send mail (indeed, even fetchmail is probably better off using procmail as its mail transport agent), but on the other hand it is not a bad idea to run Sendmail in the background using a -q 15m argument to prevent mail from getting stuck in the queue forever. The basic method should be: begin by disabling everything except syslog, crond, and xinetd, and then enable other services where the need is clear and the security implications have been thoroughly examined.

Monitoring Network Traffic

Often a network or system administrator wants to quickly get a look at the actual network traffic on a given host. This desire could be the result of suspicious behavior of certain system functions or strange hardware performance. Indeed, any number of possible turns of events could raise the question, "What's on the wire?" When this happens one does not want to muck around in log files or in the reports generated by, say, intrusion detection system (IDS) software; a quick, direct, and immediate glimpse of traffic on the network is what is needed. The following subsections discuss several tools that should be on every system, tcpdump and trafshow.

tcpdump

tcpdump is the elder statesman of packet sniffers. In practice, it is often the first utility you turn to when you want to get a look at traffic on your network. The basic syntax for packet sniffing on a given interface is simple indeed (the actual IP addresses and hostnames have been obfuscated, which is the practice throughout this chapter):

```
# tcpdump -i eth1
tcpdump: listening on eth1
03:22:36.579707 arp who-has xx.yy.139.202 tell xx.yy.139.1
03:22:36.589707 arp who-has xx.yy.139.214 tell xx.yy.139.1
03:22:36.609707 arp who-has xx.yy.139.220 tell xx.yy.139.1
03:22:36.679707 possum.holler.com.1025 > proxy1.big.huge_internet.domain:
16297+ PTR? aaa.bbb.67.10.in-addr.arpa. (44) (DF)
03:22:37.979707 arp who-has zz.qq.14.210 tell zz.qq.14.1
03:22:38.619707 arp who-has xx.yy.139.226 tell xx.yy.139.1
03:22:38.629707 arp who-has xx.yy.139.229 tell xx.yy.139.1
03:22:38.669707
8 packets received by filter
0 packets dropped by kernel
```

You need to be root to perform the action shown in the section on tcpdump.

Type **Ctrl+C** to kill the sniffing session.

tcpdump is noteworthy for two reasons: the binary file format it uses to store packets, known as *tcpdump format* and used by many network utilities (including snort, discussed later in this section) and its optional use of the Berkeley Packet Filter (BPF) language for specifying with dizzying precision exactly which packets to sniff and which to ignore.

The following example directs `tcpdump` to listen for 100 packets (`-c 100`) on the eth1 interface (`-i eth1`) and store them in an output file named `my_sniffed_packets` in `tcpdump` format (`-w my_sniffed_packets`):

```
# tcpdump -c 100 -i eth1 -w my_sniffed_packets
```

The packets so collected can be played back using `tcpdump` and printed to the screen or redirected to a text file, as shown in the following example:

```
# tcpdump -r my_sniffed_packets > my_packets_text
```

Although the binary tcpdump format is faster and recommended for capturing packets on busy interfaces, `tcpdump` can redirect its output to text files. Its man page gives several examples and variations on these themes.

trafshow

`trafshow` produces a nice color coded display that updates in real time to reflect changes in the traffic across a given interface. The color coding is by network protocol, and hostname lookup can be toggled off and on without quitting the application. `trafshow` is ideal for running constantly in a small xterm in a corner of the display, perhaps with the window's sticky button on so it appears on every desktop (if you are using a window manager that supports multiple or virtual desktops).

Firewall Theory

The term *firewall* has suffered the fate of most ideas that gain too much popularity: its meaning has become, if not totally debased, at least considerably muddied. For some, a firewall is a software package they can install on a host, and, presumably, uninstall at some later date. The current rage for residential broadband Internet connections has spawned a huge market for such products, but to be fair, firewall software packages for heavy-duty server use in the back office have been around for a long time, predating their upstart home use cousins. In another common usage, the term denotes a particular host, typically one that sits between a protected internal network and an unprotected external network. These are often called *bastion hosts*.

For the purposes of this chapter, a *firewall* refers to a collection of hardware, software, and policy components designed to implement and safeguard certain relationships of trust between two networks. A dedicated firewall hardware component, for instance, might be a host containing no read/write storage capability, one that perhaps does not even have a hard drive. Firewall software comes in several flavors but this chapter focuses on two of these: packet filters, which examine network traffic at a very low level, and access controls, which permit or deny access based on high-level features such as the source or origin IP address or host name. We mention firewall *policy* here only because it is part of the overall security policy of a site, a topic dealt with in Chapter 29.

Firewall Policy

Three main topics deserve close attention under the rubric firewall policy:

◆ What gets in?

◆ What gets out?

◆ What face do you present to the world?

What gets in? What can you trust coming in from the "external world?" How do you need to specify it? By source? By protocol? By service (or port)? By content? Will these specifications vary over the course of a day? A week (or weekend)? Ever? To what extent do you fine-tune these specifications according to destination?

What gets out? All the glitz is expended on romanticizing cyber-criminals, as if they are the modern-day equivalent of the lone gunman in Dallas in 1963. However, keeping out the black hats is easier than keeping in what needs to be kept in. Losses due to proprietary information being leaked into the wrong hands are difficult to assess because most businesses are loath – many of them have shareholders – to publicize the success of such exploits. Imposing draconian restrictions on access to your internal network from the outside is not going to stir up your users nearly as much as imposing similarly severe limits on their ability to contact hosts outside the internal net.

The previous two chapters repeatedly emphasized that, given a committed, concerted attack, *any* system can be exploited and any firewall can be breached. The reverse is also true: ultimately, if someone wants to get something out of a network, they will do so. For example, one can tunnel FTP via e-mail, provided one knows how. When data to which everyone has access cannot be prevented from leaving the internal network, the problem then becomes a matter of limiting access internally to certain online resources, and that in turn has immediate effects on productivity, to mention only the most obvious fallout. François-René Rideau, author of the Linux *Firewall Piercing mini-HOWTO* (`http://www.tldp.org/HOWTO/mini/Firewall-Piercing.html`):

> "...the moral is: a firewall cannot protect a network against its own internal users, and should not even try to.
>
> "When an internal user asks your system administrator to open an outbound port to an external machine, or an inbound port to an internal machine, then you should do it for him. ... For, unless he is so firewalled as to be completely cut off from the outside world, with no ssh, no telnet, no web browsing, no e-mail, no ping, no phone line, no radio, no nothing, then *the user can and will use firewall piercing techniques to access the machines he wants ...* the net result for security will be an unaudited connection with the outside world. So either *you trust your users, after proper training and selection, or you shouldn't grant them access to the network at all. You can and you shall protect them from the outside world, but you can't protect them from themselves.*"

What face do you present to the world? Do you present your systems as an open book with ready access to your personnel and resources, or do you put on an electronic equivalent of the inscrutable poker face, revealing nothing beyond your mere presence? These questions are usually thought of as marketing issues, but they have security implications. Often there is a desire to be too open: "Hi, we're your friendly neighborhood online corporation; here is a list of all our employees along with their e-mail addresses." Probably too much information is made available in such an atmosphere, and that is a condition that itinerant social engineers never overlook. They are out looking right now!

The other extreme, the poker face, can backfire. If your online presence says in so many words: "This place is tight as a drum, and I'm not about to change that for anybody, least of all for someone like you!" what you might in reality accomplish is attracting attention by communicating unmistakably that you want to avoid it or attracting the attention of the wrong people. The always elusive middle road needs to be sought here, as in most points of contact with other human beings.

Basic Layout

Network layout, or *topology*, as it is often termed, is a sufficiently difficult and intricate topic that only a handful of ideas can be mentioned. The usual course of events is that a network or system administrator inherits a network already up and running. Occasionally the administrator might be consulted about the design of a new network that is being brought online; the administrator may even have been hired to participate in this planning. Whatever the scenario, the next three sections describe features that need to be considered in virtually all network layouts, so it behooves administrators to be aware of the variety of approaches that are available in each scenario. The discussion is only of simple examples. Many network configurations and methodologies require that special attention be given to security questions. High availability networks, VLANs (Virtual Local Area Network), and VPNs (Virtual Private Network) are examples of increasingly popular network approaches that bring with them unique challenges for the security planner.

In rough overview, a generic firewall might look like Figure 31-1. The DMZ, or Demilitarized Zone, is home to hosts that provide publicly accessible services, such as the Web server, httpd, or the FTP server, ftpd. Systems that operate in the DMZ do not benefit from the protections afforded the internal, private LAN. Totally unfettered access is provided; the public can connect without navigating any security hurdles. The bastion host stands between systems in the DMZ and the protected internal LAN. The term *firewall* is usually applied to the bastion host, but it is more accurate to use this term to refer to all systems and software that stands between the protected network and the Internet.

Designing the Firewall

The distinguishing characteristic of the bastion host is that it runs absolutely no network services and runs only the absolute minimum of other services. In some formulations this means that not even the system logger, syslogd, or the kernel logger, klogd, is running. The bastion host has a single mission, access control, typically in the form of packet filtering. Network address translation (NAT), also known as *IP masquerading*, is commonly combined with the packet filtering role because the kernel facilities that implement packet filtering are ideally suited for the rewriting of packet headers that enables NAT. Another common compromise with the ideal of a completely service-free bastion host occurs when proxy services are located on this same host.

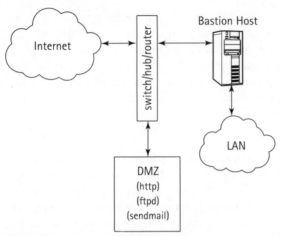

Figure 31-1: A standard firewall configuration

The idea of an empty bastion host can be expanded to include the complete absence of any writable media, such as disks, and further that the media that *is* present be composed of removable items, floppies, or CD-ROMs. The administrator ought to be familiar with some of these products, since in the event of trouble it can be a Godsend to pop a bootable floppy disk or CD-ROM into the host and bring up a preconfigured packet filter that has been designed for just such an occasion. In particular, such removable emergency firewalls can be configured to log network activity on the bastion host on writable media housed in systems inside the protected LAN. Such an arrangement calls for a good deal of care, because the tradeoff for avoiding writable media on the bastion host necessitates establishing an additional connection to the internal network, that is, a connection other than the main one that is subject to the bastion host's access control enforcement. The additional connection can also be a trouble spot when laying out intrusion detection sensors: how should you make intrusion detection sensor logs available to hosts on the safe side of the bastion host?

Not all local networks need a DMZ standing between themselves and the Internet. If the local network does not provide any services for clients accessing the network from the Internet side of things, then there is no reason to leave any systems on the public or exposed side of the bastion. In particular, systems that store their incoming e-mail on a POP or IMAP host on another network have no need for a DMZ.

The type of DMZ illustrated in Figure 31-1 presupposes that sufficient IP addresses are available for services run out of the DMZ. Also, security for hosts in the DMZ calls for some special considerations, given their relatively unprotected status. Many of the points made concerning bastion hosts apply to DMZ hosts:

- They should run a minimum of services so that, for instance, the machine running httpd is not running ftpd also.

- These machines should have no ordinary user accounts, and as few administrative accounts as possible.

- Depending on the service made available by a given host, the host access control facility should be augmented with packet filtering.

- Keeping in mind that DMZ hosts are more likely to be compromised, host access control and packet filtering should pay particular attention to outbound traffic, the intent being to prevent use of the host as a remote platform for launching attacks on yet other hosts or networks.

- Access to machines in the DMZ from hosts on the internal, protected side of the firewall must be severely curtailed.

This last point about access to the DMZ hosts raises the important *policy* question: "What assets should be placed on DMZ hosts?" The answer here is rarely self-evident, because there are varying estimates within any organization as to the cost benefit breakdown of using, for instance, a Web server in the DMZ to host not only the resources that will be publicly available, but also private, internal Web assets. Is the situation such that an added Web server within the protected LAN is cost-effective? What about e-mail? If there is an SMTP host in the DMZ, should it handle mail destined for inside the organization?

Figure 31-2 illustrates another approach to designing the DMZ. Some of the questions just raised are technically easier to solve if the DMZ is put inside the firewall. Some additional complexity is introduced by the need for a third network interface.

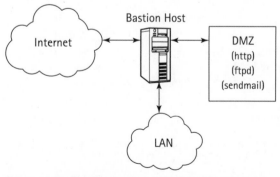

Figure 31-2: Placing a network DMZ inside a firewall

What Is an IDS Sensor?

In the context of this discussion, an *IDS sensor* is a host configured with special software and connected to an Ethernet segment whose interface device (NIC) is configured to transmit in promiscuous mode. The software is typically a package designed to sniff traffic on the segment and attempt to match up packets with known attack signatures. Like the firewall itself, these systems are fairly specialized, run no network services, have no ordinary user accounts, and in some cases have no writable media installed.

The rule of thumb for how many sensors to run is as many as possible. If limited to only one, then it should go outside the firewall. A sensor outside the firewall (in theory, at least) catches all attacks that reach the firewall. The firewall may prevent some attacks from completing the TCP handshake needed to actually enter the firewall; these putative attacks may not be seen by the sensor.

The main problem with sensors outside the firewall is so-called *false positive* responses, that is, responses that trigger the sensor outside the firewall but never develop into a full-fledged attack. A second sensor inside the firewall, or, in the case of the layout illustrated in Figure 31-1, inside the DMZ, deals less with background noise, and provides more useful information.

Finally, many security administrators prefer to monitor their IDS sensors via a second network interface card installed in each. Logging and analysis of all sensor output can then be centralized.

This approach allows hosts in the DMZ to be masqueraded (using network address translation), reducing the number of required IP addresses, theoretically, to one. On the other hand, if routable IP addresses are desired and available for DMZ hosts, then it may be convenient to place the DMZ and LAN on their own subnets.

During the Firewall Configuration sequence of the Red Hat installation, you are given the option to choose a high, medium, or no security level, as well as allow specific devices, incoming services, and ports. After installation, you can change the security level of your system by using the Security Level Configuration Tool. If you prefer a wizard-based application, refer to the "GNOME Lokkit" section of this chapter. To start the application, select Main Menu Button → System Settings → Security Level or type `redhat-config-securitylevel` at a shell prompt.

High

If you choose High, your system will not accept connections (other than the default settings) that you do not explicitly define. By default, only the following connections are allowed:

◆ DNS replies

◆ DHCP, so any network interfaces that use DHCP can be properly configured

If you choose High, your firewall will not allow the following types of connections:

◆ Active mode FTP (passive mode FTP, used by default in most clients, should still work)

◆ IRC DCC file transfers

◆ RealAudio

◆ Remote X Window System clients

If you are connecting your system to the Internet but do not plan to run a server, this is the safest choice. If additional services are needed, you can choose Customize to allow specific services through the firewall.

Figure 31-3: The Security Level Configuration Tool

Select the desired security level from the pull-down menu.

If you select a medium or high firewall, network authentication methods (NIS and LDAP) will not work.

Medium

If you choose Medium, your firewall will not allow remote machines to have access to certain resources on your system. By default, access to the following resources is not allowed:

- ◆ Ports lower than 1023 – The standard reserved ports, used by most system services, such as FTP, SSH, telnet, HTTP, and NIS.

- ◆ The NFS server port (2049) – NFS is disabled for both remote servers and local clients.

- ◆ The local X Window System display for remote X clients.

- ◆ The X Font server port – By default, xfs does not listen on the network; it is disabled in the font server.

If you want to allow resources such as RealAudio while still blocking access to normal system services, choose Medium. Select Customize to allow specific services through the firewall.

 If you select a medium or high firewall, network authentication methods (NIS and LDAP) will not work.

If you select No Firewall, you allow complete access to your system and perform no security checking. *Security checking* disables access to certain services. This should be selected only if you are running on a trusted LAN, not the Internet, or plan to do more firewall configuration later. Choose Customize to add trusted devices or to allow additional incoming services.

Selecting any of the Trusted Devices allows access to your system for all traffic from that device (that is, the trusted device is excluded from the firewall rules). For example, if you are running a local network but are connected to the Internet via a PPP dialup, you can check eth0, and any traffic coming from your local network will be allowed. Selecting eth0 as trusted means all traffic over the Ethernet is allowed, but the ppp0 interface is still firewalled. If you want to restrict traffic on an interface, leave this option unchecked.

 We do not recommend that you make a device that is connected to public networks, such as the Internet, a Trusted Device.

Allow Incoming

You can enable Allow Incoming to allow the specified services to pass through the firewall. Note that during a workstation installation, the majority of these services are not installed on the system.

◆ *DHCP* – Allows incoming DHCP queries and replies. This option enables any network interface that uses DHCP to determine its IP address. DHCP is normally enabled. If DHCP is not enabled, your computer can no longer get an IP address.

◆ *SSH* – Allows incoming SSH services. SSH (*Secure Sh*ell) is a suite of tools for logging in to and executing commands on a remote machine. If you plan to use SSH tools to access your machine through a firewall, enable this option. You need to have the openssh-server RPM installed in order to access your machine remotely, using SSH tools.

◆ *Telnet* – Allows incoming TELNET services for logging in to remote machines. TELNET communications are unencrypted and provide no security from network snooping. Allowing incoming TELNET access is not recommended. If you do want to allow inbound Telnet access, you need to install the telnet-server package.

◆ *WWW (HTTP)* – Enables incoming HTTP (Web) requests. The HTTP protocol is used by Apache and by other Web servers to serve Web pages. If you plan on making your Web server publicly available, enable this option. This option is not required for viewing pages locally or for developing Web pages. You will need to install the apache package if you want to serve Web pages. Enabling WWW (HTTP) does *not* open a port for HTTPS secure Web services). To enable HTTPS, specify it in the Other ports field.

◆ *Mail (SMTP)* – Allows incoming mail services. If you want to allow incoming mail delivery through your firewall so that remote hosts can connect directly to your machine to deliver mail, enable this option. You do not need to enable this if you collect your mail from your ISP's server using POP3 or IMAP, or if you use a tool such as Fetchmail. Note that an improperly configured SMTP server can allow remote machines to use your server to send spam.

◆ *FTP* – Allows incoming FTP service. The FTP protocol is used to transfer files between machines on a network. If you plan on making your FTP server publicly available, enable this option. You need to install the vsftpd RPM for this option to be useful.

◆ *Other ports* — Allows access to ports that are not listed in the preceding options by listing them in the Other ports field. Use the following format: `port:protocol`. For example, if you want to allow IMAP access through your firewall, specify `imap:tcp`. You can also explicitly specify numeric ports; to allow UDP packets on port 1234 through the firewall, enter `1234:udp`. To specify multiple ports, separate them with commas. You must have the iptables service enabled and running to activate the security level. Refer to the section "Activating the iptables Service" later in this chapter for details.

GNOME Lokkit

GNOME Lokkit allows you to configure firewall settings for an average user by constructing basic iptables networking rules. Instead of having to write a rule, GNOME Lokkit asks you a series of questions about how you use your system and then writes it for you in the file `/etc/sysconfig/iptables`.

You should not try to use GNOME Lokkit to generate complex firewall rules. It is intended for average users who want to protect themselves while using a modem, cable, or DSL Internet connection. To start GNOME Lokkit, type `gnome-lokkit` at a shell prompt as root. If you do not have the X Window System installed or if you prefer a text-based program, use the command `lokkit` to start the text-mode version of GNOME Lokkit.

BASIC

After starting GNOME Lokkit, shown in Figure 31-4, choose the appropriate security level for your system:

◆ *High Security* — Disables almost all network connections except DNS replies and DHCP so that network interfaces can be activated. IRC, ICQ, and other instant messaging services as well as RealAudio will not work without a proxy.

◆ *Low Security* — Disables remote connections to the system, including NFS connections and remote X Window System sessions. Services that run below port 1023 will not accept connections, including FTP, SSH, TELNET, and HTTP.

◆ *Disable Firewall* — Enables all access to services. Only choose this option if your system is on a trusted network, is not directly connected to the Internet, is behind a larger firewall, or if you write your own custom firewall rules. If you choose this option, click Next and then proceed to the "Activating the iptables Service" section. The security of your system will not be changed.

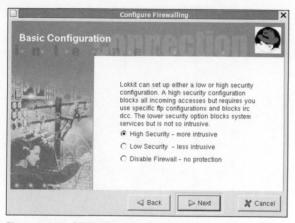

Figure 31-4: GNOME-Lokkit basic configuration

CONFIGURING LOCAL HOST ACCESS

If there are Ethernet devices on the system, the Local Hosts page (see Figure 31-5) allows you to configure whether the firewall rules apply to connection requests sent to each device. If the device connects the system to a local area network behind a firewall and does not connect directly to the Internet, select Yes. If the Ethernet card connects the system to a cable or DSL modem, it is recommended that you select No.

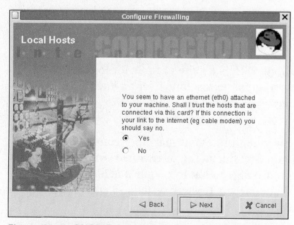

Figure 31-5: GNOME-Lokkit local hosts configuration

CONFIGURING DHCP ACCESS

If you are using DHCP to activate any Ethernet interfaces on the system, you must answer Yes to the DHCP question. If you answer no, you will not be able to establish a connection using the Ethernet interface. Many cable and DSL Internet providers require you to use DHCP to establish an Internet connection. Figure 31-6 shows the GNOME-Lokkit DHCP configuration screen.

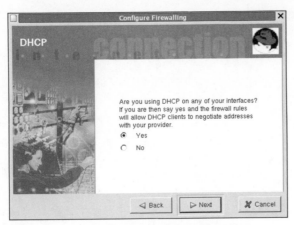

Figure 31-6: GNOME-Lokkit DHCP configuration

GNOME Lokkit also allows you to turn common services on and off. If you answer Yes to configuring services, you are prompted regarding the following options:

◆ *Web Server* – Choose this option if you want people to connect to a Web server such as Apache running on your system. You do not need to choose this option if you want to view pages on your own system or on other servers on the network.

◆ *Incoming Mail* – Choose this option if your system needs to accept incoming mail. You do not need this option if you retrieve e-mail using IMAP, POP3, or Fetchmail.

◆ *Secure Shell* – Secure Shell, or SSH, is a suite of tools for logging in to and executing commands on a remote machine over an encrypted connection. If you need to access your machine remotely through SSH, select this option.

◆ *Telnet* – TELNET allows you to log in to your machine remotely; however, it is not secure. It sends plain text (including passwords) over the network. It is recommended that you use SSH to log into your machine remotely. If you are required to have Telnet access to your system, select this option.

To disable other services that you do not need, use `serviceconf`, `ntsysv`, or `chkconfig`.

Mail Relay Services

A mail relay is a system that allows other systems to send email through it. If your system is a mail relay, someone can possibly use it to spam others from your machine. If you chose to enable mail services, after you click Finish on the Activate the Firewall page, you will be prompted to check for mail relay. If you choose Yes to check for mail relay, GNOME Lokkit will attempt to connect to the Mail Abuse Prevention System website at http://www.mail-abuse.org/ and run a mail relay test program. The results of the test will be displayed when it is finished. If your system is open to mail relay, it is highly recommended that you configure Sendmail or whatever mail transfer agent you use, to prevent it. You must have the iptables service enabled and running to activate the firewall.

To activate the Firewall, click Finish to write the firewall rules to /etc/sysconfig/iptables. This also starts the firewall by starting the iptables service. It is highly recommended that you run GNOME Lokkit from the machine, not from a remote X session. If you disable remote access to your system, you will no longer be able to access it or disable the firewall rules. Click Cancel if you do not want to write the firewall rules.

Activating the iptables Service

The firewall rules will be active only if the iptables service is running. To manually start the service, use the following command:

```
# /sbin/service iptables restart
```

To ensure that it is started when the system is booted, issue the command:

```
# /sbin/chkconfig --level 345 iptables on
```

You can also use serviceconf to activate iptables.

 You cannot run the ipchains service along with the iptables service. To make sure the ipchains service is disabled, execute the following command:

```
# /sbin/chkconfig --level 345 ipchains off
```

Firewalls and iptables

Linux comes with advanced tools for packet filtering — the process of controlling network packets as they enter, move through, and exit the network stack within the kernel. Pre-2.4 kernels relied on ipchains for packet filtering and used lists of rules applied to packets at each step of the filtering process. The introduction of the 2.4 kernel brought with it iptables (also called netfilter), which is similar to ipchains but greatly expands on the scope and control available for filtering network packets.

This chapter focuses on packet filtering basics, defines the differences between ipchains and iptables, explains various options available with iptables commands, and shows how filtering rules can be preserved between system reboots. If you require instructions for constructing iptables rules or setting up a firewall based on these rules, please see the "Additional Resources" section for more information.

 The default firewall mechanism under the 2.4 kernel is iptables, but iptables cannot be used if ipchains is already running. If ipchains is present at boot time, the kernel will issue an error and fail to start iptables. The functionality of ipchains is not affected by these errors.

Packet Filtering

Network traffic travels in units known as packets. A *network packet* is a collection of data of a specific size and format. In order to transmit a file over a network, the sending computer breaks the file into packets using the rules of the underlying network protocol, such as TCP. Each packet holds a small part of the file data. Upon receiving the transmission, the destination computer reassembles the packets into the file.

Every packet contains information that helps it navigate the network and move towards its destination. The packet can tell computers along the way, as well as the destination machine, where it came from, where it is going, and what type of packet it is, among other things. Most packets are designed to carry data, although some protocols use packets in special ways. For example, the Transmission Control Protocol (TCP) uses a SYN packet, which contains no data, but is used to initiate communication between two systems.

The Linux kernel contains the built-in ability to filter packets, allowing some of them into the system while stopping others. The 2.4 kernel's netfilter has three built-in tables or rules lists. They are as follows:

- ◆ `filter` — The default table for handling network packets.

- ◆ `nat` — This table is used to alter packets that create a new connection.

- ◆ `mangle` — This table is used for specific types of packet alteration.

Each of these tables in turn has a group of built-in chains that correspond to the actions performed on the packet by the netfilter. The built-in chains for the `filter` table include the following:

- INPUT — The INPUT chain applies to packets received via a network interface.

- OUTPUT — The OUTPUT chain applies to packets sent out via the same network interface that received the packets.

- FORWARD — The FORWARD chain applies to packets received on one network interface and sent out on another.

The built-in chains for the `nat` table are as follows:

- PREROUTING — The PREROUTING chain alters packets received via a network interface when they arrive.

- OUTPUT — The OUTPUT chain alters locally generated packets before they are routed via a network interface.

- POSTROUTING — The POSTROUTING chain alters packets before they are sent out via a network interface.

The built-in chains for the `mangle` table are as follows:

- PREROUTING — The PREROUTING chain alters packets received via a network interface before they are routed.

- OUTPUT — The OUTPUT chain alters locally generated packets before they are routed via a network interface.

Every network packet received by or sent out of a Red Hat system passes through at least one table. A packet may be checked against multiple rules within each rules list before emerging at the end of the chain. The structure and purpose of these rules may vary, but they usually seek to identify a packet coming from or going to a particular IP address or set of addresses when using a particular protocol and network service.

Regardless of their destination, packets that match a particular rule on one of the tables are designated for a particular target or action to be applied to them. If the rule specifies an ACCEPT target for a matching packet, the packet skips the rest of the rule checks and is allowed to continue to its destination. If a rule specifies a DROP target, that packet is refused access to the system, and nothing is sent back to the host that sent the packet. If a rule specifies a REJECT target, the packet is dropped, but an error packet is sent to the packet's originator.

Every chain has a default policy to ACCEPT, DROP, REJECT, or QUEUE the packet to be passed to user-space. If none of the rules in the chain apply to the packet, then the packet is dealt with in accordance with the default policy. The iptables command allows you to configure these rule lists, as well as set up new tables to be used for your particular situation.

Differences between iptables and ipchains

At first glance, ipchains and iptables appear to be quite similar. Both methods use chains of rules to decide which packets to let in or out and what to do with packets that match certain rules. However, iptables offers a much more complete and flexible means of filtering packets, giving the administrator a greater amount of control without building too much complexity into the entire system.

If you are familiar with ipchains, you need to be aware of significant differences between ipchains and iptables before attempting to use iptables. For example, with iptables, each filtered packet is processed using rules from only one chain rather than from multiple chains. To illustrate the point, a FORWARD packet coming into a system using ipchains passes through the INPUT, FORWARD, and OUTPUT chains before reaching its destination. However, iptables sends packets to the INPUT chain only if they are destined for the local system and only sends packets to the OUTPUT chain if the local system generated the packets. As a result, you have to take extra care to ensure that the rule designed to catch a particular packet in the rule actually sees the packet.

The advantage with iptables is that you now have more control over the disposition of each packet. If you are attempting to block access to a particular website, it is now possible to block access attempts from clients running on hosts that use your host as a gateway. So, for example, an OUTPUT rule that denies access will no longer prevent access for hosts that use your host as a gateway.

Another change that trips up the unwary is that the DENY target has been changed to DROP. In ipchains, packets that matched a rule in a chain could be directed to the DENY target, which silently dropped the packet. This target must be changed to DROP in iptables to have the same effect.

Sequence matters when placing options in a rule. Previously, with ipchains, how you ordered the rule options did not matter very much. The iptables command is more particular about where some options may go. For example, you must now specify the source or destination port after the protocol (ICMP, TCP, or UDP) to be used in a rule.

Finally, when specifying network interfaces to be used with a rule, you must use incoming interfaces (the -i option) only with INPUT or FORWARD chains and outgoing interfaces (the -o option) only with FORWARD or OUTPUT chains. This is necessary because OUTPUT chains are no longer used by incoming interfaces, and INPUT chains are not seen by packets moving through outgoing interfaces.

This is by no means a comprehensive list of the changes, given that iptables represents a fundamentally rewritten network filter. For more specific information, consult the Linux 2.4 Packet Filtering HOWTO and the "Additional Resources" section at the end of this chapter.

Options Used in iptables Commands

Rules that allow packets to be filtered by the kernel are put in place by running the iptables command. The options used with a given iptables rule must be grouped logically, based on the purpose and conditions of the overall rule, in order for the rule to be valid. When using the `iptables` command, you must specify the following options:

◆ Packet Type – The packet type dictates what type of packets the command filters.

◆ Packet Source or Destination – A packet's source or destination determines which packets to filter.

◆ Target – The *target* is the action taken on packets matching the type, destination, and source criteria.

UNDERSTANDING TABLES

A powerful aspect of iptables is that multiple tables of rules can be used to decide the fate of a particular packet, depending upon the type of packet being monitored and what is to be done with the packet. Thanks to the extendable nature of iptables, specialized tables can be created and stored in the `/lib/modules/ kernel-version/ kernel/net/ipv4/netfilter/` directory to meet specific goals. In this way, you can use iptables to run multiple sets of ipchains rules in specifically defined chains, each set fulfilling a particular role.

The default table, named filter, contains the standard built-in INPUT, OUTPUT, and FORWARD chains. This is somewhat similar to the standard chains in use with ipchains. However, by default, iptables also includes two additional tables that perform specific packet filtering jobs. The nat table can be used to modify the source and destination addresses recorded in packets, and the mangle table allows you to alter packets in specialized ways. Each table contains default chains that perform necessary tasks based on the purpose of the table, but you can easily set up new chains in each of the tables.

Many iptables commands have the following structure:

```
iptables [-t table] command chain param_1 opt_1 param_n opt_n
```

In this example, the `table` option allows the user to select a table other than the default filter table to use with the command. The `command` option is the heart of the rule, specifying the action to perform, such as appending a rule to or deleting a rule from a particular chain. The chain on which to operate is specified by the `chain` option. Following `chain` are pairs of parameters and options that actually define the way the rule will work and what will happen when a packet matches the rule.

When looking at the structure of an iptables command, it is important to remember that, unlike most other commands, the length and complexity of an iptables command can change based on its purpose. A simple command to remove a rule from a chain might be very short, while a command designed to filter packets from a particular subnet using a variety of specific parameters and options might be quite long. When creating iptables commands, understand that some parameters and options may create the need for other parameters and options to further specify the previous option's request. In order to construct a valid rule, this must continue until every parameter and option that requires another set of options is satisfied. Type `iptables -h` to see a comprehensive list of iptables command structures.

iptables COMMANDS

Commands tell iptables to perform a specific action. Only one command is allowed per iptables command string. With the exception of the help command, all commands must be specified using uppercase characters. The legal iptables commands are shown in the following list:

- `-A` — Appends the iptables rule to the end of the specified chain. This is the command used to simply add a rule when rule order in the chain does not matter.

- `-C` — Checks a particular rule before adding it to the user-specified chain. This command can help you construct complicated iptables rules by prompting you for additional parameters and options.

- `-D` — Deletes a rule in a particular chain by number (such as 5 for the fifth rule in a chain). You can also type the entire rule, and iptables will delete the rule in the chain that matches it.

- `-E` — Renames a user-defined chain. This does not affect the structure of the table. Rather, it just saves you the trouble of deleting the chain, creating it under the new name, and reconfiguring all of your rules for that chain.

- `-F` — Flushes the selected chain, which effectively deletes every rule in the the chain. If no chain is specified, this command flushes every rule from every chain.

- `-h` — Provides a list of helpful command structures, as well as a quick summary of command parameters and options.

- `-I` — Inserts a rule in a chain at a particular point. Assign a number to the rule to be inserted, and iptables will put it there. If no number is specified, iptables will place your command at the top of the rule list.

- `-L` — Lists all of the rules in the chain specified after the command. To list all rules in all chains in the default filter table, do not specify a chain or table. To list the rules in a specific chain in a particular table, use the syntax iptables -L chain -t table.

TIP

Powerful options for the -L command that provide rule numbers and allow more verbose rule descriptions, among others, are described in the "Listing Options" section.

◆ -N — Creates a new chain with a user-specified name.

◆ -P — Sets the default policy for a particular chain, so that when packets traverse an entire chain without matching a rule, they will be sent on to a particular target, such as ACCEPT or DROP.

◆ -R — Replaces a rule in a particular chain. You must use a rule's number after the chain's name to replace that rule. The first rule in a chain corresponds to rule number 1.

◆ -X — Deletes a user-specified chain. Deleting a built-in chain for any table is not allowed.

◆ -Z — Zeroes the byte and packet counters in all chains for a particular table.

CAUTION

Be aware of which option (-A or -I) you are using when adding a rule. The order of the rules can be very important when determining if a particular packet applies to one rule or another. Make sure when adding a rule to the beginning or end of the chain that it does not affect other rules in that chain.

iptables COMMAND PARAMETERS

Certain iptables commands, including those used to add, append, delete, insert, or replace rules within a particular chain, require parameters to construct packet filtering rule.

◆ -c — Resets the counters for a particular rule. This parameter accepts the PKTS and BYTES options to specify what counter to reset.

◆ -d — Sets the destination hostname, IP address, or network of a packet that will match the rule. When matching a network, you can use two different methods for signifying the netmask, such as 192.168.0.0/255.255.255.0 or 192.168.0.0/24.

◆ -f — Applies this rule only to fragmented packets. If the ! option is used after this parameter, only unfragmented packets will be matched.

◆ -i — Sets the incoming network interface, such as eth0 or ppp0, to use with a particular rule. With iptables, this optional parameter may be used only with the INPUT and FORWARD chains when used with the filter table, and the PREROUTING chain with the nat and mangle tables. This parameter features several useful options that may be used before specifying the name of an interface.

◆ ! — Indicates a parameter that should *not* match, meaning that any specified interfaces are specifically excluded from this rule.

◆ + — Acts as a wildcard character that matches all interfaces that match a particular string. For example, the parameter -i eth+ would apply this rule to any Ethernet interfaces on your system but exclude any other interfaces, such as ppp0. If the -i parameter is used but no interface is specified, every interface is affected by the rule.

◆ -j — Tells iptables to jump to a particular target when a packet matches a particular rule. Valid targets to be used after the -j option include the standard options, ACCEPT, DROP, QUEUE, and RETURN, as well as extended options that are available through modules loaded by default with the Red Hat iptables RPM package, such as LOG, MARK, and REJECT, among others. See the iptables man page for more information on these and other targets, including rules regarding their use. You may also direct a packet matching this rule to a user-defined chain outside of the current chain. This allows you to apply other rules against this packet, further filtering it with more specific criteria. If no target is specified, the packet moves past the rule with no action taken. However, the counter for this rule is still increased by one, as the packet matched the specified rule.

◆ -o — Sets the outgoing network interface for a particular rule, and may only be used only with OUTPUT and FORWARD chains in the filter table and the POSTROUTING chain in the nat and mangle tables. This parameter's options are the same as those of the incoming network interface parameter (-i).

◆ -p — Sets the IP protocol for the rule, which can be either icmp, tcp, udp, or all, to match every supported protocol. In addition, lesser-used protocols listed in /etc/protocols may also be used. If this option is omitted when creating a rule, the all option is the default.

◆ -s — Sets the source for a particular packet, using the same syntax as the destination (-d) parameter.

Different network protocols provide specialized matching options that may be set in specific ways to match a particular packet using that protocol. Of course, the protocol must first be specified in the iptables command, such as using -p tcp *protocol*, to make the options for the named protocol available.

TCP PROTOCOL MATCH OPTIONS

The following match options are available for the TCP protocol (-p tcp):

♦ --dport — Sets the destination port for the packet. You can use either a network service name (such as www or smtp), port number, or range of port numbers to configure this option. To browse the names and aliases of network services and the port numbers they use, view the /etc/services file. To specify a specific range of port numbers, separate the two numbers with a colon (:), such as -p tcp --dport 3000:3200. The largest valid range is 0:65535. You may also use an exclamation point character (!) as a flag after the --dport option to tell iptables to match all packets that do not use that network service or port.

♦ --sport — Sets the source port of the packet, using the same options as --dport.

♦ --syn — Applies to all TCP packets designed to initiate communication, commonly called *SYN packets*, but not to packets carrying a data payload. Placing an exclamation point character (!) as a flag after the --syn option causes all non-SYN packets to be matched.

♦ --tcp-flags — Matches TCP packets with specific bits or flags set. The --tcp-flags match option accepts two parameters that specify the flags for the various bits in a comma-separated list. The first parameter is the mask, which sets the flags to be examined on the packet.

The second parameter refers to the flags that must be set in the packet to make a match. The possible flags are ACK, FIN, PSH, RST, SYN, and URG. In addition, ALL and NONE can also be used to match every flag or none of them. For example, an iptables rule that contains -p tcp --tcp-flags ACK,FIN,SYN SYN will match only TCP packets that have the SYN flag set. As usual, ! after --tcp-flags reverses the effect of the match option, so that the second parameter's flags must not be set in order to match.

♦ --tcp-option — Attempts to match with TCP-specific options that can be set within a particular packet. This match option can also be reversed with the exclamation point character (!).

UDP PROTOCOL MATCH OPTIONS

These match options are available for the UDP protocol (-p udp):

♦ --dport — Specifies the destination port of the UDP packet, using the service name, port number, or range of port numbers. See the --dport match option in the "TCP Protocol" section for various ways to use this option.

♦ --sport — Specifies the source port of the UDP packet, using the service name, port number, or range of port numbers. See the --dport match option in the "TCP Protocol" section for various ways to use this option.

ICMP PROTOCOL

Packets using the Internet Control Message Protocol (ICMP) can be matched (-p icmp) using the option --icmp-type — Sets the name or number of the ICMP type to match with the rule. A list of valid ICMP names can be seen by typing the iptables -p icmp -h command.

Modules with Additional Match Options

Additional match options are available through modules loaded when the iptables command calls them. To use a match option module, you must load the module by name by including -m module in the iptables command. A large number of modules are available by default. It is even possible to create your own modules to provide additional match-option functionality. Many modules exist, but only the most popular ones are discussed here.

The limit module allows you to place a limit on how many packets will be matched to a particular rule. This is especially beneficial when logging rule matches so that a flood of matching packets will not fill up your logs with repetitive messages or use too many system resources.

- ◆ --limit — Sets the number of matches for a particular range of time, specified with a number and time modifier arranged in a number/time format. For example, using --limit 5/hour lets a rule match only five times in a single hour. If a number and time modifier are not used, the default value of 3/hour is assumed.

- ◆ --limit-burst — Sets a limit on the number of packets able to match a rule at one time. This option should be used in conjunction with the --limit option, and it accepts a number to set the burst threshold. If no number is specified, only five packets are initially able to match the rule.

The state module, which uses the --state match option, can match a packet with these particular connection states:

- ◆ ESTABLISHED — The matching packet is associated with other packets in an established connection.

- ◆ INVALID — The matching packet cannot be tied to a known connection.

- ◆ NEW — The matching packet is either creating a new connection or is part of a two-way connection not previously seen.

- ◆ RELATED — The matching packet is starting a new connection related in some way to an existing connection.

These connection states can be used in combination with one another by separating them with commas, such as -m state --state INVALID,NEW. To specifically match a hardware MAC address of an Ethernet device, use the mac module, which accepts `--mac-source` plus a MAC address as an option. To exclude a MAC address from a rule, place an exclamation point (!) after the `--mac-source` match option. To view other match options available through modules, see the iptables man page.

TARGET OPTIONS

Once a packet has matched a particular rule, the rule can direct the packet to a number of different targets that decide its fate and, possibly, take additional actions, such as logging the action. Additionally, each chain has a default target, which is used if none of the rules on that chain match a packet or if none of the rules that match the packet specify a target.

Only a few standard targets are available to decide what happens with the packet:

◆ `user-defined-chain` — The name of a previously created and defined chain within this table with rules that will be checked against this packet, in addition to any other rules in any other chains that must be checked against this packet.

◆ `ACCEPT` — Allows the packet to successfully move on to its destination or another chain.

◆ `DROP` — Drops the packet without responding to the requester. The system that sent the packet is not notified of the failure. The packet is simply removed from the rule that is checking the chain and discarded.

◆ `QUEUE` — Queues the packet for handling by a user-space application.

◆ `RETURN` — Stops checking the packet against rules in the current chain. If the packet with a `RETURN` target matches a rule in a chain called from another chain, the packet is returned to the first chain to resume rule checking where it left off. If the `RETURN` rule is used on a built-in chain and the packet cannot move up to its previous chain, the default target for the current chain determines the action taken.

In addition to these standard targets, various other targets may be used with extensions known as *target modules*. There are many extended target modules, most of which apply only to specific tables or situations. Other target extensions, including several that are useful with masquerading using the nat table or with packet alteration using the mangle table, can be found in the iptables man page. A couple of the most popular target modules included by default in Red Hat Linux are `LOG` and `REJECT`.

The `LOG` target logs all packets that match this rule. Since the packets are logged by the kernel, the `/etc/syslog.conf` file determines where these log entries are written. By default, they are placed in the `/var/log/messages` file. Various options can be used after the `LOG` target to specify the way in which logging occurs:

- ◆ `--log-level` – Sets the priority level of a logging event. A list of priority levels can be found in the syslog.conf man page.

- ◆ `--log-ip-options` – Logs the options, if any, set in the header of an IP packet.

- ◆ `--log-prefix` – Places a string before the log line when it is written. Accepts up to 29 characters after the `--log-prefix` option. This is useful for writing `syslog` filters for use in conjunction with packet logging.

- ◆ `--log-tcp-options` – Logs the options set in the header of a TCP packet.

- ◆ `--log-tcp-sequence` – Writes the packet's TCP sequence number.

The `REJECT` target sends an error packet back to the system that sent the packet, and then drops the packet. This target is useful if you would like to notify the system sending the matching packet of the problem. The `REJECT` target accepts the `--reject-with` type option, which allows more detailed information to be sent with the error packet. The message `port-unreachable` is the default type error given if no other option is used. For a full list of message types, see the iptables man page.

LISTING OPTIONS

The default list command, `iptables -L`, provides a very basic overview of the default filter table's current chains. Additional options provide more information and arrange that information in specific ways:

- ◆ `-v` – Displays verbose output, such as the number of packets and bytes each chain has seen, the number of packets and bytes each rule has matched, and which interfaces apply to a particular rule.

- ◆ `-x` – Expands numbers to their exact values. On a busy system, the number of packets and bytes seen by a particular chain or rule may be abbreviated using `K` (thousands), `M` (millions), and `G` (billions) at the end of the number. This option forces the full number to be displayed.

- ◆ `-n` – Displays IP addresses and port numbers in numeric format, rather than in the default hostname and network service format.

- ◆ `--line-numbers` – Lists rules in each chain with their numeric order in the chain. This option is useful when attempting to delete a specific rule in a chain, or to locate where to insert a rule within a chain.

SAVING AND RELOADING iptables RULES

Rules created with the iptables command only exist in the kernel. If you restart your system after setting up iptables rules, your rules will be lost. To make netfilter rules persistent, you need to save them to the `/etc/sysconfig/iptables` file. To do this, type the command `/sbin/service iptables save` as the root user. This causes the iptables init script to run the `/sbin/iptables-save` program and write the current iptables configuration to the /etc/sysconfig/iptables file. This file should be readable by root only, so that your packet filtering rules are not viewable by average users. The next time the system boots, the iptables init script will reapply the rules saved in /etc/sysconfig/iptables by using the /sbin/iptables-restore command.

While it is always a good idea to test a new iptables rule before committing it to the /etc/sysconfig/iptables file, it is possible to copy iptables rules into this file from another system's version of this file. This allows you to quickly distribute sets of iptables rules to many different machines.

 If you distribute the /etc/sysconfig/iptables file to other machines, you must type /sbin/service iptables restart for the new rules take effect.

Additional Resources

Following are some additional sources of information that may be helpful.

- ◆ http://netfilter.samba.org — Contains assorted information about iptables, including a FAQ addressing specific problems you may experience and various helpful guides by Rusty Russell, the Linux IP firewall maintainer. The HOWTO documents here cover subjects such as basic networking concepts, 2.4 kernel packet filtering, and NAT configurations.

- ◆ http://www.linuxnewbie.org/nhf/Security/IPtables_Basics.html — Offers a general look at the way packets move through the Linux kernel, plus an introduction to constructing simple iptables commands.

- ◆ http://www.redhat.com/support/resources/networking/firewall .html — Provides up-to-date links to a variety of packet filter resources.

- ◆ *Red Hat Linux Firewalls* by Bill McCarty (Red Hat Press/Wiley, 2003)

Summary

This chapter showed you how to begin securing entire networks of computers using a Red Hat system as a firewall. You learned how to determine what services are running and how to disable unnecessary services using a variety of tools that are part of a standard Red Hat installation. You also read how to monitor incoming network connections to make sure that incoming connections from Internet hosts are not the precursors to concerted attempts to compromise the security of your internal network. Finally, you learned a bit of basic firewall theory and then got a solid primer on creating firewalls with iptables.

Chapter 32

Detecting and Preventing Intrusions

CHAPTERS 28-31 HINT at this chapter's main topic: detecting and blocking attempted intrusions of your Red Hat Enterprise Linux–based network. This chapter revives and deepens these earlier discussions, describing methods for monitoring a Red Hat system for potential, attempted, and actual security compromises using the tools available in a standard Red Hat installation. As used in this chapter, *intrusion detection software* (IDS) refers to software packages that implement a variety of methods for monitoring a system for attempts to compromise it.

One type of IDS is file integrity software, such as Tripwire. As you learn in the next section, file integrity packages create a database of key files and file systems on a host and then compare the results of frequent integrity checks to the attributes stored in the database. The reports generated highlight changes, which may or may not indicate that a system has been compromised. Other approaches to IDS include log monitoring tools such as LogWatch and real-time monitoring of incoming network traffic using a firewall implemented with ipchains or iptables. The sections titled "Using LogWatch," "Detecting Intrusions with ipchains," and "Detecting Intrusions with iptables," respectively, illustrate how to configure each of these tools to enhance the IDS component of your Red Hat system's security.

Using Tripwire

Tripwire is not for everyone – that is, not every host on your network should be running or needs to run Tripwire. If the host is used for developmental work or as a testing platform, then it is likely that important system files are altered or replaced on a fairly regular basis. More generally, *any* system whose key system files and binaries are subject to frequent modification is unsuitable for IDS systems that rely on file integrity. This qualification notwithstanding, one central problem needs to be considered when deciding whether or not to install and run Tripwire on a given machine: Without such a tool, it is impossible to prove that a system has *not* been compromised. This dilemma leaves you with few options for machines not so equipped if the suspicion or even slight likelihood of compromise is raised, and only one of those options, reformatting the hard drive, is safe. In some cases, this is not a large problem, but in others, reformatting a drive is out of the question. Machines that are used to test operating system installation programs or otherwise used as laboratory testbeds barely notice that they are being reformatted, again, on any given day. Other systems, those with a fair amount of configuration detail implemented, are not so easy to replace, even with a decent set of backups. During and after an attack, a Tripwire check affords a degree of confidence when it is essential that time not be wasted on systems that are still intact.

 Tripwire is not the only file integrity software available for Red Hat systems. Another popular package is AIDE, an acronym for *Advanced Intrusion Detection Environment*. AIDE's home page on the Web is `http://www.cs .tut.fi/~rammer/aide.html`.

Tripwire helps ensure the integrity of critical system files and directories by comparing changes made to them relative to an initial baseline snapshot taken when Tripwire was first installed and initialized. These comparisons include file locations, creation and modification dates, file sizes, and other data. Tripwire can be config- ured to send alerts to designated users via e-mail if particular files are altered and to perform automated integrity checking via a cron job. Using Tripwire for intru- sion detection and damage assessment also reduces the recovery time following a system compromise because it reduces the number of files you must restore to repair the system to a known secure state. For maximum reliability, install Tripwire and create the initial snapshot before the system is at risk from intrusion (that is, before it is connected to a network). The following steps outline how to install, ini- tialize, and use Tripwire:

1. Install Tripwire, customize the policy and configuration files, and run the configuration script.

2. Initialize the Tripwire database of critical system files to monitor, based on the contents of the Tripwire policy file created in Step 1.

3. Run a Tripwire integrity check to compare the new database with the actual system files, looking for missing or altered files.

4. Examine the Tripwire report file and note integrity violations.

5. Take appropriate security measures if monitored files have been altered inappropriately. You can either replace the originals from backups or reinstall the affected programs.

6. Update the Tripwire database file. Valid integrity violations, such as intentionally edited files or updated programs, should be flagged to be ignored as violations in future reports.

7. Update the Tripwire policy file to change the list of files Tripwire monitors or to change how it treats integrity violations, regenerate a signed copy of the policy file, and then update your Tripwire database.

To change the list of files Tripwire monitors or how it treats integrity violations, update the supplied policy file (/etc/tripwire/twpol.txt), regenerate a signed copy (/etc/tripwire/tw.pol), and update the Tripwire database. For more information, see the section "Updating the Tripwire Policy File," later in this chapter. Refer to the appropriate sections within this chapter for detailed instructions on each step.

Installing and Configuring Tripwire

By far, the easiest way to install Tripwire is to use the up2date command. Just execute up2date tripwire and follow the prompts. After you have installed the Tripwire RPM, complete the following steps to initialize the software:

1. Customize the local configuration file: /etc/tripwire/twcfg.txt.

2. Customize the policy text file: /etc/tripwire/twpol.txt.

3. Run the Tripwire installation script to configure Tripwire for your system.

4. Initialize the Tripwire database.

5. Perform the initial integrity check.

6. Place the system in production.

Admittedly, you will find it rather tedious to get Tripwire running, but consider the tedium a tradeoff against needing to reinstall and reconfigure an entire system because you are unsure what a black hat has done if the system is compromised.

CUSTOMIZING THE CONFIGURATION FILE

Although you are not required to edit this sample Tripwire configuration file, you may find it necessary for your situation. For instance, you might want to alter the location of Tripwire files, modify e-mail settings, or change the level of detail for reports. The following list shows the required user-configurable variables in the /etc/tripwire/twcfg.txt file:

◆ POLFILE — Specifies the location of the policy file; the default value is /etc/tripwire/tw.pol.

◆ DBFILE — Specifies the location of the database file; the default value is /var/lib/tripwire/$(HOSTNAME).twd.

◆ REPORTFILE — Specifies the location of the report files. The default value is set to /var/lib/tripwire/report/$(HOSTNAME)-$(DATE).twr.

◆ SITEKEYFILE — Specifies the location of the site key file; the default value is /etc/tripwire/site.key.

◆ LOCALKEYFILE — Specifies the location of the local key file; the default value is /etc/tripwire/$(HOSTNAME)-local.key.

 If you edit the configuration file and leave any of the preceding variables undefined, the configuration file will be invalid. If this occurs, when you execute the tripwire command, it reports an error and exits.

The rest of the configurable variables, shown in the following list, are optional.

◆ EDITOR — Specifies the text editor called by Tripwire. The default value is /bin/vi.

◆ LATEPROMPTING — If set to true, this variable configures Tripwire to wait as long as possible before prompting the user for a password, thereby minimizing the amount of time the password is in memory. The default value is false.

◆ LOOSEDIRECTORYCHECKING — If set to true, this variable configures Tripwire to report if a file within a watched directory changes and not to report the change for the directory itself. That is, any changes to the directory file will not be reported, though changes to directory contents will be reported. This limits redundancy in Tripwire reports. The default value is false.

◆ SYSLOGREPORTING — If set to true, this variable configures Tripwire to report information to the syslog daemon via the user facility. The log level is set to notice. See the syslogd man page for more information. The default value is false.

◆ MAILNOVIOLATIONS — If set to true, this variable configures Tripwire to e-mail a report at a regular interval regardless of whether or not any violations have occurred. The default value is true.

◆ EMAILREPORTLEVEL — Specifies the level of detail for e-mailed reports. Valid values for this variable are 0 through 4. The default value is 3.

◆ REPORTLEVEL — Specifies the level of detail for reports generated by the twprint command. The default value is 3 but can be overridden on the command line.

◆ MAILMETHOD — Specifies which mail protocol Tripwire should use. Valid values are SMTP and SENDMAIL. The default value is SENDMAIL.

◆ MAILPROGRAM — Specifies which mail program Tripwire should use. The default value is /usr/sbin/sendmail -oi -t.

After editing the sample configuration file, you need to configure the sample policy file.

For security purposes, you should either delete or store in a secure location any copies of the plain-text /etc/tripwire/twcfg.txt file after running the installation script or regenerating a signed configuration file. Alternatively, you can change the permissions so that it is not world-readable. However, if the box *is* compromised, changing the permissions will not serve you well, so we encourage you not to store the plain-text policy file on the disk.

EDITING THE POLICY FILE

Although doing so is not required, you should edit the heavily commented sample Tripwire policy file, /etc/tripwire/twpol.txt, to take into account the specific applications, files, and directories on your system. Relying on the unaltered sample configuration from the RPM does not adequately protect your system. Modifying the policy file also increases the usefulness of Tripwire reports by minimizing false alerts for files and programs you are not using and by adding functionality, such as e-mail notification. Notification via e-mail is not configured by default. See the section "Tripwire and E-mail" for more on configuring this feature. If you modify the sample policy file after running the configuration script, see the section "Updating the Tripwire Policy File" for instructions on regenerating a signed policy file.

RUNNING THE INSTALLATION SCRIPT

As the root user, type /etc/tripwire/twinstall.sh at the shell prompt to run the configuration script. The twinstall.sh script will ask you for site and local passwords. These passwords are used to generate cryptographic keys for protecting Tripwire files. The script then creates and signs these files. When selecting the site and local passwords, consider the following guidelines:

◆ Use at least eight alphanumeric and symbolic characters, but for each password do not exceed 1,023 characters.

◆ Do not use quotes in a password.

◆ Make the Tripwire passwords completely different from the root password or any other password for the system.

◆ Use unique passwords for both the site key and the local key.

The site key password protects the Tripwire configuration and policy files. The local key password protects the Tripwire database and report files.

 There is no way to decrypt a signed file if you forget your passwords. If you forget the passwords, the files are unusable, and you will have to run the configuration script again.

Encrypting its configuration, policy, database, and report files enables Tripwire to protect them from being viewed by anyone who does not know the site and local passwords. This means that even if intruders obtain root access to your system, they will not be able to alter the Tripwire files to hide their tracks. Once encrypted and signed, the configuration and policy files generated by running the twinstall.sh script should not be renamed or moved.

Selecting Passphrases

Tripwire files are signed or encrypted using cryptographic keys that protect the configuration, policy, database, and report files from being viewed or modified except by users who know the site and/or local passphrases. As a result, should intruders somehow obtain root access to your system, they can't alter the Tripwire files to hide their activities unless they know the passphrases.

Thus, selecting good passphrases is vital. Good passphrases have the following characteristics:

◆ They contain a mixture of uppercase and lowercase alphanumeric and symbolic characters but do not use single or double quotes.

◆ They are between 8 and 1,023 characters.

◆ They are completely different from the root password for the system.

And good system administrators take the following precautions:

◆ Assign different passphrases for the site key and the local key.

◆ Store the passphrases in a secure location, and *do not* store them on the system they protect; someone who compromises the system may be able to discover and use them. As an additional precaution, you might want to save additional copies of the passphrases on a floppy disk that stays in a locked drawer.

The site key passphrase protects the site key, which is used to sign Tripwire configuration and policy files. The local key signs Tripwire's database and report files. Keep in mind that there is no way to decrypt a signed file if you forget your passphrase. If you forget the passphrases, the files are unusable and you have to run the configuration script again, which also reinitializes the Tripwire database.

INITIALIZING THE TRIPWIRE DATABASE

When initializing its database, Tripwire builds a collection of file-system objects based on the rules in the policy file. This database serves as the baseline for integrity checks. To initialize the Tripwire database, use the following command:

```
# /usr/sbin/tripwire --init
```

This command can take several minutes to run. Once you finish these steps successfully, Tripwire has established a baseline snapshot of the file system. The baseline is necessary to check for changes in critical files. After initializing the Tripwire database, run an initial integrity check as described in the "Performing an Integrity Check" section. This check should be done prior to connecting the computer to the network and putting it into production. After completing the initial integrity check, you are free to place the system into production.

Using Tripwire

There are a number of activities you should perform on a routine basis if you intend to take advantage of Tripwire's capabilities. These activities include performing an integrity check, reviewing reports, examining Tripwire's database, and updating the policy file and the database as you add, delete, and modify files on the file system.

PERFORMING AN INTEGRITY CHECK

By default, the Tripwire RPM adds a shell script named `tripwire-check` to the `/etc/cron.daily/` directory. This will automatically run an integrity check once per day. You can run a Tripwire integrity check at any time by typing the following command:

```
# /usr/sbin/tripwire --check
```

During an integrity check, Tripwire compares the current state of file-system objects with the properties recorded in its database. Violations are printed to the screen, and an encrypted copy of the report is created in `/var/lib/tripwire/` `report` directory. You can view the report using the `twprint` command as described in the next section, "Viewing Tripwire Reports." If you want to be notified by e-mail when certain types of integrity violations occur, you can configure this in the policy file. See the section "Tripwire and E-mail" for instructions on how to set up and test this feature. The /usr/sbin/twprint command is used to view encrypted Tripwire reports and databases.

VIEWING TRIPWIRE REPORTS

To view a Tripwire report, use the twprint -m r command, which displays the contents of a Tripwire report in clear text. You must, however, tell twprint which report file to display. A twprint command for printing Tripwire reports looks similar to the following:

```
# /usr/sbin/twprint -m r --twrfile /var/lib/tripwire/report/name.twr
```

The -m r option in the command directs twprint to decode a Tripwire report. The --twrfile option directs twprint to use a specific Tripwire report file. The name.twr argument specifies the name of the Tripwire report that you want to see. The name component is composed of the name of the host that Tripwire checked to generate the report, plus the creation date and time. You can review previously saved reports at any time. Simply type ls /var/lib/tripwire/report to see a list of Tripwire reports. Tripwire reports can be rather lengthy, depending upon the number of violations found or errors generated. A sample report starts off like this:

```
Tripwire(R) 2.3.0 Integrity Check Report

Report generated by:          root
Report created on:            Mon Sep  1 04:04:42 2003
Database last updated on:     Sun Aug 31 16:19:34 2003


===============================================================
Report Summary:
===============================================================
Host name:                    bubba.possum.holler.org
Host IP address:              10.0.0.1
Host ID:                      None
Policy file used:             /etc/tripwire/tw.pol
Configuration file used:      /etc/tripwire/tw.cfg

Database file used:      /var/lib/tripwire/some.host.com.twd
Command line used:            /usr/sbin/tripwire --check


===============================================================
Rule Summary:
===============================================================
---------------------------------------------------------------
Section: Unix File System
---------------------------------------------------------------
```

Rule Name	Severity Level	Added	Removed	Modified
Invariant Directories	69	0	0	0
Temporary directories	33	0	0	0
* Tripwire Data Files	100	1	0	0
Critical devices	100	0	0	0
User binaries	69	0	0	0
Tripwire Binaries	100	0	0	0

VIEWING THE TRIPWIRE DATABASE

You can also use twprint to view the entire database or information about selected files in the Tripwire database. This is useful for seeing just how much information Tripwire is tracking on your system. To view the entire Tripwire database, type:

```
# /usr/sbin/twprint -m d --print-dbfile | less
```

This command generates a large amount of output, the first few lines appearing similar to the following:

```
Tripwire(R) 2.3.0 Database

Database generated by:              root
Database generated on:              Mon Sep  1 13:56:42 2003
Database last updated on:           Mon Sep  1 16:19:34 2003


===============================================================
Database Summary:
===============================================================
Host name:                  bubba.possum.holler.org
Host IP address:            10.0.0.1
Host ID:                    None
Policy file used:           /etc/tripwire/tw.pol
Configuration file used:    /etc/tripwire/tw.cfg
Database file used:         /var/lib/tripwire/some.host.com.twd
Command line used:          /usr/sbin/tripwire -init


===============================================================
Object Summary:
===============================================================
---------------------------------------------------------------
# Section: Unix File System
---------------------------------------------------------------

              Mode        UID      Size       Modify Time
              ------      -------  ------      ---------------
  /           drwxr-xr-x  root (0)  XXX        XXXXXXXXXXXXXXXXX
  /bin        drwxr-xr-x  root (0)  4096       Mon Jan  8 08:20:45 2003
```

```
/bin/arch        -rwxr-xr-x    root (0)    2844   Tue Dec 12 05:51:35 2002
/bin/ash         -rwxr-xr-x    root (0)   64860   Thu Dec  7 22:35:05 2002
/bin/ash.static  -rwxr-xr-x    root (0)  405576   Thu Dec  7 22:35:05 2002
```

To see information about a particular file that Tripwire is tracking, such as /etc/hosts, use the following command:

```
# /usr/sbin/twprint -m d --print-dbfile /etc/hosts
```

The output will look similar to the following:

```
Object name:        /etc/hosts

Property:                          Value:
- - - - - - - - - - - -            - - - - - - - - - -
Object Type                        Regular File
Device Number                      773
Inode Number                       216991
Mode                               -rw-r--r--
Num Links                          1
UID                                root (0)
GID                                root (0)
```

See the twprint man page for more options.

UPDATING THE TRIPWIRE DATABASE

If you run an integrity check and Tripwire finds violations, you will first need to determine whether the violations discovered are actual security breaches or the product of authorized modifications. If you have recently installed an application or have edited critical system files, Tripwire will correctly report integrity-check violations. In this case, you should update your Tripwire database so those changes are no longer reported as violations. However, if unauthorized changes have been made to system files and generate integrity-check violations, you should restore the original file from a backup, reinstall the program, or, if the breach is severe enough, completely reinstall the operating system.

To update its database so it accepts valid policy violations, Tripwire first cross-references a report file against the database, then integrates into it valid violations from the report file. When updating the database, be sure to use the most recent report. Use the following command to update the Tripwire database, where name is the name of the most recent report file:

```
/usr/sbin/tripwire --update --twrfile /var/lib/tripwire/report/name.twr
```

Tripwire will display the report file using the default text editor specified on the EDITOR line of the Tripwire configuration file. This gives you an opportunity to deselect files you do not wish to update in the Tripwire database.

It is important that you change only authorized integrity violations in the database.

All proposed updates to the Tripwire database start with an [x] before the file name, similar to the following example:

```
Added:
[x] "/usr/sbin/longrun"

Modified:
[x] "/usr/sbin"
[x] "/usr/sbin/cpqarrayd"
```

If you want to specifically exclude a valid violation from being added to the Tripwire database, remove the [x]. To accept any files with an [x] beside them as changes, or to edit files in the default text editor, vi, type i and press Enter to enter insert mode and make any necessary changes. When finished, press the Esc key, type :wq and then press Enter. After the editor closes, enter your local password, and the database will be rebuilt and signed. After a new Tripwire database is written, the newly authorized integrity violations will no longer show up as warnings.

Updating the Tripwire Policy File

If you want to change the files Tripwire records in its database, change email configuration, or modify the severity at which certain violations are reported, you need to edit your Tripwire policy file. First, make whatever changes are necessary to the sample policy file, /etc/tripwire/twpol.txt. If you deleted this file (as you should whenever you are finished configuring Tripwire), you can regenerate it by issuing the following command:

```
# twadmin --print-polfile > /etc/tripwire/twpol.txt
```

A common change to this policy file is to comment out any files that do not exist on your system so that they will not generate a "file not found" error in your Tripwire reports. For example, if your system does not have a /etc/smb.conf file, you can tell Tripwire not to try to look for it by commenting out its line in twpol.txt with the # character as in the following example:

```
#    /etc/smb.conf   -> $(SEC_CONFIG) ;
```

Next, you must generate a new, signed `/etc/tripwire/tw.pol` file and generate an updated database file based on this policy information. Assuming `/etc/tripwire/twpol.txt` is the edited policy file, use this command:

```
# /usr/sbin/twadmin --create-polfile -S site.key /etc/tripwire/twpol.txt
```

 We cannot overstate the importance of protecting the `site.key` file. It is, quite literally, the key to Tripwire's integrity checking. If the Bad Guys get hold of it, all of Tripwire's security is worthless; the key file ensures that unauthorized changes to Tripwire's database files will be detected.

You will be asked for the site password. Then, the `twpol.txt` file will be encrypted and signed. It is important that you update the Tripwire database after creating a new `/etc/tripwire/tw.pol` file. The most reliable way to accomplish this is to delete your current Tripwire database and create a new database using the new policy file. If your Tripwire database file is named `bubba.possum.holler.com.twd`, type this command:

```
# rm /var/lib/tripwire/bubba.possum.holler.com.twd
```

Then type the following command to create a new database using the updated policy file:

```
# /usr/sbin/tripwire --init
```

To make sure the database was correctly changed, run the first integrity check manually and view the contents of the resulting report. See the sections "Running an Integrity Check" and "Viewing Tripwire Reports" for more on doing these tasks.

Tripwire and E-mail

You can configure Tripwire to send an e-mail to one or more accounts if a specific type of policy is violated. In order to do this, you need to figure out what policy rules should be monitored and who should get the e-mail when those rules are broken. Note that on large systems with multiple administrators, you can have different sets of people notified depending on the types of violations.

Once you have determined whom to notify and what rule violations to report to them, edit the `/etc/tripwire/twpol.txt` file, adding an `emailto=` line to the rule directive section for each appropriate rule. Do this by adding a comma after the `severity=` line and putting `emailto=` on the next line, followed by one or more e-mail addresses. More than one email address can be specified if the addresses are separated by semicolons. For example, if two administrators, Johnray and Bob, need to be notified if a networking program is modified, change the Networking Programs rule directive in the policy file to look like this:

```
(
      rulename = "Networking Programs",
      severity = $(SIG_HI),
      emailto = johnray@domain.com;bob@domain.com

)
```

After changing the policy file, follow the instructions in the section "Updating the Tripwire Policy File" to generate an updated, encrypted, and signed copy of the Tripwire policy file.

To test Tripwire's email notification configuration, use the following command:

```
# /usr/sbin/tripwire --test --email your@email.address
```

A test e-mail will immediately be sent to the e-mail address by the Tripwire program.

Updating the Tripwire Configuration File

If you want to change Tripwire's configuration file, first edit the sample configuration file, /etc/tripwire/twcfg.txt. If you deleted this file, which you should whenever you finish configuring or reconfiguring Tripwire, you can regenerate it by issuing the following command:

```
# twadmin --print-cfgfile > /etc/tripwire/twcfg.txt
```

Tripwire will not recognize any configuration changes until the configuration text file is correctly signed and converted to /etc/tripwire/tw.pol with the twadmin command. Use the following command to regenerate a configuration file from the /etc/tripwire/twcfg.txt file:

```
/usr/sbin/twadmin --create-cfgfile -S site.key /etc/tripwire/twcfg.txt
```

Since the configuration file does not alter any Tripwire policies or files tracked by the application, it is not necessary to regenerate the Tripwire database.

Tripwire File Location Reference

Before working with Tripwire, you should know where important files for the application are located. Tripwire stores its files in a variety of places depending on their roles. Within the /usr/sbin directory you will find the following programs:

- ◆ `tripwire`
- ◆ `twadmin`
- ◆ `twprint`

Inside the `/etc/tripwire` directory, you will find the following files:

- ◆ `twinstall.sh` — The initialization script for Tripwire.
- ◆ `twcfg.txt` — The sample configuration file supplied by the Tripwire RPM.
- ◆ `tw.cfg` — The signed configuration file created by the `twinstall.sh` script.
- ◆ `twpol.txt` — The sample policy file supplied by the Tripwire RPM.
- ◆ `tw.pol` — The signed policy file created by the `twinstall.sh` script.
- ◆ key files — The local and site keys created by the `twinstall.sh` script, which ends with a `.key` file extension.

After running the `twinstall.sh` installation script, you will find the following files in the `/var/lib/tripwire` directory:

- ◆ The Tripwire database — The database of your system's files, which has a `.twd` file extension.
- ◆ Tripwire reports — The `/var/lib/tripwire/report` directory is where Tripwire reports are stored.

The following list describes the roles Tripwire's files play.

- ◆ `/etc/tripwire/tw.cfg` — The encrypted Tripwire configuration file, which stores system-specific information, such as the location of Tripwire data files. The `twinstall.sh` installer script and `twadmin` command generate this file using the information in the text version of the configuration file, `/etc/tripwire/twcfg.txt`.

  After running the installation script, the system administrator can change parameters by editing `/etc/tripwire/twcfg.txt` and regenerating a signed copy of the `tw.cfg` file using the `twadmin` command. See the section "Updating the Tripwire Configuration File" for more information on how to do this.

- ◆ `/etc/tripwire/tw.pol` — The active Tripwire policy file is an encrypted file containing comments, rules, directives, and variables. This file dictates the way Tripwire checks your system. Each rule in the policy file specifies a system object to be monitored. Rules also describe which changes to the object to report and which to ignore.

System objects are the files and directories you wish to monitor. Each object is identified by an object name. A property refers to a single characteristic of an object that Tripwire software can monitor. Directives control conditional processing of sets of rules in a policy file. During installation, the sample text policy file, `/etc/tripwire/twpol.txt`, is used to generate the active Tripwire policy file.

◆ After running the installation script, the system administrator can update the Tripwire policy file by editing `/etc/tripwire/twpol.txt` and regenerating a signed copy of the `tw.pol` file using the `twadmin` command. See the section "Updating the Tripwire Policy File" for more information on how to do this.

◆ `/var/lib/tripwire/`*`host_name`*`.twd` — When first initialized, Tripwire uses the signed policy file rules to create this database file. The Tripwire database is a baseline snapshot of the system in a known secure state. Tripwire compares this baseline against the current system to determine what changes have occurred. This comparison is called an integrity check.

◆ `/var/lib/tripwire/report/`*`host_name-report_date-report_time`* `.twr` — When you perform an integrity check, Tripwire produces report files in the /var/lib/tripwire/report/ directory. The report files summarize any file changes that violated the policy file rules during the integrity check. Tripwire reports are named using the following convention: *`host_name-report_date-report_time`*`.twr`. These reports show the differences, if any, between the Tripwire database and your actual system files.

Additional Tripwire Information

Tripwire can do more than what is covered in this chapter. Refer to these additional sources for more information about Tripwire.

◆ `/usr/share/doc/tripwire-version-number` — An excellent starting point for learning about how to customize the configuration and policy files in the `/etc/tripwire/` directory.

◆ Refer to the man pages for `tripwire`, `twadmin`, and `twprint` for help using those utilities.

◆ `http://www.tripwire.org/` — The home of the Tripwire Open Source Project, where you can find the latest news on the application, including a helpful FAQ.

◆ `http://sourceforge.net/project/showfiles.php?group_id=3130` — The SourceForge project site contains links to the latest official documentation from the Tripwire project.

Using LogWatch

LogWatch is a highly customizable and easy to use log monitoring system. It parses your system log files for a given period of time to create a report covering the areas that interest you. Its reports can be as succinct or as detailed as you want. By default, Red Hat configures LogWatch to run daily as a cron job (see /etc/cron.daily/ 00-logwatch), but it can also be run from the command line. The LogWatch "executable" is actually a Perl script, /usr/sbin/logwatch. logwatch's syntax is:

```
logwatch [--detail level] [--logfile name] [--print] [--mailto addr]
[--archives] [--range range] [--save filename] [--service name]
```

As you can see from the syntax listing, logwatch can be run without any arguments, in which case, it uses the default values listed in /etc/log.d/logwatch.conf, which are defined in terms of the options listed in the syntax listing. Table 32-1 lists the options and their descriptions.

TABLE 32-1 LOGWATCH COMMAND LINE OPTIONS

Option	Description
--detail level	Defines the degree of report detail; level must be one of high, med, or low
--logfile name	Prints report based on the log specified in name; multiple names can be specified
--service name	Prints report for the service specified in name; multiple names can be specified
--print	Displays report to stdout instead of sending e-mail
--mailto addr	E-mails report to the recipient specified in addr
--archives	Includes archived log files in the report in addition to current log files
--save filename	Saves the report to the file specified in filename
--range range	Defines the date on which to report; range must be one of yesterday, today, or all

The default options and values in /etc/log.d/logwatch.conf are:

◆ `mailto = root`

◆ `range = yesterday`

◆ `detail = low`

◆ `service = all`

These options correspond to invoking `logwatch` using the following command:

```
# logwatch --mailto root --range yesterday --detail low --service all
```

LogWatch uses a set of filters, also written in Perl, for extracting information from the various log files on a Red Hat system. These filters are stored in three separate directories:

◆ `/etc/log.d/scripts/shared` — Filters common to many services and/or logfiles.

◆ `/etc/log.d/scripts/logfiles` — Filters specific to just particular logfiles.

◆ `/etc/log.d/scripts/services` — Actual filter programs for the various services.

The list of services on which LogWatch can report can be determined by reviewing the list of files in `/etc/log.d/conf/services`, which contains configuration files defining how LogWatch processes the corresponding log entries. LogWatch currently processes log entries for the services in the following list.

automount	kernel	samba
cron	modprobe	secure
ftpd-messages	mountd	sendmail
ftpd-xferlog	named	sshd
identd	pam	sshd2
in.qpopper	pam_pwdb	syslogd
init	proftpd-messages	

The type of information LogWatch reports varies from service to service and depends on the argument provided to the `--detail` option. For example, the log information generated for the `sendmail` service is the same for all values of `--detail`:

```
# logwatch --service sendmail --detail low --range today --print
```

```
################### LogWatch 2.1.1 Begin ####################
```

```
-------------------- sendmail Begin -----------------------
641360 bytes transferred
81 messages sent
-------------------- sendmail End -----------------------


##################### LogWatch End ########################
# logwatch --service sendmail --detail high --range today --print

################## LogWatch 2.1.1 Begin ####################

-------------------- sendmail Begin -----------------------
641360 bytes transferred
81 messages sent
-------------------- sendmail End -----------------------


##################### LogWatch End ########################
```

As you can see, LogWatch reports the same data for both `low` and `high`: the total number of bytes sendmail processed and the number of messages it sent. However, the story is different for the `kernel` service, as shown in the following:

 TIP   You can obtain more detailed information about mail traffic using the `mailstats` command. In order to use it, make sure that the file `/var/log/sendmail.st` exists. If it does not, execute `touch /var/log/sendmail.st` as the root user.

```
# logwatch --service kernel --detail low --range today --print

################## LogWatch 2.1.1 Begin ####################

##################### LogWatch End ########################
# logwatch --service kernel --detail high ==range today --print

################## LogWatch 2.1.1 Begin ####################

-------------------- Kernel Begin -----------------------

4 Time(s): Directory sread (sector 0x17) failed
2 Time(s): end_request: I/O error, dev 02:00 (floppy), sector 19
5 Time(s): end_request: I/O error, dev 02:00 (floppy), sector 23
1 Time(s): end_request: I/O error, dev 02:00 (floppy), sector 24
```

```
1 Time(s): end_request: I/O error, dev 02:00 (floppy), sector 26
1 Time(s): end_request: I/O error, dev 02:00 (floppy), sector 364
1 Time(s): end_request: I/O error, dev 02:00 (floppy), sector 372
1 Time(s): end_request: I/O error, dev 02:00 (floppy), sector 373
1 Time(s): end_request: I/O error, dev 02:00 (floppy), sector 400
1 Time(s): end_request: I/O error, dev 02:00 (floppy), sector 404
1 Time(s): floppy0: CRC error: track 0, head 1, sector 5, size 2
1 Time(s): floppy0: CRC error: track 0, head 1, sector 9, size 2
1 Time(s): floppy0: data CRC error: track 0, head 1, sector 17, size 2
4 Time(s): floppy0: data CRC error: track 0, head 1, sector 2, size 2
1 Time(s): floppy0: data CRC error: track 0, head 1, sector 6, size 2
1 Time(s): floppy0: data CRC error: track 0, head 1, sector 7, size 2
2 Time(s): floppy0: data CRC error: track 0, head 1, sector 9, size 2
1 Time(s): floppy0: sector not found: track 0, head 1, sector 2, size 2
1 Time(s): floppy0: sector not found: track 0, head 1, sector 3, size 2
1 Time(s): floppy0: sector not found: track 0, head 1, sector 5, size 2
10 Time(s): floppy0: sector not found: track 0, head 1, sector 6, size 2
1 Time(s): floppy0: sector not found: track 0, head 1, sector 7, size 2


 --------------------- Kernel End -------------------------


##################### LogWatch End ########################
```

LogWatch's output when the detail level is high indicates that a disk used in the floppy drive is beginning to fail. To get the maximum benefit from LogWatch, consider changing the default detail level in /etc/log.d/logwatch.conf to high.

Detecting Intrusions with ipchains

After a thoughtfully designed and rigorously observed security policy, a packet filtering firewall, based on ipchains or iptables, is one of the strongest layers in a site's security. This section describes how to configure a firewall using *ipchains*, to facilitate detecting intrusion attempts. On its own, ipchains cannot detect intrusions *per se*. But if you use ipchains in conjunction with LogWatch or another log monitoring tool, you can determine what kind of intrusions blackhats are attempting, how often, on what ports, and so forth.

The key to using ipchains for intrusion detection is using its -l option to tell the kernel to log a packet that matches a rule. Although you would not ordinarily want to log packets, logging *denied* packets is a very useful way to get an idea of the kind of undesirable traffic coming into your system. For example, suppose you have the following rule:

```
# ipchains -l -A forward -i ppp0 -j DENY
```

This `ipchains` invocation appends (`-A`) a rule to the forward chain (`forward`), directing that packets on the ppp0 interface (`-i ppp0`) to jump (`-j`) should be denied (`DENY`). The `-l` causes the kernel to log each packet matching this rule to the system log. The log entry resembles the following:

```
Sep  1 23:01:21 bubba kernel: Packet log: forward DENY ppp0 PROTO=6
192.168.0.3:1896 207.46.131.71:80 L=40 S=0x00 I=55238 F=0x4000 T=127 (#1)
```

The log entry is intended more for networking gurus than for those of us who are merely mortal, but, despite its opacity, the output does contain useful information. It breaks down like so:

- `forward` is the chain containing the rule that matched the packet and generated the log entry.

- `DENY` (deny) is what the rule said to do to the packet.

- `ppp0` is the interface name. The packet could be either an incoming or an outgoing packet because the forward chain contained the matching rule.

- `PROTO=6` means that the packet used protocol 6, which maps to the TCP protocol (protocol 1 would be the ICMP protocol and 17 UDP).

- `192.168.1.3:1896` means that the packet's source IP address was 192.168.21.3, port 1896.

- `207.46.131.71:80` indicates that the packet's destination IP address was 207.46.131.71, port 80 (the HTTP port).

- `L=40` means that the packet's total length was 40 bytes.

- `S=0x00` tells you that the Type of Service (ToS) field was `0x00`. Dividing this value (0) by 4 converts it to the ToS value ipchains uses, which, in this case, is still 0.

- `I=55238` is the IP ID.

- `F=0x4000` is the 16-bit fragment offset plus flags. A value starting with `0x4` or `0x5` means that the Don't Fragment bit is set.

- `T=127` indicates that the packet's Time To Live (TTL) is 127. Recall from Chapter 26 that a packet's TTL usually starts at 15 or 255 and that it is decreased by 1 for each hop it takes.

- `(#1)` identifies the rule number that generated the log entry.

By default, `ipchain`'s log messages go to `/var/log/messages /var/log/messages`. So, to detect attempted intrusions, add the `-l` option to each ipchains rule that you want to monitor; then configure LogWatch to use a high level of detail for kernel messages. That is, set `detail = high` in `/etc/log.d/logwatch.conf`. Now, when you run LogWatch, the kernel portion of the generated report should resemble the following:

```
# logwatch --server kernel --detail high --range today --print
-------------------- Kernel Begin ------------------------


Denied packets from host2.mydomain.dom (192.168.0.4).
  Port netbios-ns        (udp,ppp0,forward): 6 packet(s).
Total of 6 packet(s).

Denied packets from bubba.possum.holler.org (192.168.0.3).
  Port domain    (udp,ppp0,forward): 42 packet(s).
  Port http      (tcp,ppp0,forward): 4 packet(s).
Total of 46 packet(s).



-------------------- Kernel End ------------------------
```

Notice how LogWatch summarizes the denied packet traffic on a per-host and per-port basis. For example, `bubba.possum.holler.org`, at IP address 192.168.0.3, sent 42 packets to the domain port (these are probably DNS messages of some sort) using the UDP protocol on the ppp0 interface. The forward chain generated each of 42 log entries LogWatch detected. Although LogWatch's report provides a good deal of summary information, you might also want to analyze the traffic in detail. To do so, use a grep command to search for entries containing the string `Packet log` in the `/var/log/messages` file for the day in question. For example:

```
# grep 'Packet log' /var/log/messages
...
Oct 15 00:10:51 host2 kernel: Packet log: forward DENY ppp0 PROTO=17
192.168.0.4:137 198.60.22.2:137 L=96 S=0x00 I=3096 F=0x0000 T=127 (#1)
```

Based on the information generated by the combination of ipchain's `-l` option of LogWatch's reporting capability, you can decide how best to respond to attempts to access your network.

Detecting Intrusions with iptables

To detect intrusions using iptables, you can use the procedure described for ipchains, taking into account iptables' richer logging features. In particular, it enables you to use various options to control how iptables logs packets. This functionality is provided by the iptables log module.

The task you must accomplish is to modify your iptables rules to log traffic that should not get through. You can also set a prefix on these log entries to make them easy to identify and set a log level or facility (or both) to further refine the log entry and make it easy to identify in the system log.

The key components for intrusion detection using iptables are to use the new LOG target (`-j LOG`), the `--log-level` *level* option to set the logging level, and the `--log-prefix` *prefix* option to set the log entry prefix. Consider the following rule:

```
# iptables -A FORWARD -p tcp -j LOG --log-prefix "SAMPLE LOG RULE"
```

This rule appends a rule to the forward chain (`-A FORWARD`) that creates a log entry for TCP (`-p TCP`) packets traversing the forward chain, prefixing each entry with the string SAMPLE LOG RULE. The following log entry represents what such an entry might look like:

```
Oct 15 01:43:32 host2 kernel: SAMPLE LOG RULEIN=eth0 OUT=ppp0 SRC=192.168.0.3
DST=130.236.130.55 LEN=48 TOS=0x00 PREC=0x00 TTL=127 ID=30691 DF PROTO=TCP
SPT=2001 DPT=80 WINDOW=8192 RES=0x00 SYN URGP=0
```

Configure LogWatch using the same procedure described in the previous section to create a summary report listing the logged packet traffic.

Summary

This chapter described methods for monitoring a Red Hat system for attempted, potential, and actual security compromises using the tools available in a standard Red Hat installation. After learning how to configure Tripwire and interpreting its reports, you learned how to set up LogWatch to monitor log files for a wide variety of unusual conditions. You also learned how to log firewall activity, using both ipchains and iptables, and how to use LogWatch to monitor these log entries.

Chapter 33

Troubleshooting and Problem Solving

IN THIS CHAPTER

◆ Red Hat installation problems

◆ File system problems

◆ Networking problems

◆ NFS problems

EVEN THE BEST-LAID PLANS rarely survive contact with reality, and Red Hat Enterprise Linux is no exception. This chapter describes various problems that can occur with various subsystems and features of Red Hat Enterprise Linux and suggests possible solutions to the problem. Obviously, we cannot cover everything that might go awry, but we'll cover the problems *we* had and how we solved them. If our crystal ball is working, we may even be able to foresee and help prevent a few problems.

Despite the work and testing that go into preparing each release of Red Hat Enterprise Linux, unanticipated problems inevitably emerge. Most of these problems result from one of three situations:

◆ Testing Red Hat Enterprise Linux for compatibility with every piece of hardware is simply not possible.

◆ Given the range of hardware available, any given combination of two components, for example, a SCSI disk controller and a SCSI disk, may result in subtle but maddening incompatibilities.

◆ As a result of the rapid rate of hardware revisions, drivers written for earlier revisions of your hardware might not support the latest hardware version.

This chapter is intended to help you troubleshoot and solve the most common configuration challenges you might encounter installing and using Red Hat Enterprise Linux. In particular, the sections in this chapter help you resolve problems related to installation, the file system, networking, and booting the system. A final section addresses a few common problems that do not fit into other categories.

Solving Installation Problems

The situations discussed in this section include problems with not being able to log in to the system after it has been installed, the most common hardware-related gotchas, and installing Red Hat Linux on a laptop.

Unable to Log in After Installation

One of the most common problems when installing Red Hat Enterprise Linux is not being able to log in after the post-installation reboot. If you did not create a user account during the installation, you must log in as root and create a user account. Similarly, if you forget the user account password you created during installation, log in as the root user and reset the password using this procedure:

1. At the console or in a terminal window, type the command passwd user, replacing *user* with the user account name.

2. Type a new password and press Enter.

3. Retype the password and press Enter.

4. Log out, and then log back in as the new user, providing the password you just set.

If you forget the root password, reboot and follow these steps:

1. Restart the system.

2. At the GRUB boot prompt, select the kernel image you want to boot, and type e (for edit).

3. Using the cursor keys, place the cursor on the line that begins with the word kernel, and type e a second time. This opens a GRUB shell session.

4. At the GRUB shell prompt, which should resemble the following:

   ```
   grub edit> kernel /vmlinux-2.4.22-1 ro root=LABEL=/
   ```

   Press Space and type single init=/bin/sh. The modified line should now look like the following:

   ```
   grub edit> kernel /vmlinux-2.4.22-1 ro root=LABEL=/ single
   init=/bin/sh
   ```

5. Press Enter, which returns you to the same screen you saw in Step 2.

6. Type b to boot the system with the modified kernel command line. The single option causes the kernel to boot in single user mode; the init=/bin/sh option bypasses the normal boot procedure, causing the kernel to boot to a bash shell prompt. The prompt should look like:

```
init-2.05b#
```

7. At the prompt, type `passwd root` and follow the prompts to reset root's password.

8. Finally, type `shutdown -r now`; the system reboots and recognizes the new password.

Hardware-related Installation Problems

The tips in this section should help you solve the most common hardware-related problems people encounter when installing Red Hat Enterprise Linux.

UNABLE TO MOUNT THE CD-ROM AFTER INSTALLATION

On some systems, the CD-ROM fails to mount after a new installation. Apparently, this is an installer bug. The symptom is that after completing a new installation or upgrading an existing Red Hat Linux installation, the `mount` utility issues an error message similar to `dev/cdrom not a valid block device`, followed by a failed mount and, in some cases, a system crash. To solve this problem, boot the system using the boot disk you created during installation, and then execute the following command as root:

```
# /sbin/depmod -ae
```

You should also download and install the latest kernel errata. For complete details, see the bug report and solution description in the document `http://www.redhat.com/support/errata/RHSA-2001-142.html`.

IDE CD-ROM NOT DETECTED

A similar CD-ROM installation problem is that an IDE CD-ROM is not detected, making CD-ROM installations impossible. The issue here is either that the CD-ROM is on an IDE channel that the system's BIOS does not know about, or that the kernel does not recognize the results of a hardware probe for IDE CD-ROMs. The ideal solution is to tell the kernel where to find the CD-ROM at the boot LILO `boot:` prompt using the following procedure.

 TIP You can also use this procedure if an IDE CD-ROM appears to lock up in the middle of an installation.

1. Boot the system using the boot disk you created for the installation.

2. When you see

```
boot:
```

or

```
LILO:
```

type `linux hdX=cdrom` and press Enter.

X should be a or b if the CD-ROM is on the primary (first) IDE channel or c or d if the CD-ROM is on the secondary (second) IDE channel.

If the kernel *still* fails to recognize the CD-ROM and you have sufficient free disk space, you can attempt to install Red Hat Linux from the hard drive using the following procedure:

1. Make sure you have a DOS partition that is formatted as a FAT16 or FAT32 (DOS/Windows or Windows 95, respectively) partition.

2. Execute the following commands to copy the necessary files from the CD-ROM to the hard drive:

```
mkdir C:\RedHat
mkdir C:\RedHat\base
mkdir C:\RedHat\RPMS
mkdir C:\RedHat\instimage
copy E:\RedHat\base C:\RedHat\base
copy E:\RedHat\RPMS C:\RedHat\RPMS
copy E:\RedHat\instimage C:\RedHat\instimage
```

These commands assume your CD-ROM drive is the E: drive under DOS/Windows and that the free disk space exists on the DOS/Windows C: drive. Adjust the drive letters accordingly if necessary.

3. Start the installation using the boot disk you created earlier and, when prompted, select the hard drive installation method.

NO SOUND AFTER INSTALLATION

If you do not have sound support after installation, check the boot log (/var/log/ boot.log) for messages resembling the following:

```
Sep  1 23:15:11 bubba rc.sysinit: Finding module dependencies:  succeeded
Sep  1 23:15:11 bubba modprobe: Using /lib/modules/2.4.7-10/misc/sound.o
Sep  1 23:15:11 bubba modprobe: insmod: a module named sound already exists
Sep  1 23:15:11 bubba rc.sysinit: Loading sound module (sb):  failed
Sep  1 23:15:11 bubba modprobe: insmod: insmod
/lib/modules/2.4.7-10/misc/sound.o failed
Sep  1 23:15:11 bubba modprobe: insmod: insmod sb failed
Sep  1 23:15:11 bubba rc.sysinit: Loading midi module (awe_wave):  succeeded
```

Next, use the /sbin/lsmod command to determine which, if any, sound modules are loaded. For example,

```
# /sbin/lsmod
Module                 Size  Used by
ide-cd                23628   0  (autoclean)
soundcore              2596   0  (autoclean) (unused)
lockd                 31176   1  (autoclean)
sunrpc                52964   1  (autoclean) [lockd]
eepro100              19844   1  (autoclean)
agpgart               18600   0  (unused)
```

If the output resembles that shown, run the redhat-config-soundcard sound card configuration program to set up your sound card.

SOLVING LAPTOP VIDEO PROBLEMS

Laptop installations are typically the most difficult type of installation to perform because the companies that build laptop computers often use proprietary hardware or modify standard PC components in order to shoehorn desktop PC functionality into the confines of a laptop or to meet weight, power, or functionality requirements. Aggravating such practical concerns, these engineering decisions are rarely publicly documented in order to protect trade secrets. As a result, you often have to use a trial-and-error method and rely on the experiences of others.

A few laptop manufacturers actively support Linux. IBM, for example, preinstalls Linux on a select group of laptop computers, and certain dedicated Linux hardware vendors do the same. The lack of support *is* frustrating, but until manufacturers can be bothered to develop Linux drivers for their products at the same time as they develop Windows drivers, installing Linux on a laptop computer will continue to be a challenge.

While attempting a graphical Red Hat Linux installation from either the CD-ROM or a floppy disk, you may see the laptop screen go blank and you cannot continue. In this case, attempting a text-based installation might work — trying to force a graphical installation rarely works if the installer cannot use your video hardware. With *some* laptops, the graphical installer *might* work if you type the following parameter at the boot: prompt:

```
boot: linux vga=2
```

Similarly, you can try all of the possible VGA modes using the following parameter:

```
boot: linux vga=ask
```

Before giving up completely, have a look at the authoritative reference for Linux and laptops, the Linux Laptop Web site at `http://www.linux-on-laptops.com/`.

THE SIGNAL 7 AND SIGNAL 11 PROBLEMS

Perhaps the most confusing problem people run into when installing Red Hat Enterprise Linux is an error message resembling `fatal signal 11` or `fatal signal 7`. Signal 11s and signal 7s are errors indicating a hardware problem in memory or on the system's data bus. Red Hat Linux does not cause such errors. Rather, it brings such problems to light because the Linux kernel typically pushes hardware to the fullest extent of its capabilities, much more so than DOS or Windows, often revealing substandard hardware.

How should you proceed? The first thing to do is perform memory testing using memtest86, which is included on the Red Hat installation boot disk. Instructions for using memtest86 on the boot disk are included in the release notes. If memtest86 indicates hardware trouble, take your computer to a repair shop and ask them to test the RAM and, possibly, the CPU cache, on a hardware tester.

Meanwhile, check to see if you have the latest installation image from Red Hat. If the latest image still fails, the problem may be hardware related. Common suspects include bad RAM chips or defective CPU cache memory. Try turning off the CPU cache in the BIOS and see if the problem goes away. Likewise, try swapping memory around in the system's memory slots to see whether the error is slot or memory related. If that does not solve the problem, the Signal 11 Web site, `http://www.bitwizard.nl/sig11/`, may be able to help you.

Solving File System Problems

The tips in this section help you solve common problems you might encounter when working with Linux files and file systems.

Cannot Delete a File

If you cannot delete, move, or rename a file, use the `ls -l` command to verify that you have permission to do so. If you receive an error message resembling `rmdir: `dirname': directory not empty` when using `rmdir` to delete a directory, either delete the files in the directory before retrying the `rmdir` command or use `rm -r` to delete the directory and its contents. For example

```
$ rmdir images
rmdir: `images': directory not empty
$ rm -r images
```

A common question is how to delete a file that has a name beginning with a minus (-). Suppose, for example, a file in your home directory is named `-foo`. The command `rm -foo` fails and generates the following error:

```
$ rm -foo
rm: invalid option -- o
```

This problem occurs because most Linux commands interpret a minus sign followed by a letter as a command option, and anything following that as an argument to the command. So, the argument to the `rm` command, `-foo`, looks like invalid syntax, not a filename. The solution is to use two minus signs (`- -`) between `rm` and `-foo`. Most Linux commands interpret two minus signs standing alone as the end of all options; everything afterward is interpreted as an argument. So, to remove the file named `-foo`, try `rm -- -foo`, as follows:

```
$ rm -- -foo
```

TIP   To delete a file that has a name beginning with `-`, you can also use the following:

```
$ rm -- '-foo'
```

Similarly, to delete a file name that contains spaces, you can use a command similar to the following:

```
$ rm -- '-a file name containing spaces'
```

Commands with Multiword Arguments

If you pass an argument made up of multiple words to a command and get an error message stating, in part, `No such file or directory`, enclose the argument between weak quotes (" ") and try again. Remember that most shells use spaces and tab characters to distinguish between commands, options, and arguments. For example, the following command generates an error message before showing its result:

```
$ grep Kurt Wall /etc/passwd
grep: Wall: no such file or directory
/etc/passwd:kwall:x:500:500:Kurt Wall:/home/kwall:/bin/bash
```

Enclosing `Kurt Wall` within weak quotes solves the problem:

```
$ grep "Kurt Wall" /etc/passwd
/etc/passwd:kwall:x:500:500:Kurt Wall:/home/kwall:/bin/bash
```

Accessing Windows File Systems

If you get an error message that the VFAT (Virtual File Allocation Table) file system, the Windows file system, is not supported when using the `mount` command to mount a DOS/Windows floppy disk, log in as the root user and execute the following command:

```
# /sbin/modprobe vfat
```

This command loads the necessary modules that Red Hat Linux needs in order to provide support for DOS/Windows file systems.

Working with Floppy Disks

If you get a `device busy` error message when trying to unmount a floppy disk with the `umount` command, make sure your current directory is not located on the floppy disk (use the `pwd` command). Red Hat Linux cannot unmount a file system or disk of any sort if a process is using it, which includes having a current working directory located anywhere on the file system.

If you cannot use the `cd` command to change your current working directory, execute the following command to see the process IDs (PIDs) of any processes using the mount point:

```
# fuser /file-system-name
```

Next, use the following command:

```
# ps -p pid
```

Replace `pid` with the PIDs from the previous command, to see what process or processes are still using the file system.

If you accidentally remove a floppy disk from a mounted drive without first unmounting it, in many cases you can simply reinsert the floppy disk and execute the appropriate `umount` command to unmount the drive properly.

Cannot Mount a Partition

If you are unable to mount one or more partitions after an upgrade, the problem could be due to the use of partition labels. Red Hat Linux uses partition labels to help prevent problems that occur when moving hard drives around in a system. For example, if / is on `/dev/sdb` and a new drive is added to the system with a lower SCSI ID, the drive that was previously `/dev/sdb` becomes `/dev/sdc`. This change causes the mount command to generate errors when it tries mount /. Partition labels address this problem because `mount` tries to mount the partition identified by its labels as / instead of trying to mount `/dev/sdb1` and expecting it to be /. The idea is great in theory as long as you keep partition labels less than 16 characters.

Avoiding File-system Checks at Each System Reboot

If you constantly have to run `fsck` each time you boot your system, the most likely suspect is that your partitions are not being unmounted properly when you last shut down the machine. The most important thing you can do is make sure that you are shutting down the machine properly. Shutdown is done through one of two methods:

◆ If you are in text mode – run level 3 – you should log in as root and type the following command:

```
# sync;sync;sync;shutdown -r now
```

◆ If you are using the graphical login – run level 5 – click System → Halt. Eventually, you see a line that reads Power Down, indicating it is safe to turn off the machine.

In either case, if you are running APM, Linux tries to stop the machine using the BIOS.

Getting a Zip Drive to Work

To get an Iomega Zip drive attached to a parallel port to work, use the following procedure:

1. Edit `/etc/conf.modules` and add the following lines:

```
alias parport_lowlevel parport_pc
alias scsi_hostadapter ppa
```

2. Log in as root and run the following command:

```
# modprobe ppa
```

If you are having problems with an IDE Zip drive, first check to make sure there is a disk in the drive and make sure you are mounting it as partition 4 instead of 1; for example, `/dev/hdc4` instead of `/dev/hdc1`. The reason for this is that Macintosh uses partition 4 for its data partition and has problems if data is on another partition.

Solving Networking Problems

If you are unable to access hosts on a network, make sure you have at least one name server listed in `/etc/resolv.conf`. If an external system cannot connect to your system, remember the order in which the `hosts.allow` and `hosts.deny` files are read and applied. The program that starts Internet services consults `/etc/hosts.allow` first. If TCP wrappers does not find a matching rule, it applies the first matching rule, if any, in `/etc/hosts.deny`. If neither file contains a match, access is granted.

If you performed an upgrade of Red Hat Linux from an earlier version, it may appear that the upgrade did not preserve the contents of your network service configuration files. This is not the case, however. The configuration files were renamed with the extension `.rpmsave` and can be found in the network service's directory. For example, you might find that the old `/etc/httpd/conf/httpd.conf` file was renamed `/etc/httpd/conf/httpd.conf.rpmsave`. Changes should be copied to the new version of the configuration file.

◆ Files with an `.rpmorig` extension are configuration files not in an RPM package that was upgraded or installed.

◆ Files with an `.rpmsave` extension are configuration files that were in an RPM package that was upgraded or installed.

◆ Files with an `.rpmnew` extension indicates the new version of a file installed by an upgraded package.

Affected network services configuration files include, but are not limited to:

◆ `/etc/httpd/conf/httpd.conf`

◆ `/etc/samba/smb.conf`

◆ `/etc/sendmail.cf`

◆ `/etc/named.conf`

◆ `/etc/dhcpd.conf`

To avoid unfortunate accidents and needless panic or confusion, remember to back up your data before upgrading or installing the latest version of Red Hat Linux.

Getting Online with a Modem

If you are having trouble getting your modem to work, first verify that it is supported by checking the Hardware Compatibility List at `http://hardware.redhat.com/`. Next, see if the modem is being detected by the system and make sure that it does not conflict with other resources. You can check this using the following commands:

```
# cat /proc/ioports
0000-001f : dma1
0020-003f : pic1
0040-005f : timer
0060-006f : keyboard
0070-007f : rtc
```

```
00a0-00bf : pic2
00c0-00df : dma2
00f0-00ff : fpu
0170-0177 : ide1
01f0-01f7 : ide0
0220-022f : soundblaster
02f8-02ff : serial(auto)
0330-0333 : MPU-401 UART
0376-0376 : ide1
03c0-03df : vga+
03f6-03f6 : ide0
03f8-03ff : serial(auto)
d000-d07f : eth0
d800-d807 : ide0
d808-d80f : ide1
# cat /proc/interrupts
          CPU0
  0:    1296380        XT-PIC    timer
  1:      30736        XT-PIC    keyboard
  2:          0        XT-PIC    cascade
  5:          1        XT-PIC    soundblaster
  8:          1        XT-PIC    rtc
  0:      73593        XT-PIC    eth0
  2:     159669        XT-PIC    PS/2 Mouse
  3:          1        XT-PIC    fpu
  4:     246863        XT-PIC    ide0
  5:     584998        XT-PIC    ide1
NMI:          0
```

One example of a resource conflict is that your modem and some other device share an interrupt. COM1 (/dev/ttyS0) and COM3 (/dev/ttyS3) try to share the same interrupt unless told otherwise. Eliminate the conflict by setting a jumper for one of the devices that causes it to use another IRQ. Next, use minicom to see if you can communicate with the modem. The following Web pages help you configure a PPP connection:

◆ http://www.redhat.com/support/docs/tips/PPP-Client-Tips/
   PPP-Client-Tips.html

◆ http://www.redhat.com/support/docs/tips/Network-Config-Tips/
   Network-Config-Tips.html

If setserial shows your modem's UART as unknown, as you see in the following example, the kernel has not detected your serial port or the modem attached to it:

/dev/ttyS2, UART: unknown, Port: 0x03f8, IRQ: 10

This problem usually occurs because your PC's BIOS is set up to expect a Plug and Play (PnP) operating system. To solve the problem, reboot the PC and, as it powers up, press the key that permits you to access the system's BIOS. Typically, this is a function key, such as F2, but the exact key depends on your PC's BIOS. In the setup screen, locate the option for PnP operating system (often labeled "Plug & Play O/S") and turn off that option. Then save the BIOS settings and exit. Doing so causes the PC to reboot. This time, when Red Hat Linux boots, the kernel should be able to detect the PC's serial port correctly.

If your serial ports are correctly detected but the modem does not respond, make sure that /dev/modem is linked to the proper device file in /dev. An unresponsive modem is especially common with PCI modem cards, which typically do not use COM1 (/dev/ttyS0) or COM2 (/dev/ttyS1) by default. For example, suppose dmesg | grep ttyS shows the following:

```
ttyS02 at port 0x6800 (irq = 10) is a 16550A
```

In this case, execute the following command to make sure that /dev/modem is linked to the proper device file:

```
# ln -sf /dev/ttyS2 /dev/modem
```

If your modem does not appear to be detected, use the Windows Device Manager to obtain the modem's IRQ and I/O address, and compare those values to the values the setserial command reports for that port.

At present, some modems simply do not work with Linux. These are so-called "WinModems," which, in order to function, rely on the Windows operating system and a special, Windows-specific device driver. WinModems, also called *software modems*, rely on a device driver, rather than hardware, to function. In this case, your only recourse is to replace the modem with a hardware modem.

If you can connect to your ISP but are unable to surf the Web, or Netscape complains that it cannot connect to remote hosts, the problem is most likely unconfigured or misconfigured DNS (Domain Name Server) information. You need to specify your ISP's DNS servers in the /etc/resolv.conf file. Contact your ISP for this information and edit the file to include those settings. For example:

```
search example.com
nameserver 24.8.89.15
nameserver 24.8.89.16
```

What to Do if the Boot Process Hangs

A network problem exists if your system boots but then seems to hang when starting sendmail, the Sendmail daemon; httpd, the Apache Web server daemon; or smb, the Samba daemon. The most common cause is that Linux cannot resolve the host name to an IP address. The apparent hang is a pause while the kernel waits for the name resolver to time out — the boot process *will* eventually complete. To solve this problem, wait until you can log in; then log in as root to investigate and solve the problem. If you are attached directly to a network with a functioning DNS server, make sure the file `/etc/resolv.conf` has the correct values for your system's DNS server(s). Make sure that the values are correct. If you are using Red Hat Linux on a system attached to a network without a DNS server, or if your Red Hat system is destined to be the DNS server, edit the `/etc/hosts` file and insert your system's IPaddress and name to have the host name and IP address so that the lookups occur correctly. The format of the `/etc/hosts` file is:

```
127.0.0.1       localhost.localdomain localhost
192.168.0.1     bubba.somedomain.com bubba
```

Replace `bubba.somedomain.com` with the proper name of your system and the IP address with the IP address of your system.

Using two Ethernet Cards

To use two Ethernet cards in your Red Hat Linux system, first ensure that both cards are supported. Next, if the two cards use different drivers, you need to set up the second network interface and edit the `/etc/modules.conf` file to load the proper driver for the second card. If the two cards use the same driver, you may need to recompile your kernel, but several modules now allow for multiple cards. It may be that you just need to use boot arguments, such as:

```
boot: linux ether=11,0x300,eth0 ether=5,0x340,eth1
```

This option can be made permanent so that you do not have to reenter it every time your system boots. See the LILO configuration option `append=` in the `lilo.conf` man page. The Ethernet HOWTO is an excellent source of information for configuring multiple Ethernet cards in the same system. It can be found at `http://www.redhat.com/mirrors/LDP/HOWTO/Ethernet-HOWTO.html`.

Solving NFS Problems

In addition to performance degradation, you might encounter other problems with NFS that require resolution. This section discusses some of the typical difficulties system administrators have with NFS and how to resolve them. These tips are only a starting point.

 The Linux NFS-HOWTO on the NFS Web page at `http://nfs.sourcefource.net/nfs-howto/` dedicates an entire section to troubleshooting NFS.

First up are apparent problems that, in reality, are red herrings. Log messages resembling the following are annoying but harmless:

```
kernel: fh_verify: bubba/users: permission failure, acc=4, error=13
kernel: nfs: server localhost not responding, still trying
kernel: nfs: task 18273 can't get a request slot
kernel: nfs: localhost OK
nfslock: rpc.lockd startup failed
kmem_create: forcing word size alignment - nfs_fh
```

The first message occurs when the NFS setattr() RPC call fails because an NFS client is attempting to access a file to which it does not have access. This message is harmless, but many such log entries might indicate a systematic attempt to compromise the system.

The next three messages represent client attempts to contact the NFS server that are timing out. When such timeouts occur, the NFS client reduces the number of concurrent requests it sends in order to avoid overloading the server, which results in these messages. Although such messages are usually harmless, if they persist, you might want to investigate possible saturation of the network or the NFS server.

The rpc.lockd startup failure message almost always occurs when older NFS startup scripts try to start newer versions of rpc.lockd manually – these attempts fail because the kernel NFS server daemon, knfsd, starts the locking daemon automatically. To make the failure message go away, edit the startup scripts and remove statements that attempt to start lockd manually. The final error message occurs if the kernel detects that an NFS file handle is 16 bits, rather than 32 bits or a multiple thereof.

Would that all error messages were as harmless as these! A log message resembling the following, while not dire, demands timely attention:

```
nfs warning: mount version older than kernel
```

This message means exactly what it says: the version of the mount command that you are using is older than the kernel version. So, the solution is to upgrade the mount package in order for mount to recognize any additional options or features of the new kernel.

If you transfer very large files via NFS, and NFS eats all of the available CPU cycles, causing the server to respond at a glacial pace, you are probably running an older version of the kernel that has problems with the fsync() system call that accumulates disk syncs before flushing the buffers. This issue, primarily a problem with 2.2 kernels and early 2.4 kernels, is reportedly fixed in newer 2.4 kernel releases, so upgrading your kernel might solve the problem.

Similarly, if you execute commands on an NFS exported file system that do not result in large data transfers from server to client (such as an ls command) and have no problem, but then nevertheless cause severe response problems with large data transfers (such as a cp command), you may be using rsize= or wsize=

parameters on the client that are larger than the `rsize=` or `wsize=` parameters on the server. Reduce these values on the client side to see if performance recovers. Also make sure that the firewall for the client and the server permits fragmented packets to pass through. NFS uses packet fragmentation, so firewalls that deny or drop fragmented packets force constant retransmission of data. Reportedly, this is especially a problem on Linux systems still using the 2.2 packet filter, ipchains. Either switch to iptables or rewrite the ipchains filters to accept fragmented packets; performance should improve almost immediately.

If you are unable to see files on a mounted file system, check the following items:

1. Make sure that the file system *is*, in fact, mounted. If the file system is not mounted, mount it. Use one of the following commands to verify that the file system is mounted:

   ```
   # cat /proc/mounts
   # mount -f
   ```

2. If the file system is mounted, make sure that another file system is not mounted on top of it. If you have layered a file system on top of an export, unmount and remount both, making sure to mount them on separate mount points.

3. Make sure the client has read privileges to the specified files by verifying the file system permissions on the server, the client's mount point, and that the mount options in `/etc/fstab` or specified on the command line are correct on the client.

If you cannot mount an exported directory, the most common error message is:

```
mount failed, reason given by server: Permission denied
```

This error message means that the server thinks the client does not have access to the specified export. In this case, do one or more of the following:

◆ Review the export specifications in `/etc/exports` on the server, making sure that they are correct and that the client is mounting the export the same way it is exported. For example, an NFS client cannot mount an exported directory read/write (the `-o rw` option to the `mount` command) if that directory is exported from the server read-only (using the `-o ro` option to the `mount` command).

◆ On the server, execute the following command:

   ```
   # exportfs -ar
   ```

   This command makes sure that any changes made to /etc/exports since the exports were first exported are updated in the server's exports table and propagated out to NFS clients.

◆ Look at the contents of /var/lib/nfs/xtab to review the complete list of all of the export options applied to a given export. If they are incorrect, edit /etc/exports accordingly and then rerun the exportfs -ar command to update the server's export table with the proper options.

Solving Boot Problems

If you try to shut down or reboot your Red Hat system using the commands reboot, halt, shutdown -r now, or shutdown -h now and the shutdown process starts to execute correctly but then the display blanks and the system hangs, the only way to recover is to power cycle the system and then try some of the following workarounds. The problem is that at the point the system appears to hang, control of the hardware has been handed back from Linux to the firmware — it is up to the firmware (software embedded in key system hardware components) to reboot the system correctly. Fortunately, Linux enables you to select multiple ways to reboot the system in order to fix, or at least sidestep, buggy or broken BIOSes or hardware.

At the LILO: boot prompt, you can specify:

reboot=X,Y

X can be one of hard or bios.

◆ hard — Uses the CPU's reset instruction to restart the system.

◆ bios — Uses a BIOS routine (sometimes called a *BIOS vector*) to restart the system.

Y can be one of warm or cold.

◆ warm — A *warm boot* is the type of reboot invoked when you press Ctrl+Alt+Delete.

◆ cold — A *cold boot* is the type of boot invoked by power cycling the system.

So if you boot with the following command, Linux reboots by the BIOS vector with a warm reboot:

LILO: linux reboot=bios,warm

The goal is to find the right combination of X and Y that triggers the bugs in the system BIOS. Once you have found this magic sequence, use LILO's append= option to pass these parameters to the kernel each time you boot the system by adding it to /etc/lilo.conf as shown in the following example:

```
append="reboot=bios,warm"
```

Rerun /sbin/lilo -v to write the change to your boot device.

If your system installed without incident until it tried to write LILO information to the MBR (Master Boot Record), at which point the installer complained that it could not write to the MBR, the MBR may be locked by the BIOS. You need to access your system's BIOS and verify that the MBR is not write-protected. Similarly, disable any virus scan enabled in the BIOS that may interfere with writing to the MBR. If neither of these situations applies, you may already have another boot loader in the MBR that conflicts with LILO. If you know the MBR is not write-protected, try the following steps to install LILO to the MBR:

1. Boot the system to Linux. If your system cannot boot into Linux from the hard drive, boot using your boot floppy.

2. Type vmlinuz root=/dev/hdXX at the LILO: prompt, replacing hdXX with the correct location of your Linux root partition.

3. When your system is finished booting, log in as root and check /etc/lilo.conf to make sure everything is correct. An example /etc/lilo.conf is shown in the following listing:

```
boot=/dev/hda
map=/boot/map
install=/boot/boot.b
prompt
timeout=50
message=/boot/message
default=linux

image=/boot/vmlinuz-2.4.7-10
    label=linux
    initrd=/boot/initrd-2.4.7-10.img
    read-only
    root=/dev/hda5
```

Type man lilo.conf for more information about configuring /etc/lilo.conf.

4. When you are sure that /etc/lilo.conf is properly configured, execute the following command to test the configuration:

```
# /sbin/lilo -v -v -t
```

If you receive any errors, stop and verify that the /etc/lilo.conf file is correctly configured. If the lilo command works correctly, remove the -t option and rerun the command:

```
# lilo -v -v
```

5. Finally, reboot the system:

```
# sync;sync;sync;shutdown -r now
```

These steps install LILO to your MBR properly and enable you to boot without using a boot disk.

If you have trouble booting Windows from your second hard disk /dev/hdb after installing Red Hat Linux on the first hard disk, /dev/hda, the problem is that Windows expects to boot from the first hard disk. The symptom of this problem is that if you select Windows at the boot prompt, all you see is:

```
Starting....
```

Then the system locks up. To fix this problem, trick Windows into believing that it is the first drive in the system by modifying the /etc/lilo.conf file so that the entry for Windows looks like the following:

```
other=/dev/hdb1
    label=dos
    table=/dev/hdb
    map-drive = 0x80
    to = 0x81
    map-drive = 0x81
    to = 0x80
```

Rerun LILO so that your changes take effect:

```
#/sbin/lilo -v -v
```

Another common LILO problem is seeing only the following when the system boots:

```
LI
```

This means that LILO is having problems loading itself. A couple of possible situations may be causing this. You may have installed LILO above cylinder 1024 on your hard drive. (The kernel needs to reside entirely below cylinder 1023 on the drive.) If this is the case, you need to create a /boot partition that resides in these limits, and then reinstall LILO. You may also need to go into your system's BIOS and make certain that logical block addressing (LBA) mode is enabled. If LBA is off, you need to repartition and reinstall.

To remove LILO from the MBR, you can use one of the following commands. From Linux, execute the following command to replace the MBR with an earlier saved version of the MBR:

```
# /sbin/lilo -u
```

From DOS, Windows 95, or Windows NT you can use the `fdisk` command to create a new MBR using the `/mbr` option. This rewrites the MBR to boot only the primary DOS partition:

```
C:\> fdisk /mbr
```

Solving Miscellaneous Problems

The tips suggested in this section address the hodgepodge of problems and challenges you might face using Red Hat Enterprise Linux.

Getting Sound to Work

If you are having trouble getting sound to work in Red Hat Linux, you usually need only log in as root and run the `redhat-config-soundcard` command. If this does not work, some of the methods suggested next may help you narrow down or solve the problem.

Disable Plug and Play on the card via jumpers or card configuration tools that work from Windows or DOS.

If `redhat-config-soundcard` is not configuring the sound card correctly, or at all, try:

```
# /usr/sbin/redhat-config-soundcard --noautoconfig
```

This command lets you manually specify the plug and play values for the card. The values from Windows probably works if it is the only plug and play device in the machine, but examine the output from the following four commands to make sure you are not running into a resource conflict with another device in the system:

```
$ cat /proc/interrupts
$ cat /proc/ioports
$ cat /proc/dma
$ cat /proc/pci
```

You can also try using `redhat-config-soundcard`, and then edit `/etc/modules.conf` to use the correct values. Your `/etc/modules.conf` file will have a couple of lines that resemble the following:

```
alias sound sb
options sb irq=7 io=0x320 dma=3,5
```

Finally, you can also edit /etc/modules.conf, delete any lines that refer to your sound card, reboot, and then try to use redhat-config-soundcard again to configure your sound card.

If the card is not a plug and play card *and* you know its settings, you can set them manually by editing */etc/modules.conf*. For example

```
alias sound sb
alias midi opl3
options opl3 io=0x388
options sb io=0x220 irq=5 dma=1,3 mpu_io=0x330
```

You may need to go through one or more of these procedures several times to get good values. Essentially, this trial-and-error process is what redhat-config-soundcard does automatically, but, unfortunately, redhat-config-soundcard does not work for all sound cards.

Using Screensavers and Power Management

To disable screen blanking, turn off your screen saver. In text mode, the kernel turns on the screen blanker after 15 minutes, but you can disable this using the following command:

```
# setterm -powersave off -blank 0
```

If you hear disk drives speed up or other sounds, this is most likely APM (Advanced Power Management) starting up the system after idle time. You can disable APM from starting at boot time by logging in as root and typing redhat-config-services. Deselect APM, exit edhat-config-services, and reboot the machine. APM is one of the few Red Hat Linux services that require a system restart to make it take effect — APM is a low-level kernel function, so a full reset is needed.

Starting the X Window System

What should you do if you run startx and get a black screen? To get out of the black screen mode, try pressing Ctrl+Alt+Backspace. This keystroke combination causes the X server to exit if possible. If it does not work, reboot the system and reconfigure the X Window System using redhat-config-xfree86 after making sure that all your video hardware is compatible. You may want or need to obtain the latest version of XFree86 from http://www.redhat.com/support/errata/. Upgrading X is fairly simple, but an upgrade HOWTO is available at the Red Hat Web site at http://www.redhat.com/support/docs/howto/XFree86-upgrade/XFree86-upgrade.html.

If you get an error message resembling `errno 111` when you run `startx`, an X client (any X program except the X server itself running on your XFree86 X system, such as terminal window or even the window manager) tried to connect to the X server but failed to do so for some reason. Unfortunately, you ordinarily see only the last few lines of the error message. To see the complete message, execute the following command:

```
$ X -probeonly >& startx.out
```

This command creates a file named `startx.out` that contains the complete error message. Review the text of the error message carefully for clues concerning the real problem X is having.

Summary

This chapter offered numerous tips and techniques for overcoming commonly encountered problems installing, configuring, and using Red Hat Enterprise Linux. You first read about how to solve installation problems, such as not being able to use some RAID cards and not being able to mount a CD-ROM after the post-installation reboot. Next, you learned how to work around problems accessing files and using Windows file systems. After you explored ways to resolve difficulties getting online using a modem, you read about disabling power management and working through problems starting the X Window System.

Appendix

What's on the CD-ROM?

This appendix provides you with information on the contents of the CD that accompanies this book. For the latest and greatest information, please refer to the "Using the CD" section.

◆ System requirements

◆ Using the CD

◆ What's on the CD

◆ Troubleshooting

System Requirements

Make sure that your computer meets the minimum system requirements listed in this section. If your computer doesn't match up to most of these requirements, you may have a problem using the contents of the CD.

◆ PC with a Pentium processor running at 120 MHz or faster

◆ At least 64 MB of total RAM installed on your computer

◆ Ethernet network interface card (NIC)

◆ Modem with a speed of at least 28,800 bps

◆ A CD-ROM drive

Using the CD

The purpose of this CD is to boot to a working system with access to your file system to let you fix problems that are preventing your system from booting normally. To boot from the CD, follow these steps:

1. Place the rescue CD into your system CD-ROM drive and boot your system.

2. Follow the on-screen instructions to boot into rescue mode.

What's on the CD

The CD is a bootable rescue CD that boots a small Linux environment and attempts to recognize and mount any Red Hat Enterprise Linux installation to allow routine or emergency maintenance.

Troubleshooting

If you have difficulty booting or using any of the materials on the companion CD, try the following solutions:

◆ **Turn off any anti-virus software that you may have running.** Installers sometimes mimic virus activity and can make your computer incorrectly believe that it is being infected by a virus. (Be sure to turn the anti-virus software back on later.)

◆ **Close all running programs.** The more programs you're running, the less memory is available to other programs. Installers also typically update files and programs; if you keep other programs running, installation may not work properly.

◆ **Reference the ReadMe:** Please refer to the ReadMe file located at the root of the CD-ROM for the latest product information at the time of publication.

If you still have trouble with the CD, please call the Wiley Product Technical Support phone number: (800) 762-2974. Outside the United States, call 1 (317) 572-3994. You can also contact Wiley Product Technical Support at www.wiley.com/techsupport. Wiley Publishing, Inc., will provide technical support only for installation and other general quality control items; for technical support on the applications themselves, consult the program's vendor or author.

To place additional orders or to request information about other Wiley products, please call (800) 225-5945.

Index

Symbols and Numerics

* (asterisk)
    as Bash positional parameter, 663
    as Bash wildcard, 655–656
@ (at sign) as Bash positional parameter, 663
\ (backslash) in directory names (MS-DOS), 40
` (backtick) for Bash command substitution, 658–659
, (comma) in device names, 105
{ } (curly braces) for Bash command blocks, 658
> (greater than symbol) for redirecting I/O (Bash), 679–682
< (less than symbol) for redirecting I/O (Bash), 679–682
(number sign)
    as Bash positional parameter, 663
    for ks.cfg file comments, 70
( ) (parentheses) in device names, 105
% (percent sign)
    %packages command (Kickstart), 72
    %pre and %post sections of ks.cfg file, 70, 73–74
? (question mark) as Bash wildcard, 655–656
" (quotation marks) for Bash strong quotes, 659
' (single quotes) for Bash weak quotes, 659
/ (slash)
    in directory names, 40
    root (/) directory, 117–118
[ ] (square brackets) for Bash set operators, 656–657
* (star)
    as Bash positional parameter, 663
    as Bash wildcard, 655–656
2600 Web site, 817

A

A (IP address) records, 428
About dialog box, 754
Accelerated Graphics Port (AGP) slot, 30
Access Control Lists (ACLs), 696
access rules for NIS server, 326
Account Wizard (Mozilla Mail), 454–456
accounts. *See* groups; user accounts
acct file, 157
ACLs (Access Control Lists), 696
Add a new print queue dialog box
    for local printers, 233–234
    Networked CUPS (IPP) screen, 234–235
    Networked JetDirect screen, 239
    Networked Novell (NCP) screen, 238–239
    Networked Unix (LPD) screen, 235–236
    Networked Windows (SMB) screen, 236–238
Add NFS Share dialog box, 306–308
Address Resolution Protocol (ARP), 254
adduser program, 623
Advanced Intrusion Detection Environment (AIDE), 876
Advanced Maryland Automatic Network Disk Archiver. *See* AMANDA
Advanced Power Management (APM) system, 127–128, 185, 196, 916
AFP (AppleTalk Filing Protocol), 364–366. *See also* connecting to Apple networks
afpd program (AppleTalk), 364–366
AGP (Accelerated Graphics Port) slot, 30
AIDE (Advanced Intrusion Detection Environment), 876
Alert Icon program (RHN), 559–561
aliases
    device, 260, 282–283
    e-mail, 178, 444–445, 451
    newaliases command, 445, 451
    Sudo, 698, 699
aliases configuration file, 178, 444–445
Allow Incoming security level, 857–858
AMANDA (Advanced Maryland Automatic Network Disk Archiver)
    Amanda.conf options (table), 787–788
    .amandahosts file, 793–794
    amdump commands, 794
    client configuration, 793–794
    commands, 785–786
    compression types, 792
    configuring, 787–793

continued

continued

continued

continued

continued

continued

GNU GENERAL PUBLIC LICENSE

Version 2, June 1991
Copyright © 1989, 1991 Free Software Foundation, Inc.
59 Temple Place, Suite 330, Boston, MA 02111-1307, USA
Everyone is permitted to copy and distribute verbatim copies of this license document, but changing it is not allowed.

Preamble

The licenses for most software are designed to take away your freedom to share and change it. By contrast, the GNU General Public License is intended to guarantee your freedom to share and change free software — to make sure the software is free for all its users. This General Public License applies to most of the Free Software Foundation's software and to any other program whose authors commit to using it. (Some other Free Software Foundation software is covered by the GNU Library General Public License instead.) You can apply it to your programs, too.

When we speak of free software, we are referring to freedom, not price. Our General Public Licenses are designed to make sure that you have the freedom to distribute copies of free software (and charge for this service if you wish), that you receive source code or can get it if you want it, that you can change the software or use pieces of it in new free programs; and that you know you can do these things.

To protect your rights, we need to make restrictions that forbid anyone to deny you these rights or to ask you to surrender the rights. These restrictions translate to certain responsibilities for you if you distribute copies of the software, or if you modify it.

For example, if you distribute copies of such a program, whether gratis or for a fee, you must give the recipients all the rights that you have. You must make sure that they, too, receive or can get the source code. And you must show them these terms so they know their rights.

We protect your rights with two steps: (1) copyright the software, and (2) offer you this license which gives you legal permission to copy, distribute and/or modify the software.

Also, for each author's protection and ours, we want to make certain that everyone understands that there is no warranty for this free software. If the software is modified by someone else and passed on, we want its recipients to know that what they have is not the original, so that any problems introduced by others will not reflect on the original authors' reputations.

Finally, any free program is threatened constantly by software patents. We wish to avoid the danger that redistributors of a free program will individually obtain patent licenses, in effect making the program proprietary. To prevent this, we have made it clear that any patent must be licensed for everyone's free use or not licensed at all.

The precise terms and conditions for copying, distribution and modification follow.

TERMS AND CONDITIONS FOR COPYING, DISTRIBUTION, AND MODIFICATION

0. This License applies to any program or other work which contains a notice placed by the copyright holder saying it may be distributed under the terms of this General Public License. The "Program", below, refers to any such program or work, and a "work based on the Program" means either the Program or any derivative work under copyright law: that is to say, a work containing the Program or a portion of it, either verbatim or with modifications and/or translated into another language. (Hereinafter, translation is included without limitation in the term "modification".) Each licensee is addressed as "you".

   Activities other than copying, distribution and modification are not covered by this License; they are outside its scope. The act of running the Program is not restricted, and the output from the Program is covered only if its contents constitute a work based on the Program (independent of having been made by running the Program). Whether that is true depends on what the Program does.

1. You may copy and distribute verbatim copies of the Program's source code as you receive it, in any medium, provided that you conspicuously and appropriately publish on each copy an appropriate copyright notice and disclaimer of warranty; keep intact all the notices that refer to this License and to the absence of any warranty; and give any other recipients of the Program a copy of this License along with the Program.

   You may charge a fee for the physical act of transferring a copy, and you may at your option offer warranty protection in exchange for a fee.

2. You may modify your copy or copies of the Program or any portion of it, thus forming a work based on the Program, and copy and distribute such modifications or work under the terms of Section 1 above, provided that you also meet all of these conditions:

   a) You must cause the modified files to carry prominent notices stating that you changed the files and the date of any change.

   b) You must cause any work that you distribute or publish, that in whole or in part contains or is derived from the Program or any part thereof, to be licensed as a whole at no charge to all third parties under the terms of this License.

   c) If the modified program normally reads commands interactively when run, you must cause it, when started running for such interactive use in the most ordinary way, to print or display an announcement including an appropriate copyright notice and a notice that there is no warranty (or else, saying that you provide a warranty) and that users may redistribute the program under these conditions, and telling the user how to view a copy of this License. (Exception: if the Program itself is interactive but does not normally print such an announcement, your work based on the Program is not required to print an announcement.)

   These requirements apply to the modified work as a whole. If identifiable sections of that work are not derived from the Program, and can be reasonably considered independent and separate works in themselves, then this License, and its terms, do not apply to those sections when you distribute them as separate works. But when you distribute the same sections as part of a whole which is a work based on the Program, the distribution of the whole must be on the terms of this License, whose permissions for other licensees extend to the entire whole, and thus to each and every part regardless of who wrote it.

Thus, it is not the intent of this section to claim rights or contest your rights to work written entirely by you; rather, the intent is to exercise the right to control the distribution of derivative or collective works based on the Program.

In addition, mere aggregation of another work not based on the Program with the Program (or with a work based on the Program) on a volume of a storage or distribution medium does not bring the other work under the scope of this License.

3. You may copy and distribute the Program (or a work based on it, under Section 2) in object code or executable form under the terms of Sections 1 and 2 above provided that you also do one of the following:

   a) Accompany it with the complete corresponding machine-readable source code, which must be distributed under the terms of Sections 1 and 2 above on a medium customarily used for software interchange; or,

   b) Accompany it with a written offer, valid for at least three years, to give any third party, for a charge no more than your cost of physically performing source distribution, a complete machine-readable copy of the corresponding source code, to be distributed under the terms of Sections 1 and 2 above on a medium customarily used for software interchange; or,

   c) Accompany it with the information you received as to the offer to distribute corresponding source code. (This alternative is allowed only for noncommercial distribution and only if you received the program in object code or executable form with such an offer, in accord with Subsection b above.)

The source code for a work means the preferred form of the work for making modifications to it. For an executable work, complete source code means all the source code for all modules it contains, plus any associated interface definition files, plus the scripts used to control compilation and installation of the executable. However, as a special exception, the source code distributed need not include anything that is normally distributed (in either source or binary form) with the major components (compiler, kernel, and so on) of the operating system on which the executable runs, unless that component itself accompanies the executable.

If distribution of executable or object code is made by offering access to copy from a designated place, then offering equivalent access to copy the source code from the same place counts as distribution of the source code, even though third parties are not compelled to copy the source along with the object code.

4. You may not copy, modify, sublicense, or distribute the Program except as expressly provided under this License. Any attempt otherwise to copy, modify, sublicense or distribute the Program is void, and will automatically terminate your rights under this License. However, parties who have received copies, or rights, from you under this License will not have their licenses terminated so long as such parties remain in full compliance.

5. You are not required to accept this License, since you have not signed it. However, nothing else grants you permission to modify or distribute the Program or its derivative works. These actions are prohibited by law if you do not accept this License. Therefore, by modifying or distributing the Program (or any work based on the Program), you indicate your acceptance of this License to do so, and all its terms and conditions for copying, distributing or modifying the Program or works based on it.

6. Each time you redistribute the Program (or any work based on the Program), the recipient automatically receives a license from the original licensor to copy, distribute or modify the Program subject to these terms and conditions. You may not impose any further restrictions on the recipients' exercise of the rights granted herein. You are not responsible for enforcing compliance by third parties to this License.

7. If, as a consequence of a court judgment or allegation of patent infringement or for any other reason (not limited to patent issues), conditions are imposed on you (whether by court order, agreement or otherwise) that contradict the conditions of this License, they do not excuse you from the conditions of this License. If you cannot distribute so as to satisfy simultaneously your obligations under this License and any other pertinent obligations, then as a consequence you may not distribute the Program at all. For example, if a patent license would not permit royalty-free redistribution of the Program by all those who receive copies directly or indirectly through you, then the only way you could satisfy both it and this License would be to refrain entirely from distribution of the Program.

   If any portion of this section is held invalid or unenforceable under any particular circumstance, the balance of the section is intended to apply and the section as a whole is intended to apply in other circumstances.

   It is not the purpose of this section to induce you to infringe any patents or other property right claims or to contest validity of any such claims; this section has the sole purpose of protecting the integrity of the free software distribution system, which is implemented by public license practices. Many people have made generous contributions to the wide range of software distributed through that system in reliance on consistent application of that system; it is up to the author/donor to decide if he or she is willing to distribute software through any other system and a licensee cannot impose that choice.

   This section is intended to make thoroughly clear what is believed to be a consequence of the rest of this License.

8. If the distribution and/or use of the Program is restricted in certain countries either by patents or by copyrighted interfaces, the original copyright holder who places the Program under this License may add an explicit geographical distribution limitation excluding those countries, so that distribution is permitted only in or among countries not thus excluded. In such case, this License incorporates the limitation as if written in the body of this License.

9. The Free Software Foundation may publish revised and/or new versions of the General Public License from time to time. Such new versions will be similar in spirit to the present version, but may differ in detail to address new problems or concerns.

   Each version is given a distinguishing version number. If the Program specifies a version number of this License which applies to it and "any later version", you have the option of following the terms and conditions either of that version or of any later version published by the Free Software Foundation. If the Program does not specify a version number of this License, you may choose any version ever published by the Free Software Foundation.

10. If you wish to incorporate parts of the Program into other free programs whose distribution conditions are different, write to the author to ask for permission. For software which is copyrighted by the Free Software Foundation, write to the Free

Software Foundation; we sometimes make exceptions for this. Our decision will be guided by the two goals of preserving the free status of all derivatives of our free software and of promoting the sharing and reuse of software generally.

NO WARRANTY

11. BECAUSE THE PROGRAM IS LICENSED FREE OF CHARGE, THERE IS NO WARRANTY FOR THE PROGRAM, TO THE EXTENT PERMITTED BY APPLICABLE LAW. EXCEPT WHEN OTHERWISE STATED IN WRITING THE COPYRIGHT HOLDERS AND/OR OTHER PARTIES PROVIDE THE PROGRAM "AS IS" WITHOUT WARRANTY OF ANY KIND, EITHER EXPRESSED OR IMPLIED, INCLUDING, BUT NOT LIMITED TO, THE IMPLIED WARRANTIES OF MERCHANTABILITY AND FITNESS FOR A PARTICULAR PURPOSE. THE ENTIRE RISK AS TO THE QUALITY AND PERFORMANCE OF THE PROGRAM IS WITH YOU. SHOULD THE PROGRAM PROVE DEFECTIVE, YOU ASSUME THE COST OF ALL NECESSARY SERVICING, REPAIR OR CORRECTION.

12. IN NO EVENT UNLESS REQUIRED BY APPLICABLE LAW OR AGREED TO IN WRITING WILL ANY COPYRIGHT HOLDER, OR ANY OTHER PARTY WHO MAY MODIFY AND/OR REDISTRIBUTE THE PROGRAM AS PERMITTED ABOVE, BE LIABLE TO YOU FOR DAMAGES, INCLUDING ANY GENERAL, SPECIAL, INCIDENTAL OR CONSEQUENTIAL DAMAGES ARISING OUT OF THE USE OR INABILITY TO USE THE PROGRAM (INCLUDING BUT NOT LIMITED TO LOSS OF DATA OR DATA BEING RENDERED INACCURATE OR LOSSES SUSTAINED BY YOU OR THIRD PARTIES OR A FAILURE OF THE PROGRAM TO OPERATE WITH ANY OTHER PROGRAMS), EVEN IF SUCH HOLDER OR OTHER PARTY HAS BEEN ADVISED OF THE POSSIBILITY OF SUCH DAMAGES.

END OF TERMS AND CONDITIONS